Cisco® PIX™
Firewalls

Richard A. Deal

McGraw-Hill/Osborne

New York Chicago San Francisco
Lisbon London Madrid Mexico City Milan
New Delhi San Juan Seoul Singapore Sydney Toronto

The McGraw·Hill Companies

McGraw-Hill/Osborne
2100 Powell Street, 10th Floor
Emeryville, California 94608
U.S.A.

To arrange bulk purchase discounts for sales promotions, premiums, or fund-raisers, please contact **McGraw-Hill/Osborne** at the above address. For information on translations or book distributors outside the U.S.A., please see the International Contact Information page immediately following the index of this book.

Cisco® PIX™ Firewalls

7890 FGR FGR 0198765

ISBN 0-07-222523-8

Publisher
Brandon A. Nordin
Vice President & Associate Publisher
Scott Rogers
Acquisitions Editor
Francis Kelly
Project Editor
Julie M. Smith
Acquisitions Coordinator
Martin Przybyla
Technical Editor
Ole Drews Jensen
Copy Editor
Brian MacDonald
Proofreaders
Susie Elkind
Brian Galloway
Pat Mannion

Indexer
Valerie Perry
Computer Designers
George Toma Charbak
Tara A. Davis
Jean Butterfield
John Patrus
Illustrators
Sue Albert
Melinda Moore Lytle
Michael Mueller
Jackie Sieben
Series Design
Lyssa Wald
Peter F. Hancik
Cover Series Design
Jeff Weeks

This book was composed with Corel VENTURA™ Publisher.

To Natalie, my loving wife

ABOUT THE AUTHOR

Richard has over 15 years experience in the computing and networking industry including networking, training, systems administration, and programming. Over the last five years, Richard has operated his own company, called The Deal Group, Inc., which provides network consulting and training services nationwide. Richard holds many certifications from Cisco, including CCNA, CCDA, CCNP, and CCDP, and has taught numerous official Cisco classes for the past six years. Richard has developed private security classes for various training companies as well as Cisco test preparation software for QuizWare (http://www.quizware.com). He has written numerous books on Cisco products, including *CCNA Secrets Revealed!*, *CCNP Switching Exam Cram*, *CCNP Cisco LAN Switch Configuration Exam Cram*, and *CCNP Remote Access Exam Prep*.

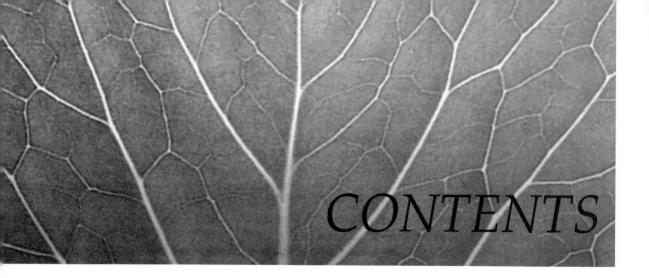

CONTENTS

Part V   VPNs and the PIX Firewall

ACKNOWLEDGMENTS

This book would not have been possible without the support of my wife Natalie. A book of this size is very time-consuming, especially when you have to balance a book, a job, and, most importantly, a family. My wife provided endless encouragement to keep me writing when I was pressed to meet deadlines for the book.

Thanks to Ole Drews Jensen for providing excellent feedback and encouragement on the technical content of this book. I would be more than happy to work with Ole again on my next book project.

It was also a pleasure working with the team at McGraw-Hill, especially the book's editor Franny Kelly and his assistants Martin Przybyla and Emma Acker. To project editor Julie Smith, I owe a debt of gratitude, especially when I was verbose and overshot the length of the book by 100 pages—thanks for your help! And the copy editor, Brian MacDonald, for helping me correct grammar problems that even Microsoft Word couldn't detect.

Best wishes to all! And cheers!
Richard

INTRODUCTION

The writing of this book was very enjoyable for me. Up until this point, all of the books I wrote were focused on passing Cisco certification exams. This book, however, allowed me to focus all my attention on the use of Cisco PIX firewalls in network design and implementation. Instead of having to worry about keeping my writing within a certain page count, or limiting my discussion to the list of exam topics, McGraw-Hill gave me free reign on developing a first-class book on the use of Cisco PIX firewalls.

Firewalls, as a technology, have been around for over a decade. However, it wasn't until the explosion of the Internet that the use of firewalls has become commonplace in corporate and small offices, and even home environments (I use a PIX 501 for my home office and ZoneAlarm on my laptop). I'm continually amazed at the number of times that my home office network is scanned and probed by curious people and hackers on the Internet. As you will see in Chapter 1, there are many types of firewalls and firewall products available in the marketplace; and choosing the appropriate firewall product can be a confusing and daunting task.

Because of the number of products available on the market, I have decided to limit the focus of this book to Cisco's PIX firewall family. This is not to say that Cisco's solution is always the best solution—in any type of network design, you need to choose the appropriate product to solve your company's specific security problems. Cisco does make an excellent firewall product, and exceeds or ties in market share with Check Point's and Nokia's firewalls. I have taken on the task of writing this book for the following reasons:

- Security is a very hot topic right now because of the events that happened on September 11, 2001, as well as the explosive growth of Internet services offered by companies.
- Cisco is the market share leader in enterprise networking solutions, and therefore, you are likely to run into PIX firewalls in your job.
- There are not any really good and focused books on Cisco's PIX firewall products.
- I have my networking roots in Cisco products and have never seen a networking company offer a better set of enterprise products and top-notch technical support.

THE INTENDED AUDIENCE

The objective of this book is to provide you with an understanding of the functions of a firewall, an overview of Cisco's PIX firewall family, the features available on the PIX firewall, including those in the most recent operating system versions, and the configuration of the PIX firewall. The concepts and configurations provided in this book are not for people thinking about a career in computer networking, but for people who are using PIX firewalls to secure their internal networks. This book can easily be read by not only network administrators, engineers, and technicians, but also networking sales persons and managers.

WHAT THIS BOOK COVERS

In this book, I make no assumptions about your skill level with PIX firewalls, and I have attempted to present every subject in a clear and easy-to-understand layout. I've separated the book into different sections in order to make the presentation of the material easier to understand, and to provide a step-by-step progression in setting up your PIX firewall. This book contains five parts.

Initially I had planned on including a sixth part, which would be a preface to this book. This part would have contained an overview of security and of Cisco's wide range of security products. However, because of the amount of material I wrote on the PIX itself, I have decided to remove these chapters and place them on my web site (http://home.cfl.rr.com/dealgroup/). There are certain places in the book where I have omitted information that pertains to end-of-life PIX models or configuration tasks not commonly performed. If you are interested in this information, I have made a note of it in the respective chapters and point you to my web site where you read this information at your leisure.

Part I—Introduction to Firewalls and Cisco Hardware Solutions

In the first Part of the book, I define what a firewall is. As you will see, a firewall can be much more than a simple packet-filtering device, even though this is where the roots of firewall solutions began back in the early 1990s. Understanding what a firewall is, what it is meant to do, and the different functions a firewall can perform is important when you are designing a network that requires a firewall component—choosing the appropriate firewall product ensures that you are meeting your company's security needs as well as getting the most functionality for your money. I discuss firewall functions such as packet filtering, stateful filtering, address translation, proxy services, and many others. Each function is covered in enough detail to provide you with a thorough understanding of how it works and where and when it should be used.

I finish this part by thoroughly covering the different PIX models that Cisco has available, as well as an overview of the features provided by the operating system of the PIX. While I was writing this book, I was fortunate enough to have access to Cisco's latest major software release for the PIX, 6.2. Therefore, most of the features available in 6.2, as well as other releases of the PIX operating system, are covered throughout the other parts of this book.

Part II—PIX Setup and Traffic Filtering

Part II begins the process of configuring a PIX firewall. I start out assuming that you have never seen the command-line interface of a PIX firewall, and begin discussing its use and the basic commands needed to get the PIX up and running.

The main reason companies use firewalls is for their filtering abilities. I thoroughly discuss the PIX's packet filtering abilities in this Part, including Cisco's old methods (conduits and outbound filters) and new methods (access control lists). Because some of the configurations can be very complicated, throughout this book I have included copious examples of PIX configurations.

Because of the stateful filtering nature of the PIX firewall, I thoroughly cover how the PIX handles traffic as it flows between different interfaces. I also discuss the address translation features of the PIX firewall, including dynamic and static, and Network Address Translation (NAT) and Port Address Translation (PAT). Because each environment is unique in the use of address translation, I cover many examples using the PIX firewall, including the following:

- You are using private addresses in your network.
- You are using public addresses in your internal network.
- You are using both public and private addresses in your internal network.
- You need to translate some addresses, but only based on the destination that they are trying to reach.
- Your ISP has given you a single public IP address.
- You have overlapping network numbers.

Part III—Advanced PIX Features

In Part III, I look beyond the packet filtering and address translation features of the PIX to focus on some of the advanced features that the PIX has for filtering traffic and handling connections. I start out by discussing the PIX's ability to filter web content with third-party server software. This feature allows you to restrict the kind of web content that an internal user can download to their desktops.

The second chapter in this part covers the issues that various applications pose to stateful firewalls and how the PIX can deal with these problems using the Protocol Fixup feature. As you will see, many applications, especially those that are multimedia-based, sometimes go through a bizarre and non-standardized process in setting up connections to other devices. This chapter will clear up a lot of the mystery surrounding these types of connections and how the PIX deals with them in a stateful firewall environment.

The last chapter in this part focuses on the PIX's IDS abilities. As you will see, the PIX is not a full-blown IDS appliance—it is limited in the number and types of attacks that it can detect. However, for SOHO environments, or to provide additional security for a networking with IDS appliances, the PIX's IDS features provide a decent and complimentary solution.

Part IV—PIX Management

In Part IV, I cover topics that allow you to manage your PIX, as well as using your PIX to ease management tasks of your network. I begin this section with an overview of Cisco's PIX Device Manager (PDM) product. PDM is a very easy-to-use GUI-based alternative to configuring a PIX firewall. I also discuss how to set up a PIX so that it can be remotely configured and monitored using SNMP.

The PIX contains a robust logging feature, and allows you to log information to its console, an internal buffer, or an external syslog server. I discuss how to set this function up, as well as how to add timestamps to the your messages. Because timing is used in other places besides logging, like Certificate Authorities (CAs) with Virtual Private Networks (VPNs), it is important to understand how you configure the date and time on the PIX. I discuss how this can be done manually as well as dynamically with the Network Time Protocol (NTP).

I then move into the AAA section, which covers some advanced security concepts. With AAA, you can control who can log into the PIX, what they can do on the PIX, and when they can do it. You can extend this function to devices that want to set up connections through the PIX, which provides you an additional level of security.

The next two chapters discuss the maintenance of the PIX itself. I discuss how you can break into a PIX firewall if you have lost or forgotten its passwords. I then move on to cover the various methods of upgrading the operating system on a PIX, installing PDM, and entering an activation key, which is used for activating certain features on the PIX.

The last chapter in this part covers the DHCP and PPPoE features of the PIX firewall. The PIX can be both a DHCP server and a client. As a DHCP server, it can assign IP addressing information to devices on the inside of a network. As a DHCP client, the PIX can dynamically acquire its IP addressing information for its external information when it is connected to an ISP. PPPoE is new in version 6.2 of the PIX operating system—I discuss its function as well as its configuration on a PIX. An advanced addressing feature of the PIX allows it to take certain addressing information received from an ISP and pass it to internal DHCP clients.

Part V—VPNs and the PIX

The last Part of this book focuses on using the PIX to set up VPN connections. This Part starts off with an overview of VPNs, including their different types, such as IPSec, L2TP, and PPTP. Because VPNs are very complicated when setting up secure connections, I discuss all of the components that are involved, including ISAKMP, IKE, Diffie-Hellman, hashing functions, encryption algorithms, transform sets, security associations, and many others.

The last chapter of this book discusses how you set up site-to-site and remote access (to stand-alone devices like PCs) connections from your PIX firewall. As you will see, setting up VPN connections on your PIX is probably one of the most difficult configurations that you'll perform. To help you with the configuration, I explain all of your options as well as give you many configuration examples.

FINAL WORDS

Even though I discuss many of the components and configurations of the PIX firewall, it is impossible to cover every type of configuration and network scenario in a single book. Therefore, I have periodically placed additional PIX information on my web site (http://home.cfl.rr.com/dealgroup/). Throughout various chapters, I make references to this additional PIX material. I also highly recommend that you use Cisco's web site (http://www.cisco.com) as well as various Usenet news groups as additional resources. I cannot begin to count the number of times that I have found the answer to a question in either of these two places. Because of the value of this information, I've rarely had to call TAC at Cisco to help with a PIX configuration issue.

I wish you the best in your networking endeavors and hope that this book helps make your job easier when it comes to using Cisco's PIX firewalls.

Cheers!

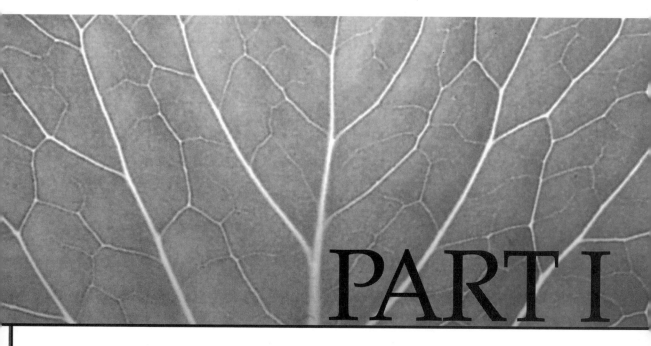

PART I

Introduction to Firewalls and Cisco Hardware Solutions

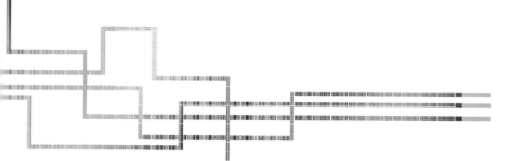

CHAPTER 1

Firewall Basics

Firewalls have evolved from a simple packet-filtering technology to a multipurpose device that includes the abilities to examine traffic for intrusion detection, scan for viruses in Java applets and ActiveX scripts, filter web traffic based on content, provide IP address translation with network address translation (NAT) and port address translation (PAT), and perform packet filtering. Most people assume that firewalls are devices that corporations use to protect their data assets, but firewalls are becoming popular with home users who have high-speed Internet access or dialup connections. This chapter will explain what a firewall is, and outline the many types of firewalls available in the marketplace.

OVERVIEW OF FIREWALLS

Firewalls are used in today's networks to prevent the exploitation of weaknesses in the TCP/IP protocol stack, as well as to enforce your company's business and security policies. They allow you to implement a centralized, yet secure, security solution for giving users necessary access to the resources in your network.

What is a Firewall?

Firewalls come in all shapes, sizes, and types. A firewall can be something as simple as a perimeter router that performs packet filtering as packets come into (and, possibly, leave) your network, or it can be something as sophisticated as a device that not only performs packet filtering, but looks at the weaknesses in various TCP/IP protocols, like SMTP, TCP, and others, and uses mechanisms to close these weaknesses to hackers. Even more powerful firewalls can examine traffic for its contents and make filtering decisions based on your company's policies. For example, you might have a policy in your company that prohibits the downloading of pornography; a content-filtering firewall can examine what traffic is being downloaded to your users' desktops and filter this information based on what is and is not allowed.

Early History of Firewalls

When I first started working with network security at the beginning of the 1990s, the term *firewall* didn't even exist. Firewalls were not really considered important in company networks until the explosion of the Internet in the mid-1990s and the high demand to have Internet access, even for company personnel. Because of the exposure to security threats in today's networks, the word *firewall* has become almost a household word. So what is a firewall?

If you had asked me this question in the late 1980s, I would have answered that a firewall is a device used in construction to prevent the spread of fire throughout a building. Of course, today, the term firewall has a completely different meaning. When I worked with my first firewall product in 1993, the TIS Firewall Toolkit, it was a simple packet filtering device that would run on most Unix platforms. I used it to protect my high-end Unix servers from attacks, especially those from the Internet. If you look at a firewall today, however, packet filtering is typically only one of many features that a firewall includes. Therefore, defining a firewall is a difficult task.

Simple Definition

Generically speaking, a firewall is a device, or a group of devices, that helps you implement your security policies to protect your company against network *traffic* threats. Simply put, a firewall allows you to control traffic between networks. Note that I did not say between the Internet and your company, because many, if not most, of the threats that you'll face as a security administrator will actually start from *inside* your company— not the hackers out on the Internet. Also, firewalls are not exclusive to TCP/IP traffic, but to other protocols as well.

Choosing a Firewall

One of the most difficult decisions that you'll need to make is what type of firewall to use for your network security. Throughout this chapter, you will see that there are many types of firewalls. Some firewalls are dedicated devices, and some run on a file server or a router platform. Some firewalls provide generic traffic filtering, and others provide stateful filtering. Some firewalls allow a transparent connection for a user, and others have a user perform an authentication process before allowing access. Some firewalls work at layer 4 of the OSI Reference model (transport), and some work at layer 7 (application).

To make this situation even more complex, there is usually not a clear-cut line that separates one product from another because a product can include functions from several categories. Therefore, it is sometimes difficult to classify a product in a specific category. One of the things that you need to do is determine the functions that you need in a firewall and then find a product that meets or exceeds these abilities. Here are some general factors that you should consider when choosing a firewall:

- How many devices do you need to protect?
- How many segments need to be directly connected to the firewall?
- What resources do you need to protect in your network?
- What applications do your users use?
- What Internet resources do your users need access to?
- What internal resources do Internet users need access to?
- How much traffic will the firewall have to handle?
- Will you be using private addresses in your network, and do you need address translation?
- Do you need to protect data between different sites?
- Are you concerned about weaknesses in the TCP/IP protocol stack?
- Do you worry about your users' productivity and how surfing the Internet will affect this?
- Are you concerned about the content of material that your users will download to their desktops?
- Does your network have to support multimedia traffic?

- Do you need to authenticate users before allowing them access into or out of your network?
- How many firewalls do you need?

This is by no means an all-inclusive list; but it at least points you in the right direction and helps you begin thinking about the functions, features, and your company's needs when considering a firewall solution.

I have had many network administrators, data processing managers, and CIOs ask me what type of firewall provides the best solution. Unfortunately, the answer to this question is almost always different based on how you answer the questions in the list. In some instances, I recommend a PIX or Nokia firewall product, in other instances, Checkpoint running on a Windows NT/2000. And sometimes, for small or home office (SOHO) environments, I might even recommend a router with basic filtering abilities. To make it even more complex, I might even recommend more than one solution: a PIX *and* a router with filtering abilities. As you can see, understanding your company's needs directly affects the security solution, including the firewall component or components, you choose to implement.

Firewall Components

A firewall does not necessarily have to be a single device. A better way of thinking of a firewall is to see it as a device or a group of devices that work together to control your network traffic. A good firewall system typically includes the following components:

- Perimeter router
- Main firewall
- Virtual private network (VPN)
- Intrusion detection system (IDS)

Please note that I use the word *components* here, and not *devices*. In a firewall system, these components could be located in separate devices, as is shown in Figure 1-1, or they can be combined into a single device, as is shown in Figure 1-2.

Perimeter Router Component

The function of the perimeter router is to provide the connection to the Internet: translating the data link layer media types from LAN to WAN. It might also perform more functions, like packet filtering, BGP routing, or VPN connections.

Main Firewall Component

The main firewall component is responsible for controlling traffic between the two networks, where typically one of the networks is external to your company and the other is the subnets that make up your company's network. Note, however, that many companies use firewalls internal to their network, where they are securing/controlling traffic between different divisions and departments. I'll use the typical use of a firewall system and apply it to your Internet connection in this chapter.

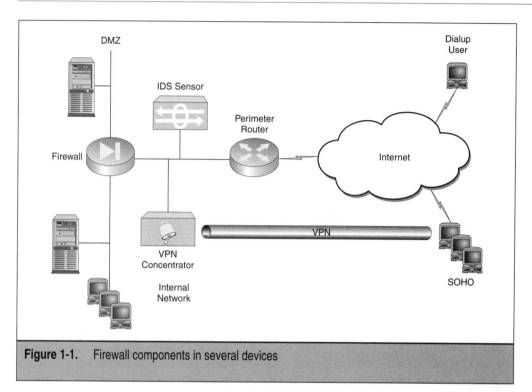

Figure 1-1.   Firewall components in several devices

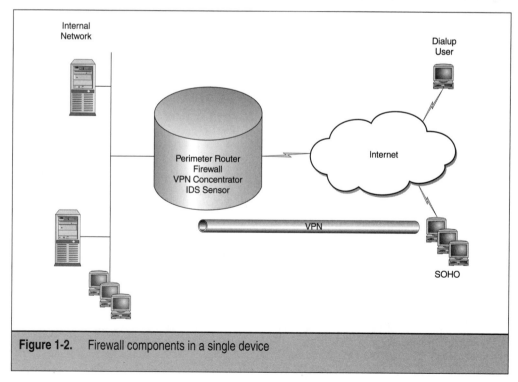

Figure 1-2.   Firewall components in a single device

VPN Component

If you have users or other offices who will be using the Internet to connect to the central site of your company, you might want to consider implementing a VPN component in your firewall system. A VPN allows you to protect your traffic from eavesdroppers.

IDS Component

Another major component of a firewall system is intrusion detection. The main firewall component will control traffic (filtering) based on the policy rules that you configure on it—no more, no less. To understand the kinds of threats that your network is facing, and to deal with new security threats that are popping up on a daily basis, you need to understand exactly what traffic is being sent into your network, as well as its intentions.

Most traffic is sent through a firewall system with a legitimate purpose: send an e-mail, access a web page, resolve a host name, download a file via FTP, telnet into a resource, and so on; however, not all traffic sent into your network has these intentions. An example of bad intentions would be reconnaissance by a hacker, an attempt to gain unauthorized access to your systems, or an attempt to halt, or at the very least, limit the level of service that your resources provide. Because of these problems, you need an intrusion detection component that can detect threats, and possibly automatically reconfigure your firewall system to block this traffic.

Additional Components

Newer firewalls will typically include additional services besides those that are necessary in a firewall system. These can include Dynamic Host Configuration Protocol (DHCP), application content filtering, and other services.

DHCP is used to assign IP addressing information to networking devices, and is an extension to the BOOTP protocol. A DHCP server can assign an IP address, subnet mask, default gateway address, WINS server address, and DNS server address to a client. Some firewalls, like PIX, support this ability, which is useful in a home, SOHO, or branch office environment.

Some firewalls also support, or can integrate with, content filtering technologies. This ability allows a firewall to examine the actual data at the application layer and make filtering decisions based on this information. An example of this function is when a firewall can examine e-mail attachments for viruses, and remove them if it finds them. Another example of this function is when a firewall examines web downloads for Java applets and ActiveX scripts and filters them. One of the limitations of content filtering, however, is that the application data must be in clear text; if it is compressed or encrypted, the firewall will not be able to decipher the contents, and will not be able to make a filtering decision.

TIP When you are using VPNs in your network and have a content filtering firewall, I recommend that the termination of the VPN occur before the firewall so that the firewall can decipher the application-layer data inside the packets.

Firewall Management

Even the most well-designed and implemented firewall solution is prone to security weaknesses. There is no such thing as a completely secure network. The weakest link in any security solution is the people who administer and use it. The second weakest link is the configuration of the equipment. Your firewall system must be carefully configured such that it enforces your security policies, yet is not so complex that you are not sure whether or not your solution is solving or creating security problems.

A good example of this happened in the mid-1990s when I was teaching an advanced Cisco router course in Dayton, Ohio. One of the components that I covered during the class was the use of Cisco access-lists, or ACLs, and how to configure them on Cisco routers. ACLs are not simple to understand or configure. A student had a question about the ACL that his company used on their perimeter router and asked me to look at it. The student then proceeded to pull out seven pages worth of ACL commands, all of which comprised a single list applied to one interface—the one connected to the Internet.

Given this situation, unless you happen to have an IQ of 200, there is absolutely no way of knowing for certain whether or not this ACL is accomplishing what it was intended to. To make matters worse, if you absolutely know that it works correctly, and then go in and insert a new command into the middle of the list, testing this *new* configuration is almost impossible.

The goal, therefore, is to make the firewall system as simple as possible to eliminate configuration mistakes that might inadvertently open your system up to security threats. Also, a good firewall solution will not put all of its defenses in one device. As an example, in Figure 1-2, if the router performing all of the firewall components becomes compromised, your entire network is now open to a hacker.

A good firewall solution will instead use a *layered* approach. Figure 1-1 shows a good example of this. With the design shown in Figure 1-1, the perimeter router and the firewall could both be controlling traffic, providing you with two lines of defense. Even if a hacker is lucky enough to get past the perimeter router, he still has to face your firewall component installed behind the router.

CONTROLLING TRAFFIC

As I mentioned earlier in this chapter, a firewall is a device or a group of devices that control the flow of traffic between networks. This traffic doesn't necessarily have to be associated with the Internet, but can be between divisions or departments within the same company, or between two companies that do a lot of business together.

In very large companies, it is very common to see a firewall being used to protect sensitive areas from internal users. As an example, a company might use a firewall to protect the devices that contain its research and development efforts, its accounting system, or a financial database. In this example, firewalls can be used to complement other methods of security.

This section describes the OSI Reference Model and how firewalls interact with the OSI Model when they perform their traffic control functions.

OSI Reference Model

The OSI Reference Model is a conceptual model developed by the International Standards Organization (ISO). The OSI Reference Model is used to describe the basic process of how data is transformed from a user entering information at a keyboard to how it is represented in a physical form on a piece of wire that connects networking devices together. There are seven layers in the OSI Reference model: application, presentation, session, transport, network, data link, and physical. Figure 1-3 portrays the layers of the OSI Reference Model.

The application, presentation, and session layers are typically integrated into the application itself. The transport, network, data link, and physical layers affect the transmission of traffic between networking devices. Here is a brief list of what each layer in the OSI Reference Model is responsible for:

- **Application:** Provides the command-line or graphical interface that a person uses to enter or retrieve data
- **Presentation:** Defines how information is presented to the user
- **Session:** Establishes, monitors, and tears down connections between networking devices
- **Transport:** Provides for a reliable or unreliable transfer of data between networking devices
- **Network:** Provides a logical network topology by using logical addresses, like IP or IPX
- **Data Link:** Provides for hardware addressing for networking devices on a segment as well as how networking devices communicate on a segment
- **Physical:** Handles all physical characteristics of a network connection

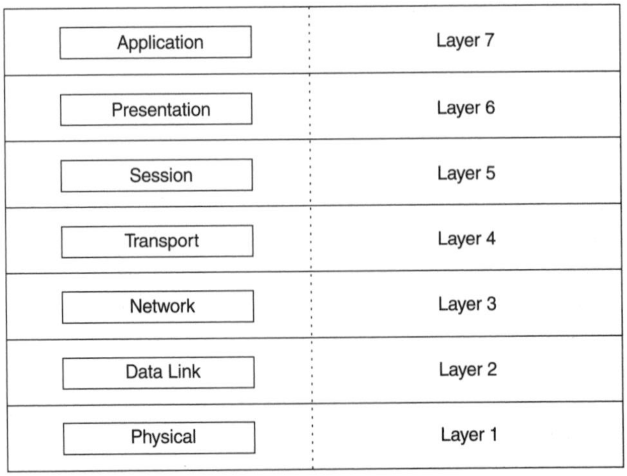

Application	Layer 7
Presentation	Layer 6
Session	Layer 5
Transport	Layer 4
Network	Layer 3
Data Link	Layer 2
Physical	Layer 1

Figure 1-3.   The OSI Reference Model describes the transformation of data.

Firewall Layers

There are many types of firewalls available in the commercial market. Probably one of the best ways of understanding these different types of firewalls is to see how they interact with the OSI Reference Model. Some firewalls work at layer 2, some work at layer 4, and some even work at layer 7. How a firewall interacts with the various layers of the OSI Reference Model reveals a lot about its behavior. For instance, if a firewall is capable of performing user authentication, it will need to interact with layer 7. However, if a firewall interacts with layers 3 or 4, it typically will not deal with specific users, but with devices and the protocols that are used between these devices.

TYPES OF FIREWALLS

As I mentioned in the last section, there are many types of firewalls, each with their own set of unique functions and abilities. The follow sections discuss some of the more common implementations of firewalls, including packet filtering firewalls, stateful firewalls, application gateways or proxy firewalls, hybrid firewalls, address translation firewalls, and host-based and personal firewalls.

PACKET FILTERING FIREWALLS

The most general and prolific form of firewall is packet filtering firewall. This type of firewall is basically a *router* that can perform filtering on packets. Because of its function, packet filtering firewalls typically perform filtering at the network layer (layer 3) of the OSI Reference model, and sometimes the transport layer (layer 4). Figure 1-4 displays the layers at which the packet filtering firewall functions. A good example of a packet filtering firewall is a Cisco router using access control lists (ACLs).

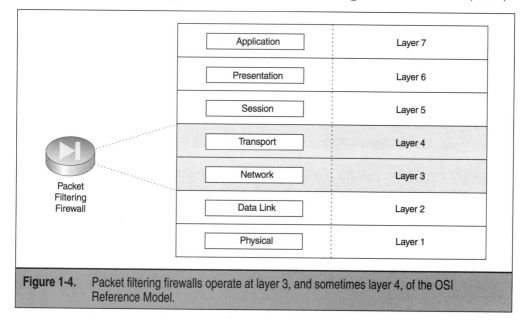

Figure 1-4.   Packet filtering firewalls operate at layer 3, and sometimes layer 4, of the OSI Reference Model.

Functions of a Packet Filtering Firewall

Because a packet filtering firewall works at the network layer, it can filter on the following information inside a packet:

- Source IP address
- Destination IP address
- IP Protocol type, like ICMP, TCP, UDP, and others
- Protocol specific information, like the type of ICMP message (echo, echo reply, destination unreachable, and so on and so forth), which allows them to deal with certain types of DoS attacks

Many packet filtering firewalls can also examine layer 4 information and filter on connection mechanics. This includes information like port numbers of applications for TCP and UDP. Some examples of port numbers are 23 for telnet, 25 for e-mail, and 80 for web traffic.

A packet filtering firewall uses a list to group its policies together for filtering of packets. Typically these lists are then applied to an interface on the firewall, which includes the direction for filtering. For example, a list might be applied on the first Ethernet interface on a packet filtering firewall in the inbound direction (as traffic comes into the firewall).

Advantages of Packet Filtering Firewalls

Packet filtering firewalls have two main advantages when compared to other firewall types:

- Their packet filtering is very quick
- Their filtering policy definitions are very flexible

Because packet filtering firewalls typically only look at layer 3 of the OSI Reference Model, they can perform their functions very quickly. In addition, defining policies is simple, yet flexible, because the types of information that the packet filtering firewall examines are limited: IP addressing, protocols, and protocol information.

Filtering Process

The basic process of filtering of a packet filtering firewall is a straightforward process, as is shown in Figure 1-5.

The first step that the packet filtering firewall performs is to determine if it has a filter applied in the appropriate direction on the firewall's interface. As an example, if the packet is entering the interface, is there an inbound filter applied to the interface? Or, if the packet is leaving the interface, is there an outbound filter applied to the interface? If there isn't an appropriate filter applied, then the firewall will typically allow the packet.

When there is an applied policy on the interface the second step that the packet filtering firewall performs is to compare the packet contents with the filtering rules. Depending on the firewall, the filtering process might look for the first match, the most

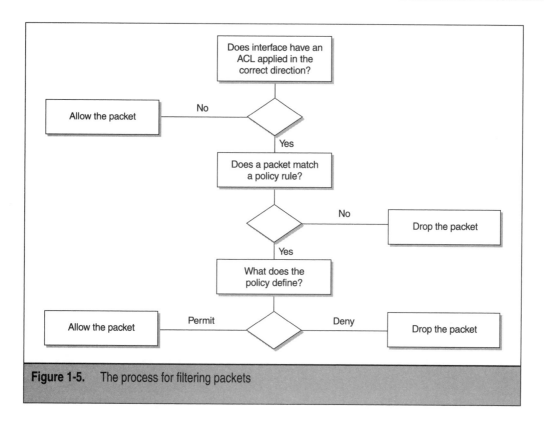

Figure 1-5.   The process for filtering packets

restrictive match, or any match—this is all dependent on the vendor's implementation. For example, with Cisco routers, ACLs are processed top-down, and the router looks for the first match in the list.

If there is no match, the packet filtering firewall will typically drop the packet; but this is dependent on the vendor's implementation. In the case of Cisco routers, if there is no match on any of the entries in the policy list, the router will drop the packet. Cisco calls this process *implicit deny* because there is not a physical entry in the policy list that has this as a process.

If the packet filtering firewall finds a match in the policy list, it will then execute the policy defined in the list entry: either permit or deny the packet. When denying a packet, a firewall has two options: it can drop the packet silently, or notify the source that the packet has been dropped.

Location of a Packet Filtering Firewall

With these advantages, a packet filtering firewall is most often used at the perimeter of a network: on a perimeter, or boundary, router. In this deployment, the perimeter router can prevent some types of network threats and attacks and drop unwanted or undesirable traffic, and let another type of firewall inside the network handle more advanced filtering functions. Figure 1-6 shows an example of the deployment of a packet filtering firewall.

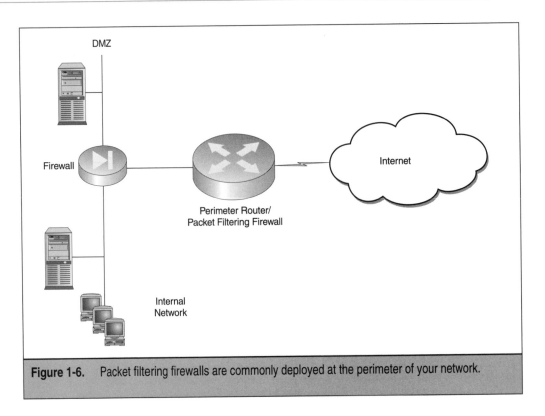

Figure 1-6.   Packet filtering firewalls are commonly deployed at the perimeter of your network.

Disadvantages of Packet Filtering Firewalls

Because they only examine layer 3 packets and layer 4 segments, packet filtering firewalls have limitations and disadvantages:

- **Cannot prevent application layer threats and attacks**   Packet filtering firewalls do not examine application layer information to perform their filtering. Thus they are open to attacks that might involve certain types of commands in an application, like those used by FTP, SMTP, and other applications. Likewise, they are susceptible to application layer attacks, like e-mail viruses and bombs, worms, Trojan horses, and Java applets and ActiveX scripts, to name a few.

- **No user authentication**   Because a packet filtering firewall doesn't perform at the application layer, it typically doesn't offer user authentication. User authentication allows a firewall to prompt a user for an account name and password before allowing a connection. A packet filtering firewall can only filter on the source IP address of a networking device—not the actual user using the networking device.

- **Limited logging abilities**   Because this type of firewall only examines source and destination IP addresses, protocol type, protocol information, and sometimes transport layer information, you are limited in what you can capture in your logs.

- **Vulnerable to certain TCP/IP protocol weaknesses** Just because packet filtering firewalls filter information at layers 3 and 4, this does not mean that they are impervious to attacks at these layers. Some layer 3 and layer 4 protocols are susceptible to certain kinds of attacks. As an example, layer 3 is susceptible to IP spoofing attacks, where the hacker changes his source IP address to an address that is allowed by the firewall, thus defeating the firewall's filtering policies. Or, as another example, TCP uses a three-way handshake to set up a connection: a hacker can take advantage of this and create a DoS attack by flooding your network with TCP SYNs (with no intention of completing the connection setup).

- **Can be complex to configure** Packet filtering firewalls are also not very user-friendly in their configuration. Packet filtering rules can become very complicated, based on a combination of source and destination addresses (or range of addresses), protocols, protocol information, and port numbers that you specify for your filtering rules. A misconfiguration in a single rule entry could easily expose your network to a wide range of effects.

 SECURITY ALERT! You should have a thorough understanding of how IP protocols function and IP applications communicate before implementing your filtering rules.

Because of these limitations, packet filtering firewalls are used as just one of many components in a firewall system design. Likewise, for certain environments like SOHO, home use, and firewall appliances, packet filtering firewalls provide a low-cost solution with some measure of protection against security threats and attacks.

STATEFUL FIREWALLS

Many people are confused by the differences between a stateful firewall and a packet filtering firewall because of their similarities. A stateful firewall is very similar to a packet filtering firewall in that stateful firewalls typically filter packets at layers 3 and 4 of the OSI Reference Model. However, one major difference between a packet filtering firewall and a stateful firewall is that a stateful firewall adds *awareness* about the connections occurring at layer 4, the transport layer of the OSI Reference Model.

Functions of a Stateful Firewall

A stateful firewall is different from a packet filtering firewall because a stateful firewall will maintain information about the connections that traverse through it, while a packet filtering firewall does not. As an example, a packet filtering firewall allows or denies packets based on its filtering rules—it doesn't look to see if these packets are part of a process that is setting up, maintaining, or tearing down a connection.

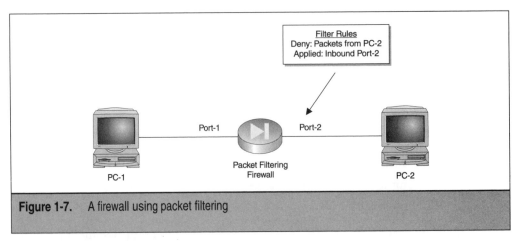

Figure 1-7. A firewall using packet filtering

Packet Filtering Firewall Example

Let's look at an example that will illustrate the differences between these two types of firewalls. Figure 1-7 shows a packet filtering firewall that has a defined rule set that specifies the following:

- Drop traffic if the source is PC-2
- Apply this rule to traffic as it enters Port-2 of the firewall

Assume that PC-2 tries to send traffic to PC-1, as is shown in Figure 1-8.

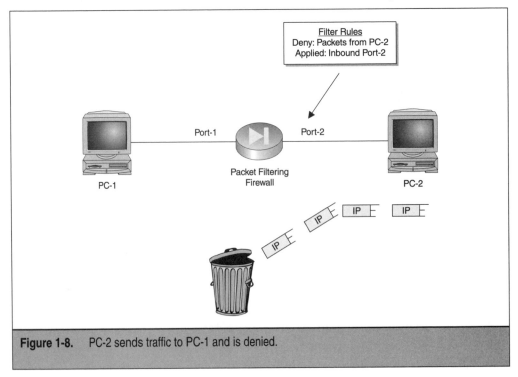

Figure 1-8. PC-2 sends traffic to PC-1 and is denied.

When this traffic reaches the firewall, the traffic is dropped (thrown away into the rhetorical data trashcan) because the rule set of the firewall states that for inbound traffic on Port-2, if the source is PC-2, then the traffic is dropped.

Now look at this from PC-1's perspective: PC-1 wants some data from PC-2. PC-1 sends his request to PC-2, who responds back with the requested data. As shown in Figure 1-9, when the packet firewall sees this traffic, it examines its rule set and determines that because the *source* of the traffic is PC-2, then it will drop the traffic.

The problem with both of these examples is that the policy should be the following: drop traffic if it originates from PC-2, but allow traffic from PC-2 if it is in *response* to another device's request. Unfortunately, packet filtering firewalls cannot perform this function because they do not look at the actual nature of the connection.

Stateful Firewall Example

Let's use the same example that was shown in Figure 1-9, where a user on PC-1 wants to get data on PC-2. With a stateful firewall, if the connection is allowed through the firewall, the firewall will add a temporary connection entry that will allow return traffic to the source. In Figure 1-10, you can see that PC-1 sends its request to PC-2.

The stateful firewall sees the connection request, realizes that there is no filtering rule that prohibits traffic from PC-1 to PC-2, and adds a temporary filtering policy to its policy applied to Port-2. This entry states that if traffic is returning from PC-2 to PC-1

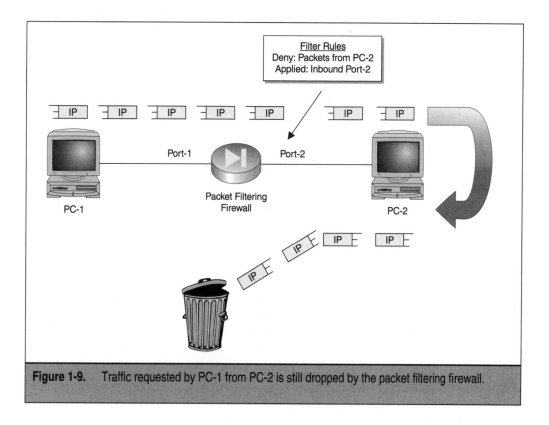

Figure 1-9.   Traffic requested by PC-1 from PC-2 is still dropped by the packet filtering firewall.

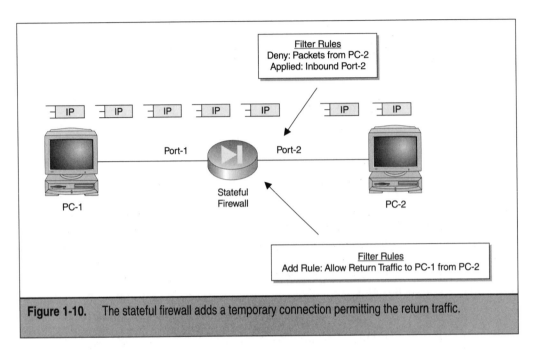

Figure 1-10. The stateful firewall adds a temporary connection permitting the return traffic.

on this same connection (same TCP or UDP port numbers), the connection will be allowed. When PC-2 receives the request and responds with the data back to PC-1, the stateful firewall examines the packets and compares them to its filtering table, as is shown in Figure 1-11.

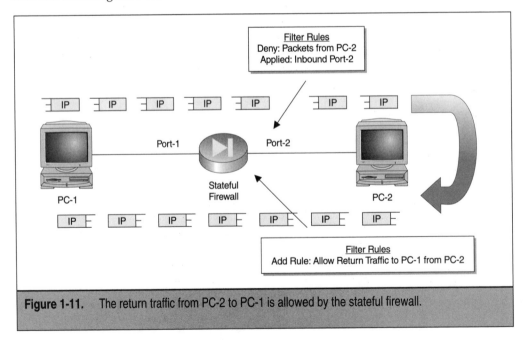

Figure 1-11. The return traffic from PC-2 to PC-1 is allowed by the stateful firewall.

As you can see in Figure 1-11, there is a temporary entry in the stateful firewall's filtering table that was created by the initial connection that states that returning traffic for this connection, and this connection only, will be allowed; however, any other traffic will be dropped. In this example, PC-1 is successfully able to receive its requested data.

So, if PC-1 is allowed to communicate with PC-2 at this point, can PC-2 set up a connection and retrieve data from PC-1? If PC-2 tries to establish a *new* connection, where the TCP/UDP port numbers are different, or the destination IP address is different, the connection request will be dropped by the stateful firewall; it will only allow traffic for the existing connection with the original IP addresses and the original TCP/UDP port numbers—any deviation by PC-2 will cause the stateful firewall to drop the packets, as illustrated in Figure 1-9.

Connection State Table

Let's detail this example a little bit further. In the example shown in Figure 1-10, assume that PC-1's IP address is 192.168.1.1 and PC-2's IP address is 192.168.2.1 and that PC-1 is attempting a telnet connection, which uses a destination port number of 23. When PC-1 telnets to PC-2, it chooses a source port number for the connection greater than 1,023 that is not currently being used on PC-1, and uses a destination port number of 23 to signify a telnet connection. When this telnet packet reaches the firewall, it records this information in a *connection state* table. The table looks like that shown in Table 1-1.

The stateful firewall will then use this information for returning traffic: if the returning traffic from PC-2 has a source IP address of 192.168.2.1 with a source port of 23 and a destination address of 192.168.1.1 with a destination port of 1,024, then the firewall will permit the traffic because of the original entry in the state table.

The stateful firewall will remove the entry from the state table once the connection has finished or after a connection is idle for a maximum period of time. The stateful firewall can usually determine that a connection has terminated by examining the packets flowing between the two devices. As an example, with TCP, there is a defined method for how the devices will terminate the connection—special TCP segments are sent indicating the teardown of the connection (FIN). If the firewall sees these segments, it knows that the connection is no longer in use and removes the entry from the state table. In this instance, PC-2 could try to trick its way past the firewall by using the old information, but because there is no temporary entry in the connection state table, the stateful firewall would drop the packets from PC-2.

Source IP Address	Source Port Number	Destination IP Address	Destination Port Number	IP Protocol
192.168.1.1	1024	192.168.2.1	23	TCP

Table 1-1.   A Connection State Table

Packet Filtering Firewall Solution

With a packet firewall, you could get around this problem by allowing certain port numbers through the firewall. For instance, with most TCP/UDP connections, when a source chooses a source port number, the number is greater than 1,023 and the destination port number is a well-known number that is typically less than 1,023. Therefore, to allow this traffic to flow from PC-1 to PC-2 and then back to PC-1, you could set up a filter on the packet filtering firewall to allow traffic from PC-2 if the destination port number is greater than 1,023 (responding back to PC-1's port) and the source port number is less than 1,023.

 SECURITY ALERT!   The problem with this approach, however, is that you are creating a very large security hole because you don't really know if the traffic coming from PC-2 is a response from PC-2 or a new connection, possibly even a DoS attack with high port numbers assigned for the destination port number in the TCP/UDP segments.

Advantages of a Stateful Firewall

As you have seen from the last few sections, a stateful firewall is more secure than a packet filtering firewall because a stateful firewall maintains information about the state of connections and allows the responses to "permitted" sources to return from the destination back to the source. In this sense, stateful firewalls are said to be *aware* of layer 4 information. You could call a stateful firewall a *super* packet filtering firewall because of this enhanced feature of being aware of connections. Also, unlike packet filtering firewalls, a stateful firewall does not have to explicitly permit all high-numbered ports to allow this process to occur, thus providing a much more secure solution.

Disadvantages of a Stateful Firewall

Stateful firewalls do have a downside to them, just like any security solution. Stateful firewalls must process and maintain more information. Imagine if you had a very large network with 20,000 users, and at any given point in time, you had a total of 5,000 connections active out to the Internet. A stateful firewall would have to add and maintain these connections in its state table, which requires a lot of processing and additional memory compared to a packet filtering firewall, which might have a small list of policy filtering commands. Because of the added processing and memory requirements, stateful firewalls cost more than packet filtering firewalls.

APPLICATION GATEWAYS (PROXY FIREWALLS)

Application gateway firewalls, often referred to as proxy firewalls, combine the filtering function of packet filtering firewalls with layer 7 access control. Figure 1-12 displays the layers at which the application gateway functions:

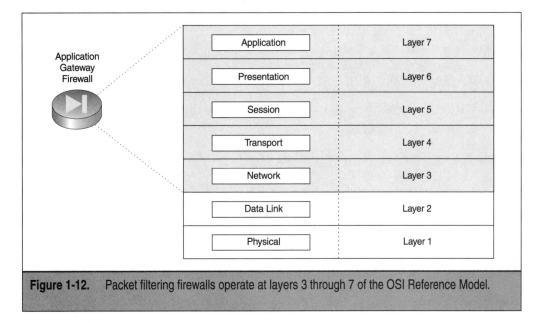

Figure 1-12. Packet filtering firewalls operate at layers 3 through 7 of the OSI Reference Model.

With an application gateway firewall, a user must be authenticated for each session before the firewall will permit access to the service for the user. Many application gateway firewalls are used to provide user authentication for specific types of applications, and other application gateway firewalls can provide authentication for many types of applications. Application gateways that provide user authentication for specific applications are often referred to as *dedicated proxy* firewalls, or *proxy* firewalls for short. Here are some examples of application gateways:

- E-mail proxy
- Web proxy
- FTP proxy
- Telnet proxy
- DNS proxy
- Finger proxy
- LDAP proxy
- Usenet News proxy

Authentication Methods

When you are using an application gateway, a user establishes a connection to the gateway firewall, such as an FTP connection, and then the application gateway firewall authenticates the user's access. This authentication process occurs in software at layer 7 of the OSI Reference Model and can be in the form of any of the following authentication mechanisms:

- User account name and password
- Source address authentication
- Hardware/software-based token card authentication
- Biometric authentication

Basically, any method of authentication used to access a network resource can be used by an application gateway to perform its own authentication on the user.

One weakness of packet filtering and stateful firewalls is that because they only work at the network/transport layer, their authentication can only be based on the source and destination addresses of the connection as well as the connection type—they can't look at the person who is actually requesting a connection. By only examining the source or destination address, a packet filtering or stateful firewall becomes susceptible to spoofing or masquerading attacks. An application gateway doesn't necessarily look at just the source or destination device; it also looks at information about a user requesting the application access, making a connection application gateway less susceptible to spoofing attacks. In a simple example, two users could use the same machine to request access to an application. Based on the user authentication information, one might be permitted while the other could be denied.

The following sections give a brief overview of the authentication methods that are commonly used by application gateways.

User Account Name and Password Authentication

With a user account name and password method, the user is prompted for a username and a corresponding password. This information is then compared to the application gateway's internal username database or an external database, like NetWare's NDS directory structure, an Oracle database, or a security server's database.

Source Address Authentication

In source address authentication, the application gateway compares the source address to a list of permitted source addresses. The application gateway might have multiple lists—one for each type of application that you wish to authenticate.

Token Card Authentication

With token card authentication, the user uses a special card that creates a one-time key that is synchronized with a token card server. The user enters the key value shown on the card (which is valid for only a short period of time) and the application gateway forwards this key to the token card server for validation.

Biometric Authentication

With biometric authentication, some type of physical information from the user is used, like a fingerprint, an eye retinal scan, the sound of the user's voice, or some other mechanism that is shown to be unique to each person. The application gateway takes this information from the user and forwards it to a biometric server for validation.

Types of Application Gateway Firewalls

Application gateway firewalls fall into one of two categories:

- Connection
- Cut-Through

The next two sections will cover these two types of application gateway firewalls, including how they function, their advantages, and their disadvantages.

Connection Gateway Firewalls

A connection application gateway has a user open up an application connection to the application gateway firewall. The application gateway firewall then authenticates the user, where the firewall will not only verify the identity of the user, but also whether or not the user is allowed to access this application at the requested destination, as is shown in Figure 1-13.

If the user is permitted, the connection application gateway will open up a new connection to the destination, acting as a go-between, or a proxy, between the user's initial connection and the connection that the application gateway built to the destination. In this example, there are actually two connections, and the gateway is responsible for handling the transfer of traffic between the two distinct connections.

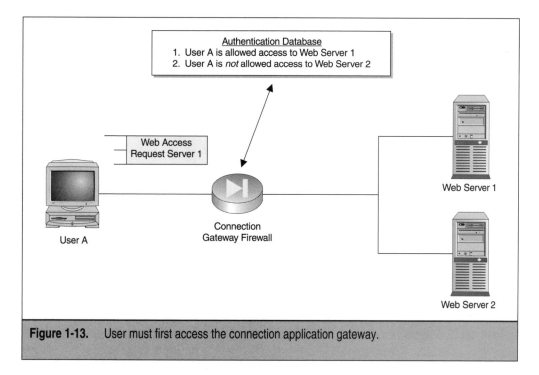

Figure 1-13. User must first access the connection application gateway.

If the user is denied, the connection between the user and the application gateway is dropped.

Advantages of connection gateway firewalls include detailed logging capabilities and filtering of application data. Because a connection gateway is always processing information at layer 7 of the OSI Reference Model, it has a much better ability to log all data for a transaction when compared to a packet filtering or stateful firewall, since these devices only process information at layer 3, or possibly layer 4: Every command and keystroke typed in by a user is seen by the connection gateway.

Also, unlike firewalls that only work at layer 3 or 4, because a connection gateway firewall sees all application layer data passing back and forth between the user and the application process, the firewall can perform filtering of actual data content. This filtering could include executing certain commands or access to certain resources. For example, a user accessing a web service can be restricted to accessing only certain web pages by the filtering rules on the application gateway. Or, for web downloads, some users might be permitted to access Java applets and ActiveX scripts, and others might be denied this function. As another example, users accessing an FTP server might be restricted in what directory structures they can access. Because the connection gateway sees all application layer traffic that passes back and forth between the source and destination, you can be very creative in your filtering policies.

Figure 1-14 shows an example of a connection gateway firewall that is used for FTP access.

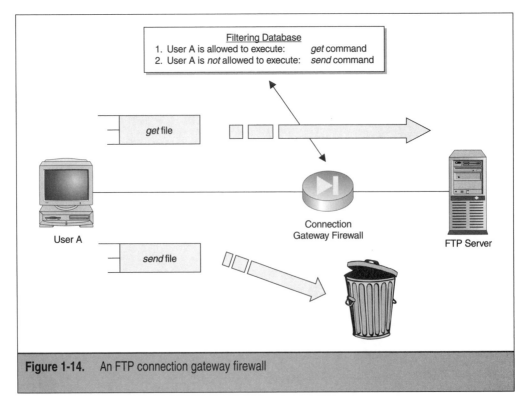

Figure 1-14. An FTP connection gateway firewall

In this example, if User A performs a `get` command to retrieve a file from the FTP server, he is permitted to execute the command by the connection gateway firewall. However, if the user attempts to put a file on the FTP server with the `send` command, the connection gateway firewall will intercept this request and drop it.

Given all of the advantages of connection gateway firewalls, they do have some big disadvantages:

- **They are very slow in processing traffic:** Because connection application gateways might handle all seven layers of the OSI Reference Model of the traffic for the two connections, as well as bridge the traffic between the two connections, they tend to be very slow and have serious scalability problems—the more users who use the application gateway, the slower that their connections become.

- **They are typically limited to a specific application or a small set of applications:** Most of the connection application gateways that vendors develop also happen to be application specific: they will typically work with a single application, like web services, telnet, or FTP. Therefore, if you require this type of security for telnet and web traffic, for example, you will typically need to purchase two different application gateways: one for telnet, and one for web connections. Some connection application gateway products support more than one application, but even then, the number of applications is limited to a small number, like two or three.

- **They sometimes require special software to be loaded on clients:** Another problem with many connection application gateway products is that they either require you to install and configure special application client software on your user's devices, or, at the very least, require you to reconfigure your users' existing applications.

Cut-Through Gateway Firewalls

With a cut-through gateway firewall, the first process is very similar to that of a connection gateway firewall: the user first authenticates to the application gateway. However, if the user is successful, the gateway firewall performs either one of these mechanisms in order to complete the connection:

- Allow the user to complete the connection by himself
- The gateway will build the second half of the connection and bind it to the first half

Unlike a connection gateway firewall that will always process user traffic at the application layer (because it acts as a bridge between the two connections), with either of these two methods, there is a single connection that the cut-through gateway can then process at layer 3 or 4 of the gateway firewall. Figure 1-15 shows an example of this.

Cut-through gateway firewalls offer some advantages over connection gateway firewalls. One of their main advantages over connection gateway firewalls is that even

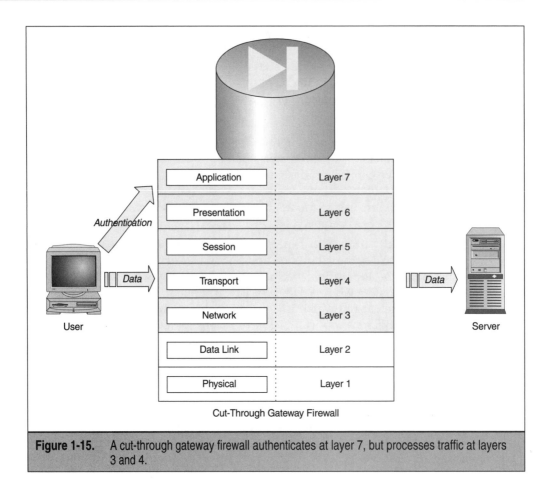

Cut-Through Gateway Firewall

Figure 1-15. A cut-through gateway firewall authenticates at layer 7, but processes traffic at layers 3 and 4.

though the authentication process happens at layer 7, all subsequent traffic between the user and the service is processed at layers 3 and 4, providing a huge boost in throughput.

Plus, because only the authentication piece needs to be handled by the cut-through gateway firewall, it can typically handle the authentication for many types of applications, and is not normally limited like a connection gateway firewall. Also, because many applications support common access methods, like a command-line interface or a GUI interface, the cut-through gateway firewall can use an authentication method that usually will not require you to modify any of the user's applications. As an example, Cisco's PIX firewall supports a cut-through gateway function for telnet, FTP, and HTTP connections, and for all of these, no modification is necessary to the user's applications.

However, given these advantages, a cut-through gateway firewall does have its down sides. Where a cut-through gateway firewall gains in throughput, it loses filtering functionality. Because the cut-through firewall only deals with the application layer during the authentication phase, it typically will not be able to filter application layer information—only information at layers 3 and 4 of the OSI Reference Model. And because the cut-through gateway is only dealing with layer 4 and below, it cannot capture the same kinds of detailed information that a connection gateway firewall can in its logging function.

Address Translation Firewalls

Most people in the networking business would not consider address translation a "firewall" solution. Address translation, however, was originally developed to solve two main problems:

- Handling a shortage of IP addresses
- Hiding network addressing schemes

People most commonly think of address translation as a solution to solve the first of these two problems: shortage of IP addresses. As you will see in the following sections, however, an address translation firewall can be used to improve the security of your network.

Address Depletion

During the huge growth of the Internet in the early 1990s, a shortage of IP addresses was foreseen at an early stage and plans were made to deal with this problem. The long-term solution to this problem was a revamped TCP/IP protocol stack, called IPv6, which was to replace the current implementation of TCP/IP, IPv4. Current IP addresses are 32 bits in length, but the new IPv6 implementation would be 128 bits long, creating hundreds of millions of additional addresses.

RFC 1918

Even though IPv6 has been standardized, not many companies implement it, including ISPs. The main reason that this standard hasn't been embraced is because of the success of the short-term solution that was developed to solve the address shortage problem: address translation. RFC 1918, by the Internet Engineering Task Force (IETF), is a document that was created to help deal with this problem.

In IP communications, every device needs an IP address, even for communications on the same network segment. To prevent the current address space from becoming depleted, RFC 1918 set aside a range of reserved addresses, which are shown in Table 1-2.

Address Class	Range of Addresses
A	10.0.0.0–10.255.255.255
B	172.16.0.0–172.31.255.255
C	192.168.0.0–192.168.255.255

Table 1-2.   RFC 1918 Reserved Addresses

With the number of addresses listed in Table 1-2, any company's addressing needs can be easily met. The A class address of 10.0.0.0 alone has over 17 million IP addresses.

These addresses, however, have one major limitation: they are reserved for use within the confines of a single company. Because of this limitation, they are referred to as *private addresses*. You cannot use them when trying to communicate with devices outside of your company—they can only be used for communication within your company. If you send packets with private addresses to your ISP, your ISP either may filter them or may not be able to route the private network numbers. In either case, packets with private IP addresses are dropped. Therefore, this presents a connectivity problem. If most of the networking devices in your network are using private addresses, how can you use them for internal communications while still allowing these devices to access resources outside of your network?

RFC 1631

RFC 1631 is an IETF document that solves the problem of internal-only addresses by creating a solution called network address translation (NAT). Address translation allows you to change an IP address in a packet from one address to another. Addresses that are allowed for communications on the Internet are commonly referred to as *public* addresses. For a connection to take place between devices across the Internet, the source and destination addresses need to be from the public address space. Address translation allows you to translate a private address to a public address, or, for that matter, from any address to any other address.

Here are some very common situations where you might need to use address translation:

- The ISP that you are using did not assign you enough public IP addresses for all of your internal machines, forcing you to use a private addressing solution.

- Your current network is using public addresses, but you have changed ISPs and your ISP will not support your old public address space.

- You are merging together two companies, which have a private address space that overlaps (for example both companies are using network address 10.0.0.0).

- You need to assign the same IP address to multiple machines so that users on the Internet see a web server farm as a single logical computer.

Address Translation Types

Address translation comes in a variety of formats, including network address translation (NAT) and port address translation (PAT), as well as dynamic and static address translation. The following sections cover the process of how these work, as well as how you can use them in a firewall solution.

Address Translation Terms

In the next few sections I will be using many terms to describe the various methods that are used to perform address translation. The following list defines some of the common terms used to describe locality and address types for address translation:

- **Inside**   Networks located on the inside of your company that will have their addresses translated
- **Outside**   Networks located outside of your network, with valid public addresses
- **Inside local IP address**   An inside device with an assigned private IP address
- **Inside global IP address**   An inside device with a registered public IP address
- **Outside global IP address**   An outside device with an registered public IP address

Table 1-3 lists some of the common address translation methods. The next two sections discuss the various implementations of NAT and PAT.

Network Address Translation (NAT)

There are two basic implementations of NAT:

- Static
- Dynamic

The following two subsections cover these two implementations.

Static NAT   In static NAT, a manual translation is created in the NAT device that maps a single IP address to a different IP address. Typically static NAT is used to translate addresses in packets as they come from the outside of your network to the inside of your network, where the translation is performed on the destination IP address in the IP packet. A typical example of using static NAT is shown in Figure 1-16.

In this example, Internet users want to access a web server that is internal to your network. You have decided to implement a common addressing scheme, using private addresses on all of your internal devices. This poses problems for Internet users because

Translation Method	Explanation
Simple	One IP address is translated to a different IP address
Extended	One IP address and TCP/UDP port number are mapped to a different IP address and, possibly, port number
Static	A manual address translation is performed between two addresses, and possibly port numbers
Dynamic	An address translation firewall automatically performs address translation between two addresses, and possibly port numbers
Network Address Translation (NAT)	Only IP addresses are translated (not port numbers)
Port Address Translation (PAT)	Many inside IP addresses are translated to a single IP address, where each inside address is given a different port number for uniqueness

Table 1-3.   Common Address Translation Methods

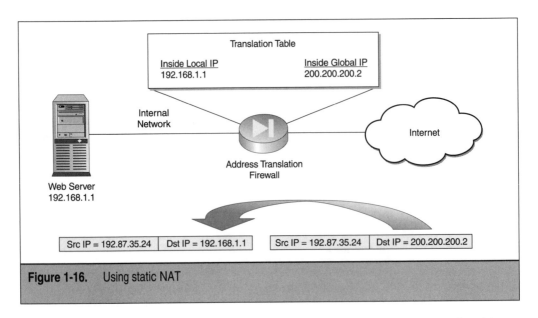

Figure 1-16.   Using static NAT

they can't use a private address in the destination field of an IP packet. To solve this problem, you can use static NAT. To the outside world, you give the appearance that your web server has a public address, when in reality it has a private address assigned to it. To accomplish this feat, your DNS server will advertise the public address as the address to use to reach the web server. The Internet users place this address in the destination field of an IP packet in order to reach your web server. When the packet reaches your network, you have another problem: your web server is actually using a private address—not the public address that the Internet users are trying to access. To solve this second problem, you use an address translation firewall, which translates the destination public IP (global) address to the private (local) address that your web server is using. Likewise, as traffic returns from the web server and is sent back to the user that requested it, the address translation firewall replaces the web server's private source address with the public address in the translation table. One nice function of this process is that the address translation process is transparent to the devices at the endpoint of the connection.

For the address translation firewall to perform the translation, however, you will have to build a static entry in the firewall's translation table. For each service with a private address that outside users need to access inside your network, you need to create a separate translation entry. Therefore, if you have 50 servers that Internet users need to access, you will need to create 50 static translation entries.

Dynamic NAT   Let's take a look at a different example. Normally, when users on the inside of your network attempt to access resources on the outside of your network, you will not use static NAT to translate private source addresses to public source addresses—the problem with static translations is that you must manually configure each one. Instead, you would typically use dynamic address translation to solve this problem.

To use dynamic address translation, you will need to create an address pool on your address translation firewall that contains a list of available public addresses. When a user attempts to access the outside network, and they have a private address in the source address field of their packet, the address translation firewall will automatically choose a public address in the address pool that is not currently being used and assign it to this user. The address translation firewall will then add an entry to its translation table with this user's private address as an inside local IP address and the assigned public address from the pool as the inside global IP address. The translation firewall will also use this translation entry to translate the user's source IP address (private) to the global address listed (public).

When traffic returns from the Internet to the user, the address translation firewall will look at the destination IP address in the returning packet and compare it to its translation table. If it finds the match in the table, it will then perform the translation, replacing the public IP address (global inside) with the private address that is assigned on the users machine (local inside).

Port Address Translation (PAT)

One limitation of NAT, whether static or dynamic, is that it only provides a one-to-one translation. In other words, each device inside your network that wants to access the Internet will have to have either a *unique* static or dynamic public address assigned to it by the address translation firewall. As an example, if you had 10,000 devices inside your network, you would need to also have 10,000 public addresses if all of these devices decided to access the Internet at the same time. If you only had 5,000 public addresses, then you would be limiting your network by only allowing half of your devices to access the Internet at any given point in time—the others wouldn't be able to because of their untranslated private address.

To solve this problem, you can use an address translation firewall that supports *address overloading*. Address overloading is just one of many terms used to describe this solution. Another name is port address translation (PAT), and some RFCs use the term Network address port translation (NAPT).

Sharing the Same IP Address   PAT basically allows many machines to share the *same* IP address. At first, this sounds like it would create pandemonium—imagine 1,000 machines having their local IP addresses changed to the same public address. When all the requests return to your network, there would be mass confusion because there would be a single public IP address, but the firewall wouldn't know which of the 1,000 internal machines the traffic should be returned to. PAT solves this problem by using the source port number of the machine—if two machines are using the same port number, the address translation firewall performing PAT will change one of the port numbers in order to make it unique. When the address translation firewall builds its entry in the translation table, it will contain four items:

- Inside local IP address (private)
- Inside local port number (original port number)
- Inside global IP address (public)
- Inside global port number (new port number)

PAT Example As an example, assume that the two PCs shown in Figure 1-17 execute a telnet connection, where both PCs choose a source port number of 10,000 and both devices are connecting to the same telnet server on the Internet, 201.201.201.1.

Notice that in this example, both PCs have their local IP addresses changed to the same global IP address: 200.200.200.2. Also notice that even though both PCs originally have the same source port number (local), the address translation firewall changes one of them to make the identity of each of these connections unique. In the table you can see that PC-A's source port number remains 10,000 when PC-A's information is translated, but PC-B's source port number is changed to 10,001. The address translation firewall then examines the returning telnet traffic and compares this information to what it has in its translation table. That way, the firewall will be able to successfully forward the correct telnet packets to the correct internal PCs when it reverses its translation process.

Because the port number field in a TCP or UDP header is 16 bits in length, you could theoretically represent 65,536 internal machines with a single public address. In reality, however, this limit is capped to about 4,000 internal devices sharing a single public address.

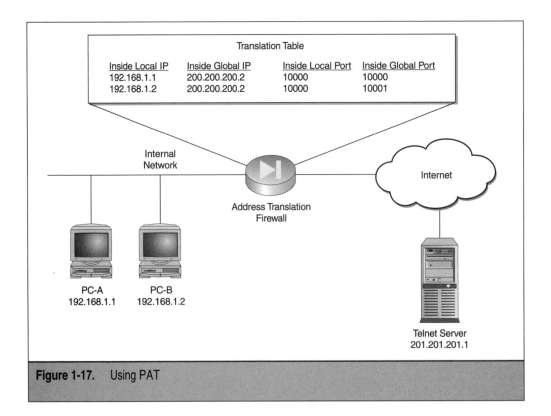

Figure 1-17. Using PAT

Please note that NAT and PAT are not mutually exclusive—in most production environments that implement address translation, both are commonly used:

- PAT is used to allow your inside users access to the Internet
- Static NAT is used to assign public IP addresses to services that Internet users will be accessing

Port Address Redirection   The example in the previous section showed PAT working dynamically—the address translation firewall dynamically chose unique port numbers. There are situations, however, when you need to statically map port numbers. Take the example where your ISP assigns you a single public IP address that you must use for all of your machines, including the Internet servers that outside users need to access. Unfortunately, PAT will not solve this problem.

Imagine that your ISP has assigned you an IP address of 200.200.200.1 and that you need to assign this address to your address translation firewall's interface, which is connected to the ISP. You can still use PAT to allow your internal users to access outside services, but you have a dilemma when outside users try to access an internal web or e-mail server. If an outside user tries to access your e-mail server by sending an e-mail to 200.200.200.1 at port 25, the address translation firewall would see this and assume that this traffic was meant for itself (which it obviously is not).

To rectify this problem and have the address translation firewall forward the e-mail to the real e-mail server in your internal network, you would use a combination of static NAT and static PAT, which is referred to as a single definition—*port address redirection* (PAR). PAR allows you to statically redirect traffic sent to a specific destination IP address, like the address translation firewall in this example, to the internal e-mail server's address. For that matter, if the e-mail server was using port 30 instead of 25, the address translation firewall could translate the port number correctly.

Address Translation Firewalls and Security

Given all of this information concerning address translation, you are probably asking how this relates to security and firewall functions. One advantage of using private IP addresses on your internal machines is that you are logically separating your private network from the public network. For the public network to access your internal resources, the traffic from the public network must pass through an address translation firewall. In this sense, the address translation device is a choke point—it is a central point where you can easily implement your security policies, where you can allow the traffic by translating it, or not allow it by dropping it.

Address translation firewalls also provide access control for your internal users when they try to access the public network—they need to have their addresses translated to public addresses before your ISP will router their traffic. Therefore, you can implement security policies that affect traffic not only in the incoming direction, but also the outgoing direction as well. Implemented correctly, address translation firewalls can give you complete control over your traffic flow.

Advantages of Address Translation

As I mentioned at the beginning of this section, the two main advantages of address translation firewalls are that they give you an almost inexhaustible amount of addresses (over 17 million) that you can use however you see fit inside your internal network and they allow you to protect (or hide) your network infrastructure. Moreover, if you need to move to a different ISP, you will not have to change your internal addresses; you only need to change your configuration on your address translation device to use your new ISP's assigned public addresses. This makes the management of your addressing much simpler.

You also have much tighter control over your security because all traffic entering or leaving your network must pass through the address translation firewall. As an example, if you have a network segment that you do not want outside users to access, you can simply make sure that your address translation firewall does not have an entry for this network in its translation table.

Disadvantages of Address Translation

Every solution has disadvantages, and address translation firewalls are no exception. The three main problems with address translation are:

- Adds a delay to packet streams
- Makes troubleshooting more difficult
- Doesn't work with all applications

Address translation adds a delay to your users' data connections—the address translation process takes additional processing in addition to what is normally performed on a packet, and thus the connection data rate will be slower. These changes include not only translating the source and destination addresses and port numbers, but also the computation of new checksums for the packets or segments. Therefore, if you have large amounts of data that must constantly be translated, you should determine which devices are creating these large data streams and consider assigning these machines' addresses from your scarce public address space.

Another problem with address translation is that when you experience problems with a data connection, it becomes more difficult to track down the real source and destination of a connection. You can even take this one step further and look at this from a security perspective: If it's hard to track the source and destination, it becomes much harder to determine who is creating a security threat. In this sense, address translation provides automatic masquerading.

Probably one of the most difficult issues to deal within address translation is that not all applications will work, or work correctly, when address translation is performed on their connections. For example, some applications embed IP addresses and port numbers in the application layer data, which many address translation firewalls do not examine and thus do not translate. Therefore, if a device uses this information to try to access a resource, the device would be stopped at the address translation firewall because the firewall wouldn't have the correct information in its translation table. NetBIOS is an example of a protocol that is notorious for doing this in applications that use it. Multimedia applications are another example where address translation, and more specifically PAT, can cause the application to stop working. Therefore, you might have to disable NAT or PAT for certain devices based on the applications that they use. You will definitely want to examine which problematic applications your address translation firewall can handle correctly.

HOST-BASED FIREWALLS

A host-based firewall is a firewall solution that uses firewall software installed on a computer system. With a host-based firewall, the firewall software is used to protect not only the contents on the computer, but also the operating system itself. This software can be used to protect both servers as well as users' desktops. When this software is used to protect a user's computer, the solution is commonly referred to as *personal* firewall.

Host-Based Firewall Abilities

Host-based firewalls typically do not have the same capabilities that other firewall solutions have. Instead, they are built to provide protection to a computer and its operating system at a reasonable cost. Host-based firewalls provide access control functions that are used to restrict certain kinds of access to a computer. These access control functions are similar to what a packet filtering or stateful firewall performs, but usually with less filtering and auditing capabilities.

Because they lack some of the advanced security features of more advanced firewalls, host-based firewalls and personal firewalls are therefore used in SOHO environments, by telecommuters, or even by casual Internet users. For these environments that need to access corporate offices, many host-based firewalls have VPN capabilities that allow for protected connections between the user's computer and a remote site.

Advantages of Host-Based Firewalls

One advantage of host-based firewalls is that they can be used in tandem with other firewall systems, including application gateways, address translation firewalls, packet filtering firewalls, and stateful firewalls. You can use host-based firewalls to harden the operating system on a computer to provide additional protection to the applications and data running on the computer. You should never assume that using other firewall types will provide complete protection to the systems sitting behind these firewalls. Instead, you should assume the worst and do your best to protect these systems with additional tools.

In some SOHO environments, a host-based firewall might be the only cost-effective solution because the user might be connecting to the Internet using his own PC with a DSL or cable modem, as is shown in Figure 1-18.

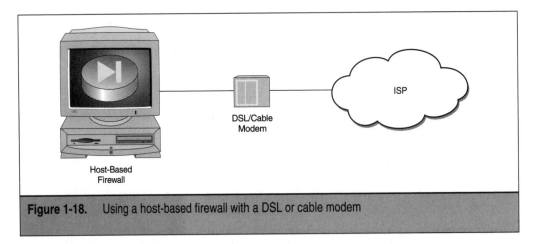

Figure 1-18.   Using a host-based firewall with a DSL or cable modem

In this solution, the user might not be able to afford a separate firewall solution, which could cost hundreds, if not thousands, of dollars. Or a SOHO might be using a server that provides Internet connectivity, and a host-based firewall solution adds little cost to protecting the server itself, as well as the handful of clients behind it.

Disadvantages of Host-Based Firewalls

Because host-based firewalls are implemented in software, they affect the network performance of your computer. Therefore, if your PC receives a lot of network traffic, a host-based firewall might not be a good solution for your environment.

Another disadvantage of host-based firewalls is that you need to administer each host that you load the firewall software on. For example, if you decide to protect your server farm with host-based firewall software, and you have 20 servers in your server farm, you need to administer 20 firewalls, which might become cost-prohibitive as well as creating extra administrative support. Every time you need to change your security policies, you will need to update the configuration on each of these host-based firewalls. In this example, it might be cheaper to buy a single firewall solution, like a stateful firewall, and place your server farm behind this stateful firewall.

Also, maintaining the consistency of security policies with many of your servers, and possibly SOHO and telecommuters who have host-based firewall solutions installed, may become difficult, if not impossible. If SOHO and telecommuters are using the Internet to access the corporate site, and they are responsible for maintaining their host-based systems, you might be creating a security weakness that a hacker can exploit to gain access to these systems, and thus use this as a stepping-stone on his way to hacking into computers at your corporate site.

Therefore, when you are considering solutions for a host-based firewall system, you should seriously consider what management capabilities are included in the system, including centralization of management. Likewise, you should also examine the firewall's ease-of-configuration and management abilities—if SOHO environments will be responsible for configuring and managing the firewall, it will need to be easy to install and maintain, which means that it might have to sacrifice security features for ease-of-use.

Hybrid Firewalls

For the last few years, because of the increased need for security and the demand in the marketplace to create more market share by security vendors, many firewall solutions have appeared that contain a mixed set of firewall abilities, and it is therefore difficult to classify these firewall products into a single category. Actually, most firewall products that you see in the marketplace today have a mixture of abilities.

As an example, Cisco introduced their first firewall solution in the early 1990s by including access control functions in their router product line. This new feature was called access-lists, or ACLs for short, and allowed the router to perform packet filtering functions at layers 3 and 4. This feature was slowly enhanced until, about a few years ago, Cisco developed a version of their IOS code that included stateful firewall features. To make their router line more robust, this IOS code also includes a limited ability to detect intrusions as well as perform a cut-through proxy for FTP, telnet, and HTTP connections, NAT and PAT functions, and VPN capabilities. Figure 1-2 shows an example of a hybrid firewall.

In today's choice of firewall solutions, you should determine what features will meet your company's needs and then find a firewall product that will meet, or exceed, these requirements.

FIREWALL DESIGN

Designing a firewall system is not an easy task. Not only does its success depend on the strength of your security policy, but it also depends on the security systems that you decide to use as well as the design that you create for these systems. One important item that will definitely impact the design of your security solution is the current design of your network. A poorly designed network can make your task of designing a security solution an impossibility. Therefore, when you are designing a network, one component of this design should include the firewall system that will be used to protect it.

The design will typically use a segmentation approach, where you will break your network into components that can be easily monitored and defended. You should almost think of this as a chess game—you should always be anticipating your opponent's next move and stay one step ahead of him. In the case of network security, you should always keep abreast of the latest security news in networking and take a proactive approach in dealing with security issues and problems.

Basic Guidelines

When you are designing a network with a firewall system, you should remember that there is no single solution that will solve every problem—each situation will have its own set of problems. However, there are four basic guidelines that you should follow:

- Use the onion defense
- Users are threats too
- Use a product for what it is intended for
- Use the KISS principle

The Onion Defense

The onion defense in network design involves a security solution that has multiple layers of protection included in it. As a simple example, look at what many kings and queens did when they were protecting their families and subjects. Their first line of defense usually included a moat that surrounded a high stone wall, which was their second line of defense. Manning the wall would be archers, spearmen, knights, and foot soldiers. And inside this wall would be a castle made of stone, which would again be protected by many of the king's army.

When you are creating a security solution, you should use the onion defense. Having only one layer in your defense can leave you defenseless if this single security obstacle is breached. As an example, if the king only protected his people with a moat, and the invaders where somehow able to cross the moat, it would be fairly easy for the invaders to take over the king. Even if the moat was very deep and very wide, this single security obstacle, if breached, could be devastating.

Take this example to heart when designing your security solution. This is not to say that you must build layer after layer after layer into your security solution, but you should definitely have more than one layer in your defense system. As an example, you might have Internet traffic examined by an IDS sensor, filtered by a perimeter router, and passed through a firewall before it can access any of your company's internal resources.

Users Are Threats Too

You also need to remember that most security threats, especially the ones that can be the most damaging, will occur from *within* your network. It is impossible to create a completely secure solution, and it can become very costly to try to protect every asset that your company has. However, you should take measures that will allow your company to perform its business, as well as make a profit and keep you in a good job, but lessen the likelihood of your users creating serious security threats.

Even if your internal users do not pose a threat, if a hacker somehow gets past your perimeter defenses and reaches the inside of your network, your company's networking devices and computer data are completely exposed. Therefore, you should take additional security measures for important assets by using secure authentication methods as well as securing your servers with protection like host-based firewalls.

Use a Product for What It Is Intended

When implementing your solution, you need to be careful about your choice of products that you use to secure your network—buy the product that solves your particular security concern and use it for only that purpose.

As an example, Cisco routers with the IOS Firewall Feature set support all of the following security features: packet filtering, stateful filtering, intrusion detection, address translation, VPNs, auditing, and many others. Note that even though Cisco has the best routing products on the market, this does not mean that the Cisco's routers are always the best security solution. As an example, even though they have IDS abilities, there are much, much better products on the market that can detect attacks against your network. Likewise, just because Cisco's routers can perform stateful firewall functions does not make them the best stateful firewall on the market—they happen to perform this process much more slowly than many other stateful firewall products.

Therefore, never try to fit a product into your security solution—design your security solution first, and then find products that will meet the design requirements of this solution.

Use the KISS Principle

The last guideline is probably the one that is not followed most often. There is an acronym in the English language that succinctly describes it: KISS. KISS stands for *keep it simple, stupid*. When you are creating your security solution, do not get fancy, creating tens of layers of defenses, using sophisticated security products. If you make your security solution complex, it becomes very difficult to not only verify its function, but also to configure and maintain it. If it is very complex to set up, you are probably leaving yourself open to making configuration mistakes, which can lead to security holes. Likewise, if it requires a lot of training and a lot of maintenance, it will cost more and is more likely to break down without you noticing.

For example, many companies, when they are considering a stateful firewall product for their network, focus on selection criteria like security features, throughput, and management abilities. These are important items, but sometimes I have recommended a firewall product to a company because their employees have had previous experience with it from other jobs. In this case, the firewall might not be the best-performing solution, and it might not have the most security features, but the network administrators have experience with it and feel comfortable working with it. In this environment, your administrator will be less likely to make mistakes and will be able to use the product to create a solid line of defense.

Segmentation and the DMZ

As I mentioned in the previous section, using the onion defense provides you with a layered approach to your network defenses. One of the most common forms of implementing the onion defense is the use of a DMZ (demilitarized zone). A DMZ is an area in your network that creates a buffer between the public network and your internal network. Typically, services that you want the public network to access are placed within the DMZ. You would commonly find services like your web and FTP servers, a public e-mail server, and a DNS server in a DMZ.

Layered Security

To reduce security threats, each of these areas is assigned a security level, from low to high. As an example, the public network might be assigned a low security level, the DMZ a medium security level, and your internal network a high security level. Your firewall system is then used to enforce your security policies. Most firewall systems use the following *default* rules when it comes to traffic traveling between the different security levels:

- Allow traffic if it travels from a high-security-level segment to a segment with a lower security level

- Deny traffic if it travels from a low-security-level segment to a segment with a higher security level

- Deny traffic if it travels between two segments with the same security level

With these rules, if you want traffic to go between segments where it is denied by default, you must explicitly configure a firewall rule that will permit it.

Figure 1-19 illustrate these traffic flow rules. In this example, traffic is allowed to travel between the following segments by default:

- Internal network to DMZ

- Internal network to Internet

- DMZ to Internet

In other words, the chain of trust is from higher to lower, not lower to higher. For traffic to travel between the Internet and the DMZ, the Internet and the internal network, or the DMZ and the internal network, you need to configure security policies in your firewall system to permit this.

NOTE   When allowing traffic to go from a lower-security-level segment to a higher one, you should be very specific as to the type of traffic that is allowed.

For example, for Internet users to access the web server in the DMZ, your firewall system should only allow the Internet users access to the IP address of the web server and, even more specifically, TCP segments that have port 80 specified. All other traffic

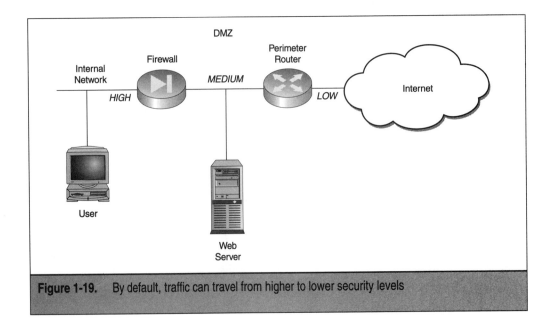

Figure 1-19.   By default, traffic can travel from higher to lower security levels

should be dropped. For instance, if someone from the Internet tries to telnet to the web server, these packets should be dropped by your firewall system.

This design also provides a layered defense. If a hacker is somehow able to compromise a device in the DMZ, your internal networks would still have another layer of security because the firewall's rules would, by default, not allow traffic from the lower-security-level segment to the higher one.

DMZ Implementations

DMZs come in many types of designs. You can have a single DMZ, multiple DMZs, DMZs that separate the public network from your internal network, and DMZs that separate traffic between internal networks. The following sections show some of these implementations.

Public DMZs   Figure 1-19 shows an example of a single public DMZ implementation. In this example, all your public services are placed on the DMZ segment and the DMZ, internal network, and public network are separated by a firewall system. In this case, the firewall system consists of a firewall and a perimeter router.

This is only one example of a DMZ implementation, however. A more common approach to a single public DMZ is shown in Figure 1-20. In this example, a single firewall is used to provide the segmentation, instead of a firewall and perimeter router.

The solution shown in Figure 1-20 can actually be expanded to include multiple public DMZs, based on your security needs. For instance, you might be providing Internet services for other companies by providing application hosting functions. In this situation, each company would have its own public DMZ, as is shown in Figure 1-21. This is a very common practice for many ISPs that offer hosting or application services for companies.

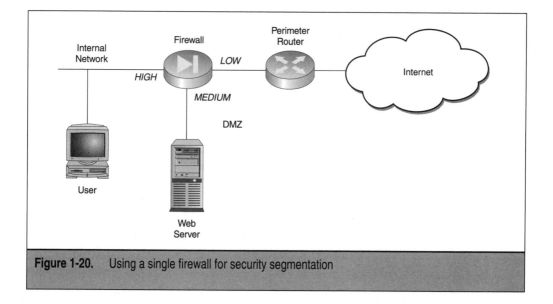

Figure 1-20.   Using a single firewall for security segmentation

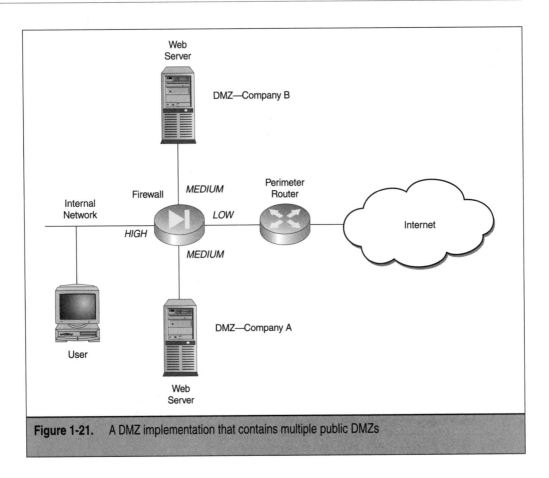

Figure 1-21.   A DMZ implementation that contains multiple public DMZs

Internal DMZs   Most people assume that DMZs are used to provide a buffer zone between a public network and your internal network. However, DMZs can also by used to protect different parts of your internal network from each other. In large companies, this is a common practice, especially between different divisions. This design philosophy allows you to *compartmentalize* your network. Figure 1-22 shows an example of the use of an internal DMZ.

Advantages of internal DMZs include the following:

- Allows you to control traffic between compartments
- A security problem that occurs in one compartment is localized

Each compartment is usually assigned the same security level, which causes the firewall system to only allow traffic between compartments if you explicitly allow it. This gives you absolute control of the traffic that travels between the various compartments. Another advantage of this design is that if one compartment becomes compromised, the rest of the company's network is still protected by the firewall system.

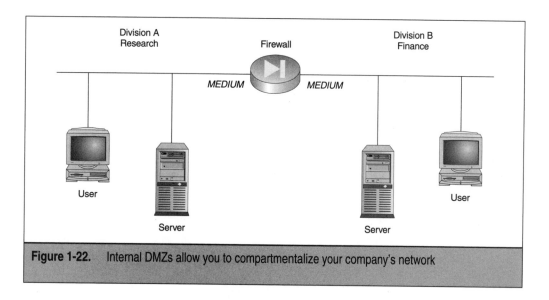

Figure 1-22. Internal DMZs allow you to compartmentalize your company's network

Placement of Firewall Components

When it comes to designing secure networks and the placement of your security products, there is no one template or boiler plate that will work in every company—every situation is different. In this section, I will look at two examples, each of which has advantages and disadvantages with their designs.

Example 1: Basic Firewall Solution

Figure 1-23 shows the first design example. In this example, there is a perimeter router with packet filtering abilities. This router provides you with your first line of defense. It should only allow two types of traffic:

- Resources that your users requested from Internet services
- Traffic from the Internet that is headed to the services in your DMZ

Other than these two items, the perimeter router should drop everything.

On the segment between the perimeter router and the stateful firewall is an IDS sensor, which provides your second line of defense. This sensor examines all traffic and determines if any attacks are being attempted against your network, or even attacks that originate from your network.

The stateful firewall provides your third line of defense. It implements most of your security policies that affect traffic as it travels between the Internet, your DMZ, and your internal network. With your stateful firewall, just like with your perimeter firewall, you should deny everything and then only allow specific types of traffic to specific resources.

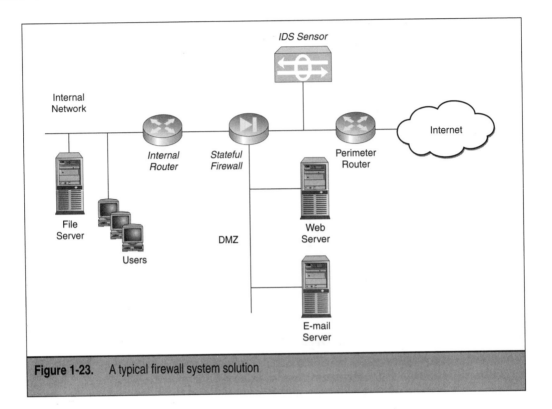

Figure 1-23.   A typical firewall system solution

The fourth line of defense is the internal router, which has packet filtering abilities. This is a good example of an onion defense—you have multiple layers, and if the first layer becomes compromised, you still have multiple layers behind the first, protecting your company's assets.

Example 2: Elaborate Firewall Solution

In this example, I will take the firewall solution shown in Figure 1-23 and improve upon it, as shown in Figure 1-24.

In the design shown in Figure 1-24, there are many more layers involved in the protection of your network. The first difference between the two designs is that the design in Figure 1-24 uses a router firewall for the perimeter router—this is a router with stateful firewall features, providing you additional protection over a normal packet filtering firewall. Likewise, the internal router includes stateful firewall abilities, or can possibly be replaced with a full-fledged stateful firewall.

The servers on the DMZ have been hardened by having host-based firewall software installed on them. This allows you to not just add additional protection for these services, but also gives you more intrusion detection capabilities by giving you additional auditing information about the types of traffic, as well as their traffic patterns, that are trying to access resources on the servers.

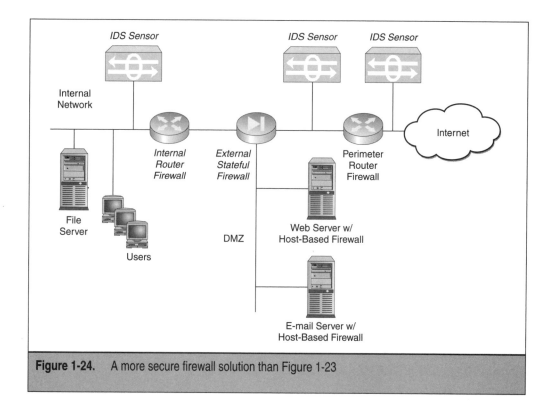

Figure 1-24.   A more secure firewall solution than Figure 1-23

Also notice that there are three IDS sensors—one monitors traffic before it hits your network, another monitors traffic between the perimeter router firewall and the stateful firewall, and a third monitors traffic on the inside of your network. This design allows you to monitor the effectiveness of each of your firewall components and make the necessary adjustments to your security solution. It is important to remember that security is an ever-evolving process. Obviously, the main advantage that this solution has over the one shown in Figure 1-23 is that it is definitely more secure; however, the main disadvantage of this solution is that it costs more to implement and maintain.

FURTHER STUDY

Web Sites

For an introduction to firewalls, read the *Guidelines on Firewalls and Firewall Policy* at http://csrc.nist.gov/publications/nistpubs/800-41/sp800-41.pdf.

CHAPTER 2

PIX Firewall Family

C isco's PIX firewall family is a set of stateful firewall products ranging from the 501, which was developed for Small-Office/Home Office (SOHO) environments, to the 535, which was developed for large enterprise networks or ISP sites. All of these products use the same operating system and management tools, easing your implementation and monitoring tasks. Because all the PIX family firewalls use the same operating system, the major difference between the models is scalability and performance. The low-end 501 can handle up to 50 devices, and the high-end 535 can handle 500,000 connections. The focus of this chapter is to cover some of the important features of the PIX firewall family as well as the firewalls themselves.

PIX FEATURES

The PIX firewall family can best be described as hybrid firewalls. The PIX firewalls offer many features discussed in Chapter 1, as well as many others, including the following:

- Secure, real-time, proprietary operating system—Finesse Operating System (FOS)
- Stateful firewall using the Adaptive Security Algorithm (ASA)
- Sequence Number Randomization (SNR) to secure TCP connections
- Cut-Through Proxy for authenticating telnet, HTTP, and FTP connections
- Default security policies to ensure maximum protection
- Virtual private network (VPN) abilities
- Intrusion detection system (IDS)
- Address translation using NAT and PAT
- Dynamic Host Configuration Protocol (DHCP) in both client and server mode

These are just some of the features of the PIX firewall. The following sections provide an overview of some of these major features of the PIX firewall family. The features that I don't cover in this chapter are covered in later chapters.

Finesse Operating System

The heart of the PIX firewall is the Finesse Operating System (FOS). It implements the actual firewall functions that the PIX hardware performs. In this sense, it is somewhat similar to the IOS of Cisco routers, or what Microsoft Windows 2000 or XP is to PCs. The FOS is a proprietary operating system.

Firewall Applications

Some firewall products run on top of an operating system; these solutions are commonly called *firewall applications*. One disadvantage that firewall applications have compared a proprietary operating system is that the firewall vendor must deal with two software products in creating a firewall: the operating system and the firewall application. This process can often lead to a less secure system. This is especially true when you consider all the security threats that have been directed specifically at Unix and Microsoft operating systems.

An example of a firewall product that uses firewall applications is CheckPoint. This is not to say that CheckPoint's firewall is a worse solution than a firewall product that uses a proprietary operating system. However, there are many more things a firewall vendor like CheckPoint will have to do to ensure that the firewall provides a secure solution.

Here are some of the main advantages of firewall applications:

- Easy to install and maintain
- Runs on a wide variety of PC/server platforms

Proprietary Operating Systems

Proprietary operating systems provide a security advantage over firewall applications—there is only one system, instead of two, that a vendor has to be concerned about in providing a secure firewall solution. Another huge advantage of proprietary operating systems is scalability. Because a proprietary operating system can be customized to a specific hardware platform, this firewall system can provide extremely fast packet filtering abilities.

Off-the-shelf operating systems like Unix and Microsoft Windows are general-purpose operating systems that were developed to perform many tasks, but not all of these tasks are performed at an optimal performance level. Using a general operating system affects the performance of the packet filtering and firewall functions of the firewall application. To provide for scalability, you must load your firewall application on very expensive server platforms.

Using a proprietary operating system in a firewall solution also makes it much more difficult for hackers to penetrate the firewall. Hackers are very familiar with the functions of common operating systems like Unix and Microsoft products, which makes it a little bit easier to attack the firewall application. However, when vendors use a proprietary operating system to implement their firewall solution, a hacker will have little or no knowledge about the functions and processes of the operating system, making it very difficult for the hacker to compromise the firewall solution.

There are some disadvantages to using a proprietary operating system. First, because the operating system is proprietary, your security personnel will have to learn the new system. Many of your personnel will already have experience with Unix or NT/2000, and thus their learning curve in implementing the firewall application solutions will be shortened.

Also, because firewall applications are developed for a specific operating system platform like Unix or Windows NT/2000, your security personnel will already be familiar with the interface that is employed by the firewall. A good example of this is CheckPoint's firewall solution—it has a very good, intuitive GUI interface, which makes configuration easy, and also reduces the likelihood of making mistakes and opening up unintended holes in your firewall system.

Here are some of the main advantages of using proprietary OSs for firewalls:

- They tend to be more secure than firewall applications.
- They provide for better scalability and packet filtering speeds because the operating system is customized directly to work with specific hardware.

Command-Line Interface of the PIX Firewall Family

Because the PIX firewalls use the same operating system—the FOS—the configuration of Cisco's PIX firewalls is simplified. You have a choice of three configuration methods in configuring your PIX firewall:

- Command-Line Interface (CLI)
- PIX Device Manager (PDM)
- Cisco Secure Policy Manager (CSPM)

The CLI implemented on the PIX is somewhat similar to Cisco's IOS-based router CLI. As you will see in later chapters, however, there are many differences between the CLIs of both platforms. The PDM is an HTML-based tool that allows you to remotely manage the PIX with a web browser. CSPM is a complete management package that allows you to manage your security policies for PIX and router firewalls as well as your Cisco IDS devices, like the 4200 series sensors and the DSM card for the Catalyst 6000 series switches, and Cisco VPN devices, which include the PIX, IOS-based routers, 3000 VPN concentrators, and VPN clients.

As you can see, you have many options available to you in order to configure your PIX and implement your security policies. This book primarily focuses on the CLI of the PIX firewalls, but Chapter 9 covers the graphics-based PDM.

Adaptive Security Algorithm

The PIX is a *stateful* firewall. A stateful firewall adds and maintains information about a user's connection. The Adaptive Security Algorithm (ASA) implements the stateful function of the PIX firewall by maintaining connection information in a connection and translation table, referred to as an *xlate table*. The PIX firewall uses these tables to enforce its security policies for users' connections. Here is some of the information that a stateful firewall keeps in its connection table:

- Source IP address
- Destination IP address
- IP protocol (like TCP or UDP)
- IP protocol information, such as TCP/UDP port numbers, TCP sequence numbers, and TCP flags

---

NOTE   PIX provides a stateful process for TCP and UDP traffic only.

Stateful Firewall Example

Figure 2-1 is a simple example that explains the stateful process. These are the steps shown in Figure 2-1:

1. A user on the inside of your network performs an HTML request from a web server on the outside of your network.

2. As the request reaches the PIX firewall, the PIX takes the user's information, such as the source and destination address, the IP protocol, and any protocol information (such as the source and destination port numbers for TCP), and places this data in the connection table.

3. The PIX forwards the user's HTTP request to the destination web server.

Figure 2-2 shows the returning traffic from the HTTP server. These are the steps as the traffic returns from the web server:

1. The destination web server sends the corresponding web page back to the user

2. The PIX intercepts the connection response and compares it to the entries that it has in its xlate table

    A. If a match is found in the connection table, the returning packet(s) is permitted.

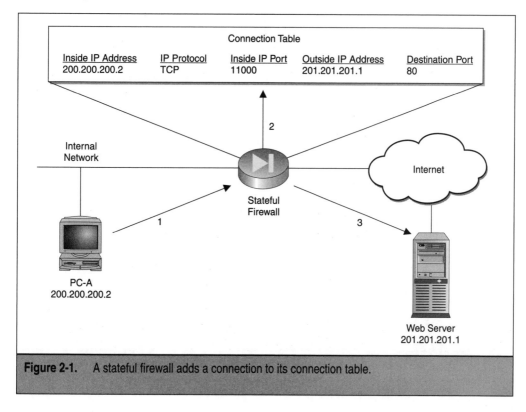

Figure 2-1. A stateful firewall adds a connection to its connection table.

B.   If a match is not found in the connection table, the returning packet(s) is dropped.

A stateful firewall maintains this connection table. If it sees a connection tear-down request between the source and destination, the stateful firewall removes the corresponding connection entry. If a connection entry is idle for a period of time, the entry will timeout, and the stateful firewall will remove the connection entry.

Differences between Stateful and Packet Firewalls

The example in the previous section shows the difference between a stateful firewall and a packet firewall. A stateful firewall is *aware* of the connections that pass through it. Packet firewalls, on the other hand, don't look at the state of connections, but just at the packets themselves.

A good example of this are the extended access lists (ACLs) that Cisco routers can use. With these ACLs, the router will only look at the following information:

• Source IP address
• Destination IP address

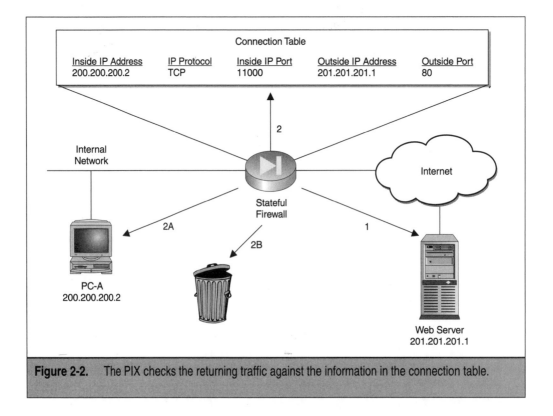

Figure 2-2.   The PIX checks the returning traffic against the information in the connection table.

- IP Protocol
- IP protocol information, like TCP/UDP port numbers or ICMP message types

At first glance, because the information is the same as that which a stateful firewall examines, it looks like a packet filtering firewall performs the same functions as a stateful firewall. However, a Cisco router doesn't look at whether this is a connection setup request, an existing connection, or a connection tear-down request—it just filters packets as they flow through the interface.

Some people might argue that the `established` keyword for router ACLs implements the stateful function found in a stateful firewall; however, this keyword only looks for certain TCP messages in segments, like FIN, ACK, RST, and others, and allows them through. Again, the router is *not* looking at the state of the connection itself, just information found inside the TCP segment.

Sequence Number Randomization

The PIX includes a security feature called Sequence Number Randomization (SNR), which is implemented by the ASA. SNR is used to protect you against reconnaissance and session hijacking attacks by hackers. One problem with the TCP protocol is that most TCP/IP protocol stacks use a fairly predictable method when using sequence numbers—a sequence number in a TCP segment indicates the number of bytes sent. With many connection types, a hacker can use this information to make predictions concerning the next set of data to be sent, and thus the correct sequence number. Sophisticated hackers will then use this information to perform a session hijacking.

The PIX's SNR feature fixes this problem by randomizing the TCP sequence numbers that the TCP/IP application put in the TCP segment. The PIX will place the old sequence number as well as the new sequence number in its connection table. As traffic is returned from the destination, through the PIX, back to the source, the PIX looks for this information and changes it back for acknowledgment purposes.

For example, a segment might pass through the PIX where the sequence number is 578 in the TCP segment, as shown in Figure 2-3. The SNR changes this sequence number to a random number, 992 in this case, and forwards the segment to the destination. The destination is unaware of this change, and acknowledges to the source the receipt of the segment, using an acknowledgment number of 993. The PIX, upon receiving the reply, undoes the SNR process by changing the 993 value to 579, so that the source device is not confused. Remember that the TCP acknowledgement process has the destination increase the sequence number by one, and uses this as the acknowledgment number.

SECURITY ALERT!   To both the source and destination devices, the SNR process is transparent. Cisco highly recommends that you do *not* disable this feature. Disabling SNR opens up your network to TCP session hijacking attacks.

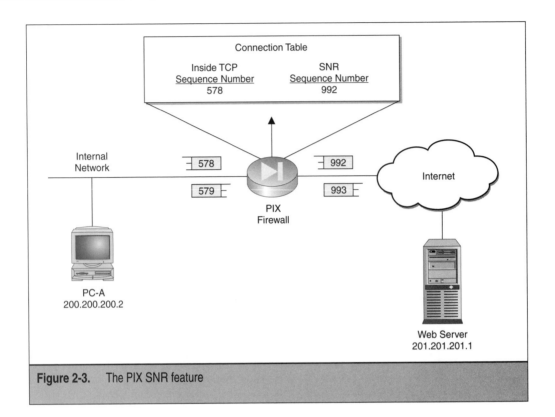

Figure 2-3.   The PIX SNR feature

Cut-Through Proxy

As you saw in the previous section, the ASA implements many security features of the FOS besides the stateful firewall functions of the PIX. Another ASA enhancement is the Cut-Through Proxy (CTP) feature. CTP allows the PIX to intercept incoming and outgoing connections and authenticate them before they are permitted. These connections are not authenticated by the PIX itself, but by an external security server, such as Cisco's Cisco Secure Access Control Server (ACS). Cisco supports both the TACACS+ and RADIUS protocols for authentication.

The CTP feature on PIX can authenticate the following applications:

- FTP
- HTTP
- Telnet

When the ASA is configured for CTP, it first authenticates connections before permitting them through the firewall. Figure 2-4 illustrates the steps that occur for CTP:

1. User *Pong* initiates an FTP to 200.200.200.2.

2. The PIX firewall intercepts the connection and checks for an entry in its connection and xlate tables—if there is an existing entry, the PIX permits the connection (step 4A).

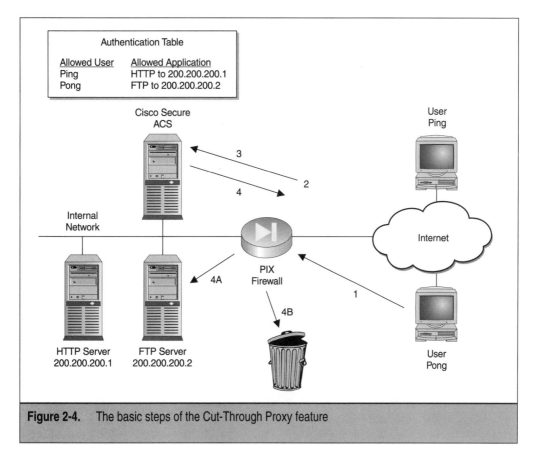

Figure 2-4. The basic steps of the Cut-Through Proxy feature

3. If the PIX does not find an entry, it will prompt the user *Pong* for a username and a password, and forward this information to the security server for authentication.

4. The security server examines its internal authentication table for the username and password and what service this user is allowed access to—the security server sends either an *allow* or *deny* message to the CTP of the PIX.

   A. If the PIX receives an *allow* message, it adds the user's connection information to the xlate table and permits the connection.

   B. If the PIX receives a *deny* message, it drops the user's connection, or, possibly, re-prompts the user for another username/password combination.

Once the user has been authenticated, all traffic will be processed by the PIX at layers 3 and 4 of the OSI Reference Model. This is different than your traditional Application layer proxy, where all traffic, from the authentication phase to the user's actual data traffic, is processed at layer 7 of the OSI Reference Model. With CTP, the authentication phase is processed at layer 7, but data traffic is processed at layers 3 and 4.

NOTE Cut-Through Proxy authenticates the connection at the application layer, but processes the subsequent data stream at layers 3 and 4.

One problem that the CTP feature has is that it is susceptible to eavesdropping, because the username and password are sent across the network in clear text. If a hacker happens to be eavesdropping on the connection while the username and password are being transferred to the PIX, he could use this information to gain unauthorized access to your internal network. You could remove this weakness by either using one-time passwords (OTP) or using a smartcard system where the smartcard-generated key is only valid once. Another problem with the CTP process is that the user might have to authenticate twice: once via CTP, and then again at the actual server.

Policy Implementation

The PIX ASA is responsible for implementing and enforcing your security policies. The ASA uses a tiered hierarchy that allows you to implement multiple levels of security. To accomplish this, each interface on the PIX is assigned a security level. The ASA uses these security levels to enforce its policies. For example, the interface connected to the public network has the lowest security level, whereas the interface connected to the inside network has the highest security level. Here are the three default security policy rules for traffic as it flows through the PIX:

- Traffic flowing from a higher-level security interface to a lower one is permitted.
- Traffic flowing from a lower-level security interface to a higher one is denied.
- Traffic flowing from one interface to another with the same security level is denied.

Figure 2-5 shows a simple example of what is and is not allowed. In this example, the internal user, when he initiates a connection to a web server on the Internet, is permitted out. Also, the ASA adds a connection in its xlate table so that the returning traffic from the external web server will be permitted back to the user—once the user terminates the connection, the entry will be removed from the xlate table. At the bottom of the picture in Figure 2-5, a user on the Internet is trying to access a web server on the inside of the network. The ASA rules on the PIX automatically drop this traffic by default.

The three rules in the previous list are the default rules. You can create exceptions to these rules for the ASA, which generally fall into two categories:

- Allowing access based on a user account
- Allowing access based on a filter

For example, a user from the Internet who is trying to access an FTP server on the inside of your network is, by default, denied the connection. There are a couple of methods that you could use to open up a small hole in the PIX firewall to allow this connection:

- Set up CTP to allow the user's connection
- Use a conduit or access-list to open up a temporary hole

If only a handful of outside users need access to the FTP server, CTP is an excellent method to use. However, if this is a public FTP server where people from the Internet are constantly accessing files in the server, and these people could be anyone in the world, CTP doesn't provide a scalable solution.

Instead, you can use either a conduit or an access-list to open up a temporary hole in the ASA to allow FTP traffic to the specific FTP server on the inside of your network. In this sense, you are creating an *exception* to the ASA's default security policy, which is to deny all inbound traffic by default. Both of these exception rules are discussed in Chapters 4 and 5.

One limitation of conduits is that they are only applicable when traffic is flowing from a lower-level interface to a higher one. If traffic is flowing from a higher-level interface to a lower one, Cisco uses either *outbound filters* or ACLs. This is discussed in Chapter 5.

NOTE   Conduits and outbound filters are Cisco's older implementation on PIX to filter traffic between interfaces. Both of these methods have been supplanted on PIX by ACLs. This book covers both sets of methods because many PIX implementations still have the older commands.

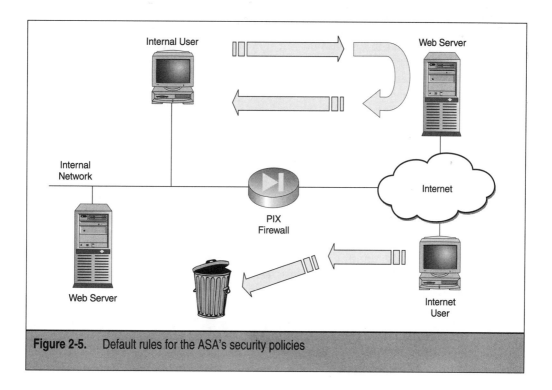

Figure 2-5.   Default rules for the ASA's security policies

Fault Tolerance

Cisco's PIX firewalls support two forms of fault tolerance: failover and stateful failover. Not all PIXs support failover. For failover to function properly, you need to meet the following requirements:

- Use a PIX 515, 520, 525, or 535 model.
- Use identical PIX models running the same version of software.
- Connect the PIXs together with a serial failover cable (this is not necessary in version 6.2 of the FOS).

With failover fault tolerance, one PIX is the primary PIX and is responsible for forwarding traffic. The secondary PIX is in a standby mode and passively monitors the primary PIX. The standby PIX does *not* forward any user traffic, and thus cannot perform any type of load balancing. All configuration changes are performed on the primary PIX and these are automatically copied to the standby unit. When there is a problem with the primary PIX, the standby PIX promotes itself to the primary role, which typically takes 30 to 45 seconds.

Chassis Failover

Failover provides chassis redundancy: if the primary PIX in the failover configuration fails, the standby PIX will begin processing traffic. Not all of the information maintained on the primary PIX is replicated to the standby PIX, like the tables the ASA builds. This type of failover is disruptive for communications that were being transported by the primary PIX because this information is not synchronized between the primary and standby PIXs. Therefore, this type of failover is not stateful—users have to reestablish their connections. The requirements for a chassis failover configuration are the same as those mentioned in the previous section. An example of a non-stateful (chassis) failover setup is shown in the top part of Figure 2-6.

Stateful Failover

A stateful failover configuration is basically the same as a chassis failover—the two main differences are that a stateful failover setup requires a dedicated Fast Ethernet connection between the primary and standby unit and the state information on the primary is synchronized with the standby. The LAN connection is used to synchronize the primary's xlate and address tables with the standby unit. As with a chassis failover, the standby unit monitors the primary unit, and when it sees that the primary is not functioning correctly, the standby unit promotes itself to the primary role. When it does this, the cutover should be completely transparent to the users and their connections because the state table on the standby is the same as that on the primary. An example of a stateful failover setup is shown in the bottom part of Figure 2-6.

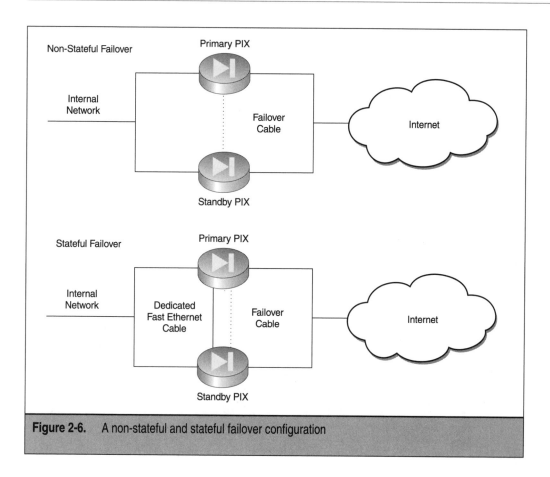

Figure 2-6.   A non-stateful and stateful failover configuration

PIX FOS 6.2

Cisco's newest operating system is version 6.2, and contains many enhancements and scalability features over the 6.1 version of the FOS. Here is a list of some of the 6.2 features:

- **PPPoE**   PPP over Ethernet functionality provides improved ISP compatibility.

- **Hardware VPN client functionality**   PIXs can now act as hardware-based VPN clients, allowing the dynamic download of security policies to your PIXs, simplifying your VPN deployment.

- **Bi-directional NAT**   PIX allows NAT from higher-security-level to lower-security-level interfaces as well as from lower-security-level interfaces to higher ones, simplifying overlapping address issues.

- **LAN-based failover**   PIX can now perform failover using LAN connections instead of using the failover serial cable, which allows the two PIXs in the failover configuration to be separated by long distances.
- **N2H2's Sentian web filtering addition**   The PIX now supports N2H2's product as an additional web content filtering solution. Sentian, along with WebSense, are the two official web content filtering products that Cisco's PIX supports.
- **Additional PAT support**   PAT is now supported for Session Initiative Protocol (SIP) and H.323v2 protocols.

These are just some of the many features available in Cisco's 6.2 PIX operating system.

PIX HARDWARE

Cisco offers a variety of platform solutions in the PIX firewall series of products. From the low-end 501 to the high-end 535, Cisco has a PIX that caters to small office Internet access as well as large internetwork designs and implementations. The hardware architecture of the PIX firewalls is similar to that of a PC—it uses a PCI bus structure with Intel-compatible processors and NICs. If you open up the case of the larger PIX models, especially the 520, you would see that it looks almost like the inside of a normal PC. Of course, Cisco has tuned this architecture and the FOS to provide you with optimal performance for stateful firewall functions. The following sections cover each of these models in more depth.

PIX Licensing

Before I discuss the hardware of Cisco's PIX firewalls, it is important to discuss Cisco's licensing scheme. Cisco uses a license scheme that restricts the abilities of the PIX. When you purchase a PIX firewall, you need to make two purchases: one for the hardware itself and one for the software and its licensing. This can become a bit complicated because licenses fall into two categories—restricted and unrestricted—and for restricted licenses, there are three components that you may or may not have activated.

License Types

The software licensing is broken into multiple areas: encryption capabilities, failover support, number of interfaces supported, and number of connections allowed. The PIX supports two types of encryption: DES and 3DES. I will discus these encryption algorithms in more depth in Chapter 16. DES and 3DES are used for encryption of VPN IPSec connections. A DES or 3DES license is also necessary if you will be using the PIX Device Manager (PDM) to manage your PIX. PDM uses HTTPS as a transport and DES is needed in order to create the protection key and protect the connection. You also need a DES or 3DES license for SSH connections. Prior to version 6.0 of the FOS, you had to purchase these licenses.

However, starting with version 6.0 and the introduction of the PDM management software, Cisco started shipping the DES license free with every PIX. Today, if you have a PIX running with older software and wish to upgrade it to version 6.*x* and take advantage of PDM, you can contact Cisco for a free DES license key. There is one restriction for the free DES license key—your PIX must still be under warranty or you must be under an up-to-date maintenance contract with Cisco.

NOTE   When activating a license for your PIX, you will need to give Cisco the serial number of your PIX as well as additional information. Cisco will use this to generate a unique key to unlock the feature for your specific PIX. You will not be able to use this key on other PIXs because their serial numbers are different. Likewise, this key can only be used to unlock the specific feature or features that you have paid for.

The failover license is necessary if you wish to connect two PIXs together and perform either non-stateful or stateful failover. If you do not currently have a license for failover, and wish to add it for your PIXs, it is a simple matter of paying Cisco the necessary money, and Cisco will then give you a key that you can use to unlock the failover feature.

Some PIXs, such as the 515, support multiple interfaces. However, if you buy the 515, you need to be aware that by default, it only supports three interfaces, even though it has the capacity to support six. If you need more than three interfaces, you will need to purchase an additional license key from Cisco to support the additional interfaces. Cisco also limits the number of interfaces on higher PIX models with a restricted license.

A limited license is typically indicated by the letter *R* in the software license. A limited license indicates that you have not purchased all of the features for your PIX. However, if your license is indicated by the letters *UR*, this indicates that you have an unrestricted license and thus have access to all of the features of your PIX—encryption, failover, and connections.

Connection Licenses

The licensing scheme that Cisco uses for connections is different based on the model of PIX that you purchase. For example, the 501 PIX uses a model based on number of machines, whereas the other PIXs use a model based on number of connections.

PIX 501 Connection License   The PIX 501 uses a connection license based on the number of machines that you want to allow access through your PIX. There are two licenses:

- 10-User
- 50-User

In either situation, the PIX 501 keeps track of the machines that send traffic through the PIX based on their addressing information. Once the PIX reaches the license limit, it will not allow any more machines to send traffic through the PIX. One annoying problem with this function is that the process the 501 uses to keep track of machines is not dynamic. In other words, the PIX doesn't restrict connections based on a total of 10 or 50 machines, but an absolute restriction.

With absolute restriction, once the PIX has seen the *first* 10 or 50 machines, it will not let traffic travel through the PIX for any other machines, even if the first set of machines are *not* transmitting traffic. Therefore, if you have an office with 60 PCs and a 50-user license, only the first 50 PCs that send traffic through the PIX will be allowed—the last 10 PCs will have their traffic dropped by the PIX. You can get around this by rebooting the PIX, which will cause it to erase its table of learned addresses, but you are still stuck with the absolute limit.

Therefore, you need to carefully consider your licensing needs with the PIX 501. If you need more than 50 user connections, you are better off buying a 506 model or higher. As you will see in the next section, the other PIXs (including the 506) are more lenient in their licensing.

Other PIXs Connection License   For models other than the PIX 501, Cisco uses a license scheme based on the number of *connections*, not devices. Because the license scheme is based on connections, it is important to understand what the PIX considers a connection. Basically, a connection is a session layer or socket connection based on the combination of the following:

- Source IP address
- Destination IP address
- TCP or UDP protocol
- TCP/UDP source port number
- TCP/UDP destination port number

At first glance, a PIX like the 520, which can support 256,000 connections, seems like it would never run out of connections. However, Cisco's definition of a connection might cause problems with supporting all of the connections for your users and the outside public.

As an example, take a look at a simple web page download. The download of a single web page requires a single connection. However, embedded in this web page might be a multitude of pictures (GIF or JPG files), sound, and video clips—each one of these requires a separate connection to transmit to your user's desktop. Therefore, what seems like a simple download can easily involve dozens of connections. Multiply the number of these connections by the maximum number of users that might travel through the PIX at any given time, and you could easily use up your connection licenses.

There is one major difference, though, between the 501 PIX that uses a user license scheme and the rest of the PIXs that use a connection license scheme. With a user license limit, it's the first set of users that are allowed access through the PIX. Once you have reached your license limit, no additional users will be allowed, even if the first set of users are not sending any traffic. With a connection-based license scheme, the PIX only monitors open connections—once a connection is done and is torn down, the PIX will no longer count this as a connection towards your license limit.

Therefore, when you look at the example of downloading a web page, the opening of dozens of connections to display the web page correctly only counts against your license limits until the download completes. Once the download completes, these connections are freed up for other users and devices to use.

Because of the dynamic nature of a connection-based license scheme, it is very important to understand your traffic patterns so that you can purchase the right PIX with the appropriate connection license limit. Of course, you can always upgrade your connection license to a higher number by purchasing a license with a higher number of connections. Note, however, that there are *physical* constraints for licensing. In other words, the PIX itself is restricted in the number of connections it can physically support by its hardware. For example, the PIX 520 can only support 256,000 connections before it runs out of gas. Therefore, you need to know not only the number of connections, but also the physical capabilities of the PIX model that you are considering purchasing.

PIX 501

The PIX 501 is Cisco's newest smallest PIX and is about the size of an external modem. This tiny firewall is directly geared at the SOHO environment. It supports either 10 or 50 user's devices and has a maximum data throughput of 10 Mbps. Like its bigger brothers, it can also support VPN connections and has a VPN throughput of about 3 Mbps.

NOTE With a restricted license, the throughput of the PIX 501 is throttled.

Table 2-1 shows the hardware characteristics of the 501. The PIX 501 has an AMD 133Mhz processor with 16MB of RAM and 8MB of flash. Flash is used to store the FOS and PDM images as well as the configuration file of the PIX.

NOTE The PIX 501 does not support failover.

Front of the PIX 501 Chassis

Figure 2-7 shows a picture of the front of a PIX's 501 chassis. As you can see, the front of the chassis contains no interfaces or buttons, only LEDs.

Table 2-2 lists a description of the LEDs found on the front of the 501's chassis.

Characteristic	Value
Processor	AMD 133 MHz
RAM	16MB
Flash	8MB
Interfaces	1 10BaseT port and a 4-port 10/100 integrated switch
Failover support	No

Table 2-1. Hardware Characteristics of the PIX 501

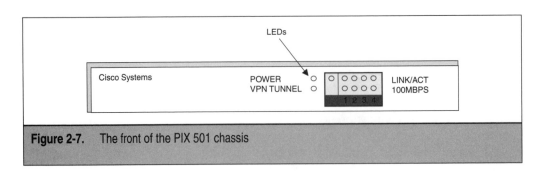

Figure 2-7.   The front of the PIX 501 chassis

Note that there is a colored box around five sets of LEDs (LINK/ACT and 100 Mbps) these represent the five ports of the 501. The first port has no 100 Mbps LED because this port only operates at 10 Mbps—this port is meant to connect to your ISP, or to a router that is connected to your ISP. The other four ports have two LEDs—these ports refer to the 4-port 10/100 integrated switch on the rear of the 501 chassis. Physically, these are separate ports on the PIX; however, from a configuration perspective, these four ports are treated as one logical port. These ports are connected to your internal devices.

Rear of the PIX 501 Chassis

Figure 2-8 shows an illustration of the rear of the PIX 501 chassis. On the left side is the integrated 4-port switch, where the ports are numbered from 4 down to 1. Each of these ports requires a Category-5 cable with an RJ-45 connector. Logically, these ports are represented by the physical interface name of *ethernet1* in the PIX's configuration. The port labeled *0* is the 10BaseT port. It also requires a Category-5 cable with an RJ-45 connector. This port is given a name of *ethernet0* in the PIX's configuration and is connected to the outside network.

LED	Meaning
POWER	Green when the 501 is powered up
VPN TUNNEL	Green when at least one VPN tunnel is active
LINK/ACT	Solid green when a physical layer link is established Flashing green when traffic is passing through the interface Off if there is no physical layer connection
100 MBPS	Green if the port is operating at 100 Mbps Off if the port is operating at 10 Mbps

Table 2-2.   LEDs on the Front of the PIX 501

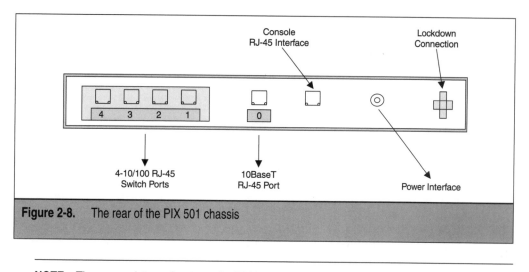

Figure 2-8. The rear of the PIX 501 chassis

NOTE   The nomenclature of ports on the PIX is somewhat similar to that used by Cisco routers.

To the right of the *ethernet0* port is an RJ-45 console interface. This interface is used to gain access to the CLI of the PIX. The serial cable used for the console port is included with the PIX, and is the same cable used for router console connections: a flat ribbon cable (rolled) with an RJ-45 connector at both ends. Cisco also includes a terminal adapter that converts the RJ-45 connector to a DB-9 connector, which you can plug into the serial port of your PC and use a terminal emulation package like HyperTerm to access the CLI.

To the right of the console port is the power interface—the actual power supply is not built into the PIX, but is encased in an external brick. You need to plug the external power supply into this port of the PIX.

The last component on the rear of the 501 chassis is a lock-down mechanism, which is located on the right side of the chassis. This is used to secure the 501 to the physical location around it. Because the 501 is so small (almost small enough to fit into the inside breast pocket of your jacket), Cisco has included this feature so that someone doesn't slip the PIX into their pocket and literally walk off with it. You can attach a lock-down cable to this port and then secure it to a desk or large shelving unit.

PIX 506

The PIX 506 is directed at branch office/remote office environments. The PIX 506 comes in two different models: 506 and 506E. The 506 has been discontinued by Cisco, and has been supplanted by the 506E. The size of the chassis for these two PIXs is about the size of the 1600 series Cisco router. The chassis of both PIXs—506 and 506E—is the same: the difference between the two PIXs is performance. Specifically, the 506E model was built to handle increased VPN performance. Table 2-3 shows the hardware characteristics that the 506 and 506E have in common.

Characteristic	Value
RAM	32MB
Flash	8MB
Interfaces	2 10BaseT ports
Failover support	No

Table 2-3. Common Hardware Characteristics of the PIX 506 and 506E

Table 2-4 shows the differences between the 506 and 506E PIX models.

As you can see, the main difference between the two models is VPN performance—the 506E is specifically built for VPN functions. The 506E does have a faster processor than the regular 506; however, the data throughput is the same for the two models. Another thing to note is that the 506 and higher models of the PIX use a different licensing scheme than the 501, as I pointed out in the "PIX Licensing" section of this chapter. The 506 bases its licensing scheme on connections, not devices.

Front of the PIX 506 Chassis

Figure 2-9 shows an illustration of the front of a PIX 506 chassis. There are three LEDs on the front panel of the 506:

- **Power**   Indicates if there is power to the PIX
- **Active**   Indicates whether the FOS is loaded
- **Network**   Indicates traffic activity on the ports

Characteristic	506	506E
Processor	Intel Pentium MMX 200 MHz	Intel Pentium Celeron 300 MHz
Connection limits	10,000	10,000
Data throughput	20 Mbps	20 Mbps
VPN throughput	20 Mbps for DES and 10 Mbps for 3DES	20 Mbps for DES and 16 Mbps for 3DES
VPN peers	25	25

Table 2-4. Comparison of the PIX 506 and 506E

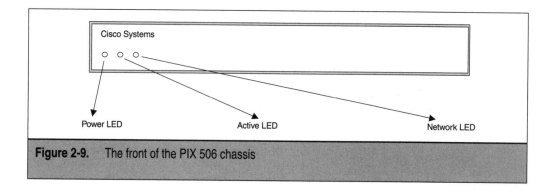

Figure 2-9. The front of the PIX 506 chassis

Table 2-5 shows the status of these LEDs.

Rear of the PIX 506 Chassis

Figure 2-10 shows an illustration of the rear of a PIX 506 chassis. On the left side of the rear chassis are two 10BaseT ports with RJ-45 interfaces. The left port should be connected to the inside of your network, and the right port should be connected to the outside of your network. For configuration purposes, the PIX uses the following nomenclature for these ports:

- Inside *ethernet1*
- Outside *ethernet0*

To the left and right of each port is an LED. The left LED indicates activity on the port, and the right one indicates a physical layer connection.

LED	Status
Power	Off if the PIX is powered off Green if the PIX is powered on
Active	Off if the FOS is loading Green if the FOS has completed loading
Network	Off if traffic is not passing through the PIX Flashing green if traffic is passing through the PIX

Table 2-5. LEDs on the Front of the PIX 506

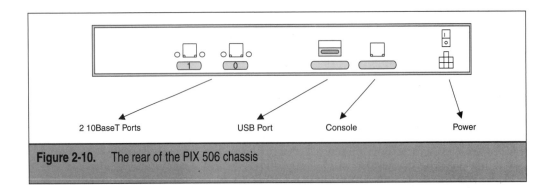

2 10BaseT Ports   USB Port   Console   Power

Figure 2-10. The rear of the PIX 506 chassis

To the right of the two 10BaseT ports is a USB port, which is currently not used by the PIX. This interface is reserved for future enhancements. To the right of the USB port is an RJ-45 console port, which has the same characteristics as the console port on the PIX 501.

On the far right of the rear of the PIX 506 is the power switch and the power receptacle. The power switch is located at the top, and the outlet is beneath the switch. The 506, like the 501, uses an external power brick for its power. You'll need to connect the power brick to this interface and use the switch to turn on the 506.

PIX 515

The PIX 515 is directed at small- to medium-sized businesses. Like the 506, the 515 comes in two different models: the 515 and the 515E. The 515 is an end-of-life product and has been replaced by the 515E. The chassis is the same for both of these PIXs; the major difference is that the 515E has increased throughput and processing for VPN connections. Table 2-6 shows the hardware characteristics that the PIX 515 and 515E have in common.

Characteristic	Value
RAM	32MB with a restricted license (R) 64MB with an unrestricted license (UR)
Flash	16MB
Interfaces	3 10/100 Ethernet interfaces with a restricted license (R) 6 10/100 Ethernet interfaces with an unrestricted license (UR)
Failover support	Yes, with a failover license

Table 2-6. Common Hardware Characteristics of the PIX 515 and 515E

There are two types of interface cards that you can add to the 515 chassis:

- 1-port 10/100 Ethernet card
- 4-port 10/100 Ethernet card (requires an Unrestricted license)

The PIX 515 and 515E do have their differences, though, as is shown in Table 2-7. As you can see from Table 2-7, the 515E has both an increased data and VPN performance. Once reason the 515E has a markedly different VPN performance over the 515 is that it uses a special hardware card called a VAC (VPN Accelerator Card).

PIX 515 Licensing

The 515 has three categories of licensing:

- Restricted
- Unrestricted
- Failover

The Restricted (R) license allows you to populate the 515 with up to three 10/100 Ethernet interfaces. By default, every 515 comes with two 10/100 Ethernet ports. The restricted license only requires 32MB of RAM.

If you upgrade to the Unrestricted (UR) license, you will need to increase your RAM to 64MB. If you buy a 515 with an UR license, it automatically comes with 64MB of RAM. The UR license includes the VAC as well as support for up to six 10/100 Ethernet interfaces. The UR allows you to perform both DES and 3DES encryption for VPN connections. The UR includes the failover feature; however, you can buy the failover license with a 515 that has an R license if you only need the failover capability. Table 2-8 shows the differences between the R and UR licenses.

Characteristic	515	515E
Processor	Pentium Pro 200 MHz	Intel Celeron 433 MHz
Connections	100,000	125,000
Data throughput	170 Mbps	188 Mbps
VPN throughput	10 Mbps	63 Mbps
VPN connections	1,000	2,000

Table 2-7.   Comparison of the PIX 515 and 515E

Characteristic	Restricted (R)	Unrestricted (UR)
RAM	32MB	64MB
Maximum ports	3	6
3DES	No	Yes
Failover	No (can be added)	Yes

Table 2-8. Comparison of the R and UR Licenses for the PIX 515

Front of the PIX 515 Chassis

The front of the 515 and 515E chassis only contain LEDs. Like the PIX 506, there are three LEDs on the front panel of the 506:

- Power   indicates if there is power to the PIX
- Active   indicates whether the FOS is loaded
- Network   indicates traffic activity on the ports

Table 2-9 shows the status of these LEDs.

Rear of the PIX 515 Chassis

Figure 2-11 shows the rear of the 515/515E chassis. On the left side there are two slots, one on top of the other. These are used to add additional interfaces to the PIX. To the right of this is a slot that is used for the VAC on the 515E. Below the VAC slot are two 10/100 Ethernet interfaces. The left interface is the inside interface, and the right interface is the outside interface. Every PIX 515 has these fixed interfaces. Both of these interfaces have three LEDs, as is shown in Table 2-10.

To the right of two 10/100BaseT ports is a USB port, which is currently not used by the PIX. This interface is reserved for future enhancements. Above the USB port is a DB-15 serial interface that is used for failover communications between the primary

LED	Status
Power	Off if the PIX is powered off Green if the PIX is powered on
Active	Off if the FOS is loading Green if the FOS has completed loading
Network	Off if no traffic is passing through the PIX Flashing green if traffic is passing through the PIX

Table 2-9. LEDs on the Front of the PIX 515

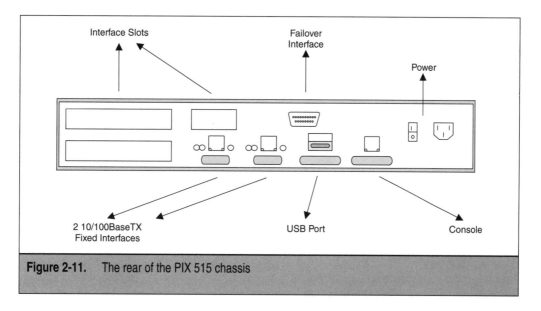

Figure 2-11. The rear of the PIX 515 chassis

and standby PIX. This is a proprietary cable and should be ordered from Cisco if you will be configuring your PIXs for failover. To the right of the USB port is an RJ-45 console port, which has the same characteristics as the console port on the PIX 501. On the right-hand side of the chassis is the power switch and power outlet.

Port Nomenclature of the PIX 515

The two fixed interfaces on the PIX 515 are labeled *ethernet0* for the outside interface (the one on the right) and *ethernet1* for the inside interface (the one on the left). The naming conventions are used for configuring your PIX 515. The naming conventions for interfaces in the slots are as follows:

- Lowered numbered interfaces are in the top slots and higher ones in the bottom slot

- Interfaces are numbered left-to-right

LED	Location	Description
100	Far left of the port	If off, the interface is set to 10Mbps If green, the interface is set to 100Mbps
Link	Directly to the left of the port	If off, there is no physical layer connection If green, there is a physical layer connection
FDX	Right of the port	If off, the port is set to half-duplex If green, the port is set to full-duplex

Table 2-10. The Port LEDs on the PIX 515

The top part of Figure 2-12 shows an example where the two slots have single-port cards. The port in the top slot is labeled *ethernet2* and the port in the bottom is *ethernet3*. The bottom part of Figure 2-12 shows an example where a slot has a 4-port 10/100 Ethernet card. The port on the left is labeled *ethernet2* and the port on the right of the slot is labeled *ethernet5*.

PIX 525

The PIX 525 replaces the PIX 520, which used to be Cisco's enterprise-line firewall. Like its predecessor, the 525 is directed at providing stateful firewall solutions for enterprise networks, but provides more functionality. For information on the PIX 520, please visit my web site (http://home.cfl.rr.com/dealgap/). Table 2-11 shows the hardware characteristics of the PIX 525.

Unlike the PIX 520, the 525 can support up to eight interfaces. However, you need a UR license to use all eight interfaces. With an R license, you are limited to six interfaces. Another difference between the 525 and the 520 is that the 525 also supports Gigabit Ethernet—you can place up to three Gigabit Ethernet interfaces into the chassis of the 525.

Table 2-12 shows the performance capabilities of the PIX 525.

Like its smaller sister, the PIX 525 supports the VAC interface. With the VAC, the 525 supports a VPN connection throughput of 70 Mbps, whereas without the VAC, the 525 must perform software-based VPN encryption, limiting its throughput to 31 Mbps.

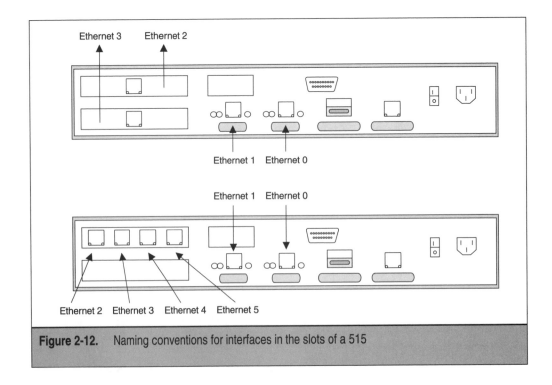

Figure 2-12.   Naming conventions for interfaces in the slots of a 515

Characteristic	Hardware Description
Processor	Intel Pentium III 600 MHz
RAM	256MB
Flash	16MB
Maximum interfaces	8
Failover support	Yes

Table 2-11.   Hardware Characteristics of the PIX 525

Front of the PIX 525 Chassis

Figure 2-13 shows the front of the 525 chassis. There are only two LEDs on the front panel of the 525:

- **Power**   Indicates if there is power to the PIX
- **Active**   If this LED is green, the unit is the primary unit in a failover configuration. If it is off, either the PIX is a standalone unit or is the standby unit in a failover configuration.

Rear of the PIX 525 Chassis

Figure 2-14 shows the rear of the PIX 525 chassis. The rear of the chassis on the 525 is actually more similar to the 515 than it is to the 520 model. On the left side are three slots that will currently accept any of the following cards:

- 1-port 10/100 Ethernet
- 4-port 10/100 Ethernet
- 1-port Gigabit Ethernet

To the right of these slots are two fixed 10/100 Ethernet interfaces. The left interface is the inside interface, and is referred to as *ethernet1*. The right interface is the outside interface, and is referred to as *ethernet0*. The nomenclature for the ports in the three slots is the same as the PIX 515.

Capability	Capability Information
Connections	280,000
Data throughput	370 Mbps
VPN throughput	31 Mbps or 70 Mbps
VPN connections	2,000

Table 2-12.   The Performance Capabilities of the PIX 525

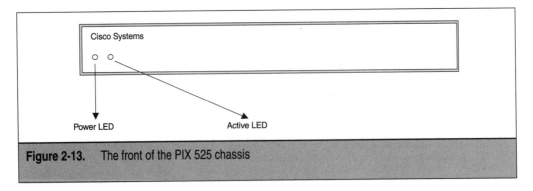

Figure 2-13.   The front of the PIX 525 chassis

To the right of the two fixed 10/100BaseTX interfaces is a USB port, which is currently not used by the 525. Next to this port is an RJ-45 console port that allows you to access the CLI of the 525. Above these two ports is the DB-15 failover port. At the far right side of the chassis are the power outlet and the power switch.

PIX 535

The PIX 535 is Cisco's high-end firewall and is directed at high-end service provider networks. Table 2-13 shows the hardware characteristics of the PIX 535. The PIX 535 supports the greatest number of interfaces: ten. However, you need a UR license to use all ten interfaces. With an R license, you are limited to six interfaces. The PIX 535's hardware supports over 6GB of RAM; however, the PIX FOS limits this to 1GB of actual use.

Table 2-14 shows the performance capabilities of the PIX 535.

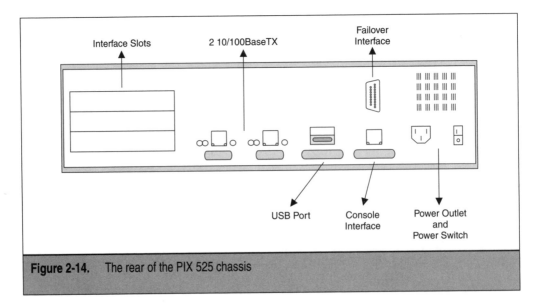

Figure 2-14.   The rear of the PIX 525 chassis

Characteristic	Hardware Description
Processor	Intel Pentium III 1.0 GHz
RAM	1GB
Flash	16MB
Maximum interfaces	8
Failover support	Yes

Table 2-13. Hardware Characteristics of the PIX 535

The PIX 535 supports the optional VAC interface. With the VAC interface, the 535 can support VPN encryption speeds for data at a rate of 100 Mbps.

Front of the PIX 535 Chassis

The front of the PIX 535 looks the same as the 525, containing only two LEDs:

- **Power**   Indicates if there is power to the PIX
- **Active**   If this LED is green, the unit is the primary unit in a failover configuration. If it is off, either the PIX is a standalone unit or is the standby unit in a failover configuration.

Rear of the PIX 535 Chassis

Figure 2-15 shows the rear of the PIX 535 chassis. The rear of the chassis on the 535 is unique in all of the PIX models. On the far left, there is a DB-15 failover interface that has the same specifications as the failover interface of the other PIX models. Below this is an RJ-45 console interface and to the right of this is a USB port (currently not used).

In the middle of the chassis are nine slots for your interface cards. These cards are the same cards used by the PIX 525: 1-port and 4-port 10/100 Ethernet and 1-port Gigabit Ethernet. Unlike the 525, there are no fixed Ethernet ports in the chassis of the 535. On the far right are two power supplies (and their outlets), as well as the power switch. The power supplies are modular and can be removed; they are also hot swappable.

Capability	Capability Information
Connections	500,000
Data throughput	1.7
VPN throughput	100 Mbps
VPN connections	2,000

Table 2-14. The Performance Capabilities of the PIX 535

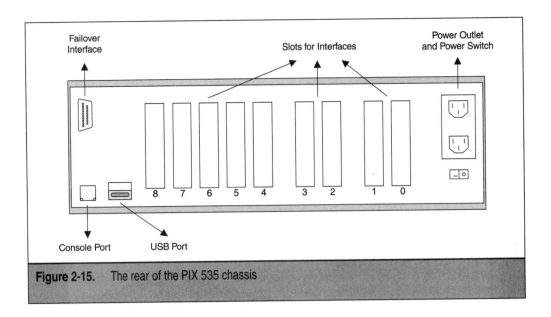

Figure 2-15.   The rear of the PIX 535 chassis

PIX 535 Port Nomenclature and Architecture

The slots of the PIX 535 are numbered from right to left: 0 through 8. The interfaces are numbered from the lowest slot number to the highest. If there is more than one port in a slot, the interfaces are numbered from top to bottom. As an example, the very first interface in slot 0 is *ethernet0*. If there were a single interface in slot 0 and a 4-port 10/100 Ethernet card in slot 1, the interface in slot 0 would be referred to as *ethenet0*, and the interfaces in slot 1 would be *ethernet1*, *ethernet2*, *ethernet3*, and *ethernet4*, from top to bottom.

Figure 2-16 shows an illustration of the architecture used by the PIX 535. As you can see, the slots are separated into three groups, where each group is connected to a separate bus:

- Slots 0 and 1 are connected to bus 0, which is a 64-bit/66 MHz PCI bus
- Slots 2 and 3 are connected to bus 1, which is a 64-bit/66 MHz PCI bus
- Slots 4 through 8 are connected to bus 2, which is a 32-bit/33 MHz ISA bus

The placement of interface cards in the chassis of the 535 *can* affect the PIX's performance. All Gigabit Ethernet cards should be put into bus 0 and bus 1—putting them into bus 2 will cause them to not operate. All 10/100 cards and the VAC can be placed into any of the three buses; however, if you put these cards into either bus 0 or bus 1, the bus will be reconfigured to operate at *33 MHz*, which will affect the throughput of any Gigabit Ethernet cards that are also plugged into these buses.

NOTE   Placement of cards in the slots of the 535 can affect the performance of your PIX.

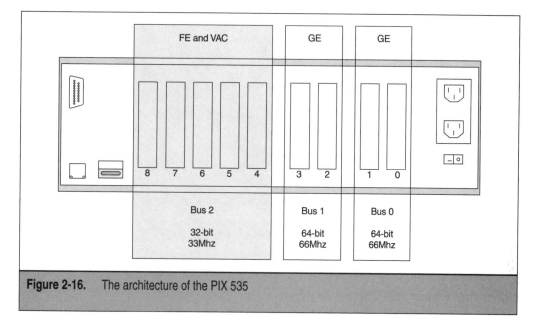

Figure 2-16.   The architecture of the PIX 535

COMPARISON OF PIX MODELS

To help you understand some of the differences between all the PIX models, Table 2-15 shows a comparison.

FURTHER STUDY

Web Sites

For an overview of Cisco PIX models, features, and FOS versions, visit http://www.cisco.com/warp/public/cc/pd/fw/sqfw500/.

PIX Model	Placement	Connections	Data Throughput	VPN Throughput
501	SOHO	10–50 Users	10 Mbps	3 Mbps
506	Branch/Remote Office	10,000	20 Mbps	10 Mbps
506E	Branch/Remote Office	10,000	20 Mbps	20 Mbps
515	Small-to-Medium Office	128,000	147 Mbps	10 Mbps
515E	Small-to-Medium Office	128,000	188 Mbps	63 Mbps
520	Enterprise	256,000	240 Mbps	20 Mbps
525	Enterprise	280,000	360 Mbps	70 Mbps
535	Service Provider	500,000	1.0 Gbps	100 Mbps

Table 2-15.   Comparison of PIX Models

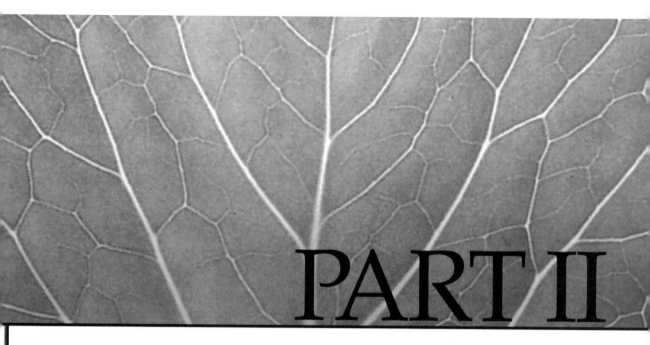

PART II

PIX Setup and Traffic Filtering

CHAPTER 3

The PIX Command-Line Interface and Basic Configuration

The last chapter focused on the features of Cisco's PIX firewall and the various PIX models in Cisco's firewall lineup. Starting with this chapter and continuing through the remainder of this book, I will focus on how to configure your PIX to meet the requirements outlined in your security policy. This chapter will focus on accessing your PIX, becoming familiar with the command-line interface (CLI) of the PIX, and creating a very basic configuration for your PIX. If you have configured Cisco IOS-based routers, the configuration of the PIX, as you will see, is somewhat similar.

ACCESS TO THE PIX

Cisco offers three main methods for configuring your PIX:

- Command-Line Interface (CLI)
- PIX Device Manager (PDM)
- Cisco Secure Policy Manager (CSPM)

The following sections provides an overview of these access methods.

Console Access

The most popular method of configuring the PIX is by using the CLI. The CLI is somewhat similar to that used by Cisco's IOS-based routers. If you have configured Cisco routers before, configuring PIX will be fairly easy. To gain access to the CLI, you can use one of the following access methods:

- Console port
- Telnet
- Secure Shell (SSH)

For console access, you need to connect one end of Cisco's ribbon serial cable to the console interface of the PIX, and the other end to an RJ-45-to-DB9 terminal adapter that you'll attach to the serial port of your PC. On your PC, you'll need to run a software package like HyperTerm, TinyTerm, or some other program that performs terminal emulation. In your terminal emulation program, you'll need to use the settings shown in Table 3-1 for access to the PIX's console port.

You can also access the CLI of the PIX via telnet and SSH. For security reasons, Cisco denies both of these types of remote access—you must perform some configuration tasks to allow these access methods. Of these two methods, SSH is more secure because SSH encrypts information between your PC and the PIX. I will discuss the configurations of these two modes of access to the PIX later on in this chapter.

Setting	Configuration
Baud Rate	9600bps
Data Bits	8
Stop Bits	1
Parity	None
Flow Control	None

Table 3-1.   Terminal Emulation Settings for PIX Console Access

Other Access Methods

Cisco supports two GUI-based products that allow you to configure and manage your PIX. The PIX Device Manager (PDM) is used as an alternative to using the CLI. Many administrators are very familiar with GUI-based interfaces, and don't feel comfortable working with the FOS-style CLI. For these individuals, Cisco offers the PDM software. PDM offers an easy-to-use web browser-based GUI that lets you not only configure your PIX, but also manage it. With PDM, you can perform complex configuration tasks and gather important statistics. Chapter 9 covers the use of the PDM.

Cisco also offers an alternative GUI product called the Cisco Secure Policy Manager (CSPM). CSPM is more of a management tool than a configuration tool. One problem that larger internetworks face is the management of policies, especially security policies. If you have 50 perimeter routers and 20 PIXs, ensuring that all of these security devices have the appropriate security policies applied to them can become a daunting task. CSPM allows you to create your security policies from a single management platform and then have these policies applied to the appropriate device or group of devices. With CSPM, you can create separate sets of policies based on the location and traffic flowing through these devices.

NOTE   In this sense, CSPM is not a tool that you would use to configure your PIX, but to manage the security polices on your PIX.

COMMAND-LINE INTERFACE

The focus of most of this book will be centered on the CLI of the Finesse Operating System (FOS). As you will see throughout this book, the CLI that the FOS uses is very similar to that of Cisco's IOS-based routers. However, be forewarned that there *are* differences between the CLIs of these operating systems. In other words, you will see many of the same commands used on both products. There are just as many commands, as well as other items, that make the two CLIs distinctly unique, however.

PIX Bootup Sequence

The PIX bootup sequence is similar to the bootup of any networking device. The PIX first loads its BIOS, performs some diagnostic checks on its hardware components, and then loads the FOS, as is shown in this code.

```
CISCO SYSTEMS PIX-501
Embedded BIOS Version 4.3.200 07/31/01 15:58:22.08
Compiled by morlee
16 MB RAM

PCI Device Table.
Bus Dev Func VendID DevID Class              Irq
 00  00   00   1022   3000  Host Bridge
 00  11   00   8086   1209  Ethernet           9
 00  12   00   8086   1209  Ethernet          10

Cisco Secure PIX Firewall BIOS (4.2) #6: Mon Aug 27 15:09:54 PDT 2001
Platform PIX-501
Flash=E28F640J3 @ 0x3000000

Use BREAK or ESC to interrupt flash boot.
Use SPACE to begin flash boot immediately.
Reading 2470400 bytes of image from flash.
16MB RAM
Flash=E28F640J3 @ 0x3000000
BIOS Flash=E28F640J3 @ 0xD8000
mcwa i82559 Ethernet at irq  9  MAC: 0008.e3c7.f7a1
mcwa i82559 Ethernet at irq 10  MAC: 0008.e3c7.f7a2

      -----------------------------------------------------------------
                          ||         ||
                          ||         ||
                         ||||       ||||
                     ..:||||||:..:||||||:..
                     c i s c o S y s t e m s
                     Private Internet eXchange
      -----------------------------------------------------------------
                        Cisco PIX Firewall

Cisco PIX Firewall Version 6.1(2)
```

```
Licensed Features:
Failover:        Disabled
VPN-DES:         Enabled
VPN-3DES:        Disabled
Maximum Interfaces:     2
Cut-through Proxy:      Enabled
Guards:          Enabled
Websense:        Enabled
Inside Hosts:    10
Throughput:      Limited
ISAKMP peers:    5


****************************** Warning ******************************
Compliance with U.S. Export Laws and Regulations - Encryption.

This product performs encryption and is regulated for export
by the U.S. Government.

This product is not authorized for use by persons located
outside the United States and Canada that do not have prior
approval from Cisco Systems, Inc. or the U.S. Government.

This product may not be exported outside the U.S. and Canada
either by physical or electronic means without PRIOR approval
of Cisco Systems, Inc. or the U.S. Government.

Persons outside the U.S. and Canada may not re-export, resell
or transfer this product by either physical or electronic means
without prior approval of Cisco Systems, Inc. or the U.S.
Government.
****************************** Warning ******************************

Copyright (c) 1996-2000 by Cisco Systems, Inc.

            Restricted Rights Legend

Use, duplication, or disclosure by the Government is
subject to restrictions as set forth in subparagraph
(c) of the Commercial Computer Software - Restricted
Rights clause at FAR sec. 52.227-19 and subparagraph
(c) (1) (ii) of the Rights in Technical Data and Computer
Software clause at DFARS sec. 252.227-7013.


            Cisco Systems, Inc.
```

```
                    170 West Tasman Drive
                    San Jose, California 95134-1706

...................
DHCP command failed
outside interface address added to PAT pool

Cryptochecksum(changed): 9de0ec38 9d35bba0 c4054269 e0bade5a
Type help or '?' for a list of available commands.
pixfirewall>
```

This code is an example of the bootup sequence from a PIX 501. You can see some basic information about your PIX, like the version of its BIOS, the version of the FOS, and the abilities enabled for your PIX.

The 501 in this code has the following features enabled: VPN with DES, Cut-Through Proxy, Guards (like Mail Guard and DNS Guard), WebSense for HTML content filtering, a 10 user license, limited throughput, and a maximum of five IPSec/ISAKMP peers for VPN connectivity. Note that for the PIX 501, Cisco restricts the throughput of the PIX with a restricted license; with an unrestricted license, the interfaces are handled at wire speeds.

Once the PIX has completed booting, you are presented with the CLI prompt, `pixfirewall>`, as is shown at the bottom of this code.

CLI Modes

The PIX supports different levels of access to the FOS. These levels, and the user prompts that go with them, are shown in Table 3-2.

As you can see from the levels of access and user prompts listed in Table 3-2, you would think that you were dealing with a Cisco router. Like a Cisco IOS-based router, the PIX has three main levels of access: *User EXEC*, *Privilege EXEC*, and *Configuration* modes.

User EXEC Mode

User EXEC mode is the first mode that you are presented with once you log into the PIX. You can tell that you are at this mode by examining the prompt: the prompt will

Level of Access	User Prompt
User EXEC mode	`pixfirewall>`
Privilege EXEC mode	`pixfirewall#`
Configuration mode	`pixfirewall(config)#`
Monitor mode	`>`

Table 3-2. The Levels of Access to the PIX

contain the name of the PIX, which defaults to `pixfirewall`, and is followed by the >
symbol. The following is an example of gaining access to *User EXEC* mode:

```
Type help or '?' for a list of available commands.
pixfirewall>
```

Within any of the access modes of the PIX CLI, you can pull up context-sensitive
help by either typing in the `help` command or entering a ?, like this:

```
pixfirewall> ?
enable          Enter privileged mode or change privileged mode
                    password
pager           Control page length for pagination
quit            Disable, end configuration or logout
pixfirewall>
```

On a Cisco IOS-based router, *User EXEC* mode allows you to execute a limited
number of basic management and troubleshooting commands. However, from *User
EXEC* mode on a PIX, your only real options are to enter *Privilege EXEC* mode or to
log out of the PIX.

To log out of the PIX while at *User EXEC* mode, use the `exit` or `quit` command,
like this:

```
pixfirewall> exit
Logoff
```

Privilege EXEC Mode

Privilege EXEC mode is a level of access one step above *User EXEC* mode. Access to this
mode gives you complete access to your PIX. To gain access to this mode, you first must
access *User EXEC* mode and then type in the `enable` command, as shown here:

```
pixfirewall> enable
Password:
pixfirewall#
```

You will *always* be prompted for the *Privilege EXEC* password, even if one is
not configured. As you can see from this example, the CLI prompt changes from
`pixfirewall>` to `pixfirewall#`, indicating that you are now at *Privilege EXEC*
mode. To view the commands that you can use in *Privilege EXEC* mode, either type
in the `help` command or enter a ?. Because you are at *Privilege EXEC* mode, you will
see a couple of screens with commands that you can execute—much more than at
User EXEC mode.

To go back to *User EXEC* mode, use the `disable` command, as shown here:

```
pixfirewall# disable
pixfirewall>
```

As you can see, the prompt changed from a # to a >. If you want to log out of the PIX, from either *User* or *Privilege* EXEC mode, use the `exit` or `quit` command.

Configuration Mode

Configuration mode is used to enter most of your PIX configuration implementations and changes. To enter Configuration mode, you'll need to execute the `configure terminal` command from *Privilege EXEC* mode, as shown here:

```
pixfirewall# configure terminal
pixfirewall(config)#
```

Notice that the prompt changed from # to (config)# when you entered the `configure terminal` command, indicating that you are now in *Configuration* mode. To view the commands that you can execute at Configuration mode, enter the `help` command or `?`.

If you see the message `<--- More --->` show up at the bottom of the screen, there is more information than can fit into one screen. Pressing the ENTER key will scroll down through the output one line at a time; pressing the space bar will scroll the information down one screen at a time.

TIP   There are two interesting points to make about the output between the *Privilege EXEC* and *Configuration* mode commands. First, unlike the IOS routers, you *can* execute *Privilege EXEC* commands in *Configuration* mode on a PIX. Second, there are no sub-configuration modes used by PIX—all PIX configuration commands are executed at the `(config)#` prompt. There is one exception to subconfiguration modes in 6.2 of the FOS—I discuss this in Chapter 5.

To exit *Configuration* mode, either enter the `exit` command or press CTRL-Z, like this:

```
pixfirewall(config)# exit
pixfirewall#
```

Note that the prompt changed back to #, indicating your return to *Privilege EXEC* mode.

Monitor Mode

Monitor mode is similar to *ROMMON* on a Cisco IOS-based router—it is typically used to perform the password recovery procedure, and to perform low-level troubleshooting tasks and certain types of upgrades. To access *Monitor* mode, you'll first need to reboot your PIX. As the PIX boots up, you'll see a message that states "Use BREAK or ESC to interrupt flash boot." Press one of these keys within 10 seconds of seeing this message and you'll be taken into *Monitor* mode, as is shown in this code:

```
CISCO SYSTEMS PIX-501
Embedded BIOS Version 4.3.200 07/31/01 15:58:22.08
Compiled by morlee
```

```
16 MB RAM

PCI Device Table.
Bus Dev Func VendID DevID Class              Irq
 00  00  00   1022   3000  Host Bridge
 00  11  00   8086   1209  Ethernet          9
 00  12  00   8086   1209  Ethernet          10

Cisco Secure PIX Firewall BIOS (4.2) #6: Mon Aug 27 15:09:54 PDT 2001
Platform PIX-501
Flash=E28F640J3 @ 0x3000000

Use BREAK or ESC to interrupt flash boot.
Use SPACE to begin flash boot immediately.
Flash boot interrupted.
0: i8255X @ PCI(bus:0 dev:17 irq:9 )
1: i8255X @ PCI(bus:0 dev:18 irq:10)

Using 1: i82557 @ PCI(bus:0 dev:18 irq:10), MAC: 0008.e3c7.f7a2
Use ? for help.
monitor>
```

Notice that at the end of this code, the prompt now reads `monitor>`. To see the commands that you can execute at *Monitor* mode, enter the `help` command or `?`.

NOTE   While in Monitor mode, the PIX will not pass any traffic between interfaces; you must have the PIX load the FOS to accomplish this.

To have the PIX load the FOS and continue with the bootup process, either re-power the PIX or execute the `reload` command.

Cisco IOS Router and PIX CLI Comparison

So far in this chapter, the CLI that PIX uses appears to be very similar to what Cisco's IOS-based routers use. Here are some of the differences between the PIX and IOS-based router CLI:

- With the PIX, you can execute `show` commands at both *Privilege EXEC* and *Configuration* modes.
- *User EXEC* mode on PIX has a very limited set of commands that you can execute compared to IOS-based routers.
- The IOS-based routers support subconfiguration modes within *Configuration* mode.

Given these differences, however, these two products have many CLI features in common:

- Context-sensitive help
- Command abbreviation
- History recall
- CLI editing features

The following sections cover the basics of these PIX CLI features.

Context-Sensitive Help

I have already covered the `help` and `?` commands to pull up help at each access level. In addition to seeing a list of commands available to you at each access level, you can also access help for a specific command. Cisco refers to this process as *context-sensitive* help. The context-sensitive help available to you from the CLI of the PIX is not as feature-rich as that of IOS-based routers. You can pull up help for a command by typing in the command, and following it by a space and a ?, like this:

```
pixfirewall(config)# access-list ?
usage: [no] access-list <id> deny|permit <protocol> <sip> <smask>
               [<operator> <port> [<port>]] <dip> <dmask>
               [<operator> <port> [<port>]]
           access-list <id> deny|permit icmp <sip> <smask>
               <dip> <dmask> [<icmp_type>]
pixfirewall(config)# access-list
```

In this example, I was in *Configuration* mode when I pulled up help for the `access-list` command. Notice that after the help output is displayed, the command that you typed in is redisplayed on the command line.

One limitation of the PIX context-sensitive help feature is that you can only pull up the syntax of a command. With Cisco IOS-based routers, you can get a listing of parameters for a command and what each parameter does. Currently, the PIX does not support this handy configuration feature.

Command Abbreviation

Another nice feature of the PIX CLI is that you can abbreviate commands and command parameters to their most unique characters. For example, to go from *User EXEC* to *Privilege EXEC* mode, you use the `enable` command. The `enable` command can be abbreviated to `en`. When you enter a ? at a *User EXEC* prompt, you'll notice that there are two commands at *User EXEC* mode that start with the letter *e*: `enable` and `exit`. Therefore, you cannot abbreviate the `enable` command to the letter *e*. If you would attempt to, the PIX would give you an error message.

The command abbreviation feature is not just restricted to PIX commands, but also applies to the parameters for these commands. As an example, to access *Configuration* mode, you can enter con t, which is short for `configure terminal`. Another useful abbreviation is when you are entering a wildcard for an IP address or subnet mask: 0.0.0.0 can be abbreviated to just the number 0.

NOTE: On IOS-based routers, you can type in part of a command or parameter and hit TAB to have the router fill in the rest of the command or parameter. Unfortunately, the PIX CLI does not support this feature.

History Recall

Each of the access levels of the PIX stores the commands that you previously executed—these commands can be recalled, edited, and then executed. The history recall feature works the same as that on IOS-based routers. Table 3-3 lists the control sequences to recall commands.

To view the commands that you have executed at an access level, move to that access level and execute the `show history` command, like this:

```
pixfirewall(config)# show history
  en
  con t
  exi
  co t
  con t
  exit
  show history
  conf t
  term
  show history
pixfirewall(config)#
```

One interesting point to make about this example is that from *Configuration* mode, you can see commands that you executed in both *Configuration* mode and *Privilege EXEC* mode.

Control Sequence	Explanation
CTRL-P	Recall the last command
Up Arrow	Recall the last command
CTRL-N	From a previous command in the history list, recall a more recent one
Down Arrow	From a previous command in the history list, recall a more recent one

Table 3-3.   Control Sequences for the History Feature

Control Sequence	Description
CTRL-A	Takes you to the beginning of the command line
CTRL-E	Takes you to the end of the command line
ESC-B	Takes you back one word at a time on the command line
ESC-F	Takes you forward one character at a time on the command line
CTRL-B	Takes you back one character at a time
Left Arrow	Takes you back one character at a time
CTRL-F	Takes you forward one character at a time
Right Arrow	Takes you forward one character at a time
CTRL-D	Deletes the character that the cursor is on
Backspace	Deletes the character that is to the left of the cursor
CTRL-R and CTRL-L	Redisplay the current line
CTRL-U	Erase the current line and put the cursor at the beginning
CTRL-W	Erase the word the cursor is on

Table 3-4.   Control Sequences for Editing

CLI Editing Features

When you use the history recall feature, you may want to edit the contents of a recalled command. The control sequences used by the PIX are the same as those used by IOS-based routers. These sequences are listed in Table 3-4.

If you see a $ sign at the beginning of a command line when you are performing your editing functions, this indicates that the complete command cannot fit in the display and that there are more letters to the left of the $. By default, you can have up to 512 characters on a command line—any extra characters are ignored.

SETUP SCRIPT UTILITY

The PIX supports a small scripting utility that enables you to create a very basic configuration on the PIX and store that configuration in flash. With the exception of the PIX 501, 506, and 506E, every PIX comes without a configuration. When you boot up a new PIX, or if you erase the configuration file with the `write erase` command and reboot the PIX, the PIX will start up the setup script utility automatically.

NOTE   The basic configuration included on the PIX 501s and 506s allows them to dynamically acquire an IP address from the ISP as well as acting as a DHCP server for the internal interface that your users are connected to. The PIX 501 will perform PAT with the single address that your ISP has assigned you.

To start up the script manually, go to *Configuration* mode and enter the `setup` command, as shown here:

```
pixfirewall(config)# setup
Pre-configure PIX Firewall now through interactive prompts [yes]?
Enable password [<use current password>]:
Clock (UTC):
  Year [2002]:
  Month [Apr]:
  Day [13]:
  Time [11:08:23]:
Inside IP address [192.168.1.1]:
Inside network mask [255.255.255.0]:
Host name [pixfirewall]:
Domain name:
Name required
Domain name: dealgroup.com
IP address of host running PIX Device Manager:

The following configuration will be used:
Enable password: <current password>
Clock (UTC): 11:08:23 Apr 13 2002
Inside IP address: 192.168.1.1
Inside network mask: 255.255.255.0
Host name: pixfirewall
Domain name: dealgroup.com

Use this configuration and write to flash?
```

The script prompts you for your configuration parameters. If an entry appears in brackets ([ ]), you can press ENTER to accept this default value. If a default value is not listed, you must enter a parameter. One limitation of the script is that if you make a mistake, there is no way of going back to the previous question. Of course, once you get done answering these questions, you can answer "no" to the question "Use this configuration and write to flash?" and start the script over again. As you will see throughout this book, most configuration tasks require you to enter the actual command (because the script lacks most configuration tasks). Because of this, most seasoned PIX veterans never bother using the `setup` command but manually perform this process by entering the appropriate PIX commands in *Configuration* mode.

CONFIGURATION FILES

The PIX uses flash memory to store the FOS, the PDM, and its configuration file. Like the IOS-based routers, whenever you make configuration changes, these changes affect only the configuration that is in RAM—the configuration that the PIX is actively using. You must manually enter a command to copy the configuration to flash in order to save it. This section covers the commands that you can use to manipulate your configuration file.

The configure Commands

The `configure` commands are used to affect a configuration change on your PIX. Table 3-5 lists the `configure` commands.

The `configure` and `write` (covered in the next section) commands work at either *Privilege EXEC* or *Configuration* mode. Note that these commands are basically the old-style commands used by the IOS-based routers.

The write Commands

The `write` commands are used to either save, view, or remove your configuration file. Table 3-6 lists the `write` commands.

One miscellaneous command that you should know is the `reload` command. Use this command in either *Privilege EXEC* or *Configuration* mode to reboot your PIX. In much older versions of the FOS, some changes in the PIX's configuration required a reboot; today, this is not true.

Command	Explanation
`configure memory`	Merges your configuration from a configuration file in flash to RAM.
`show configure`	Views your configuration file in flash.
`configure terminal`	Enters configuration mode.
`configure net` `TFTP_server's_IP:filename`	Merges your configuration file in RAM with a configuration file from a TFTP server.
`configure floppy`	Merges your configuration file in RAM with a configuration file from the floppy drive (applicable only for the PIX 520).
`configure factory-default`	Restores the default factory configuration file to a PIX 501, 506, or 506E—this command is not applicable for any other PIX model.

`configure http[s]://`
`[username:password@] location`
`[:port_number] / http_pathname`
	Merges your configuration file in RAM with a configuration from a file from a web server.

Table 3-5. The configure Commands

Command	Explanation
write memory	Saves your active configuration file in RAM to flash.
write terminal	Views your configuration file in RAM.
write net *TFTP_server's_IP:filename*	Saves your configuration file in RAM to a TFTP server.
write floppy	Saves your configuration file in RAM to the floppy drive on a PIX 520 (use the DOS `format` command to prepare it).
write erase	Erases your saved configuration file in flash.
write standby	Copies the configuration file from RAM on this PIX to the standby PIX's RAM when failover has been configured.

Table 3-6. The write Commands

BASIC PIX CONFIGURATION COMMANDS

This section covers some of the commands that you use to create a basic configuration for your PIX firewall. Some of these commands are the same, or similar to those found on an IOS-based router; other commands, however, are quite different. In most situations, if you need to undo a configuration command, you will either preface the command with the no (which is what you would do on an IOS-based router) or clear parameter.

> **NOTE** The PIX is limited to a configuration file that is smaller than 350KB—that is, a configuration file with a little more than 350,000 characters. This is true for any PIX model, from the 501 up to the 535. On a Unix system, you can use the wc to count the number of characters in your configuration file. On a Windows machine, you can use an application like Microsoft Word to see the actual character count.

Configuring the Passwords

The PIX supports two levels of passwords: one for access to *User EXEC* mode via telnet and one for access to *Privilege EXEC*. You configure these passwords in either *Privilege EXEC* or *Configuration* mode. These passwords are encrypted when stored in RAM or flash to protect you from eavesdropping attacks. To configure the telnet password, use the passwd command:

```
pixfirewall# passwd password
```

Note that the command for changing a password is really spelled with the letters *or* missing. The password is case-sensitive and can be any combination of characters and numbers. The limit to the length of the password is 16 characters. The default password is *cisco* for telnet access.

SECURITY ALERT!   The default telnet password is *cisco*—you'll definitely want to change this! *User EXEC* access via the console port does not use this password. Actually, there is no password for console access unless you implement AAA, which is discussed in Chapter 11.

To set the *Privilege EXEC* password, use the `enable password` command:

```
pixfirewall# enable password password
```

It is highly recommended that you configure a *Privilege EXEC* password because there is no default password. This command is somewhat similar to the IOS-based routers, except that this command automatically encrypts the password. The password is case-sensitive and can be any combination of characters and numbers. The length of the password is limited to 16 characters.

 SECURITY ALERT!   There is no default Privilege EXEC password—it is highly recommended that you configure one.

Configuring the Interface

Now that you have set up passwords for your PIX, you are ready to proceed with the configuration of the PIX's interfaces. Typically, this will be a three-step process:

1. Assign the physical properties to the interface.
2. Give the interface a logical name.
3. Verify your interface's configuration.

Assigning Physical Properties to an Interface

To assign physical properties to an interface on a PIX, you need to use the `interface` *Configuration* mode command:

```
pixfirewall(config)# interface hardware_name hardware_setting
```

The *hardware_name* parameter specifies the actual physical interface, like *ethernet0*, *ethernet1*, and so on and so forth. You can abbreviate these names to first letter of the interface type followed by the number of the interface. For example, *ethernet0* can be entered as *e0*. This is true for any PIX command that uses physical interface names. The *hardware_setting* parameter specifies the hardware setting that you wish to assign to the interface. Table 3-7 lists these settings.

NOTE   Not all parameters can be used for every interface type. By default, all interfaces on the PIX are enabled. If you disable an interface, use the `interface` command with a configured hardware setting to enable it.

Parameter	Description
aui	Half-duplex 10Base5
bnc	Half-duplex 10Base2
10baset	Half-duplex 10BaseT
10full	Full-duplex 10BaseT
100basetx	Half-duplex Fast Ethernet
100full	Full-duplex Fast Ethernet
auto	Auto-sense the speed and duplexing on a 10/100 card
1000basesx	Half-duplex Gigabit Ethernet
1000xsfull	Full-duplex Gigabit Ethernet
1000auto	Auto-negotiation of duplexing for Gigabit Ethernet
4mbps	Token Ring 4 Mbps
16mbps	Token Ring 16 Mbps (the default)
shutdown	Disables the interface

Table 3-7.   Hardware Settings for the `interface` Command

Remember that the PIX does not have any subconfiguration modes. This fact can be seen with the `interface` command. On a Cisco IOS-based router, using the `interface` command would take you into *Interface Configuration* mode.

Naming an Interface

Most PIX commands do not use the physical interface name when performing configurations and monitoring tasks. Instead, they use the logical name given to a physical interface. The `nameif` *Configuration* mode command is used to assign the logical name to an interface:

```
pixfirewall(config)# nameif hardware_name logical_name security_level
```

The *hardware_name* parameter specifies the actual physical interface, like ethernet0, ethernet1, and so forth. The logical name is the name that you use to refer to the interface. By default, ethernet0 is named *outside* and ethernet1 is named *inside*. Each interface has a security level, which can range from 0 to 100. The format of this parameter is to use the word `security` followed by the security level (number). You can abbreviate the word `security` to `sec`. An example of a security level of 50 would be `sec50`. The *outside* interface defaults to 0 and the *inside* interface defaults to 100.

NOTE   If your first two interfaces are Ethernet, the PIX will automatically create their names and levels for you.

PIX's ASA uses the security levels to enforce its security policies. Here are the rules that the ASA uses:

- Traffic from a higher to a lower level is permitted, by default, unless you have restricted traffic with an ACL or outbound filter.

- Traffic from a lower to a higher level is denied, by default, unless you explicitly permit it by either configuring statics and conduits (or ACLs), discussed in Chapters 4 and 5, or configure Cut-through Proxy authentication, discussed in Chapter 11.

- Traffic from the same level to the same level is always restricted.

SECURITY ALERT!   By default, traffic from the *inside* interface of your PIX to any other interface on the PIX is permitted. However, traffic from the *outside* interface of your PIX is automatically dropped when going to any other interface unless you explicitly permit it.

Let's look at an example to illustrate this process. Figure 3-1 shows a network that I use throughout the rest of this chapter.

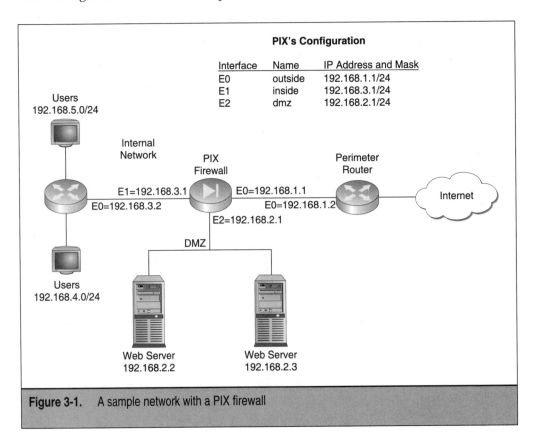

Figure 3-1.   A sample network with a PIX firewall

In this example, the PIX has three interfaces: an external, an internal, and a DMZ interface. With the PIX's ASA in action, here are the data connections that are, by default, permitted:

- Traffic from the inside interface to the DMZ.
- Traffic from the inside interface to the outside.
- Traffic from the DMZ interface to the outside.

If the traffic originates from any other source than the ones listed here, and is going to any other destination through the PIX, the PIX will automatically deny it.

Assigning an IP Address to the Interface

Once you have named your interfaces, you are ready to assign IP addresses to them. Without an IP address on an interface, the PIX will *not* process traffic on the interface. To assign an IP address to an interface on your PIX, use the ip address *Configuration* mode command:

```
pixfirewall(config)# ip address logical_interface_name ip_address [subnet_mask]
```

With this command, you must give the logical name of the interface that you created with the nameif command (or the default name of the interface). If you omit the IP address, it defaults to 127.0.0.1, which means that the PIX will not process traffic on the interface. If you omit the subnet mask, it defaults to the A, B, or C class subnet mask that corresponds to the network number of the IP address.

Verifying Your Interface Settings

Now that you have set up your interfaces, you are ready to verify your settings by using show commands.

TIP   Remember that show commands can be executed at either *Privilege EXEC* or *Configuration* mode.

To examine the configuration of your interface, use the show interface command:

```
pixfirewall# show interface
interface ethernet1 "inside" is up, line protocol is up
  Hardware is i82559 ethernet, address is 0008.e3c7.f7a2
  IP address 192.168.1.1, subnet mask 255.255.255.0
  MTU 1500 bytes, BW 10000 Kbit full duplex
        136 packets input, 14842 bytes, 0 no buffer
        Received 136 broadcasts, 0 runts, 0 giants
        0 input errors, 0 CRC, 0 frame, 0 overrun, 0 ignored, 0 abort
        0 packets output, 0 bytes, 0 underruns
        0 output errors, 0 collisions, 0 interface resets
        0 babbles, 0 late collisions, 0 deferred
```

```
       0 lost carrier, 0 no carrier
       input queue (curr/max blocks): hardware (128/128) software (0/1)
       output queue (curr/max blocks): hardware (0/0) software (0/0)
```

The format of the output of this command is very similar to the same command used on IOS-based routers. One important item to point out is the first line, where the status is shown for both the physical and data link layers respectively. In this example, both of these layers are functioning correctly. Here are the status values of the interface:

- If you see up and up, both the physical and data link layers are functioning correctly.
- If you see up and down, there is a data link layer problem.
- If you see down and down, there is a physical layer problem.
- If you see administratively down and down, the interface has been manually disabled.

The show interface command displays all of the interfaces on the PIX. If you are only interested in seeing the status of a single interface, enter the command followed by the physical name of the interface, like *ethernet0*.

You can use either the show interface or show ip [address] command to view the IP configuration of your PIX's interfaces:

```
pixfirewall(config)# show ip
System IP Addresses:
        ip address outside 192.168.1.1 255.255.255.0
        ip address inside 192.168.3.1 255.255.255.0
        ip address dmz 192.168.2.1 255.255.255.0
Current IP Addresses:
        ip address outside 192.168.1.1 255.255.255.0
        ip address inside 192.168.3.1 255.255.255.0
        ip address dmz 192.168.2.1 255.255.255.0
```

The System IP Addresses are the IP addresses assigned to the active PIX when you have failover configured. If this PIX were the standby unit, it would assume these addresses on the interface when a failover occurred. The Current IP Addresses are the IP addresses currently being used on the interface. Failover is discussed in Chapter 12.

To perform detailed troubleshooting, the PIX supports debug capabilities similar to IOS-based routers. Once you have assigned an IP address to an interface on the PIX, you can verify its accessibility by pinging it from another machine on the same subnet. On the PIX, first enter the debug icmp trace command to enable debugging for ICMP traffic. Then go to another machine on the same subnet, and ping the PIX's interface. Your output will look something like this:

```
pixfirewall# debug icmp trace
ICMP trace on
Warning: this may cause problems on busy networks
```

```
pixfirewall#
1: ICMP echo request (len 32 id 2 seq 256) 192.168.1.2 > 192.168.1.1
2: ICMP echo reply (len 32 id 2 seq 256) 192.168.1.1 > 192.168.1.2
3: ICMP echo request (len 32 id 2 seq 512) 192.168.1.2 > 192.168.1.1
4: ICMP echo reply (len 32 id 2 seq 512) 192.168.1.1 > 192.168.1.2
5: ICMP echo request (len 32 id 2 seq 768) 192.168.1.2 > 192.168.1.1
6: ICMP echo reply (len 32 id 2 seq 768) 192.168.1.1 > 192.168.1.2
7: ICMP echo request (len 32 id 2 seq 1024) 192.168.1.2 > 192.168.1.1
8: ICMP echo reply (len 32 id 2 seq 1024) 192.168.1.1 > 192.168.1.2
```

The output of the command is fairly readable: there were four echo requests from the machine and four replies from the PIX. To turn off the debug for ICMP, preface the above command with the no parameter: no debug icmp trace.

TIP   Unfortunately, you have to turn off each debug item that you have enabled individually. On IOS-based routers, you can enter undebug all or no debug all to turn off all debug processing, but the PIX doesn't support these commands.

Configuring Routing

There are two methods you can use to get routing information into your PIX: static routes and the Routing Information Protocol (RIP). The PIX needs some basic routing information to take incoming packets and forward them out of the appropriate interface. The following two sections cover the use of static routes and the RIP routing protocol, and how to configure them on your PIX.

Routing Limitations and Recommended Configurations

It is important to point out that your PIX is *not* a full-functioning router. You can manually configure static routes on your PIX to help it forward traffic, or you can have the PIX passively listen to RIP routing updates and incorporate the routing information into the PIX's local routing table. The PIX, however, will never forward routing traffic between its interfaces. Therefore, if you have a PIX sitting between two routers, and you want these two routers to share routing information, you need to build a tunnel between the two routers and tunnel the routing information between them by encapsulating the routing updates in IP packets, or TCP or UDP segments. From the PIX's perspective, it doesn't examine the encapsulated routing update, only the IP packet itself. If you are using Cisco routers, it is a common practice among networking administrators to use the GRE tunneling protocol to tunnel the routing information. I briefly discuss GRE tunnels in Chapter 16.

For small networks, you should use a default route pointing to the router off of the *outside* interface and static routes pointing to your networks off of your remaining PIX interfaces. For large networks, you should use a default route pointing to the router off of the *outside* interface and use RIP on your remaining interfaces.

SECURITY ALERT! RIP version 1 has no security mechanism built into it, and thus can be easily spoofed. Therefore, you should use RIP version 2 on your PIX and the routers connected to your PIX.

Configuring Static Routes

Once you enter an IP address on your PIX's interface, the PIX automatically creates a static route for the specified network number. This is referred to as a *connected route*. Once you are done configuring your interfaces IP addresses, the PIX will know about all of the directly connected networks. However, the PIX doesn't know about networks more than one hop away from itself. To solve this problem, one option is to configure static, or default, routes. Use the `route` *Configuration* mode command to create your static routes, as shown here:

```
pixfirewall(config)# route logical_name network_number subnet_mask
                           next_hop_IP_address [hop_count]
```

The first parameter you must enter is the logical name of the interface where the route exists. If you refer back to Figure 3-1, for 192.168.4.0/24 and 192.168.5.0/24, this would be the *inside* interface. Next, you follow it with the network number and the subnet mask. For a default route, enter 0.0.0.0 for the network number, or 0 for short, and 0.0.0.0 for the subnet mask, which can also be abbreviated to 0. After the network number and subnet mask, specify the router that the PIX will forward the traffic to in order to get the traffic to the correct destination. Again, for the 192.168.4.0/24 and 192.168.5.0/24 networks, the next-hop address is 192.168.3.2. You can also add a hop count to rank static routes when your PIX is connected to more than one router and you want the PIX to know about both routing paths.

> **NOTE** The PIX will not load-balance between multiple paths—it will only use one. If the hop count is different, the PIX will use the path with the lower hop count. If the hop count is the same, the PIX will use the first `route` command that you entered.

To remove a static route from your PIX's configuration, use the `clear route` command:

```
pixfirewall(config)# clear route [logical_name network_number
                          [subnet_mask next_hop_IP_address]]
```

If you don't specify a specific route, all of the routes will be removed from the PIX's routing table. The only exceptions are the routes that the PIX automatically adds when you assign an IP address to an interface.

Configuring RIP

As I mentioned in the "Routing Limitations and Recommended Configurations" section, the PIX is not a router—it does not forward routing updates that it receives.

However, you can have your PIX incorporate RIP routing updates into its local routing table. To configure RIP, use the `rip` *Configuration* mode command:

```
pixfirewall(config)# rip logical_name default|passive [version [1|2]]
                          [authentication [text|md5 key (key_id)]]
```

You must first specify the logical name of the interface where PIX will run RIP, like *inside*. The `default` parameter causes the PIX to broadcast a default route on the interface to other devices. The `passive` option has the PIX listen to RIP routing updates and incorporate them into its own routing table.

The default `version` is 1—you can override this by having your router process RIPv2 updates. RIPv2 was introduced in PIX FOS 5.3. It supports both broadcast and multicasting; however, for multicasting the interface NIC must be an Intel 10/100 and Gigabit—if it isn't, the NIC will only process local broadcast packets.

The `authentication` parameter allows you to set up authentication for RIPv2 devices. You have two choices for authentication—send the authentication in clear text (`text`) or encrypt the authentication (`md5`). It is highly recommended to use the MD5 hash function and not clear text for authentication. When specifying MD5, you need to specify the encryption key, which can be up to 16 characters in length, as well as the key identification number, which can be a number between 1 and 255. Note that on your routers you will need to match these values. I'll discuss MD5 in more depth in Chapter 16.

If you need to remove RIP from your configuration, use the `clear rip` *Configuration* mode command.

Verifying Your Routing Configuration

To see the routes in your PIX's routing table, use the `show route` command:

```
pixfirewall# show route
        inside 192.168.30 255.255.255.0 192.168.31 1 CONNECT static
        outside 192.168.10 255.255.255.0 192.168.3 11 1 CONNECT static
        dmz 192.168.2.0 255.255.255.0 192.168.2.1 1 1 CONNECT static
```

In this example, you can see the three static routes that the PIX automatically created (`CONNECT`) when you specified your IP addresses for each of the interfaces.

If you only want to see the RIP routes (if you've configured RIP), use the `show rip` command.

```
pixfirewall# show rip [logical_interface_name]
```

To troubleshoot problems with RIP, use the `debug rip` command:

```
pixfirewall# debug rip [logical_interface_name]
```

MANAGEMENT COMMANDS

This section rounds out the basic PIX configuration commands. In the following sections, I cover how to assign your hostname and domain name to your PIX as well as allowing access to the PIX for management purposes. I also cover some basic testing and monitoring tools that you can use on your PIX.

Configuring Host and Domain Names

By default, the name of your PIX defaults to `pixfirewall`. You can change this with the `hostname` *Configuration* mode command:

```
pixfirewall(config)# hostname name_of_your_PIX
```

The name that you give your PIX only has local significance. The only visible effect of executing this command is that your prompt will include the new name, like this:

```
pixfirewall(config)# hostname pokey
pokey(config)#
```

To assign a domain name to your PIX, use the `domain-name` command:

```
pixfirewall(config)# domain-name your_PIX's_domain_name
```

Permitting IP Access to the PIX

By default, the only access that the PIX allows is on the console port—HTTP, telnet, and SSH access are denied. The following sections show you how to enable these types of access to the PIX.

Enabling HTTP PDM Access

Permitting HTTP access is necessary if you want to manage your PIX using PDM. This requires you to configure two commands:

```
pixfirewall(config)# http server enable
pixfirewall(config)# http client_IP_address [subnet_mask] [interface_name]
```

The `http server enable` command starts a scaled-down web server process on the PIX. The `http client_IP_address` command specifies the machines that are allowed access to the PIX. you can specify a specific IP address, where the mask defaults to 255.255.255.255, or you can specify a network number and subnet mask. If you specify a logical interface name, the client machine will only be allowed access if it comes into the PIX from this interface. If you omit the interface name, all internal interfaces are permitted. These commands are discussed in more depth in Chapter 9.

NOTE   When accessing PDM from a browser on your workstation, make sure to type `https://<ip-address>` in the URL field. If you only type the IP address or the IP address with `http://` in front, you will not get access to the PIX.

Enabling Telnet Access

To allow telnet access to the PIX, you need to configure two commands. First, you must assign a telnet password with the `passwd` *Privilege EXEC* command discussed in the "Configuring the Passwords" section of this chapter. Second, you must specify the IP addresses that are allowed access to the PIX with the `telnet` *Configuration* mode command:

```
pixfirewall(config)# telnet IP_address [subnet_mask] [interface_name]
```

If you omit the name of the interface, access from any internal interfaces is permitted. You can list up to 16 hosts or networks with multiple `telnet` commands.

If you want to allow telnet access from all internal machines, use the following syntax:

```
pixfirewall(config)# telnet 0 0 inside
```

Remember that you can abbreviate 0.0.0.0 as 0. To allow access from only a specific internal network segment, use this syntax:

```
pixfirewall(config)# telnet 192.168.4.0 255.255.255.0 inside
```

If you want to allow telnet access from only a specific machine, use this configuration:

```
pixfirewall(config)# telnet 192.168.5.2 255.255.255.255 inside
```

Note that you can enter the `telnet` command multiple times to set your telnet access policies.

To see your telnet access policies, use the `show telnet` command:

```
pixfirewall# show telnet
    192.168.4.0 255.255.255.0 inside
    192.168.5.2 255.255.255.255 inside
```

The default timeout for idle telnet sessions is five minutes. You can change this with the `telnet timeout` command:

```
pixfirewall(config)# telnet timeout number_of_minutes
```

The time can range from one to sixty minutes. To see the configured timeout, use the `show telnet timeout` command.

To see who is currently logged into the PIX via telnet, use the `who` command:

```
pixfirewall# who
1: From 192.168.1.7
2: From 192.168.1.2
```

The first number is the session ID, and is unique for each logged in user. You can also see this display with the `show who` command.

You can terminate a telnet connection by using the `kill` command:

```
pixfirewall# kill session_ID
```

You can view the session IDs by using the who command. When terminating a session, the PIX allows the telnet user to permit any currently executing command and then, without warning, terminates the user's connection.

Enabling SSH Access

Secure shell (SSH) allows a user to establish a pseudo console connection via a remote secure shell connection. One limitation of using telnet is that you cannot telnet to the PIX from the *outside* interface. You can get around this limitation by using SSH. SSH basically provides an encrypted connection between the client and the PIX.

To allow for SSH access, you must configure the following on your PIX:

- Define a hostname
- Define a domain name
- Generate a public/private RSA key combination
- Specify the addresses allowed to access the PIX via SSH

I have already talked about assigning a hostname and domain name to the PIX previously in this chapter. The public/private RSA key combination is used to secure the connection for the secure shell. To create your keying information, use the ca generate rsa key command:

```
pixfirewall(config)# ca generate rsa key modulus_size
```

To execute the above command, you must first install either a DES or 3DES activation key, if one has not already been installed. The modulus size can be 512, 768, 1024, or 2048. The larger the size, the more secure the connection will be. To see the public key created by the ca generate rsa key command, use the show ca mypubkey rsa command, like this:

```
pixfirewall(config)# show ca mypubkey rsa

% Key pair was generated at: 18:45:09 Apr 15 2002

Key name: pixfirewall.dealgroup.com
 Usage: General Purpose Key
 Key Data:
  307c300d 06092a86 4886f70d 01010105 00036b00 30680261 00b0ec90 f5eee13a
  37c49a2c ceae73b2 7db88f0a abdd0977 cc98a8b8 8cd087bc a020765b a6aeaf9d
  5c635f4a 607e7fe0 347cd422 3400b5cd a6859592 dd707e0c d2340a51 06d310ff
  7e6791aa ef6dd5dc c8ce77f6 845d264c ea702a9d 37b622e8 21020301 0001
pixfirewall(config)#
```

Use the command `ca save all` to store RSA key pairs in flash memory. I discuss RSA and public/private keys in more depth in Chapters 16 and 17.

Once you have created your public key, you can now specify the addresses permitted to establish SSH connections to the PIX. Use the `ssh` command to specify permitted addresses:

```
pixfirewall(config)# ssh ip_address [subnet_mask] [interface_name]
```

If you omit the subnet mask, it defaults to 255.255.255.255, no matter what class of address that you enter. The default idle timeout for SSH sessions is five minutes. To alter this value, use the `ssh timeout` command:

```
pixfirewall(config)# ssh timeout minutes
```

To see your configured timeout, use the `show ssh timeout` command.

To see what users have current SSH connections to the PIX, use the `show ssh sessions` command:

```
pixfirewall# show ssh sessions
Session ID      Client IP      Version Encryption      State   Username
     0          192.168.1.2    1.5     DES             6       pix
```

To disconnect a session, use the `ssh disconnect` command:

```
pixfirewall# ssh disconnect session_id
```

You can show the session ID number with the `show ssh sessions` command.

When you establish an SSH connection to the PIX, you will first see the following information in your SSH session:

```
pixfirewall(config)# .
pixfirewall(config)# .
```

The `.` does not affect the SSH session, but is used as an indicator to show you that the PIX is generating a server key or is decrypting a message. In other words, the PIX is busy setting up the connection. After this set up, the PIX will prompt you to enter a username, where you will enter the username of *pix*, and then the telnet password that was configured with the `passwd` command—remember that the default telnet password is *cisco*.

Testing Connections

To verify that you have IP connectivity, you can use two basic troubleshooting commands: `ping` and `show arp`. The following two sections cover these PIX commands.

ping

To test whether or not you have a connection with other IP devices, you can execute the ping command:

```
pixfirewall# ping [logical_interface_name] IP_address
```

The interface_name parameter allows you to specify which interface's IP address to use as the source of the ping. If you omit the name, it will default to the name of the interface that the PIX will use to reach the destination.

The following is an example of the ping command:

```
pixfirewall(config)# ping 192.168.7.200
        192.168.7.200 response received -- 0ms
        192.168.7.200 response received -- 0ms
        192.168.7.200 response received -- 0ms
```

If you cannot ping a destination, verify that the PIX's interfaces are up, and that you have the correct IP addresses assigned to them. You can use the show interfaces and show ip commands to verify this. For the *outside* interface, ICMP traffic is blocked by default in the ingress (inbound) direction if the ICMP traffic is not coming from the directly connected subnet. Chapter 5 covers the commands that you can use to allow ICMP traffic inbound on the *outside* interface. You can also use the debug icmp trace command to see the actual ICMP packets.

IP ARP

The IP ARP protocol resolves an IP address (layer 3) to a MAC address (layer 2). MAC addresses are used for communications between devices on the same segment or subnet, that is, the same LAN medium. Any time the PIX initiates connections or receives connection requests to itself, it will add the IP and MAC addresses to its local ARP table. To view the PIX's ARP table, use the show arp command. as shown here:

```
pixfirewall# show arp
        inside 192.168.7.200 00e0.9871.b91e
```

Currently there is one entry in the PIX's ARP table: a device with an IP address of 192.168.7.200 that is off of the *inside* interface. You can clear the entries in the ARP table with the clear arp *Privilege EXEC* command.

By default, the PIX keeps addresses in the ARP table for four hours (14,400 seconds). You can modify the timeout for ARP entries with the arp timeout command:

```
pixfirewall(config)# arp timeout seconds
```

To view the timeout that you have configured, use the show arp timeout command.

You can manually add or remove an entry from the ARP table by using the PIX *Configuration* mode commands shown here:

```
pixfirewall(config)# arp interface_name IP_address MAC_address [alias]
pixfirewall(config)# no arp interface_name IP_address
```

You need to specify the name of the interface that the device is off of, as well as the device's IP and MAC addresses. If you add the `alias` parameter, the entry will become a permanent entry in the ARP table, even upon a reboot of the PIX. If you need to disable proxy ARP, use the `sysopt` command :

```
pixfirewall(config)# sysopt noproxyarp
```

VIEWING PIX INFORMATION

The PIX supports a multitude of `show` commands. Many of these commands are the same commands that you would execute on an IOS-based router to see the same kinds of information. The following sections will cover some common `show` commands, including `show version`, `show memory`, and `show processes`.

PIX Characteristics

To display the hardware and software characteristics of your PIX firewall, use the `show version` *Privilege EXEC* command. The information that you can see from this command is similar to the `show version` command on an IOS-based router. With this command, you can see the following information about your PIX firewall:

- FOS software and PDM versions
- Uptime since last reboot
- Type of processor
- Amount of RAM and flash
- Interfaces
- Licensed features
- Serial number
- Activation key
- Timestamp showing when configuration was last changed

The following is an example of the `show version` command:

```
pixfirewall# show version

Cisco PIX Firewall Version 6.1(2)
Cisco PIX Device Manager Version 1.1(2)

Compiled on Mon 31-Dec-01 08:44 by morlee
```

```
pixfirewall up 1 hour 42 mins

Hardware:   PIX-501, 16 MB RAM, CPU Am5x86 133 MHz
Flash E28F640J3 @ 0x3000000, 8MB
BIOS Flash E28F640J3 @ 0xfffd8000, 128KB

0: ethernet0: address is 0008.e3c7.f7a1, irq 9
1: ethernet1: address is 0008.e3c7.f7a2, irq 10

Licensed Features:
Failover:        Disabled
VPN-DES:         Enabled
VPN-3DES:        Disabled
Maximum Interfaces:    2
Cut-through Proxy:     Enabled
Guards:          Enabled
Websense:        Enabled
Inside Hosts:    10
Throughput:      Limited
ISAKMP peers:    5

Serial Number: 406091733 (0x183477d5)
Activation Key: 0xbbdb185f 0xc57ebacc 0x5c47ef1b 0x59a2a66e
pixfirewall#
```

Available Memory

The PIX uses RAM to store many components, including its active configuration, the
translation table, the connection table, the ARP table, and many other tables. Because
RAM is an important resource that the PIX uses to enforce its security policy, you
should periodically check how much memory is free on the PIX. To view this information,
use the show memory *Privilege EXEC* command:

```
pixfirewall# show memory
16777216 bytes total, 5980160 bytes free
pixfirewall#
```

Processes Running on the PIX

To see the processes that are currently running on the PIX, use the show processes
Privilege EXEC command, as shown here:

```
pixfirewall# show processes

      PC        SP       STATE     Runtime    SBASE       Stack Process
   Lsi 80078c6e 8081e850 8046afa8       0 8081d890 4008/4096 arp_timer
```

```
Lsi 8007c1ef 80841944 8046afa8      0 80840988 3928/4096 FragDBGC
Lwe 8000be20 80844e38 8046e6c8      0 80843f78 3760/4096 dbgtrace
Lwe 8015d3f2 80846fb4 804486a8      0 80845008 8092/8192 Logger
Hwe 80160783 8084a060 80448958      0 808480a0 8092/8192 tcp_fast
Hwe 8016070a 8084c0ec 80448958      0 8084a130 8032/8192 tcp_slow
Lsi 800c84c2 80857038 8046afa8      0 80856078 4008/4096 xlate clean
Lsi 800c83e8 808580c4 8046afa8      0 80857108 3988/4096 uxlate clean
```

Processes on the PIX are basically lightweight threads that require very few instructions for execution. The Runtime column displays the number of milliseconds that the process has been running. The Stack column indicates the number of bytes used by the process and the total size of the process itself. The Process column displays the actual PIX thread/process that is running.

NETWORK CONFIGURATION EXAMPLE

In this section, I will go over a basic PIX configuration, using the network shown in Figure 3-1. This code shows the basic configuration for the PIX shown in Figure 3-1.

```
pixfirewall#    passwd NoEntry
pixfirewall#    configure terminal
pixfirewall(config)#    hostname pix
pix(config)#    enable password OpenSaysMe
pix(config)#
pix(config)#    interface ethernet0 10full
pix(config)#    interface ethernet1 10full
pix(config)#    interface ethernet2 10full
pix(config)#
pix(config)#    nameif ethernet0 outside sec0
pix(config)#    nameif ethernet2 dmz sec50
pix(config)#    nameif ethernet1 inside sec100
pix(config)#
pix(config)#    ip address outside 192.168.1.1 255.255.255.0
pix(config)#    ip address dmz 192.168.2.1 255.255.255.0
pix(config)#    ip address inside 192.168.3.1 255.255.255.0
pix(config)#    telnet 0 0 inside
pix(config)#
pix(config)#    route outside 0.0.0.0 0.0.0.0 192.168.1.2 1
pix(config)#    route inside 192.168.4.0 255.255.255.0 192.168.3.2 1
pix(config)#    route inside 192.168.5.0 255.255.255.0 192.168.3.2 1
pix(config)#
pix(config)#    exit
pix#
pix#    write memory
```

```
Building configuration...

Cryptochecksum: 21657c19 e04a2a24 e502173c 8626e76d

[OK]
pix#
```

The first command that I executed in this code is to assign a telnet password of *NoEntry*. After this, I changed the hostname of the PIX to *pix* and a *Privilege EXEC* password of *OpenSaysMe*. I then hard-coded the interface settings to 10BaseT full-duplex. The `nameif` commands assigned the names to the interfaces as well as the security levels. I included interfaces *ethernet0* and *ethernet1* in this example, even though these are the default values. Each interface has been assigned an IP address based on those in Figure 3-1. Once IP is configured, I wanted to be able to telnet into this PIX, so I am allowing any internal machine telnet access. Next, I configured one default route and two static routes. Finally, I saved the PIX's configuration—remember that you can execute the `write memory` command at either *Privilege EXEC* or *Configuration* mode.

There are actually quite a few more things that you will need to do in order to pass traffic through your PIX firewall. This chapter, as well as this example, only focused on the basics—preparing your PIX so that you can implement your security polices. The following chapters will deal with traffic as it flows through the PIX.

FURTHER STUDY

Web Sites

For information about putting a simple configuration on your PIX and performing basic management tasks, visit: http://www.cisco.com/univercd/cc/td/doc/product/iaabu/pix/pix_62/config/index.htm.

CHAPTER 4

Traffic Flow Through the PIX and Address Translation

In the last chapter, I talked about some of the PIX commands to create a basic configuration for your PIX firewall. By default, however, traffic will not flow through the PIX. There are certain settings that you will have to configure on the PIX to allow traffic to flow from lower security level interfaces to higher ones as well as for traffic to flow from higher security level interfaces to lower ones. This chapter focuses on these two traffic flows, and discusses addressing issues and address translation. The next chapter covers filters and access control lists, which you can use to further refine the traffic flow through your PIX.

PROTOCOL OVERVIEW

Before I begin discussing the commands that allow traffic to flow through the PIX, you first need to have a good understanding of the mechanics of the two most-often used protocols, TCP and UDP. This is important because the PIX treats these traffic streams differently in its stateful packet filtering process implemented by the ASA.

Overview of TCP

TCP, the Transmission Control Protocol, is a connection-oriented protocol. This means that before any transfer of data can take place, certain connection items will have to be negotiated in order to set up the connection. To perform this negotiation, TCP will go through a three-way handshake.

In the first part of the three-way handshake, the source sends a TCP SYN segment, indicating the desire to open up a connection (SYN is short for *synchronize*). Each TCP segment sent contains a sequence number. When the destination receives the TCP SYN, it acknowledges this with its own SYN as well as an ACK (short for *acknowledgment*). The ACK portion indicates to the source that the destination received the source's SYN. The source then sends an ACK segment to the destination indicating that the connection setup is complete. Of course, during this three-way handshake, the devices are negotiating parameters like the window size, which restricts how many segments a device can send before waiting for an acknowledgement from the destination. Also during the transmission of actual data, the source and destination acknowledge the receipt of received segments from the other device.

The TCP setup process is often referred to as a *defined state machine* because a connection is opened first, data is sent, and the connection is torn down upon completion of the data transaction.

Outgoing Connection Requests

You may be asking what this has to do with a stateful firewall like the PIX. First, understand that, when connections are being set up, traffic flows in two directions through the PIX . Assume that you have a user on the inside of your network who initiates a TCP connection to a device on the outside of your network. Because TCP has a defined set of rules for setting up a connection, it is easy for the PIX to understand what is happening in the connection setup process. In other words, it is easy for the PIX to inspect this traffic. As I discussed in Chapter 1, a stateful firewall keeps track of the *state* of a connection.

In this example, the PIX sees the outgoing SYN and realizes that this is a setup request from an inside user. Because it is a stateful firewall, the PIX will add an entry in its connection table so that the SYN/ACK from the destination will be permitted back in, and the inside user will be able to complete the connection. The PIX will then permit traffic to flow back and forth between these two machines for only this connection (unless the inside user opens up another connection to this destination).

Likewise, TCP goes through a well-defined process when tearing down a connection. When the PIX sees the tear-down process, the PIX knows that the connection is being terminated, and will remove the connection from its connection table. Therefore, once the entry is removed from the PIX's connection table, if the outside destination device tries to send traffic through the PIX using the old connection parameters, the PIX would drop the traffic.

Incoming Connection Requests

Because it is a stateful firewall, the PIX drops all TCP traffic that tries to enter your network, by default. To allow this traffic, you will have to explicitly permit the TCP connection types that you want.

 SECURITY ALERT! By default, PIX *denies* all traffic flowing that originates from a lower security level interface and is trying to reach a higher security level interface.

One problem that TCP has, however, is that it is very predictable, which sometimes plays into the hands of hackers. For instance, a hacker might attempt to send a flood of TCP SYNs to an internal device, pretending to try to set up TCP connections. The real intention of the hacker, however, is to not complete the three-way handshake for each of these TCP SYNs, but to keep on sending SYNs to tie up resources on the internal machine. As I discuss in Chapter 8, the PIX has intrusion detection system (IDS) capabilities that you can configure to prevent these kinds of attacks.

Overview of UDP

UDP, the User Datagram Protocol, is a connectionless protocol and has no defined state machine. This means that there is no preliminary negotiation between the two devices that will be communicating. Instead, a device just starts sending UDP segments when it wishes to communicate with another device. There is no defined process as to how this should occur. Likewise, there is typically no signal indicating the end of the actual UDP transmission. UDP itself also has no built-in flow control to regulate the flow of traffic between two machines. Because of these limitations, UDP is typically used only to send a small amount of information between devices.

A good example of this is the DNS protocol—used when a device needs to resolve a hostname to an IP address. The device sends a DNS query (UDP segment) to a DNS server, and the server responds with a single reply. In this example, using UDP is a more efficient process than TCP because only two segments need to be sent.

Outgoing Connection Requests

Let's look at another example to illustrate one of the problems that the PIX has with its stateful nature and UDP traffic. In this example, assume that the user is performing a TFTP to a device outside of your network. When the user initiates the TFTP connection, the PIX performs its stateful process and adds a temporary connection in its connection table to allow any UDP segments from the destination TFTP device to return through the PIX.

The problem is that once the user has completed the TFTP, the PIX has no idea that the connection has completed. Of course, you don't want the PIX to keep this temporary entry in the connection table after the transmission has completed. To solve this problem, the PIX uses a less-than elegant solution—it keeps track of the idle time for the UDP connection. Once the PIX sees no traffic for the idle time period, it will remove the connection. This is not a very clean solution because this might be a valid idle period while the two UDP devices are performing other processes, and will resume their communication shortly. In this example, the PIX might remove the temporary connection from its state table, and when the device on the outside of your network resumes its transmission, the PIX will drop the traffic because it is no longer allowing it.

Note that some UDP applications are more predictable than TFTP, like DNS. In a DNS example, where a user is initiating a DNS query, there should be one and only one response coming back from the DNS server. In this situation, it makes sense to remove the connection from the connection table once the PIX sees the returning DNS reply. The PIX does this by default. This feature is called DNS Guard, and is discussed in Chapter 8.

 SECURITY ALERT! The PIX treats UDP as a stateful connection, like TCP. However, because there is not a defined connection tear-down process, the PIX will examine the idle period of a UDP connection to determine when it should be removed from the connection table. This process makes inbound UDP sessions susceptible to IP Spoofing and session replay attacks.

Incoming Connection Requests

As I mentioned earlier, because the PIX is a stateful firewall, it will not allow any traffic into your network if the source of the traffic is located on the outside of your network. You will have to explicitly permit this traffic to allow the UDP connection. Since UDP is connectionless, dealing with incoming connections opens you up to more of a security risk. When a UDP connection terminates, the PIX might not know this and thus keep the connection in the connection table. A sophisticated hacker could exploit an IP spoofing attack, which uses a source address of the outside device of the original UDP connection. The PIX would be unable to identify the intrusion, and would then reset its idle timer and allow the spoofed traffic into your network.

Also, because UDP doesn't use any type of connection setup when initiating a traffic stream, the PIX has problems dealing with UDP segments that are trying to come into your network through the PIX. In other words, the PIX has problems differentiating between the start, continuation, and ending of a UDP connection. Therefore, a hacker could be performing a session replay attack, which replays some of the same UDP segments that the hacker saw in an earlier transmission. From the PIX's perspective, this appears to be a continuation of the original UDP data stream.

The PIX treats UDP like TCP. When a user from the inside of the network generates a DNS request, the PIX adds the connection information to the xlate table, and allows the reply from the external DNS server. However, realize that UDP doesn't use any type of connection setup when sending information. This presents a problem for connections originating from the outside: How does the PIX know that this is the beginning and continuance of a connection and not the same repeated information? The PIX can sometimes determine this with its Protocol Fixup feature, which I cover in Chapter 7. In most instances, though, the PIX cannot make this determination.

And Then There's ICMP

ICMP has some characteristics that are very similar to UDP: it's connectionless, and it has no flow control. Therefore, the PIX has the same problems dealing with ICMP traffic as it does when dealing with UDP traffic.

The PIX does treat ICMP traffic differently than UDP traffic, however: it is not treated as a stateful connection. For example, if a user on the inside of your network pings a device on the outside of your network, the PIX does not add a temporary entry in its connection table for the returning ICMP traffic. Therefore, if you want to allow any type of ICMP traffic into your network, whether returning ICMP traffic, or ICMP traffic that originates from the outside world, you need to explicitly permit it through the PIX to the inside of your network.

NOTE   The PIX treats ICMP traffic as non-stateful. By default, the PIX drops all ICMP traffic as it tries to enter your network.

TRANSLATIONS AND CONNECTIONS

Before I continue, I want to differentiate between two terms commonly used when dealing with traffic that flows through the PIX: *translation* and *connection*. A *translation* is an IP-address-to-IP-address mapping when a connection is a TCP or UDP session. The PIX uses translations to perform network address translation (NAT) and port address translation (PAT). You use NAT and PAT when you have deployed private addresses in your internal network, and you need to translate these addresses to a public address space before they leave your network. Please refer to Chapter 1 for more information on NAT and PAT. A *connection*, on the other hand, is basically a TCP or UDP session. A connection specifies all of the parameters used to send traffic to a device, like the source and destination IP addresses, the IP protocol, the application port numbers, and other information.

Translations

The PIX supports up to 65,536 simultaneous translations in its translation table. You can use up to 256 global address pools for translation. These pools contain the public address space that the PIX uses when translating the internal IP private addresses to public address. You can have a single pool with 65,536 addresses, or 256 pools with 256 addresses each.

Connections

As I mentioned, the PIX refers to a connection as a TCP or UDP session. The number of sessions supported by a PIX depends on the model, as well as the connection license that you have purchased for the PIX. Table 4-1 states these limits, which were discussed in Chapter 2.

As I mentioned in Chapter 2, the PIX 501 uses a user license scheme, instead of a connection license scheme. With user licensing, the PIX only allows the first set of users, up to the license limit, through the 501; any additional users are not permitted, even if any of the first set of users are not sending any traffic. You can get around this problem by rebooting the PIX, after which it will, again, allow the first set of users. A better solution is to purchase a higher-end PIX that uses connection licensing.

For PIX models that use connection licensing, the PIX keeps track of the device's connections, not the devices themselves. When a device starts a connection, it counts against the license limit, and the PIX subtracts this connection from the total available connections. Once the connection has been terminated, the PIX adds one to its count of available connections. This is more flexible than the user licensing scheme, because all of the devices are allowed to transmit traffic—only the number of connections is checked.

PIX Model	License Limits
501	10 to 50 users
506/506E	10,000 connections
515/515E	125,000 connections
520	256,000 connections
525	280,000 connections
535	500,000 connections

Table 4-1. The License Limits of the Various PIX Models

ADDRESS TRANSLATION

One of the many issues that you will have to deal with in your network is the assignment of addresses to all of your networking devices. Because of the shortage of public addresses, in many cases, you will have to use private addresses to assign to your internal networking devices. As you will see in the following sections, however, private addresses, even though they allow all of your devices to communicate via IP, also create problems. I will first provide an overview of private addresses and outline the pros and cons of using private addresses, and then I will discuss how the PIX deals with the translation of IP addresses.

Private Addresses

To address the shortage of addresses, and to accommodate the growing need for connecting companies to the Internet, the Internet Engineering Task Force (IETF) developed RFC 1918. Table 4-2 lists the private addresses assigned in RFC 1918.

As you can see from the addresses listed in Table 4-2, you should have more than enough addresses to meet any company's internal address needs. Each of the devices in your network can be given a unique address. RFC 1918, however, defines one restriction: a packet containing a private address in either the source or destination IP address fields cannot be forwarded to a public network.

Imagine two companies, Company A and Company B, that both use 10.0.0.0/8 for their internal addressing, try to communicate to each other , as shown in Figure 4-1. Obviously, this will create many problems because both companies may have overlapping network issues—each company might be using the same subnet numbers. In this situation, the overlapping subnets would not be able to communicate with each other. For example, both companies might have a 10.1.1.0/24 subnet, as shown in Figure 4-1. Within their own companies no connectivity issues arise, but as soon as these two subnets need to reach each other, they will not be able to. The boundary router between these two networks will have a dilemma when trying to reach 10.1.1.0/24— does it forward traffic to Company A or Company B?

Network Address Translation

To solve the problem of overlapping addresses, as well as to address the problem of using private addresses and accessing a public network, the IETF developed RFC 1631,

Address Class	Addresses
A	10.0.0.0–10.255.255.255
B	172.16.0.0–172.31.255.255
C	192.168.0.0–192.168.255.255

Table 4-2.   The Private Addresses Specified by RFC 1918

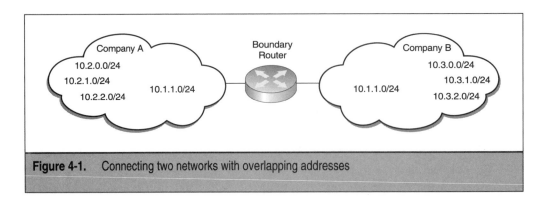

Figure 4-1.   Connecting two networks with overlapping addresses

which defines the process of address translation. This allows you to translate a private address in an IP packet header to another address—either public or private. Here are some common examples where you might need to deploy NAT:

- You are merging two networks together that have an overlapping address space. You need to make it appear that the overlapping network numbers are unique to the two different sides.

- Your ISP has assigned you a very small number of public addresses and you need to provide many of your machines access to the Internet.

- You were assigned a public address space by your ISP, and when you changed ISPs, your new ISP will not support your assigned address space.

- You have critical services on a single machine, and you need to duplicate these resources across many machines. However, you need to make it appear that all of the machines that contain these resources appear as a single entity.

As you will see in the next few sections, using NAT to solve these problems has advantages and disadvantages.

Advantages of Using NAT

One of the main advantages of NAT is that you have an almost inexhaustible number of private addresses at your disposal: over 17 million. This includes one class A network number, sixteen class B network numbers, and 256 class C network numbers. When you use private addresses, if you change ISPs, you will not have to re-address your network—you only have to change your translation rules on your translation device. Because all traffic must pass through your translation device to reach your devices with private addresses, you have strict control over:

- What resources, like the Internet, the external users can access on the inside of your network

- Which users on the inside of your network are allowed access to the Internet

Disadvantages of Using NAT

As you have seen, NAT solves many addressing problems, but not all of them. In fact, it actually introduces some new problems. First, when address translation is performed by your address translation device, it will have to change the IP addresses in the IP packet header and possibly even the port numbers in TCP or UDP segment headers. Because of this, the address translation device will have to perform additional processing not only to handle the translation process, but to also compute new checksums for the packets, putting an additional burden on the translation device.

Another problem that NAT introduces deals with troubleshooting network problems. Because NAT changes the source and/or destination IP addresses in the packet headers, it becomes more difficult to troubleshoot the network problems. When you examine the addresses in the packet header, you don't know whether you are dealing with the addresses that these machines have assigned on them, or the addresses that they have been translated to by an address translation device. This also makes it easier for a hacker to hide his own identity.

Not all applications work with address translation. Most translation devices only perform address translation for addresses in the IP packet header. Some applications embed IP addresses in the data payload, which an address translation device cannot catch. If a receiving device uses the IP address in the data payload, it wouldn't be able to reach the transmitter of the packet. Figure 4-2 shows an example of this process. In this example, a machine on the right (172.16.1.1) sends a packet to a machine on the left (200.200.200.1). Inside the payload, the 172.16.1.1 device embeds its own IP address. When this IP packet reaches the NAT device, the NAT device translates the addressing

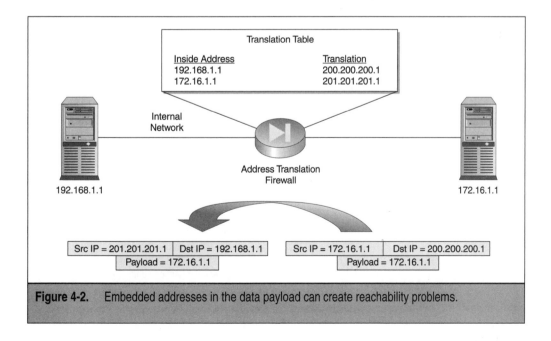

Figure 4-2.   Embedded addresses in the data payload can create reachability problems.

information in the packet header based on the rules defined in the NAT device's translation table. However, the translation device is not smart enough to figure out that there is also an IP address embedded in the payload—172.16.1.1's own IP address. When the half-translated packet reaches the destination (192.168.1.1), if the destination tries to use 172.16.1.1 to return a reply instead of 201.201.201.1, the translation device will be confused and not be able to forward the packet correctly.

NAT Terms and Definitions

The device that performs address translation can take on many forms. This device can be a firewall, a router, a proxy gateway, or even a file server. Cisco's routers, as of IOS 11.2, and the PIX firewall both support NAT. For a better understanding of the commands used on the PIX to configure address translation, you must first understand some of the terms that are commonly used in address translation. Many of these terms I already discussed in Chapter 1.

In addition to the terms discussed in Chapter 1, there are terms that describe the different forms of address translation employed by address translation devices, as shown in Table 4-3.

Examples of Address Translation

As you can see from Table 4-3, there are different types of address translation that can be performed by an address translation device. In this section, you'll look at two examples: one that uses NAT and one that uses PAT.

NAT Example

NAT, as I mentioned earlier, performs a one-to-one address translation. Typically you use static translation when you have a server that you want external users to reach from the Internet. For your internal users, however, you will typically create a pool of IP addresses and let the translation device randomly assign a global address to the device (dynamic NAT). In this example, I'm going to assume that a user on the inside

NAT Translation type	Definition of Translation Type
Simple translation	A single IP address is mapped to another IP address.
Extended translation	A single IP address and TCP/UDP port are mapped to another address and port number.
Static translation	The address translation is manually configured by an administrator.
Dynamic translation	The address translation is performed dynamically by a address translation device.
Port address translation (PAT)	Each device that has its address translated is translated to the same IP address. To keep each of these connections unique, the source port number of the connection is also changed.

Table 4-3.   Different Types of Address Translation

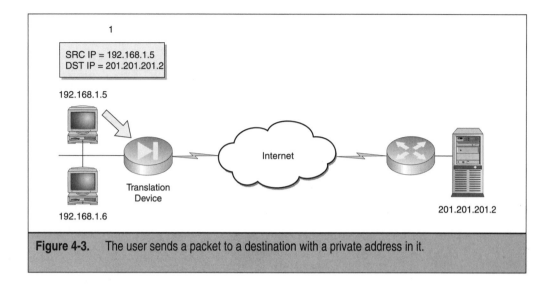

1

SRC IP = 192.168.1.5
DST IP = 201.201.201.2

192.168.1.5

Internet

Translation
Device

192.168.1.6

201.201.201.2

Figure 4-3.   The user sends a packet to a destination with a private address in it.

of your network is going to access resources on the outside of your network. Figure 4-3 illustrates this example.

In this example, assume that the user on 192.168.1.5 is trying to access 201.201.201.2. In Figure 4-3, you can see the actual transmission from 192.168.1.5. The translation device receives the packet from 192.168.1.5, determines if it needs to perform translation (and does it if necessary), and forwards the packet on its way to the destination. As you can see in Figure 4-4, the address translation device sees the incoming packet and compares it to its address translation rules.

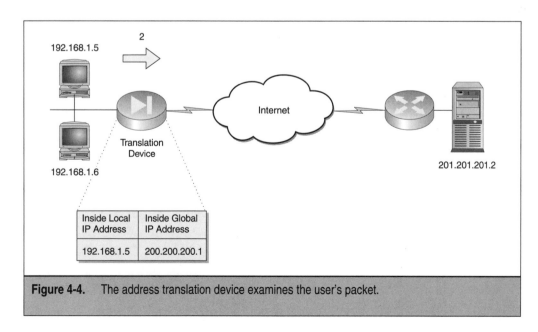

192.168.1.5

2

Internet

Translation
Device

192.168.1.6

201.201.201.2

Inside Local IP Address	Inside Global IP Address
192.168.1.5	200.200.200.1

Figure 4-4.   The address translation device examines the user's packet.

Because the packet matches its rule in its address translation policy, the address translation device translates the source IP address in the packet from 192.168.1.5 to 200.200.200.1, which is a global IP address. This process can be seen in Figure 4-5. Note that if you have configured a static translation for the internal user, the address translation device will know exactly how to translate the source address—this entry will already be in the address translation table. However, if you are using dynamic translation, the address translation device will pick an unused address from its address translation pool, assign the address to the user, and then add this entry to the address translation table.

In Figure 4-6, you can see that the destination (201.201.201.2) has received the packet. From the destination's perspective, the source appears to have an address of 200.200.200.1. This is transparent both to the local user and the destination.

When the destination sends the response back to the user, it uses the global IP address that it saw in the translated packet: 200.200.200.1. This process can be seen in Figure 4-7.

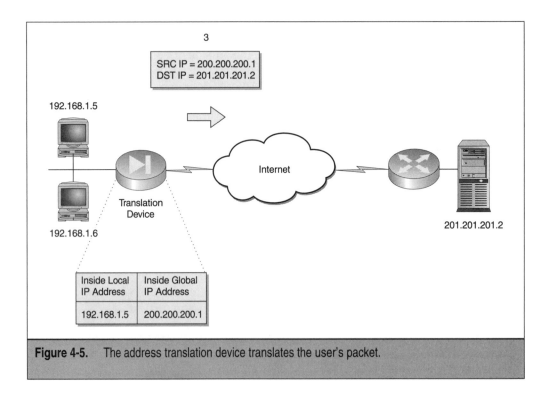

Figure 4-5. The address translation device translates the user's packet.

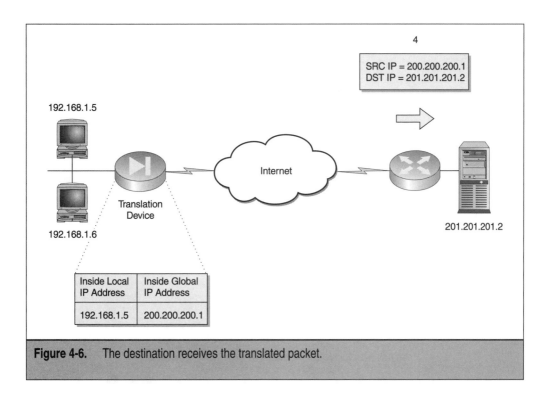

Figure 4-6.   The destination receives the translated packet.

In Figure 4-8, the address translation device receives the packet and examines its address translation policy. After determining that it needs to translate the packet, it examines its address translation table to see how to perform the translation. It sees the entry for 200.200.200.1 and changes this global destination IP address to a local address of 192.168.1.5 and forwards the packet to the inside user.

NOTE   The address translation process is transparent to the source and destination devices.

PAT Example

With PAT, an address translation device will possibly change both the packet's IP address and the TCP or UDP segment's port number. This example examines a situation in which your ISP assigned you a single IP address, and you need to use this one

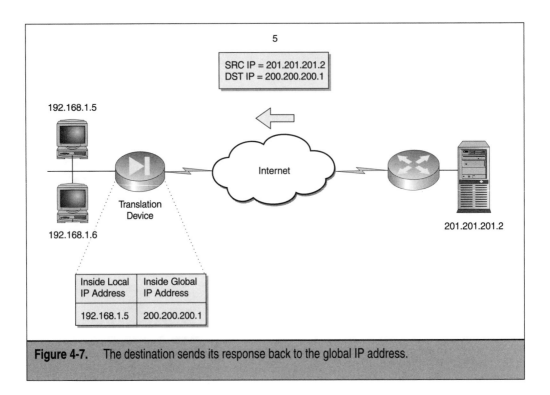

Figure 4-7. The destination sends its response back to the global IP address.

address for all of your users' connections to the Internet. In this example, the user at the 192.168.1.5 device sends a packet to 201.201.201.2, as shown in Figure 4-9.

In Figure 4-10, the address translation device receives the packet. It compares the packet information to its internal address translation policies and determines whether it needs to perform address translation on the packet. In this example, there is a policy match, so the translation device performs its address translation, and changes the local address of 192.168.1.5 to 200.200.200.1. In this instance, the source port number of 1,024 is unused in the address table, so the address translation device leaves it as is. Note that the address translation device adds an entry to its address translation table so that it can handle the returning traffic for this device.

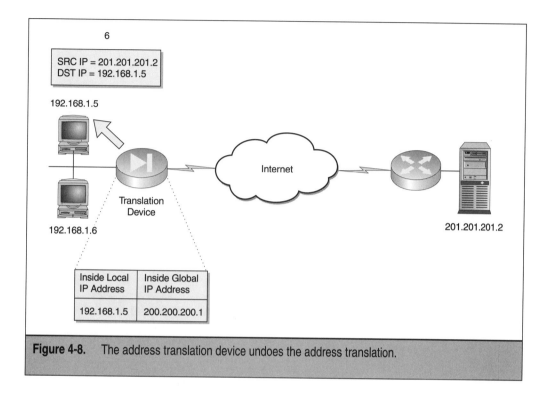

Figure 4-8. The address translation device undoes the address translation.

In Figure 4-11, the destination receives the translated packet. Again, the translation process is transparent to both the source and destination devices.

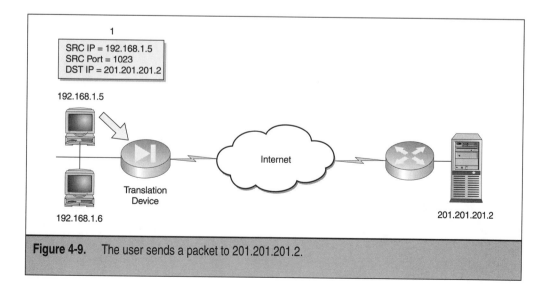

Figure 4-9. The user sends a packet to 201.201.201.2.

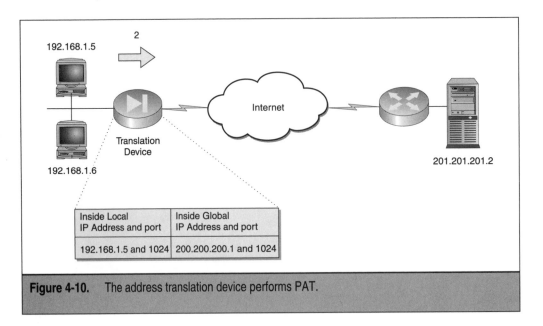

Figure 4-10. The address translation device performs PAT.

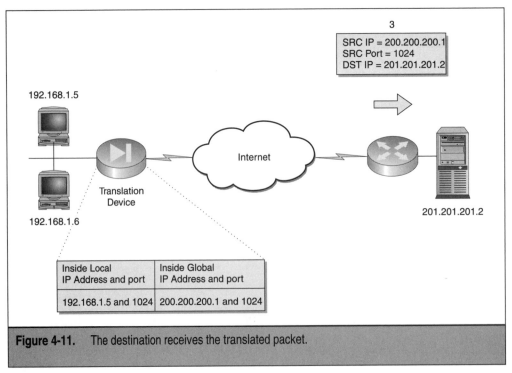

Figure 4-11. The destination receives the translated packet.

When the destination device sends its reply, it uses a destination IP address of 200.200.200.1 and a destination port of 1,024. When the translation device receives the inbound packet, it determines that address translation should be performed, and then looks for a match in its address translation table. It sees a match, changes the destination IP address to 192.168.1.5, and leaves the destination port number the same. This process is shown in Figure 4-12.

To illustrate the implementation of PAT, assume that 192.168.1.6 also sends a packet to 201.201.201.2 with a source port of 1,024, as shown in Figure 4-13.

The address translation device receives the packet, determines that there is an address translation policy match, and then creates an entry in its address translation table for the user's connection. In this instance, the same global IP address is used for the translation of the source IP address. However, because there is already a source port 1,024 in the address translation table, the address translation device assigns a source port of 1,025 for the user's connection, as shown in Figure 4-14. The translation of the source port number allows the destination device to differentiate between the connections from 192.168.1.5 and 192.168.1.6, and also allows the address translation device to undo its translation for returning traffic from 201.201.201.2.

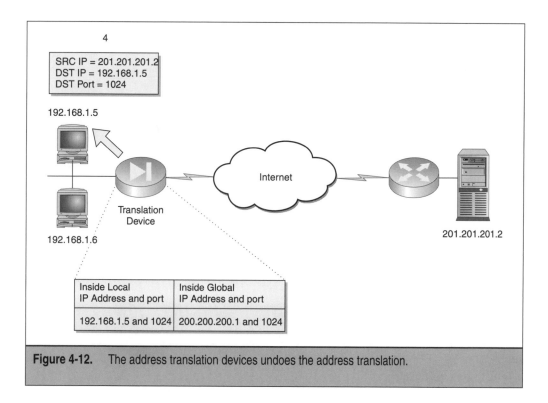

Figure 4-12. The address translation devices undoes the address translation.

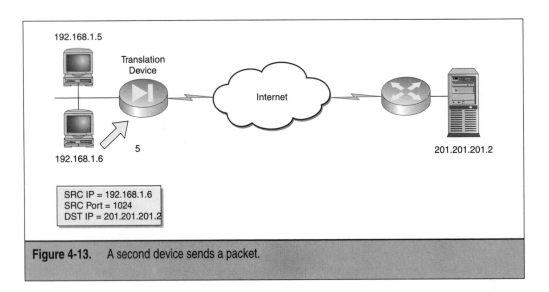

Figure 4-13. A second device sends a packet.

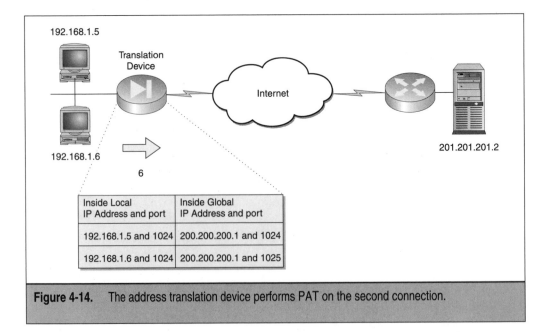

Figure 4-14. The address translation device performs PAT on the second connection.

CONFIGURING YOUR PIX FOR INSIDE-TO-OUTSIDE ACCESS

The security levels of the interface affect how the PIX deals with traffic. As I mentioned in Chapter 3, the nameif command allows you associate a security level with an interface. Traffic is allowed to freely travel from a higher level interface to a lower one, but it is, by default, prohibited from traveling from a lower level interface to a higher one.

One problem with this traffic flow, however, is that the PIX assumes that you are using private addresses on the inside of your network, and that these addresses must be translated to a public address space. Therefore, you need to either configure address translation or disable address translation to allow traffic to flow through the PIX from a higher security-level interface to a lower-security-level interface. This requires you to configure two sets of commands: global and nat. The following two sections cover the use of these commands, and then I will show you some examples of configurations using NAT and PAT for traffic flowing from higher-security-level interfaces to lower ones.

NOTE   The PIX *always* assumes that traffic needs to be translated when passing through the PIX, even though you might not need address translation.

Defining the Address Pool

One of the first things that you need to define when performing NAT or PAT is the pool of addresses that the PIX will use when performing its translation. The PIX performs address translation on the source IP address in the packet, changing the local address to a global address defined in its address pool. To create your global address pools, use the global *Configuration* mode command:

```
pixfirewall (config)# global [(logical_interface_name)] pool_number
                    first_IP_address[-last_IP_address]
                    [netmask subnet_mask]
```

The first parameter is the logical name of the interface. The logical interface is defined with the nameif command. When packets travel through the interface specified, they are translated using the addresses listed in this pool. If you omit the *logical_interface_name*, it defaults to *outside*.

The *pool_number* is used to specify which internal address(es) will be translated when exiting this interface. Basically, this is a pointer to the PIX's nat command. I discuss the use of the nat command in the next section, which allows you to specify the internal addresses that will be translated.

SECURITY ALERT!   Any time you add, change, or delete a `global` command, you should clear the translation table with the `clear xlate` command in order for your changes to take effect.

Address Pools and NAT

After the *pool_number* parameter comes your list of addresses. You can specify a range of addresses, like `192.168.1.1-192.168.1.10`, or you can specify a network number with its subnet mask, with the `netmask` parameter, for example: `192.168.1.0 netmask 255.255.255.0`. This example tells the PIX that all addresses from network 192.168.1.0 should be used for address translation, with the exception of the first address (the network number itself) and the last address (the directed broadcast). You could also specify this address range using the following syntax: `192.168.1.1-192.168.1.254`. Both of these methods produce the same result.

By default, when you have more than one address listed in your address pool, the PIX performs NAT on its packets. The first device's packet through the PIX is assigned the first address in the pool, the second device is assigned the second address, and so on. This assignment process continues until the PIX reaches the last address. At that point, the PIX performs translation tasks by using PAT with the last address. This ensures that all of your internal devices can participate in the address translation process and have their traffic flow through the PIX.

Address Pools and PAT

If you only want your PIX to perform PAT instead of NAT, just specify a single IP address in your global address pool, such as 192.168.1.250. The PIX then uses this address, and performs PAT on all of the packets by replacing their source address with this global address, and changing the source port numbers in the packets to ensure uniqueness for each internal device.

With PAT on a PIX, you can support 64,000 internal devices. Therefore, if you have more than 64,000 devices, you should specify more than one `global` command, where each `global` command has a single IP address in it. For example, if you need to support 70,000 devices through your PIX, you need two global addresses for PAT. Remember that you shouldn't list these two global addresses in a single `global` command, because the PIX will perform NAT on the first address and PAT on the second. Instead, create two `global` commands with the same pool number, where each `global` command has a single address in its pool.

PAT on an Interface Address

There is a special form of the `global` command that allows you to use an IP address on the PIX when performing address translation:

```
pixfirewall(config)# global (logical_interface_name) pool_number interface
```

Notice that with the syntax of the global command here, the address pool has been replaced by the interface parameter. This tells the PIX to use the IP address of the interface specified by the *logical_interface_name* as the global IP address when translating internal source IP addresses. Typically, this process is used in the following two situations:

- Your PIX is directly connected to your ISP (typically via a DSL/cable modem connection), and your ISP assigns you only one public IP address that you must use on the interface of the PIX that connects directly to the ISP. You would have to configure this address on its outside interface. Of course, you have just used up your one available public address, so you have nothing left for your global address pool. You can overcome this limitation by using this address for your global pool as well by configuring the syntax of the global command using the interface parameter.

- Your PIX is directly connected to your ISP, and your ISP uses DHCP to dynamically assign your PIX an IP address. Your PIX could have a different IP address each time it boots up and dynamically acquires its outside interface's IP address via DHCP. The problem of using the regular global syntax is that you must know the global address to use in the pool. You could get around this by manually changing the address each time the PIX boots up and acquires its new address. A much simpler solution is to use the interface parameter.

Defining the Addresses to Translate

The function of the global command is to define the pool of addresses (or single address) for the PIX to use when it is translating the source IP address of packets as they flow from higher-security-level interfaces to lower-level interfaces. In other words, it defines the global addresses that a local address will be changed to. What the global command does not define is the actual internal devices upon which address translation should be performed—that is, the local addresses. The nat *Configuration* mode command accomplishes this feat. The syntax of the nat command is:

```
pixfirewall (config)# nat [(logical_interface_name)] pool_number
                       local_IP_address [subnet_mask
                       [outside] [dns] [norandomseq]
                       [timeout hh:mm:ss]
                       [maximum_connection_limit
                       [embryonic_connection_limit]]]
```

Any time you add, change, or delete a nat command, you should clear the translation table with the clear xlate command.

Interface Name

The first parameter in the nat command is the logical name of the interface. The logical interface is defined with the nameif command. You specify the interface name where the local devices are located for which you want to perform address translation. If you omit the *logical_interface_name*, it defaults to *inside*.

Pool Number

The *pool_number* parameter is used to specify which global address pool(s) to use when performing the source IP address translation for the internal devices—converting the local address to a global address. This number associates this command with the *global* command discussed in the last section. To take this one step further, the interface name specified in both the *nat* and *global* commands specifies when address translation should be performed.

For instance, assume that your PIX has three interfaces: *inside*, *outside*, and *dmz*, and that you have configured a *nat* command for your users, and associated this with the *inside* interface. Also assume that you have configured a *global* command with your pool of global addresses and associated this with the *outside* interface. Therefore, any time traffic flows from the *inside* interface that matches the local addresses in the *nat* command, and will exit the *outside* interface, the PIX will use the address pool in the corresponding *global* command to translate the source IP address in the packet.

If, however, an internal user off of the PIX's *inside* interface sends a packet that is destined to the PIX's dmz interface, the PIX would not perform address translation on it, because there is no corresponding *global* command for the dmz interface with a pool number that matches the *nat* command for the *inside* interface. To allow traffic from the *inside* interface to the dmz interface, you'll need an additional *global* command for address translation between these two interfaces.

Addresses to Translate

After the *pool_number* parameter is the local IP address that you want the PIX to perform address translation on. Note that if you don't have the address of a device specified in the *nat* command, traffic from this device will not be able to travel from a higher-security-level interface to a lower-level one. If you specify a network number for the *local_IP_address* parameter, follow this with the *netmask* parameter and the *subnet_mask* of this network—this tells the PIX that it is translating addresses for an entire subnet or network.

For example, if you only configure 192.168.1.1 as an address and omit the mask, the PIX assumes that the mask is 255.255.255.255—a specific host. However, if you configure a network number of 192.168.1.0 as the local address, and a subnet mask of 255.255.255.0, this configuration tells the PIX that any local address of network 192.168.1.0 should be translated. If you want all your addresses to be translated, then use a local address of 0.0.0.0 and a subnet mask of 0.0.0.0; or, you can abbreviate this as 0 0.

Disabling NAT for a Group of Users

As I mentioned earlier, the PIX expects you to use NAT to move traffic from a higher-level interface to a lower-level one. However, there may be instances when NAT, or PAT, is not necessary. For instance, perhaps a part of your network, or perhaps even your entire network, is using public IP addresses. In this instance, you have no need to perform NAT or PAT on these addresses. However, by default, the PIX assumes that you need NAT, and will not let traffic flow between higher- and lower-level interfaces unless you configure NAT for these addresses. Likewise, you might be creating a VPN tunnel through the PIX to a remote site, and you want the remote site to look like a logical extension to your addressing design. In this instance, you don't want your PIX to perform address translation for traffic traversing the VPN tunnel between the two sites.

To get around these problems, the PIX supports a special NAT pool number, labeled 0. By giving a pool number of 0 to a list of addresses in a `nat` command, you are telling the PIX not to translate these addresses, but to still allow them to access lower-level interfaces. For example, if you configure `nat (inside) 0 0 0` on your PIX, you would be telling it that any address (the second and third 0's) from the *inside* interface should not be translated, but should still be allowed access to lower-level interfaces. If you had a PIX with four interfaces—*inside, dmz1, dmz2,* and *outside*—and your entire network used public IP addresses, and you did not need to perform NAT/PAT, you could configure the following on your PIX:

```
pixfirewall(config)#  nat (inside) 0 0 0
pixfirewall(config)#  nat (dmz1) 0 0 0
pixfirewall(config)#  nat (dmz2) 0 0 0
```

This configuration ensures that higher-level interfaces can send traffic to a lower-level interface and address translation will not be performed on these packets.

Besides specifying the actual network and mask of the devices that you wish to disable NAT for with the `nat` command, you can use a different approach, an access list, by using the following syntax:

```
pixfirewall(config)#  nat [(interface_name)] 0 access-list acl_name
```

I will discuss access lists in Chapter 5. One restriction with the entries in the access list is that you cannot specify a port number—only a source and destination IP addresses. Likewise, you cannot specify a protocol type, except for IP itself—TCP and UDP are invalid. This is an example of an *invalid* configuration:

```
pixfirewall (config)#  access-list no-nat permit tcp
                       192.168.1.0 255.255.255.0
                       0.0.0.0 0.0.0.0
pixfirewall(config)#  nat (inside) 0 access-list no-nat
```

As you can see, the access list contains the `tcp` parameter, making it invalid for NAT. The following is an example of a valid configuration:

```
pixfirewall (config)#  access-list no-nat permit ip
                       192.168.1.0 255.255.255.0
                       0.0.0.0 0.0.0.0
pixfirewall(config)#  nat (inside) 0 access-list no-nat
```

Any traffic from 192.168.1.0 that is headed for any destination will not be translated. One unique thing about access-lists on the PIX, as you will see in Chapter 5, is that their format is the same as an access list on an IOS-based router, except that you give the access list a name, and you use a subnet mask instead of a wildcard mask.

> ⚠️ **SECURITY ALERT!**   ACLs on a PIX use a *subnet* mask, not a wildcard mask like IOS-based routers.

Using access lists for restricting NAT gives you more flexibility because you can specify not only the source address, but also what destination the source address is reaching. The network in Figure 4-15 illustrates a situation where you might want to disable traffic from a particular network, depending on what destinations devices are trying to reach. In this example, you definitely want to perform NAT on internal users' packets from 172.16.1.0/16, when their traffic is destined to the outside interface of the PIX. You might want to disable NAT when traffic flows from the internal users to the *dmz* interface, however.

Other Command Options

Table 4-4 lists some additional parameters that you can specify when configuring your nat command.

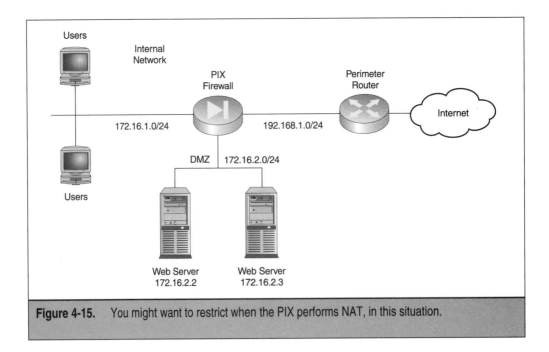

Figure 4-15.   You might want to restrict when the PIX performs NAT, in this situation.

Parameter	Meaning
`outside`	Performs a reverse NAT—from the outside interface to another interface on the PIX.
`dns`	Has the PIX alias DNS reply when returning from a DNS server to an internal device listed in the NAT local address pool.
`norandomseq`	Turns off the TCP Sequence Number Randomization feature— you should do this if another firewall is already randomizing TCP sequence numbers. Otherwise, you should leave this feature enabled to help prevent hackers from hijacking TCP sessions.
`timeout`	Specifies the length of time that an idle connection will remain in the translation table.
`maximum_connection_limit`	Limits the maximum number of connections allowed for the devices listed in the `nat` command for the specified interface.
`embryonic_connection_limit`	Limits the maximum number of half-open connections allowed for the devices listed in the `nat` command for the specified interface.

Table 4-4.   Additional NAT Command Parameters

Verifying Address Translation

There are three basic commands that you should use to verify your address translation configuration and operation:

- `show global`
- `show nat`
- `show xlate`

The `show global` command displays the `global` commands that you have configured on your PIX:

```
pixfirewall(config)# show global
global (outside) 1 200.200.200.10-200.200.200.30 netmask 255.255.255.0
```

The `show nat` command displays the `nat` commands you have configured:

```
pixfirewall(config)# show nat
nat (inside) 1 0.0.0.0 0.0.0.0 0 0
```

I will discuss the `show xlate` command at the end of this chapter.

Address Translation Examples

In this section I cover some network examples that use NAT and PAT to allow users to access resources from higher-security-level interfaces to lower ones. These examples are not all inclusive, but I have included examples of situations that you will commonly come across when setting up a PIX.

Configuration Example Using Only NAT

To illustrate the implementation of NAT on a Cisco PIX firewall, take a look at a few configuration examples. In the first example, I'll use the network shown in Figure 4-16.

In the network illustrated in Figure 4-16, I have the PIX employ NAT for address translation for all internal addresses, using a global pool of addresses from 199.199.199.0/24. This is the PIX's configuration:

```
pixfirewall(config)# ip address outside 192.168.1.1 255.255.255.0
pixfirewall(config)# ip address inside 192.168.2.1 255.255.255.0
pixfirewall(config)#
pixfirewall(config)# route outside 0.0.0.0 0.0.0.0 192.168.1.2 1
pixfirewall(config)# route inside  192.168.3.0 255.255.255.0 192.168.2.2 1
pixfirewall(config)# route inside  192.168.4.0 255.255.255.0 192.168.2.2 1
pixfirewall(config)#
pixfirewall(config)# global (outside) 1 199.199.199.0 netmask 255.255.255.0
pixfirewall(config)# nat (inside) 1 0 0
```

As you can see, the configuration has two `ip address` commands for its two interfaces, and one default route and two static routes (for the internal networks off of the internal router). Below this are the PIX's address translation commands. The `global` command specifies a network number to use when translating the internal local source IP addresses before forwarding them out of the *outside* interface. The `nat` command specifies that all internal addresses on the *inside* interface should be translated. The pool number of 1 ties the `nat` and `global` commands together.

Configuration Example Using Both NAT and PAT

In this PIX address translation example, I'll use the same network diagram pictured in Figure 4-16. However, instead of using NAT on all internal addresses, I'll use a combination of both NAT and PAT. This is the configuration:

```
pixfirewall(config)# ip address outside 192.168.1.1 255.255.255.0
pixfirewall(config)# ip address inside 192.168.2.1 255.255.255.0
pixfirewall(config)#
pixfirewall(config)# route outside 0.0.0.0 0.0.0.0 192.168.1.2 1
pixfirewall(config)# route inside  192.168.3.0 255.255.255.0 192.168.2.2 1
pixfirewall(config)# route inside  192.168.4.0 255.255.255.0 192.168.2.2 1
pixfirewall(config)#
```

```
pixfirewall(config)# global (outside) 1 199.199.199.1-199.199.199.125
pixfirewall(config)# global (outside) 2 199.199.199.126
pixfirewall(config)# nat (inside) 1 192.168.3.0 255.255.255.0
pixfirewall(config)# nat (inside) 2 192.168.4.0 255.255.255.0
```

The major differences between this example and the NAT-only example are the
`global` and `nat` commands. In this example, there are two `global` commands.
The first `global` command, for pool number 1, specifies that the PIX should perform
NAT using addresses from 199.199.199.1 through 199.199.199.125. The second `global`
command, for pool 2, specifies only a single IP address, 199.199.199.126, indicating that
PAT should be performed with this address.

The two `nat` commands following these `global` commands specify the internal
addresses that will be translated using NAT. The first `nat` command refers to the first
global address pool, and will translate all source addresses from 192.168.3.0/24 to
199.199.199.1 through 199.199.199.125. The second `nat` command will translate
all source addresses from 192.168.4.0/24 to a single address in the second global pool
(199.199.199.126), and the PIX will only perform PAT on these addresses. By using
different pool numbers in the `nat` and `global` commands, you can control which
internal addresses will be translated with which global pool.

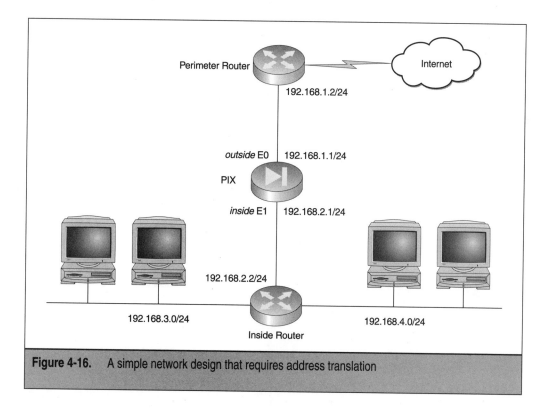

Figure 4-16.   A simple network design that requires address translation

Configuration Example Using PAT and Disabling NAT

In this configuration example, I'll use the network diagram pictured in Figure 4-17. As you can see, the internal network contains a mixture of both private and public IP addresses. In this example, I will set up a configuration that will translate the internal private addresses, but will leave the internal public addresses alone.

The following is the configuration that accomplishes this dual configuration:

```
pixfirewall(config)# ip address outside 192.168.1.1 255.255.255.0
pixfirewall(config)# ip address inside 192.168.2.1 255.255.255.0
pixfirewall(config)#
pixfirewall(config)# route outside 0.0.0.0 0.0.0.0 192.168.1.2 1
pixfirewall(config)# route inside  192.168.3.0 255.255.255.0 192.168.2.2 1
pixfirewall(config)# route inside  199.199.199.128 255.255.255.128 192.168.2.2 1
pixfirewall(config)#
pixfirewall(config)# global (outside) 1 199.199.199.1
pixfirewall(config)# global (outside) 1 199.199.199.2
pixfirewall(config)# nat (inside) 1 192.168.3.0 255.255.255.0
pixfirewall(config)# nat (inside) 0 199.199.199.128 255.255.255.128
```

The 192.168.3.0 subnet uses pool 1 for its address translation. Pool 1 has two `global` statements, each with a single IP address. The PIX will perform PAT with both of these addresses for devices from this internal network number. The

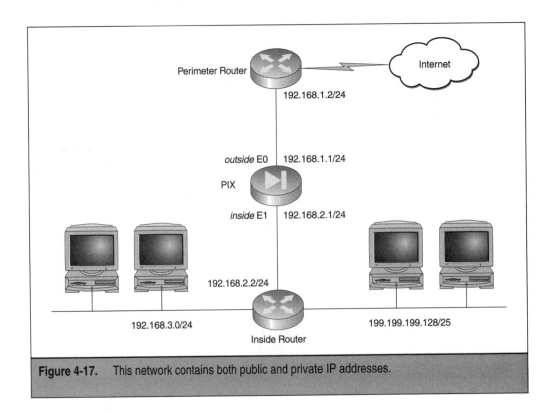

Figure 4-17.   This network contains both public and private IP addresses.

second `nat` command disables address translation for all internal addresses from the 199.199.199.128/25 subnet by using the pool number of 0.

Configuration Example Using PAT and an Interface

In this configuration example, I'll use the network diagram pictured in Figure 4-18. The PIX is directly attached to the ISP, and the ISP has assigned a single public IP address to the PIX, which must be used on the *outside* interface.

The following is the configuration that will allow the PIX to use the single IP address on its outside interface while also using the address to perform PAT for the devices on the inside of the network:

```
pixfirewall(config)# ip address outside 199.199.199.2 255.255.255.252
pixfirewall(config)# ip address inside 192.168.2.1 255.255.255.0
pixfirewall(config)#
pixfirewall(config)# route outside 0.0.0.0 0.0.0.0 199.199.199.1 1
pixfirewall(config)# route inside  192.168.3.0 255.255.255.0 192.168.2.2 1
pixfirewall(config)# route inside  199.199.199.128 255.255.255.128 192.168.2.2 1
pixfirewall(config)#
pixfirewall(config)# global (outside) 1 interface
pixfirewall(config)# nat (inside) 1 0 0
```

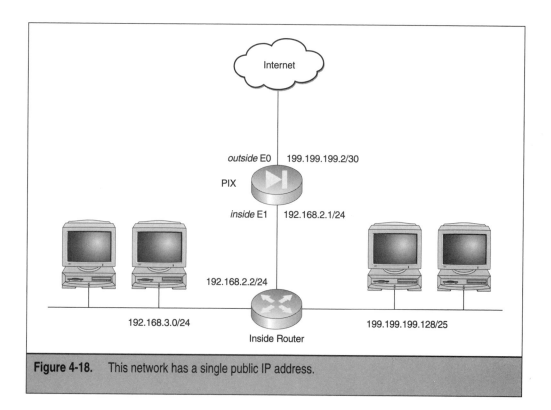

Figure 4-18.   This network has a single public IP address.

In this example, the `nat` command specifies that all internal addresses use the address pool configured in the `global` command for pool 1. The corresponding `global` command, however, doesn't specify a pool of addresses, but refers to the *outside* interface. One advantage of this process is that if the ISP is not statically assigning you the public address, but is using DHCP to assign you the address, you don't need to worry about what address is eventually assigned on the outside interface because the `interface` parameter causes the PIX to use the currently assigned address, whether it's statically assigned or dynamically assigned.

Also note that there is an internal segment using 199.199.199.128/26 as an address space—this is also translated because the `nat` command specifies all addresses. If you don't want to enable NAT for these addresses, you'll need another `nat` command associated with pool 0.

TRAFFIC ENTERING YOUR NETWORK

The `nat` and `global` commands are typically used to perform address translation as traffic travels from higher-security-level interfaces to lower-level ones. As I mentioned in Chapter 3, the ASA allows traffic to flow from higher-level to lower-level interfaces by default. When you have traffic traveling in the opposite direction (from a lower-level interface to a higher-level one), you'll be faced with two issues:

- The PIX still expects address translation to be performed on this inbound traffic.
- The PIX automatically drops this traffic based on its interface rules and stateful nature.

You need to perform two tasks to allow traffic to pass from lower-level interfaces to higher-level ones. To solve the first issue, you need to configure `static` commands to perform the address translation. To solve the second issue, you need to configure either `conduit` or `access-list` commands to open up holes in the ASA's algorithm. Cisco now focuses on using access lists, not conduits, to enforce security policies on the PIX because it relates to traffic flowing between interfaces. I will cover the use of both of these commands. In this chapter I cover the use of conduits, and I cover the use and implementation of ACLs in the next chapter.

Setting Up Address Translations

Using dynamic NAT with the `global` and `nat` commands creates problems for external machines accessing resources inside your network. For example, imagine that you have a web server located on your DMZ segment, that you want users on the Internet to be able to access. If you use dynamic NAT to assign the web server an address, the external users would not know which dynamic address the PIX assigned the server. To solve this dilemma, you will typically use static NAT. Static NAT simplifies access for Internet users when they want to access publicly-accessible services that your company offers.

Figure 4-19 shows a simple example of a network using static NAT. In this illustration, there are two servers located on the DMZ segment: 192.168.2.2, which is a web server, and 192.168.2.3, which is an e-mail server. In this example, the outside world uses a destination address of 200.200.200.1 to access the web server. When the PIX sees this IP address on the *outside* interface, it translates it to 192.168.2.2, which is the address physically configured on the web server. The nice thing about this process is that it is transparent to both the Internet users and the web server itself. This is also true for the e-mail server. One other point to make with this static translation is that the host addresses do not have to match in the translation process. For the e-mail server, the outside host address is 200.200.200.2, but its internal address ends in .3. The following section covers the configuration of static translations on the PIX.

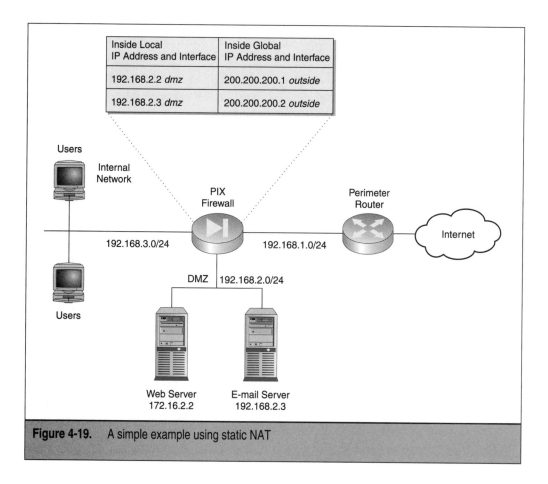

Figure 4-19. A simple example using static NAT

Static Translations

To configure static NAT translations, use the `static` command on the PIX:

```
pixfirewall (config)# static [(internal_interface_name, external_interface_name)]
                      global_IP_address local_IP_address
                      [dns] [netmask subnet_mask]
                      [maximum_connections [embryonic_limit]] [norandomseq]
```

You can optionally specify the interfaces that are associated with the traffic flow for the static address translation. The first interface is the one with the higher security level, and the second interface is the one with the lower security level. If you omit the interface names, it defaults to (`inside, outside`).

After the interface names comes the static translation. The first address that you specify is the global IP address that the devices on the lower-level interface use to reach the internal device. In the example in Figure 4-19, this is 200.200.200.1 for the web server and 200.200.200.2 for the e-mail server. The second address is the address physically assigned to the device located off of the higher-security-level interface. Again, using the example in Figure 4-19, the address for the web server is 192.168.2.2, and for the e-mail server, it is 192.168.2.3.

NOTE   The interface names and the addresses listed in the `static` command are reversed, which has created a lot of confusion for network administrators setting up static translations!

If all the devices on a segment need a static translation, you don't need to create a separate `static` command for each device. Instead, you can list a network number for the public and private IP addresses, and then follow this with the `netmask` parameter and subnet mask used by the internal subnet. The PIX will drop all inbound packets with a destination IP address that is a network number or broadcast address. To help the PIX differentiate between these addresses and host addresses, you must configure the `netmask` parameter.

In the example in Figure 4-19, if you wanted a static translation for all machines on 192.168.2.0/24, you could specify the following for your configuration: `200.200.200.0 192.168.2.0 netmask 255.255.255.0`. This causes the PIX to perform a one-to-one static translation automatically. For example, the global address of 200.200.200.1 would match to the local (internal) address 192.168.2.1, the address 200.200.200.2 would match to 192.168.2.2, and so on.

⚠ SECURITY ALERT!   Remember that the PIX requires address translation to pass packets between interfaces. Even if you have public addresses assigned to your internal devices, you still need to configure a static translation.

For an example, imagine that you have a DMZ with servers that have public addresses assigned to them. You still need to configure a static translation(s) for these addresses. When you configure your `static` command, you need to specify the public address twice: as the global address, *and* as the local address. This satisfies the PIX's requirement for a static translation. The strange thing about this process is that, in reality, you are translating the destination address to the same destination address.

After the static translation information, you have some optional parameters that you can specify. These parameters are also used by the `nat` command, and are described in Table 4-4. To view the static translations you have created, you can use the `show` `static` command.

NOTE The PIX always processes address translations using your `static` commands first, before using a translation created by a `nat/global` configuration.

Port Redirection

A newer feature in the PIX is the ability to redirect traffic sent to one destination IP address and port number to a different address. For example, you might have a single IP address assigned to you by your ISP, and this address must be assigned to the *outside* interface of the PIX. The problem with this situation is that when you assign the public address to the PIX's *outside* interface, any traffic directed to this IP address will be processed by the PIX. Alternately, the ISP might not even assign this address statically, but use DHCP to assign it.

The `static` command is used to redirect traffic destined to a specific port to a different internal machine. This ability allows you to advertise a single IP address to the world for all of your Internet services, like DNS, e-mail, FTP, and WWW, and have the PIX split this traffic out to separate internal servers.

The PIX allows you to get around this problem by using a variation of the `static` command:

```
pixfirewall (config)# static [(internal_interface_name, external_interface_name)]
                      tcp|udp global_IP_address|interface
                      local_IP_address local_port_number
                      [netmask subnet_mask]
                      [maximum_connections [embryonic_limit]] [norandomseq]
```

Port Redirection Parameters   The beginning of the `static` command, where you specify the interfaces involved, is the same as a one-to-one translation mentioned in the previous section. After this information you must specify the IP protocol: either `tcp` or `udp`. Next comes the public IP address that outsiders use to access resources on the inside of your network. Note that you can use the `interface` parameter instead, which causes the PIX to perform the translation on whatever address is assigned on the interface specified by the *external_interface_name* parameter. You must then specify the internal address (*local_IP_address*) that the traffic will be directed to.

To perform the port redirection, you need to specify the port number to redirect with the *local_port_number* parameter—this is the destination port number in the TCP or UDP segment. If you want to direct web traffic to one internal machine and e-mail traffic to another machine, you can easily accomplish this with two static commands: one command redirects port 80 traffic to the web server, and the other command redirects port 25 traffic to the e-mail server. The rest of the parameters are basically the same as described in the previous section.

Port Redirection Example   Let's look at a simple example to illustrate how you can use port redirection. For this example, I'll use the network shown in Figure 4-20.

In this example, your ISP has assigned you a single public IP address—199.199.199.2/30—which you must assign to the outside interface of your PIX. However, you want users on the Internet to access the Web and e-mail servers located on the inside of your network. To accomplish this, you can configure two static commands: one for the web server, and one for the e-mail server, like this:

```
pixfirewall(config)#  ip address outside 199.199.199.2 255.255.255.252
pixfirewall(config)#  ip address inside 192.168.1.1 255.255.255.0
pixfirewall(config)#
pixfirewall(config)#  static (inside, outside) tcp interface
                         192.168.1.2 80
pixfirewall(config)#  static (inside, outside) tcp interface
                         192.168.1.3 25
```

The first static command redirects TCP port 80 traffic sent to the IP address assigned to the outside interface of the PIX to the web server at 192.168.1.2. The second static command redirects e-mail traffic to 192.168.1.3.

Note that the PIX is still performing its translation process, because it will replace the destination IP address in the packet (199.199.199.2) with either 192.168.1.2 or 192.168.1.3 before forwarding the packet to the appropriate server on the inside of the network. Also, remember that you must configure either a conduit or access-list to open a hole in your firewall by the ASA, which I'll talk about a little bit later in this chapter.

Reverse NAT and Address Overloading

As I mentioned earlier in this chapter, the global and nat commands are typically used to translate the source IP addresses in packets as they travel from higher-security-level interfaces to lower-level ones. Version 6.2 and higher of the FOS support dynamic address translation from lower-security-level interfaces to higher-level ones. Cisco refers to this feature as *Outside NAT*. In reality, it is basically NAT, but from lower-to higher-security-level interfaces. Here are some of the advantages of Outside NAT:

- It allows you to connect overlapping networks between different interfaces of the PIX—using the same network number off of two different interfaces.
- It handles routing issues where you have the same network number off of more than one interface on the PIX.

- It automatically handles translation of addresses in DNS replies from DNS servers between the interfaces where dynamic translation is performed.

Given all of these advantages, the Outside NAT feature does have one limitation—it does not work with the Internet Locator Service (ILS) when the PIX has its Protocol Fixup feature enabled to deal with the quirks of ILS. I discuss the Protocol Fixup feature in Chapter 7.

When performing Reverse, or Outside, NAT, you have two choices for translation:

- Dynamic translations using the `global` and `nat` commands
- Static translation using `static` commands

Once you have configured Reverse NAT, when the PIX receives a packet on a less-secure interface that is destined for a more-secure interface, the PIX first examines its xlate table for an existing entry. If the PIX can't find an existing translation entry, it examines the address translation policies that you have configured to determine if it can create a translation in the xlate table. If a policy is found (a matching `static` or `nat`/`global` command), then the PIX will add the entry to the xlate table. The following two sections show you how to configure both address translation policies.

Configuring Dynamic Reverse NAT   Configuring dynamic Reverse NAT requires the use of the `global` and `nat` commands. I'll use the network depicted in Figure 4-21 to illustrate an example where you can use dynamic Reverse NAT.

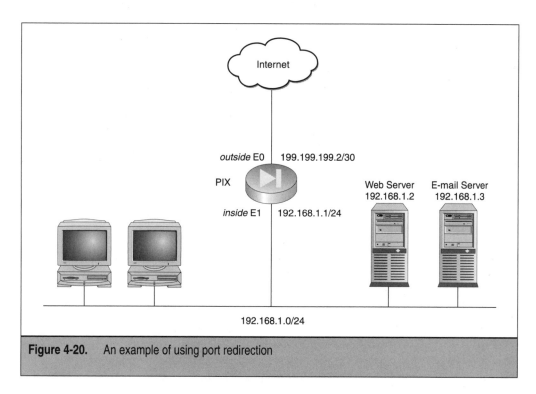

Figure 4-20.   An example of using port redirection

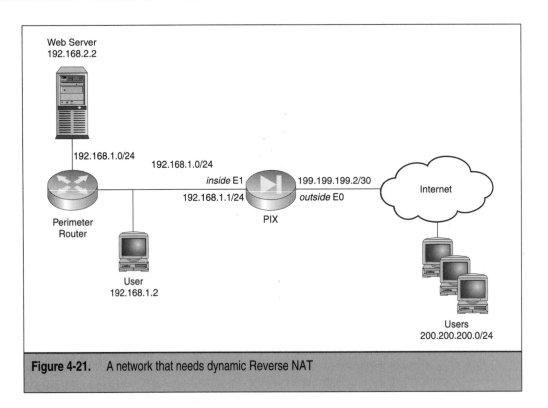

Figure 4-21. A network that needs dynamic Reverse NAT

In the example shown in Figure 4-21, the *inside* router has a policy that drops all traffic heading to 192.168.2.0/24 with the exception of traffic originating from 192.168.1.0/24. To simplify the filtering rules for this internal router, you don't want to configure any additional `access-list` commands to allow any other traffic. However, there is one minor problem: you also want to allow access from a group of users located across the Internet. These machines have an address from network 200.200.200.0/24. You can accommodate this by configuring the following code on your PIX:

```
pixfirewall(config)#  ip address outside 199.199.199.2 255.255.255.252
pixfirewall(config)#  ip address inside 192.168.1.1 255.255.255.0
pixfirewall(config)#
pixfirewall(config)#  route outside 0.0.0.0 0.0.0.0 199.199.199.1 1
pixfirewall(config)#  route inside  192.168.2.0 255.255.255.0 192.168.1.3 1
pixfirewall(config)#
pixfirewall(config)#  nat (outside) 1 200.200.200.0 255.255.255.0 outside
pixfirewall(config)#  global (inside) 1 192.168.1.24-192.168.1.254
```

Notice the `outside` parameter at the end of the `nat` command—this specifies that any device with a source address from network 200.200.200.0/24 will be translated to an address from the address pool in the `global` command. From the machines on the inside of the PIX, these packets appear to originate from 192.168.1.0/24, which makes the filtering rules on the router between 192.168.1.0/24 and 192.168.2.0/24 simple to configure.

Configuring Static Reverse NAT—Overlapping Addresses   One common problem of merging companies together today is that many companies use private addresses to assign IP addresses to their internal machines. The problem of using private addresses is that many of these companies use the same private address—10.0.0.0/8, 172.16.0.0/16, and 192.168.1.0/24 are the most commonly used ones. Therefore, when it comes time to directly connect the merging companies together, you have an issue where many of the network numbers used in one company are also being used in the other company, as is shown in Figure 4-22.

As you can see in this example, the two routers on each network don't know that there are other devices with the same network number, but on a different segment— these routers make routing decisions based solely on the best path to a destination. For example, Company A's router might actually be learning about 172.16.1.0/24 from Company B's router; however, the router's metric structure will tell it that what it is directly connected to is the best path—thus, Company A's router will always used the directly connected choice versus the network located in Company B. Of course, a user from 172.16.2.0/24 in Company A might legitimately be trying to reach a device in 172.16.1.0/24 in Company B, but the router in Company A will route it to the segment in Company A.

NOTE   One important item to point out about Figure 4-22 is that the network numbers on the PIX's interface *cannot* overlap. Each interfaces on your PIX needs to be associated with a unique subnet.

To solve this overlapping address problem, you can trick the two networks. For example, from Company A's perspective, you can make Company B appear to have

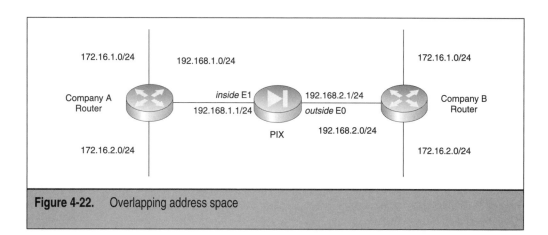

Figure 4-22.   Overlapping address space

an address space of 172.18.0.0/24. From Company B's perspective, you can make Company A appear to have address from 172.17.0.0/24. A logical view of this process is shown in Figure 4-23.

There are two commands that you can use to configure this solution:

- `alias`
- `static` (new in FOS 6.2)

The following two sections cover the use of these commands to handle overlapping addresses.

Using the alias command   Prior to FOS release 6.2, you would use the `alias` command to solve overlapping address problems. The syntax of this command is:

```
pixfirewall (config)#  alias [(interface_name)]
                       internal_IP_address external_IP_address
                       [subnet_mask]
```

The `interface_name` is the name of the interface on the *inside* of your network where you have overlapped addresses. If you omit this name, it defaults to inside. As an example, you might have randomly chosen a public network number when setting up your network, but you now need to connect to the network on the Internet where this address is assigned. You could readdress your network, but this might take days and days to accomplish.

Another solution would be to use `global` and `nat` commands to set up dynamic translation to change your source IP addresses to a different public address space that your ISP has assigned to you. However, there is one problem with this solution. Assume that you have used 200.200.200.0/24 to address your network, and you obviously don't own this address space. You have inherited this network from another administrator who,

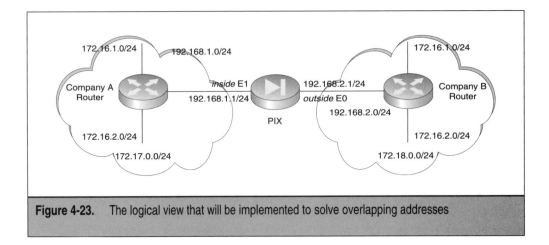

Figure 4-23.   The logical view that will be implemented to solve overlapping addresses

knowing no better, randomly chose an address space, subnetted it, and then laid out the subnets and assigned appropriate addresses to the machines in the network. The main problem here is that when your internal devices perform a DNS lookup that goes out to the Internet and a response comes back in with a destination IP address of 200.200.200.0/24, your internal machines are going to assume that the destination is not out on the Internet but local to the network. Therefore, your internal devices cannot access the devices that really have that public address space assigned to them.

As an interim solution while you are re-addressing your network, you could use the alias command to fix the DNS problem that I just described. The *external_IP_address* is the address out on the Internet that you are trying to reach, but you can't because you are also using it in your own internal network. The *internal_IP_address* is the address that you want the *external_IP_address* changed to, so it appears as a unique network number to the devices inside your internal network. Optionally, you can specify a network number for both of these addresses and then specify the appropriate subnet mask—this causes a complete network translation.

Take a look at a coding example using Figure 4-24. In this example, you are using 200.200.200.0/24 for your internal addressing, but your ISP has assigned you 201.201.201.0/24.

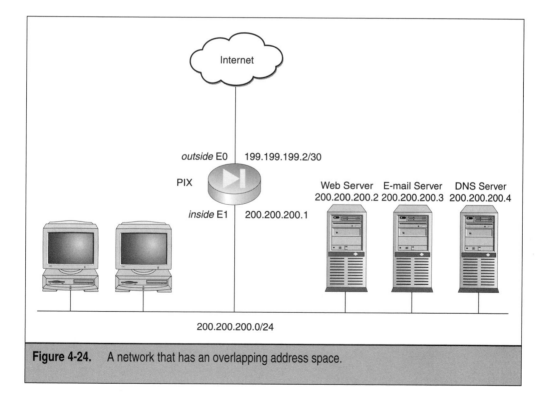

Figure 4-24.   A network that has an overlapping address space.

You would configure your PIX like this:

```
pixfirewall(config)#  alias (inside)  200.200.200.0 201.201.201.0
                      255.255.255.0
pixfirewall(config)#  static (inside, outside) 201.201.201.0 200.200.200.0
                      netmask 255.255.255.0
```

After you have configured the alias command, your PIX will perform two tasks:

1. When the PIX receives an internal packet destined to 201.201.201.0/24, which is what this example is pretending is assigned to the outside network, the PIX will change this destination address to 200.200.200.0/24. Then the ISP and other Internet routers will be able to route it correctly to the network that has been officially assigned this number.

2. When an internal DNS user performs a DNS look up that goes out to the Internet and returns with a reply of 200.200.200.0/24, the PIX will intercept the DNS reply and replace the address with one from 201.201.201.0/24—therefore, your internal devices assume that the destination is actually on the outside of your network.

As you can see from the second task, the PIX automatically interacts with DNS servers to ensure that the entire process is transparent to your internal users as well as users out on the Internet that have been assigned this address space.

The static command allows Internet users to access your internal devices. Remember that your ISP has assigned you 201.201.201.0/24—this command causes your PIX to translate the destination IP addresses of 201.201.201.0/24 to 200.200.200.0/24, which is what your internal devices have assigned to them.

There is one other important item to point out with the example in Figure 4-24. If you have an internal DNS server that is supplying addresses to both the inside and outside users, you will want to use the 200.200.200.0/24 addresses in the "A" (address) DNS records. The PIX will intercept these to send out an address from 201.201.201.0/24 based on your alias/static entries. You might find, however, that you need to have a backup DNS server located at your ISP. Obviously you can't be advertising 200.200.200.0/24 for your internal machines, because you don't own 200.200.200.0/24, plus these "A" records are not going through your PIX, because external Internet users could be accessing the ISP's DNS server for address resolution. To get around this problem, you need to ensure that the ISP's DNS server gets "A" records with an address of 201.201.201.0/24 for your internal machines. Actually, in this instance, you could even have your internal clients use the ISP's DNS server for resolution to local machines, because the PIX will intercept the response and change the 201.201.201.0/24 to 200.200.200.0/24.

Once you have added, changed, or modified an alias command, execute the clear xlate command to clear the PIX's translation table. To view your alias configuration, use the show alias command. This command displays the alias commands that you have configured on your PIX.

For the PIX to intercept DNS messages correctly, you have to disable proxy ARP on your PIX. To disable proxy ARP on your PIX, use this command:

```
pixfirewall(config)# sysopt noproxyarp internal_interface_name
```

You can disable the DNS aliasing with this command:

```
pixfirewall(config)# sysopt nodnsalias
```

You might want to disable DNS aliasing if your DNS server is already handling the problem, or if some other device in the network is performing the aliasing already.

Using the static command   Version 6.2 of the FOS for the PIX allows you to use the `static` command to solve overlapping addressing issues. One advantage of using the `static` command is that it gives you more flexibility and control over address translation, because you specify two interfaces where the address translation is to take place. The problem with the `alias` command is that you can only specify a single interface.

I'll use the same example that I worked with in the last section, shown in Figure 4-24. The internal network is using 200.200.200.0/24, which this company doesn't own. Their ISP has assigned them the C-class address of 201.201.201.0/24. These are the static commands necessary to handle the overlapping address issue:

```
pixfirewall(config)# static (outside, inside) 200.200.200.0
                            201.201.201.0 netmask 255.255.255.0
pixfirewall(config)# static (inside, outside) 201.201.201.0
                            201.201.201.0 nermask 255.255.255.0
```

The first `static` command translates outside source IP addresses from 200.200.200.0 to 201.201.201.0, which makes them appear unique when external devices from 200.200.200.0/24 try to access internal resources. In addition, as your internal devices send replies back to these devices, the `static` command will change the destination IP address from 201.201.201.0/24 back to 200.200.200.0/24.

The second `static` command translates the host address of 201.201.201.0 (what the Internet users are trying to access) to 200.200.200.0 (what you have physically assigned to your internal users).

Allowing Traffic from Lower-Level to Higher-Level Interfaces

Now that you have set up your address translation to satisfy the PIX's need for address translation from lower-level interfaces to higher-level ones with the `static` command, you must now open up a hole in the PIX's firewall to allow this inbound traffic. To have the ASA open up a hole, you can use one of two commands:

- `conduit`
- `access-list`

Cisco has been pushing their user base to move from conduits to access lists. In this chapter I will focus on the implementation of conduits, and in the next chapter I will discuss the use of access-lists.

Configuring Your Conduits

The syntax for configuring a conduit is shown here:

```
pixfirewall(config)# conduit permit|deny protocol_name
                           inside_global_IP_address inside_global_subnet_mask
                               [operator port_#_or_name[-port_#_or_name]
                           outside_IP_address outside_subnet_mask
                               [operator port_#_or_name[-port_#_or_name]
pixfirewall(config)# conduit permit|deny icmp
                           inside_global_IP_address inside_global_subnet_mask
                               [icmp_message]
                           outside_IP_address outside_subnet_mask
                               [icmp_message]
```

The first conduit command listed is for IP, TCP, and UDP traffic, and the second command is for ICMP traffic. As you can see from the syntax, the configuration of conduits is somewhat similar to that of configuring access-lists on IOS-based routers.

Unlike ACLs, you do not need to activate conduits on an interface—they apply to *all* traffic going from a lower-level interface to a higher-level one. As you will see in the next chapter, ACLs give you more granularity because they are applied to interfaces.

You can create up to 8,000 conduit commands on the PIX. However, you should note that how the PIX processes these commands is very important in ensuring that you don't open a huge hole that hackers could exploit.

SECURITY ALERT   Conduits are processed in the order that you enter them in your PIX configuration—if you permit everything with the first conduit command, and drop traffic with following conduit commands, the PIX stops processing when a packet's contents match the conduit command in the first statement. Therefore, the order in which you enter your conduit commands is *extremely* important—a misconfigured conduit command could leave your network in a vulnerable state.

Conduit Protocol Parameters

After the conduit command comes the action that you wish to perform—permit or deny. Next comes the protocol that you will be performing filtering on. This can either be a name, like tcp, or a number, like 6. For a list of assigned protocol numbers for IP, visit this site: www.iana.org/assignments/protocol-numbers.

Conduit Address Parameters

When you are configuring addresses, there are two important items to remember. First, the *inside_global_IP_address* is not a source address, nor is the address physically assigned to the devices inside of your network—it's the global address assigned by the `static` command for how the outside world views the destinations inside of your network. The first thing that the PIX does is to compare the incoming packet to its list of conduits. The PIX performs its comparison process by examining the source of the packet, which matches up with the *outside_IP_address* parameter, and the destination of the packet, which matches up with the *inside_global_IP_address* parameter, as well as any protocol information, such as TCP/UDP ports or ICMP message types. At this point, the PIX hasn't performed its address translation—it performs address translation *after* processing all of the conduits. Therefore, the internal address you specify is what the user on the lower-level interface is using as the destination IP address. If the PIX doesn't find a match on any `conduit` statements, it drops the packet.

The second item dealing with addresses is the subnet mask that follows the inside and outside addresses. The first time that I ran into conduits on the PIX, I was pleasantly surprised that Cisco has finally started moving away from wildcard masks and moving toward subnet masks for filtering purposes. Too many times when I was teaching Cisco classes, students would be confused over how to configure a wildcard mask for an ACL on an IOS-based router. If you are used to configuring wildcard masks on Cisco routers, the masks that you enter for the inside global and outside addresses are subnet masks.

The addressing nomenclature for dealing with a specific host address or any host address is the same as that with ACLs on a Cisco router. For a specific host, use the keyword `host` followed by the host address, making sure that you omit the subnet mask. For example, to specify a host of 192.168.1.1, you could use either one of the following two methods:

- `host 192.168.1.1`
- `192.168.1.1 255.255.255.255`

If you want to match on any host, you can use the keyword `any` to represent the address and subnet mask. For example, you could use either of the following two syntaxes:

- `any`
- `0.0.0.0 0.0.0.0` (which can be abbreviated to 0 0)

Conduit Port Parameters

After the address, you can list specifics concerning the IP protocol. For example, for TCP and UDP, you can specify an operator and the port name or number, or a range of numbers. Operators include `eq` (equal to), `neq` (not equal to), `lt` (less than), and `gt` (greater than). To specify a range of port numbers/name, enter the beginning and ending port numbers or names and separate them with a hyphen with no spaces between the hyphens and the ports. If you omit the port information, the PIX assumes that you are talking about all ports for the specified protocol. For information about valid port numbers, visit `www.iana.org/assignments/port-numbers`.

For ICMP traffic, you can specify an ICMP message type (either by name or number). If you omit the message information, the PIX assumes that you are talking about all ICMP messages. Remember that for ICMP traffic, the PIX is not stateful. Therefore, if you want ICMP replies to your users' traffic and tests, you'll need to explicitly permit it with either a `conduit` or `access-list` command. For information about ICMP parameters, visit `www.iana.org/assignments/icmp-parameters`.

Checking Your Conduits

After making any changes to conduits on your PIX, be sure that you execute the `clear xlate` command to ensure that all traffic flowing through the PIX is using your new policies. If you want to view the conduits that you have just created, use the `show conduit` command.

 SECURITY ALERT! Any time you make changes to conduits on your PIX, execute the `clear xlate` command in order for the PIX to start using your changes.

Examples of Using Statics and Conduits

To help you better understand the use and configuration of the `static` and `conduit` commands, I have put together a simple example. To help with this example, I will use the network shown in Figure 4-25. In this example, the network has two internal segments—192.168.3.0/24 and 192.168.4.0/24—and one DMZ segment that has a public address assigned to it—200.200.200.0/29.

The PIX configuration to set this up is shown here:

```
pixfirewall(config)#  nameif ethernet0 outside sec0
pixfirewall(config)#  nameif ethernet1 inside sec100
pixfirewall(config)#  nameif ethernet2 dmz sec50
pixfirewall(config)#
pixfirewall(config)#  ip address outside 192.168.1.1 255.255.255.0
pixfirewall(config)#  ip address inside 192.168.2.1 255.255.255.0
pixfirewall(config)#  ip address dmz 200.200.200.1 255.255.255.248
pixfirewall(config)#
pixfirewall(config)#  route outside 0.0.0.0 0.0.0.0 192.168.1.2 1
pixfirewall(config)#  route inside  192.168.3.0 255.255.255.0 192.168.2.2 1
pixfirewall(config)#  route inside  192.168.4.0 255.255.255.0 192.168.2.2 1
pixfirewall(config)#
pixfirewall(config)#  global (outside) 1 200.200.200.9-200.200.200.254
                         netmask 255.255.255.0
pixfirewall(config)#  nat (inside) 1 0 0
pixfirewall(config)#
pixfirewall(config)#  static (dmz, outside) 200.200.200.2 200.200.200.2
pixfirewall(config)#  static (dmz, outside) 200.200.200.3 200.200.200.3
pixfirewall(config)#
pixfirewall(config)#  conduit permit tcp host 200.200.200.2 eq 25 any
pixfirewall(config)#  conduit permit tcp host 200.200.200.3 eq 80 any
pixfirewall(config)#  conduit permit icmp any any
```

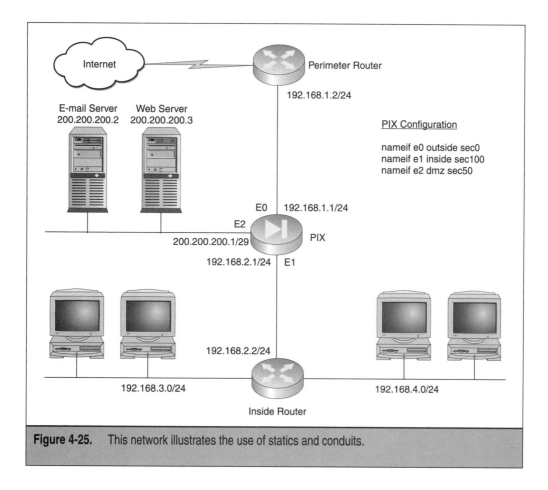

Figure 4-25.   This network illustrates the use of statics and conduits.

The first two sections contain the interface names and IP addresses. The section with the route commands contains the static routes. The global and nat commands set up address translation for the internal subnets, 192.168.2.0/24, 192.168.3.0/24, and 192.168.4.0/24, and specify that the address translation used ranges from 200.200.200.9 to 200.200.200.254.

There are two static commands for the web server and e-mail server located off of the dmz interface. Note that the global and local IP addresses listed in the static command are the same because these machines have public addresses assigned to their interfaces. The configuration of these static commands obviously doesn't perform an address translation, but it does satisfy the PIX's requirement for address translation configuration. Also note that the static commands only specify translation between the *outside* and *dmz* interfaces. Therefore, by default, traffic will not be able to originate from the *dmz* interface on the PIX and travel to the *inside* interface—instead, devices on the *inside* interface will have to initiate the traffic and have the PIX create the dynamic address translations. If you wanted this to occur, you would need to configure a global command for the *dmz* interface for the internal users. Note that the IP address assigned to the dmz has a subnet mask of 255.255.255.248—this will allow the web and e-mail servers to differentiate traffic on the local subnet from the translated addresses.

Following the two static commands are some `conduit` commands. The first `conduit` command allows any traffic from a lower-level interface if it is destined for port 25 (SMTP) on 200.200.200.2. Likewise, the second command allows any traffic from a lower-level interface if it is destined to port 80 on 200.200.200.3. These two conduits allow external traffic to the specific resources on the dmz interface of the PIX. The third `conduit` command allows all ICMP messages from lower-level interfaces to higher ones.

Note that the IP address listed in the first two `conduit` commands is the publicly reachable address. In this instance, this is not an issue because the internal servers are using public addresses. However, if they had been using private addresses, you want to make sure that the `conduit` commands refer to the public address that you assign to them in the `static` commands—remember that conduits are processed before `static` commands, and that the external Internet users use the public addresses to reach these services.

NOTE   `conduit` commands are processed before `static` commands, so make sure that you specify the global address as the internal address—not the address physically assigned to your internal device.

VIEWING THE PIX'S TRANSLATIONS AND CONNECTIONS

Once you have configured your address translation with your `global`, `nat`, and `static` commands, and configured your holes in the firewall with your `conduit` commands, you are now ready to use `show` commands to verify your configuration. The following sections cover these commands.

Viewing Active Translations

One of the more important commands that you will use when troubleshooting problems with connections is the `show xlate` command. This command shows the translations that you manually configured with the `static` command, as well as those the PIX dynamically created based on your `nat` and `global` commands.

The syntax of the `show xlate` command is:

```
pixfirewall# show xlate [detail] [global|local IP_address1[-IP_address2]
                   [netmask subnet_mask]] gport|lport port[-port]]
              [interface interface_name_1 [,interface_name_2]
                 [,interface_name_x]]
              [state static [,dump] [,portmap] [,norandomseq]
                 [,identity]]
```

Typing `show xlate` by itself lists the entire translation table. Table 4-5 explains the rest of the parameters for this command:

An example of the output of the `show xlate` command is shown here:

```
pixfirewall#  show xlate
Global 200.200.200.10 Local 172.16.7.80 nconns 1 econns 0
Global 200.200.200.11 Local 172.16.7.81 nconns 3 econns 0
```

In this example, the global address is the address that external devices use to access the internal device, displayed as the local address. For example, if someone from the outside world wanted to access 172.16.7.80, they would use a destination address of 200.200.200.10. There are two other items in this display of interest: `nconns` refers to the number of connections that is currently open to this address and `econns` refers to the number of half-open, or embryonic, connections to this device.

The following is an example using the `detail` parameter with the `show xlate` command:

```
pixfirewall(config)#  show xlate detail
3 in use, 3 most used
Flags: D - DNS, d - dump, I - identity, i - inside, n - no random,
       o - outside, r - portmap, s - static
TCP PAT from inside:172.16.7.80/1026 to outside:200.200.200.1/1024 flags ri
UDP PAT from inside:172.16.7.80/1028 to outside:200.200.200.1/1024 flags ri
ICMP PAT from inside:172.16.7.80/21505 to outside:200.200.200.1/0 flags ri
```

In this example, there are three PAT connections. Notice the flags listed at the end. The `r` indicates that this is a port map (PAT) connection and the `i` indicates an inside address.

Parameter	Explanation
detail	Displays the translation type as well as the interfaces the connection traverses.
global|local	Displays only the global or local addresses in the output.
gport|lport	Displays translations for the specified `global` or `local` port number(s).
interface	Displays only the translations for the specified interfaces.
state	Displays the connections by their state. You can also limit the output of the display by specifying the state(s) that you are interested in: translations configured by the `static` command (`static`); transactions being removed (`dump`); translations configured with PAT by `global` command (`portmap`); translations defined by the `nat` or `static` command with the `norandomseq` parameter (`norandomseq`); or translations defined with the `nat 0` configuration (`identity`).

Table 4-5.   The Parameters for the show xlate Command.

Clearing the Xlate Table

Any time that you make changes that affect the translation table, you should execute the `clear xlate` command. Executing this command will enforce the new changes. In some old versions of the PIX FOS, you sometimes had to reboot the PIX in order to enforce your changes. Any time that you execute any command in the following list, you will need to clear the translation table:

- `access-list`
- `alias`
- `apply`
- `conduit`
- `global`
- `interface`
- `ip address`
- `nameif`
- `nat`
- `outbound`
- `static`

The syntax of the `clear xlate` command is shown here:

```
pixfirewall# clear xlate [global|local IP_address[-IP_address]
                         [netmask subnet_mask]
                         local_port[-local_port]|global_port[-global_port]]
                         [interface name_of_interface1[,interface2,...]
                         [state static[,dump][,portmap][,norandomseq]
                             [,identity]]
```

If you don't specify any parameters, all translations will be cleared from the translation table. Of course, you can be specific about the entry from the table that is to be cleared. Note that if you attempt to clear a static entry from the xlate table, one that was placed there with a `static` command, it will reappear immediately. Refer to Table 4-6 for an explanation of these parameters.

Viewing the Connection Table

The PIX keeps track of the connections going through it by placing a connection's information in a connection table. The PIX allows traffic from a lower-level-security interface to a higher-level one if there is a corresponding entry in the connection table. There are two basic ways that an entry is placed in the connection table:

- A connection is added when a TCP or UDP connection is initiated from a higher-level interface to a lower one—this allows the return traffic to the device.

- A connection is added when either a conduit or access-list is configured.

To see the connections in the connection table, use the show conn command. The syntax of this command is:

```
pixfirewall# show conn [detail] [count]
                   [foreign|local IP_address_1[-IP_address_2]]
                      [netmask subnet_mask] [protocol tcp|udp|protocol]
                      [fport|lport port_1[-port_2]]
                   [state [up [,finin] [,finout] [,http_get] [,sip]
                      [,smtp_data] [,smtp_banner] [,smtp_incomplete]
                      [,nojava] [,data_in] [,data_out]
                      [,sqlnet_fixup_data] [,conn_inbound] [,rpc]
                      [,h323] [,dump]]
```

Typing show conn by itself lists the entire connection table. Table 4-6 explains the rest of the parameters for this command:

An example of the output of the show conn command is shown here:

```
pixfirewall# show conn
6 in use, 6 most used
TCP out 202.202.202.1:80 in 192.168.1.5:1404 idle 0:00:00 Bytes 11391
TCP out 202.202.202.1:80 in 192.168.1.5:1405 idle 0:00:00 Bytes 3709
TCP out 202.202.202.1:80 in 192.168.1.5:1406 idle 0:00:01 Bytes 2685
TCP out 202.202.202.1:80 in 192.168.1.5:1407 idle 0:00:01 Bytes 2683
```

In this output, the internal host (in) 192.168.1.5 accessed an external web server (out) at 202.202.202.1.

Parameter	Explanation
detail	Displays the translation type as well as the interfaces the connection traverses.
count	Displays only the number of connections in the table—this can help you figure out if you have purchased the right connection license.
foreign|local	Displays only the specified foreign or local addresses.
protocol	Displays only the specified IP protocol.
fport|lport	Displays translations for the specified foreign or local port number(s).
state	Displays the connections by their state. You can also limit the output of the display by specifying the state(s) that you are interested in.

Table 4-6.   The Parameters for the show conn Command.

An example of the output of the `show conn detail` command is shown here:

```
pixfirewall#(config)#   show conn detail
1 in use, 2 most used
Flags: A - awaiting inside ACK to SYN, a - awaiting outside ACK to SYN,
       B - initial SYN from outside, D - DNS, d - dump,
       E - outside back connection, f - inside FIN, F - outside FIN,
       G - group, H - H.323, I - inbound data, M - SMTP data,
       O - outbound data, P - inside back connection,
       q - SQL*Net data, R - outside acknowledged FIN,
       R - UDP RPC, r - inside acknowledged FIN, S - awaiting inside SYN,
       s - awaiting outside SYN, U - up
TCP outside:202.202.202.32/23 inside:192.168.1.10/1026 flags UIO
```

In this example, at the top of the display is a table explaining the flags that you may see at the end of a connection entry. Below this is a TCP telnet connection that was initiated by 192.168.1.10 (`inside`) to 202.202.202.32 (`outside`). Its flags indicate that it is active, and allows both inbound and outbound transfer of data.

FURTHER STUDY

Web Sites

To see the RFC defining private addresses, visit www.ietf.org/rfc/rfc1918.txt.

To see the RFC defining address translation, visit www.ietf.org/rfc/rfc1631.txt.

To see the IP protocol numbers that you can use for `conduit` commands, visit www.iana.org/assignments/protocol-numbers.

To see the TCP/UDP port numbers that you can use for `conduit` commands, visit www.iana.org/assignments/port-numbers.

To see the ICMP message types that you can use for `conduit` commands, visit www.iana.org/assignments/icmp-parameters.

For more information about configuring address translation on your PIX, visit www.cisco.com/univercd/cc/td/doc/product/iaabu/pix/pix_62/config/index.htm.

CHAPTER 5

Filtering Traffic with Outbound Filters and Access-Lists

In the previous chapter, I talked about some of the PIX commands to perform address translation, like `global`, `nat`, and `static`, as well as the `conduit` command, which has the ASA open a hole in the firewall to allow traffic to flow from lower-security-level interfaces to higher-level ones. In this chapter, I cover two topics. The first deals with filtering traffic from higher-security-level interfaces to lower ones. By default, the PIX allows traffic to flow freely from higher levels to lower levels. I will discuss how you can create outbound filters with the `outbound` command to restrict this traffic.

The second topic of this chapter is access control lists, or what Cisco refers to as *ACLs* (pronounced *ackles*). Cisco introduced ACLs in FOS 5.3, and ACLs have been pushed by Cisco as the future direction of filtering on the PIX. Today, ACLs can handle both of the functions that conduits and outbound filters provide.

FILTERING OUTBOUND TRAFFIC

In Chapter 4 I covered the use of the `global` and `nat` commands to perform address translation as traffic moves from higher-security-level interfaces to lower-level ones. If you recall, address translation is required by the PIX, even if you are using public addresses. Of course, you can disable this function by using the `nat 0` command. In either case, however, once you have configured or disabled address translation, all traffic, by default, is allowed to move from the higher-level interface to the lower-level ones.

You may want to restrict this traffic flow, but this will require some configuration on your part by first building an outbound filter and then activating it. The next sections cover the use of the `outbound` command to create your outbound filter and the `apply` command to activate your filter.

Overview of Outbound Filters

Outbound filters are used to filter traffic from higher-security-level interfaces to lower-level ones. Like conduits, outbound filters are similar to ACLs on IOS-based routers. As I mentioned in the last section, all traffic from higher-level interfaces to lower ones is allowed, by default. This is a function of the implementation of the ASA's security policies, and the stateful nature of the PIX. You can create outbound filters to restrict this access. For example, you might want to restrict which users, or subnets, are allowed Internet access.

Configuring Outbound Filters

Configuring outbound filters is somewhat similar to creating ACLs on an IOS-based router. You need to take two steps to create and activate your filters:

1. Create your outbound filtering commands.
2. Activate your outbound filter on an interface.

Of course, the commands are slightly different on a PIX than on an IOS-based router. On an IOS-based router, to create an IP ACL, you use the `access-list` command, and to activate it, you use the `ip access-group` command on an interface.

On a PIX, you use two completely different commands. To create your filters, you use the `outbound` command. To activate your filter for an interface, you use the `apply` command. The next two sections cover the commands for creating and activating outbound filters.

Configuring Your Outbound List

To configure an outbound filter, use the `outbound` command. You can have up to 1,599 `outbound` commands in a list. The syntax for the `outbound` command is:

```
pixfirewall(config)# outbound list_number permit|deny |except
                     IP_address [subnet_mask]
                     [java|port_number[-port_number]] [protocol_name]
```

The `list_number` parameter uniquely identifies an outbound filter and also groups together the commands in the filter. This number is similar to an ACL number on an IOS-based router.

Following the `list_number` parameter is the action you want to have the PIX perform when a packet's contents matches the conditions listed in the `outbound` command. The `permit` keyword permits the packet, the `deny` keyword drops the packet, and the `except` keyword creates an exception to the most recent `outbound` command in the outbound filter.

After the condition is the IP address or network number that you want to permit or deny. This can be a single IP address or a subnet or network number. For the `subnet_mask` variable, enter the subnet mask of the bits that you want to match.

 SECURITY ALERT!   Please note that the mask used in an outbound filter is *not* a wildcard mask like that used with ACLs on IOS-based routers, but a **subnet** mask.

Following the address and subnet mask, you list the port numbers or names (or a range of port numbers/names) that you want to examine. The port names include the following: `dns`, `ftp`, `h323`, `http`, `ident`, `nntp`, `ntp`, `pop2`, `pop3`, `rpc`, `smtp`, `snmp`, `snmptrap`, `sqlnet`, `telnet`, and `tftp`. By default, all Java applets are permitted when you allow HTTP traffic. If you want to allow HTTP traffic, but deny Java applets, then use the keyword `java`. If you want to match on all ports, use a port number of 0—this is the default if omitted.

After the port number, enter the IP protocol. These can be `ah`, `esp`, `icmp`, `ip`, `tcp`, or `udp`. If you omit the protocol name, it defaults to either `tcp` or `ip`. If you enter a port number, then the protocol defaults to `tcp`; otherwise, it defaults to `ip`. You can also enter a number for the protocol instead of a name. A protocol number of 0 is the default protocol—`tcp`. For filtering Java applets, you do not need to specify a protocol name.

To list your outbound commands, use the show outbound command. To remove a single entry in a list, preface the specific outbound command with the no parameter. To delete all of your outbound filters on your PIX, use the clear outbound command.

Activating Your Outbound List

To activate an outbound filter on one of the PIX's interfaces, use the apply command:

```
list_number
pixfirewall(config)# apply [(interface_name)] list _number
                          outgoing_src|outgoing_dst
```

The name of the interface is an internal interface of the PIX where you want to filter traffic from—in other words, as traffic comes into this interface of the PIX and travels to a lower-security-level interface, you want to filter it with an outbound list. This interface name is the logical name of the interface specified by the nameif command. If you omit the name of the interface, it defaults to *inside*. You'll need to specify which outbound list is applied to the interface with the *list_number* parameter.

One interesting thing to point out about the outbound command is that you only enter a single IP address—there is no reference in the outbound command pertaining to whether this is the source address in the packet or the destination address in the packet when the PIX performs its filtering. To affect whether this is a source or destination address, use one of the two following parameters in the apply command:

- outgoing_src   This parameter has the PIX examine the local source IP address, the destination port, and the protocol in the IP packet header.
- outgoing_dst   This parameter has the PIX examine the destination IP address, the destination port, and the protocol in the IP packet header

Whether you specify the address as a source or destination address, the port number the PIX examines is *always* the destination port number in the TCP or UDP segment.

Once you have applied the outbound filter, use the show apply command to see which outbound filters have been applied to the interfaces of your PIXs. To remove a single application of an outbound list, preface the specific apply command with the no parameter. To delete all of your applied outbound filters on your PIX, use the clear apply command.

Outbound Filter Processing on the PIX

Outbound filters are processed by the PIX in sequential order based on their list number—1, 2, 3, and so on. Within a list, the PIX will automatically sort entries from most specific to least specific. Take a look at the following example of a presorted outbound filter:

```
pixfirewall(config)# outbound 1 deny 0 0 0
pixfirewall(config)# outbound 1 permit 192.168.1.0 255.255.255.0 23 tcp
pixfirewall(config)# outbound 1 deny 192.168.1.1 255.255.255.0 23 tcp
```

I assume that you have entered the commands in the order shown here. In this example, the least specific entry is at the top of the list, and the most specific entry is at the bottom. However, the PIX will take these `outbound` commands for outbound filter 1 and sort them by the number of bits in the mask when you are looking for a match—the more bits in the mask, the more specific the match. Given this, the following code shows the order of how the PIX will sort the entries after you have entered them (a postsorted outbound filter):

```
pixfirewall(config)# outbound 1 deny 192.168.1.1 255.255.255.0 23 tcp
pixfirewall(config)# outbound 1 permit 192.168.1.0 255.255.255.0 23 tcp
pixfirewall(config)# outbound 1 deny 0 0 0
```

As you can see in this example, the process that the PIX uses here is very different from ACLs on an IOS-based router.

Therefore, because the PIX sorts commands within a list, one of the first entries you should put in your list (so that you don't forget) is to either permit everything or deny everything. If you have a statement that permits everything, then you can add your `deny` statements to drop the specific traffic that your security policy dictates. If you have a statement that denies everything, then you can create your specific `permit` statements.

Like IOS-based ACLs or PIX conduits, as soon as the PIX finds a match, it stops processing the rest of the list. Therefore, the number of each outbound filter is important. Another thing to point out is that if the PIX goes through all of the `outbound` commands in each list, and doesn't find a match, it will *permit* the packet. This is different from ACLs and conduits, which have an implicit deny at the end of their configuration. You need to remember that the PIX, by default, allows traffic from higher-security-level interfaces to lower-level ones—therefore, if the PIX cannot match a packet to a filtering statement, it will *permit* the packet.

 SECURITY ALERT!   You do not need a `permit` statement in an outbound filter to permit all packets because this is the default behavior of the PIX when traffic passes from higher-security-level interfaces to lower-level ones.

NOTE   You need to clear the address translation table with the `clear xlate` command after making any changes to outbound filters or their application to an interface.

Examples of Filtering with Outbound Filters

To help illustrate the use of outbound filters on the PIX, let's take a look at a few examples. The following sections show three short examples with outbound filters.

An Outbound Filter with a Two-Interface PIX

For the first example, I'll keep it simple by using a PIX that has only two interfaces—*inside* and *outside*. I'll use Figure 5-1 to help illustrate this example. In this example there

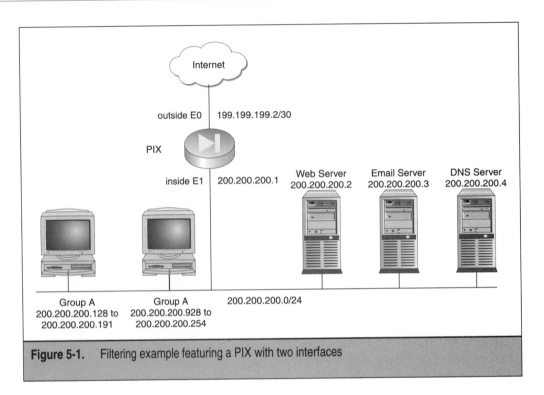

Figure 5-1. Filtering example featuring a PIX with two interfaces

is an internal network with some servers, as well as two groups of users: Group A and Group B. Here are the security policies that I am going to enforce in this example:

- Allow all traffic outbound from the servers
- Allow all traffic outbound from the Group A users
- Deny all traffic outbound from the Group B users except for HTTP, FTP, telnet, and DNS traffic.

Listing 5-1 shows the configuration of this filtering policy using outbound filters.

Listing 5-1
```
pixfirewall(config)#  outbound 1 deny 0.0.0.0 0.0.0.0 0 ip
pixfirewall(config)#  outbound 1 permit 200.200.200.2 255.255.255.255 0 ip
pixfirewall(config)#  outbound 1 permit 200.200.200.3 255.255.255.255 0 ip
pixfirewall(config)#  outbound 1 permit 200.200.200.4 255.255.255.255 0 ip
pixfirewall(config)#  outbound 1 permit 200.200.200.128 255.255.255.192 0 ip
pixfirewall(config)#  outbound 1 permit 200.200.200.192 255.255.255.192 80 tcp
pixfirewall(config)#  outbound 1 permit 200.200.200.192 255.255.255.192 21 tcp
pixfirewall(config)#  outbound 1 permit 200.200.200.192 255.255.255.192 20 tcp
pixfirewall(config)#  outbound 1 permit 200.200.200.192 255.255.255.192 23 tcp
```

```
pixfirewall(config)#  outbound 1 permit 200.200.200.192 255.255.255.192 53 udp
pixfirewall(config)#  apply (inside) 1 outgoing_src
```

In Listing 5-1, I filled in all of the optional parameters, even though they weren't required. For instance, for the first entry listed in the outbound filter, I could have easily typed outbound 1 deny 0 0 and the PIX would have changed this to the line that I typed in.

More Than One Outbound Filter

For the next example, I'll take the network shown in Figure 5-1, and add some additional security policies. In addition to the security policies mentioned previously, Group B should be allowed to access any device in network 131.108.0.0/16. One of the problems of the example shown in Listing 5-1 is that outbound filter 1 is looking at source addresses, not destination addresses. To accommodate this, you need to create an additional filter that has the PIX look at destination IP addresses.

Of course, as mentioned earlier, the PIX processes these lists sequentially—so the problem with the example in Listing 5-1 is that if there is no match, all traffic should be dropped. To solve this problem, you can take one of either two approaches:

- Remove the first entry in outbound filter 1 (the entry that denies all traffic) and create a second filter that allows traffic to destination 131.108.0.0/16 and then denies everything else.

- Delete outbound filter 1 and create two outbound filters—the first filter permits traffic going to destination 131.108.0.0/16, and the second mirrors the outbound filter in Listing 5-1.

Listing 5-2 shows the second solution that meets these specifications.

Listing 5-2
```
pixfirewall(config)#  clear apply
pixfirewall(config)#  clear outbound
pixfirewall(config)#
pixfirewall(config)#  outbound 1 permit 131.108.0.0 255.255.0.0 0 ip
pixfirewall(config)#
pixfirewall(config)#  outbound 2 deny 0.0.0.0 0.0.0.0 0 ip
pixfirewall(config)#  outbound 2 permit 200.200.200.2 255.255.255.255 0 ip
pixfirewall(config)#  outbound 2 permit 200.200.200.3 255.255.255.255 0 ip
pixfirewall(config)#  outbound 2 permit 200.200.200.4 255.255.255.255 0 ip
pixfirewall(config)#  outbound 2 permit 200.200.200.128 255.255.255.192 0 ip
pixfirewall(config)#  outbound 2 permit 200.200.200.192 255.255.255.192 80 tcp
pixfirewall(config)#  outbound 2 permit 200.200.200.192 255.255.255.192 21 tcp
pixfirewall(config)#  outbound 2 permit 200.200.200.192 255.255.255.192 20 tcp
pixfirewall(config)#  outbound 2 permit 200.200.200.192 255.255.255.192 23 tcp
pixfirewall(config)#  outbound 2 permit 200.200.200.192 255.255.255.192 53 udp
pixfirewall(config)#
pixfirewall(config)#  apply (inside) 1 outgoing_dst
pixfirewall(config)#  apply (inside) 2 outgoing_src
```

In this example, I assumed that you were on the same PIX and you only wanted to make the changes. Therefore, the two `clear` commands remove the outbound filters and their application on the PIX. The first outbound filter allows traffic going to 131.108.0.0/16 based on the `apply` command at the end of the example: `outgoing_dst`. Therefore, if any traffic from the inside network attempts to reach this destination, it is permitted. Again, remember that lists are processed sequentially. To get to the second list, you need to ensure that you don't have a `deny` statement that drops everything in the first list.

The second outbound filter is exactly the same filter used in Listing 5-1—the only difference is that its list number is 2. Therefore the PIX will process this after list 1. To recap, if any traffic (Group A users, Group B users, or the servers) is destined for 131.108.0.0/16, the PIX will permit it; however, if there is no match in the first outbound, filter, the PIX uses the second applied filter (list number 2) to enforce your security policies. The second filter basically denies everything except for the traffic originating from the servers, traffic originating from Group A, and traffic originating from Group B if it is HTTP, FTP, telnet, or DNS queries.

An Outbound Filter with a Three-Interface PIX

Now I'll use a more complicated example to show how tricky it can become when dealing with outbound filters. In this example, let's use a PIX that has three interfaces. Figure 5-2 shows the example network.

The configuration shown in Listing 5-3 shows the address translation configuration on the PIX before you configure any outbound filters.

Listing 5-3
```
pixfirewall(config)#  global (outside) 1 200.200.200.0 netmask 255.255.255.0
pixfirewall(config)#  nat (inside) 1 0 0
pixfirewall(config)#  nat (middle) 1 0 0
```

In this example, I am assuming that there are no services located inside this network that Internet users need to access. Instead, I'll just focus on filtering traffic between the internal interfaces of the PIX (*middle* and *inside*) and the external interface (*outside*). Before I actually start explaining the filters, take a look at the address translation listed in Listing 5-3. The `global` command translates addresses when packets exit the *outside* interface for both internal interfaces (middle and inside). By default, 192.168.5.0/24 is *not* allowed to communicate to 192.168.3.0/24 and 192.168.4.0/24 because there are no statics or conduits configured to allow this (remember that the middle interface has a lower security level than the *inside* interface).

For this filtering example, assume the following filtering policies:

1. 192.168.2.0/24 should be allowed to access 192.168.1.0/24, but not the Internet.

2. 192.168.3.0/24 should not be allowed to access any devices on lower-level interfaces.

3. 192.168.4.0/24 should be allowed access to all lower-level interfaces.

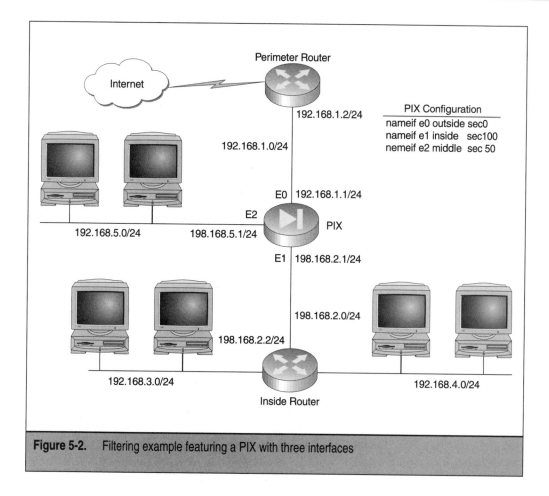

Figure 5-2. Filtering example featuring a PIX with three interfaces

Listing 5-4 shows the necessary configuration to accomplish our filtering policies.

Listing 5-4
```
pixfirewall(config)# outbound 1 deny 192.168.3.0.255.255.255.0 0 ip
pixfirewall(config)#  apply (inside) 1 outgoing_src
pixfirewall(config)#
pixfirewall(config)#  outbound 2 permit 192.168.1.0 255.255.255.0 0 ip
pixfirewall(config)#  apply (inside) 2 outgoing_dst
pixfirewall(config)#
pixfirewall(config)#  outbound 3 deny 0.0.0.0 0.0.0.0 0 ip
pixfirewall(config)#  outbound 3 permit 192.168.4.0 255.255.255.0 0 ip
pixfirewall(config)#  apply (inside) 3 outgoing_src
```

The first outbound filter denies all traffic from 192.168.3.0/24 based on the `outgoing_src` in the `apply` command. This filter satisfies the second filtering requirement. The second outbound filter allows traffic to reach 192.168.1.0/24 (with the exception of 192.168.3.0/24, which was filtered in the first filtering list) based on the `outgoing_dst` in the `apply` command. This command satisfies the first half of the first requirement. The third outbound filter denies all traffic with the exception of traffic with a source address of 192.168.4.0/24. Therefore, the second half of the first policy—denying Internet access to users on 192.168.2.0/24—is achieved. Likewise, all traffic from 192.168.4.0/24 is permitted to all segments.

As you can see from this example, the configuration of the `outbound` commands to accomplish our filtering policies was not a simple task. You need to have a very good understanding of how the PIX processes outbound filters to implement your security polices. Probably the biggest drawback of using outbound filters is that they limit you to examining only a source address *or* a destination address—you can't look at both simultaneously. Therefore, there are some filtering policies that you will not be able to implement with outbound filters.

 SECURITY ALERT!   Because outbound filters can only look at either the source IP address or the destination address (not both simultaneously), there are certain types of traffic that you might not be able to filter. In addition, the configuration of outbound filters can be very complex.

ACLs AND THE PIX

Beginning with FOS 5.3, Cisco introduced ACLs to standardize the implementation of filters on the PIX. Conduits and outbound filters had some major limitations in their filtering abilities. Cisco ported their ACL technology from their IOS-based routers to the PIX platform.

As you will see throughout this section of the book, PIX ACLs have many components in common with Cisco's ACL router implementation. For example, there are two steps that you'll have to go through in order to set up and activate your ACLs—create the ACL and apply it to an interface. In this sense, PIX ACLs are somewhat similar to outbound filters—as you will see, though, ACLs provide you with a lot more flexibility in their filtering abilities than outbound filters. The follow sections cover the implementation of ACLs and some enhancements introduced in FOS 6.2, like TurboACLs and object groups.

Comparing ACLs and Conduits/Outbound Filters

ACLs on Cisco IOS-based routers and the PIX firewalls are very similar in their function, processing, and configuration. The future direction of filtering on the PIX is the use of ACLs. ACLs, like conduits, can have the ASA open up holes in the firewall to allow traffic to flow between lower-security-level interfaces and higher-level ones. ACLs are more flexible than conduits because they can also be used to filter traffic from higher-level interfaces to lower-level ones, performing the function of outbound filters.

Cisco is attempting to move to a more uniform command-line interface across its networking products, which you can see with the ACL commands on the PIX. Because most filtering enhancements made by Cisco are implemented with ACLs, Cisco recommends that you migrate from the use of conduits and outbound filters to ACLs in your PIX's configuration. Table 5-1 compares ACLs with conduits and outbound filters.

One major difference with PIX ACLs is that you can perform filtering on traffic entering a specific interface. This gives you a lot more flexibility in filtering since you are not limited to the flow of traffic *between* interfaces, as is the case with conduits and outbound filters. In other words, ACLs don't examine the security levels of interfaces involved in the traffic flow—just the packet contents and the traffic entering an interface that has the ACL applied to it. Since ACLs can be used for filtering of traffic between higher- and lower-level interfaces, and vice versa, they work in tandem with `static` commands, since static address translation is required for traffic from a lower-level interface to a higher one. Like conduits and outbound filters, but unlike Cisco router ACLs, PIX ACLs use a *subnet* mask to match on IP addresses.

SECURITY ALERT!   Cisco still supports conduits and outbound filters for backwards compatibility; however Cisco highly recommends that you don't mix the two types of filtering: use ACLs, *or* use conduits and outbound filters—not both. If you have both, the PIX processes ACLs before the conduits or outbound filters. Also remember that ACLs use *subnet masks*, not wildcard masks, when matching on a packet's addressing contents.

Configuring and Activating ACLs

The configuration of ACLs on your PIX is very similar to that of configuring ACLs on an IOS-based router. The configuration process involves two steps: Create your filtering rules with the `access-list` command and activate your filtering rules on an interface with the `access-group` command. The following sections cover the configuration of ACLs.

Component	ACLs	Conduits	Outbound Filters
Traffic Filtering	Applied to traffic flowing through an interface	Applied to traffic flowing from lower-security-level interfaces to higher-level ones	Applied to traffic flowing from higher-security-level interfaces to lower-level ones
Requires a `static` command	For lower-to-higher access	Yes	No
Masking	Subnet mask	Subnet mask	Subnet mask
Filtering limitations	None	Filters on *all* traffic from lower to higher interfaces—not traffic specific to an interface	Can only filter on the source *or* destination address—not both simultaneously

Table 5-1.   Comparing ACLs with Conduits and Outbound Filters

Creating Your Filtering Rules

To configure your filtering rules with ACLs, use the `access-list` command:

```
pixfirewall(config)# access-list ACL_ID [deny|permit] IP_protocol
                     source_IP_address source_subnet_mask
                         [operator port_number]
                     destination_IP_address destination_subnet_mask
                         [operator port_number]
                                    -or-
pixfirewall(config)#   access-list ACL_ID [deny|permit] icmp
                       source_IP_address source_subnet_mask
                       destination_IP_address destination_subnet_mask
                       [ICMP_message_type]
```

The following sections will cover the parameters in the commands shown in this syntax.

ACL Identification   On the PIX, each ACL is differentiated from other ACLs by a unique identifier—this identifier can be either a name or a number. Following the `ACL_ID` is the action that you want the PIX to take when there is a match on a condition listed in the ACL command: either `permit` or `deny`. If there is a match on a `permit` statement, the PIX forwards the traffic normally. However, if there is a match on a `deny` statement, the PIX drops the packet and generates the following message:

```
%PIX-4-106019: IP packet from source_address to destination_address,
               protocol protocol received from interface interface_name
               deny by access-group acl_ID
```

 SECURITY ALERT!   At the end of every access-list on the PIX is an implicit `deny` statement—this *drops* all traffic that is not matched on a previous statement. This statement is invisible when you look at the ACL with a `show` command.

Therefore, if you want to see messages concerning the PIX dropping packets, you should manually add a `deny` statement at the very end of your ACL that drops all traffic: `access-list ACL_ID deny ip any any`. Cisco highly recommends that you don't log these messages to the console, but to a syslog server instead, because a very busy network could easily flood the console and cause the PIX to perform extra processing.

TIP   Cisco recommends that you log ACL matches to the PIX's internal buffer or an external syslog server.

ACL Protocols   There are two basic formats of the `access-list` command, as you saw. The first command is used by any IP protocol, and the second one is specific for ICMP traffic. To differentiate the two types, you need to specify either the name or number of the IP protocol that is to be filtered after the `permit` or `deny` parameter. Here are some common protocol names that you can specify: `icmp`, `ip`, `tcp`, and `udp`.

If you want to match on any IP traffic, specify the protocol as `ip`. For a complete listing of IP protocol numbers, visit www.iana.org/assignments/protocol-numbers.

ACL Addresses and Masks   Following the IP protocol designation, you need to specify the source IP address and subnet mask that you want to match on. As you have found out with conduits and outbound filters, ACLs on the PIX use a subnet mask, not a wildcard mask, to match on part or all of the IP address listed in the ACL command. Remember that ACLs require both a source address and subnet mask as well as a destination address and subnet mask.

The addressing nomenclature for dealing with a specific host address or any host address is the same as that with ACLs on a Cisco router. For a specific host, use the keyword `host` followed by the host address, making sure that you omit the subnet mask. For example, to specify a host of 192.168.1.1, you could use either one of the following two methods:

- `host 192.168.1.1`
- `192.168.1.1 255.255.255.255`

If you want to match on any host, you can use the keyword `any` to represent the address and subnet mask. For example, you could use either of the following two syntaxes:

- `any`
- `0.0.0.0 0.0.0.0`—this can be abbreviated to 0 0

NOTE   Remember that the PIX processes filter functions like ACLs before any address translation is performed, so you should place the address the PIX will see in the packet in the ACL statement.

ACLs and TCP and UDP Traffic   Once you have entered your IP address and subnet mask for protocols like TCP and UDP, you can specify an operator and a port number or name to be specific about the traffic that is to be filtered—this is also true for the destination address and subnet mask. You can specify an operator and the port name or number, or a range of numbers. Operators include `eq` (equal to), `neq` (not equal to), `lt` (less than), and `gt` (greater than). To specify a range of port numbers or names, enter the beginning and ending port numbers or names and separate them with a hyphen with no spaces between the hyphens and the ports. If you omit the port information, the PIX assumes that you are talking about all ports for the specified protocol and address.

Here is a list of TCP/UDP port names that you can use on the PIX: `dns`, `ftp`, `h323`, `http`, `ident`, `nttp`, `ntp`, `pop2`, `pop3`, `rpc`, `smtp`, `snmp`, `snmptrap`, `sqlnet`, `telnet`, and `tftp`. Of course, you can always use a port number if the PIX doesn't support the name of the port that you are trying to specify. For information about valid port numbers, visit www.iana.org/assignments/port-numbers.

ACLs and ICMP Traffic   For ICMP traffic, you can specify an ICMP message type (either by name or number). If you omit the message information, the PIX assumes that you are talking about all ICMP messages. Remember that for ICMP traffic, the PIX is not stateful. Therefore, if you want ICMP replies to your users' traffic and tests, you need to explicitly permit it with an ACL applied on the interface where the returning replies are received.

Here is a list of ICMP message names that you can use on the PIX: `alternate-address`, `conversion-error`, `echo`, `echo-reply`, `information-reply`, `information-request`, `mask-reply`, `mask-request`, `mobile-redirect`, `parameter-problem`, `redirect`, `router-advertisement`, `router-solicitation`, `source-quench`, `time-exceeded`, `timestamp-reply`, `timestamp-request`, `unreachable`, and others. For information about ICMP parameters, visit `www.iana.org/assignments/icmp-parameters`.

ACL Maintenance   You need to execute the `clear xlate` command any time that you add, change, or delete an ACL or its application to have the PIX enforce your new security policies correctly and not rely on what the PIX currently has in its translation and connection tables. To remove an ACL entry, precede the command with the `no` parameter. To view your configured ACL commands, use the `show access-list` command. To delete an ACL, use the `clear access-list` command. You will need to specify the *ACL_ID* to delete a specific list—if you omit the *ACL_ID*, all ACLs on the PIX are deleted.

For detailed troubleshooting of ACLs on the PIX, use the `debug` command:

```
pixfirewall#  debug access-list all|standard|turbo
```

The `standard` keyword displays information from non-turbo, or standard-configured ACLs. The `turbo` keyword displays debugging information from TurboACLs, which I'll discuss later in this chapter. The `all` keyword shows debugging information from both turbo and non-turbo ACLs. To turn off debugging for ACLs, preface the `debug` command with the `no` parameter.

Activating Your Filtering Rules

Once you have created your ACL, you need to activate it on an interface. The following is the syntax of the `access-group` command that you need to use to activate your ACL:

```
pixfirewall(config)#  access-group ACL_ID in interface interface_name
```

The *ACL_ID* specifies which ACL you are activating. Currently, you can only specify `in` for the direction of traffic when filtering—this refers to traffic entering the interface. After the `interface` parameter, you need to specify the name of the interface on the PIX where this ACL is to be activated. You can only have one ACL applied to an interface. To remove an ACL applied to an interface, precede the `access-group` command with the `no` parameter.

ACL Configuration Examples

To help illustrate the use of ACLS, let's take a look at some examples. I'll start out easy with an example of a PIX that has two interfaces and proceed to one with three interfaces.

PIX with Two Interfaces: Example 1

I'll start out with a simple example by considering a PIX that only has two interfaces. Take a look at the network shown in Figure 5-3. In this example, the internal network is using a private class address (192.168.1.0/24) and has been assigned the following public address space: 200.200.200.0/29. Here are the security policies that you need to set up with ACLs:

- Allow all outbound traffic (this is the default).
- Restrict inbound traffic to only the internal servers.

Listing 5-5 shows the address translation and ACL configuration of the PIX firewall.

Listing 5-5

```
pixfirewall(config)#  global (outside) 1 200.200.200.1
pixfirewall(config)#  nat (inside) 1 0 0
pixfirewall(config)#  static (inside, outside) 200.200.200.2 192.168.1.2
pixfirewall(config)#  static (inside, outside) 200.200.200.3 192.168.1.3
pixfirewall(config)#  static (inside, outside) 200.200.200.4 192.168.1.4
pixfirewall(config)#
pixfirewall(config)#  access-list PERMIT_IN permit tcp
any  host 200.200.200.2 eq 80
pixfirewall(config)#  access-list PERMIT_IN permit tcp
any  host 200.200.200.3 eq 25
pixfirewall(config)#  access-list PERMIT_IN permit udp
any  host 200.200.200.4 eq 53
pixfirewall(config)#  access-list PERMIT_IN deny ip any any
pixfirewall(config)#
pixfirewall(config)#  access-group PERMIT_IN in interface outside
```

I would like to point out a few things before I discuss the ACL configuration in Listing 5-5. First, notice that the PIX is performing PAT (using 200.200.200.1) when users' traffic heads out to the Internet. Also, there are three `static` commands to perform the address translation for the three internal servers.

Take a look at the ACL named PERMIT_IN in Listing 5-5; the first line allows TCP traffic from any source if it is headed to 200.200.200.2, and only if this traffic is for port 80, the web server process running on the web server. Notice that I used the public address as the destination address. Remember that ACLs are processed before address translation is performed (the `static` and `global` commands). One other thing to point out about the ACL is that I have added a `deny any any` statement at the end of the ACL—this is not necessary because there is an implicit `deny` at the end of every ACL; however, I want the PIX to create a log message for each dropped packet, which this statement accomplishes. The last thing done in this configuration is the activation of the PERMIT_IN ACL on the outside interface, which filters traffic as it comes in from the Internet.

PIX with Two Interfaces: Example 2

In this example, I want to expand on the example in Figure 5-3 and Listing 5-5. Assume that you have two groups of internal devices, as is depicted in Figure 5-3: GroupA

(192.168.1.128-192.168.1.191) and GroupB (192.168.1.192-192.168.1.254). Here are the filtering rules that to set up for GroupA:

- Denied access to all devices on network 131.108.0.0/16.
- Denied access to the following web servers: 210.210.210.0/24.
- Allowed access to all other Internet sites.

Here are the filtering rules to set up for GroupB:

- Allowed access to all devices in network 140.140.0.0/16.
- Allowed access to the following web servers: 210.210.210.5/32 and 211.211.211.3/32.
- Denied to all other Internet networks.

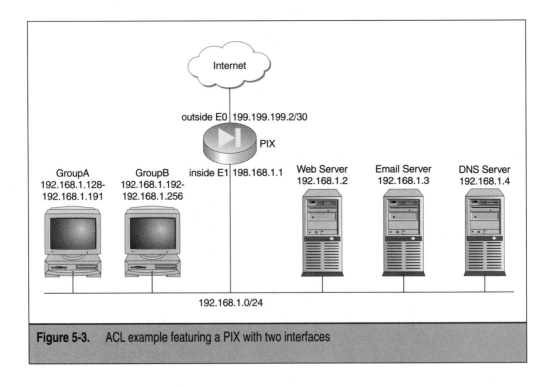

Figure 5-3. ACL example featuring a PIX with two interfaces

I'll assume that the inbound policies remain the same; therefore, I can build upon the example in Listing 5-5. Listing 5-6 shows the commands to accomplish the policy restrictions:

Listing 5-6
```
pixfirewall(config)#  access-list PERMIT_OUT deny ip
                          192.168.1.128 255.255.255.192
                          131.108.0.0 255.255.0.0
pixfirewall(config)#  access-list PERMIT_OUT deny tcp
                          192.168.1.128 255.255.255.192
                          210.210.210.0 255.255.255.0 eq 80
pixfirewall(config)#  access-list PERMIT_OUT permit ip
                          192.168.1.128 255.255.255.192 any
pixfirewall(config)#
pixfirewall(config)#  access-list PERMIT_OUT permit ip
                          192.168.1.192 255.255.255.192
                          140.140.0.0 255.255.0.0
pixfirewall(config)#  access-list PERMIT_OUT permit tcp
                          192.168.1.192 255.255.255.192
                          host 210.210.210.5 eq 80
pixfirewall(config)#  access-list PERMIT_OUT permit tcp
                          192.168.1.192 255.255.255.192
                          host 211.211.211.3 eq 80
pixfirewall(config)#  access-list PERMIT_OUT deny ip
                          192.168.1.192 255.255.255.192  any
pixfirewall(config)#
pixfirewall(config)#  access-group PERMIT_OUT in interface inside
pixfirewall(config)#  access-list PERMIT_OUT permit ip
                          host 192.168.1.2 any
pixfirewall(config)#  access-list PERMIT_OUT permit ip
                          host 192.168.1.3 any
pixfirewall(config)#  access-list PERMIT_OUT permit ip
                          host 192.168.1.4 any
pixfirewall(config)#
```

In Listing 5-6, I've broken up the ACL called PERMIT_OUT into two sections—one for GroupA and one for GroupB. Remember that ACLs are processed top-down, and the order of your statements does matter. One other item to point out is that the source IP addresses listed in the ACL statements are the addresses before translation, because the PIX processes ACLs before any address translation policies.

Take a look at GroupA's statements first. The very first entry in the ACL denies all IP traffic from 192.168.1.128/26 if it is destined for 131.108.0.0/16. The second statement denies all traffic from 192.168.1.128/26 if it is destined for TCP port 80 on any web server in network 210.210.210.0/24. The third statement allows any other IP traffic from 192.168.1.128/26 to go anywhere else on the Internet.

In GroupB's configuration (the second half of the ACL), the first permit statement (after GroupA's statements) allows any IP traffic from 192.168.1.192/26 to 140.140.0.0/16. The second and third statements allow all traffic from 192.168.1.192/26 to reach the two web servers: 210.210.210.5 and 211.211.211.3. Below this are three statements that allow traffic from the internal servers out. The last statement in the

ACL denies any other traffic from 192.168.1.192/26. The last part of the configuration in Listing 5-6 shows the application of the ACL (PERMIT_OUT) to the inside interface as traffic comes into this interface.

PIX with Three Interfaces

To help you understand how flexible ACLs are compared to conduits and outbound filters, I'll show a more complicated example: you have a PIX that has three interfaces and you want to control traffic between these interfaces, as shown in Figure 5-4:

Listing 5-7 shows just the address translation configuration of this PIX .

Listing 5-7
```
pixfirewall(config)# global (outside) 1 200.200.200.10-200.200.200.253
                             netmask 255.255.255.0
pixfirewall(config)# nat (inside) 1 0 0
pixfirewall(config)# nat (dmz) 1 0 0
pixfirewall(config)# static (dmz, outside) 200.200.200.1 192.168.5.5
pixfirewall(config)# static (dmz, outside) 200.200.200.2 192.168.5.6
pixfirewall(config)# static (inside, dmz) 192.168.5.0 192.168.5.0
                             netmask 255.255.255.0
pixfirewall(config)# access-list NO_NAT permit ip
                         192.168.2.0 255.255.255.0
                         192.168.5.0 255.255.255.0
pixfirewall(config)# access-list NO_NAT permit ip
                         192.168.3.0 255.255.255.0
                         192.168.5.0 255.255.255.0
pixfirewall(config)# access-list NO_NAT permit ip
                         192.168.4.0 255.255.255.0
                         192.168.5.0 255.255.255.0
pixfirewall(config)# nat (inside) 0 access-list NO_NAT
```

Explanation of the Basic Configuration   Before I go into the configuration of the ACLs, I will first discuss what the network in Figure 5-4 and the configuration shown in Listing 5-7 is doing. As you can see from this example, you are dealing with a PIX that has three interfaces—*outside*, *dmz*, and *inside*. The *outside* interface is connected to the router, which, in turn, is connected to the ISP. There is a default route pointing to this interface. The *dmz* interface has some user devices, as well as two servers: an e-mail server and a web server. The *inside* interface is connected to an internal router, which, in turn, is connected to two subnets: 192.168.3.0/24 and 192.168.4.0/24. There are two static routes configured for these two subnets.

There is one global command and two nat commands. I'll look at these from the perspectives of both the *inside* interface and the *dmz* interface. If a device from the inside interface tries to access a device on the dmz interface, it will not have its address translated—this is based on the very last static command in the configuration. If a device on the inside interface tries to access the Internet, its address is translated to a public address: 200.200.200.10 through 200.200.200.253.

If a device on the *dmz* interface tries to access a device on the outside interface, its addresses will be translated to the same public address space as the devices on the inside interface. The exceptions to this translation are the two Internet servers. There are two

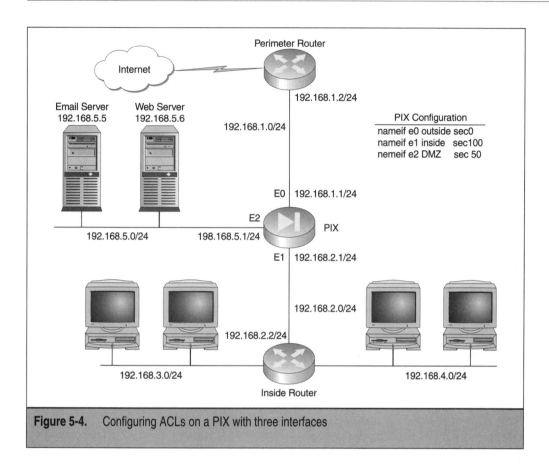

Figure 5-4. Configuring ACLs on a PIX with three interfaces

static commands—(dmz, outside)—that perform the address translation statically. These static commands change the e-mail server's address from 192.168.5.5 to 200.200.200.1, and the web server's address from 192.168.5.6 to 200.200.200.2.

The last static command defines the address translation for these192.168.5.0/24 devices when they initiate a connection to the *inside* interface, or, for that matter, when devices on the *inside* interface try to access these two services. This configuration logically disables translation between the *dmz* and *inside* interfaces for these two servers.

Configuring Filtering Policies   Now that I have discussed the basic configuration of the PIX shown in Listing 5-7, I'll talk about configuring some filtering policies for this PIX. As I mentioned in the previous section, the two servers located on the *dmz* interface need to access the internal network. Here's a list of all of the policies that need to be implemented for users on the DMZ segment:

- Users should not be allowed to access anything on 192.168.1.0/24.
- Device 192.168.5.5 and 192.168.5.6 should be allowed access to 192.168.2.0/24.

- Devices on the DMZ segment should be allowed to access any destination on the Internet.

Here's a list of the policies that need to be implemented for internal users:

- Users should be allowed access to the e-mail and web server on 192.168.5.0/24, but not to other devices on this segment.
- Users should not be allowed access to 192.168.1.0/24.
- Devices on 192.168.2.0/24 and 192.168.3.0/24 should be allowed access to any destination on the Internet.
- Devices on 192.168.4.0/24 should only be allowed access to 131.108.0.0/16, 140.140.0.0.16, and 210.210.210.0/24 out on the Internet.

Here's a list of all of the policies that need to be implemented for external users trying to access resources in your network.

- Users should be allowed access specifically to the e-mail server.
- Users should be allowed access specifically to the web server.
- All other types of access should be denied.

To enforce these polices, you need to create three ACLs and apply them to the three respective interfaces of the PIX. Listing 5-8 shows the configuration of the policies for the DMZ:

Listing 5-8
```
pixfirewall(config)#  access-list DMZ deny ip
                           any  192.168.1.0 255.255.255.0
pixfirewall(config)#  access-list DMZ permit ip
  host 192.168.5.5
  192.168.2.0 255.255.255.0
pixfirewall(config)#  access-list DMZ permit ip
  host 192.168.5.6
  192.168.2.0 255.255.255.0
pixfirewall(config)#  access-list DMZ deny ip
  any  192.168.2.0 255.255.255.0
pixfirewall(config)#  access-list DMZ deny ip
  any  192.168.3.0 255.255.255.0
pixfirewall(config)#  access-list DMZ deny ip
  any  192.168.4.0 255.255.255.0
pixfirewall(config)#  access-list DMZ permit ip
  192.168.5.0 255.255.255.0  any
pixfirewall(config)#  access-list DMZ deny ip any any
pixfirewall(config)#
pixfirewall(config)#  access-group DMZ in interface dmz
```

Listing 5-8 is fairly straightforward. The first ACL statement denies access to the 192.168.1.0/24 segment—notice that I used the keyword any for the source address—this applies to any source address originating from the *dmz* interface. This prevents spoofing attacks. The second and third ACL statements allows all IP traffic from 192.168.5.5 and

192.168.5.6 to travel to 192.168.2.0/24—this is denied by default because of the security levels of the two interfaces involved. The fourth, fifth, and sixth ACLs deny any traffic from the DMZ headed to the three internal subnets. This prevents other devices on the *dmz* interface from accessing resources on 192.168.2.0/24, and also prevents any device on this segment from accessing the two networks on the internal router: 192.168.3.0/24 and 192.168.4.0/24. The reason that these statements are needed is the statement that follows this (the seventh statement), which allows traffic from any device on 192.168.5.0/24 to go anywhere—you need to deny the specifics before you permit everything. The second to the last statement in the configuration drops all packets. I've added this so that I can see a log of all dropped packets—this greatly facilitates troubleshooting connectivity problems when the PIX is dropping packets based on its filter(s). The last command in this configuration is activation of the ACL on the *dmz* interface.

Here is an interesting question: based on the this ACL, if a device from 192.168.3.0/24 accesses the web server, and the web server responds back, is the return permitted through the firewall? One important item to point out about these filtering policies is that the PIX will be performing two tasks to determine if the traffic is allowed or dropped. The PIX first looks into its connection table to see if there is a connection already there. In this situation, the device from 192.168.3.0/24 initiated the connection, and because the DMZ is a lower-security-level interface, and there is no ACL configured on the inside interface, the PIX permits the connection and adds the temporary connection to its connection table. Thus, when the return comes back through the PIX, the PIX examines its table, sees the entry that was just created, and allows the response back to the 192.168.3.0/24 network. The only time the ACL is used is when there is no entry in the connection table—then the PIX examines the ACL to determine whether or not a hole in the firewall should be opened to allow the traffic. If you wanted to deny this traffic, you would need to create an ACL and apply it to the inside interface.

SECURITY ALERT The PIX uses the connection table first to determine access, and if an entry is not there, then it looks at the security level of the interfaces involved. If the flow is from a higher-level interface to a lower-level one, the packet is allowed by default unless an ACL is applied inbound on the higher interface—then the PIX uses the ACL to determine access. If the flow is from a lower-level to a higher-level interface, an ACL must be applied inbound on the lower interface, and must explicitly permit the traffic before the PIX will allow it to the higher interface.

Go ahead and look at the configuration for the filtering policies for the internal users, shown in Listing 5-9.

Listing 5-9
```
pixfirewall(config)#
                               any  host 192.168.5.5 eq 25
pixfirewall(config)# access-list INTERNAL permit tcp
  any  host 192.168.5.6 eq 80
pixfirewall(config)# access-list INTERNAL deny ip
  any  192.168.5.0 255.255.255.0
pixfirewall(config)# access-list INTERNAL deny ip
  any  192.168.1.0 255.255.255.0
```

```
pixfirewall(config)#  access-list INTERNAL permit ip
   192.168.2.0 255.255.255.0  any
pixfirewall(config)#  access-list INTERNAL permit ip
   192.168.3.0 255.255.255.0  any
pixfirewall(config)#  access-list INTERNAL permit ip
   192.168.4.0 255.255.255.0
   131.108.0.0 255.255.0.0
pixfirewall(config)#  access-list INTERNAL permit ip
   192.168.4.0 255.255.255.0
   210.210.210.0 255.255.255.0
pixfirewall(config)#  access-list INTERNAL deny ip any any
pixfirewall(config)#
pixfirewall(config)#  access-group INTERNAL in interface inside
```

The first and second commands allow all users on the *inside* interface to access the web and e-mail server on 192.168.5.0/24, and the third statement denies all other internal traffic to this nework. The fourth statement denies all internal traffic destined to 192.168.1.0/24. The fifth and sixth statements allow 192.168.2.0/24 and 192.168.3.0/24 to access any other network. The seventh and eighth statements allow devices from 192.168.4.0/24 to 131.108.0.0/16 and 210.210.210.0/24. Any other traffic not matching any of the `permit` statements in this list will be dropped. The last statement in the configuration activates the ACL on the *inside* interface.

Listing 5-10 shows the configuration for the filtering policies that affect the external users (the ones on the Internet, or located on 192.168.1.0/24):

Listing 5-10
```
pixfirewall(config)#
   any 200.200.200.1 eq 25
pixfirewall(config)#  access-list EXTERNAL permit tcp
   any 200.200.200.2 eq 80
pixfirewall(config)#  access-list EXTERNAL deny ip any any
pixfirewall(config)#  access-group EXTERNAL in interface outside
```

Of the three ACLs, the one for the external users is the simplest. The first and second statements allow internal users access to the e-mail and web servers on 192.168.5.0/24—notice that the destination addresses are the public addresses, because this is what the PIX sees. The third statement drops all traffic and the last statement activates the ACL on the *outside* interface.

As you can see from this example, the configuration of ACLs can be a very complex process. You should *always* test any changes you make to your ACLs to ensure that you are not inadvertently opening up any unnecessary holes in your PIX firewall.

PIX and Windows Domains Example

One of the most common problems that I am asked to help with in the configuration of firewalls is allowing authentication and domain access in a Windows NT or 2000 environment. Because this is a very common problem, I've added an example to illustrate the configuration that you must create on your PIX. Actually, the filtering configuration is easy; however, remember that by opening up your firewall to allow domain access, you are opening up a security hole that may allow hackers to take advantages of holes in your PDC or BDC.

Overview of the Windows Example   To illustrate the configuration, I'll use the network shown in Figure 5-5. In this example, devices on network 201.201.201.0/24 need to access the Windows Internet Naming Service (WINS) server (200.200.200.2) as well as the Windows server (200.200.200.3). In this example, I'll look at the traffic flow between USERA (201.201.201.1) and both the WINS (WINS1) and file server (FILE1). I need to configure two things: static translation for the external access, and an ACL to allow the NT/2000 functionality to work with WINS.

For the purpose of this example, I will show you the configuration for Windows NT. As shown in Figure 5-5, the host USERA will access resources on the inside of the network—specifically WINS1 (200.200.200.2) and FILE1 (200.200.200.3). I'll assume that USERA is part of the domain specified on WINS1; however, this doesn't have to be true in order to allow USERA access to the Windows NT services in 200.200.200.0/24. I'll also assume that the PDC (Primary Domain Controller) is WINS1.

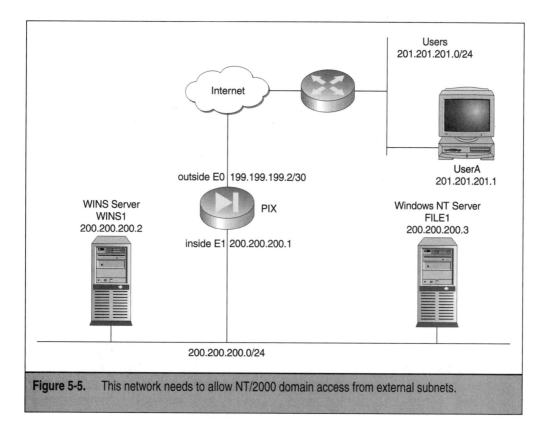

Figure 5-5.   This network needs to allow NT/2000 domain access from external subnets.

USERA can use one of two methods in order to access resources, or files, from his desktop, through the PIX firewall:

- Using the Universal Naming Convention (UNC) by entering: `\\resource_name`
- Double-clicking on the resource in the Network Neighborhood

As you can see, the firewall itself will be transparent to USERA; in other words, USERA doesn't have to do any extra in order to access resources on the 200.200.200.0/24 network.

Basic PIX Configuration   First, take a look at the PIX's address translation configuration in Listing 5-11:

Listing 5-11
```
pixfirewall(config)# nat (inside) 0 0.0.0.0 0.0.0.0
pixfirewall(config)# static (inside, outside) 200.200.200.0 200.200.200.0
  netmask 255.255.255.0
```

In this example, the internal network is using a public address (200.200.200.0). Therefore, the `static` command uses the same public address in the global and local address parameters.

Traffic to Permit   Before I begin with the configuration of the ACL, there are a couple of things that I need to discuss. As you probably know, Microsoft is a big fan of using the NetBIOS protocol for handling networking functions. However, setting up a filter to allow NetBIOS traffic is not the only traffic that you need to permit through your PIX. Plus, depending on whether you are using NT or 2000, the list of ports that you must allow will differ—with Windows 2000, you must allow some of the same ports (but not all of them), and quite a few different ports.

Table 5-2 shows the ports you will probably need to allow if you are using Windows NT.

Table 5-3 shows the ports you will probably need to allow if you are using 2000.

Client Ports	NT Server Port	Name of Service
TCP/1024-65535	TCP/135	Remote Procedure Calls (RPCs)
UDP/137	UDP/137	NetBIOS Name
UDP/138	UDP/138	NetBIOS Netlogon and Browsing
TCP/1024-65535	TCP/139	NetBIOS Session
TCP/1024-65535	TCP/42	WINS Replication

Table 5-2.   The List of Ports You Need to Allow for Windows NT

Client Ports	2000 Server Port	Name of Service
TCP/1024-65535	TCP/135	RPCs
TCP-UDP/1024-65535	TCP-UDP/389	LDAP
TCP/1024-65535	TCP/636	LDAP SSL
TCP/1024-65535	TCP/3268	LDAP GC
TCP/1024-65535	TCP/3269	LDAP GC SSL
TCP-UDP/53,1024-65535	TCP-UDP/53	DNS
TCP-UDP/1024-65535	TCP-UDP/88	Kerberos
TCP/1024-65535	TCP/445	SMB

Table 5-3.   The List of Ports You Need to Allow for Windows 2000

NOTE   If you are using RPCs, there might be additional protocols and ports that you will have to permit through your firewall. Chapter 9 will discuss problematic protocols, like RPCs, and how the PIX can deal with them in a secure fashion.

ACL Configuration   To create an ACL to allow USERA to browse resources on 200.200.200.0/24, you must understand what USERA's machine does before the actual browse process takes place. First, USERA's machine registers itself using the NetBIOS name server. The UDP segment created by this process uses 137 as both the source and destination port number. USERA's machine then uses Netlogon to search for a domain controller. It uses another UDP segment to accomplish this, using 138 as both the source and destination port number.

Once the machine is registered and logged in, USERA can begin his browsing for resources. When establishing a connection to a resource, USERA's machine sets up a TCP connection, with a random port number above 1,023 as the source and 139 as the destination.

Now that you understand the basic process, I'll configure the ACL. Listing 5-12 shows the necessary code to allow anyone from 201.201.201.0/24 to access Windows resources on network 200.200.200.0.

Listing 5-12
```
pixfirewall(config)# access-list windows permit udp
    201.201.201.0 255.255.255.0
    host 200.200.200.2 eq 137
pixfirewall(config)# access-list windows permit udp
```

```
     201.201.201.0 255.255.255.0
     host 200.200.200.2 eq 138
pixfirewall(config)#  access-list windows permit tcp
     201.201.201.0 255.255.255.0
     host 200.200.200.2 eq 139
pixfirewall(config)#  access-list windows permit udp
     201.201.201.0 255.255.255.0
     host 200.200.200.3 eq 137
pixfirewall(config)#  access-list windows permit udp
     201.201.201.0 255.255.255.0
     host 200.200.200.3 eq 138
pixfirewall(config)#  access-list windows permit tcp
     201.201.201.0 255.255.255.0
     host 200.200.200.3 eq 139
pixfirewall(config)#  access-list windows permit icmp any any
pixfirewall(config)#  access-group windows in interface outside
```

The first three ACL commands in Listing 5-12 allow access to the WINS1 server, and the next set of three ACL commands allows access to the FILE1 server. I've also allowed ICMP traffic with this ACL to verify that USERA can ping the internal resources—this is used to ensure that the devices have initial connectivity, and simplifies troubleshooting. If you know that USERA can ping the internal servers, but can't browse, then the problem doesn't relate to network connectivity, but possibly your filter or WINS/PDC setup.

TIP   If you have other internal networks that you want external users to access, you need to create the appropriate entries in your ACL, and set up the necessary static address translations with the `static` command.

Additional Issues   If you are using DHCP to assign IP addresses to devices on the inside of your network, you will have three choices to solve connectivity problems (remember that your devices could have different IP addresses each time that they boot up). Your first choice is to specify the keyword *any* as a destination address in your ACL configuration. Obviously, the problem with this approach is that you are opening up a fairly big hole in your firewall—someone performing spoofing has access to all of your internal Windows resources. The second solution is to hard-code IP addresses on these internal resources, which might require a lot of work on your part. Your third choice is to not allow external access to your Windows resources unless they are coming in via a VPN connection. I will discuss the PIX and VPNs in Chapters 16 and 17.

Make sure that your internal WINS server sends both the translated address as well as the internal IP address to the WINS client. Remember that if you are using private addresses on the inside of your network, and the client is using the global public address in the `static` command, the WINS server needs to send the public address to the client. Of course, the WINS server is also sending addresses to internal clients with the private address. To solve this problem, have the WINS server send both addresses.

If client receives a "The Network Path was Not Found" error message dialog when trying to access a resource, you should perform the following steps:

- Turn on debugging on the PIX for ACLs—make sure that the last statement in the ACL is deny ip any any so that you can see if the PIX is inadvertently dropping some of the client's packets, thus causing the failure.

- If the WINS server has multiple NICs, or multiple IP addresses, make sure that the PIX has a static address translation for each of these addresses. Also verify that the ACL on the PIX is allowing access to each of these addresses on the WINS server.

- Verify that the WINS server is actually responding to the client's request—remember that if the client doesn't get a response, it resorts to using local broadcasts for resolution, which obviously the PIX is not going to see. You might want to use a protocol analyzer to verify this, or configure an ACL on the PIX for the inside interface that has one statement—permit ip any any—and then turn on debugging to see the matches. On a production PIX in a busy environment, this is not really recommended.

TurboACLs

TurboACLs are a new feature introduced in PIX FOS 6.2. TurboACLs are a logical extension of normal ACLs. With a normal ACL, the PIX treats the entries in the ACL as a linked list, which it processes in a linear fashion starting with the first entry, then the second entry, and so on. Obviously, the more commands in the ACL, the longer it takes the PIX to process the commands. If the PIX is lucky, it will find a match in the first few statements; however, the PIX might have to process the entire list to decide whether to allow or drop the packet.

TurboACLs are a feature that is used to reduce the time that it takes to find a match on a statement in an ACL and therefore either permit or deny the packet. The PIX accomplishes this by compiling the normal ACL to speed up the searching for a match on an ACL statement.

Requirements for and Issues with TurboACLs

The following are the list of items required in order to use TurboACLs:

- FOS 6.2.
- Minimum of 2.1MB of flash and 1MB of flash for every set of 2,000 ACL statements.

Starting in FOS, TurboACLs allow the PIX to improve performance when searching for a match in very large ACLs. TurboACLs don't provide any real benefit for small ACLs—

once you have 19 or more entries in an ACL, you should consider using TurboACLs to speed up the PIX's searching performance. For shorter ACLs, the time it takes to find a match with a TurboACL is about the same as a normal ACL using a linear search. Cisco allows you to turn on TurboACLs for all ACLs, and then disable the turbo functionality on a per-ACL basis.

NOTE   When you enable TurboACLs globally on your PIX, the PIX will only compile normal ACLs that have 19 or more entries in them.

One drawback of using TurboACLs is that they are very memory-intensive when compiling and were developed by Cisco specifically for the higher-end PIXs like the 525 and 535, where you might be required to configure a few thousand ACL statements to enforce your security policies. Because of these flash memory requirements, the smaller-end PIXs, like the 506, might have issues using TurboACLs and other features such as the PIX Device Manager (PDM).

Because of these flash memory issues, the PIX 501 does not support the TurboACL feature—the PIX 501 only has 8MB of flash. Cisco assumes that you will be using PDM to manage the 501, which is true for many novices to the PIX firewall. However, once you become familiar with configuring the PIX with the CLI, you have no real need for the GUI-based PDM. It would be a nice feature if Cisco allowed you to use TurboACLs on the 501 if you removed PDM from flash on the 501.

One last item to point out is that whenever you add, change, or delete an entry in an ACL that is a TurboACL, the PIX must take the normal ACL and recompile it. This puts a heavy load on the processor of the PIX and might slow down your traffic for a small period of time.

Configuring TurboACLs

To enable TurboACLs, use this command:

```
pixfirewall(config)# access-list compiled
```

When you enter this command, any ACL on your PIX that has 19 or more entries in it will be compiled into a TurboACL (assuming that it has not already been compiled). To disable the TurboACL feature, precede the above command with the no parameter—this disables TurboACLs for all ACLs on your PIX. By default, TurboACLs are *disabled* on the PIX.

If you want to enable or disable TurboACLs for one specific ACL, use this command:

```
pixfirewall(config)# [no] access-list ACL_ID compiled
```

When you specify a particular ACL, remember that the PIX will *only* compile ACLs that have 19 or more statements.

Verifying TurboACL Configurations

Once you have enabled the TurboACL feature, you can use the `show access-list` command to verify your configuration, and to see the flash usage for your compiled ACLs:

```
pixfirewall#  show access-list
TurboACL statistics:
ACL                     State       Memory(KB)
--------------------  ----------- ----------
CHECK                   Operational  2
Shared memory usage: 2046 KB
access-list compiled
access-list CHECK turbo-configured; 19 elements
access-list CHECK permit tcp any host 192.168.1.2 (hitcnt=0)
access-list CHECK permit udp any host 192.168.1.6 eq dns (hitcnt=10)
```

The example shown here is an abbreviated output—many of the ACL commands are not listed. You can see at the top of the display that there is one ACL called CHECK that is using 2MB of flash memory. This ACL has been compiled, and has 19 ACL commands in it. The first two commands are displayed. Notice that at the end of each command listing is a `hitcnt` value—this indicates the number of matches on the ACL statement.

OBJECT GROUPING

Another enhancement added in FOS 6.2 is the ability to group objects together to simplify the configuration of complex filtering policies with conduits, outbound filters, and ACLs. Cisco calls this feature *Object Grouping*. Object Grouping allows you to create groups that you apply your filtering polices to, thereby reducing the number of filtering commands that you have to enter. This eases your implementation and also ensures that you apply the same policy to every device when a policy needs to be applied across a group of devices.

Object Grouping allows you to create the following objects:

- Client devices
- Server devices
- Types of services (TCP and UDP port numbers; that is, applications)
- ICMP message types
- Networks

Once you have created your various groups of objects, you can then include them in your filtering commands to permit or deny packets based on matches in the Object Groupings.

Advantages of Object Groups

I'll outline some situations where Object Groupings does or doesn't make sense. For example, if you need to define a filtering policy that denied traffic from 192.168.1.1 to 192.168.2.2 for telnets, you could easily accomplish this with a single filtering command. However, if you have a list of ten clients trying to access three servers for both telnet and e-mail, the filtering configuration becomes very complex. You could use Object Groupings to create a client group for the ten clients, a server group for the three servers, and a server group for telnet and e-mail; and then use these groupings in a single filtering command.

Another nice feature of Object Grouping is that you can embed an object group within another object group. As an example, you might have two client object groups, and you want to create a filter that includes both of these groups. To solve this problem, you can create a third object group, and include the first two client object groups within this new group.

TIP   When you take advantage of Object Grouping, you can reduce the number of filtering commands needed in an ACL, conduit, or outbound filter.

Syntax for Grouping Objects

The syntax for creating an object group is very simple, as shown here:

```
pixfirewall(config)#  object-group type_of_object group_ID [protocol_name]
```

There are four different object types that you can specify for the *type_of_object* parameter. Table 5-4 lists the valid object types.

Once you have specified an object type, you need to follow it with an ID for the group—this is a number that groups together the various object types that you will create. If you specified `service` as the type of object, you need to tell the PIX which protocols are to be included in the list of applications. Your options are `tcp`, `udp`, or `tcp-udp` (for both).

Subconfiguration Modes

One very interesting thing occurs when you enter the `object-group` command— you'll be taken to a *Subconfiguration* mode. In Chapter 3, I mentioned that one major difference between the IOS-based routers and the PIX is that all of the commands for the PIX are executed at a single level in *Configuration* mode. This is true with the one exception of the newly introduced `object-group` command. When you enter this command, you'll be taken into an appropriate subconfiguration mode. Your prompt

Object Type	Explanation
`icmp-type`	Specifies a grouping of ICMP messages.
`network`	Specifies a grouping of hosts and/or subnets/networks.
`protocol`	Specifies a group of IP protocols, like IP, ICMP, TCP, UDP or other IP protocols
`service`	Specifies a group of TCP or UDP applications, or both.

Table 5-4.   Available object types for Object Grouping

will change, indicating the change in modes. These are the prompts for the modes
listed in Table 5-4, in their respective order:

```
pixfirewall(config-icmp-type)#
pixfirewall(config-network)#
pixfirewall(config-protocol)#
pixfirewall(config-service)#
```

You will actually list your objects—client devices, networks, protocols, application
services, and ICMP message types, within the appropriate *Subconfiguration* mode. If
you are used to Cisco's IOS-based router interface, this will be nothing new to you.

Descriptions

When you are in a *Subconfiguration* mode, you can still execute `show`, `config`, and
`write` commands. There is also one command, `description`, that is common to all
types of object groups. The `description` command allows you to enter up to 200
characters as a description for an object group. The syntax of the `description`
command is:

```
pixfirewall(config-protocol)# description descriptive_text
```

In this example I'm in *Protocol Subconfiguration* mode; however, this command works in
all *Subconfiguration* modes for Object Grouping.

Nesting Object Groups

Another command common to all Object Groups is the `group-object` command. The
`group-object` command allows you to add a previously created group to a group of
the same type. The syntax of this command is:

```
pix(config-protocol)# group-object group_ID
```

To use the `group-object` command, you need to create an object group with your included services, protocols, networks, or ICMP message types. You can then create a new object group of the same type and use the `group-object` command to reference your already created object group. You need to use the *group_ID* number of the previous group when using the `group-object` command.

Exiting a Subconfiguration Mode

To exit a *Subconfiguration* mode when you are within an object group, you can type either `exit` or `quit`; or, if you execute a *Global Configuration* mode command, such as `ip address` or `static`, when you are in a *Subconfiguration* mode, you will automatically be taken out of *Subconfiguration* mode and placed into *Global Configuration* mode.

Object Groups for Networks

You can create an object group to specify host addresses and network numbers that you use in your filter commands. To create a network object group, use the commands shown here:

```
pixfirewall(config) object-group network group_ID
pixfirewall(config-network)#  network-object host host_address
pixfirewall(config-network)#  network-object network_address subnet_mask
```

The first command, `object-group network`, creates a network object group and takes you into the *Network Subconfiguration* mode. The second and third commands allow you to specify the devices in the object group—the first is for a specific host and the second is for a network or subnet number.

Object Groups for Protocols

You can create an object group for IP protocols that you use in your filter commands. To create a protocol object group, use these commands:

```
pixfirewall(config) object-group protocol group_ID
pixfirewall(config-protocol)#  protocol-object protocol_name_or_number
```

The first command, `object-group protocol`, creates a protocol object group and takes you into the *Protocol Subconfiguration* mode. The second command allows you to specify the IP in the object group. You can specify a protocol name, like `ip`, `tcp`, `udp`, or `icmp`, or you can give the IP protocol number instead, like 6 for TCP or 17 for UDP.

Object Groups for Services

You can create an object group for TCP and UDP applications that you use in your filter commands. To create a services object group, use these commands:

```
pixfirewall(config)# object-group service group_ID tep/udp/tcp-udp
pixfirewall(config-service)#  port-object eq port_number/name
pixfirewall(config-service)#  port-object range first_port last_port
```

The first command, `object-group service`, creates a services object group and takes you into the *Service Subconfiguration* mode. You need to specify either TCP, UDP, or both protocols—this refers to the types of ports within this object group. The second command, the one with the `eq` parameter, specifies a specific port number (or name) in the Object Group. You can also specify a `range` of port numbers—you need to use the keyword `range` followed by the first number in the list and the last number.

Object Groups for ICMP Messages

You can create an object group for ICMP messages that you use in your filter commands. To create an ICMP object group, use these commands:

```
pixfirewall(config-icmp-type)#  icmp-object ICMP_message
```

The first command, `object-group icmp-type`, creates an ICMP message type object group and takes you into the *ICMP Subconfiguration* mode. The second command specifies the ICMP message type (like the ICMP number) in the object group.

Examining Your Object Groups

Once you have configured your object groups, you can display them with the `show object-group` command. The following is the syntax of this command:

```
pixfirewall#  show object-group [protocol|network|service|icmp-type]
pixfirewall#  show object-group id group_ID
```

If you only type in the `show object-group` command and do not specify any parameters, the PIX will display all of your object groups. You can limit this by specifying a specify type of object group, or a specific object group. Here's an example of this command:

```
object-group network web_servers
  description: This is a list of Web servers
  network-object host 200.200.200.2
  network-object host 200.200.200.9
object-group network trusted_web_servers
  network-object host 192.199.1.7
  network-object 201.201.201.0 255.255.255.0
  group-object web_servers
```

In this example, there are two object groups. The first one is called `web_servers`, and contains two hosts: 200.200.200.2 and 200.200.200.9. The second object group is called `trusted_web_servers`, and contains one host (192.199.1.7), one network (201.201.201.0/24) and one embedded, or nested, object group called `web_servers`.

NOTE If you use a `show` command to display your filters, such as `show access-list`, the PIX will not display the object group configuration, but instead will display the *expanded* configuration—the PIX will replace the object references with the actual IP protocols, addresses/ network numbers, and services.

Deleting Object Groups

To remove all object groups on your PIX, use the `clear object-group` command. Optionally, you can remove all of the object groups of a specific type by adding the type to the end of the `clear object-group` command. The following is the syntax of this command:

```
pixfirewall# clear object-group [protocol|network|services|icmp-type]
```

If you only want to remove a specific object group, use this syntax:

```
pixfirewall(config)# no object-group group_ID
```

NOTE You cannot delete an object group that is currently being referenced by another PIX command, such as an ACL or a conduit.

Using Object Groups with ACLs

To help you understand how Object Groups are used by filtering commands, I'll now examine how they are used by ACLs on the PIX. As I mentioned earlier in this chapter, there are two forms of the ACL command: one for ICMP traffic and one for all other types of IP traffic. The following is the syntax for these two commands if you use object groups:

```
pixfirewall(config)# access-list ACL_ID deny|permit icmp
                     source_address_and_mask|
                          object-group network_object_group_ID
                     destination_address_and_mask|
                          object-group network_object_group_ID
                          [icmp_type|object-group
icmp_type_object_group_ID]

pixfirewall(config)# access-list ACL_ID deny|permit
                     IP_protocol|
                          object-group protocol_object_group_ID
                     source_address_and_mask|
```

```
object-group network_object_group_ID
                            [operator source_port|
                                  object-group service_object_group_ID]
                       destination_address_and_mask|
                            object-group network_object_group_ID
                            [operator destination_port|
                                  object-group service_object_group_ID]
```

As you can see, you can use object groups where they suit you. For example, you could list a network object group for the source address information, but list a specific host address for the destination—you can mix and match object groups and specific ACL protocol information based on your configuration needs.

To help illustrate the use of Object Groups with ACLs, I'll use the network shown in Figure 5-6. In this example, I will allow outside access to the internal servers, but only for web and FTP access to the specific servers.

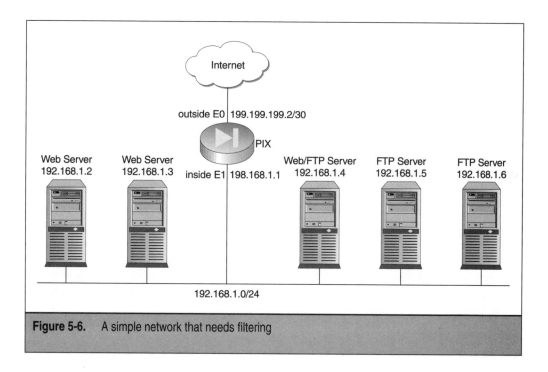

Figure 5-6. A simple network that needs filtering

The following is the configuration, including address translation, for the PIX:

```
pixfirewall(config)#  global (outside) 1 200.200.200.1 netmask 255.255.255.0
pixfirewall(config)#  nat (inside) 1 0 0
pixfirewall(config)#  static (inside, outside) 200.200.200.2 192.168.1.2
pixfirewall(config)#  static (inside, outside) 200.200.200.3 192.168.1.3
pixfirewall(config)#  static (inside, outside) 200.200.200.4 192.168.1.4
pixfirewall(config)#  static (inside, outside) 200.200.200.5 192.168.1.5
pixfirewall(config)#  static (inside, outside) 200.200.200.6 192.168.1.6
pixfirewall(config)#
pixfirewall(config)#  object-group network web_servers
pixfirewall(config-network)#  network-object host 200.200.200.2
pixfirewall(config-network)#  network-object host 200.200.200.3
pixfirewall(config-network)#  network-object host 200.200.200.4
pixfirewall(config-network)#  exit
pixfirewall(config)#  object-group network ftp_servers
pixfirewall(config-network)#  network-object host 200.200.200.4
pixfirewall(config-network)#  network-object host 200.200.200.5
pixfirewall(config-network)#  network-object host 200.200.200.6
pixfirewall(config-network)#  exit
pixfirewall(config)#  access-list PERMIT_IN permit tcp
                      any  object-group web_servers eq 80
pixfirewall(config)#  access-list PERMIT_IN permit tcp
                      any  object-group ftp_servers eq 21
pixfirewall(config)#  access-list PERMIT_IN deny ip any any
pixfirewall(config)#  access-group PERMIT_IN in interface outside
```

There are two network object groups here, one for web servers and one for FTP servers. There are two ACL statements that allow access to these web servers and FTP servers, but deny everything else. If you didn't use object groups, you would need six statements for the servers and then the deny any if you wanted to log all dropped packets.

ICMP TRAFFIC AND THE PIX

To round off this chapter, the last topic that I will cover is ICMP traffic, and how the PIX deals with it. There are two issues concerning ICMP—ICMP traffic passing *through* the PIX and ICMP traffic directed *at* the PIX. The next sections deal with these two topics.

ICMP Traffic Through the PIX

As I mentioned Chapter 4, ICMP traffic is *not* stateful. ICMP messages, by default, are permitted when traveling from a higher-security-level interface to a lower-level one. However, ICMP traffic is denied, by default, from a lower-security-level interface to a higher-level one, even if it is an ICMP message response to a user's ICMP query. To allow ICMP traffic to travel from a lower-level to a higher-level interface, you need to configure a `static` translation and either a conduit or an ACL. The `static` command is only necessary for traffic originating from a lower security level interface.

Typically, you should allow the following ICMP message types into your network to help provide some basic management and troubleshooting abilities for your internal devices: echo reply, source quench, unreachable, and time exceeded. For external devices to test connectivity to your network, you might also want to permit the ICMP echo message, but I would definitely restrict what internal computers that devices on the Internet can generate pings to.

I'll use the network shown in Figure 5-6 to illustrate what the ACL would look like to allow returning ICMP traffic to your users. I'll build upon the example that I started in the previous section. Here's an example of the configuration to allow returning ICMP traffic:

```
pixfirewall(config)#  object-group icmp-type icmp_traffic
pixfirewall(config-icmp-type)#  icmp-object echo-reply
pixfirewall(config-icmp-type)#  icmp-object source-quench
pixfirewall(config-icmp-type)#  icmp-object unreachable
pixfirewall(config-icmp-type)#  icmp-object time-exceeded
pixfirewall(config-icmp-type)#  exit
pixfirewall(config)#  object-group network ALL_servers
pixfirewall(config-network)#  group-object web_servers
pixfirewall(config-network)#  group-object ftp_servers
pixfirewall(config-network)#  exit
pixfirewall(config)#  access-list PERMIT_IN permit tcp
                   any  object-group web_servers eq 80
pixfirewall(config)#  access-list PERMIT_IN permit tcp
                   any  object-group ftp_servers eq 21
pixfirewall(config)#  access-list PERMIT_IN permit icmp
                   any  any object-group icmp_traffic
pixfirewall(config)#  access-list PERMIT_IN permit icmp
                   any  object-group ALL_servers  echo
pixfirewall(config)#  access-list PERMIT_IN deny ip any any
pixfirewall(config)#  access-group PERMIT_IN in interface outside
```

I've created two object groups—one for allowing ICMP returning traffic, and one that puts the web and FTP servers into a network group so that you can specifically allow echoes to them. The first two entries in the ACL are the same as in the previous section. The two entries after those are new. The first one allows ICMP traffic from anywhere, and to anywhere if it matches the ICMP message types in the `icmp_traffic` object group. The entry after this allows any echoes from anywhere if they are destined to the devices specified in the `ALL_servers` object group.

ICMP Traffic Directed at the PIX

Until version 5.2.1 of the FOS, any ICMP traffic destined to any of the interfaces of the PIX would be allowed, and the PIX would automatically respond back. One unfortunate drawback of this process is that a hacker could use ICMP to learn that the PIX firewall was there, and possibly learn some basic information about it. Up until version 5.2.1, you could not disable this function and make the PIX invisible to other devices. Starting with version 5.2.1, you now have the option of making the PIX *stealthy*—you can control how the PIX itself will respond to ICMP messages, or prevent them altogether. This feature is sometimes referred to as *stealth PIX*.

Restricting ICMP Traffic Directed at the PIX

To control ICMP messages destined to an interface on the PIX, use the `icmp` command:

```
pixfirewall(config)#  icmp permit|deny
                      source_IP_address source_subnet_mask
                      [ICMP_message_type] interface_name
```

You must specify a source IP address and a subnet mask. Unlike a conduit or ACL, there is no destination IP address, because the PIX itself is the destination.

You can qualify which ICMP messages are allowed or denied by entering a value for the *ICMP_message_type* parameter. The message types can be entered as either a name or a number. See the ACL list configuration in this chapter for a list of message types. If you omit the message type, the PIX will assume that you want to allow or deny all ICMP messages. The last parameter is the name of the interface for which you want to restrict ICMP messages.

The PIX processes the `icmp` commands top-down for an interface. In other words, when the PIX receives an ICMP packet destined to one of its interfaces, checks to see if there are any `icmp` commands associated with the interface. If there are none defined for the interface, the PIX processes the ICMP message. If there is an ICMP list, the PIX processes the commands based on the order in which you entered them. If the PIX goes through the entire list, and doesn't find a match, the PIX drops the ICMP message. To remove your `icmp` commands that you have configured, use the `clear icmp` command.

NOTE   Like ACLs and conduits, there is an implicit deny at the end of the `icmp` command list—therefore, if you use the `icmp` command, you should at least specify one `permit` statement per interface unless you want your PIX to be completely invisible.

ICMP Example

Now, let's take a look at an example on how to use the `icmp` command to restrict ICMP messages directed at the PIX's interface. In this example, you want to be able to test connectivity from the PIX to other destinations on the Internet, and you only want the PIX to process certain ICMP packets to aid in connectivity testing—all other ICMP messages should be dropped. Here's an example of how to accomplish this:

```
pixfirewall(config)#  icmp permit any echo-reply outside
pixfirewall(config)#  icmp permit any information-reply outside
pixfirewall(config)#  icmp permit any mask-reply outside
pixfirewall(config)#  icmp permit any parameter-problem outside
pixfirewall(config)#  icmp permit any source-quench outside
pixfirewall(config)#  icmp permit any time-exceeded outside
pixfirewall(config)#  icmp permit any timestamp-reply outside
pixfirewall(config)#  icmp permit any unreachable outside
pixfirewall(config)#  icmp deny any outside
```

As you can see, there are only certain items that are permitted—basically ICMP replies to ICMP messages that the PIX generates, as well as any error messages.

FURTHER STUDY

Web Sites

To see the IP protocol numbers you can use for filtering commands, visit www.iana.org/assignments/protocol-numbers.

To see the TCP/UDP port numbers you can use for filtering commands, visit www.iana.org/assignments/port-numbers.

To see the ICMP message types you can use for filtering commands, visit www.iana.org/assignments/icmp-parameters.

For more information about configuring filtering on your PIX, visit www.cisco.com/univercd/cc/td/doc/product/iaabu/pix/pix_62/config/index.htm.

For information allowing access to Windows NT and 2000 domain components, visit support.microsoft.com/default.aspx?scid=kb;EN-US;Q179442.

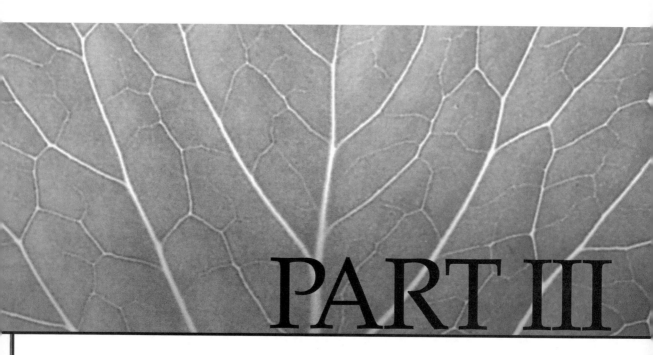

PART III

Advanced PIX Features

CHAPTER 6

Web Traffic Filtering

In Chapter 5, I talked about some of the advanced filtering abilities of the PIX, including ACLs. One limitation of ACLs is that they can only filter on the network and transport layers of the OSI Reference Model—they cannot filter on content information. For instance, one type of attack that hackers like to use is to create malicious Java or ActiveX applets that users will download and run. This traffic is downloaded using HTTP port 80. The problem with ACLs is that an ACL can either permit or deny port 80 traffic, which includes the applets embedded within the connection—ACLs cannot filter just the applets.

Likewise, ACLs have issues when dealing with the filtering of web content. Imagine that you have a security policy that prohibits the downloading of pornographic material. Because web information is changing on a daily basis, you would have to continually find these sites and add them to your ACL configuration, which is an unmanageable process.

The PIX firewall has two solutions to these problems. The first solution is the ability of the PIX to filter on Java and ActiveX scripts that are embedded in HTTP connections. The second solution for filtering content allows the PIX to work with third-party content filtering software to filter HTTP traffic. This chapter focuses on these two solutions.

HTTP TRAFFIC

Before I actually begin discussing filtering of web content information, I first need to discuss how the PIX deals with HTTP traffic. By default, the PIX assumes that HTTP traffic is using TCP and port 80. Of course, many web serves don't use this port number for their TCP connections. Some use 8,000, 8,080, or other port numbers. However, when the PIX is inspecting traffic for HTTP connections, by default, it only examines port 80.

You can change this behavior by modifying the PIX's Protocol Fixup feature for HTTP traffic. The Protocol Fixup feature, sometimes referred to as the Application Inspection feature, examines traffic on specific connections and even sometimes modifies that traffic. I've devoted Chapter 7 to this subject. However, because the Protocol Fixup feature is used for HTTP traffic, and you need to add additional ports to the PIX's inspection list, I will briefly discuss application inspection for HTTP traffic.

As I mentioned, application inspection for HTTP is only enabled for port 80 by default. To add additional ports, use the following command:

```
pixfirewall(config)#  fixup protocol http [port_#[-port_#]]
```

You can add additional ports by placing the port number at the end of the `fixup protocol http` command. If you want to enter a range of ports, just separate the beginning and ending port numbers with a dash. If the port numbers are not sequential, just enter the `fixup protocol http` command again with the new port number—whenever you re-execute this command, it adds additional port numbers to the existing list. If you want to remove port numbers from the inspection list, preface the command with the no parameter. If you enter `no fixup protocol http` without specifying any port number, this disables application inspection for HTTP traffic completely.

NOTE   By adding additional port numbers, you are allowing the PIX to examine these connections for Java and ActiveX scripts as well as web content information.

FILTERING JAVA APPLETS AND ACTIVEX SCRIPTS

Most web sites today use Java applets and ActiveX scripts to add additional functionality to their web services. These mechanisms can take the form of animated pictures, multimedia presentations, and many other types of web effects. Although these tools provide many advantages to web developers, in the wrong hands they can be used to gather information about a computer, or damage the contents on a computer.

One solution to this problem is to use the filtering abilities built into a user's web browser. Almost every web browser includes these filtering abilities, like current versions of Netscape's Navigator and Communicator and Microsoft's Internet Explorer. There are typically two problems with this type of filtering, however. First, you must ensure that every user's desktop configuration is the same and stays the same, which means that you'll have to place some type of software on each user's PC to lock down these settings and prohibit the user from changing them. Second, the configuration settings for filtering in most browsers are not a simple matter. For example, I use Internet Explorer 6.0, and there are almost a dozen different settings for Java and ActiveX—for the novice and intermediate user, an incorrect setting might open a user's desktop to attack by these multimedia tools.

The PIX firewall can filter on both embedded Java applets and ActiveX scripts without any additional software or hardware components. This allows you to prevent the downloading of malicious applets and scripts to your users' desktops while still allowing users to download web content. One advantage of using the PIX is that it provides a central point for your filtering policies. However, the filtering can only be done based on a web server's IP address. Therefore, you do not have some of the filtering abilities that a browser or content filtering engine has, but you can use the PIX in combination with other tools, like secure browser settings and a content filtering engine, to provide the maximum security for your network. The following two sections discuss how to filter Java applets and ActiveX scripts on your PIX firewall.

 SECURITY ALERT!   When the PIX is filtering Java applets and ActiveX scripts, if the HTML object tag is split across multiple IP packets, the PIX will not be able to filter the applet or script.

Configuring Java Filters

There are actually two methods of filtering Java applets on your PIX: the `outbound` filter and the `filter java` command. The `outbound` command is the old way of filtering Java applets—I briefly discussed this in Chapter 5. This command is no longer supported starting in FOS 6.2. The `filter java` command replaces the `outbound` command. I'll discuss the configuration of both of these methods in the following sections.

outbound Command

If you are going to use outbound filters to filter Java applets, use these commands:

```
pixfirewall(config)#  outbound list_number permit|deny|except
                              IP_address [subnet_mask] [port_#[-port_#]]
                              java
pixfirewall(config)#  apply (interface_name) list_number
                              outgoing_src|outgoing_dst
```

Chapter 5 explains the parameters for these commands, so I will only focus on the important ones in this chapter. In the outbound command, you list the addresses that you want to allow or disallow. Remember to specify java at the end of this command. Then activate the filter with the apply command. If you specify outgoing_src, the PIX examines the source addresses listed in the outbound filter as packets go from higher-level to lower-level interfaces. If you specify outgoing_dst, the PIX examines the destination addresses listed in the outbound filter as packets go from higher-level to lower-level interfaces. Remember that you can have more than one outbound filter applied to an interface and that you need to use the clear xlate command after making outbound filter changes.

Here is an example that would prevent all internal users from downloading Java applets:

```
pixfirewall(config)#  outbound 1 deny 0 0 java
pixfirewall(config)#  apply (inside) 1 outgoing_src
```

Remember that you can abbreviate 0.0.0.0 as 0. This is an extreme example of filtering, but it protects you against all Java applets.

> **SECURITY ALERT!**   There are two major limitations of using outbound filters on your PIX. First, it is very difficult, as I explained in Chapter 5, to filter on both source and destination addresses with outbound filters. Second, this type of filter is used when traffic initiates from a higher-level interface to a lower-level one—you can't use it in reverse.

filter java Command

The newer method of filtering Java applets is to use the filter java command:

```
pixfirewall(config)#  filter java port_number[-port_number]
                              internal_IP_address subnet_mask
                              external_IP_address subnet_mask
```

This is the only command that you need to configure to filter applets. One thing that you'll notice is that you do not need to activate the filter on an interface, as in the case of outbound filters—the filter java command is automatically applied to traffic entering any interface on the PIX. The second difference between this method and outbound filters is that you can specify the HTTP port numbers for the PIX to examine for Java applets. In the previous example, you would have to use the Protocol Fixup feature for HTTP to add additional ports. With the `filter java` command, you specify additional ports within the above command. You can specify either the port number or name (like `http`). The third difference with this method is that it allows you to specify both the source and destination IP addresses, whereas outbound filters restrict you to a single address (source *or* destination). Like ACLs, the `filter java` command uses subnet masks for matching on a single address, a range of addresses, or all addresses.

For example, if you wanted to filter all Java applets for HTTP connections, you would use the following syntax:

```
pixfirewall(config)#  filter java 80 0 0 0 0
                           -or-
pixfirewall(config)#  filter java http 0 0 0 0
```

Configuring ActiveX Filters

In addition to being able to filter Java applets, you can also filter ActiveX scripts using the `filter activex` command:

```
pixfirewall(config)#  filter activex port_number[-port_number]
                           internal_IP_address  subnet_mask
                           external_IP_address  subnet_mask
```

The syntax of the `filter activex` command is the same as the `filter java` command, and behaves in the same manner. If you want to filter all ActiveX scripts, use this example:

```
pixfirewall(config)#  filter activex 80 0 0 0 0
                           -or-
pixfirewall(config)#  filter activex http 0 0 0 0
```

As you can see, filtering ActiveX scripts is no different from filtering Java applets—both are easy to set up.

FILTERING WEB CONTENT

One major concern of many companies connected to the Internet today is the type of information that their employees are downloading to their desktops. Quite a few studies have been done, and, on average, between 30 and 40 percent of a company's Internet traffic is non-business in nature. In some instances, the information that employees download can be offensive to other employees. This information can range from pornography to political and religious material. A lot of the downloaded content is not offensive, but can use up expensive bandwidth, like stock quotes and real-time audio and video.

The PIX, in and of itself, doesn't have the ability to make filtering decisions based on web content. However, the PIX can work with third-party products to provide comprehensive web filtering features. The following sections cover how the PIX and web filtering products interact, the third-party web filtering products that the PIX supports, and web filtering configuration on the PIX.

Web Filtering Process

In order to filter web content, the PIX must interoperate with an external web content server. Figure 6-1 shows the actual interaction.

In Figure 6-1, a user sends an HTML request to an external web server (Step 1). The PIX then does two things in Step 2:

- Forwards the HTML request to the web content filtering server
- Forwards the HTML request to the actual web server

In Step 3, the web content filtering server compares the URL request to its internal policies and sends back the action to the PIX. The PIX then enforces the action on the returning traffic (Step 4). If the web content filtering server says to deny the traffic, the PIX drops the traffic. If, however, the web content filtering server says to permit the traffic, the PIX forwards the traffic to the internal user (Step 5).

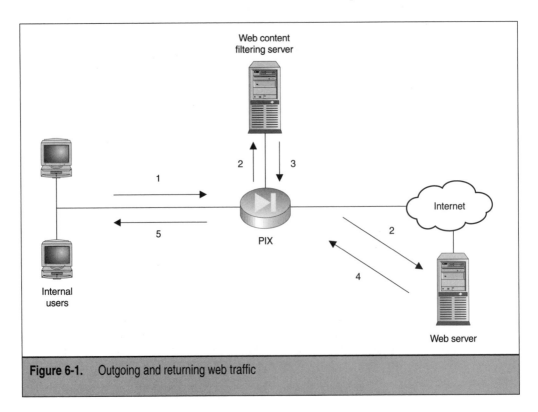

Figure 6-1.   Outgoing and returning web traffic

As you can see from this explanation, the PIX doesn't actually filter the outbound content. This allows enough time for the web content filtering server to send back an action to the PIX before the external web server replies back to the user, thereby introducing little, if any, delay in the user's traffic stream. However, if the web content filtering server is handling thousands of requests, your users may experience delay in their traffic stream.

 SECURITY ALERT! One limitation of web content filtering is that the PIX cannot filter URLs that contain FTP or HTTPS connections.

Cisco supports two web content filtering products: Websense and Sentian. The next two sections have a brief overview of these products.

Websense

Until FOS 6.2, Cisco only supported Websense's Websense Enterprise web content filtering product. The PIX has supported this product since FOS 5.3. Websense actually works with a bunch of third-party firewall and proxy appliances, including Check Point Firewall-1, Cisco's Content Engine, CyberGuard, iPlanet's Web Proxy Server, Microsoft's ISA Server, SonicWALL, and many others. Websense has the ability to filter more than 3.5 million web sites and 800 million web pages in over 44 languages. It has over 75 customized categories from adult content to MP3, gambling, and even shopping. You can set up filters to always block certain categories or sites on an individual or group basis or base blocking on time limits and quotas. Websense is currently supported on Windows NT and 2000 servers as well as Sun Solaris and Red Hat Linux.

There are three main components to Websense: Reporter, Master Database, and Webcatcher. The Reporter component is a tool that allows you to create reports. You can use these reports to evaluate how your employees are using the Internet, and how often, as well as how much bandwidth they consume. The Master Database is the heart of Websense. It contains a list of all web sites and pages. You can purchase a maintenance agreement from Websense that will allow you to download the newest web information every week. On average, Websense adds about 25,000 sites per week. Webcatcher allows Websense to automatically add unrecognized web sites to the Master Database as well as forward this information to Websense in order for them to correctly categorize the information in their next weekly update.

In the last section, I explained how, generically, a web content filtering server interacts with the PIX. When the PIX and Websense interact, there is one additional step that takes place. Websense can only filter information based on IP addresses—not fully qualified domain names (FQDNs). Therefore, before the PIX forwards the URL to the Websense server, the PIX performs a DNS lookup to resolve the name to an IP address. Remember that the PIX has already allowed the request from the user to proceed to the destination web server. When the PIX gets the DNS reply back, it forwards the resolved URL to Websense and then waits for the Websense server's response.

Sentian

Cisco added support for N2H2's Sentian web content filtering product in FOS 6.2. N2H2's product runs on Microsoft Windows NT and 2000 servers as well as Red Hat Linux. As a general comparison between Sentian and Websense, most tests have found Sentian to respond faster and provide better scalability (it supports load balancing across multiple servers); however, Websense has been around for quite some time and has a large install base—and it has a very intuitive GUI interface, making it easier to manage.

Sentian is actually broken into five components, each of which can be installed on the same or different servers:

- **Administration**   Provides the GUI interface and is used to administer your filtering policies
- **Internet Filtering Protocol (IFP)**   Stores all of your users' and groups' filtering settings, including the general block and allow lists
- **Filter**   Downloads the web content information from N2H2 periodically, and interacts with third-party products, like the PIX, to filter web content
- **Log**   Stores the web activity data from filtering functions
- **Reporting**   Uses the logging information from the Log component to create reports

The interaction between Sentian and Cisco's PIX firewalls is basically the same as that between Websense and the PIX.

Configuring Web Filtering

Web content filtering on the PIX allows you to filter web information for users accessing web resources on the outside of your network. There are two things that you must configure:

1. Identify the web content filtering server
2. Specify the traffic to have filtering performed on it

There are other configuration tasks that you can complete, but these are optional. The following sections cover the web content filtering commands of the PIX.

Server Identification

The first thing that you need to configure is the identity of the web content filtering server that the PIX will use with the url-server command. If you are connecting to a Websense server, the syntax is as follows:

```
pixfirewall(config)#  url-server [interface_name] vendor websense
                      host server_IP_address
                      [timeout seconds]
                      [protocol TCP|UDP version 1|4]
```

If you omit the name of the interface, it defaults to *inside*. The timeout value defaults to five seconds—if the PIX doesn't get a reply back within five seconds, it will contact the second Websense server, if you have configured one. You might want to increase this time out period if the Websense server is located at a remote site from the PIX. The default protocol is TCP, but can be configured for UDP if you are running version 4 of Websense. The default version is 1.

If you are connecting to a Sentian server, the syntax is as follows:

```
pixfirewall(config)#  url-server [interface_name] vendor n2h2
                          host server_IP_address[port port_number]
                          [timeout seconds] [protocol TCP|UDP]
```

The configuration of Sentian is very similar to Websense. One difference is that you can specify a port number for the TCP or UDP connection. The default port number is 4005.

Traffic Filtering Policies

Once you have identified the web content filtering servers that your PIX will use, you must now identify which traffic the PIX will perform web filtering on. The command to identity the traffic to be filtered is the filter url command:

```
pixfirewall(config)#  filter url port_number[-port_number]
                          user_IP_address user_subnet_mask
                          webserver_IP_address webserver_subnet_mask
                          [allow] [proxy-block]
```

You must specify either the name (http) or port number(s) to have the PIX examine them. The default port number for web traffic is 80. I recommend that you put in all common port numbers used by web servers, including 8080. Next, you enter your internal users' IP addresses and masks that you want to perform filtering on—if you want all users, specify 0.0.0.0 0.0.0.0, or 0 0, as the user information. This is then followed by the external web servers' addressing information. To filter content to any web server, specify 0.0.0.0 0.0.0.0, or 0 0.

There are two optional parameters at the end of the filter url command. The allow parameter affects how the PIX will react if it doesn't get a reply back from the filtering server. By default, if the PIX doesn't get a reply back, it denies the user access to the web server. You can override this by specifying the allow parameter. When you configure this parameter, the PIX waits for a response from the content filtering server—if it doesn't get a reply back, the PIX allows the web traffic. This allows your users to still access the Internet in the event that the web content filtering server is not reachable. The proxy-block parameter causes the PIX to drop all web requests to proxy servers.

You can override your filtering policies by using the following command:

```
pixfirewall(config)#  filter url except
                          user_IP_address user_subnet_mask
                          webserver_IP_address webserver_subnet_mask
```

Instead of a port number or name as in the previous example, you can use the `except` parameter. This creates an exception to your PIX's filtering function. For instance, you might want to filter on all traffic except the management subnet. In this case, you would specify something like this:

```
pixfirewall(config)#  filter url 80 0 0 0 0
pixfirewall(config0#  filter url except 192.168.1.0 255.255.255.0 0 0
```

In this example, all web traffic will be filtered by the web content filtering server with the exception of 192.168.1.0/24.

Long URLs

One problem that the PIX had in FOS 6.1 and earlier dealt with long URL names. If a URL was 1,160 characters or longer, the PIX wouldn't process it—in effect, allowing the connection. This sounds like it wouldn't be a problem, because most URLs are fewer than 80 characters. However, many CGI-BIN scripts and backend programs have information embedded in a URL passed to them—this information, in certain cases, might be very long, which creates a problem with the PIX. As of FOS 6.2, this limit has been increased to 4,000 characters (for Websense only). However, you might not want to send all of these extra characters to the content filtering server, or even deny users access to these long URLs.

You can change the PIX's behavior with long URLs by using the following command:

```
pixfirewall(config)#  filter url longurl-truncate|longurl-deny|
                      cgi-truncate
```

The `longurl-truncate` parameter tells the PIX to send only the hostname/IP address portion of the URL to the content filtering server for evaluation. The `longurl-deny` command has the PIX deny the user's web connection if the URL is longer than the maximum permitted. The `cgi-truncate` parameter behaves the same as the `longurl-truncate` parameter with the exception that this parameter only applies to CGI-BIN script requests embedded in a URL.

Caching URL Information

One of the issues of using a web content filtering server, as I pointed out earlier, is that it can introduce a delay in the user's web traffic stream as the PIX and filtering server interact in order to enforce your web access policies. You can have the PIX cache information received by a filtering server so that, the next time a user accesses the same server, the PIX can use its local cache to perform the filtering policy instead of forwarding the request to the filtering server. The advantage of this approach is that your users' throughput will increase. The downside of this approach is that the web content filtering server is not seeing the traffic and therefore cannot log it. If you are gathering information about user's web habits, then you would not be able to log all of a user's connection information.

Caching, by default, is disabled on the PIX. To enable it, use the following command:

```
pixfirewall(config)# url-cache dst|src_dst size cache_size
```

You have two choices on how to cache information. If you specify the `dst` parameter, the PIX caches information based only on the destination web server address—you should only choose this option if *all* your internal users have the same access policies. If your internal users have different access policies, specify the `src_dst` parameter—this causes the PIX to cache both the source and destination addresses. The cache size can range from 1 to 128KB.

Buffering Web Server Replies to Users

As I mentioned at the beginning of this section, when the PIX receives a user's web request, it simultaneously forwards it to the content filtering server as well as the external web server. One problem that might occur is that the external web server reply to the user's request might come back to the PIX *before* the content filtering server's action that the PIX should take. If this should occur, the PIX automatically drops the user's web request.

To prevent this from happening, you can buffer the external web server's reply until the PIX receives the action from the filtering server. By default, this feature is disabled. To enable it, use the following command:

```
pixfirewall(config)# url-block block block_buffer_limit
```

This command limits the number of blocks URLs can use. The limit is specified in number of blocks. The default buffer size is 1KB.

To configure the amount of memory available for buffering long or pending URLs, use the following command:

```
pixfirewall(config)# url-block url-mempool memory_size
```

The memory can be specified as a value from 2KB to 10,240KB.

As I mentioned earlier, in FOS 6.2, you can increase the size of URLs for Websense to 4,000 characters—however, the default is 1,159 characters. To increase the size for Websense URLs, use the following command:

```
pixfirewall(config)# url-block url-size URL_characters
```

You can enter a value from 2,000 to 4,000 characters. Remember that this command only applies to Websense server connections—Sentian is restricted to 1,159 characters for URL lengths.

Verifying Your Configuration

Once you have set up your web content filtering configuration, you can use various `show` commands to verify your configuration. To view the web content filtering servers that

you have configured with the url-server command, use the show url-server
command:

```
pixfirewall#  show url-server
url-server (outside) vendor n2h2 host 10.1.1.5 port 4005
        timeout 5 protocol TCP
url-server (outside) vendor n2h2 host 10.1.2.5 port 4005
        timeout 5 protocol TCP
```

In this example, there are two Sentian filtering servers that have been configured on
this PIX. You can see more information by adding the stats parameter:

```
pixfirewall(config)#  show url-server stats
URL Server Statistics:
----------------------
Vendor                         n2h2
URLs total/allowed/denied      4000/3783/217

URL Server Status:
------------------
10.1.1.5               UP
10.1.2.5               DOWN
```

In this example, there are two Sentian servers. You can see that out of a total of
4,000 URL requests, 3,783 were allowed and 217 were denied.

To view your filtering commands, use the show filter command:

```
pixfirewall(config)#  show filter
filter url http 0.0.0.0 0.0.0.0 0.0.0.0 0.0.0.0
```

In this example, all internal user web traffic to any external web server will be
examined.

If you have enabled caching of URL information on your PIX that it received
from the content filtering server, you can view the caching statistics with the show
url-cache stats command:

```
pixfirewall(config)#  show url-cache stats
URL Filter Cache Stats
----------------------
    Size :          1KB
 Entries :           36
  In Use :           22
 Lookups :          241
    Hits :          207
```

In this example, the cache size has been set to 1KB. The *Entries* item specifies the
total number of cached entries that can fit in the cache based on the configured size.
In this example, only 36 entries can be cached. The *In Use* item specifies the number of
entries that are currently cached (22). The *Lookups* entry specifies the number of times

the PIX has looked in the cache for a match, and the *Hits* entry shows the number of times the PIX found a match in the cache.

To view statistics about URL information received from external web servers that is being temporarily buffered by the PIX, use this command:

```
pixfirewall(config)# show url-block block stat
URL Pending Packet Buffer Stats with max block 1
-----------------------------------------------------
Cumulative number of packets held:          53
Maximum number of packets held (per URL):   1
Current number of packets held (global):    0
Packets dropped due to exceeding url-block buffer limit:  78
Packet drop due to retransmission:          0
```

As you can see in this example, 53 packets were held up because the PIX was waiting for a response from the web content filtering server. You will want to keep tabs on the number of packets being dropped because they exceeded the buffer limit—if this is continually increasing, you will want to increase the block size for buffering. To clear the statistics, use the `clear url-block block stats` command.

The `show perfmon` command shows you performance information for many important components of the PIX, including web content filtering performance. Here is an example:

```
pixfirewall(config)# show perfmon


PERFMON STATS:      Current       Average
Xlates              0/s           0/s
Connections         0/s           2/s
TCP Conns           0/s           2/s
UDP Conns           0/s           0/s
URL Access          0/s           2/s
URL Server Req      0/s           2/s
<--output omitted-->
```

With this command, you should focus on the *URL Server Req* entry, which displays the number of lookups the PIX forwarded to the web content filtering server.

URL Filtering Example

To help illustrate the configuration example, I'll use the network shown in Figure 6-2. This example uses Websense for a web content filtering solution.

The following listing focuses only on the filtering commands for this set up:

```
pixfirewall(config)# url-server (inside) vendor websense
                     host 192.168.1.2 protocol tcp version 4
pixfirewall(config)# filter url 80 0 0 0 0
pixfirewall(config)# filter url 8080-8099 0 0 0 0
pixfirewall(config)# url-cache dst 128
```

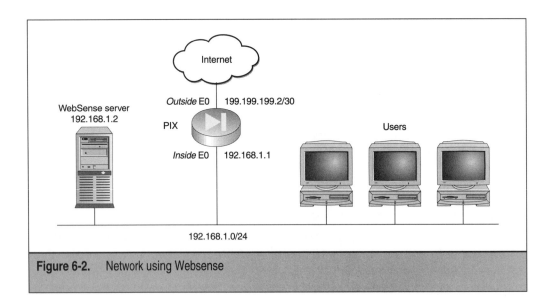

Figure 6-2. Network using Websense

In this example, the `url-server` command specifies that the server is a Websense server and the connection is using TCP. Any web traffic on port 80 or 8080 through 8099 will be examined for filtering. The PIX can cache information returned by the Websense server using 128KB of memory. As you can see from this example, the set up of web filtering on the PIX is easy.

FURTHER STUDY

Web Sites

For information about Websense products, visit: www.websense.com.

For information on integrating the PIX and Websense together, visit: www.websense.com/support/documentation/setup/setuppix.pdf.

For information about N2H2's Sentian product, visit: www.n2h2.com.

For more information about configuring web filtering on your PIX, visit: www.cisco.com/univercd/cc/td/doc/product/iaabu/pix/pix_62/config/index.htm.

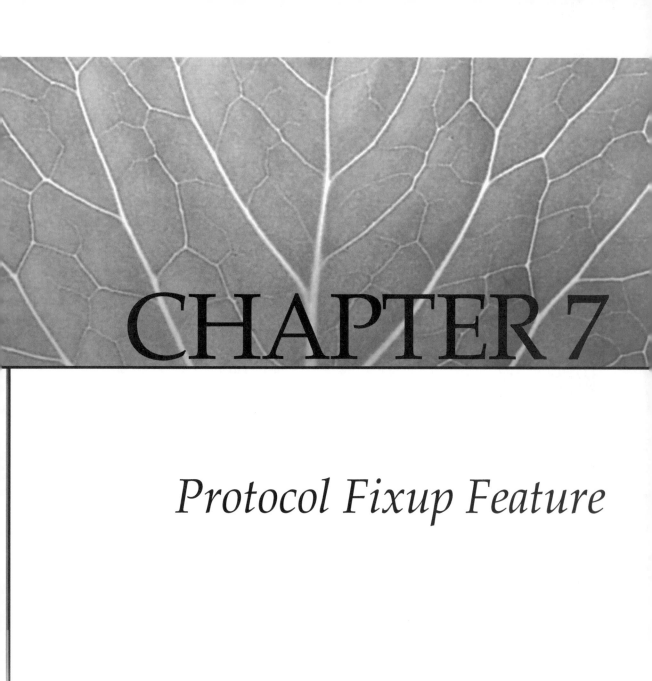

CHAPTER 7

Protocol Fixup Feature

In Chapters 4, 5, and 6, I discussed address translation, including NAT and PAT as well as filtering traffic as it flows through the PIX. Obviously, you need these types of features in a firewall to provide function and security. However, not every protocol or application fairs well in an environment that uses NAT/PAT or where a stateful firewall is filtering traffic. This chapter will cover some of these problematic protocols and applications and how the PIX can *fix* many of the issues with these protocols to deal with address translation and stateful filtering.

ISSUES WITH PROTOCOLS AND APPLICATIONS

Many applications, especially multimedia applications, have problems whenever address translation is performed on the contents of packets or filtering is performed on traffic. Many of these applications use random port numbers for their connections, and/or assign these port numbers dynamically across an existing connection. For a translation firewall, this presents a lot of problems.

If the firewall is performing address translation, it must look for the negotiated dynamic port number during the connection negotiation to make sure that it does address translation with this port number. Likewise, if an application opens up a control connection that is used to create and manage random data connections, a stateful firewall will have problems with allowing the additional data connections for the devices trying to communicate. The next two sections cover these two problems in more depth.

Port Numbering Issues

The first problem deals with how applications, especially multimedia applications, create and manage connections. For example, setting up a telnet connection is a simple and straightforward process. A user's PC requests a telnet connection to a destination. On the user's PC, an unused source port number above 1,023 is chosen. The destination port number in the transport segment is 23. This information is sent to the telnet server. The telnet server knows that this is a telnet connection by looking at the destination port number (23), and knows how to process it. Likewise, the telnet server knows how to respond back by using the original source port number as the destination port in the response, and the source IP address as the destination address in the response.

Telnet Example

The top part of Figure 7-1 shows a simple example of a telnet connection. In this example, the user's laptop on the left chose a source port number of 1,024 and, because this is a telnet connection, used a destination port number of 23. When the segment arrives at the telnet server, the server looks at the destination port number, which is 23, and knows that a telnet process needs to handle it. It examines its list of processes to see if this particular process for this user already exists. Because this is a new connection, the server won't find a process and therefore will create one. The server also knows how to respond back by using the same information that it found in the IP packet header (source IP address) and the TCP segment header (source port number). For a

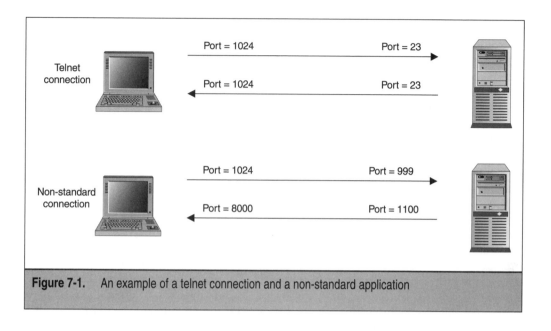

Figure 7-1.   An example of a telnet connection and a non-standard application

stateful firewall, it is very easy to deal with this type of connection because the port numbers and mechanics of the connection setup are well defined and easy to determine.

Non-Standard Protocols and Applications

Of course, not every protocol, nor every application, follows the mechanics of a simple telnet connection, where the port numbers are standardized and there is a single connection for the flow of management and data information. Some protocols use more than one connection to handle the flow of information, and do not, necessarily, follow any predefined standards. With some of these additional connections, the source opens up the additional connections, while with other applications, it's the destination that opens additional connections. And, sometimes, *both* devices initiate additional connections. To make matters worse, each of these protocols and applications has different methods for choosing port numbers for these additional connections—sometimes they are specifically defined, sometimes they fall within a pre-defined range, and sometimes they are completely random. For a stateful firewall, these issues present a lot of problems.

Let's look at a simple example, shown in the bottom part of Figure 7-1, to illustrate the problem that these kinds of protocols and applications pose to a stateful firewall. In this example, I'll invent an imaginary application called *problem*. The problem application uses two connections for transmitting information between the source and destination. A source device initiates the connection, chooses a random port number greater than 1,023, and uses a well-defined port number, 999, as the destination port. During the setup of this initial connection, the destination device randomly chooses an open port on its box for the source of the second connection, a port number greater than 1,023, and asks the source device which port number it should use as the destination on the source device for the second connection (again, a port number greater than 1,023).

You can see that for the first connection, the source chose 1,024 as the source port number, and is using 999 as the destination port number, which alerts the destination that this traffic is for the problem application—the 999 port number has been preconfigured on both devices to indicate that this is an application connection. The destination negotiates with the source device for the second connection's parameters, which include the port number to be used on the originating source device (8,000). The problem application server chooses 1,100 as its source port number. The main problem with this example is that there might be a stateful firewall between the two devices.

Client on the Inside   Let's look at this example from the perspective of a stateful firewall between these two devices. In the first example, assume that the user initiating the connection is on the inside of the network and the problem application server is on the outside of the network. The stateful firewall adds the 1,024/999 connection when the user initiates the connection to the remote server. However, when the remote problem server tries to establish the second connection inbound, the stateful firewall will deny it by default, because from its perspective, this is a different connection than the first one. To allow this second connection, you would have to configure a conduit or ACL that would allow all traffic above source port 1,023, since this is what the problem server uses for a source port, and all traffic above destination port 1,023. Obviously, this is a serious security concern if you have to open up a complete range of ports to allow your users to access this application.

Client on the Outside   Let's now reverse the network and assume that the user is on the outside of the network and the problem server is on the inside. In this example, the initial connection of the user would be denied—you would have to configure an ACL or conduit to allow the initial connection for the user's inbound traffic to the server (to port number 999). When the server sets up the second connection, because the traffic would be flowing from a higher-level interface to a lower-level one, it would be permitted and the stateful firewall would automatically add the appropriate connection information in its connection table.

As you can see from the example of the problem application, protocols and applications that set up connections in a non-standard way present some unique problems for stateful firewalls.

Address Translation Issues

Let's look at the second major problem that non-standard applications and protocols can present in an environment that involves a firewall. Many firewalls use NAT, PAT, or both to perform address translation. Some applications and protocols are known to embed not only IP addresses in the data payload, but also port numbers. The most notorious protocol known to embed addressing information in the payload is NetBIOS, but it is only one of many protocols and applications that are known to do this.

Firewall Issues

Embedding addressing information in the data payload can create problems for address translation devices, such as firewalls. Typically, an address translation device only translates addresses in the IP header and port numbers in the TCP and UDP segment headers—any addressing information embedded in the payload is ignored. Of course, this can cause a connection to break if an application is embedding addressing information that the source and destination are using for their connections, especially if these devices are using the information embedded in the payload to reply to a connection instead of what is in the actual packet and segment headers.

Address Translation Example

Let's look at an example of how embedded addressing information can cause a problem with a network device performing address translation. I'll use the network shown in Figure 7-2 to illustrate the issues of address translation and embedded addresses. In the network shown in Figure 7-2, the device with an address of 192.168.1.1 is trying to connect to a service on port 999 on server 192.1.1.1. The source embeds its own IP address in the payload, which the destination will use to return traffic to the source.

Here are the steps that occur for the connection interaction between 192.168.1.1 and 192.1.1.1:

1. The user device (192.168.1.1) creates an IP packet/segment, which it will use to connect to the service (port 999) on the destination server (192.1.1.1).

2. The address translation device translates the source address and source port numbers—notice that the payload information, which contains the source device's IP address, is not translated.

3. The destination server returns the response using a destination address of 192.168.1.1 instead of the global address—it uses the address embedded in the payload.

4. The address translation device looks at its translation table, doesn't see a global address of 192.168.1.1, and drops the packet.

This is just a simple example where an address translation device can cause a connection to not function properly, or at all. There are many applications that embed IP addresses, as well as port numbers, that the destination device should use for continuing communications. Probably the most well known of these is IP ARP (Address Resolution Protocol). Most address translation devices already know about the most common applications that perform these kinds of stunts, and automatically translate the addressing information in the payload, but an address translation device might not be able to handle every application, or every protocol, that it sees.

 SECURITY ALERT!   Because of issues with how connections are set up with certain protocols and applications, the port numbers that are used by these connections, and the use of address translation, take care when allowing this type of traffic into your network.

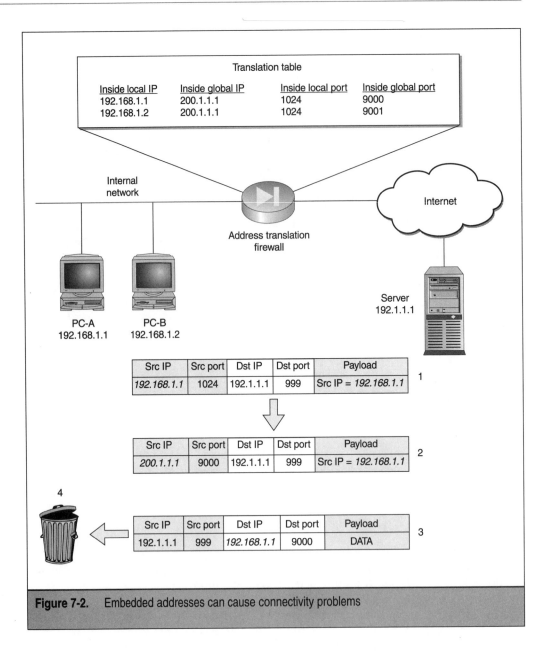

Figure 7-2. Embedded addresses can cause connectivity problems

ESTABLISHED CONNECTIONS

One of the issues discussed in the "Port Numbering Issues" section earlier in this chapter is that sometimes a source device will open up a connection to a remote machine, and then the remote machine will open up another connection back to the source. In most instances, the port numbers used for this second connection are random, or fall within a wide range of numbers. There are two basic methods that you can use to deal with this issue:

- Configure the established command to allow the second connection.
- Use the *Protocol Fixup* feature of the PIX, commonly called *application inspection*.

The remainder of this chapter will deal with these two solutions. I'll start first, though, with the older of the two solutions, the established command.

Syntax of the established Command

The purpose of the established command is to allow a second connection to be set up on ports other than the first connection (which was initially permitted). One restriction of this command is that it doesn't work with PAT—it only works with NAT or no address translation. Typically, the PIX's application inspection feature is used to deal with these kind of issues; however, as you will see later on in this chapter, the application inspection feature only works with certain applications and protocols. The established command can be used for applications and protocols not supported by the application inspection feature of the PIX.

The syntax of the established command is the following:

```
pixfirewall(config)#  established destination_protocol
                        [original_source_port_number]
                        [original_destination_port_number]
                        [permitto protocol port[-port]]
                        [permitfrom protocol port[-port]]
```

The *destination_protocol* is the protocol for the original connection that was permitted when a source device established a connection to a destination device. This refers to the initial outbound connection. Optionally, you can limit the scope of established connections by also specifying the source and destination port numbers. If you use 0 as a port number, it is treated as a wildcard and matches on all port numbers.

The permitto and permitfrom parameters apply to a new connection that the destination device is trying to build *back* to the source. The permitfrom parameter refers to the external device and the permitto to the internal device. Note that you can specify a different protocol than the one originally used by the first connection—for example, the first connection might use TCP, while the second connection uses UDP.

 SECURITY ALERT!   If you omit the permitto and permitfrom optional parameters, all new connections that the outside device opens up back to the source (any port numbers) are permitted. Therefore, I strongly recommend that you enter values for these parameters.

To view you configuration of established commands, use the *Privilege EXEC* show established command. To remove a specific established command, use the keyword no in front of the established command. To remove all of your established commands, use the clear established command.

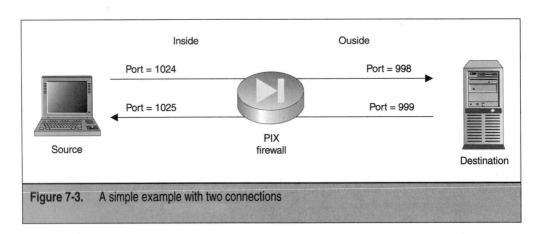

Figure 7-3. A simple example with two connections

Simple Example of the established Command

To help you understand the syntax of the `established` command, take a look at the network example shown in Figure 7-3. In this example, the inside source is establishing a connection to an outside destination. I'll assume that this is a TCP connection. The port numbers are 1,024 on the source and 998 on the destination. Once this connection is established, the destination opens up another connection back to the source, where the port numbers are 999 at the destination and arbitrary at the source (in our example, the source chose 1,025). This connection is a UDP connection.

One method of allowing this second inbound connection would be to set up an ACL or conduit—the problem with this approach is that the PIX, when looking at the ACL or conduit, is not examining whether or not this new connection is part of the setup process of a previous connection. Therefore, if you didn't know the addresses of the devices, or the port numbers in the second connection, you would have to open up a fairly big hole in your firewall to allow this second connection.

A better solution is to use the `established` command. The following is a solution for the example depicted in Figure 7-3:

```
pixfirewall(config)#  established tcp 0 998 permitto udp 1024-65535
                           permitfrom udp 999
```

In this example, if an internal user opens up a TCP connection to port 998 to an external device, then the external device is allowed to open up a new connection back to the internal user, and only the internal user, if the protocol for the connection is UDP, the source port on the external user is 999, and the destination port on the internal user is 1,024 through 65,535.

APPLICATION INSPECTION

As you can see from the last section, certain protocols and applications present special cases to the PIX, and have to be handled differently than connections that operate using a standard connection method, like telnet. As I mentioned in Chapter 2, the PIX uses the ASA (Adaptive Security Algorithm) to implement the stateful function of the firewall.

Another of ASA's functions is to implement the *Protocol Fixup* feature—this feature handles issues with non-standard connections, as well as embedded addresses and port numbers. For those applications that require special inspection because of these issues, the ASA fixes problems with these protocols so that a user doesn't have to worry about application issues, and the process is transparent to the user. Likewise, the ASA fixes these problems such that you are only opening a tiny hole in the PIX firewall to allow just the connection itself between the user and the resource on the service instead of opening up the firewall to a wide range of addresses and ports.

Functions of Application Inspection

One of the functions of the ASA and application inspection is to have the PIX examine certain applications and protocols for embedded addressing information. This allows the PIX to locate embedded addressing information in a user's payload, fix it, and then recompute any checksums for the data, segment, or packet. Another function of application inspection is to determine if an application or protocol uses multiple connections. If it does, the ASA will look for the port numbers that are negotiated for these additional connections and place an entry in the connection table to allow these additional connections.

Steps for Application Inspection

There are three items that affect traffic flowing through the PIX:

- **ACLs**   Filtering rules
- **Connections**   xlate and connection table information
- **Inspection**   Application inspection rules

The PIX uses all three of these to determine what to do with traffic that comes into a particular interface. In the following sections, I'll look at two situations that affect traffic through the PIX: traffic from higher-level to a lower-level interfaces and traffic from lower-level to higher-level interfaces.

Higher-Level to Lower-Level Interface   Let's first deal with an example where traffic is flowing from a higher-level interface to a lower-level one. I'll use the network shown in Figure 7-4 to illustrate the first part of the process.

The PIX goes through the following steps when application inspection is configured for a particular application or protocol:

1. When a user initiates an outbound connection, the PIX checks its ACLs on the internal interface to verify that the user is allowed to proceed with the connection.

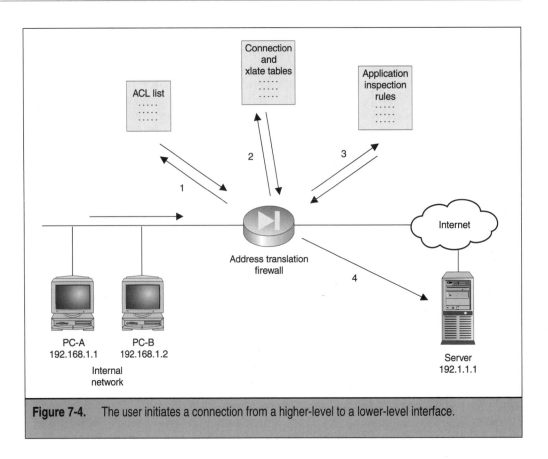

Figure 7-4.   The user initiates a connection from a higher-level to a lower-level interface.

2. If the user is allowed, the PIX adds an entry containing the user's connection details to its xlate and connection tables.

3. If application inspection is enabled for the specified protocol or application that the user is using for this connection, the PIX monitors the connection and adds any additional connections (related to the first connection) to the xlate and connection tables.

4. The packet is forwarded to the destination.

    The PIX takes the following steps, shown in Figure 7-5, for the traffic returning from the server:

5. The destination returns a response.

6. The PIX examines the packet and compares it to its connection table—if it finds a response, it performs address translation on the response and forwards it to the inside of the network; otherwise it looks at its ACL on the outside interface to determine if the packet is permitted or not.

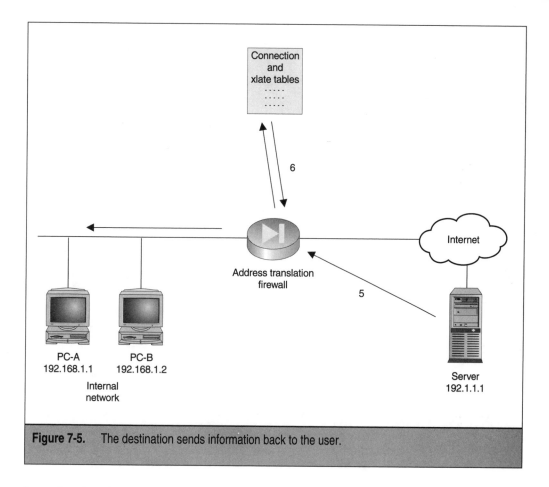

Figure 7-5. The destination sends information back to the user.

Lower-Level to Higher-Level Interface   Let's reverse the situation and assume that the traffic is originating on the outside of the network and is trying to reach a service on the inside of the network. I'll use Figure 7-6 to illustrate the process.

1. When a user initiates an inbound connection, the PIX checks its connection table to see if this is an already established connection.

2. Because this is a new connection, the PIX looks for an entry in its ACL for the external interface.

3. If an entry is found in the ACL, the PIX then determines if application inspection is configured for this connection and monitors it, creating any additional connections in the connection table for these connections and any application or protocol fixes that are necessary.

4. Any returning traffic from the user, unless prohibited by an ACL on the internal interface, is permitted by default.

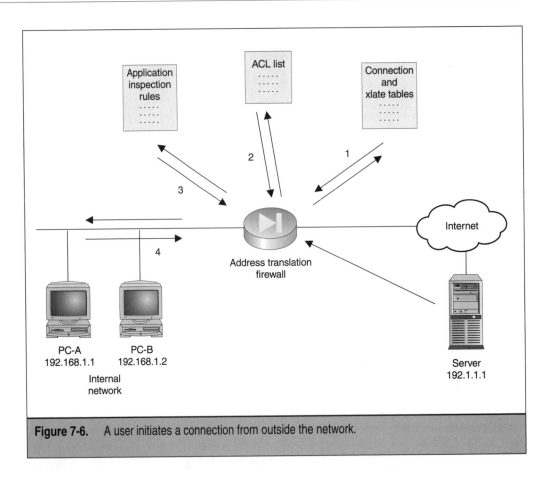

Figure 7-6.   A user initiates a connection from outside the network.

Example of Application Inspection

In the example in Figure 7-3, if the client was on the inside of the network and the server on the outside, the connection that the server initiated would be denied because there isn't a connection in the connection table to allow the traffic to flow from the outside to the inside interface (from a lower-level interface to a higher-level one). With application inspection, the PIX looks at the user's original connection, determines that application inspection is required, searches for information on the original connection about additional connections that are to be set up, and then dynamically adds these to the connection table.

Therefore, given the example in Figure 7-3, with application inspection, the PIX would determine that a second connection was being set up and add the parameters of this second connection to its connection table. When the server initiates the second connection, the PIX would allow the connection into the network, but only to the original inside user.

Limitations of Application Inspection

Application inspection is enabled on the PIX, by default, for quite a few applications and protocols. Note, however, that application inspection, unfortunately, does not support every protocol, nor does application inspection support NAT or PAT with certain types of applications. The PIX uses application inspection on a set of applications on their default port numbers; however, you can add additional port numbers if your application is using a different port number other than the default. Table 7-1 lists the supported applications and their specifics.

As you can see from Table 7-1, the PIX supports many protocols and applications for application inspection; however, this list is not all-inclusive. Sometimes you can

Application	Ports	NAT/PAT Support	Restrictions
CU-SeeMe	UDP 7648	None	None
DNS	UDP 53	Both	Doesn't change PTR records
FTP	TCP 21	Both	None
H.323	TCP 1720	Both (6.2 PAT)	None
H.323 RAS	UDP 1719 and UDP 1718	Both (6.2 PAT)	Gatekeeper TCP Control
HTTP	TCP 80	Both	MTU limitations with stripped ActiveX/Java applets
ICMP	--	Both	None
ILS LDAP	--	PAT	New in 6.2
NetBIOS over IP	--	None	None
NetBIOS Name Service	UDP 137	None	No support for WINS
NetBIOS Domain Service	UDP 138	Both	None
RSH	TCP 514	Both	None
RTSP	TCP 554	None	No HTTP clocking
SCCP Skinny	TCP 2000	NAT	TFTP uploads not supported
SIP	TCP 5060 and UDP 5060	Both (6.2 PAT)	None
SMTP	TCP 25	Both	None
SQL*Net	TCP 1521	Both	Supports v1 and v2
Sun RPCs	UDP and TCP 111	None	None
VDOLive	TCP 7000	NAT	None
Windows Media (Netshow)	TCP 1755	NAT	Support for TCP or UDP streaming over HTTP
XDMCP	UDP 177	None	None

Table 7-1.   Applications Supported for Application Inspection

configure the PIX, in a secure manner, to deal with protocols and applications not listed in Table 7-1 by using the established command; but in many instances, you'll have one of two choices:

- Open up the firewall on a broad range of ports, turn off address translation to allow the connection, or both (least secure).
- Don't allow access to the application (most secure).

As you can see from these two choices, it's almost an all-or-nothing proposition if application inspection or the established command won't deal with your protocol's or application's specific issues. Cisco, however, is continually adding applications to their application inspection feature, so an application that is not supported today may be supported in the near future.

APPLICATION INSPECTION CONFIGURATION

In this section, I'll cover the commands for configuring application inspection on the PIX. I will then spend some time covering the connection mechanics that some of these protocols and applications implement to help you understand the issues that you face in dealing with connectivity. Please note that some features of application inspection are security-related, like DNS and SMTP, instead of dealing with dynamic connections or embedded addresses and port numbers. For the applications where the PIX uses application inspection to deal with security issues, I will discuss their mechanics and configuration in Chapter 8.

Configuring application inspection is a fairly simple process. Certain applications are enabled by default on the PIX for application inspection. You can disable these protocols and enable other protocols. Also, if you have an application that is running on a non-standard port, you can add this port for inspection. The following sections show the syntax for the basic application inspection command.

Basic Command Syntax

The following is the syntax for the application inspection command:

```
pixfirewall(config)# fixup protocol protocol_name
                            [port_number[-port_number]]
```

As you can see from the command name itself, fixup protocol, Cisco is referring to fixing or dealing with issues pertaining to protocols (or applications). Cisco refers to this feature as either the *application inspection* or *protocol fixup* feature. The first parameter, protocol_name, refers to the name of the protocol or application that the PIX is inspecting. The port or range of port numbers refers to the ports that the application is using for connectivity—this is typically the destination port when the user makes a connection.

Protocol Name	Parameter Name	Default Port Number
FTP	ftp	21
H323	h323 h225	1720
H323 RAS	h323 ras	1718 and 1719
HTTP	http	80
ILS LDAP	ils	389
RSH	rsh	514
RTSP	rtsp	554
SMTP	smtp	25
SQL*Net	sqlnet	1521
SIP	sip	5060
SCCP (Skinny)	skinny	2000

Table 7-2.   Default Protocol Parameters for Application Inspection

Table 7-2 lists the protocols/applications that are enabled by default on the PIX for application inspection, as well as the default port numbers.

Adding, Changing, and Removing Port Numbers

You can change the port numbers for all of the protocols in Table 7-2, except for RSH. However, you can always add additional ports to RSH as well as any of the other above listed applications. For instance, you might have web servers running on both port 80 and 8090. To add the additional port, use this command:

```
pixfirewall(config)#  fixup protocol http 8090
```

The PIX will now inspect both port 80 and port 8090 for HTTP traffic. Please note that not every protocol supports multiple ports. To add port numbers that are not contiguous, re-execute the fixup protocol command, specifying the non-contiguous port number or numbers. It is important to point out that this command does *not* overwrite currently added ports, but adds ports to the list that is to be inspected for the protocol—the exception to this are protocols that only support a single port number. In this instance, the port number is overwritten by the command that you most recently entered. I will discuss the particulars of each protocol as you proceed throughout the rest of this chapter.

To remove a port number for application inspection of a protocol, precede the fixup command with the no parameter. As an example, to remove the port that I just added, I would use this command:

```
pixfirewall(config)#  no fixup protocol http 8090
```

As you can see, it is very simple to remove a port number from inspection. To disable inspection completely for a protocol, keep removing the specific entries for a protocol. As an example, after the configuration performed just performed, HTTP is being inspected on one port—80. To remove inspection completely for HTTP, you'll need to enter one command, specifying port 80.

If you have made many additions for port numbers for application inspection, and you want to set application inspection back to the default port numbers, use the `clear fixup` command.

> **SECURITY ALERT!** Once you have made your changes, you need to execute the `clear xlate` command to ensure that your current connections will have inspection applied to them.

Verifying Your Configuration

To check your configuration of which protocols are being inspected, use the `show fixup` command:

```
pixfirewall#  show fixup
fixup protocol ftp 21
fixup protocol http 80
fixup protocol h323 h225 1720
fixup protocol h323 ras 1718-1719
fixup protocol ils 389
fixup protocol rsh 514
fixup protocol rtsp 554
fixup protocol smtp 25
fixup protocol sqlnet 1521
fixup protocol sip 5060
fixup protocol skinny 2000
```

In this example, eleven protocols are enabled—these are the default applications enabled for application inspection.

APPLICATION INSPECTION FOR FTP

To help understand the application inspection feature of the PIX and how it interacts with certain protocols, in the next few sections I will go through most of the protocols supported by the Protocol Fixup feature and discuss their mechanics as well as how the PIX deals with them. Let's start with FTP first, because it is one of the more common protocols that is used.

Mechanics of FTP Connections

FTP is one of the oldest IP applications, and was designed to move files between different networked computers. FTP, interestingly enough, is unlike normal connections such as telnet and e-mail. FTP actually uses two connections—one is a command connection used by the user to enter FTP commands, and the other connection is used for the actual transfer of files. FTP supports two different modes—*standard* and *passive*—and based on the mode, the setup of two connections and transfer of data are slightly different. The next two sections explain these two different modes for FTP.

Standard Mode

To better help you understand how connections get set up with *standard* FTP, let's use the top part of the illustration shown in Figure 7-7. When a user wants to initiate an FTP connection, the user sets up a *command* connection first. The user uses the command connection to execute commands, like get and send. When the user device opens a command connection, it chooses a free source port number greater than 1,023 and uses a destination port number of 21. Whenever the user attempts to either get or send a file, the FTP server opens a second connection, called a *data* connection, which is used for the file transfer. The server gets from the client (via the command connection) a port number greater than 1,023 that is not being used on the client, and the server uses that port as the destination and a source port of 20.

To better help you understand some of the issues with standard-mode FTP, let's take a look at situations where there is a PIX firewall between the client and FTP server. The next two sections explain the connectivity issues when the client is on the inside of the network versus the outside of the network.

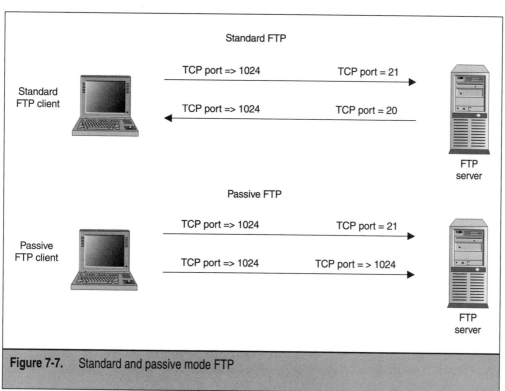

Figure 7-7. Standard and passive mode FTP

Client on the Inside of the PIX When the client is on the inside of the network and initiates an FTP connection to an FTP server on the outside of the network, the PIX allows the connection by default, because the connection is traveling from a higher-level interface to a lower-level one. A problem exists, however, when the client attempts to send or retrieve a file and the server tries to initiate a data connection back to the inside client.

With the application inspection feature, the PIX expects this data connection to be built, and looks for a file transfer command within the command connection. When the PIX sees the data transfer command, it dynamically adds the connection entry in the connection table with the appropriate information—this includes the client's port number that it shared with the FTP server. Therefore, you don't have to worry about the inbound connection coming from the FTP server.

Without the application inspection feature, you would have to configure a conduit or ACL to specifically allow this second connection. The problem with this is that you don't really know which client, or possibly even which server—you would basically have to permit traffic from any device (the FTP server) heading to anywhere (the clients), if the source port number is 20. Obviously, this opens a fairly large hole in your PIX firewall. If you disable application inspection for FTP, you'll have to manually configure this type of conduit or ACL entry to allow standard mode FTP connections.

Client on the Outside of the PIX In this example, let's assume that the client is on the outside of your network, and the FTP server is on the inside. For the initial client connection to work, you need to configure a conduit or ACL that will allow traffic heading to the FTP server for TCP port 21—without this, no type of FTP connection can be made. Once the command connection has been established, when the client attempts to retrieve a file, the server initiates the data connection back to the client.

In this situation, because the data connection is coming from a higher-level interface and is exiting a lower-level interface, the PIX permits it by default, unless you have an ACL or outbound filter that prohibits this connection. Therefore, in this example, application inspection doesn't come into play.

Passive Mode

Just as in standard mode for FTP, *passive mode* has two connections: command and data. The bottom part of Figure 7-7 shows an example of the setup of these two connections. The command connection in passive mode is established in the same manor as standard FTP: the user device chooses an open port greater than 1,023 as a source port and uses a destination port of 21. Whenever a data connection is needed, the user device establishes the connection to the server—this is the opposite of standard-mode FTP. For this data connection, the user device again chooses an open port number greater than 1,023 as a source port, but acquires from the FTP server what port number to use for the destination port, a number greater than 1,023. This number is negotiated on the command connection.

Client on the Inside of the PIX When the client is on the inside of the network and initiates an FTP connection to an FTP server on the outside of the network, the PIX allow the connection by default because the connection is traveling from a higher-level interface to a lower-level one. This is also true for the data connection. Therefore, both of these connections will be able to be established unless you are filtering with ACLs or outbound filters.

Client on the Outside of the PIX   In this example, assume that the client is on the outside of your network and the FTP server is on the inside. For the initial client connection to work, you need to configure a conduit or ACL that will allow traffic heading to the FTP server for TCP port 21—without this, no type of FTP connection is possible.

Once the command connection has been established, when the client attempts to retrieve or send a file, the client will attempt to establish a data connection to the server. Assuming that application inspection is enabled for FTP, the PIX automatically looks at the FTP commands that the user is entering on the command connection, as well as the connection information being negotiated, and dynamically creates an entry in the connection table for the data connection. However, if you've disabled application inspection for FTP, you will have to manually add a conduit or ACL to allow traffic to your FTP server at TCP ports greater than 1,023 as well as the first filter statement for port 21 that I already mentioned.

Command Syntax for Application Inspection of FTP

Now that you have a basic understanding of the two modes for FTP as well as their specific issues, let's talk about the command for application inspection for FTP. As I mentioned earlier, application inspection for FTP is enabled by default. The syntax for the application inspection command for FTP is as follows:

```
pixfirewall(config)# fixup protocol ftp [strict] [port_number]
```

The default command connection port is 21, but you can add additional ports. To disable application inspection for FTP, precede the command with the no parameter.

strict Parameter

The use of the `strict` parameter prevents any embedded FTP commands in HTTP connections. The exception to this is the 227 command by a server and the PORT command by a client. By default, embedded FTP commands in web connections are permitted. Here are some additional items that the `strict` parameter causes the PIX to perform:

- Checks to make sure that all dynamically negotiated ports are above 1,023.
- Verifies that all commands end in <CR><LF> as per the RFC—if not, the TCP connection is closed.
- Verifies that there are exactly five commas in the PORT and PASV commands—if not, the TCP connection is closed.
- Checks that PORT commands are generated by clients, not servers—if the command is from a server, the PIX denies the connection.

- Checks that PASV commands are generated by servers, not clients—if the command is from a client, the connection is denied.

- Checks the size of the RETR and STOR commands—if they are not correct, the PIX logs a message and terminates the connection.

When application inspection is enabled, the PIX automatically inspects the packet payload and performs NAT on addressing information. Here are the four tasks that application inspection performs for FTP traffic:

- Performs NAT on embedded addresses.

- Keeps track of the FTP command and response sequence.

- Dynamically creates the data connection by examining PORT and PASV commands.

- Records an audit trail of activities performed

Auditing Functions of FTP Application Inspection

When application inspection is enabled for FTP, every time a file is either sent to or retrieved from an FTP server, an audit record is generated with a message ID of 302002. Likewise, the log message will contain the username, source and destination IP addresses, any addresses translated by NAT, and the file operation.

APPLICATION INSPECTION FOR RSH

RSH (remote shell) was designed for Unix systems to alleviate the hassles of having to authenticate every time you logged into another system. One problem with telnet is that you must always enter a username and password when accessing a remote system. With RSH, you log into one machine, and then you can remotely start up a shell process on a different machine without having to again enter a username and password. On the remote Unix system, there is an .rhosts file that contains a list of IP addresses of devices that are allowed to perform RSH. This greatly simplifies accessing remote resources.

Today, most people don't use RSH because it is very insecure—all traffic going across the connection is susceptible to eavesdropping, and it is very easy to execute a spoofing attack to start up a shell on a remote system with this process enabled. Because of these inherent security problems with RSH, most people use SSH (secure shell), which I discussed in Chapter 3.

 SECURITY ALERT!   You should not allow RSH traffic through your PIX because it is susceptible to spoofing attacks.

Mechanics of RSH Connections

To help illustrate how RSH connections are established between a client and a server, I'll use the example shown in Figure 7-8. When setting up an RSH connection (which uses TCP), the client device chooses a source port number greater than 1,023 that is not currently being used. The destination port number is the well-known port 514. This connection is known as a *command connection,* and is used to emulate the CLI of the shell.

Once the command connection is established, the RSH server sets up another TCP connection, called an *error connection*, back to the client. The error connection is used to transmit errors related to the shell. The server asks the client on the command connection which free port number (greater than 1,023) the client is assigning to this connection for the destination port number, and the server chooses a port number greater than 1,023 as a source port number. The server then builds this connection to the client. As you can see, this process is very similar to standard-mode FTP.

Client on the Inside of the PIX

When the client is on the inside of the network and initiates an RSH connection to an RSH server on the outside of the network, the PIX allows the connection by default because the connection is traveling from a higher-level interface to a lower-level one. A problem exists, however, when the server attempts to set up the error connection back to the client.

With the application inspection feature, the PIX expects this error connection to be built by the server, and looks for the port numbers negotiated by the devices on the command connection. When it sees this information, the PIX dynamically adds a connection entry in the connection table with the appropriate information—this includes the client's port number that it shared with the RSH server.

Without the application inspection feature, you would have to configure a conduit or ACL to specifically allow this error connection. The problem with this is that you

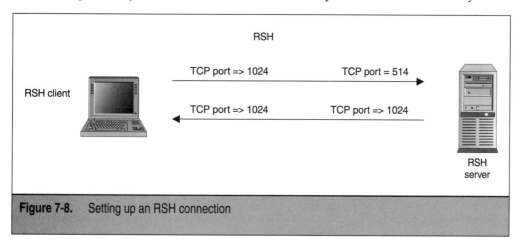

Figure 7-8.   Setting up an RSH connection

don't really know which client, or possibly even which server—you would basically have to permit traffic from any device (the RSH server) heading to anywhere (the clients). The other problem you face is that you would have to open up all source and destination port numbers greater than 1,023 for the error connection—obviously, this is a major security problem. If you disable application inspection for RSH, you'll have to manually configure this conduit or ACL entry to permit the error connection.

Client on the Outside of the PIX

In this example, let's assume that the client is on the outside of your network, and the RSH server is on the inside. For the initial client connection to work, you need to configure a conduit or ACL that will allow traffic heading to the RSH server for TCP port 514—without this, no type of RSH connection can be made. Once the command connection has been established, the server establishes the second connection (error) back to the client.

In this situation, because the error connection is coming from a higher-level interface and is exiting a lower-level interface, the PIX permits it by default, unless you have an ACL or outbound filter that prohibits this connection. Therefore, in this example, application inspection doesn't come into play.

Command Syntax for Application Inspection of RSH

Now that you have a basic understanding of the connection setup for RSH, let's talk about the command for application inspection for RSH. As I mentioned earlier in this chapter, application inspection for RSH is enabled by default. The syntax for the application inspection command for RSH is as follows:

```
pixfirewall(config)#  fixup protocol rsh [port_number]
```

You cannot change the original port number of 514 for the command connection, but you can always add additional ports to RSH. To disable application inspection for RSH, precede the command with the no parameter.

APPLICATION INSPECTION FOR SKINNY

Skinny Client Control Protocol (SCCP), or Skinny for short, is a Cisco-simplified protocol for implementing Voice over IP (VoIP) with Cisco's IP Phones and Cisco's CallManager server. Skinny is interoperable with other H.323 devices. Support for application inspection of Skinny is new in FOS 6.0. Currently, the PIX understands version 3.1.1 of Skinny. When the PIX is performing its application inspection of Skinny, it examines Skinny signals to determine if there are embedded addresses that need to be translated, and translates them. It also looks for the call setup of an audio connection and dynamically adds this connection to the PIX's connection table.

NOTE   Skinny application inspection supports NAT, but not PAT.

Mechanics of Skinny Connections

To help illustrate how Skinny connections are established between an IP Phone client and the CallManager server, as well as connections between IP Phone clients, I'll use the example shown in Figure 7-9. When an IP Phone first boots up, it uses DHCP to acquire its IP addressing information, which includes its IP address and subnet mask, a default gateway, a DNS server address, and a TFTP server address. With version 6.2 of the PIX firewall, the PIX supports DHCP options 150 and 166, which allow the PIX to send the TFTP server address to DHCP clients, including Cisco's IP Phones. I discuss DHCP in Chapter 15.

When the IP Phone client sets up the first connection (which uses TCP) to the CallManager server, the client chooses a port number greater than 1,023 that is not currently being used. The destination port number is port 2,000. This connection is a *signaling connection* and is used by the client to send signaling information, like a call setup or teardown request of audio phone connections. Across this signaling connection, the client indicates which UDP port it will use to handle the processing of voice packets (phone connections). After connecting to the CallManager server, the client uses TFTP to download its configuration instructions from the TFTP server, which usually resides on the CallManager server (as shown in Figure 7-9).

Once the signaling connection is established, the IP Phone client can make phone calls. When the client makes a phone call, it uses the signaling connection to signal the CallManager server of the call setup request to a destination phone. The source client uses its chosen UDP port number (greater than 1,023) for this *audio connection*. The CallManager then contacts the destination party, acquires the chosen destination UDP

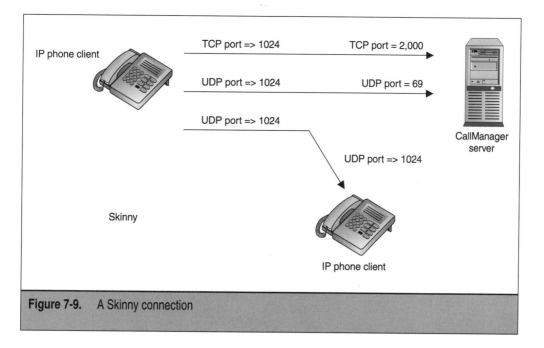

Figure 7-9.   A Skinny connection

port number (greater than 1,023) from the destination, along with the destination's IP address, and then notifies the source client of this connection information so that the source can now complete the audio connection to the destination phone.

Client on the Inside of the PIX

When the client is on the inside of the network and initiates a signaling connection to a CallManager server on the outside of the network, the PIX allows the initial TFTP connection (UDP 69) and the signaling TCP connection by default, because both connections are traveling from a higher-level interface to a lower-level one. This is also true for the audio connection if the destination IP phone is on the outside of your network. Therefore, all of these connections will be able to be established unless you are filtering traffic with ACLs or outbound filters. In this case, the only role that application inspection plays is handling any embedded NAT addresses. The PIX accomplishes this by examining the signaling information in the signaling connection.

Client on the Outside of the PIX

In this example, let's assume that the IP Phone client is on the outside of your network, and the CallManager server and destination IP phone are on the inside. For the initial client connections (TFTP and signaling) to work, you need to configure a conduit or ACL that will allow traffic heading to the TFTP server for UDP port 69 and the CallManager server for TCP port 2,000—without this, no type of VoIP connection is possible. In most cases, the TFTP server function will be running on the same platform as CallManager.

Once the signaling connection has been established, the client can make and receive phone calls. When the client makes a phone call, it uses the signaling connection to tell the CallManager to contact the remote end to acquire the connection parameters for the connection (like the UDP port number the destination will use). The CallManager server sends this information to the client, and the client then establishes the connection using this information.

One problem with this scenario is that the IP Phone that the source is calling is probably not the CallManager station itself, but an IP Phone with a different IP address. The second problem is the dynamic destination port number. With Skinny application inspection, the PIX examines the signaling information on the signaling connection and uses this information to dynamically create an entry in the connection table to permit this traffic. If the destination address (the IP phone on the inside network) is using a NAT-translated address, the PIX ensures that it changes the local address to a global address when dealing with the outside client.

Issues with Skinny

If you disable application inspection for Skinny, you will face many hurdles. The first is that if you are using NAT, and the IP phone initiating the connection is on the outside of the network and the destination IP phone is on the inside of the network, the call will not complete because the CallManager is sending the local address, and not the global address, to the external device.

Another problem is that even if you are using addresses that aren't translated by NAT (public addresses) on the inside of your network, you will still face another issue with external IP Phones that wish to establish connections to inside IP phones—you don't know what UDP port numbers to open up for the audio connections. Of course, if you are the administrator of CallManager, you've preassigned the ports for use, and thus you know the range; however, opening up a whole range of ports on a PIX, or all ports above 1,023 if you're not sure of the UDP port numbers, is very risky and exposes you to all kinds of security threats.

One item that I pointed out in the last section was that a Cisco IP Phone uses TFTP to download its configuration. Typically, the TFTP server is running on the same device as CallManager. However, there is one serious problem with this TFTP connection and the information that is downloaded from the server to the IP Phone—the PIX currently does not translate any embedded NAT-translated addresses inside the downloaded TFTP file. Therefore, if the CallManager and IP Phone are on different interfaces of the PIX, and you are using NAT, you won't be able to set up phone connections. The only way around this issue today is to disable NAT on your PIX for all IP Phone devices.

Another issue with Skinny and the PIX is that Skinny gateway devices, like a voice conferencing bridge, might fragment VoIP packets. When the PIX performs application inspection for Skinny, it examines each packet and drops any bad packets. From the PIX's perspective, the SCCP checksums found for the complete packet won't match the contents of each of the fragments, thus causing the PIX to drop the packets. Therefore, at least for version 6.2 and earlier of the PIX FOS, you should make sure that there is no intermediate device that is performing fragmentation on Skinny packets.

Command Syntax for Application Inspection of Skinny

Now that you have a basic understanding of the connection setup for Skinny, let's talk about the command for application inspection. As I mentioned earlier in this chapter, application inspection for Skinny is enabled by default. The syntax for the application inspection command for Skinny is shown here:

```
pixfirewall(config)#  fixup protocol skinny [port_number[-port_number]]
```

The default port number for the CallManager connection is TCP 2,000—you can change this if you've changed it in your VoIP implementation. You can also specify a range of TCP port numbers for application inspection of Skinny. To disable application inspection for Skinny, precede the command with the no parameter.

APPLICATION INSPECTION FOR SIP

The Session Initiation Protocol (SIP), specified in IETF's RFC 2543, is a VoIP protocol that defines how audio connections are set up between audio-capable IP devices. SIP's main function is to handle the call setup process between IP devices. SIP works with the Session Description Protocol (SDP), which is defined in RFC 2327. SDP is responsible for assigning the ports for the voice (audio) connections that the VoIP devices use. Application inspection for SIP was introduced in FOS 6.0.

Mechanics of SIP Connections

Both SIP and Skinny are VoIP protocols; as you will see in this section, however, the way they set up connections is slightly different. To help illustrate how SIP connections are established between a VoIP client and a VoIP gateway, as well as setting up phone connections between VoIP clients, I'll use the example shown in Figure 7-10.

When the client sets up the first connection (which can use either TCP or UDP), the client device chooses a port number greater than 1,023 that is not currently being used. The choice of protocols is based on the configuration and implementation of the VoIP solution: the client will be configured to use one or the other. The destination port number is port 5,060. This connection is a *signaling connection* and is used by the VoIP client to send signaling information, like a call setup or teardown request of audio phone connections, to the VoIP gateway device.

Once the signaling connection is established, the VoIP client can make phone calls. When the client makes a phone call, it uses the signaling connection to signal the VoIP gateway of the call setup request to a destination phone. The source client chooses a UDP port number (greater than 1,023) for this *audio connection* and notifies the gateway of its choice. The VoIP gateway then contacts the destination party, acquires the destination UDP port number (greater than 1,023) that is to be used for the incoming call connection from the destination, along with the destination's IP address, and then

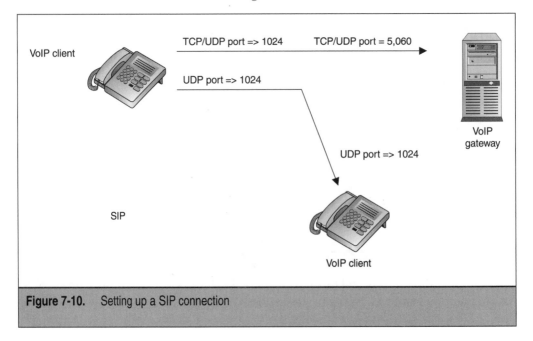

Figure 7-10.   Setting up a SIP connection

notifies the source client of this connection information so that the source can now complete the audio connection to the destination phone.

As you can see from the previous example, the connection set up process is very similar to Skinny. In the next two sections, I will cover the connection process based on whether the client is on the inside of the firewall or the outside.

Client on the Inside of the PIX

When the VoIP client is on the inside of the network and initiates a signaling connection to a VoIP gateway and IP VoIP destination client on the outside of the network, the PIX allows the signaling TCP or UDP connection at port 5,060 by default because the connection is traveling from a higher-level interface to a lower-level one. This is also true for the audio connection. Therefore, both of these connections will be able to be established unless you are filtering with ACLs or outbound filters. In this case, the only role that application inspection plays is handling any NAT-translated addresses, changing local addresses to global addresses. The PIX accomplishes this by examining the signaling information in the signaling connection.

Client on the Outside of the PIX

In this example, let's assume that the source VoIP client is on the outside of your network, and the VoIP gateway and destination VoIP client are on the inside. For the initial client signaling connection to work, you need to configure a conduit or ACL that will allow traffic heading to TCP or UDP port 5,060—without this, no type of VoIP connection is possible.

Once the signaling connection has been established, the client can make and receive phone calls. When the client makes a phone call, it uses the signaling connection to tell the VoIP gateway to contact the remote end to set up the connection parameters for the connection (like what port number the destination will use to accept the connection). The VoIP gateway sends this information to the source client, and then the client establishes the connection using this information.

One problem with this scenario is that the VoIP client that the source is calling is probably not the VoIP gateway itself, but some other VoIP client with a different IP address. The second problem is the dynamic destination port number used for this connection. SIP application inspection solves this problem. With SIP application inspection, the PIX examines the signaling information on the signaling connection and uses this information to dynamically create an entry in the connection table to permit the second connection. Likewise, if the destination address (the VoIP client on the inside network) is using a NAT-translated address, the PIX ensures that it changes the local address to a global address when dealing with the outside client.

Issues with SIP

If you disable application inspection for SIP, you will face many hurdles, as is the case with Skinny. The first is that if you are using NAT, and the VoIP client initiating the connection is on the outside of the network and the destination is on the inside of the network, the call will not complete because the VoIP gateway is sending the local address of the internal client to the external device instead of the global address.

Another problem is that even if you are using addresses that aren't translated by NAT (public addresses) on the inside of your network, you will still face another issue with external VoIP clients that wish to establish connections to inside VoIP devices—you don't know what UDP port numbers to open up for the audio connections. Of course, if you are the administrator of the VoIP gateways, you've preassigned the ports for use, and thus you know the range; however, opening up a whole range of ports on a PIX, or all ports above 1,023 if you're not sure of the UDP port numbers, is very risky and exposes you to all kinds of security issues.

There is another caveat with SIP that deals with placing calls on hold. Assume there is an audio connection between an internal VoIP phone and an external VoIP phone, and the external phone wants to put the current phone call to the internal client on hold. In order to do this, the external client will have to contact the VoIP gateway on port 5,060. If the gateway is located on the inside of the firewall, the connection is denied by default. You can solve this problem by either setting up an ACL to allow the inbound traffic, or using the `established` command, which is more secure. The following is the syntax for the `established` command:

```
pixfirewall(config)# established udp 5060 permitto udp 5060
                       permitfrom udp 0
```

This configuration allows a UDP connection on port 5,060 to the VoIP gateway if a UDP connection already exists from that phone to an inside phone.

Command Syntax for Application Inspection of SIP

Now that you have a basic understanding of the connection setup for SIP, let's talk about the command for application inspection for SIP. As I mentioned earlier in this chapter, application inspection for SIP is enabled by default. The syntax for the application inspection command for SIP is shown here:

```
pixfirewall(config)# fixup protocol sip [port_number[-port_number]]
```

The default port number for the VoIP gateway connection is UDP 5,060—you can change this if you've changed it in your VoIP implementation. You can also specify a range of UDP port numbers for application inspection of SIP. To disable application inspection for SIP, precede the command with the `no` parameter. Note that this command disables inspection for SIP TCP connections—there is currently no way of disabling inspection for SIP UDP.

NOTE PAT is now supported for SIP application inspection in FOS 6.2—prior to 6.2, only NAT was supported.

APPLICATION INSPECTION FOR MULTIMEDIA USING RTSP

Multimedia applications pose many of the same problems for firewalls that I have discussed so far in this chapter. One of the main reasons that multimedia applications are difficult to deal with is that there is no single unifying standard that defines how they should be implemented. Each vendor, instead, has developed their own implementation method for their applications. The following are some of the problems you have to deal with concerning multimedia applications and firewalls:

- Some multimedia applications embed IP addresses and port numbers in the payload, which can cause problems with environments that have deployed NAT, PAT, or both.

- Some multimedia applications use the same port number for both the source and destination, which makes it more difficult to determine which is initiating a session.

- Some multimedia applications use TCP for connections, and others use UDP. Some applications use a combination of protocols for their connections.

- Some multimedia applications use dynamic port numbers for their additional connections, which creates filtering problems because the actual port numbers can come from a very large range of numbers.

Here is a simple example that illustrates the problems that you will face. RealAudio's clients open up a TCP connection to port 7070 on a RealAudio server. The RealAudio server then opens up a UDP connection from port 6970 to 7170 to the client.

As you can see from the above list of problems, dealing with multimedia applications in a firewall environment is not an easy task. The best solution to use in dealing with multimedia applications is the PIX's application inspection feature. The application inspection feature of the PIX handles the translation of embedded NAT-translated addresses, as well as opening up a hole in the firewall for just the additional connections between the clients and servers.

Mechanics of RTSP Connections

Many applications use the Real-Time Streaming Protocol (RTSP) to implement the communication infrastructure to transmit information between multimedia devices. RTSP is defined in RFC 2326. RTSP is used by many multimedia applications to control the delivery of information, which includes video and audio, as well as data, in a real-time fashion. It supports both TCP and UDP for control and information streaming processes.

The PIX's application inspection feature does not work with every multimedia application. As I mentioned earlier, not every vendor implements these multimedia applications in the same manner. Currently, Cisco officially supports the following multimedia applications:

- Apple QuickTime
- Cisco IP/TV
- RealNetworks RealAudio, RealPlayer, and RealServer

In addition to these multimedia applications, other multimedia applications may work, depending on how the vendor implemented them. A work-around for those applications not supported by the application inspection feature is to use conduits, ACLs, or the `established` command to open up the necessary holes in your PIX firewall to allow connectivity. As you will see in the next few sections, the holes that you need to open might be very large—the advantage of the application inspection feature for multimedia is that the PIX only opens up holes for the connections requested between the communicating devices.

Types of Multimedia Connections

There are typically three connections established between a client and a server when RSTP is used:

- **Control connection**   This channel, which is bidirectional, allows the client and server to communicate with each other concerning the setting up and tearing down of multimedia connections. RSTP defines the mechanics as to how this connection is set up and the messages that traverse it. In most instances, the connection uses TCP, and the port that terminates at the server is 554.

- **Multimedia connection**   This is a unidirectional connection from the server to the client. The actual content information, like audio or video, is sent across the connection to the client. In almost all cases this is a UDP connection. One problem with this connection is that there are no real standards regarding how port numbers should be chosen. There are two protocols that define the setup and delivery of information across this connection: Real-Time Transport Protocol (RTP) and Real Data Transport Protocol (RDT). RTP is based on a standard and RDT was developed by RealNetworks. I'll discuss these protocols in a few moments.

- **Error connection**   This is a UDP connection that can be unidirectional or bidirectional. It is used by the client to request the resending of missing information from the server. Sometimes it is also used for synchronization purposes to ensure that video and audio streams don't experience jitter problems.

Depending on whether you are using RTP or RDT for the multimedia connection, the connection setup process is different. Therefore, I've included the next two sections to help describe the connection setup process for each. As I mentioned when I discussed the *multimedia connection*, the use of UDP port numbers is application-specific. In the examples that follow, therefore, I've assumed that the multimedia software running on the client is Real Networks' RealPlayer, which is accessing Real Networks' G2 RealServer.

Standard RTP Mode

In this section I will use an example to show you how RTSP, using RTP, sets up connections between a RealPlayer client and a RealServer. I'll use the top part of the illustration shown in Figure 7-11 to illustrate the example.

The first connection set up between the RealPlayer client and RealServer is the control connection. RealNetworks only supports TCP for this. Actually, every multimedia application that I've dealt with that uses RTSP runs RTSP across TCP, even though RFC 2326 supports both TCP and UDP. This control connection allows the client and server to communicate with each other and establish parameters for the multimedia connections—no actual multimedia traffic traverses this connection. The client chooses a port number greater than 1,023, and the server is listening on 554, which is defined in RFC 2326.

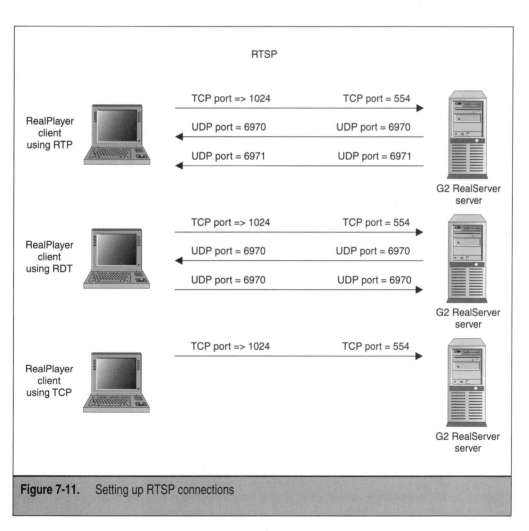

Figure 7-11.   Setting up RTSP connections

When the client requests multimedia information, the server and client negotiate the port numbers for this UDP connection. In the RealPlayer configuration, the default port numbers range from 6,970 to 7,170. However, you can easily change this in the client's configuration. There are two restrictions that RTP places on this port number:

- The port number must be an even (not odd) number.
- The port number cannot be a well-known port number—it must be greater than 1,023.

This is a unidirectional connection—only the server can send the multimedia information on this connection to the client. The server builds this connection to the client.

The second UDP connection set up uses RTCP (Real-Time Control Protocol). This is a bidirectional connection that the client uses to synchronize the multimedia connection as well as to request any missing UDP segments from the multimedia connection. The restriction on this port number is that it must be one number greater than that used by RTP—therefore, it will always be an odd number. Like the last UDP connection, the server builds this connection to the client.

In the next two sections I will cover the connection process based on whether the client is on the inside of the firewall or the outside.

Client on the Inside of the PIX (RTP)   When the RTSP client is on the inside of the network and initiates a signaling connection to an RTSP server on the outside of the network, the PIX allows the signaling TCP (or UDP) connection at port 554 by default, because the connection is traveling from a higher-level interface to a lower-level one.

The second connection, the multimedia RTP UDP connection, is initiated by the server to the client. With the RTSP application inspection feature, the PIX examines the RTSP control messages to determine the port numbers being used on the two sides, and dynamically adds this connection to the connection table. One restriction with the application inspection feature for RTSP is that the PIX cannot handle any NAT-translated addresses in the control messages of the RTSP TCP connection—therefore, you need to disable NAT for multimedia to work.

Likewise, the third UDP connection, RTCP, is built from the server to the client. Again, the application inspection feature causes the PIX to dynamically add this connection to the connection table.

If you disable application inspection for RTSP, you need to create two conduits for the two UDP server connections, or use the `established` command. Each multimedia application should define what this port number, or range of port numbers is. In many cases, if you happen to be the administrator of the multimedia application, you can change these numbers to suite your environment. If your multimedia application uses a range of port numbers, unfortunately the hole that you create in your firewall will have to cover this range. In a worst-case scenario, where any port above 1,023 can be used, you basically have to open up your firewall to all these ports, which is not a recommended security practice.

Client on the Outside of the PIX (RTP)   In this example, assume that the RTSP client is on the outside of your network and the RTSP server is on the inside. For the initial client signaling connection to work, you need to configure a conduit or ACL that will allow traffic heading to TCP (or UDP) port 554—without this, no type of RTSP connection is possible.

Because the RTSP server sets up the RTP and RTCP UDP connections, and these connections are going from a higher-level to a lower-level interface, you don't need to do anything special on the PIX. You could disable application inspection for RTSP, and the connections would still work.

RealNetworks' RDT Mode

In this section I will use an example to show you how RTSP, using RDT, sets up connections between a RealPlayer client and a RealServer. I'll use the middle part of the illustration shown previously in Figure 7-11 to illustrate the example.

The first connection that is set up between the RealPlayer client and the RealServer is the control connection. RealNetworks only supports TCP for this. This control connection allows the client and server to communicate with each other and establish parameters for the multimedia connections—no actual multimedia traffic traverses this connection. The client chooses a port number greater than 1,023, and the server is listening on 554, which is defined in RFC 2326. This connection is the same connection discussed in the last section.

When the client requests multimedia information, the server and client negotiate the port numbers for two simplex UDP connections. A *simplex connection* is a unidirectional connection—you can either send or receive, but not both. The server builds one simplex connection to the client, and the client builds the other simplex connection to the server. Even though these are two distinct connections, the same port numbers can be used for both connections (remember that they're simplex connections) or different port numbers can be used. In the example shown in Figure 7-11, I used the same port number for these connections.

In the next two sections I will cover the connection process based on whether the client is on the inside of the firewall or the outside.

Client on the Inside of the PIX (RDT)   When the RTSP client is on the inside of the network and initiates a signaling connection to an RTSP server on the outside of the network, the PIX allows the signaling TCP (or UDP) connection at port 554 by default, because the connection is traveling from a higher-level interface to a lower-level one.

The second connection, the multimedia RDT UDP connection, is initiated by the server to the client. With the RTSP application inspection feature, the PIX examines the RTSP control messages to determine the port numbers being used on the two sides, and dynamically adds this connection to the connection table. Remember that NAT is not supported with RTSP. Because the third UDP connection is built from the client to the server, it is automatically permitted.

If you disable application inspection for RTSP, you need to create one conduit for the simplex UDP server connection, or use the `established` command. Each multimedia application should define what this port number, or range of port numbers is. In many cases, if you happen to be the administrator of the multimedia application, you can change these numbers to suite your environment.

Client on the Outside of the PIX (RDT)   In this example, assume that the RTSP client is on the outside of your network and the RTSP server is on the inside. For the initial client signaling connection to work, you need to configure a conduit or ACL that will allow traffic heading to TCP (or UDP) port 554—without this, no type of RTSP connection is possible.

Because the RTSP server sets up the UDP RDT simplex connection, and this connection is going from a higher-level to a lower-level interface, you don't need to do anything special on the PIX because the connection is permitted by default.

For the second simplex UDP connection from the client to the server, the PIX determines the port numbers for the connection by examining the RTSP messages in the RTSP TCP connection, and dynamically adds the connection to the connection table. If you disable application inspection for RTSP, you need to add a conduit or ACL, or use the `established` command, to allow this arbitrary UDP connection.

TCP with Either RTP or RDT

As you saw in the last two sections, RTP and RDT use UDP for the multimedia connections. There is an option of using TCP for the multimedia connections instead of UDP. One of the advantages of using TCP is that there is only a single connection used to transmit all data—both control and multimedia information. Therefore, pushing this connection through a firewall is fairly simple. However, because TCP adds delay in the multimedia stream, this type of connection is not commonly used for real-time connections.

In this section I will use an example to show you how RTSP, using TCP for either RTP or RDT, sets up connections between a RealPlayer client and a RealServer. I'll use the bottom part of the illustration shown in Figure 7-11 to illustrate the example.

The first, and only, connection that is set up between the RealPlayer and RealServer is the *control/data connection*. This control connection allows the client and server to communicate with each other as well as to transmit multimedia data across it—this is unlike RTP and RDT mode, where a separate connection is used for the multimedia data.

Because there is only a single TCP connection, dealing with this in an environment that uses a firewall is fairly simple. If the client is on the inside of the network and the server is on the outside, there is nothing special you have to do to allow the traffic to flow from the higher-level interface to the lower-level one. If the client is located on the outside of the network and the server is on the inside, you need to build a conduit or ACL to allow TCP traffic destined to port 554 to the internal RTSP server.

Issues with RTSP

Just like any protocol that the PIX deals with when using application inspection, the PIX is limited in what it can do with the connections. Here is a list of some of the more important restrictions of RTSP and application inspection:

- The PIX cannot fix embedded NAT addresses in RTSP messages—there are usually other ways, within the RTSP application itself, to get around this problem.
- The PIX cannot fix embedded port addresses (PAT) in RTSP messages.

- The PIX cannot fix RTSP messages through UDP ports.

- RTSP supports multicasting of the UDP multimedia connection—the PIX never forwards a broadcast or multicast; therefore this type of connection is not supported through the PIX.

- RTSP supports the embedding of RTSP messages within HTTP—the PIX cannot inspect these embedded messages.

Command Syntax for Application Inspection of RTSP

Now that you have a basic understanding of the connection setup for RTSP and the PIX's limitations, let's talk about the command for application inspection. As I mentioned earlier in this chapter, application inspection for RTSP is enabled by default. The syntax for the application inspection command for RTSP is as follows:

```
pixfirewall(config)#  fixup protocol rtsp [port_number]
```

The default port number for the RTSP control connection is 554—you can change this if you've changed it in your RTSP server implementation. Likewise, other multimedia applications might use a number other than 554. For example, if you are using Cisco's IP/TV, you need to add port 8,554 to you list of ports to inspect. To disable application inspection for RTSP, precede the command with the no parameter.

APPLICATION INSPECTION FOR H.323

H.323 is an ITU-T standard for the bi-directional exchange of voice, video, and data. H.323 is something of a hybrid protocol in that it supports video as well as audio connections. In this sense, it handles multimedia in addition to audio. As you will see in the following sections, like most multimedia applications, H.323 is a more difficult protocol to deal with than simple VoIP connections. Unlike SIP, Skinny, or FTP, H.323 sets up many connections between two devices. The following sections cover the components of H.323, how connections are set up, and how the application inspection feature for H.323 on the PIX functions.

H.323 Overview

H.323 is actually a group of standards that defines the communication process between two H.323 devices. H.323 includes the following group of standards:

- **H.225**   Registration, admission, and status

- **H.235**   Call signaling

- **H.245**   Control signaling

- **Q.931**   Messaging

- **TPKT**   Packet headers

- **ASN.1**   Encoding packets

For call setup and control TCP is used; for the audio/video connections UDP is used. As you can see, this is similar to RTSP. Unlike RTSP, H.323 uses two TCP connections and one or more UDP connections. The first connection is a TCP connection to port 1,720. The remaining connections use UDP and TCP, but the port numbers are typically random (above 1,023). This, obviously, causes problems in environments that use firewalls. H.323 uses ASN.1 (Abstract Syntax Notation) to encode its packets, which makes application inspection difficult when deciphering the packet information.

There are also two versions of H.323—v1 and v2. All PIX FOS's support v1; you need at least 5.2 to support v2. As you can see from my previous statements and the list of standards incorporated into H.323, the application inspection feature of the PIX for H.323 was not simple to implement.

Supported Applications

Because each vendor adds its own mechanisms above and beyond H.323, and because of the complexities of H.323 itself, the PIX does not support every H.323 multimedia application. However, here is a list of supported H.323 multimedia applications:

- Cisco Multimedia Conference Manager
- CU-SeeMe's Meeting Point and CU-SeeMe Pro
- Intel Video Phone
- Microsoft NetMeeting
- VocalTec's Internet Phone and Gatekeeper

Other H.323 multimedia applications might work with the PIX's application inspection feature, but Cisco officially supports only these applications.

Types of H.323 Devices

Before I begin discussing the setup of connections with H.323, let's first discuss the two types of devices that can be involved in the connection setup process: *terminals* and *gatekeepers*. An H.323 terminal is an endpoint in the H.323 connection. It is a client that is responsible for making connections. This can be something as simple as software running on a PC or a dedicated hardware appliance like an IP phone. One requirement of all H.323 terminals is that they must support voice communications—other types of communications, like video and data, are optional.

An H.323 gatekeeper is a central point for all multimedia calls, and provides call control services to the terminals that register with it. Its two main functions are to perform address translation (which can be NAT or telephone number-to-IP address translation) and bandwidth management. Note that the gatekeeper is not necessary to set up connections directly between two terminals—if the two terminals that want to communicate know each others' addressing information, they can set up the connection directly. This is different from Skinny and SIP.

A gatekeeper is not necessary, but it does make it easier to deploy multimedia services on a large scale. A gatekeeper is the central repository for addressing information—terminals register their addressing information with the gatekeeper, and the gatekeeper gives this information to querying terminals. In this sense, it functions something like a hybrid PBX/DNS server. H.225 defines the Registration, Admission, and Status (RAS) protocol that the terminals and gatekeepers use to communicate with each other.

Mechanics of H.323 Connections

There are three basic ways that a connection can be made between two terminals:

- A terminal can contact a gatekeeper for address translation information and then set up the connection directly to the destination terminal—this requires both terminals to be registered with the gatekeeper.

- A terminal can contact a gatekeeper and have the gatekeeper handle the call signaling and control information between the two terminals—this requires both terminals to be registered with the gatekeeper.

- A terminal that knows the destination terminal's address can set up the connection directly.

Table 7-3 summarizes the connection types and port numbers used by H.323 applications.

The next few sections cover the interaction of the terminal with the gatekeeper and interaction between the two terminals.

Protocol	Port	Description
UDP	1,718	Multicast to discover the gatekeepers on a segment
TCP	1,719	RAS connection used to register terminal information with the gatekeeper
TCP	1,720	H.225 signaling connection used to set up and tear down connections
TCP	1,024–65,535	H.245 control connection
UDP	1,024–65,535	RTP audio connection
UDP	1,024–65,535	RTP video connection
UDP	1,024–65,535	RTCP synchronization connection

Table 7-3. Connections and Port Numbers for H.323 Applications

Finding and Connecting to a Gatekeeper

As I mentioned previously, a gatekeeper is not necessary to establish a multimedia connection between two terminals; however, it does help centralize and simplify your multimedia deployment. There are two basic methods of contacting a gatekeeper:

- The terminal uses an auto-discovery process to find the gatekeeper.
- The terminal has the gatekeeper's IP address hard-coded in its local configuration.

I'll use the illustration in Figure 7-12 to demonstrate the two connections that might be used to initiate a connection to the gatekeeper.

If the terminal doesn't know the gatekeeper's IP address, it will send a multicast to 224.0.1.41 (well-known multicast address). This is a UDP multicast with a port number of 1,718. Obviously, if the terminal is on one side of a PIX firewall, and the gatekeeper is on the other side, this process will fail—the PIX never forwards broadcasts or multicast packets. Therefore, you would have to use the second solution—hard-code the IP address of the gatekeeper on the terminal client.

Once the terminal knows the IP address of the gatekeeper, the terminal sets up a direct UDP connection to the gatekeeper—this is the second connection shown in Figure 7-12. The source port of the terminal is a random port above 1,023, and the destination port is 1,719. When this connection is established, the terminal then registers its information with the gatekeeper. This information includes the identity of the terminal (like an ID, name, E.164 phone number, or some other type of alias) and the IP address of the terminal. Therefore, when other terminals want to contact this terminal, they can use the destination terminal's alias (which is static) to find the destination's IP address to set up a multimedia connection. In this sense, the registration process is somewhat like WINS or dynamic DNS.

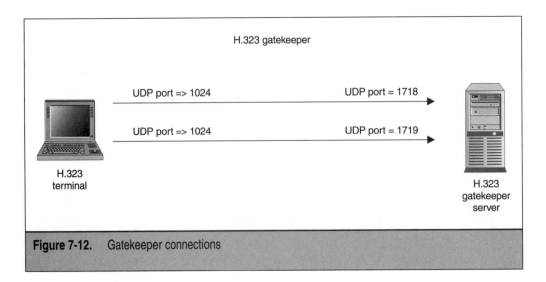

Figure 7-12.   Gatekeeper connections

Terminal on the Inside of the PIX   When the terminal is on the inside of the network and initiates a signaling connection to a gatekeeper server on the outside of the network, the PIX allows the RAS UDP connection by default at port 1,719, because the connection is traveling from a higher-level interface to a lower-level one. Application inspection on the PIX takes care of translating any embedded NAT-translated addresses in this RAS connection.

If you disable application inspection for RAS, you need to ensure that you are not performing NAT on your PIX for the terminal(s) in question. Otherwise, the terminal will register its local address, which is not visible to the outside world.

Terminal on the Outside of the PIX   In this example, assume that the terminal is on the outside of your network, and the gatekeeper server is on the inside. For the initial client signaling connection to work, you need to configure a conduit or ACL that allows traffic heading to UDP port 1,719—without this, no type of gatekeeper connection is possible.

Using Only Terminals to Establish Connections

Let's start out simple and examine the connection set up between two terminals without a gatekeeper involved in the process. In this situation, the source terminal must know the address of the destination terminal. I'll use the illustration shown in Figure 7-13 as an example.

The source terminal first opens up a TCP connection with a source port number greater than 1,023 and a destination port number of 1,720. This connection is used for call setup and signaling between the two terminals (this is defined in the H.225

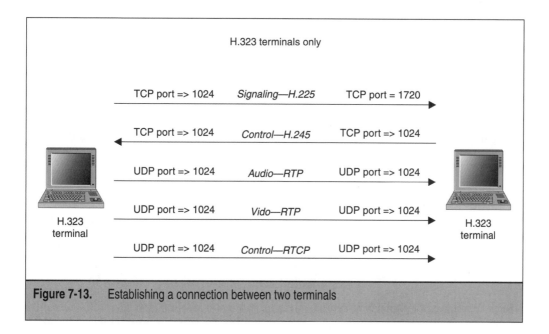

Figure 7-13.   Establishing a connection between two terminals

standard). This connection is the signaling connection, and is used to set up multimedia connections between the two terminals. The Q.931 ITU-T standard is used to implement signaling for setting up and tearing down connections on this connection (ISDN also uses Q.931 for the same purpose). On the signaling connection, the two parties negotiate the port numbers to use for the second TCP connection.

The called party (destination terminal) initiates the second TCP connection back to the source. Both of the port numbers for this connection are dynamically chosen above 1,023 by both parties. This connection is called the *call control connection* and its mechanics are defined in H.245. This connection handles the multimedia connections that are set up, including which audio and video codecs will be used.

Up to three UDP connections will be established from the source terminal to the destination, assuming that this is a video-conference call:

- Audio using RTP
- Video using RTP
- Control using RTCP

The source terminal opens up all three of these UDP connections—the actual ports are negotiated between the two sides on the signaling connection. These port numbers are random numbers greater than 1,023 not currently being used by any other connections on the respective terminals. The source then sets up the three connections to the destination. Notice that the protocols used for these UDP connections are the same ones that RTSP supports in standard RTP mode.

NOTE   This example only applies to video conferencing. Additional UDP connections and TCP connections can be set up between the multimedia devices—each application is unique in this regard.

Source Terminal on the Inside of the PIX   When an H.323 terminal is on the inside of the network and initiates a signaling connection to a terminal on the outside of the network, the PIX allow the TCP connection to port 1,720 by default, because the connection is traveling from a higher-level interface to a lower-level one. To set up the second TCP connection, the PIX looks at the information in the signaling connection with application inspection to detect the port numbers for the second connection, originated by the outside terminal, and dynamically adds this connection to the connection table. For the UDP multimedia connections added after this, because they originate from the terminal on the inside of the network, the PIX permits them by default.

If you disable application inspection for H.323, you need to ensure that you are not performing NAT on your PIX for the terminal(s) in question. Otherwise, the terminal will register its local address, which is not visible to the outside world. Worse, you have to open up a very wide range of TCP ports (1,023 through 65,535) in order to allow the inbound H.245 TCP connection from the outside terminal. Of course, you could always use the established command to limit the size of the hole in your firewall.

Source Terminal on the Outside of the PIX   In this example, assume that the H.323 terminal is on the outside of your network and the destination terminal is on the inside. For the initial client signaling connection to work, you need to configure a conduit or ACL that will allow traffic heading to TCP port 1720—without this, no type of signaling connection is possible. The H.245 TCP connection from the inside machine to the outside machine is permitted by default. However, the set of UDP connections that get set up next from the outside terminal to the inside terminal are denied by default—with application inspection for H.323, the PIX dynamically adds these connections by searching for the negotiated ports in the signaling connection. Likewise, application inspection handles any NAT-translated addresses in the signaling connection.

If you disable application inspection for H.323, H.323 connections will be denied by default—you need to add an additional conduit to allow all UDP port numbers above 1,023 through the PIX, or, better yet, use the `established` command to allow the multimedia UDP connections.

Using a Gatekeeper for Address Translation Only for Terminal Connections

Now let's complicate the process by throwing a gatekeeper into a network scenario. In this situation, the terminals will use the Gatekeeper for registration only, and will set up any other connections directly between themselves. This process is commonly referred to as *direct mode*. I'll use the illustration in Figure 7-14 as an example.

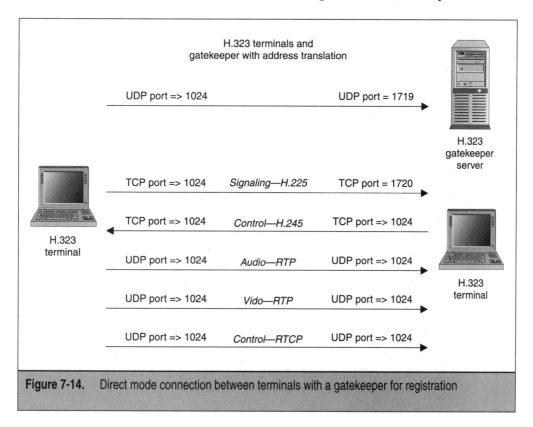

Figure 7-14. Direct mode connection between terminals with a gatekeeper for registration

Each terminal sets up a direct UDP connection to the gatekeeper—this is the first connection shown in Figure 7-14. The source port of the terminal is a random port above 1,023, and the destination port is 1,719. When this connection is established, the terminal then registers its addressing information with the gatekeeper. The terminals use this connection to perform address translation (resolving aliases to IP addresses). In this situation, the source terminal only needs to know the alias of the destination terminal to build a connection to it.

The source terminal then opens up a TCP connection to the destination terminal (not the gatekeeper), where the source terminal's source port number is greater than 1,023, and the destination port number is 1,720. This connection is used for call setup and signaling between the two terminals (this is defined in standard H.225). On this connection, the two parties negotiate the port numbers to use for the second TCP connection. This connection is the *control connection,* and is used to set up multimedia connections between two terminals.

The rest of the connections are established in exactly the same manner as described in the previous section on building connections directly between two terminals. All of the issues mentioned in the "Finding and Connecting to a Gatekeeper" and "Using Only Terminals to Establish Connections" sections apply to the connections being set up in this section.

Using a Gatekeeper for Address Translation and Signaling and Control for Terminal Connections

The last mode that can be used for setting up multimedia connections between terminals involves a gatekeeper, like the last section, but in this instance, the gatekeeper plays a more involved role. In this situation, both the signaling (H.225) and control (H.245) connections from the terminals are set up between the terminals and the gatekeeper, not between each other. This scenario is often referred to as *routing mode.* I'll use the illustration shown in Figure 7-15 to help with the explanation of the setting up of the connections.

Each terminal sets up a direct UDP connection to the gatekeeper—this is the first connection shown in Figure 7-15. The source port of the terminal is a random port above 1,023, and the destination port is 1,719. When this connection is established, the terminal then registers its information with the gatekeeper. The terminals use this connection to perform address translation (resolving aliases to IP addresses).

Each terminal then opens up a TCP connection to the gatekeeper (not the destination terminal), where the source terminal's source port number is greater than 1,023 and the destination port number is 1,720. This connection is used for call setup and signaling—the gatekeeper acts as a go-between (this is defined in standard H.225). On this connection, each terminal/gateway pair negotiates the port numbers for the H.245 control connection. The gatekeeper then builds this TCP connection back to the terminal. Remember that the source and destination port numbers for this are random numbers above 1,023.

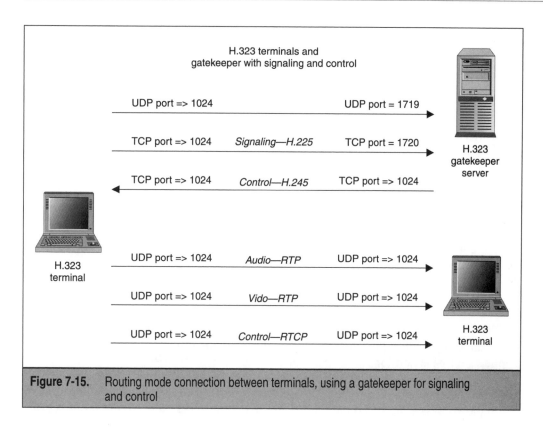

Figure 7-15. Routing mode connection between terminals, using a gatekeeper for signaling and control

Once these connections have been established between the two respective H.323 terminals and the gatekeeper, the terminals can now request connections to be set up. These UDP multimedia connections, unlike the last two TCP connections, are not built to the gatekeeper, but instead are built directly between the terminals themselves. This port information is negotiated on the TCP connections via the gatekeeper, and then the UDP connections are created from the calling party (source terminal) to the called party (destination terminal).

Source Terminal on the Inside of the PIX   As you can see, the setup of these connections is not a simple process. Depending on where all of these devices are located relative to the firewall, application inspection is not a simple process for the PIX firewall. For example, if the source terminal is on the inside of the firewall, and the gateway and destination terminal are on the outside, here is what would happen with application inspection enabled:

1. The two initial connections to the gatekeeper are permitted (1,719 and 1,720) because they originate on the inside.

2. The H.245 TCP connection from the gatekeeper is allowed via application inspection—the PIX examines the TCP 1,720 signaling connection for the port numbers, and dynamically adds this connection to the connection table.

3. The UDP multimedia connections are permitted because they originate from the inside of the network.

Source Terminal on the Inside of the PIX   If the source terminal is on the outside of the network, and the gatekeeper and destination terminal are on the inside of the network, here is what would happen with application inspection enabled:

1. You need a conduit or ACL to allow the UDP 1,719 and TCP 1,720 connections since these connections originate on the outside.

2. The H.245 TCP connection from the gatekeeper to the outside terminal is allowed by default.

3. Application inspection examines the signaling connection to determine that a call is being set up between the outside and inside terminals, and dynamically adds the UDP connections to the connection table.

There are many more scenarios that I could cover here, but I think that you now understand this is not a simple process that the PIX is handling when dealing with application inspection for H.323. If you disable application inspection for H.323, you have to open up some very large holes in your PIX firewall to allow the random TCP and UDP port numbers through.

In the last few sections I dealt with H.323 in general. As I pointed out, though, each H.323 application is typically implemented differently, even though they say they follow the H.323 standard. The next few sections look at a few examples to see some of these differences.

NOTE   As of 6.2 of the FOS, the PIX supports PAT on H.323 connections.

CU-SeeMe

CU-SeeMe is a multimedia application that allows you to set up terminal-to-terminal audio, video, and data collaboration connections. CU-SeeMe clients can connect to clients of the same type, or to clients that are H.323 compatible (at least some of them). CU-SeeMe can operate in two different modes:

- **H.323 mode**   Used when a CU-SeeMe client connects to an H.323-compliant terminal

- **CU-SeeMe mode**   Used when the two devices are both CU-SeeMe devices

Cisco supports application inspection for both modes. Table 7-4 lists the protocols and ports used for H.323 mode for CU-SeeMe devices.

Protocol	Port	Description
TCP	1,720	Signaling
TCP	1,024–65,535	Call Control
UDP	1,024–65,535	Audio and video RTP and RTCP
TCP	1,503	T.120 data connections (file transfers and collaboration)

Table 7-4. Protocols and Ports for CU-SeeMe Clients in H.323 Mode

As you can see from Table 7-4, the information is the same as a normal H.323 connection, with the exception of the additional T.120 data connection. The PIX performs application inspection on TCP 1,720.

Table 7-5 lists the connections used by CU-SeeMe devices in CU-SeeMe mode.

The ports listed in Table 7-5 are used as both the source and destination ports. As you can see from these connections, this differs widely from the H.323 implementation for connections. The PIX performs application inspection on both TCP and UDP ports 7,648 and 7,649.

Netshow

Microsoft's Netshow is a multimedia implementation that allows users to receive both audio and video streams across an IP-based network. The most common client application used to view Netshow content is Microsoft's Windows Media Player. This client software connects to a Netshow server to download and process multimedia information. There are two connection modes that clients can use:

- UDP Stream
- TCP Stream

Protocol	Port	Description
TCP	7,648–7,649	Signaling connection
UDP	7,648–7,649	Call control and sending and receiving chat streams
UDP	24,032	RTP audio connections
UDP	56,800	RTP video connections

Table 7-5. Protocols and Ports for CU-SeeMe Clients in CU-SeeMe mode

In UDP Stream mode, a client connects to the server using TCP and a destination port number of 1,755. Once the client establishes the connection, the client tells the server the client UDP port number to use in order to stream the information down to the client. The server chooses a UDP port number between 1,024 and 5,000 as the source port. Once this UDP connection is established, the server streams the multimedia information to the specified port. With application inspection, the PIX allows the additional connection.

In TCP Stream mode, as in UDP stream mode, the client connects to the multimedia server using TCP 1,755. Once this connection is established, the server uses the same connection to download the multimedia stream. One advantage that this method has over UDP stream is that it is fairly easy to deal with when there is a firewall sitting between the two Netshow devices. The major drawback of TCP Stream is that because it uses TCP, it doesn't perform well with real-time multimedia streams. Since there is only a single connection, the PIX does not use application inspection on the TCP connection.

VDOLive

VDOLive is a multimedia stream protocol that allows users to receive real-time video and audio via an IP-based network. VDOLive was developed by VDOnet Corporation. It uses a TCP connection for control messages and a UDP connection for the multimedia streams. Table 7-6 lists the port numbers involved with these connections.

As you can see from Table 7-6, managing VDOLive through a normal firewall isn't too difficult. The application inspection feature of the PIX monitors the TCP session and allows only the negotiated UDP connection to be dynamically added to its connection table for the connection from the server to the client. The PIX also performs any necessary address translation of addresses in the TCP 7,000 connection.

Command Syntax for Application Inspection of H.323

Now that you have a basic understanding of the connection setup for H.323, let's talk about the command for application inspection for H.323. As I mentioned earlier in this chapter, application inspection for H.323 is enabled by default. The syntax for the application inspection commands for H.323 is:

```
pixfirewall(config)#  fixup protocol h323 ras   [port_number[-port_number]]
pixfirewall(config)#  fixup protocol h323 h225 [port_number[-port_number]]
```

Protocol	Client Port	Server Port	Description
TCP	1,024–65,535	7,000	Control messages and signaling
UDP	1,024–65,535	7,001	Multimedia streams

Table 7-6.   Protocols and Ports for VDOLive

The first command performs application inspection for H.323 RAS (connections to a gatekeeper server). The default port numbers are 1,718 and 1,719—you can change this if you've changed it on your H.323 gatekeeper devices. To disable application inspection for H.323 RAS, precede the first command with the no parameter.

The second command performs application inspection for H.323 signaling connections (h225 parameter). The default port number for the H.323 signaling connection is 1,720—you can change this if you've changed it in your H323 client/server implementation. To disable application inspection for H.323 signaling, precede the command with the no parameter.

NOTE Because of space constraints, I was not able to cover all of the application inspection features for the protocols supported by the PIX. ICMP, XDMCP, ILS, and SQL*Net have been omitted from this chapter. However, if you visit my web site (http://home.cfl.rr.com/dealgroup/), you will find information concerning these protocols and the application inspection feature there.

FURTHER STUDY

Web Sites

For a quick overview of IP-based applications, visit RFC 1180 at www.ietf.org/rfc/rfc1180.txt.

For information on the FTP protocol in RFCs 412, 413, and 430, visit www.ietf.org/rfc.

For information concerning FTP and firewalls, examine RFC 1579 at www.ietf.org/rfc/rfc1579.txt.

For information on the operation of RSH clients, visit linuxcommand.org/man_pages/rsh1.html.

For information on the operation of RSH servers, visit linuxcommand.org/man_pages/rshd8.html.

For information on ICMP, visit www.nic.mil/ftp/rfc/rfc792.txt.

For NAT issues with ICMP, visit RFC 3022 at www.ietf.org/rfc/rfc3022.txt.

For more information on X Window and XDMCP, examine RFC 1013 at www.ietf.org/rfc/rfc1013.txt.

For information on Cisco's SCCP Skinny protocol, visit www.omicron.ch/images/fluke/VOIP.pdf.

For information on setting up connections with SIP, visit www.cisco.com/univercd/cc/td/doc/product/voice/c_ipphon/sip7960/sipadm30/appbcf.htm.

For information on RTSP and its implementation, visit RFC 2326 at www.ietf.org/rfc/rfc2326.txt.

For an excellent explanation of RTSP, visit Real Networks at docs.real.com/docs/proxykit/rtspd.pdf.

For a nice overview of H.323, visit www.tmcnet.com/articles/comsol/0100/0100cc.htm.

For details on the implementation and operation of H.323, visit www.networkcomputing.com/netdesign/1003videoconf.html.

Here is an excellent document on the implementation and operation of H.323: www.sh.lsumc.edu/h323/tech/H323blueprint.pdf.

Here is another excellent document on the implementation and operation of H.323: www.strongsec.com/zhw/KSy_VoIP_2.pdf.

For an overview of H.323 issues with firewalls, visit www.surfnet.nl/innovatie/surfworks/showcase/h4.html.

Here is a good resource on the CU-SeeMe client product: www.fvc.com/software/pdf/whitepaper_firewall.pdf.

Here is a good reference for allowing multimedia traffic through a firewall: www.cyber.ust.hk/handbook4/03b_hb4.html.

For an overview of SQL*Net, visit www.oriolecorp.com/SQLNet.html.

For information on ILS, LDAP, and Microsoft's NetMeeting, visit nsa2.www .conxion.com/support/guides/sd-6.pdf.

Cisco Secure PIX Firewalls

Table of Contents

Stateful Firewall

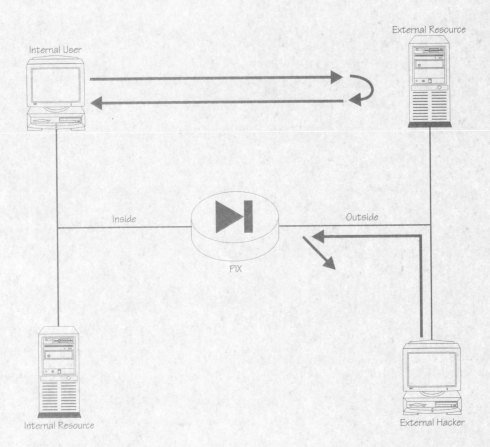

As a stateful firewall, the PIX is aware of the connection information for packet trains. By default, the PIX allows outgoing traffic, and the returning replies to this traffic, for TCP and UDP, as is shown at the top of this figure. All other traffic is treated as non-stateful. Also, the PIX will not allow returning ICMP traffic nor new connections into your network unless you explicitly permit then with conduits or access control lists, as is shown at the bottom of the above figure.

Web Content Filtering

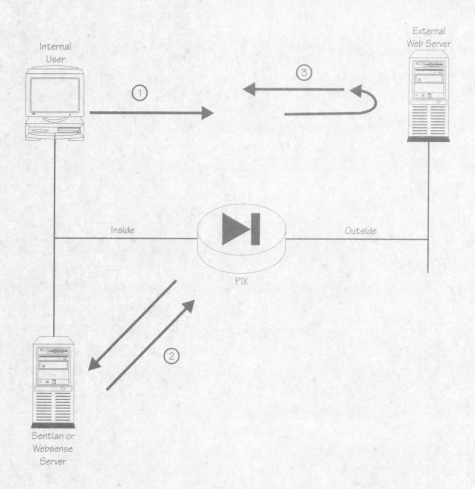

The PIX can filter web content with the help of a third-party web content filtering server, like N2H2's Sentian or Websense's Websense Server. When internal users attempt to download web pages, the PIX verifies web access with the web content filtering server, which returns a reply to the PIX. Based on the server's reply, the PIX will either permit or deny the returning web pages from the external web server.

Protocol Fixup

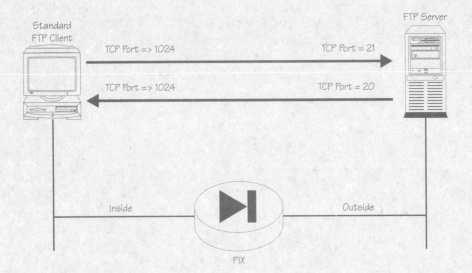

Certain protocols and applications present special problems to firewalls like the PIX. Some applications embed addressing and port information in the payload, some use a non-standard method of setting up connections, some have inherent security problems, and some applications have all three of these problems. Because of this, they have to be handled differently than connections that operate using a standard connection method (such as telnet). Luckily, the PIX's Protocol Fixup Feature allows the PIX to deal with these issues in many of the applications that employ these methods. For example, if it's necessary to have a standard FTP connection for control information and a separate inbound connection for data transfers, the PIX will automatically allow the inbound connection once the outbound connection has been established.

Intrusion Detection System

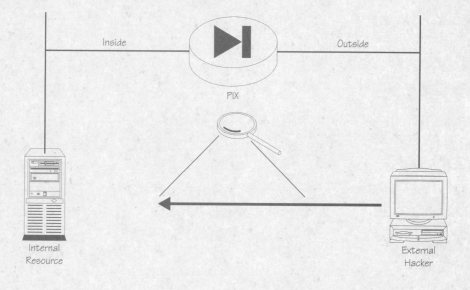

Inside

Outside

PIX

Internal
Resource

External
Hacker

Cisco's PIX firewall has a scaled-down version of an Intrusion Detection System
built into it. The IDS abilities allow the PIX to detect over 50 of the most
common types of attacks. Once an attack is detected, the PIX can log the
attack as well as drop the offending packets or close the connection.

Cut-Through Proxy

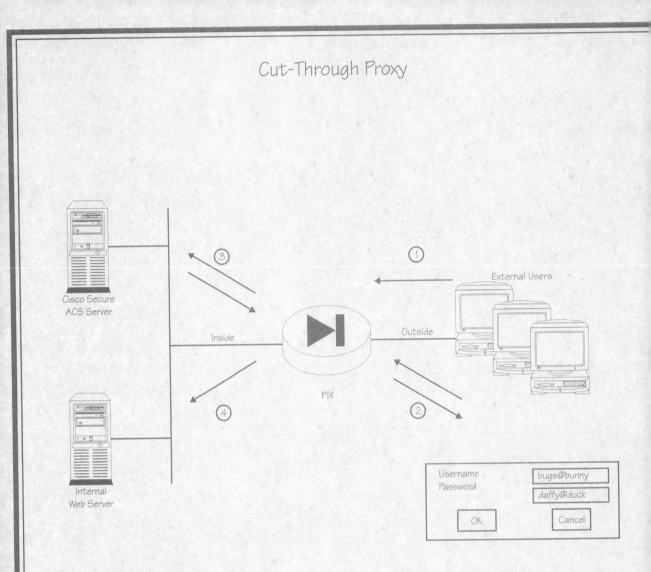

Cut-Through Proxy (CTP) is a security feature on the PIX that performs an additional level of authentication. With Cut-Through Proxy, an external user initiates either a telnet, FTP, or HTTP connection to a resource on the inside of your network. The PIX intercepts the connection request and responds back to the external user with a username and password prompt. The user then fills in this information and forwards it to the PIX. When the PIX receives the account information, it then forwards this information to an internal security server like Cisco Secure ACS. The security server verifies the account information and then tells PIX to either permit or deny the initial connection request. If the connection is permitted, the PIX allows the connection to complete to the internal server.

Failover

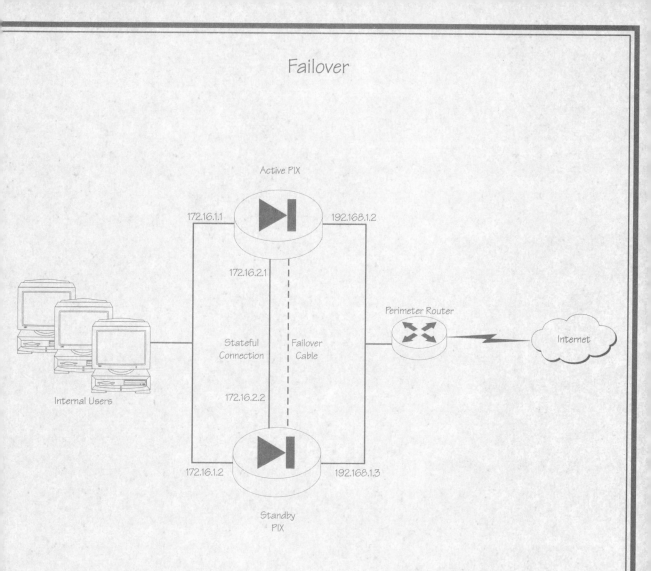

Active PIX

172.16.1.1   192.168.1.2

172.16.2.1

Perimeter Router

Stateful   Failover
Connection   Cable   Internet

Internal Users

172.16.2.2

172.16.1.2   192.168.1.3

Standby
PIX

Starting with the PIX 515 model and higher, Cisco's PIX supports a failover feature. In failover, there is an active PIX which forwards traffic, and a standby PIX that verifies the status of the active PIX. If the active PIX fails, the standby PIX will start forwarding traffic. Cisco supports two modes for failover: non-stateful and stateful. In a non-stateful failover, the active PIX shares its connection information with the standby PIX. Therefore if the active PIX fails, any existing user connections will still be forwarded normally by the standby PIX.

VPNs and IPSec

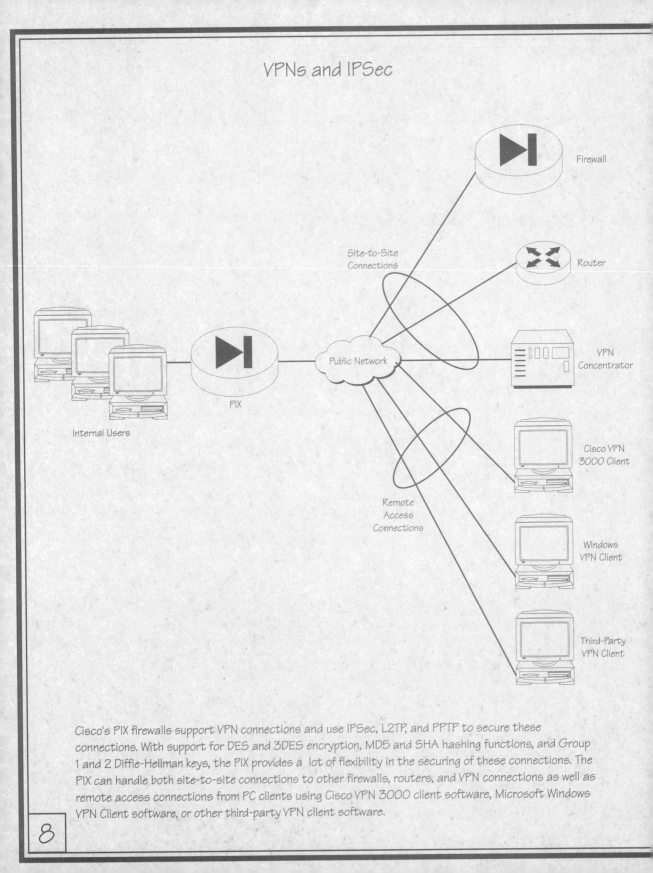

Cisco's PIX firewalls support VPN connections and use IPSec, L2TP, and PPTP to secure these connections. With support for DES and 3DES encryption, MD5 and SHA hashing functions, and Group 1 and 2 Diffie-Hellman keys, the PIX provides a lot of flexibility in the securing of these connections. The PIX can handle both site-to-site connections to other firewalls, routers, and VPN connections as well as remote access connections from PC clients using Cisco VPN 3000 client software, Microsoft Windows VPN Client software, or other third-party VPN client software.

CHAPTER 8

Attack Guards, IDS Features, and Spoofing Protection

In the last chapter, I talked about the application inspection feature of the PIX and how you use it to deal with problematic applications—those that set up additional connections (sometimes with random ports) as well as sometimes embedding addressing information in the data payload of these connections. Actually, the application inspection feature has additional benefits besides those of fixing applications so that the traffic for these applications can pass through the PIX firewall. As you will see from this chapter, the application inspection feature also has security advantages.

To begin this chapter, I will discuss some of the *Attack Guard* features of the FOS—some of these actually use application inspection to enhance the security of your PIX, like SMTP, for instance. I will also discuss the Intrusion Detection System (IDS) abilities of the PIX and how you can use the PIX to detect and thwart hacking attacks against your network. Lastly, I will cover a feature on the PIX that you can use to help protect against spoofing attacks.

ATTACK GUARD FEATURES

As you know, there are many IP applications that have had security issues in the past. Probably the most well known of these applications is Sendmail, which uses SMTP to deliver e-mail between IP devices. This is not to say that Sendmail is a bad program. However, hackers tend to zero in on applications that are widely used, like Sendmail, Microsoft's IIS, and the Apache web server. By spending their time finding security holes in these well-used applications, hackers are expanding their possibilities when they finally do find a weakness.

Imagine if you found a security hole in Sendmail that allowed you to gain administrator access to a server. If there are 100,000 machines on the Internet that use Sendmail, you've just developed an ability to compromise *all* of these machines. Therefore, you can see why hackers spend a lot of time looking for weaknesses and security holes in commonly used applications.

To help deal with some of these threats in commonly used applications and protocols, Cisco has developed a set of Attack Guard features. These features cannot prevent all attacks against your network, but they do deal with some of the most common forms of attacks. Table 8-1 lists the Attack Guard features that Cisco has developed for the PIX. As you can see from the list in Table 8-1, each Guard feature is given a unique name. The following sections cover each of these Guard features.

Attack Guard Name	Description
DNS Guard	Reduces the likelihood of DNS spoofing of DNS server replies.
Mail Guard	Restricts the SMTP commands that can be executed by an SMTP connection.
Flood Guard	Prevents TCP flood attacks, and ensures that there are enough resources to handle AAA functions.
Fragment Guard	Prevents IP fragment flood attacks.

Table 8-1. The PIX's Attack Guard Features

DNS Guard

The DNS Guard feature of the PIX firewall has two main functions:

- It helps reduce the likelihood of a hacker spoofing DNS replies from a DNS server.
- It translates the DNS A-records for the PIX `alias` command.

The next two sections cover these two functions.

Preventing Spoofing of DNS Server Replies

One of the functions of the DNS Guard PIX feature is to allow only a single DNS reply to a user's DNS address resolution request. An example will help explain this Guard feature—I'll use the network shown in Figure 8-1 to help illustrate this example. In Figure 8-1, a user generates a DNS query to resolve a fully-qualified domain name (FQDN) to an IP address. As this passes through the PIX, the PIX adds a connection in its connection table for this user's UDP request. When the DNS server receives the query, it responds back with the translated address.

The issue with this process is that a user device might generate multiple DNS queries if the DNS server is slow in responding, and thus multiple replies might legitimately be expected from the DNS server. If a hacker sees the first DNS reply, it can generate its own set of replies to the user's requests.

Even in a stateful environment where the PIX knows that with a DNS connection there are only two packets—a query and a reply—and the PIX closes the connection after it sees the first reply, a hacker could hijack the remaining DNS connections by spoofing the DNS server's own responses. The PIX, as soon as it sees the spoofed reply, would assume that this is the end of the session and terminate it—thus, the user would never see the legitimate DNS server reply because the PIX prematurely closed the connection.

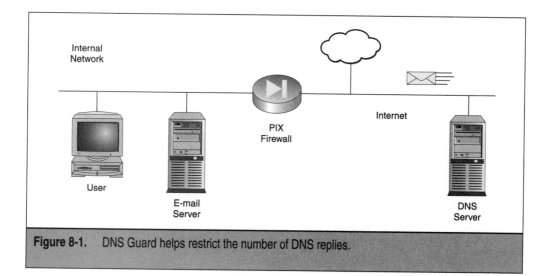

Figure 8-1. DNS Guard helps restrict the number of DNS replies.

These "extra" DNS spoofed replies might cause confusion for the client—should the client use the first "real" response from the DNS server or the other responses which contain a different address?

The DNS Attack Guard feature of the PIX prevents spoofing problems by closing the conduit as soon as it sees the first DNS reply to the user's request. This feature prevents two problems. First, it prevents the session hijacking of the DNS server's additional responses. Second, it prevents DoS (Denial of Service) DNS attacks. If the PIX allowed the temporary UDP conduit to remain in the connection table for a predetermined amount of time, a hacker could flood the user with a whole bunch of spoofed DNS replies.

Translating DNS A-Records for the PIX alias Command

The second function of DNS Guard is to translate DNS A-records for `alias` command configurations. DNS application inspection allows the PIX to handled embedded NATed addresses. And as of FOS 6.2, DNS Guard also supports embedded PATed addresses.

Implementing DNS Guard

DNS Guard for the PIX is implemented by using the application inspection feature that I discussed in Chapter 7. One limitation of DNS Guard is that it is always enabled—there is no command to disable it.

NOTE   DNS Guard is always enabled—you cannot disable it.

Mail Guard

Sendmail uses the Simple Mail Transport Protocol (SMTP) to deliver e-mail between IP devices. Many of these security issues deal with the commands used to implement SMTP and the interaction between SMTP devices. To deal with the weaknesses in SMTP, Cisco has developed the Mail Guard feature for the PIX. Cisco implements the Mail Guard feature with the application inspection feature discussed in the last chapter. With SMTP connections, the PIX examines the SMTP commands executed on TCP port 25 connections (by default).

Application Inspection

With the Mail Guard feature, the PIX examines *all* SMTP commands executed on mail connections. The application inspection process only allows the seven commands defined in section 4.5.1 of RFC 821. These commands are described in Table 8-2. If the PIX sees an SMTP command that is not listed in Table 8-2, the PIX denies the command. Actually, the PIX converts the SMTP command to a NOOP command.

For some e-mail servers that are not fully compliant with RFC 821, like Microsoft's Exchange, when the PIX generates a NOOP for commands other than the seven listed in Table 8-2, the Exchange server will revert to a minimal SMTP connection configuration.

SMTP Command	Description
DATA	Signifies the actual e-mail message that is to be sent.
HELO	Announces the identity of an e-mail device.
MAIL	Starts the e-mail transaction, signifies the beginning of a new e-mail, and indicates who the e-mail message is from in the FROM: field.
NOOP	Indicates that no action is to be taken other than the receiver sending an OK reply.
QUIT	Closes an SMTP connection.
RCPT	Indicates who the e-mail message is to be forwarded to in the TO: field.
RSET	Indicates that the current e-mail transaction is to be aborted.

Table 8-2.   SMTP Commands Allowed by the Mail Guard Feature

One problem with this approach is that you have just lost a lot of the added functionality of Microsoft's Exchange application; however, your e-mail connection is now more secure.

 SECURITY ALERT!   I recommend that you leave the Mail Guard feature enabled unless it causes your e-mail system to not function properly.

For other e-mail servers, the prevention of any SMTP commands, besides the seven listed in Table 8-2, can cause problems—you might not be able to receive your e-mails. In this instance, you will probably have to disable the Mail Guard feature. The down side of this is that you have opened a larger hole in your firewall that a hacker might be able to exploit. ESMTP is an example of a mail protocol where you might have to disable Mail Guard in order for your e-mail server to function properly. ESMTP clients generate a EHLO (slightly different from a HELO) to signify an ESMTP connection; the PIX, obviously, does not allow this. Some of these clients are smart enough to send a HELO message and use SMTP instead of ESMTP; however, many clients assume that the e-mail server is not functioning and drop the connection attempt.

NOTE   Currently there is no ability to add or remove the commands in Table 8-2 for application inspection—it's an all-or-nothing proposition.

Another function of the application inspection process of Mail Guard is that the PIX examines the actual sequence of SMTP commands as well as the format of these commands. If the PIX sees an SMTP command that is not formatted correctly, or with invalid codes or parameters, like a pipe symbol (|), the PIX will either remove or replace the offending information, or generate a NOOP message.

Implementing Mail Guard

As I mentioned earlier, the PIX implements the Mail Guard feature using application inspection. This feature is enabled by default and listens to TCP port 25. To disable Mail Guard or to change the port number, use the `fixup protocol` command:

```
pixfirewall(config)# fixup protocol smtp [port_number[-port_number]
```

To disable the Mail Guard feature, precede the command with the `no` parameter. If your e-mail server is running on a TCP port other than 25, you can add additional ports with this command. Use the `show fixup` command to verify that Mail Guard is enabled.

In addition to ensuring that you have application inspection enabled, you also need to perform the following tasks:

- Create a static translation for your internal e-mail server
- Add an ACL entry for your internal e-mail server
- Allow the IDENT protocol for your e-mail server

To help explain the configuration of Mail Guard, I'll use the network shown previously in Figure 8-1, where the email server has an internal IP address of 10.0.0.2. To allow the e-mail connection, your PIX configuration should look like this:

```
pixfirewall(config)# static (inside, outside) 200.200.200.2
                         10.0.0.2 netmask 255.255.255.255 0 0
pixfirewall(config)# access-list restrict permit tcp
                         any host 200.200.200.2 eq smtp
pixfirewall(config)# access-list restrict permit tcp
                         any host 200.200.200.2 eq 113
pixfirewall(config)# access-group restrict in interface outside
pixfirewall(config)# fixup protocol smtp 25
```

The `static` command performs address translation for the e-mail server. From the Internet's perspective, the e-mail server has an IP address of 200.200.200.2. Internally, however, it has an address of 10.0.0.2. There are two ACL commands in this configuration. The first ACL command allows e-mail traffic on port 25 to the internal e-mail server, and the second command allows IDENT connections. This command is not necessary in most cases, but some devices still use the obsolete IDENT to verify the identity of a device. If you don't have this ACL entry, some connections may fail, or, in some implementations, the connection process will be very slow—the IDENT will timeout and then the connection will proceed anyway. This ACL, called `restrict`, is then enabled for the external interface of the PIX. The last command enables Mail Guard—this is enabled by default and isn't necessary in your configuration.

TIP   In the case of quite a few applications, like FTP and SMTP, you may have to allow IDENT into your network in order for Internet users to interact with your services. If you are experiencing abnormal delays with the set up of connections, or connections are failing, you will want to use a protocol analyzer to determine if IDENT is the culprit, and, if so, create an ACL statement to allow this traffic.

Flood Guard

There are many DoS (Denial of Service) forms of attacks. One of the most common is to flood a machine with hundreds or thousands of packets. A more ingenious hacker, though, will attempt to disguise their flooding attack by making the packets look like a part of an existing connection. These attacks not only tie up resources on a machine, but also affect your network's bandwidth. Cisco has developed two solutions to deal with flooding in the Flood Guard feature. The first handles TCP SYN flood attacks, and the second ensures that AAA (Authentication, Authorization, and Accounting) functions can still occur on the PIX in times of high traffic loads (unintentional or intentional). The following two sections cover these two aspects of the Flood Guard feature.

Flood Guard for TCP SYN Attacks

A good example of a flood DoS attack is when a hacker pretends to set up a TCP connection to a remote device. TCP uses a three-way handshake to set up a connection, like this:

1. The source sends a SYN to the destination.
2. The destination responds back with a SYN/ACK.
3. The source responds with an ACK.

One weakness in the way TCP handles the three-way handshake is that the destination is expecting the source to send a final ACK. Hackers sometimes exploit this weakness by flooding a service with TCP SYNs, with no thought of completing the connection. These connections are sometimes referred to as *embryonic* connections, or half-open connections. The problem with half-open connections is that they tie up ports and resources on a service (as well as the PIX itself) that cannot be used by legitimate services. Eventually these half-open connections will time out; but in the meantime, they disrupt your level of service.

Configuration of Flood Guard for TCP SYN Flooding   To deal with TCP SYN floods, Cisco had created the Flood Guard feature. Basically, the Flood Guard feature is an extension to the nat and static commands that are used to define your address translation. With these commands, you can optionally limit the maximum number of connections to a resource, as well as the number of embryonic connections.

The syntax of the `nat` and `static` commands is as follows:

```
pixfirewall(config)#  nat [(logical_interface_name)] pool_number
                      local_IP_address [subnet_mask
                      [outside] [dns] [norandomseq]
                      [timeout hh:mm:ss]
                      [maximum_connection_limit
                      [embryonic_connection_limit]]]
pixfirewall(config)#  static [(internal_interface_name, external_interface_name)]
                      global_IP_address local_IP_address
                      [dns] [netmask subnet_mask]
                      [maximum_connections [embryonic_limit]] [norandomseq]
```

The syntax of these commands was discussed in Chapter 6. If you recall, the `nat` command, used in combination with the `global` command, provides address translation abilities from higher to lower security level interfaces. In this situation, you have the ability to limit a flood of TCP SYNs as they *leave* your network. The `static` command provides address translation from lower security level interfaces to higher ones.

Because I thoroughly covered these commands in Chapter 4, I will only focus on the last three parameters of the `nat` command and the two next-to-the-last parameters of the `static` command. The `timeout` parameter specifies for how long an idle connection will remain in the translation table before being removed (used only in the `nat` command). The `maximum_connection_limit` parameter limits the maximum number of connections allowed for the devices listed in the `nat` command for the specified interface. The `embryonic_connection_limit` parameter limits the maximum number of half-open connections allowed for the devices listed in the `nat` command for the specified interface. If you omit these last two parameters, they default to a value of 0, which means that there is no limit, or rather the limit is based on whatever your connection license limit is.

NOTE   Remember that you must be very careful about defining these limits because you could be affecting legitimate traffic for networking devices.

TCP Intercept   In version 5.3 of the FOS, the TCP SYN Flood Guard feature of the PIX was enhanced. When a TCP SYN flood is occurring and the *embryonic_connection* limit has been reached, the PIX does not drop any new incoming connection requests. The problem of dropping any new connection requests is that many of these requests may be legitimate connection setup requests—it doesn't make much sense to drop all TCP connection requests, including the legitimate ones. To deal with this issue, the PIX uses a new feature called TCP Intercept.

Let's look at Figure 8-2 to illustrate the TCP Intercept feature. In this example, an Internet user is trying to access a server that is on an internal segment.

When the PIX receives the incoming TCP connection setup request from the Internet user (Step 1), it checks its maximum and embryonic connection limit. If it has not reached these limits, the connection is allowed to proceed. If the maximum connection

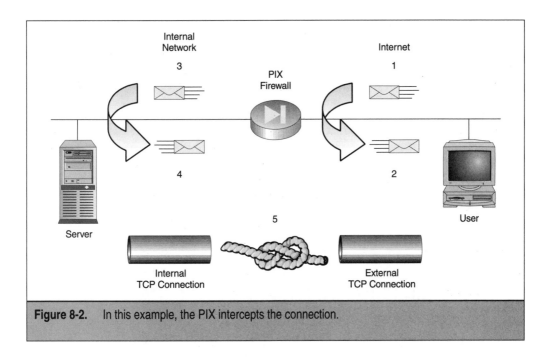

Figure 8-2. In this example, the PIX intercepts the connection.

limit is reached, the connection is dropped. However, if the connection exceeds the embryonic limit, the PIX will implement the TCP Intercept feature.

Instead of forwarding the connection setup request to the inside server, the PIX pretends to be the inside server and completes the three-way handshake with the Internet user (Step 2). If the PIX is not successful in completing the three-way handshake, no harm is done to the inside server. If the three-way handshake is successful, though, the PIX will then establish a second TCP connection to the inside server (Steps 3 and 4). Once this second TCP connection is built, the PIX will then bind the two separate connections into a single logical connection, as is shown in Step 5.

From the Internet user's perspective and the inside server's perspective, the PIX is transparent—they really think they are setting up a connection between the real end points. One limitation of TCP Intercept is that, unfortunately, any TCP parameters that are negotiated with the Internet user to the PIX and the server to the PIX are not shared between the two connections. Using the TCP Intercept feature does not require any special configuration on your part—you just need FOS 5.3 on your PIX and to define your embryonic limits for your `static` and `nat` commands.

Network and Broadcast Addresses   Another Flood Guard feature of the PIX is that if a destination address for a translation is either a network number or a broadcast address (like a directed broadcast), the PIX does not forward it. The PIX uses the subnet mask in the `static` command to determine these two addresses. When the PIX receives an inbound packet, it compares the destination address to the address(es) and subnet mask of each `static` command. If the PIX determines that the destination address is not a host address, but either a network number or directed broadcast, the PIX drops this packet. This feature is always enabled and there is no mechanism to disable it.

Configuration Example with Static Translation   Let's look at a simple example by setting limits with the `static` command. I'll build upon the example in Figure 8-1, which I covered previously in this chapter. Here is the updated version of the syntax for the `static` command:

```
pixfirewall(config)# static (inside, outside) 200.200.200.2
                     10.0.0.2 netmask 255.255.255.255 100 75
```

In this example, the e-mail server has a maximum connection limit of 100—anything above this will be dropped by the PIX. Therefore, it is very important that you set this number to a value somewhat higher than the maximum number of connections that you would ever expect to connect to the e-mail server at one time. The embryonic limit is set to 75 connections. If this PIX was running version 5.1, and the embryonic limit was reached, no new connections would be allowed until the embryonic limit dropped below 75. If this PIX was running version 5.3, once the connection limit reached 75, the PIX would use the TCP Intercept feature in setting up the connections between itself and the requesting user to verify that the connection is legitimate.

Flood Guard for AAA

The second function of the Flood Guard feature of the PIX is to ensure that user authentication resources on the PIX itself do not become exhausted, thereby creating a successful DoS attack against access to the PIX itself. Most of the authentication functions of the PIX deal with AAA, which I discuss in Chapter 11. Cisco sometimes refers to this second function of Flood Guard as *Flood Defender*.

   When connection limits on the PIX are almost exhausted, the PIX can use the Flood Guard feature to start removing these connections to allow authentication functions to occur. It does this by dropping the following TCP connections (in the specified state) in the given order:

1. Timewait
2. FINwait
3. Embryonic
4. Idle

This feature is enabled, by default. To enable it or disable it, use this command:

```
pixfirewall(config)# floodguard enable|disable
```

You can also disable Flood Guard with the `clear floodguard` command. To see the status of Flood Guard, use the `show floodguard` command.

Fragmentation Guard

Another form of DoS attack that hackers commonly use is to flood a service with hundreds or thousands of IP fragments. Unskilled hackers send a flood of fragments that are basically garbage—they cannot be reassembled into a complete packet. More skilled hackers ensure that the fragments do add up to a complete packet, but the packet itself is not meant to accomplish anything. And the most ingenious of hackers embed an attack within another attack—they might use fragments to create a DoS attack, and once the fragments are reassembled, they'll use the completed packet to implement another form of an attack.

Overview of Fragmentation Guard

The Fragmentation Guard feature of the PIX firewall is used to protect you against fragment attacks. Cisco followed the RFC 1858 recommendations for dealing with IP fragment attacks when they developed Fragmentation Guard. Fragmentation Guard only allows fragments from an existing IP connection. Within an existing connection, if a packet is fragmented, the PIX expects to receive the first fragment first— if it receives a fragment from the middle of the packet first, it drops these partial packets. To reduce fragmentation attacks, the PIX allows 100 (cannot be changed) full IP fragmented packets per second per internal destination.

Of course, there are legitimate reasons to have a lot of fragments—if the source or destination is located on different media types, fragmentation can occur. For instance, if the source is on a FDDI or token ring segment and the destination is on an Ethernet segment, most of the packets sent from the source to the destination have to be fragmented. In this instance, Fragmentation Guard could be causing the PIX to drop legitimate fragments. If you run into this situation, you should disable Fragmentation Guard.

Certain applications also create fragments. One application that might create a lot of fragmented packets is Network File System (NFS), which is a popular application in Unix to remotely share file systems (disk space).

Another issue that can cause problems with your network is that the PIX drops fragments for a packet if the PIX does not see the first fragment first, followed by the rest of the fragments that make up a completed packet. Some operating systems, like Linux, perform fragmentation by sending out the last fragment of the packet first and the first fragment last. The PIX drops all of these fragments because it doesn't see the very first fragment of the packet at the beginning of the packet train. Also, there might be a load balancing solution between the source and destination that splits the fragments across multiple paths to the destination, which could cause the first fragment of the packet to arrive after other fragments. If you are having problems with these issues, disable the Fragmentation Guard feature.

Configuring Fragmentation Guard

Unlike the other Guard features, Fragmentation Guard is disabled by default. To enable Fragmentation guard, use the `sysopt` command:

```
pixfirewall(config)#  sysopt security fragguard
```

As you can see, you cannot specify a limit of the fragments per packet, per time period, or per destination or source. Likewise, you cannot selectively enable a specific interface on the PIX—it's an all-or-nothing proposition. To disable Fragmentation Guard, precede the command with the no parameter. To determine whether or not Fragmentation Guard is enabled, use the show sysopt command.

NOTE   For more information on dealing with fragments on your PIX firewall, visit my web site at http://home.cfl.rr.com/dealgroup/.

INTRUSION DETECTION SYSTEM (IDS)

The second half of this chapter is dedicated to the IDS abilities of Cisco's PIX firewall. The first thing that you should realize is that the PIX does not contain a full-blown implementation of an IDS appliance. The PIX can detect over 50 different attacks, whereas many IDS appliances can detect hundreds of different kinds of attacks. As an example, Cisco's IDS hardware sensors, the 4210, 4230, 4250, and the IDS Module for the Catalyst 6000 series switches, can detect more than 600 different kinds of attacks. Therefore, the PIX IDS solution is fine for small office environments, but an IDS appliance should be used in large networks to detect networking attacks.

SECURITY ALERT!   The IDS solution implemented in the PIX is not a full-blown IDS implementation—it can only detect a small number of common network threats. Therefore, in larger networks, the PIX should be used in tandem with a full-fledged IDS system, like Cisco's IDS hardware sensors, for intrusion detection.

Definition of IDS

Before I begin discussing the IDS capabilities of the PIX and its configuration, I will first discuss some of the basics of IDS. In its simplest form, IDS is the ability to detect network threats and attacks. These attacks include not just those attacks that originate from the Internet and are directed at your network, but also those from internal sources.

SECURITY ALERT!   Many studies have found that, on average, about 60 percent of attacks occur from within a company's network.

There are two basic methods of developing an IDS solution: Profile-based and signature-based. Each of these has its own strengths as well as weaknesses. The following two sections cover both of these implementations.

Profile-Based IDS Implementations

In an IDS solution that uses profiles, the IDS device examines traffic activity on a segment and then compares this to what is considered normal. The word *normal*, in this instance, is a relative term. In the case of an IDS solution, *normal* is defined as the kinds and amounts of traffic that are typical for a given segment. This requires you to create traffic profiles for each segment that you wish to monitor and then incorporate these profiles into your IDS solution. Your IDS solution then compares actual traffic patterns to its loaded profiles and looks for a match—if it doesn't find a match, it considers this an anomaly and flags an alarm, indicating that the current traffic pattern might be a possible attack.

Sometimes profile-based IDS implementations are called *anomaly detection* systems because they are constantly looking for anomalies in the traffic patterns. One problem with profile-based systems is that they tend to generate a large number of false readings. In other words, the IDS solution might generate an alarm for traffic that is an anomaly, but isn't necessarily an attack.

For example, suppose that every day at 8:00 A.M. there is a spike in your traffic while users access a database application. Typically this spike levels out at about 9:00 and then declines around 11:30, as users get ready to go to lunch. However, there might be a situation where one day there is a company meeting from 8:00 to 9:00, and when the users return to their desks and access the database application, there is a huge spike in traffic. The IDS sees this spike, determines that it is not occurring between 8:00 and 9:00, and thus triggers an alarm.

Another problem with profile-based IDS solutions is that traffic patterns typically change over time, thus requiring you to continually resample your traffic patterns to ensure that you have appropriate profiles for your IDS solution. This can be a time-consuming process because you will need a profile for various periods of the day and various days of the week. Because of these issues, many IDS solutions do not use profiles.

Signature-Based IDS Implementations

The most popular type of IDS implementation are the ones that use signatures. With this type of IDS implementation, the IDS solution compares packets from a network segment to signatures, where a signature defines what is considered an attack against the network. This type of implementation is commonly called *misuse detection*. It has a smaller number of false readings than profile-based implementations. The reason for this is that most network attacks are very systematic and thus more easily detected than the profiles-based attacks. Where profiles look for *anomalies* in traffic patterns, signature-based IDS implementations compare packets to a signature, which is basically a template. The more signatures that your IDS solution has, the more attacks it can detect.

One down side of signature-based solutions is that as new types of network attacks are invented by hackers, your signature-based IDS solution might not be able to detect them. You might have to wait for your IDS vendor to develop a signature that can detect the new form of attack. With profile-based systems, a deviation, whether it is a new hacker trick or an old hacker exploit, can be detected with the same profile implementation.

From an administrator's perspective, however, it is much easier to maintain a signature-based implementation than a profile-based system. Profile-based systems, as I mentioned in the last section, require a lot of sampling and resampling to maintain current and realistic profiles. With signature-based systems, you only need to add signatures as new attacks are discovered.

Event Horizon

As you saw in the last section, each IDS implementation—profile-based and signature-based—has its own unique set of problems. They do share one common problem related to a process called an *event horizon*. An event horizon is the amount of time that it takes to detect an attack. Some types of attacks employed by hackers can be stretched out over a period of time—the longer the time period, the more difficult it is to detect the attack. One of the reasons for this is that the IDS solution has to capture the traffic over the entire period of the attack in order to determine if an attack is occurring.

For example, something like a network scan or port sweep on a network segment that takes place over a few seconds is very easy to detect with a signature-based IDS implementation. The IDS solution only needs to buffer up a small number of packets, compare these packets to its list of signatures, and trigger an alarm if a match is found. However, imagine an ingenious hacker that employs the same attack, but spreads out the sweep over three or four hours. Detecting this kind of probe is almost impossible because the IDS solution doesn't have the resources to keep all of the packets over this period as well as the horsepower to process them all in a realistic time frame.

As you can see, neither solution is an exact science. A good IDS solution should be able to detect most forms of attacks and trigger a small number of false positives. Because an IDS solution can't detect every kind of threat or attack, it is only common sense that an IDS solution be integrated into a large security design—the IDS solution is just one component in your overall security design. Your security design will contain many components, including hardened routers, IDS devices, VPNs, and, of course, firewalls.

 SECURITY ALERT!   IDS implementations are not an exact science—they are a best guess about a threat or attack against a network.

IDS Signatures

The PIX, like Cisco's routers with IDS abilities and Cisco's IDS hardware appliances, is based on a signature implementation. As I mentioned, a signature is a template containing parameters that tell an IDS solution what to look for in a stream of packets. When a match is found between actual traffic and a signature, a response is triggered. This response can be something as simple as generating an alarm, or something as advanced as having the IDS solution configure dynamic ACL entries on perimeter routers and firewalls to block offending traffic. Signatures are the heart of a signature-based IDS solution—a good set of IDS signatures should be flexible enough to detect known attacks and, in some cases, new attacks as they are developed by hackers.

Signatures can be grouped into two general classes: *Attack* and *informational* signatures. Attack signatures indicate that an attack is occurring against your network and its resources. Informational signatures don't necessarily indicate an attack. They are typically used to gather information about traffic flowing through your network as well as validating certain kinds of attacks. Each of these signature classes is broken into further subclasses.

Signature Implementations

The design of signatures involves two components—implementations and structures. There are two implementation methods for signatures: *Context* and *content*. With a context implementation, a signature only looks at the packet header of captured packets for matches—it does not look in the actual packet contents (data payload) for information. This information includes the following items in an IP packet header:

- IP source and destination addresses
- IP protocol field
- IP options
- IP fragment parameters
- IP, TCP, and UDP checksums
- TCP and UDP port numbers
- TCP flags

With a content implementation, however, a signature looks at the data payload for information that indicates an attack. As an example, a content signature might look at the SMTP commands in an e-mail transfer, or the FTP commands executed by a user, as well as the files that the user is trying to access.

Signature Structures

The structure of a signature determines how many packets the IDS solution has to examine for a particular signature when looking for network attacks. There are two basic signature structures: *Atomic* and *composite*.

An atomic structure, as its name implies, looks at a single packet for a match on a signature. For an IDS solution, this kind of comparison process is very easy to implement because after examining each packet, it can be ignored and the next packet examined. An example of an atomic structure would be a signature that looks for both the SYN and FIN flags set in a TCP segment header. Obviously this is an invalid combination of TCP flags in the TCP header; however, with an atomic structured signature, each IP packet is examined for the combination of these flags; if one is found, a response is triggered.

A composite structure for a signature has the IDS solution examine a range of packets for a match. As an example, a hacker might perform a sweep of port 25 on every device on a segment, where this sweep is contained in separate packets—one for each destination. The IDS solution would have to examine multiple packets to determine that this is a port sweep of multiple machines versus a port probe of one specific machine. As another example, a hacker might create overlapping fragments, so that when the destination tries to reassemble them, it gets error messages. A signature to detect this kind of an attack would have to examine multiple fragmented packets to determine if the fragments had overlapping offsets.

Signature Classes

When a vendor develops signatures, they will typically group them together into classes, where each class represents a type of access or attack against a network. This helps administrators determine the kind of threat against their network. There are four general classes:

- Informational
- Reconnaissance
- Access
- DoS

Informational classes of signatures, often referred to as *benign* signatures, are used to trigger on normal network activity like ICMP echo requests and TCP and UDP connection requests. These signatures are not typically used to detect a networking attack, but to give you information about how resources are being used in your network. For example, you might have a DMZ with a handful of servers on it, where you have disabled telnet on each of these devices. Therefore, if someone tries to telnet to them, this gives you some information about a possible probe against your network. Of course, it could be one of your administrators who has forgotten that telnet has been disabled.

Reconnaissance classes of signatures are rules that trigger an alarm when someone is trying to learn information about your network—including your network topology and any possible weaknesses in your networking equipment. Reconnaissance attacks include network and port scans, and DNS queries.

Access classes of signatures are rules that trigger an alarm when someone attempts to gain unauthorized access to your networking equipment, attempts to increase the privileges of an account on a resource, or attempts to access protected data. There are literally hundreds of attacks that are included under this category class. One example of an access attack is someone using Back Orifice to remotely control a Microsoft Windows-based machine. Another example of an access attack is a user trying to download a password file to run a password-cracking utility on it to discover the passwords for the accounts on a particular resource.

DoS classes of signatures are rules that trigger an alarm when a certain type of traffic activity or pattern is used to purposefully reduce your current level of service for a resource, or to cause a resource to crash. I've already discussed one form of an IDS attack in this chapter: TCP SYN floods. Just like access attacks, there are hundreds of these kinds of attacks that hackers can exploit in order to disrupt services or compromise the security of your network. One of my favorite DoS attacks is the Ping of Death—with a single mighty ping, a hacker might be able to crash your system.

Given this list of signature classes, only three really deal with network threats or attacks: reconnaissance, access, and DoS. The PIX's IDS implementation deals with just these three, whereas Cisco's hardware IDS appliances, like the 4210 and 4230, deal with all four classes.

Signature Categories and Types

Cisco uses the same signatures implementation across all of their platforms. Therefore, the signature used on a 4210 to detect TCP SYN floods is the same signature used on the PIX to detect the same kind of DoS attack. Of course, each Cisco product doesn't necessarily have all of the signatures that Cisco has developed. As I mentioned earlier, the PIX has over 50 signatures, whereas Cisco's IDS hardware appliances, like the 4210, have over 600. However, by using the same nomenclature and implementation across all of their products, Cisco has simplified the learning process when dealing with signatures.

Signature Categories

To differentiate one signature from another, Cisco gives each signature a unique number. To simplify matters, Cisco groups like signatures together by giving them numbers from the same range. Numbers from 1,000 to 19,999 are used for Cisco defined signatures and 20,000 to 50,000 are used for user-defined signatures. Table 8-3 lists the eight predefined categories of Cisco's signatures.

Signature Types

Cisco has taken the eight categories listed in the previous section and grouped them together into a more general set of categories, or what Cisco refers to as *signature types*. Cisco has four basic types of signatures:

- **General** General signatures include signatures from the following categories: 1,000, 2,000, 3,000, 4,000, 5,000, and 6,000. These are signatures that are used to detect IP, TCP, UDP, and ICMP attacks.

Signature Numbers	Explanation
1,000–1,999	Used to detect threats using IP packet header information, including IP options, IP fragments, and bad or invalid IP packets
2,000–2,999	Used to detect threats that use the ICMP protocol, like ping sweeps and ICMP traffic records
3,000–3,999	Used to detect threats that use the TCP protocol, like TCP host sweeps, TCP port scans, TCP SYN floods, TCP traffic records, FTP attacks, e-mail attacks, NetBIOS attacks, legacy web attacks, TCP session hijacking, and TCP application access
4,000–4,999	Used to detect threats that use the UDP protocol, like UDP host sweeps, UDP port scans, UDP traffic records, and UDP application access
5,000–5,999	Used to detect threats that use the HTTP protocol and are specific to web browsers and web servers
6,000–6,999	Used to detect threats that use a combination of protocols and methods, like a Distributed DoS (DDoS) attack, authentication failures, RPC attacks, and DNS attacks
8,000–8,999	Used to detect threats that look for a match in a data pattern (called a string) in the data payload of TCP connections
10,000–19,999	Used to detect ACL violations on IOS-based routers and PIX firewalls

Table 8-3.   The Eight Predefined Categories for Signatures

- **Connection** Connection signatures include signatures from the 3,000 and 4,000 categories of signatures. These signatures are used to detect TCP and UDP connections to specific port numbers, like a telnet or FTP connection to port 23 or 21 respectively.

- **String** String signatures include signatures from the 8,000 category of signatures. These signatures look for matches on specific strings in a user's TCP payload, like the words "password" or "delete all files".

- **ACL** ACL signatures include signatures from the 10,000 category of signatures. These signatures are triggered when an ACL violation occurs (a match on a `deny` statement) on a Cisco IOS-based router or PIX firewall with ACLs configured.

NOTE For a list of all of the signatures that the PIX supports, visit my web site at http://home.cfl.rr.com/dealgroup/.

The PIX and IDS

The PIX is not a full-blown IDS solution, but it does have the ability to detect many of the more common network threats and attacks. Cisco's high-end IDS solutions, like the 4210, 4230, 4250, and IDS Module (IDSM) for the Catalyst 6000 switches can interoperate with each other and can log messages to Cisco Secure Policy Manager (CSPM). The interaction with these devices is done with a Cisco proprietary protocol called PostOffice. Any communications between two IDS sensors or an IDS sensor and CSPM use the PostOffice protocol. CSPM is Cisco's management station that allows you to customize signatures, apply your policy rules, and view the alarms generated by the IDS sensors.

One limitation of the PIX is that it does not support the PostOffice protocol, and therefore messages generated by the PIX cannot be processed by CSPM. This makes managing your IDS solution more difficult. CSPM can take all of the alarms from all of the IDS hardware sensors like the 4210 and IDSM and centralize the viewing and reporting of these events.

This limitation of the PIX should not preclude you from making use of its IDS abilities, however. When a match occurs with a signature, the PIX can take one (or more) of the following actions:

- Do nothing
- Generate an alert (which can be logged to a syslog server)
- Terminate the connection, if it is still open
- Drop the packet

You have the ability to control what occurs on the PIX when a match against a signature occurs. The following sections discuss the configuration of IDS on the PIX firewall.

Configuring IDS on your PIX Firewall

As I mentioned in the previous section, the PIX can take various actions based on a match on a signature. There are two sets of policies that you can specify: global and specific. Policies are broken into two categories: attack signatures and informational signatures. You can specify separate policy actions for each set of signatures. Policies are then applied to an interface—the PIX uses these policies to detect attacks and to apply an action to take when there is a match on a specific signature. The following sections cover the configuration and activation of IDS policies on your PIX.

Configuring Your Global Policies

You can specify global policies for these actions for every signature. The PIX uses specific policies whenever possible; if a specific policy doesn't define what action to take, the global policy is used instead. To set your global policies, use the `ip audit` command:

```
pixfirewall(config)#  ip audit info|attack action [alarm] [drop] [reset]
```

The PIX allows you to separate your global policies for informational and attack signatures. When you use the `ip audit` command, you must specify which set of signatures you are setting your global policies for. You can specify one of three actions:

- `alarm`   Generates a syslog message to a syslog server.
- `drop`   Drops the packet(s).
- `reset`   Closes the connection if it is open.

The default action for all signatures is to generate an alarm when there is a match on traffic passing through the PIX. You can specify multiple actions for the PIX to take when a corresponding match is found.

You can undo your configuration by preceding the command with the no parameter. You can reset your IDS global policies back to their defaults by using the `clear ip audit` command. To view your global policies, use the `show ip audit attack` and `show ip audit info` commands.

Configuring Attack and Information Policies

Besides your global IDS policies, you can create individual, or specific, policies for actions to take on a signature match. To create an individual policy, use this command:

```
pixfirewall(config)#  ip audit name policy_name attack|info
                         [action [alarm] [drop] [reset]]
```

The *policy_name* parameter is used to group your policy statements together. This name must be unique among all of your policies. You might want to have different policies for different interfaces. In most situations, however, you'll create a single policy and use this for all external traffic coming into your PIX.

Like your global policies, you can specify separate actions for attack and informational signatures, and you can specify up to three actions for each type—`alarm`, `drop`, and `reset`. If you don't specify the `action` parameter, this individual policy will inherit the rules of the global policy.

You can undo your configuration by preceding the command with the `no` parameter. You can delete your IDS specific policies by using the `clear ip audit name` *policy_name* command. To view your specific policies, use the `show ip audit name` command.

Excluding IDS Signatures

By default, the PIX looks for a match on all signatures included in the FOS version. You can, however, exclude signatures—this limits your IDS detection abilities, but can also reduce the number of false alarms. To exclude a signature, use this command:

```
pixfirewall(config)#  [no] ip audit signature signature_number disable
```

To add a signature back into the PIX's detection, use the `ip audit signature` command preceded by the `no` parameter. To verify which signatures have been disabled, use the `show ip audit signature` command.

When a match on a signature occurs on the PIX, and the signature is enabled, the PIX creates a syslog message, in most instances. The format of the syslog message is like this:

```
%PIX-4-4000nn IDS:signature_number signature_message from IP_address to
                        IP_address on interface interface_name
```

All of the PIX's signature messages will begin with `%PIX-4-4000`. The *nn* following the 4000 is the specific syslog message number for the signature match. The *signature_number* is the actual signature number, while the *signature_message* is a description of the actual signature. Following this are the source and destination IP addresses involved with the connection as well as the interface of the PIX of the inbound connection.

Here is a simple example of a syslog message generated from a Snork attack:

```
pixfirewall#
%PIX-4-400032 IDS:4051 UDP Snork attack from 130.181.92.2 to 200.200.200.5
                        on interface outside
pixfirewall#
```

In this example, a UDP Snork attack was detected on the *outside* interface. This attack was originated from 130.181.92.2 and aimed at 200.200.200.5.

Activating Your IDS Policies

To activate an IDS policy, you must apply it to an interface of the PIX, like this:

```
pixfirewall(config)#  ip audit interface name_of_interface policy_name
```

With the `ip audit interface` command, you must specify the logical PIX interface name followed by the name of your auditing policy. When you activate a policy for an interface, the PIX audits both inbound and outbound traffic on that interface.

To remove the policy from your PIX's interface, precede the command with the `no` parameter. To see which IDS policies are activated for the interfaces of your PIX, use the `show ip audit interface` command.

PIX IDS Example

To help illustrate the use of IDS on the PIX, let's go through an example. I'll use the network shown in Figure 8-3. In this example, I will just focus on the IDS commands for the PIX. The administrator of this network has decided that for informational signatures, the PIX should only log a message on a match; but for attack signatures, the PIX should not only log a message, but also reset the connection, if one exists. Also, the following signatures should be disabled: 2000, 2001, 2004, 2005, and 2150. The IDS policy should be activated for the external interface of the PIX.

The code for this configuration is shown here:

```
pixfirewall(config)#  ip audit signature 2000 disable
pixfirewall(config)#  ip audit signature 2001 disable
pixfirewall(config)#  ip audit signature 2004 disable
pixfirewall(config)#  ip audit signature 2005 disable
pixfirewall(config)#  ip audit signature 2150 disable
pixfirewall(config)#
pixfirewall(config)#  ip audit name checkit info
pixfirewall(config)#  ip audit name checkit attack action alarm reset
pixfirewall(config)#  ip audit interface outside checkit
```

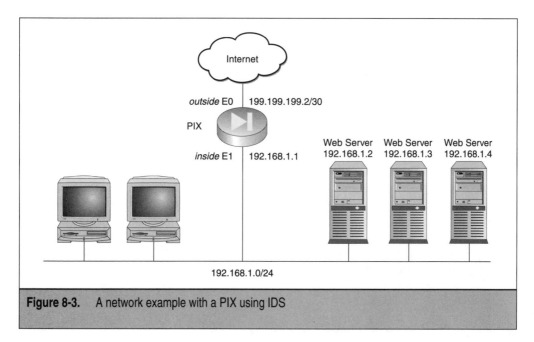

Figure 8-3.   A network example with a PIX using IDS

In this example, the `ip audit signature` commands disable the signatures in our IDS policy criteria. The first `ip audit name` command specifies that you want to examine traffic for informational attacks, and because no action is specified, it inherits the action from the global policy—this defaults to `alarm`. The second `ip audit name` command is for attack signatures and specifies two actions—generate an alarm and reset a connection—when a match occurs. These two policies are grouped together by the name `checkit`. The IDS policies are then activated on the *outside* interface with the `ip audit interface` command.

SPOOFING PROTECTION

A favorite method that hackers like to use is *masquerading*. This is where the hacker changes the source IP address in the packet to a different address. In the IP world, this process is referred to as *IP spoofing*.

A good example of IP Spoofing is an ICMP attack called the *Smurf* attack, named after the popular 1980s cartoon show. In the Smurf attack, the hacker sends an ICMP packet to a device on the inside of your network and changes the source address to a device that hacker wants to attack—this is typically another machine that is also located on the inside of your network. Through this process, when the ICMP packet arrives at the internal destination inside a network, the device responds not to the hacker, but to another machine specified by the hacker's doctored source address. From the perspective of the two internal devices, the communication looks like it is occurring locally.

Spoofing Example

Let's look at a simple example to explain spoofing. I'll use the network shown in Figure 8-4 to illustrate the example. To simplify the explanation, I'll assume that no address translation is necessary for the connections. In Figure 8-4, the hacker (199.199.199.10) creates an ICMP echo request packet with a destination address of 200.1.1.3 and a source address of 200.1.1.2 (Step 1). This is obviously a spoofed packet, because the hacker doesn't have a source address of 200.1.1.2. When the packet reaches the firewall, it allows the connection to the internal e-mail server. The e-mail server receives the packet, and responds back with an echo reply, as is shown in Step 2. Notice that the response is sent to the source address, 200.1.1.2, which is the web server. A hacker enjoys performing this kind of an attack since it becomes more difficult to pinpoint the actual culprit. In this situation, the hacker would flood one machine with a flood of packets, which would be redirected to another machine, thus creating a DoS situation against two devices.

In this example, the simplest solution to employ is to ensure that your firewall filters any inbound traffic that has a source address internal to your network. Of course, an ingenious hacker would not use a source and destination address from the same network—he would use a destination address from a different ISP's network when attacking one of your internal devices.

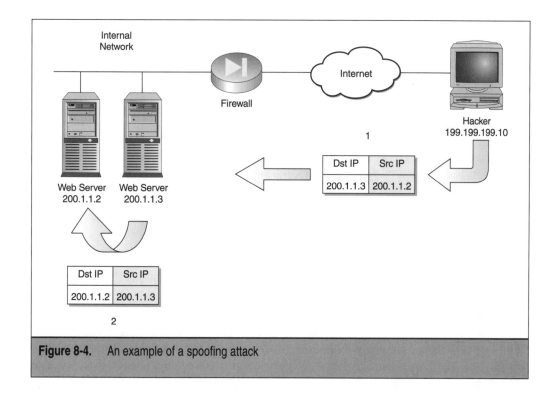

Figure 8-4.   An example of a spoofing attack

 SECURITY ALERT!   Make sure that you always filter traffic on your PIX if the inbound packets from the outside world have a source IP address that is internal to your network.

Spoofing Protection Feature of the PIX

Cisco has developed a feature for the PIX firewall to somewhat limit spoofing attacks. Cisco's anti-spoofing feature performs a route lookup on the source address. Typically, route lookups occur for the destination address. However, with a source address route lookup, the PIX is determining if there is a route available for the source address. This process of doing a route lookup on a source address is commonly referred to as *reverse path forwarding*. If there is no route available, the PIX drops the packet. This process is described in RFC 2267 to help defeat IP spoofing attacks.

Cisco supports both inbound and outbound route lookups on source IP addresses. The PIX configuration requires that a default route be configured with the `route` command on the PIX that points to the *outside* interface. For outbound traffic, the PIX checks the source IP addresses in the packets against the PIX's routing table. Because of this function, you will need to define every internal network with a static route, using the `route` command. If you don't, the PIX will assume that the source is on the outside of the network and that therefore someone on the inside is executing a masquerading attack. Of course, this is just a case of a misconfiguration—if you don't tell the PIX the location, it always assumes that the destination is off of the *outside* interface.

For inbound traffic, the PIX checks the source IP addresses in the packets to verify that there is route to the source. Again, the PIX checks its local routing table to determine the location of the source (inside or outside). The main limitation of the anti-spoofing feature is that it is mainly used to detect spoofing attacks that are originating from the *inside* of your network. For example, with the network and example shown in Figure 8-6, the PIX would be able to determine that this was a spoofing attack because 200.1.1.0/24 is on the inside of the network, but the packet coming into the network shows this source located on the outside of the network. However, an ingenious hacker will probably not use one of your addresses when using spoofing—instead, they'll use an address from a different ISP's network. Because this matches the default route on the PIX, the PIX will assume that this is not a spoofing attack.

 SECURITY ALERT! The spoofing feature of the PIX is not foolproof—it cannot detect all types of spoofing attacks.

Cisco's anti-spoofing feature doesn't necessarily check all packets, because this would be very process-intensive. Therefore, for TCP and UDP sessions, only the first, or initial, packet in the connection has the reverse route lookup done on it; all subsequent packets associated with the connection do not have the lookup done on them. For ICMP packets, however, the PIX performs a lookup for each packet. Remember that this lookup is local to the PIX—the PIX checks its own routing table to determine the location of the source.

Configuring Spoofing Protection

To set up reverse path forwarding IP spoofing protection on your PIX firewall, use the `ip verify reverse-path interface` command. By default, this feature is disabled on the PIX and requires manual activation. The syntax of the command for this feature is:

```
pixfirewall(config)# ip verify reverse-path interface interface_name
```

This command enables reverse path forwarding lookups in both the inbound and outbound directions of the specified interface. Preface the command with the no parameter to disable anti-spoofing for an interface. You can also use the `clear ip verify reverse-path interface` command to disable anti-spoofing for an interface. To completely disable anti-spoofing on your PIX, use the `clear ip verify` command.

NOTE Remember that for anti-spoofing to function correctly, you need to create a static route with the PIX `route` command for each internal route and have a default route pointing to the PIX's outside interface.

Once you have configured anti-spoofing on your PIX, you can verify your configuration and operation with either one of the two following commands:

```
pixfirewall(config)#  show ip verify [reverse-path [interface interface_name]]
pixfirewall(config)#  show ip verify statistics
```

The show ip verify command lists the PIX commands in your anti-spoofing configuration. The show ip verify statistics command displays the number of packets dropped because of detected spoofed source addresses. Here is an example of this command:

```
pixfirewall(config)#  show ip verify statistics

interface outside: 35 unicast rpf drops
interface inside: 1 unicast rpf drops
```

You can clear the statistics from the show ip verify statistics command by using the clear ip verify statistics command.

Spoofing Protection Configuration Example

To help illustrate the use of Cisco's spoofing protection feature, I'll use the network shown in Figure 8-5. In this example, I'll enable spoofing protection for both the *inside* and *outside* interfaces of the PIX.

The following is the configuration for the PIX:

```
pixfirewall(config)#  ip address outside 192.168.1.1 255.255.255.0
pixfirewall(config)#  ip address inside 192.168.2.1 255.255.255.0
pixfirewall(config)#  route outside 0.0.0.0 0.0.0.0 192.168.1.2 1
pixfirewall(config)#  route inside  192.168.3.0 255.255.255.0 192.168.2.2 1
pixfirewall(config)#  route inside  192.168.4.0 255.255.255.0 192.168.2.2 1
pixfirewall(config)#
pixfirewall(config)#  global (outside) 1 200.200.200.0 netmask 255.255.255.0
pixfirewall(config)#  nat (inside) 1 0 0
pixfirewall(config)#
pixfirewall(config)#  ip verify reverse-path interface outside
pixfirewall(config)#  ip verify reverse-path interface inside
```

There are two important things to point out in this example configuration. First, notice that there are two specific static routes and the default route. Remember that you don't need to specify a route for a directly connected interface (networks 192.168.1.0/24 and 192.168.2.0/24)—the PIX automatically adds these. As I mentioned in Chapter 3, these are referred to as *connected routes*. The second important item to point out is the two ip verify reverse-path commands for the *outside* and *inside* interfaces—these commands enable the reverse path lookup on the source addresses of packets for these interfaces. As you can see from this example, the configuration of anti-spoofing is fairly easy.

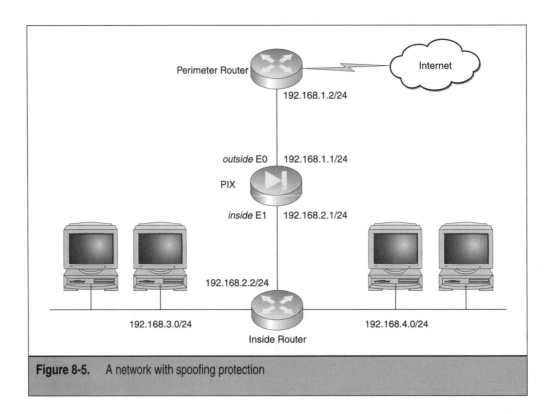

Figure 8-5.   A network with spoofing protection

FURTHER STUDY

Books

For detailed information on IDS and Cisco's implementation of IDS, read *Cisco Secure Intrusion Detection System*, Earl Carter and Rick Stiffler, Cisco Press, October 2001.

Web Sites

For information on testing the Mail Guard feature, visit www.cisco.com/warp/public/110/22.html.

For information on designing an IDS solution, visit www.cisco.com/univercd/cc/td/doc/product/iaabu/idpg/index.htm.

For information on the implementation of spoofing protection, examine RFC 2267 at www.ietf.org/rfc/rfc2267.txt.

For information on configuring the Cisco PIX firewall, visit www.cisco.com/univercd/cc/td/doc/product/iaabu/pix/pix_62/index.htm.

PART IV

PIX Management

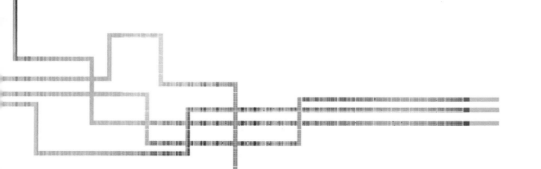

CHAPTER 9

PIX Device Manager

In the last few chapters I discussed some of the advanced features of the PIX firewall. Starting with this chapter, I will discuss the management features of the PIX, beginning with the PIX Device Manager (PDM). Throughout this book I have focused on the text-based command-line interface (CLI) of the PIX firewall when discussing configuration tasks. However, the PIX does support a GUI interface that can perform most of your configuration tasks, as well as assist you in monitoring and troubleshooting your PIX. There are three different versions of PDM: 1.0, 1.1 and 2.0. This chapter focuses on the use of PDM 2.0, which requires FOS 6.2 or higher on your PIX.

PDM OVERVIEW

PDM is not a full-blown management utility like CiscoWorks 2000; however, PDM does allow you to manage a single PIX remotely. Actually, PDM can be used to management multiple PIXs; however, its one restriction is that you can only manage a single PIX at a time. Cisco has other network management products that allow you to manage multiple PIXs simultaneously, like Cisco Secure Policy Manager (CSPM). PDM uses a web browser and Java applets to interface with a remote PIX. Certificates and HTTPS are used to provide a secure connection between your PC and the PIX, ensuring that information transferred between the two devices is undecipherable to eavesdroppers.

To ease your configuration tasks, PDM provides software *wizards* to complete many configuration tasks, like the PIX's initial configuration as well as for VPN connections (discussed in Chapters 16 and 17). In addition to using PDM for configuration tasks, you can also use it to monitor your PIX firewall. With PDM, you can create real-time graphs of information, like connection and throughput data, as well as performance statistics. You can also create historical reports for the last five days.

NOTE   If you are using CSPM to define your security policies for your PIX firewalls, any changes you make with PDM will be overwritten by CSPM the next time CSPM performs an update. However, you can still use PDM for monitoring purposes.

REQUIREMENTS FOR PDM

By default, when you buy a new 501 or 506E PIX, PDM is included with your purchase. However, you can add PDM to any PIX firewall, if you meet the minimum hardware and software requirements for your PIX and your desktop. The following sections cover the requirements necessary to install and run PDM.

PIX Requirements

PDM 2.0 is supported on all of the following PIX models: 501, 506, 506E, 515, 515E, 520, 525, and 535. By default, PDM is shipped, in the PIX's flash, with the 501, 506, and 506E models, but can easily be added to the other PIX models. As I previously mentioned, this chapter focuses on PDM 2.0, which requires FOS 6.2. If your PIX is running FOS 6.0 or 6.1, you will need to use PDM version 1.1.

For PDM to function optimally, your PIX's configuration file should be less than 100KB, which is approximately 1,500 PIX commands. A configuration file larger than this size can cause performance problems on your desktop when using PDM. To determine the size of your configuration file, use the show flashfs command:

```
pixfirewall#  show flashfs
flash file system:  version:2  magic:0x12345679
  file 0: origin:        0 length:1511480
  file 1: origin: 2883584 length:2288
  file 2: origin:        0 length:0
  file 3: origin: 3014656 length:4311804
  file 4: origin: 8257536 length:280
```

file 1 indicates the configuration file. The *length* is the size of the file in bytes. In this example, the configuration file is just a little bit bigger than 2KB.

TIP Some higher model PIXs support configuration files up to 1 or 2MB in size. Remember that PDM is really developed for small office environments where the administrator is not comfortable with Cisco's CLI.

To protect the connection between your desktop and the PIX, PDM requires that your PIX have at least a DES or 3DES license installed to implement SSL. Currently, if your PIX does not have this license, and your PIX is still under a warranty or maintenance contract with Cisco, you can obtain a free DES license. You need to install this first before you install PDM on your PIX. If you do not have a DES license, you can obtain one at the following web address: www.cisco.com/cgi-bin/Software/FormManager/formgenerator.pl?pid=221&fid=324. Cisco requires you to register your PIX before you will be given a DES license.

PDM must be installed in flash on your PIX firewall. Flash contains the FOS, PDM, and the configuration file. Because of size constraints, you must have at least 8MB of flash on your PIX. The actual installation process for PDM is described in Chapter 14.

Desktop Requirements

PDM works with Windows, Sun Solaris, and Linux. Table 9-1 lists the minimum hardware and software requirements for these platforms

On all desktop platforms, Cisco recommends that you have a monitor with a minimum of 800×600 resolution and 256 colors, but more preferably with 1024×768 resolution and 16-bit color.

Operating System	Processor	RAM	Web Browser
Windows 98, ME, XP, NT, 2000	Pentium 350Mhz	128MB	Internet Explorer 5.0, 5.5, 6.0 or Netscape Communicator 4.5 or 4.7
Solaris 2.6	SPARC chip	128MB	Netscape Communicator 4.5 or 4.7
Red Hat Linux 7.0, 7.1, 7.2 with GNOME or KDE 2.0	Pentium	64MB	Netscape Communicator 4.7

Table 9-1. Desktop Hardware and Software Requirements

Your web browser must meet the following requirements:

- The browser must be JavaScript and Java enabled—plug-in Java modules can create problems when using PDM.
- Microsoft Internet Explorer needs JDK 1.1.4 or higher.

PREPARING TO USE PDM

Once you have installed PDM on your PIX and have met the minimum software and hardware requirements on your desktop, you are now ready to use PDM. Your PIX needs a minimum configuration on it for you to access it from your desktop using PDM. You can use the *Configuration*-mode setup command to put an initial configuration on your PIX, or, if you have a PIX 501, 506, or 506E, you can use the default factory configuration.

Your third option is to use the CLI and manually enter the base configuration. You need to configure the following information on your PIX: Name, domain name, date and time, *Privilege EXEC* password, IP address and mask on the inside interface, enable PDM access, and specify which machines are allowed to use PDM to manage the PIX. Here are the commands for this base configuration:

```
pixfirewall(config)# hostname name_of_your_PIX
pixfirewall(config)# domain-name your_PIX's_domain_name
pixfirewall(config)# clock set hh:mm:ss name_of_month day year
pixfirewall(config)# enable password password
pixfirewall(config)# ip address logical_interface_name
                        ip_address [subnet_mask]
pixfirewall(config)# http server enable
pixfirewall(config)# http client_IP_address [subnet_mask]
                        [interface_name]
```

These commands were discussed in Chapter 3 (the clock command is discussed in Chapter 10).

Here is a sample configuration illustrating these commands:

```
pixfirewall(config)#  hostname bumblebee
bumblebee(config)#  domain-name dealgroup.com
bumblebee(config)#  clock set 12:00:00 July 23 2002
bumblebee(config)#  enable password KeepOut
bumblebee(config)#  ip address inside 192.168.1.1 255.255.255.0
bumblebee(config)#  http server enable
bumblebee(config)#  http 192.168.1.0 255.255.255.0 inside
```

In this example, any internal machine from network 192.168.1.0/24 is allowed to use PDM to manage the PIX.

ACCESSING PDM

Once you have put a base configuration on your PIX, you are now ready to access it via your Java-enabled web browser. Remember that PDM requires HTTPS, so you need to enter the following URL into your web browser:

```
https://PIX's_inside_interface_IP_address
```

If you are using the factory configuration on a PIX 501, 506, or 506E, the PIX's inside interface defaults to 192.168.1.1. Once you hit ENTER, PDM will start up.

A few windows will open up. Because PDM uses SSL for a secure connection, the first window that opens will prompt you to accept the certificate from the PIX. You must accept the certificate in order to access PDM. You are then prompted for the *Privilege EXEC* password of the PIX. You can implement AAA authentication instead of using this password (this is covered in Chapter 11). If you are using AAA, you must enter both a username and password. From here, your web browser will open up another window that PDM runs from—you can close the original web browser window. The second window, which handles the Java interaction between the PIX and your desktop, should *not* be closed (this is specifically stated within this window). If this is the first time you are using PDM with your PIX, the Java software will acquire the configuration of the PIX automatically.

After you log in to the PIX, you are shown the window in Figure 9-1. This is the main window for PDM and all of your configuration is done within this window. Along the top of the window are menu choices—many of these menu choices can also be executed by clicking on the appropriate icon below the menu choices.

Here are some important icons at the top of the window:

- **Circle with an arrow**   Downloads the running configuration of the PIX to PDM.
- **Floppy diskette**   Saves the running configuration on the PIX to flash.
- **Four colored boxes**   Displays an icon legend with a description of various icons.

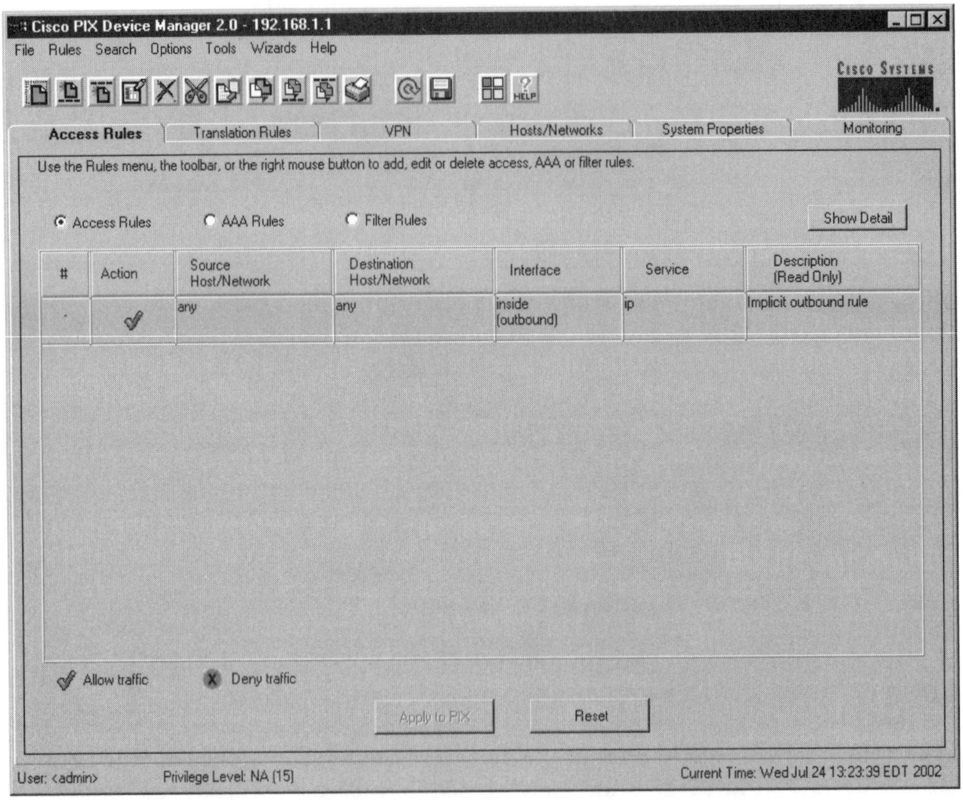

Figure 9-1. The main PDM window

- **Question mark** Brings up the appropriate help information based on the configuration tab that is in the forefront.
- **Small floppy diskette** This icon will display in the upper left-hand corner whenever you make changes to PDM and need to download these changes to the PIX.

USING PDM

Once you have brought up the main PDM screen, there are two methods that you can use with PDM: wizards and configuration tabs. The following two sections cover the configuration processes of PDM.

Wizards

Wizards provide a step-by-step process of putting a configuration on the PIX. To use wizards, click the Wizards option from the menu. There are two wizards: *Startup Wizard* and *VPN Wizard*. The Startup Wizard allows you to put an initial configuration on your PIX firewall. You'll be prompted for information like the host and domain name of your PIX, the passwords, the interface configurations, Auto Update, VPN setup, NAT information, and DHCP addressing. If you already have a configuration on your PIX, the PIX places the set values in the configuration fields, where you can accept the current values, or change them to something else.

The VPN Wizard allows you to set up a site-to-site or remote access VPN connection. I discuss VPNs in Chapters 16 and 17. As you will see in Chapter 17, using the CLI to set up VPN connections is very command-intensive. I highly recommend using the VPN Wizard to set up your VPNs because the wizard provides a very easy, step-by-step method of entering all of your VPN connection information.

Configuration Tabs

Along the top of the PDM display are various tabs that allow you to configure your PIX:

- **Access Rules**   Configure ACLs, filtering URL content, and AAA functions.
- **Translation Rules**   Configure your NAT translation rules for addresses to be translated and those that are not, as well as your static translation rules.
- **VPN**   Add, customize, or remove configuration rules for VPN connections (I highly recommend that you use the VPN Wizard to add VPN connections and use this tab to customize your VPN connection rules).
- **Hosts/Networks**   Specify the networks and hosts that are on each of the PIX's interfaces (used for routing, access rules, and translation rules).
- **System Properties**   Specify other types of configuration for your PIX, like DHCP server, connection to AAA servers, logging, IDS, and other system information.
- **Monitoring**   Create charts and tables based on statistical information on your PIX.

I will not cover all of the configuration tabs within PDM, because almost all of the configuration tasks within PDM are very easy and intuitive. I'll focus on just the *Access Rules* and *Monitoring* tabs to give you an idea how the GUI interface works.

Access Rules

The *Access Rules* tab is initially displayed when you start up PDM. There are three radio buttons for the three different sets of rules:

- **Access Rules**   access control lists

- **AAA Rules**   authentication, authorization, and accounting information for AAA
- **Filter Rules**   filtering rules for web content using N2H2 or WebSense

Clicking the appropriate radio button changes the display in the middle of the screen. The default rules displayed are Access Rules, which are the ACLs on the PIX. To the right of these radio buttons is a button labeled Show Detail—clicking this button displays detailed information about the rules below this. Once you click it, the button label changes to Show Summary—clicking this button again takes you back to the original display.

For the purpose of this example, I'll focus on how to set up an ACL using PDM. Once the Access Rules rule set is displayed, you will see an ACL or list of ACLs that are currently configured on the PIX. I find it helpful to click the Show Detail button to display ACL specifics in the display below. I'll use Figures 9-1 and 9-2 to discuss the addition of ACL statements and lists. There are various columns in the display of Figure 9-1:

- **#**   This is the order of evaluating the different rules for the access-lists. This is not an ACL number.
- **Action**   Indicates whether traffic is permitted or denied (a green checkmark icon indicates permitting traffic and a red X icon indicates denying traffic).
- **Source Host/Network**   Specifies the IP addresses of the sources initiating traffic.
- **Destination Host/Network**   Specifies the IP addresses of the destinations receiving traffic.
- **Interface**   Specifies the name of the interface where the ACL is applied and what interfaces the traffic is destined for (outbound means a lower-security-level interface whereas inbound means a higher-security-level interface).
- **Service**   Indicates the IP protocol that is to be filtered.
- **Description**   Provides a brief description of the ACL statement

The first thing to point out is that there is only one statement and one list in this example. To add new entry, perform one of the following:

- Choose Rules | Add.
- Click the Add New Rule icon in the top left corner (looks like a page with a star burst at the top-left page corner).
- Right click in the ACL display and choose Add.

All three of these functions bring up the window shown in Figure 9-2.

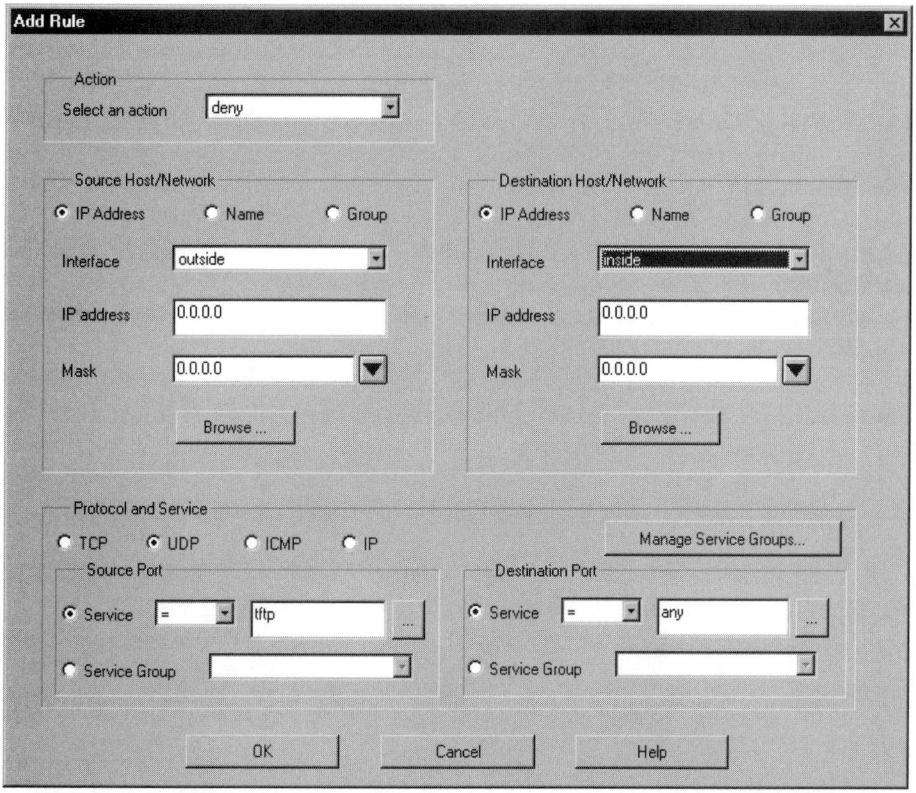

Figure 9-2. Adding an ACL rule

The process is very straightforward. At the top of the screen, choose your action from the drop-down box: permit or deny. Below this are two columns. The left column is for the source host or network, and the right column is for the destination host or network. If you are using Object Groups, you can click the Group radio button and select your configured group. The default is to specify the source and destination by IP address. It is very important that you specify the name of the interface where the source and destination device(s) are located, because this affects where the ACL will be activated. To create an Object Group, from the choose Tools | Service Groups and add the necessary groups to your PIX's configuration.

Next, enter the appropriate addressing information and then proceed to the *Protocol and Service* section beneath this. This section allows you to specify the IP protocol and protocol information. The default display is for TCP or UDP traffic. For this traffic, choose the operator or port, or you can use Object Groups by clicking the Service Group radio button and choosing the appropriate group from the drop-down box. If you choose IP as the protocol, you can then pull up a window where you can choose the appropriate IP protocol—IP itself, AH, ESP, OSPF, any, and many others. If you choose ICMP as the protocol, then you can choose a specific ICMP message, or all messages. Once you are done, click the OK button at the bottom of the screen. When you click this button, you are returned to the *Access Rules* configuration tab, where you will see your new entry.

When you add statements, PDM places the command at the bottom of the appropriate ACL based on the interface name for the source devices in the ACL statement. The display is sorted by the interface names, which represent the various ACLs. For example, there are two ACLs in Figure 9-3. In this example, I've added a statement to the default ACL (allowing all outbound traffic by default). The first ACL is for the *inside* interface,

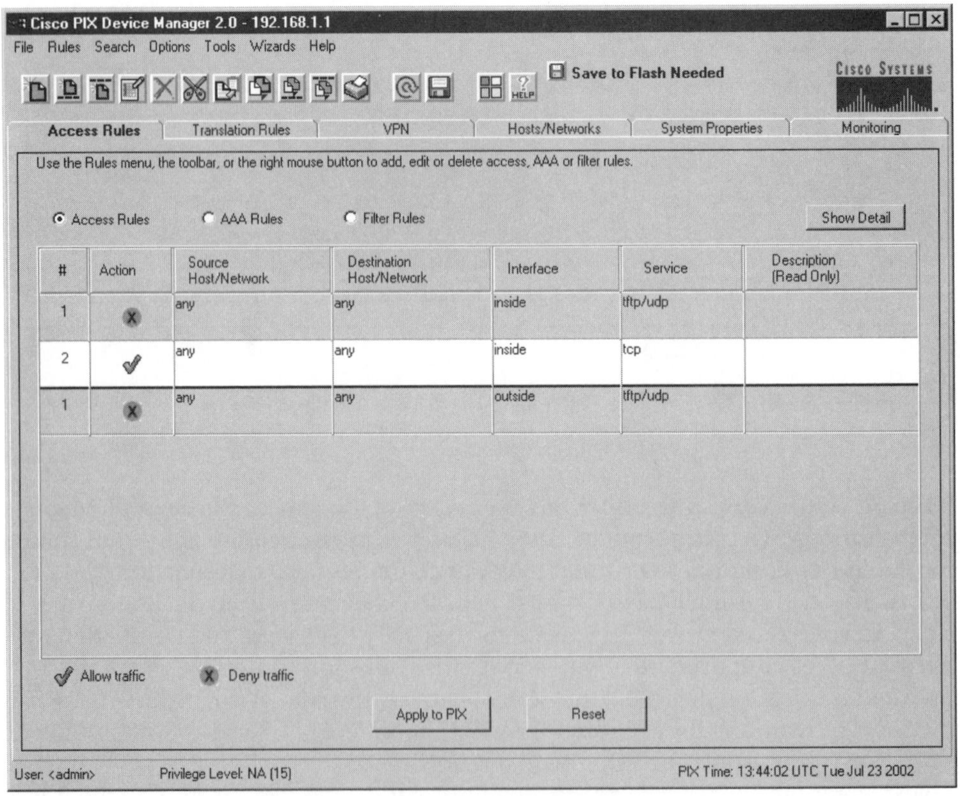

Figure 9-3. ACL example

and consists of the first two statements. The first statement denies TFTP using UDP, and the second statement permits all other traffic. The second ACL is applied to the *outside* interface, and consists of a single statement: deny TFTP UDP traffic. Remember that there is an implicit deny at the end of both of these ACLs.

Because the order of statements is important when the PIX processes an ACL, you have different options available to ordering ACL statements by using either the menu selections, the icons, or right-clicking an item and choosing an option:

- **Add** Adds a statement at the bottom of the list.

- **Insert Before** Inserts a statement before the rule that is currently selected.

- **Insert After** Inserts a statement after the rule that is currently selected.

- **Edit** Edits the current rule.

- **Cut** Removes the current rule from the list, but keeps it in a buffer.

- **Copy** Copies the current rule into a buffer.

- **Paste** Takes the rule in the buffer and adds it to the end of the appropriate ACL.

- **Paste Before** Takes the rule in the buffer and inserts it before the currently selected rule.

- **Paste After** Takes the rule in the buffer and inserts it after the currently selected rule.

- **Delete** Delete the currently selected rule.

Any time that you do something within PDM that affects the PIX's configuration, you will need to perform two tasks. First, you must have PDM push the configuration from your desktop down to the PIX by clicking the *Apply to PIX* button at the bottom of the screen. If you have made changes that you don't like, just click the *Reset* button. This causes PDM to create the appropriate PIX commands, download them to the PIX, and have the PIX execute them on the running configuration. The second thing you need to do is to have the PIX save these changes from RAM to flash by clicking the *Save to Flash Needed* icon at the top-right hand corner of the PDM screen. You can see this icon in Figure 9-3.

As you can see from this explanation, it is much easier to manipulate ACL statements using PDM than it is with the CLI of the PIX. Even though most of the time I tend to favor CLI interfaces over GUI interfaces, the PDM is an exception.

Monitoring

In addition to making it easy to configure your PIX, PDM also offers many monitoring and troubleshooting tools. There are two very handy features available from the Tools menu: Ping and Command Line Interface. The Ping option allows you to have the PIX ping a remote device. The Command Line Interface option opens up another window where you can enter either a single PIX command, or a list of PIX commands. These commands are then downloaded to the PIX, executed, and any resulting output is displayed within the Command Line Interface window. Therefore, if PDM doesn't support a GUI option to configure something on the PIX, you can use this feature and download the command directly to the PIX without having to log in to the PIX.

Another nice feature of PDM are the graphs and statistics that you can display from the Monitoring tab, as you can see in Figure 9-4. In this screen, there is a column on the left side that lists the various reporting categories. PDM groups categories together sometimes under a single heading—you can list the specific subcategories by clicking the + button to the left of the category name. As you can see in Figure 9-4, I've clicked all the plus buttons for summarized groupings. For instance, the Systems Graph category contains the following subcategories: Blocks, CPU, Failover, and Memory.

To obtain reporting information, click a category or subcategory. For example, if you click CPU from the Systems Graph category, you will have various options about the types of information and format of the information that you want to view.

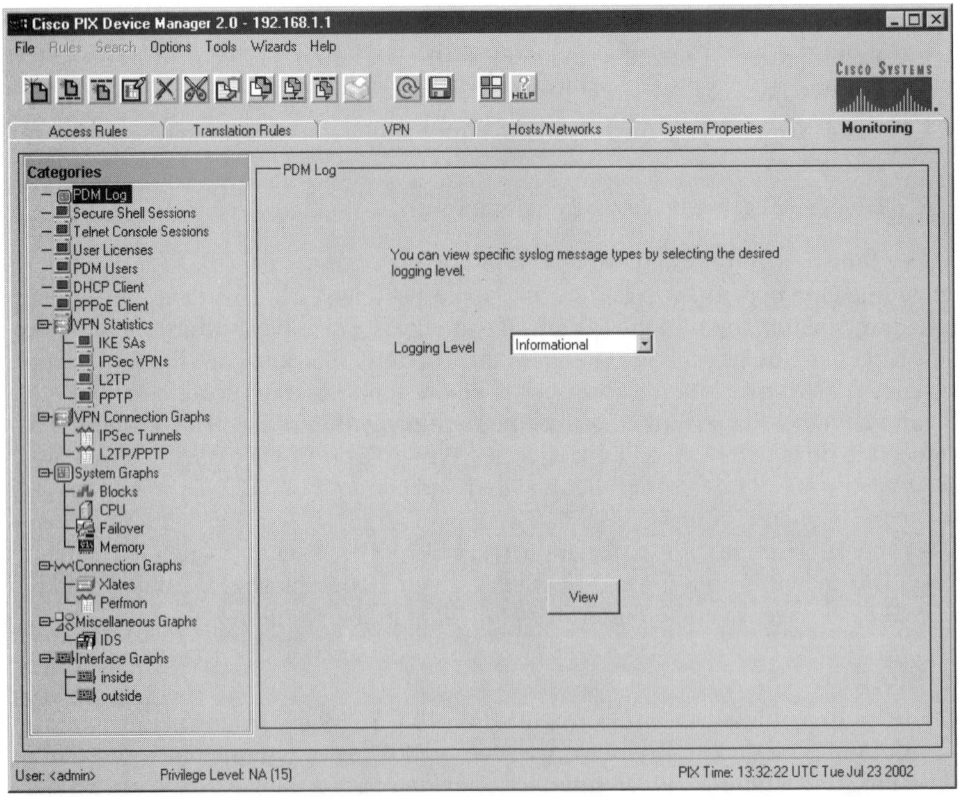

Figure 9-4. Using the Monitor tab

For CPU, there is only one graphing option: CPU Utilization. Click this to select it and then click the Add>> button to add this to the items to be graphed. Some categories allow you to graph multiple items simultaneously.

Once you have selected all of your items, click the *Graph It!* Button, and PDM creates a semi-real time graph for you, as is shown in Figure 9-5. At the bottom of the window, you can see that the reporting information is updated every 10 seconds—you can change this option from the drop-down box. Also, you can view the reporting

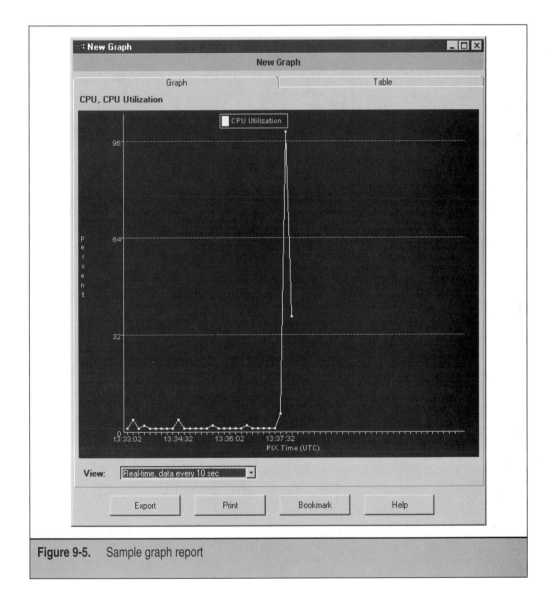

Figure 9-5.   Sample graph report

information in either a graphical or tabular display. In a tabular display, you can export the information by clicking the Export button at the bottom of the screen. As you can see, creating a report is a simple process with PDM.

FURTHER STUDY

Web Sites

For an overview of PDM, visit www.cisco.com/warp/public/cc/pd/fw/sqfw500/prodlit/pixdm_ds.pdf.

For information about installing and using PDM, visit www.cisco.com/univercd/cc/td/doc/product/iaabu/pix/pdm/index.htm.

CHAPTER 10

SNMP and Logging

In the last chapter I talked about using Cisco's PIX Device Manager (PDM) to remotely manage your PIX. PDM is a fairly new remote-based GUI manager. Prior to PDM, you could use the Simple Network Management Protocol (SNMP) to manage your PIX. The first part of this chapter is dedicated to setting up SNMP on your PIX firewall.

In addition to managing your PIX and its configuration, you will want to use the PIX's logging features to keep an audit trail of what is occurring on your PIX. You can use this information to determine security threats and attacks, as well as to keep track of administrative events. The last part of this chapter focuses on logging abilities and how the PIX keeps track of time. The time on a PIX is important for logging purposes—when the PIX logs an event, it also tags the event with the current time. Therefore, I recommend that you use a mechanism to correctly synchronize the time on your PIX to a time server. To help you with this function, the PIX supports the Network Time Protocol (NTP), which I will also cover.

SNMP

SNMP is a very old management protocol developed initially for IP-based systems. It serves two primary purposes:

- It allows for remote management of devices.

- It allows devices to send information about events or alarms to a management station—this is called an *SNMP trap*.

SNMP allows the interaction between two devices by defining a Management Information Base (MIB), which specifies how data is to be stored locally and retrieved remotely.

 SECURITY ALERT!   You should not use SNMP across an insecure network, like the Internet, because SNMP is not a very secure protocol. If you need to move SNMP information across an insecure network, make sure that you protect it by tunneling this traffic through a VPN, which I discuss in chapters 16 and 17.

SNMP MIBs

There are three implementations of SNMP—versions 1, 2, and 3. The PIX supports versions 1 and 2. There is one limitation that the PIX has concerning SNMP, however. Typically, as I mentioned at the beginning of this section, SNMP can be used to manage a device remotely. This can include the gathering of configuration and statistical information on a device, or it can include remote configuration tasks where you are changing a configuration on a device. The PIX's limitation is that all of its MIBs are read-only. This means that you cannot use an SNMP manager to change the configuration of the PIX—you can only read the MIB values. Therefore, the use of SNMP on the PIX is strictly used for only the monitoring of system events.

Besides using SNMP to access this information, the PIX offers a variety of commands that you can also use. The following sections cover these commands.

CPU Usage

Cisco has added some new MIBs for the PIX in version 6.2 of the FOS. One of the more important ones is the CPU usage of your PIX. You can have your SNMP management station periodically poll your PIX firewall for this MIB value and then use it to perform capacity planning. With this new MIB, you can view the following CPU usage information:

- CPU usage over the last five seconds
- CPU usage over the last one minute
- CPU usage over the last five minutes

You can also see this information with the show cpu usage command:

```
pixfirewall(config)#  show cpu usage
CPU utilization for 5 seconds: 2%; 1 minute: 1%; 5 minutes: 1%
```

As you can see, this PIX is not very busy.

Buffer Usage

The PIX uses buffers to store temporary data. You should monitor the buffers carefully to ensure that your PIX doesn't run out of buffer space, which would cause it to drop packets. The following is the output of the show block command, which displays buffer usage:

```
pixfirewall#  show blocks
SIZE        MAX        LOW      CNT
   4       1600       1600     1600
  80        100         98       99
 256         80         77       77
1550        780        400      502
65536         8          8        8
```

The SIZE column indicates the size of a buffer in bytes. The MAX column indicates the maximum number of allocated buffer blocks. The LOW column indicates the number of fewest available blocks since the PIX rebooted last. The CNT column indicates the number of currently available blocks.

TIP   If you ever see a 0 in the LOW column, this indicates that the PIX at some point in time ran out of buffer space and had to start dropping packets—if you continually see this problem, you should add more memory to your PIX.

Connection Usage

The show conn command is useful in determining how many connections your PIX is currently using and how many connections it has seen in use since the PIX was booted. You can use this information to determine whether or not you need to increase your connection license limit. Here is an example of the show conn command:

```
pixfirewall#  show conn
15 in use, 88 most used
```

Failover Usage

The show failover command is used to display the status of your PIX's failover configuration. The failover feature on the PIX allows a standby PIX to monitor an active PIX, and, if the active PIX or one of its interfaces fails, the standby PIX can promote itself to an active role. I discuss this command and the failover feature in more depth in Chapter 12.

Memory Usage

The show memory command is useful in determining whether or not you have enough memory in your PIX for trouble-free operation. Remember that many things take up memory in your PIX, including the following:

- Address translations
- Connections
- Conduits
- Active configuration
- ARP table
- Cached authentication information
- Cached URL information

These are just a few of the items that the PIX stores in RAM—if you have a very active PIX, and you are consistently running with only about 1MB of free RAM, you should seriously consider upgrading the memory on your PIX. The following is an example of the show memory command:

```
pixfirewall#  show memory
16777216 bytes total, 5432188 bytes free
```

SNMP Traps

As I mentioned earlier, an SNMP trap is an event that a device will log to a management station. The PIX supports the following two types of SNMP traps: Generic traps and security traps. Examples of generic traps include a bootup of the PIX, an interface changing state (up or down), or an SNMP authentication failure. Examples of security traps include syslog messages, a PIX failover event, or a *Privilege EXEC* access authentication failure.

> **NOTE**   If you have other devices on a lower-security-level interface that will be logging traps to an SNMP management station on a higher-level interface, you need to create an ACL or conduit that will allow traffic to UDP port 162. SNMP management stations, when they perform a get operation, use UDP port 161 for the connection.

Each SNMP trap that is generated will have an SNMP object ID (OID) that uniquely identifies the type of source that generated the trap—this is typically based on the hardware platform of the device.

SNMP Configuration

Configuring SNMP on your PIX is a simple process. The syntax for the PIX's SNMP commands is:

```
pixfirewall(config)#   snmp-server community key_value
pixfirewall(config)#   snmp-server host [interface_name]
                           IP_address [trap|poll]
pixfirewall(config)#   snmp-server contact name_of_contact
pixfirewall(config)#   snmp-server location PIX_location
pixfirewall(config)#   snmp-server enable traps
```

The following sections explain the use of each of these commands.

Community String

The `snmp-server community` command sets the secret key value used for SNMP communication between the PIX and the SNMP management station. This value must be the same on both sides or the PIX and management station will not interact. The value that you use for the key can be up to 32 characters in length, and is case sensitive. Also, you cannot use spaces as part of the key value. This is the only required configuration that you need to perform to enable SNMP access to your PIX—the rest of the commands are optional.

SECURITY ALERT!   The key value defaults to *public* if you don't configure it—I strongly recommend that you change this value to secure your PIX firewall.

SNMP Management Stations

If you want your PIX to send SNMP traps to a management station, you need to configure the `snmp-server host` command. Optionally, you can specify the name of the interface that the SNMP management station resides on—if you omit this, it defaults to *inside*. This is then followed by the IP address of your SNMP management station. You can specify up to 32 management stations—use a different `snmp-server host` command for each station.

There are two additional optional parameters for this command: `trap` and `poll`. If you specify `trap`, only SNMP traps will be sent to the specified management station; plus, the management station will *not* be allowed to poll (read) the SNMP MIBs on the PIX. If you specify `poll`, the opposite is true—the PIX will not send SNMP traps to the management station, but will allow the management station to poll the PIX. If you do not specify either one of these parameters, both are enabled by default.

Contacts and Locations

To specify a contact (a name of administrator or person who should be contacted in case of a problem), use the `snmp-server contact` command. The contact can be up to 127 characters in length, and spaces are permitted; however, the PIX converts multiple consecutive spaces into a single space.

To specify the location of your PIX firewall, which can help in troubleshooting issues, use the `snmp-server location` command. Like the contact, the location value can be up to 127 characters in length, and spaces are permitted, but multiple consecutive spaces are converted into a single space.

SNMP Traps

By default, the PIX does not generate an SNMP trap whenever a log message is generated. These messages, as you will see in the last half of this chapter, can be displayed to the console of the PIX, sent to a log buffer, sent to an external logging server (syslog server), or sent as a trap via SNMP. By default, these messages are not sent as SNMP traps. To enable this feature, use the `snmp-server enable traps` command. The configuration of this command is reliant on the configuration of the PIX's `logging history` command, which I will discuss in the "Logging Events" section later on in this chapter. This command specifies the level of the information that should be logged. If the level is set to `debugging`, the PIX logs everything, and thus generates an SNMP trap for every event. You might want to use this level initially for testing purposes, and then change the logging level to a more suitable parameter. One other command that you need to configure for generating SNMP traps for syslog messages is the `logging on` command, which enables the logging of messages to remote devices. This command is also discussed in the "Logging Events" section.

Resetting Your SNMP Configuration

To undo the configuration of any one of the SNMP commands, just precede the `snmp-server` command with the `no` parameter. To reset your PIX's SNMP configuration back to the factory defaults, use the `clear snmp-server` command. To verify your SNMP configuration, use the `show snmp-server` command:

```
pixfirewall#  show snmp
snmp-server host inside 192.168.1.2
snmp-server location Corporate Office
snmp-server contact Spongey
snmp-server community checkthisout
```

SNMP Configuration Example

To help explain the setup of SNMP for you PIX, I'll go through a simple example, using the network in Figure 10-1 to illustrate the setup.

The following is the base configuration to allow SNMP connectivity:

```
pixfirewall(config)#  static (inside, outside) 199.199.199.6 192.168.1.2
pixfirewall(config)#  access-list PERMIT_IN permit udp
                         host 200.200.200.2 host 199.199.199.6 eq 161
pixfirewall(config)#  access-list PERMIT_IN deny ip any any
pixfirewall(config)#  access-group PERMIT_IN in interface outside
pixfirewall(config)#
pixfirewall(config)#  snmp-server community checkthisout
pixfirewall(config)#  snmp-server location Corporate Office
pixfirewall(config)#  snmp-server contact Spongey
pixfirewall(config)#  snmp-server enable traps
pixfirewall(config)#  snmp-server host inside 192.168.1.2
```

The first thing to point out about this configuration is the ACL—it allows the remote router to send SNMP traps to the internal SNMP management station. The second thing to point out are the `snmp-server` commands that configure the PIX's SNMP configuration. The `community` parameter specifies a key value of `checkthisout`, which must also be configured on the SNMP management station (192.168.1.2). Logging of traps has been enabled (`snmp-server enable traps`) and the management station has been defined with the `snmp-server host` command.

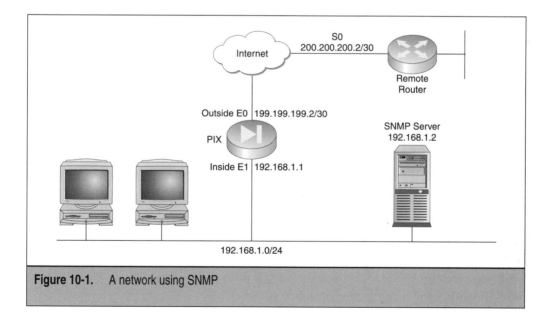

Figure 10-1. A network using SNMP

DATE AND TIME

Before I begin discussing the logging features of the PIX, I need to spend some time discussing the date and time on the PIX, because the logging features of the PIX place a date and time stamp on each event that they record. Therefore, it is important to ensure that your PIX has the correct time configured on it. There are two basic ways that you can configure the date and time on your PIX—manual and automatic. With manual configuration, you use the `clock` command to set these values.

There are two basic problems with manually setting the time on your PIX. First, the time you enter might be off slightly from the real time, which might create discrepancies amongst the logs of multiple devices. For instance, if you are looking at the log files of your IDS device and you are noticing what seems to be an attack occurring at 11:35 AM, and then you look at your PIX's log files and don't see this, you might be scratching your head. Of course, you might be looking for the wrong time in the PIX's log file because the PIX's time might be different from that of the IDS. Imagine that your PIX records about 1,000 events an hour—trying to find the event you're looking for with a 10-minute difference can be tedious.

The second problem with manually setting the time is that the battery that handles the clock on the PIX will eventually die. This means that every time the PIX boots up, it will start with the same initial date and time. For example, I have a Dell laptop whose clock battery has died and is very difficult to replace. Every time it boots up, it records a time of June 1, 1997. This could create serious problems with logging of events if this situation occurred on your PIX firewall.

One of the most common solutions implemented today to solve this problem is the use of the Network Time Protocol (NTP). NTP allows devices to automatically synchronize their date and time to the same clock source, thus guaranteeing that all of your networking devices report the same time value. The following sections cover the configuration of both manual and automatic timing configurations for your PIX firewall.

Setting the Date and Time on the PIX

Manually setting the date and time on your PIX firewall is a simple task. There are three basic settings that you should configure:

- The actual date and time itself
- The time zone that the PIX resides in
- Whether the time zone the PIX is located in uses daylight saving time

The following sections cover the configuration of these items as well as how to view the date and time configured on your PIX.

NOTE The PIX will automatically adjust its clock when a leap year occurs.

Setting the Clock

To manually set the date and time on your PIX, use the `clock set` command:

```
pixfirewall(config)#  clock set hh:mm:ss name_of_month day year
```

The `hh:mm:ss` specifies the current time—the PIX uses a 24-hour clock, so 1:00 P.M. would be 13:00. The month is specified by the actual *name* of the month—this can be abbreviated to the first three characters of the name of the month. The day is a one- or two-digit value and the year is a four-digit value between 1993 and 2035. Note that you can reverse the order of the month and day values. Here is an example of configuring the date and time:

```
pixfirewall(config)#  clock set 23:59:59 may 23 2002
```

Setting the Time Zone

To set the local time zone that your PIX resides in, use the `clock timezone` command, introduced in FOS 6.2:

```
pixfirewall(config)#  clock timezone name_of_time_zone offset_hours
                             [offset_minutes]
```

The `name_of_time_zone` parameter specifies the actual time zone name, like EST for Eastern Standard Time. You can use your own names, but it is recommended to use the common names that everyone is familiar with. The default is Universal Coordinated Time (UTC), which is the same as Greenwich Mean Time (GMT). The `offset_hours` parameter specifies the number of hours that you should offset the timing value of the PIX from UTC. Optionally, you can even specify the number of minutes to offset the time from UTC. Both the hours and minutes offset can be preceded by a plus or minus sign to determine how to offset the time—if you don't specify this operation, it defaults to +. To set the time zone back to UTC, use the `no clock timezone` command.

NOTE Setting this command only affects the display of the time—the PIX *always* keeps track of time internally by using UTC.

Setting Daylight Saving Time

As of FOS 6.2, the PIX now supports daylight saving time (DST) and time zones that support daylight saving time. By default, the PIX does not adapt to DST unless you specifically configure it. Here are the commands to configure DST:

```
pixfirewall(config)#  clock summer-time time_zone_name recurring
                             [week_of_month weekday_name month_name hh:mm
                              week_of_month weekday_name month_name hh:mm
                             [offset_value]]
```

```
pixfirewall(config)#  clock summer-time time_zone_name date
                          day month year hh:mm
                          day month year hh:mm [offset_value]
pixfirewall(config)#  clock summer-time time_zone_name date
                          month day year hh:mm
                          month day year hh:mm [offset_value]
```

The first `clock summer-time` command, the one with the `recurring` parameter, is used to specify the length of summer time for DST purposes. If you don't specify any time values, the beginning and ending dates for the summer time length default to United States rules. The `time_zone_name` allows you to specify a time zone name that the PIX displays when the summer time time zone is in effect. For instance, EDT is used for Eastern Daylight Savings Time for the east coast of the United States—this is only used for display purposes. There are two sets of dates—the first date is the beginning of summer time for DST purposes and the last date is the end of DST. The `week_of_month` parameters specify the week of the month, which can be a number from 1 to 5, or the parameter word `last` for the last week of the month. The `weekday_name` parameter is the name of the day of the week, like *Monday, Tuesday,* or *Wednesday.* The `month_name` parameter is the name of the month, like *January, February,* or *March* (which can be abbreviated to the first three characters). The `hh:mm` parameter is the actual hour and minute time that summer time begins and ends for the specified date. Finally, the `offset_value` parameter specifies how many minutes should be offset when summer time begins and ends. The default is 60 minutes.

The last two commands, the ones with the `date` parameter, can be used instead of the `recurring` command. The `time_zone_name` parameter works the same as in the recurring version of the command. The `date` parameter specifies the specific beginning and ending dates for the beginning and ending of summer time. The format of the beginning and ending date is either the day of the month (from 1 to 31), the name of the month, the four-digit year, and the actual time; or, you can start with the name of the month first, followed by the day of the month, the four-digit year, and the actual time. With the first of these two commands, the date format would be *23 May 2002,* whereas the format of the second command would be *May 23 2002.* Finally, you can optionally specify the number of minutes to offset the time for the beginning and ending of summer time—this defaults to 60 minutes if you omit it.

TIP If you are in the Northern Hemisphere, you should place the starting date first followed by the ending date for the summer time zone; however, if you are in the Southern Hemisphere (as in Australia or Brazil), you should put the ending date first followed by the starting date.

The main difference between the `date` and `recurring` commands is that the `date` command specifies just a single time period to make the adjustment, while the `recurring` command will make the adjustment every year. To remove all summer time configurations and reset the display of the clock to UTC, use the `clear clock` command.

NOTE The `clock summer-time` command only affects the display of the date and time—the PIX still keeps track of time internally using UTC.

Viewing the PIX's Current Time

To view the clock setting of your PIX, use the `show clock` command:

```
pixfirewall#  show clock [detail]
```

Without the `detail` parameter, the `show clock` command only displays the current date and time. Note that that the time includes hours, minutes, seconds, and milliseconds—the milliseconds value is new in FOS 6.2. With the `detail` parameter, the `show clock` command also displays the source of the timing. If the source is specified as *hardware calendar*, then the time is from the clock battery on the PIX's motherboard. Otherwise, it is from an external source like an NTP server, which I'll discuss in the next section. Here's an example of the use of the `show clock` command:

```
pixfirewall#  show clock
11:59:29.473 UTC Wed May 22 2002
pixfirewall#  show clock detail
11:59:32.823 UTC Wed May 22 2002
Time source is hardware calendar
```

Using NTP

Starting with FOS 6.2, Cisco has included code in the PIX to allow it to be a Network Time Protocol (NTP) client. In Cisco's NTP implementation, the PIX can obtain timing information from an NTP server running NTP version 3. NTP is a hierarchical protocol that allows devices to synchronize their internal timing. It's hierarchical in the sense that there is not necessarily one master clock source, but possibly dozens or hundreds of clock sources. This is a very common technique to ensure that you have redundancy with time servers and that one time server doesn't become overwhelmed with hundreds or thousands of devices requesting a date and time update. However, to maintain the date and time integrity—you really don't want hundreds of different time sources—NTP uses a hierarchy, as is shown in Figure 10-2.

To maintain a timing integrity, each NTP server reports to a higher-level server, and a higher-level server may have multiple servers underneath it. At the top of the hierarchy is an NTP device that uses an atomic clock, the most precise timing instrument known. This is not to say that your network requires an atomic clock source—your network, however, should have a master clock source that references an atomic clock source on the Internet. Therefore, even though there might be multiple NTP servers providing clocking for hundreds of devices, all timing is based on the same, precise time source—the device with a master clock.

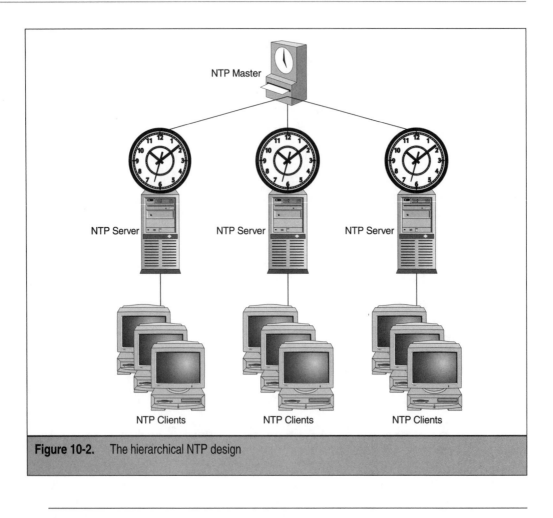

Figure 10-2. The hierarchical NTP design

NOTE NTP devices use UDP for communication. Both the source and destination port numbers are 123.

Typically, the client queries its server for the time using a unicast UDP packet. However, NTP does support a broadcast and multicast mode, where the NTP server periodically advertises the time to NTP clients. The PIX firewall currently supports only the unicast mode.

NTP Authentication

In many instances, you will be getting your clocking information from an external NTP server. As I mentioned, NTP uses UDP as a transport protocol. Of course, these two items bring up security concerns because NTP packets can be easily spoofed and NTP sessions are subject to session replay attacks. Opening up UDP port 123 in your firewall, even if it is for just one or two external NTP servers, could present a security problem.

NTP does have some built-in mechanisms to prevent security attacks. The first method, which Cisco supports on their PIX firewalls, is an authentication mechanism. The authentication mechanism operates at the application layer and is used to ensure not only that the timing information came from a specified NTP server peer, but also that the actual timing information wasn't tampered with. The timing information is protected by taking the timing information, along with a hash value, or key, and running it through the MD5 hash algorithm. This is the same algorithm that many other protocols use for authentication, like PPP's CHAP, EIGRP, and OSPF (I discuss MD5 in more depth in Chapter 16). The resulting output of this hash function is a fixed-length value. Both the original timing information and the fixed-length value are sent by the NTP server to the client. The client also needs the same key value in order to verify the integrity of the timing information. The client takes the same timing information, uses the same key value, and runs it through the MD5 hash algorithm. If the output hashed value is the same as that included in the NTP packet, then the client knows that it came from the specified source and that the timing information was not tampered with.

The second mechanism that NTP supports is the use of encryption to actually hide the time and date contents from prying eyes. One problem with authentication is that the actual timing information is sent in clear text, which leaves it open to eavesdropping. With encryption, the actual timing information is encrypted and then placed in the NTP packet. The PIX firewall doesn't support this feature within NTP; however, you could set up a VPN between the server and client to protect all traffic between these two devices. I will discuss authentication and encryption in much more depth in Chapter 16.

Configuring the PIX's NTP Client

The following two sections cover the configuration of the NTP client on a PIX firewall. As you will see, the configuration is a simple process.

Specifying the NTP Server   To specify the NTP server that the PIX should use to get the current date and time, use the ntp server command:

```
pixfirewall(config)#  ntp server server's_IP_address [key key_number]
                              [source interface_name] [prefer]
```

The first parameter that you specify is the NTP server's IP address. Optionally, you can specify a key_number parameter—this is used to indicate the authentication information used to authenticate the NTP server. If you specify this value, you will have to configure authentication information, which is discussed in the next section. You can also specify the name of the interface off of which the NTP server resides. If you do this, and an NTP packet from this server arrives on a different interface, the PIX will ignore it. The last parameter, prefer, allows you to set a preference of using this NTP time server over other servers that you have also configured on your PIX firewall. To remove a time server, precede the specified ntp server command with the no parameter.

Enabling Authentication   If you used the `key` value in the `ntp server` command, you need to configure the following commands to allow for NTP authentication:

```
pixfirewall(config)#  ntp authenticate
pixfirewall(config)#  ntp trusted-key key_number
pixfirewall(config)#  ntp authentication-key key_number md5 string
```

The `ntp authenticate` command enables authentication for NTP. Once you configure this command, the PIX will only synchronize with an NTP server if it is able to validate the NTP information sent by the server—if it can't perform the validation, the PIX will drop the NTP packets.

The `ntp trusted-key` command specifies a `key_number` value that must match that in the `ntp server` command—it basically says that this NTP server should be trusted. The `key_number` should be looked at as an index number or pointer—it can range from 1 to 4,294,967,295. This number should be in every NTP packet sent by the NTP server.

The `ntp authentication-key` command then specifies the actual string value to use for the MD5 algorithm for your NTP server or servers. The `key_number` is the same as that in the `ntp trusted-key` command. The string parameter for the MD5 value can be up to 32 characters in length. Once you execute this command, whenever you look at the PIX's configuration, you will not see the actual string value—instead, this will be replaced in your display with * * * * * * * * * whenever you execute a `write terminal`, `show configuration`, or `show tech-support` command.

You can remove any of these commands by preceding them with the `no` parameter. To completely remove your NTP configuration, including authentication, use the `clear ntp` command.

Verifying the Operation of NTP

Once you have configured NTP on your PIX, you can use three basic commands to verify the configuration and operation of NTP:

```
pixfirewall#  show ntp
pixfirewall#  show ntp associations [detail]
pixfirewall#  show ntp status
```

The `show ntp` command gives a basic overview of the NTP configuration on your PIX. The `show ntp associations` command displays information about the NTP time servers that you have configured. The `show ntp status` command displays information about the NTP clock value.

Here is an example of the `show ntp associations` command:

```
pixfirewall#  show ntp associations
      address          ref clock     st  when  poll  reach delay offset  disp
*~192.168.1.10    172.16.1.21      5    31   128   377    4.1  -5.67   3.4
+~192.168.1.20    172.16.1.21      5    28   128   377    5.2  10.21   1.4
* master (synced), # master (unsynced), + selected, - candidate, ~ configured
```

Code	Description
*	The PIX is synchronized to this NTP server
#	The PIX is in the process of synchronizing to this NTP server
+	This is an NTP server that the PIX can synchronize with
−	This is a possible NTP server that the PIX can use
~	This NTP server was statically configured and the PIX will use a unicast to connect to it

Table 10-1. Status Characters for NTP Associations

At the very beginning of each row in the output are some special characters that are briefly explained at the bottom of the display. Table 10-1 contains a more detailed explanation. In this example, 192.168.1.10 is the master clock source that the PIX is synchronizing with.

An explanation of the column headers in the show NTP associations command is shown in Table 10-2.

Optionally, you can add the detail parameter to the show ntp associations command. This will display more detailed NTP timing information for each peer.

The show ntp status command shows the current NTP clocking status of the PIX. An example of this command is shown here:

```
pixfirewall#  show ntp status
Clock is synchronized, stratum 5, reference is 192.168.1.10
nominal freq is 99.9985 Hz, actual freq is 100.0268 Hz, precision is 2**6
reference time is c02128a9.73c1954b (20:29:29.452 UTC Fri Feb 22 2002)
clock offset is -0.2414 msec, root delay is 45.37 msec
root dispersion is 22.7 msec, peer dispersion is 3.4 msec
```

Column Description	Explanation
address	The IP address of the NTP server
ref clock	The clock source that the NTP peer server is using
st	The stratum level of the clock source of the peer
when	The last time a time update was received from the peer
poll	How often the NTP server is polled for the time
reach	The reachability status, in octal, of the peer
delay	The round-trip delay, in milliseconds, to reach the peer
offset	The difference between what the NTP server says the time is and the local time of the PIX
disp	The time dispersion, or distribution

Table 10-2.   Column Headers for the show ntp associations Command

The first line of output indicates that the PIX is synchronized with the NTP server—in other words, the PIX is getting valid replies to its NTP queries. If the output said *unsynchronized*, then there is an NTP connection problem between the PIX and all of its configured NTP servers. The *stratum* reference refers to the reliability of the clock soure. A stratum level of 1 is an atomic clock. The current clocking source is 192.168.1.10—this PIX's NTP server. The rest of the information relates to the clocking information from this NTP server.

NTP Example

To help illustrate the configuration on NTP on a PIX firewall, I'll use Figure 10-3. In this example there is both an internal and external NTP server. The external NTP server is getting its clocking from the internal server.

The following is the configuration for this setup:

```
pixfirewall(config)#  static (inside, outside) 199.199.199.6 192.168.1.2
pixfirewall(config)#  access-list PERMIT_IN permit udp
                          host 201.201.201.2 eq 123
                          host 199.199.199.6 eq 123
pixfirewall(config)#  access-list PERMIT_IN deny ip any any
pixfirewall(config)#  access-group PERMIT_IN in interface outside
pixfirewall(config)#
pixfirewall(config)#  ntp authenticate
pixfirewall(config)#  ntp trusted-key 1234
pixfirewall(config)#  ntp authentication-key 1234 md5 secret+key
pixfirewall(config)#  ntp server 192.168.1.2 key 1234 source inside prefer
```

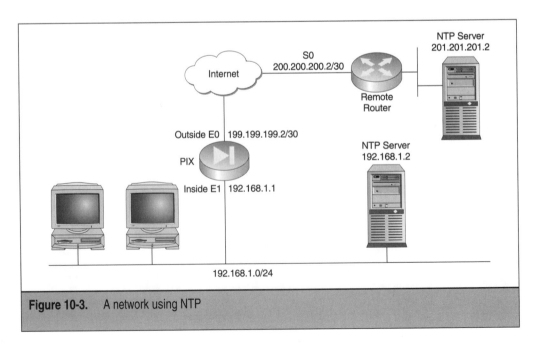

Figure 10-3. A network using NTP

The first part of the configuration sets up the basic configuration, including a `static` command for the internal server. This is necessary for the external server to get its clocking from the internal server. Notice the ACL that follows this—it allows the external NTP server to get its timing information from the internal server.

Below this is the actual NTP configuration for the PIX. I've enabled authentication for access to the internal server—192.168.1.2. The authentication key is *1234* and the authentication string is *secret+key*. As you can see from this configuration , setting up an NTP client on the PIX is simple.

LOGGING EVENTS

Now that you have a basic understanding of SNMP and timing on the PIX, I'll discuss the PIX's logging abilities. The PIX has the ability to log events to the following places:

- Console port
- Internal buffer
- Syslog server
- SNMP management station

The default logging destination is the console port of the PIX. Cisco highly recommends, however, that you either log information to the PIX's internal buffer or an external resource. Logging to the console port is very CPU-intensive, especially in a network where the PIX is processing a lot of traffic. The rest of this chapter covers the PIX's logging features and configuration.

Supported Transport Protocols for Syslog

The PIX firewall supports both the UDP and TCP protocol for logging to a syslog server. Typically, most syslog servers only support UDP for logging transactions. One limitation of UDP is that it is connectionless; therefore, messages sent by the PIX might not make it to the syslog server. For that reason, Cisco has added TCP for syslog. If your syslog server doesn't support TCP, you can freely download from Cisco's web site a syslog server Cisco developed specifically for the PIX firewall. Cisco calls this product the PIX Firewall Syslog Server. The default protocol is UDP, but you can easily change this to TCP.

 SECURITY ALERT!   UDP is more susceptible to session hijacking and spoofing than TCP, and TCP is a connection-oriented protocol. Therefore, you should use TCP as a syslog transport if it is important that you log *every* logging event to an external syslog server.

Message Categories

When the PIX generates log messages, Cisco separates the messages into four major categories, as is shown in Table 10-3.

Category	Description
System	This type of message is generated when the PIX reboots, or a user logs in or out of the PIX, or some other similar event.
Security	This type of message is generated when the PIX drops UDP packets or TCP connections.
Resources	This type of message is generated when the PIX runs out of memory or resources to support additional connections, or runs out of memory or resources for new entries in the xlate table.
Accounting	This type of message is generated for tracking information about the bytes transferred for a connection.

Table 10-3.   Message Categories for Logging

By breaking the information into categories, you can more easily parse the logging information with an external program to perform additional reporting on it.

Configuring Logging

This section covers the commands to configure logging on your PIX firewall. There are many logging options that you can configure on your PIX firewall. To make this more readable, I've broken this information into multiple sections.

Command Syntax for Logging

The following lists the logging commands that you can execute on your PIX:

```
pixfirewall(config)#  logging on
pixfirewall(config)#  logging buffered severity_level
pixfirewall(config)#  logging console severity_level
pixfirewall(config)#  logging facility facility_number
pixfirewall(config)#  logging history severity_level
pixfirewall(config)#  logging host [(interface_name)] syslog_IP_address
                          [tcp|udp[/port_#]]
pixfirewall(config)#  logging message message_ID
pixfirewall(config)#  logging monitor severity_level
pixfirewall(config)#  logging queue queue_size
pixfirewall(config)#  logging standby
pixfirewall(config)#  logging timestamp
pixfirewall(config)#  logging trap severity_level
pixfirewall(config)#  clear logging
pixfirewall(config)#  clear logging disabled
pixfirewall#  show logging
pixfirewall#  show logging disabled
pixfirewall#  show logging queue
```

Table 10-4 explains the use of these commands.

Command	Description
logging on	Turns on logging.
logging buffered	Specifies that log message be sent to the internal buffer of the PIX. You need to specify a severity level for logging, which is covered in Table 10-5.
logging console	Specifies the logging level for messages to be sent to the console of the PIX. You need to specify a severity level for logging, which is covered in Table 10-5.
logging facility	Specifies the location of the file where syslog messages will be directed to on the syslog server. There are eight facility levels supported: local0 through local7. The default is local4.
logging history	Sets the message level to send syslog traps to an SNMP management station. You need to specify a severity level for logging, which is covered in Table 10-5.
logging host	Specifies the IP address of the syslog server. You can optionally specify the interface where the syslog server is located—if you omit the name, it defaults to *inside*. You can optionally specify the transport layer protocol, which defaults to UDP. If you are logging to multiple syslog servers, you must use the same transport protocol for all of them—either TCP or UDP. You can also optionally specify the port number if you are using a different one than the standard one for syslog. The default port number is UDP 514.
logging message	Specifies which messages should be logged by the PIX. By default, the PIX logs all messages. You can precede this command with the no parameter and put in the specific message number, thereby causing the PIX to not log the specified message. Logging message descriptors can be found in the *Cisco PIX Firewall System Log Messages* section in the documentation of the PIX Firewall. You can prevent the PIX from logging all messages with the exception of one: the "%PIX-6-199002: PIX startup completed. Beginning operation" message.
logging monitor	Specifies the logging (and level) for telnet sessions—what logging messages you see when you have a telnet connection to the PIX. You need to specify a severity level for logging, which is covered in Table 10-5.
logging queue	Specifies the maximum number of messages logged to the PIX's internal buffer. This defaults to 512. If you specify 0, the PIX will keep all messages possible in its internal buffer, based on the PIX's available block memory.
logging standby	Allows a standby PIX configured with failover to log messages to a syslog server. By default, only the active (primary) PIX logs syslog messages.

Table 10-4.   The PIX Logging Commands

Command	Description
logging timestamp	This command is only used for logging to the PIX Firewall Syslog Server software. This command adds a timestamp to logging messages before sending them to the syslog server.
logging trap	Sets the logging level for messages sent to an SNMP management device. You need to specify a severity level for logging, which is covered in Table 10-5.
clear logging	Clears the logging messages in the internal buffer of the PIX.
clear logging disabled	Re-enables all logging messages that you disabled with the logging message command.
show logging	Displays the configuration of logging on your PIX. If you are logging messages to the PIX's internal buffer, it also displays these messages.
show logging disabled	Displays the logging messages that you have manually disabled.
show logging queue	Displays the number of messages in the buffer, the highest number of messages ever seen in the buffer, and the number of messages the PIX wasn't available to log to the buffer because there wasn't enough block memory.

Table 10-4.   The PIX Logging Commands (continued)

To disable a logging command or undo a configuration, precede the logging command in Table 10-4 with the no parameter.

Severity Levels

The logging buffered, logging console, logging history, logging monitor, and logging trap commands in Table 10-4 require the *severity_level* parameter. The severity level basically ranks the logging messages in order of importance. Table 10-5 shows the severity levels that can be assigned to messages.

Level Number	Name of Level	Level Description
0	Emergencies	The system is unusable.
1	Alerts	You need to take immediate action to fix the problem.
2	Critical	There is a critical condition on the PIX.
3	Errors	The PIX has experienced an error.
4	Warnings	There is a configuration or processing issue.
5	Notifications	A normal, yet significant, event has occurred.
6	Informational	A non-significant event has occurred on the PIX.
7	Debugging	Allows the PIX to log the output of debug commands, FTP commands, and web URLs.

Table 10-5.   Logging Severity Levels

The lower the number for the severity level for a logging message, the more severe the message.

Using TCP for a Transport

When you are using TCP for a transport to log messages to a syslog server, there are certain conditions that can occur that prevent the PIX from logging messages. These include the following:

- The PIX cannot access the syslog server on the configured port.
- The syslog server has been misconfigured.
- The disk drive on the syslog server is full and no more messages can be logged.

When any of these problems are fixed, unfortunately, the PIX does not automatically start to send messages to the syslog server. Instead, you need to manually enter the `logging host` command.

> **SECURITY ALERT!**   If you are using UDP as a transport for logging messages to a syslog server, and the UDP server is not available, the PIX cannot detect this. If you are using TCP as a transport and the PIX cannot log messages because of an error, once you fix the error, you have to re-enter the `logging host` command to re-enable logging.

Example Configuration

Let's take a look at an example to help illustrate the `logging` commands. I'll use the network shown in Figure 10-4 for this example. In this example there is an internal syslog server.

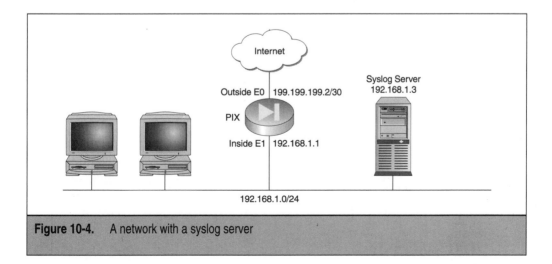

Figure 10-4.   A network with a syslog server

I'll only focus on the `logging` commands in this configuration. The following is the configuration for this setup:

```
pixfirewall(config)# logging on
pixfirewall(config)# no logging console
pixfirewall(config)# no logging monitor
pixfirewall(config)# logging buffer 2
pixfirewall(config)# logging host inside 192.168.1.3 tcp
pixfirewall(config)# logging timestamp
```

Logging is enabled, but I've disabled logging to the console and telnet sessions, and limited logging to the PIX's internal buffer to a severity level of 2 (critical errors). The example also logs messages to a syslog server (192.168.1.3) using TCP. Timestamps will be included in these logging messages.

To verify your configuration, use the `show logging` command:

```
pixfirewall# show logging
Syslog logging: enabled
Timestamp logging: enabled
Console logging: disabled
Monitor logging: disabled
Buffer logging: level critical, 0 messages logged
Trap logging: disabled
```

In this, no logging messages are listed because there are no logging messages in the internal buffer of the PIX.

FURTHER STUDY

Web Sites

For information on SNMP, examine RFCs 2571 through 2576:

- www.ietf.org/rfc/rfc2571.txt
- www.ietf.org/rfc/rfc2572.txt
- www.ietf.org/rfc/rfc2573.txt
- www.ietf.org/rfc/rfc2574.txt
- www.ietf.org/rfc/rfc2575.txt
- www.ietf.org/rfc/rfc2576.txt

For an overview of NTP, visit www.cisco.com/warp/customer/126/ntpm.html. This is an excellent document, but requires a CCO account from Cisco in order to access it.

For information on RFC 1305, which covers the implementation of NTP, visit www.ietf.org/rfc/rfc1305.txt.

For information on the syslog process, visit www.ietf.org/rfc/rfc3164.txt.

For information on the PIX's log messages, visit www.cisco.com/univercd/cc/td/doc/product/iaabu/pix/pix_62/syslog/index.htm.

For more information about configuring your PIX, visit www.cisco.com/univercd/cc/td/doc/product/iaabu/pix/pix_62/config/index.htm.

CHAPTER 11

Centralizing Security

In the last chapter, I talked about using SNMP to manage your PIX as well as the PIX's logging features. This chapter builds upon the management features that I have discussed so far. In this chapter, I'll explain how you can centralize the security of your PIX firewall with a security server, as well as some additional authentication methods for inbound connections, like Cut-Through Proxy, Virtual Telnet, and Virtual HTTP.

CENTRALIZING SECURITY

One of the major problems you face when designing your network is the management of security. In large networks, you can easily have over 1,000 networking devices to manage, including routers, switches, firewalls, file servers, and many others. Each of these devices has its own local authentication method. For instance, a PIX firewall has a telnet and a *Privilege EXEC* password. Imagine if you had to periodically change these passwords on a 1,000 devices to ensure a secure environment. Obviously, this would not be easy.

For example, I worked with a company that had about 1,200 routers. This company had many networking administrators, as well as many networking contractors working for them. They basically had three job levels within their networking division: tier 1, tier 2, and tier 3. Tier 1 and 2 administrators were granted *User EXEC* access to the routers, and tier 3 workers were allowed *Privilege EXEC* access. This sounds simple enough, but the company had a major dilemma. They would never hire a tier 3 contractor because contractors would come and go on a weekly basis, and this would mean that they would definitely have to change all of the *Privilege EXEC* passwords on all of their 1,200 routers. Instead, they only had a small staff of employees, about ten, that had tier 3 access and performed *Privilege EXEC* functions. As you can imagine, these ten employees were completely swamped with work trying to maintain the 1,200 routers.

A better solution to this problem would be to hire contractors at a tier 3 level and give them *Privilege EXEC* access. Of course, you wouldn't want to change passwords on 1,200 routers every time a tier 3 contractor left the company. To solve this problem, you could use a centralized security solution. Instead of having the routers and other networking devices perform authentication locally, you could have them forward the authentication requests to a centralized security server or servers, who would validate the user's identity and pass the results back to networking devices. This allows you to maintain user accounts at one location, making it easy to add and remove accounts. When a tier 3 contractor is hired, you would add that person to the security server, with the appropriate security access, and when the contract is terminated, it would be a simple matter of deleting the account from a single security server. Cisco actually sells a product, called *Cisco Secure ACS*, that allows you to centralize the security for your networking devices, like routers, switches, firewalls, and other networking equipment.

AAA

AAA helps you centralize your security checks and is broken into three areas: *Authentication* (who), *Authorization* (what), and *Accounting* (when). Together, all three of these areas are referred to as *AAA*.

Authentication is responsible for checking a user's identity to determine if the user is allowed access to the networking device. A user must enter a username and password to validate. Once a user has gained access to the networking device, *authorization* determines what the user can do—what commands they can execute and what privilege levels they have access to. For example, you could allow a person *Privilege EXEC* access to a router, but not allow them access to *Configuration* mode. And lastly, you can keep a record of a user's actions, like what commands they executed and when they executed them, with the *accounting* function.

Security Protocols

To implement AAA, you need a secure protocol to transport security information between the networking device and the security (AAA) server. There are three security protocols used to implement AAA:

- Kerberos
- Remote Access Dial-In User Service (RADIUS)
- Terminal Access Controller Access Control System (TACACS+)

Some of Cisco's networking devices support all three protocols; however, Cisco only supports the last two on their PIX firewalls, and for RADIUS, Cisco only supports authentication functions. The next three sections provide a brief overview of these security protocols.

Kerberos

Kerberos was developed at the Massachusetts Institute of Technology (MIT) and uses DES (40- or 56-bit keys) for encrypting information between the networking device and the security server, referred to as a Key Distribution Center (KDC). Kerberos is an open standard; however, it functions at only the application layer. This means that you need to make changes to the actual application to use Kerberos. On IOS-based routers, Cisco has included Kerberos authentication for telnet, RSH, RLOGIN, and RCP. Cisco doesn't support Kerberos on the PIX.

RADIUS

RADIUS was developed by the Livingston Corporation, which is now owned by Lucent. It is currently an open standard, defined in RFCs 2138 and 2139. However, many proprietary extensions have been added by various companies for their networking devices, making it a somewhat open standard. RADIUS supports UDP (ports 1645 and 1646) for the connection between the networking device and security server, and only encrypts the key used for authentication, but not the actual data payload, making it less secure (susceptible to eavesdropping attacks) than Kerberos or TACACS+. Probably RADIUS's biggest advantage over the other two security protocols is that, because it was developed for dialup networks like ISPs, it has a very robust accounting system.

TACACS+

TACACS was originally developed for the United States Defense Department and has been updated over the years by Cisco, resulting in an enhanced version called TACACS+. Because of the many changes Cisco has made to the protocol, it is proprietary in nature. Unlike RADIUS, TACACS+ uses TCP (port 49) for the security connection, and encrypts the entire payload contents in the security packets, making it more reliable and more secure than RADIUS. TACACS+ also supports a single connection feature—the networking device opens a single TCP connection to the AAA server, and uses this single connection for all AAA functions. This feature provides faster response times than with RADIUS, because RADIUS uses a separate UDP connection for each AAA request.

SERVER AND AUTHENTICATION CONFIGURATION

The PIX has support for AAA functionality. Normally, AAA is used to control access to the command-line interface shell of a networking device. The PIX supports this function of AAA, but also uses AAA for network access *through* the PIX, allowing users to authenticate to the PIX before their connections are allowed through it. Some examples of these AAA PIX features are Cut-Through Proxy, Virtual Telnet, and Virtual HTTP. The following sections contain an overview of how to configure AAA on your PIX.

The first thing that you will need to configure for AAA is access from the PIX to your AAA security server with the `aaa-server` commands, shown here:

```
pixfirewall(config)# aaa-server group_tag protocol
                          tacacs+|radius
pixfirewall(config)# aaa-server group_tag (interface_name)
                          host AAA_server_IP_address AAA_key
                          [timeout value_in_seconds]
```

The first command specifies which security protocol you'll use when your PIX accesses the security server: TACACS+ or RADIUS. The *group_tag* parameter is used to group your security information together, because you might have one set of security servers for authenticating command-line access and another set for authenticating Cut-Through Proxy. In most instances, you'll only need one grouping. The *group_tag* parameter must be unique among all of these parameters, and you can have up to 16 different group tags on your PIX.

Next, you must specify the security server that your PIX will use. You must specify the name of the interface where the security is located. Following this is the `host` parameter and the IP address of the security server. The *AAA_key* parameter is the key used to secure the connection between the security server and the PIX—this key must also be configured on the security server, and is case sensitive. You can configure up to 256 different security servers, where each AAA server has its own configuration command. When trying to connect to the security server, the PIX will try for five seconds, by default. If it can't reach the security server, it will try the second security server that you've configured (if you have configured another one). You can change this value with the optional `timeout` parameter. The timeout can be increased up to 30 seconds.

SHELL ACCESS

There are actually two areas that you can secure for shell access: access to the PIX itself, and the commands that the user can execute once authenticated. To use AAA, you only have to secure the shell access; securing commands is optional. To secure access to the PIX, you'll use the `aaa authentication` and `aaa authorization` commands, which I'll discuss in the next two sections.

Authenticating Shell Access

The PIX allows you to use AAA (using a security server) to provide authentication for shell access. Once you have configured your security server information with the `aaa-server` commands, you can now proceed with your shell authentication by using the `aaa authentication` command:

```
pixfirewall(config)#  aaa authentication serial|enable|telnet|ssh|http
                        console group_tag
```

The following are the methods of access that you can authenticate:

- `serial`   accessing the PIX via the console port
- `enable`   accessing *Privilege EXEC* mode
- `telnet`   accessing the PIX via telnet
- `ssh`   accessing the PIX via SSH
- `http`   accessing the PIX via PDM

The *group_tag* parameter specifies the security server and protocol to use. Once you set this up, the PIX will always use the security server for authenticating the access method you configured. If the security server cannot be reached, the PIX has a backdoor to allow you access to the CLI: enter a username of *pix* and the password you configured with the `enable password` command, which was discussed in Chapter 3. This method can only be used on the console port of the PIX.

CSNT Setup

If you want your PIX to use *Privilege EXEC* authentication using Cisco Secure ACS for NT/2000 (CSNT), you need to perform the following steps on your CSNT server (I'm assuming that you are using CSNT 3.0):

1. Click the Interface Configuration button on the left side of the screen.
2. Click the TACACS+ (Cisco IOS) button.
3. Find the Advanced Configuration Options section and click the Advanced TACACS+ features radio box.
4. Click the Submit button at the bottom.

Once you have done this, you can now tell CSNT to authenticate using CSNT's configured enable password instead of the PIX's:

1. Click the User Setup button on the left side of the screen.
2. Enter the appropriate username and click the Add/Edit button.
3. Under the TACACS+ Enable Control subsection of the Advanced TACACS+ Settings section, click the radio button labeled Max Privilege for any AAA Client, and choose level 15 from the pull-down menu.
4. Under the TACACS+ Enable Password subsection of the Advanced TACACS+ Settings section, choose the type of password CSNT will use: the user's PAP password, a password from an external database, or a password that you manually enter in this section.
5. Click the Submit button at the bottom.

Once you have done this, make sure that you have configured the aaa authentication enable command on your PIX. Your PIX should now authenticate *Privilege EXEC* access and use the password method you specified in CSNT.

If you want to restrict who can access your PIX to perform administrative functions with CSNT, perform the following within CSNT:

1. Click the Group Setup button on the left side of the window.
2. Choose the correct group name from the pull-down menu and click the Edit Settings button.
3. Scroll down to the Network Access Restrictions section.
4. Enter the appropriate information in either the Denied Calling/Point of Access Locations subsection or Permitted Calling/Point of Access Locations, depending on whether you want to deny certain people and allow the rest, or vice versa.
5. Click the Submit+Restart button.

NOTE This book only briefly covers the configuration necessary for Cisco Secure ACS 3.0 for NT/2000—the steps described in this book differ slightly depending on the version of CSNT that you are running, or the process may be completely different if you are using another product.

PIX Authentication Example

Here is a simple PIX configuration example of using shell authentication:

```
pixfirewall(config)#  aaa-server TACSRV protocol tacacs+
pixfirewall(config)#  aaa-server TACSRV (inside)
                              host 192.168.1.10 thisisasecret
pixfirewall(config)#  aaa authentication serial console TACSRV
pixfirewall(config)#  aaa authentication enable console TACSRV
pixfirewall(config)#  aaa authentication telnet console TACSRV
pixfirewall(config)#  aaa authentication ssh console TACSRV
pixfirewall(config)#  aaa authentication http console TACSRV
```

In this example, all methods of access use the *TACSRV* group tag for authentication. This group tag specifies the use of TACACS+ to the AAA security server at 192.168.1.10, where the secret key is *thisisasecret*.

Using Command Authorization

Once a user has been authenticated for shell access on the PIX, you can optionally restrict the commands that user can execute. To do this, you assign different privilege levels to the PIX's commands. One problem of giving a user *Privilege EXEC* access is that they can basically do anything that they want on the PIX. Instead, you might want to restrict the user to just troubleshooting commands. There are two ways of doing this: local to the PIX or an external security server.

To have the PIX perform command authorization itself, use this command:

```
pixfirewall(config)#  privilege [show|clear|config] level level
                              [mode enable|configure]
                              command PIX_command
```

The show, clear, and configure modifiers allow you to change the privilege level of the specified command for just that modifier—if you omit the modifier, it affects the level of the command for all three modifiers. The privilege level is a number between 0 and 15. The mode parameter affects the access mode where you are changing the privilege of the command. Last, use the command parameter followed by the command that you want to change access for. Use the show privilege all command to display your privilege configuration.

Here is a simple example of using the `privilege` command:

```
pixfirewall(config)# privilege show level 10 command access-list
pixfirewall(config)# privilege configure level 15 command access-list
pixfirewall(config)# privilege clear level 15 command access-list
```

In this example, a user at level 10 or higher can execute the `show access-list` command, and a user at level 15 can configure or delete ACLs.

As you probably recall from Chapter 3, the `enable` command is used to move from *User* mode to *Privilege EXEC* mode. When you type this command in by itself, the PIX assumes that you are using access privilege level 15. You can change this behavior using one of two methods. The first method requires some user intervention—when the user tries to access *Privilege EXEC* mode, they must use this command:

```
pixfirewall(config)# enable privilege_level
```

You then enter the appropriate password that has been configured. One option with setting the *Privilege EXEC* password on the PIX is to assign a privilege level to the password—if you omit the privilege level for the `enable password` command, it defaults to 15. Use the `show curpriv` command to see your current privilege level.

The second method is to use the `aaa authorization` command:

```
pixfirewall(config)# aaa authorization command group_tag
```

The `group_tag` parameter must match an `aaa-server` command, which determines the type of authorization performed: Only TACACS+ security servers are supported for authorization functions.

If you are using CSNT, you need to perform the following to set up external authorization on your PIX:

1. Click the Group Setup button on the left side of the window.

2. Choose the correct group name from the pull-down menu and click the Edit Settings button.

3. Scroll down to the Shell Command Authorization Set section.

4. Click the Command button and enter the command in the box.

5. Under the Arguments heading, enter any arguments that you wish to allow in the scroll box.

6. Under the Unlisted Arguments heading, click the Permit or Deny radio button to determine what will happen if the argument the user enters is not listed in the Arguments box.

7. Click the Submit button at the bottom.

8. Repeat Steps 1 through 7 for any additional commands.

9. Click the Submit+Restart button at the bottom.

Once you have listed the commands that the user is allowed to execute it, test it by having the user log in to the PIX and execute various commands, include those allowed and denied by your CSNT configuration.

NOTE When using command authorization, check your configuration and access *before* saving your configuration to flash—if you make a mistake and lock yourself out of the PIX, you can easily reboot your PIX with the old configuration file in flash.

CUT-THROUGH PROXY

The previous section discussed how to set up authentication to restrict access to the PIX itself. However, there may be circumstances where you want to authenticate connections through the PIX itself. For example, you might have a situation where using an ACL doesn't provide enough security. Remember that ACLs, discussed in Chapter 5, can only look at the layer 3 and 4 information, which can easily be spoofed. As an added security measure, you can use the PIX's Cut-Through Proxy feature, which provides application-layer authentication.

As of FOS 6.2, Cisco supports per-user ACLs that can be downloaded and applied to the PIX once a user has authenticated. This feature is supported by both TACACS+ and RADIUS with Cut-Through Proxy and Virtual Telnet and HTTP. This feature requires Cisco Secure ACS as a security server.

Cut-Through Proxy Process

With Cut-Through Proxy, the PIX receives an inbound connection from a lower level security interface. Before accepting the connection, the PIX can first authenticate it by prompting the source machine with a username and password prompt. The user must enter a username and password, which are sent to the PIX. The PIX will then forward the username and password to a security server to have the information validated. If the user is permitted, the ASA opens up a small hole in the firewall to permit the connection.

One important item to point out is that Cut-Through Proxy can authenticate both inbound *and* outbound connections. Currently, Cisco only supports Cut-Through Proxy connections for the following applications: HTTP, telnet, and FTP. As you will see in later sections, there are other methods for dealing with other applications.

Figure 11-1 shows the Cut-Through Proxy process with a security server: In Step 1, an external user attempts to access an internal web server. In Step 2, the PIX sends a username and password prompt to the user. The user then enters the AAA username and password.

One nice feature for this prompt is that the user can use the following nomenclature when entering the username and password (FTP and HTTP connections only):

```
AAA_username@internal_host_username
AAA_password@internal_host_password
```

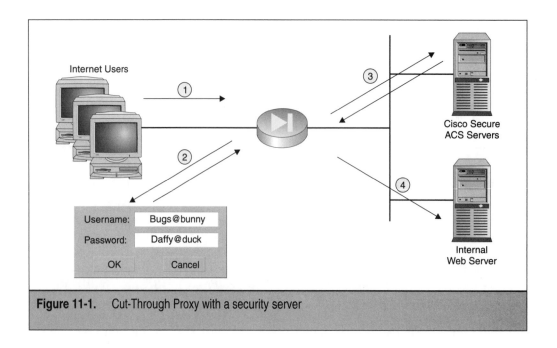

Figure 11-1. Cut-Through Proxy with a security server

The AAA username can be up to 127 characters in length, and the password can be 64 characters in length.

The PIX then takes the AAA username and password only and forwards it to the security server (Step 3) for validation. If the AAA server can validate the user, the server tells the PIX to permit the connection. Otherwise, it tells the PIX to drop the connection. If the connection is permitted, and you used the correct nomenclature, the PIX will take the internal username and password following the @ sign, and forward these to the internal server (Step 4)—this alleviates the user from having to enter a username and password twice: once for AAA and once for the internal server, providing a single login process for the user. The usernames and passwords themselves cannot contain the @ sign.

Using Cut-Through Proxy gives you more security because you are authenticating a user instead of the IP address of a device; however, please note that the username and password that the user sends to the PIX are in *clear* text, and are thus susceptible to eavesdropping. If you are concerned about this, integrate a token card system into your security server setup.

Cut-Through Proxy Authentication

To configure Cut-Through Proxy authentication, you'll need to set up your `aaa authentication` commands on your PIX as well as configure your Cisco Secure ACS security server. There are actually two versions of the authentication and authorization commands: one for FOS 4.*x* and one for FOS 5.*x* and later. This book only covers the latter. Here is the syntax of the authentication command on the PIX:

```
pixfirewall(config)#  aaa authentication include|exclude application_name
                          inbound|outbound|interface_name
                          internal_IP_address internal_subnet_mask
                          external_IP_address external_subnet_mask
                          group_tag
pixfirewall(config)#  aaa authentication match ACL_name interface_name
                          group_tag
```

The first thing you must specify is either the `include` or `exclude` parameter, which tells the PIX which applications will use Cut-Through Proxy authentication. After this, you must specify the application name that you'll authenticate. These include: `http`, `ftp`, `telnet`, or `any` (for all three applications). Next, you must specify the direction or interface where Cut-Through Proxy will be performed:

- `inbound`   from a lower to higher security level interface
- `outbound`   from a higher to lower security level interface
- *interface_name*   inbound on this interface

Following this are the inside and outside addresses that authentication should be performed for. If you want to authenticate all connections, use 0.0.0.0 0.0.0.0 0.0.0.0 0.0.0.0 or 0 0 0 0—this will cause the PIX to use Cut-Through Proxy for all of the applications that you specified for all connections. If you only want to authenticate connections to a specific web server, then list that web server as the internal address and everyone for the external address. Finally, you need to specify the *group_tag* value, which tells the PIX which security server should perform the authentication.

Optionally, you can use an ACL name with the `match` parameter to specify the traffic to be authenticated. This is shown in the second command. When you do this, the ACL can only match on HTTP, FTP, and telnet traffic. This function was introduced in FOS 5.2.

Here is a simple example of a Cut-Through Proxy configuration:

```
pixfirewall(config)#  aaa-server TACSRV protocol tacacs+
pixfirewall(config)#  aaa-server TACSRV (inside)
                          host 192.168.1.10 thisisasecret
pixfirewall(config)#  aaa authentication include http outside
                          192.168.1.12 255.255.255.255 0 0 TACSRV
```

In this example, the PIX is using TACACS+ to communicate to the security server (192.168.1.10). Cut-Through Proxy authentication is being performed for only HTTP traffic destined to 192.168.1.12 when it enters the *outside* interface. All other types of traffic will have to pass your ACL configuration in order to access the web server. One important item to point out is that the PIX first processes its ACLs *before* performing

Cut-Through Proxy. Therefore, if you want to authenticate HTTP traffic, you will need to explicitly permit HTTP traffic with an ACL on a lower security interface.

NOTE Remember that web browsers can cache usernames and passwords. Therefore, if you have configured timeouts for HTTP connections, which will cause the PIX to re-authenticate the user, the web browser might send the same information to the PIX, which will be forwarded to the security server. This can cause a problem if you are using token cards for authentication.

Cut-Through Proxy Authorization

The problem with authenticating Cut-Through Proxy connections is that you might need to specify a wide range of internal networks to allow access to, but not every inbound user should access all of these internal devices—instead, you want to refine the access to internal services for these users. Or, perhaps you don't want your users to have to authenticate to each server that they access. In the latter example, your users would authenticate once, have the PIX cache this information, and then for additional user connections, the PIX would forward the cached information to the security server for verification.

As an example, you might have the following configuration:

```
pixfirewall(config)#  aaa authentication include any outside
                          0 0 0 0 TACSRV
```

In this example, once an external user is authenticated, he can access any internal device offering FTP, HTTP, or telnet services, assuming your ACLs permit this. In many cases, this is a security problem.

However, there is a solution: you can refine a user's access using AAA authorization. Configuring Cut-Through Proxy authorization requires two steps: configure `aaa authorization` commands on your PIX and the appropriate configuration on your security server. Please note that you must first configure AAA authentication on your PIX before you can proceed with the authorization configuration. In addition to this, the PIX currently only supports TACACS+ for authorization.

Configuring Authorization

On your PIX firewall, use the following command to set up Cut-Through Proxy authorization:

```
pixfirewall(config)#  aaa authorization include|exclude application_name
                          inbound|outbound|interface_name
                          internal_IP_address internal_subnet_mask
                          external_IP_address external_subnet_mask
                          group_tag
pixfirewall(config)#  aaa authorization match ACL_name interface_name
                          group_tag
```

As you can see, the syntax of these commands is almost the same as the `aaa authentication` commands.

There are a couple of items that need to be pointed out concerning authorization. First, the PIX only supports TACACS+ for authorization. Second, if the PIX doesn't find a match in any of its authorization statements, it will implicitly permit the user's connection (assuming there is an ACL to permit this traffic). Third, besides specifying an application name (any, http, ftp, or telnet), you can also list an IP protocol number or name as well as a port number or range. When you specify a range, separate the beginning and ending port numbers by a hyphen. For example, your web servers might not be running on port 80, but on ports 8080-8081. To catch this port number, use the following syntax for the *application_name* parameter: tcp/8080-8081.

Configuring CSNT

Once you have configured authorization on your PIX, you must enable it on your security server. Here are the steps if you are using CSNT:

1. Click the Group Setup button on the left side of the screen.
2. Choose the appropriate group name from the pull-down menu and click the Edit Settings button.
3. Go to the Shell Command Authorization Set section.
4. Under the Unmatched Cisco IOS Commands heading, click the Command radio button and enter either telnet, http, or ftp in the box below the radio button. You can also specify an IP protocol and port number or numbers by using this syntax: protocol_number_or_name/port_number[-port_number]
5. If you want restrict access to certain destinations, enter the IP addresses in the text box below the Arguments heading and click the Permit radio button below this. To allow all destinations, don't enter IP addresses in this box and click the Permit radio button.
6. Click the Submit button at the bottom of the page.
7. Repeat steps 1 through 6 for each additional application.
8. Click the Submit+Restart button at the bottom of the page.

OTHER TYPES OF TRAFFIC

As I mentioned in the previous section, one limitation of Cut-Through Proxy is that it can only be used to authenticate HTTP, FTP, and telnet connections. If you have other applications that you need to authenticate, the Cut-Through Proxy feature will not be able to handle the authentication. However, you do have three other options available to you:

- Use authentication on the application server the user is trying to access.
- Use the Virtual Telnet PIX feature on the PIX.
- Use the Virtual HTTP PIX feature on the PIX.

One problem with having the application server perform the authentication is that your authentication mechanism isn't centralized—you need to set up authentication on every server where you need user authentication. Virtual Telnet and HTTP provide a more scalable solution, as you will see in the following sections, and can authenticate and authorize connections in both the inbound and outbound directions.

Using Virtual Telnet

Typically, you'll use Virtual Telnet when you need to authenticate connections *other* than HTTP, FTP, or telnet. With Virtual Telnet, the user telnets to the PIX and then supplies a username and password to pass authentication. Once authenticated, the PIX terminates the telnet session and allows the user to open up the connection. One annoyance with Virtual Telnet is that it is a two-step process for a user to connect to a resource—the user telnets into the PIX to be authenticated, and then the user opens up the application connection to the actual service.

Let's look at a simple example where you can use Virtual Telnet. You have an internal TFTP server (UDP 69). Obviously, Cut-Through Proxy can't authenticate this connection. You can authenticate this connection using Virtual Telnet, however. To accomplish this, the user first telnets to a virtual IP address on the PIX—this address must be a reachable address (on the Internet, this has to be a public address). Actually, the virtual IP address is similar to a loopback address on an IOS-based router. The PIX then prompts the user for a username and password, and then authenticates this information via Cisco Secure ACS. If the authentication is successful, the security server then examines what connections the user is allowed to set up and then passes this information to the PIX. The PIX's ASA then opens up a hole in the firewall for these connections

To set up Virtual Telnet on your PIX, use the following command:

```
pixfirewall(config)# virtual telnet global_IP_address
```

The IP address must be a public-reachable address—treat this address as a loopback address on an IOS-based router. For inbound users, this will typically be a public IP address; for outbound users, it can be either a public or a private IP address. After configuring this command, you must still configure your AAA commands.

To help illustrate the use of Virtual Telnet, I'll use the network in Figure 11-2:

Here is the code to set up Virtual Telnet for this network:

```
pixfirewall(config)# virtual telnet 200.200.200.2
pixfirewall(config)# aaa-server TACSRV protocol tacacs+
pixfirewall(config)# aaa-server TACSRV (inside)
                         host 192.168.1.2 thisisasecret
pixfirewall(config)# aaa authentication include udp/69
                         outside 0 0 0 0 TACSRV
pixfirewall(config)#
pixfirewall(config)# static (inside, outside) 200.200.200.2
                         200.200.200.2 netmask 255.255.255.255
```

```
pixfirewall(config)#  static (inside, outside) 200.200.200.3
                          192.168.1.3 netmask 255.255.255.255
pixfirewall(config)#  static (inside, outside) 200.200.200.4
                          192.168.1.4 netmask 255.255.255.255
pixfirewall(config)#  access-list INBOUND permit tcp any 200.200.200.2
                          eq 23
pixfirewall(config)#  access-group INBOUND in interface outside
```

In this example, the Virtual Telnet address is 200.200.200.2, which is internal to the PIX itself. The AAA server is 192.168.1.2, and the aaa authentication command specifies that TFTP traffic should be authenticated. Notice the very first static command as well as the ACL—these are necessary to permit the inbound telnet from an external user. Please note that you must still configure CSNT to perform authentication.

Using Virtual HTTP

Virtual HTTP is used when Cut-Through Proxy and the internal web server have difficulties communicating with each other. In many instances, if you are using Microsoft's IIS as a web server, Cut-Through Proxy will not be able to handle the interaction with the web server correctly. As I mentioned in the previous section, you are somewhat limited in passing information from the user to the web server: it has to be in a username/password format. If you need to pass more information to the web server to set up the connection, Virtual HTTP will allow this, whereas Cut-Through Proxy won't.

Virtual HTTP works by having the PIX mimic a web server. The user attempts to open up a connection to an internal web server, and the PIX intercepts the connection, as in Cut-Through Proxy. The virtual web server on the PIX authenticates the user and

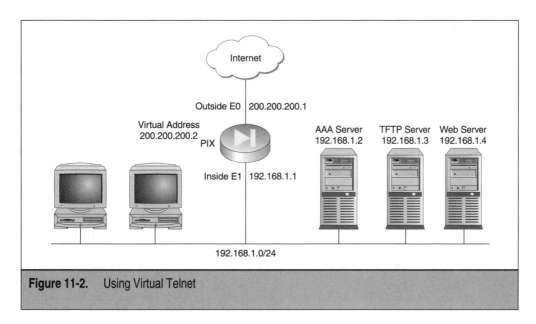

Figure 11-2. Using Virtual Telnet

then builds the connection to the internal web server. From the user's perspective, the interaction appears to be with the internal web server and not the virtual web server, making the virtual web server on the PIX seem transparent.

To set up a Virtual HTTP server on the PIX, use the following command:

```
pixfirewall(config)# virtual http global_IP_address [warn]
```

As in the case of setting up Virtual Telnet, the IP address here is internal to the PIX—use a public address for external users accessing internal resources, or a private or public address for internal users accessing external resources. The warn parameter causes the PIX to send a pop-up web window to the user notifying them that their web connection is being "redirected." Please note that you need to set up an ACL for inbound traffic to allow the user's connection to the virtual web server address (TCP 80).

The configuration of the Virtual HTTP feature is basically the same as Virtual Telnet. Using the example in the "Using Virtual Telnet" section, the only thing that you would need to change would be to remove the virtual telnet command, and replace it with virtual http. Also, you would need to change your ACL to reflect port 80 instead of 23.

Authorizing Virtual Telnet and HTTP Connections

The last two sections showed you how to set up authentication for Virtual Telnet and HTTP connections. Remember that authorization is used to refine the type of access a user is allowed, or when you don't want your users to have to authenticate to each server that they access. In the latter example, your users would authenticate once, have the PIX cache this information, and then for additional user connections, the PIX would forward the cached information to the security server for verification.

You must always configure authentication first before authorization. This is a two step process: you need to add your AAA authentication and then authorization commands on the PIX, and then configure your security server. On the PIX, here is the syntax of the aaa authorization command:

```
pixfirewall(config)# aaa authorization include|exclude
                      IP_protocol_name/port_number[-port_number]
                      inbound|outbound|interface_name
                      internal_IP_address internal_subnet_mask
                      external_IP_address external_subnet_mask
                      group_tag
pixfirewall(config)# aaa authorization match ACL_name interface_name
                      group_tag
```

The first command has almost the same syntax as the one used for Cut-Through Proxy. The major difference is that instead of specifying an application, you need to specify an IP protocol name or number, followed by a slash, and then a port name or number. For a range of ports, separate the first and last port with a hyphen. Other than that, the syntax is the same. Of course, you can always use the second command in combination with an ACL, which tells the PIX which traffic to perform authorization on.

One restriction with authorization for Virtual Telnet and HTTP is that Cisco only supports TACACS+. Remember that if a match is not found within a set of authorization commands, the PIX will permit the user's action. You also need to configure your security server. The steps for CSNT were outlined earlier in the "Cut-Through Proxy Authorization" section. The major difference is that you specify the connection by using the protocol name or number, followed by a slash, and then the port number in the Command text box.

CHANGING AUTHENTICATION PARAMETERS

There are some optional parameters that you might want to configure for AAA authentication. Some optional things that you can configure are

- Limiting the number of proxy connections per user
- Changing the authentication prompt presented by the PIX
- Changing the timeouts for authenticated connection

The following three sections cover the use and configuration of these parameters.

Limiting Proxy Connections

You can limit the number of concurrent proxy connections that a user is allowed to establish with the aaa proxy-limit command:

```
pixfirewall(config)# aaa proxy-limit #_of_connections|disable
```

For the #_of_connections parameter, you can specify a value from 1 to 128—the default is 3. The disable parameter disables limits. You can view your configured information with the show aaa proxy-limit command.

Authentication Prompts

The PIX allows you to modify the prompts used during the authentication process. If you recall from the "Cut-Through Proxy" and "Using Virtual Telnet" sections, the user is prompted for both a username and a password. You can modify what the PIX sends to the user with the following command:

```
pixfirewall(config)# auth-prompt [accept|reject|prompt] prompt_string
```

There are actually three prompts that can be involved in the password checking process:

- prompt   This text is displayed before the username and password prompt.
- accept   This text is displayed once a user has authenticated via telnet.
- reject   This text is displayed once a user has failed telnet authentication.

There are limitations on the length of the prompt, based on the application the user is accessing:

- **FTP and telnet**   235 characters
- **Microsoft Internet Explorer**   37 characters
- **Netscape Navigator**   120 characters

I recommend that you keep your prompts short so that you'll be able to support any type of application. For the actual prompt, you should not use any type of special characters; however, you are permitted to use spaces and punctuation marks. Whenever you enter a question mark or press the ENTER key, the PIX terminates the prompt. If you entered a question mark, the question mark becomes part of the prompt.

Here is a simple example of setting the prompts:

```
pixfirewall(config)#  auth-prompt prompt Full body cavity search
                               before proceeding!
pixfirewall(config)#  auth-prompt accept Hello Dave!
pixfirewall(config)#  auth-prompt reject Duh! Try again!
```

Once you have configured these prompts and your AAA configuration, you can test it. Here is an example of a user performing a Virtual Telnet:

```
Full body cavity search before proceeding!
Username: Monkey
Password: *****
Duh! Try again!

Full body cavity search before proceeding!
Username: Monkey
Password: *******
Hello Dave!
```

Authentication Timeouts

The PIX supports two different timeouts for AAA authenticated connections: idle and absolute. These timeouts affect when the PIX will terminate an AAA connection that a user has open. By default, the PIX caches this information for five minutes and then uses it to re-authenticate the user upon expiration of their connection. To set these timeouts, use the `timeout` command:

```
pixfirewall(config)#  timeout uauth hh:mm:ss [absolute|inactivity]
```

The `absolute` timeout affects the duration of a user's connection whether the user is active or idle on the connection. The `inactivity` timeout tells the PIX when to tear down a connection once it is idle for the specified length of time. To disable a timeout, set the timeout value to 00:00:00. The exception to this is for FTP and Virtual HTTP connections—setting this value to 00:00:00 will cause connectivity problems within the PIX itself. To examine your timeout values, use the `show timeout` command.

CONFIGURING ACCOUNTING

The last function of AAA is accounting. Accounting allows you to keep a record of the actions of your users, like when they successfully or unsuccessfully authenticate, what services they are accessing, or what commands they are executing. To use AAA accounting, you need a TACACS+ server—syslog and RADIUS are not supported.

The command for configuring accounting is `aaa accounting`:

```
pixfirewall(config)#  aaa accounting include|exclude accounting_service
                           inbound|outbound|interface_name
                           internal_IP_address internal_subnet_mask
                           external_IP_address external_subnet_mask
                           group_tag
pixfirewall(config)#  aaa accounting match ACL_name
                           inbound|outbound|interface_name group_tag
```

The layout of this command is almost the same as the `aaa authentication` and `aaa authorization` commands. The `include` parameter specifies what connections accounting will be enabled for—if the connection isn't included, the PIX will not capture accounting information for it. The `accounting_service` parameter specifies the type of connection, like `any`, `ftp`, `http`, `telnet`, or even by protocol and port, like `udp/69`. For the latter syntax, you can specify a range of ports by separating the beginning and ending port numbers with a hyphen (`tcp/8080-8090`).

Remember to enable accounting on your security server, if this is necessary. You can optionally use an ACL with the `match` parameter to specify the connections to gather information from.

Here is an example where all connections will have accounting enabled for them:

```
pixfirewall(config)#  aaa accounting include any inbound
                           0 0 0 0 TACSRV
pixfirewall(config)#  aaa accounting include any outbound
                           0 0 0 0 TACSRV
```

Once you have set up accounting, make sure that your security server is receiving the accounting information from the PIX.

TESTING AND TROUBLESHOOTING AAA

Now that you have configured AAA on your PIX, you will want to verify its operation. There are many show and clear commands that you can use. Table 11-1 lists the show commands. Here is an example of the show uauth command:

```
pixfirewall#  show uauth
                                Current           Most Seen
 Authenticated Users           3                 3
 Authen In Progress            0                 3
user `monkey' from 199.199.199.8 authenticated
user `cow' from 199.199.199.22 authorized to:
port 192.168.1.8/telnet 192.168.1.10/http
user `chicken' from 205.205.205.89 authorized to:
port 192.168.1.10/http 192.168.1.11/http
```

In this example, three users have been authenticated. The first user has only been authenticated, and the second two users have been authenticated and authorized. You can see the source address of the user as well as the resource that they have been authorized to access.

You can use clear commands to clear a configuration or to reset a connection. Table 11-2 lists the clear commands.

Command	Definition
show aaa-server	Displays the AAA servers, keys, and security protocols you configured
show aaa authentication| authorization |accounting	Shows the AAA PIX commands you configured
show auth-prompt [prompt|accept|reject]	Shows the authentication prompts you configured
show timeout uauth	Displays the connection timeout values configured
show virtual [http|telnet]	Shows the Virtual Telnet and HTTP configuration
show uauth	Displays the status of users' authentication process

Table 11-1. show Commands

Command	Description
clear aaa-server [*group_tag*]	Removes all of your AAA configuration commands, or just those associated with the *group_tag* that you can optionally specify
clear uauth [*user_account_name*]	Clears all authenticated connections, or just those for the specified user account

Table 11-2.   clear Commands

FURTHER STUDY

Web Sites

For a brief overview of AAA, visit www.cisco.com/univercd/cc/td/doc/cisintwk/intsolns/secsols/aaasols/c262c1.htm.

For an overview of Kerberos, visit www.cisco.com/warp/public/106/1.html.

For an overview of RADIUS, visit www.cisco.com/warp/public/cc/pd/iosw/ioft/iolk/tech/rdius_wp.htm.

For an overview of TACACS+, visit www.cisco.com/warp/public/614/7.html.

For information on CiscoSecure ACS for NT, visit www.cisco.com/univercd/cc/td/doc/product/access/acs_soft/csacs4nt/index.htm.

For more information on CiscoSecure ACS for Unix, visit www.cisco.com/univercd/cc/td/doc/product/access/acs_soft/cs_unx/csu23ug/index.htm.

For more information about configuring your PIX, visit: www.cisco.com/univercd/cc/td/doc/product/iaabu/pix/pix_62/config/index.htm.

CHAPTER 12

PIX Failover

In the last chapter, I talked about AAA and how it can be used to provide more secure access to your PIX as well as authenticating connections with the Cut-Through Proxy and Virtual Telnet and HTTP features. This chapter will focus on the redundancy features of the PIX, specifically the failover feature. With the failover feature, you can feel more secure knowing that if your primary PIX fails, a redundant PIX will step in and continue processing packets. As you will see throughout this chapter, though, there are different types of failover, and each of these types has advantages and disadvantages.

FAILOVER OVERVIEW

To use the PIX's failover feature, you need two PIXs: an *active* (or primary) PIX and a *standby* PIX. The PIX that has been assigned the primary role will actually forward traffic. The standby PIX's role is to monitor the primary PIX to ensure that it is operational. In this sense, the failover implementation of the PIX is somewhat similar to Cisco's Hot Standby Routing Protocol (HSRP), which provides router redundancy for default gateways. Figure 12-1 shows an example network with active and standby PIXs.

NOTE   The failover feature does not provide any type of load balancing—only failover capabilities. In other words, only one of the two PIXs in a failover configuration will actually forward traffic.

The PIXs' configurations are automatically synchronized, easing your configuration management. All configuration commands are executed on the active PIX and are automatically replicated to the standby PIX. Likewise, in newer versions of the FOS, certain tables stored in memory, like the xlate and connection tables, can also be synchronized between the two PIXs.

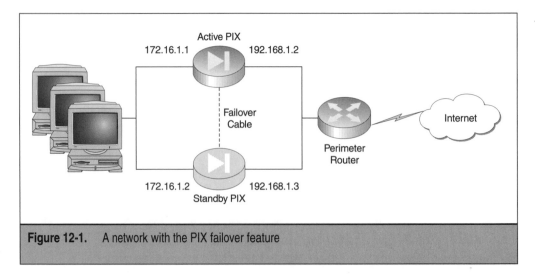

Figure 12-1.   A network with the PIX failover feature

When the standby PIX detects a failure, it promotes itself to the active role and starts forwarding traffic. Detecting a failure with the active PIX can take up to 45 seconds, depending on the type of failure. When a failure occurs, a logging message is generated. These messages have a level of 2 (critical). Figure 12-2 shows an example where the active PIX in Figure 12-1 has failed and the standby PIX has promoted itself to an active role.

Failover Requirements

The PIX failover feature is not supported on every platform. Likewise, the failover feature has strict requirements that must be met for failover to function correctly, if at all. The following sections cover these requirements.

Hardware Requirements

To set up the failover feature, the two PIXs must meet the following hardware requirements:

- Same PIX model
- Same amount of flash
- Same amount of RAM
- Same number and types of interfaces

The failover feature is not supported on every PIX model. Currently, the PIX 501, 506, and 506E models do not support failover. You need at least a PIX 515 or 515E in order to implement failover. When you implement failover, the primary and standby PIXs must be *identical* models. This means that a PIX 515 and a 520 cannot be used for a failover setup. Even a 515 and a 515E cannot be used.

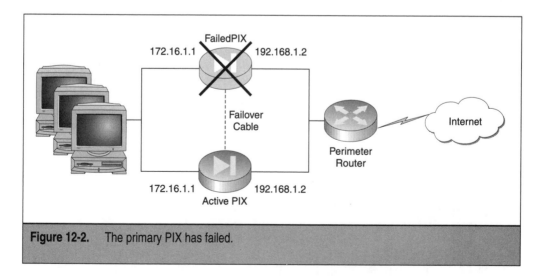

Figure 12-2.   The primary PIX has failed.

NOTE I've actually set up failover between non-identical models (515 and 520); however, Cisco doesn't officially support this configuration. If you have a problem and call TAC, they will tell you to change your hardware models so they match, and then to call them about any additional problems.

Both PIXs also need the same amount of flash and RAM. Even if the standby unit has a larger amount of flash, you should still keep these hardware components the same size. Imagine a situation where you have a primary PIX, PIX 1, with 16MB of flash and a standby unit, PIX 2, with 32MB of flash. Obviously, looking at this situation, you would think that this configuration should work. However, imagine that the PIX 1 fails and the standby PIX, PIX 2, becomes the active PIX. Throughout the course of events where you fix PIX 1, you may make many configuration additions to the active PIX (2)—so many changes that you go over the 16MB limit. When PIX 1 comes back online, it will not be able to fit the entire configuration in flash and thus failover will fail when the unit with 32MB of flash fails.

A similar situation can arise if you have a mismatch in the amount of RAM in the two PIXs and you are using the stateful failover feature of the PIX. I'll discuss the stateful failover feature later on in this chapter. In short, you should ensure that your PIX's hardware characteristics are the same.

Cisco doesn't officially say that the number and types of interfaces in the PIXs have to match. However, from personal experience, I've run into situations where the interface types did not match and this caused a problem that prevented the synchronization of the configuration files between the active and standby PIXs. In other words, if your primary PIX has three 10/100 Ethernet interfaces, I would make sure that the standby unit also has the same number and type.

TIP I highly recommend that you also make sure that the number and types of interfaces on the two PIXs match.

Software Requirements

In addition to meeting the minimum hardware requirements, there are also software requirements. To set up the failover feature, the following software requirements must be met:

- Primary PIX must have a UR license, and the standby must have an FO or UR license
- Same type of activation key type for encryption
- Same version of the FOS
- Same software configuration
- Unique IP addressing

Licensing The PIX that will initially be the primary must have an unrestricted license (UR). However, the standby PIX can have either a failover (FO) or UR license. If you try to use a restricted license (R) on one of the two PIXs, or an FO license on the two PIXs, failover will not function. The PIXs must also have the same type of activation key type for encryption—if one has a 3DES license, the other PIX must also have a 3DES license. This is important when you are using your PIXs to set up VPN connections, which I discuss in Chapter 17.

If you have purchased only a failover license for your PIX, which means that this PIX is to be used in a failover configuration as the standby PIX, and you try to run the PIX in a stand-alone configuration, the PIX will reboot itself at least one time every 24 hours. When the PIX reboots, you will see the message shown below on the console of the PIX:

```
==========================NOTICE ==========================
    This machine is running in secondary mode without
    a connection to an active primary PIX. Please
     check your connection to the primary system.
                REBOOTING....
============================================================
```

To fix this problem, either connect this unit to another PIX and make this PIX the standby unit, or purchase the appropriate license to run this PIX in a stand-alone configuration.

Operating Systems   Both the primary and standby PIXs need the same version of the FOS. This is not to say that failover will not function if the versions of the FOS are different; however, certain configurations might not be synchronized because of a software incompatibility, and this may cause failover problems.

Software Configurations   Both the primary and standby PIXs also need the same software configuration. This is automatically performed for you when you enter your commands on the active PIX—they are automatically replicated to the standby PIX. The one exception to this is the IP addressing of the two PIXs' interfaces—each interface on each PIX needs a *unique* IP and MAC address. When an interface from the active PIX is connected to the same subnet as that of an interface on the standby PIX, each IP address has to be from the same IP network number. You can see an example of this in Figure 12-1.

One important item to point out is that configuration changes that you make on your PIXs should only be done on the active PIX. Changes made to the active PIX will automatically be replicated to the standby PIX. If you make configuration changes to a standby PIX, these are *not* replicated to the active PIX, and, in most cases, you will actually be prevented from making these changes on the standby PIX.

NOTE   Make configuration changes on the active PIX—these are automatically replicated to the standby PIX.

Types of Failover Configurations

There are two methods of connecting your PIXs together to implement failover, cable-based and LAN-based, and there are two failover solutions that Cisco offers, non-stateful and stateful. The following sections discuss the types of failover configurations that Cisco offers.

Cable-Based and LAN-Based Configurations

Cable-based and LAN-based configurations define the actual cabling required between the primary and standby PIXs to set up failover. The following two sections will discuss these implementations.

Cable-Based Configuration   In a cable-based configuration, you are required to purchase a special serial-based cable from Cisco that you plug into the DB-15 failover port on each PIX. This cable connection is clocked at 115 Kbps. Actually, prior to FOS 5.2, the baud rate of this serial connection was 9.6 Kbps; however, since version 5.2, the baud rate was increased to 115 Kbps. Each end of the cable is marked: *primary* and *standby*. You need to plug the *primary* end of the cable into the primary PIX and the *standby* end of the cable into the *standby* PIX. The pin-outs at each end of the cable determine which side is which. When you connect the cable between the two PIXs, they automatically sense which end of the cable that they are plugged into and assume the related failover role.

NOTE   If you have a PIX with a failover-only license, and it is either attached to the primary end of the cable or is not connected to a cable, it might hang when trying to reboot. Remember that a PIX with a failover-only license should only be used as the standby PIX in a failover configuration.

The two PIXs use the serial cable to communicate with each other. This can include the verification that the other PIX is functioning correctly as well as synchronizing the configuration from the primary to the standby unit. If the primary PIX's power fails, the standby PIX will be able to detect this from the failover cable and promote itself to an active state.

Prior to FOS 6.2, you had no choice but to use the cable-based method of configuration. One of the issues with this configuration is that the two PIXs had to be physically near each other because the serial cable is only about six feet long.

LAN-Based Configuration   LAN-based configuration is new in FOS 6.2. With a LAN-based configuration, the two PIXs do not use the serial failover cable for communication. Instead, one interface on each PIX is used for the failover connection. One advantage that this configuration has over the cable-based configuration is that the PIXs can be farther apart than the six-foot limit of the serial cable. Basically, the LAN medium itself dictates the distance limitation. With the correct type of interface, like one that has a laser, you could stretch this connection many kilometers.

One restriction for the LAN-based configuration is that the two interfaces on the two respective PIXs must be in the same subnet—a router cannot separate them. Likewise, there must be a dedicated switch or hub connection between the two PIXs. In other words, you cannot use an Ethernet crossover cable for the connection. When Cisco uses the word *dedicated*, they mean that there cannot be any other devices in the broadcast domain. Obviously, if this was a hub connection, you could only connect the two PIXs to the hub. However, if you were using a switch, you need to make sure that interfaces of the two PIXs that you are using for a LAN-based connection are the only two devices in that VLAN. In this situation, if you had multiple devices, you need to create at least two VLANs—one for the LAN-based connection for the PIXs, and at least one for the rest of your networking devices. Figure 12-3 shows an example of a LAN-based failover connection between two PIXs.

NOTE   You cannot use an Ethernet crossover cable for the LAN-based connection; this connection must be a dedicated switch (PIXs in their own VLAN) or hub connection between the two PIXs.

Another limitation of a LAN-based configuration is that the standby PIX, because it is not connected to the active PIX by the failover cable, will not be able to directly detect a power failure. It will eventually be able to detect that the active PIX has lost power, but it does this by detecting the lack of hello messages that the primary PIX used to be generating. Therefore, it will take longer for the standby unit to promote itself to an active state.

Because the PIXs are using a LAN connection for communication, Cisco has decided to use the IP protocol to handle failover communications. Normally, in a cable-based configuration, you would erase the configuration on the standby unit, turn it off, connect it up to the primary unit, and then power up the standby unit. After you execute these steps, when the standby unit reboots, it automatically acquires all of its configuration from the primary unit via the serial failover cable. However, with a LAN-based configuration, you have to perform some configuration on the standby PIX to allow it to communicate with the primary. In this situation, you need to configure the IP addressing and interface characteristics of the interface that is to be used for the LAN-based connection. Once you have done this to establish IP connectivity, you can perform the remaining configuration on the primary PIX.

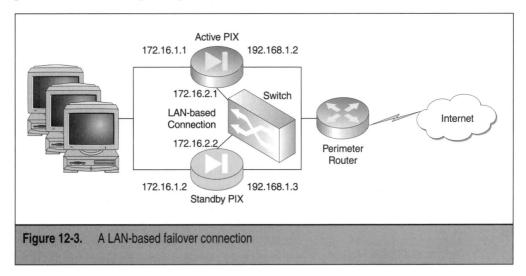

Figure 12-3.   A LAN-based failover connection

Non-Stateful and Stateful Failover Implementations

The PIX supports two types of redundancy with its failover feature: non-stateful and stateful. The basic difference between these two is that a non-stateful implementation provides basic chassis redundancy between the two PIXs, whereas a stateful failover synchronizes some of the tables in the active PIX's memory, like the xlate and connection tables, with the standby unit, thus providing a stateful nature when a failover occurs.

Non-Stateful Implementation   In a non-stateful implementation, the failover feature provides basic chassis redundancy. Any information stored in the failed PIX's memory, like the xlate table, connection table, and other information used to implement a stateful firewall are *not* synchronized between the primary and active unit. Basically, the only thing synchronized between the two PIX's in a non-stateful configuration is the configuration file on the active PIX.

If the active PIX fails in a non-stateful implementation, the standby PIX will promote itself to the active role. However, in this process, any connections that were currently using the primary PIX will fail and must be reestablished by the user via the second PIX. Please note that the user doesn't have to know anything about this second PIX—he just needs to perform a reconnect.

Stateful Implementation   With a stateful failover implementation, the information about users' connections *are* synchronized between the two PIXs. This information includes the address translation information as well as connection information. When the active PIX fails, the standby PIX has the same the connection information as the primary, allowing a seamless transition.

Compared to non-stateful failover, stateful failover provides both chassis and stateful redundancy. In very large networks, Cisco recommends that you use at least a 520 or 525 model for stateful failover—a 515 might have issues keeping up with synchronizing all of the changes in the state tables.

To implement stateful failover, you need at least version 5.1 of the FOS and a stateful license for your PIX. By default, PIX 515s and higher can do non-stateful failover. However, you must pay Cisco extra money in order to take advantage of the stateful failover feature.

Another of the requirements to set up stateful failover between two PIXs is that you need at least a dedicated FDDI, Fast Ethernet, or Gigabit Ethernet connection between the two PIXs. In other words, you cannot have a router separating the connection for these two PIXs. This is in addition to the serial cable for a cable-based implementation or an Ethernet connection for a LAN-based implementation. This connection can be one of the following types: crossover cable or a full-duplex switch connection, where the two stateful connections between the PIXs are placed in their own personal VLAN.

NOTE   You need at least a 100 Mbps dedicated connection between the PIXs to handle the synchronization of the state information.

Figure 12-4 shows an example of a stateful connection between two PIXs. This example uses a cable-based implementation of failover, where there is a dedicated stateful crossover connection between the two PIXs. In this example, this connection uses subnet 172.16.2.0/24.

The PIXs use IP packets to communicate with each other across this state connection. Cisco uses the IP protocol number of 105 to differentiate failover communication packets from other IP packets, like TCP (6) and UDP (17). Typically, it will take 15 to 45 seconds for a standby PIX to promote itself to an active role. Therefore, the cutover is not a completely seamless process. Even though this implementation synchronizes state information, the delay of the promotion of the standby PIX might cause a user connection to time out. Also, other users' connections will be in a *paused* state while the standby PIX is promoted.

Synchronizing Information Between PIXs

As I mentioned earlier, for the active PIX to synchronize with the standby PIX, both PIXs need to have the same version of the FOS as well as the same hardware characteristics. Synchronization between the two PIXs occurs under these circumstances:

- The standby PIX boots up and acquires the up-to-date configuration from the active PIX.

- A command entered on the active PIX is replicated to the standby PIX, but *not* vice versa.

- The `write standby` command forces a synchronization between the two PIXs.

- In a stateful failover configuration, a change in certain tables of the active PIX will cause a replication of this information to the standby PIX.

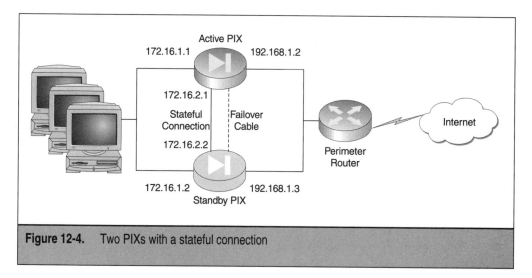

Figure 12-4.   Two PIXs with a stateful connection

Synchronization Process

When a configuration synchronization is occurring between two PIXs, you'll see two messages appear on the console: *Sync Started* and *Sync Completed*. During the actual synchronization process, you will not be able to enter any commands on your PIX. Once the synchronization has completed, and you see the *Sync Completed* message, you'll be able to execute additional commands on your PIX.

The synchronization process between the two PIXs occurs between RAM. As an example, if you are on the active PIX and execute the `access-list` command to add an ACL, this command is replicated to RAM of the standby PIX. Please note that this information is not replicated to the flash of the standby PIX. Therefore, if you power off both the active and standby PIXs at this point, this ACL would disappear from your configuration. To save the configuration, execute the `write memory` command on the active PIX. This will perform two tasks: save the configuration on the active PIX, and cause this command to *also* be executed on the standby PIX.

Remember that the synchronization occurs over either the failover serial cable or the LAN cable that you set up for failover. The exception to this is that for stateful failover, you need an additional connection to handle the synchronization of the state information, which I'll discuss in the next section.

NOTE   The synchronization process does not synchronize flash between the two PIXs—only some of the RAM contents.

Stateful Failover Synchronization

With non-stateful failover, the only thing synchronized between the two PIXs is the configuration file on the active PIX. With stateful failover, however, additional items are replicated from the active to the standby PIX. This replicated information includes the following from the active PIX:

- Configuration file in RAM
- Global address pools and the status of addresses used in the pools
- Connection table and the status of the connections, with the *exception* of HTTP port 80 traffic
- Most UDP connections, with the exception of those that have been "fixed up" with the Protocol Fixup feature
- The xlate table and the status of the translations
- Negotiated port numbers for applications that the PIX has "fixed up" with the Protocol Fixup feature
- System uptime
- System clock (the actual date and time)

The following information, however, is *not* synchronized between the two PIXs:

- The uauth table, which is used by AAA for user authentication
- The ISAKMP and IPSEC security associations (SAs)
- The routing information on the active PIX
- The ARP table on the active PIX

Therefore, when the active PIX fails and the standby PIX is promoted to an active role, the user will typically *not* have to reestablish any connections. As you can see from these lists, though, any IPSec connections will not be maintained and will have to be rebuilt. I will discuss IPSec in Chapters 16 and 17.

Failover Communication Between the PIXs

As I mentioned earlier, there are two ways of configuring the failover feature between the PIXs—using the serial failover cable or a dedicated LAN connection. The two PIXs use this failover connection to communicate with each other. The one advantage that the serial cable has over the LAN method is that a power failure on the active PIX can be immediately detected by the standby PIX and cause the standby unit to promote itself. The LAN-based connection has one advantage, though, over the serial connection: the LAN-based connection can span very large distances compared to the six-foot limitation of the serial failover cable.

Messages

The communication over the failover cable is message-based and reliable. Every message sent by a PIX has a corresponding acknowledgment (ACK) returned. If an ACK is not received within three seconds, the PIX will resend the message. If a message is retransmitted unsuccessfully five times, the standby PIX will start the promotion process to an active state. There are five basic types of messages conveyed over the failover link between the two PIXs:

- Exchange of MAC addresses
- Hello messages (keepalives)
- Which state the PIX is in—active or standby
- The status of the interfaces(s) connecting the PIXs
- The configuration file of the active PIX

Please note that state information for stateful failover is not carried across the serial- or LAN-based failover connection, but a separate dedicated LAN connection.

Stateful Failover Communication

When you have chosen to implement the stateful failover option, you need a dedicated LAN connection between the two PIXs that is clocked at least 100 Mbps. This LAN connection is in addition to other LAN connections. The active PIX uses this stateful failover LAN connection to replicate all state information between the two PIXs.

Any synchronization that is done for state information is always performed after a configuration synchronization (replicating the commands executed on the active PIX to the standby PIX). Initially, the entire state table is replicated to the standby unit. After this, only changes are shared between the active and standby units, which reduces the amount of processing the two PIXs have to handle.

The state update is UDP-like in nature in that there are no retransmissions of state information if the standby unit does not receive the update. However, if a state update is not received by the standby unit, there is an error detection mechanism that will flag the problem and report it. You can use this for monitoring purposes to determine if the link between the two PIXs is fast enough, or if you are having CPU performance problems on your PIXs that are causing this problem.

Note that because this is a LAN connection that uses IP for communicating the state information between the two PIXs, there is a slight delay in the synchronization process. Therefore, if the primary PIX fails, a very small amount of state information might not have had the chance to be replicated to the standby PIX.

Hello Packets

The two PIXs communicate with each other by sending out *hello* packets to each other over every interface, including the failover interfaces. The default period of these hello packets is 15 seconds—you can change this with the `failover poll` command, which I'll discuss in the configuration section later on in this chapter. The hello timer can range from 3 to 15 seconds. If you change the hello timer to a smaller value, the PIXs will be able to determine if there is a problem with an interface more quickly. However, if you set this timer to a very small period, you might create a situation where the standby PIX promotes itself to the active role because it thinks the active PIX has failed, when in reality, there is either a lot of LAN congestion, or the active PIX is slow in sending out its hello packets.

NOTE   Setting the hello value to a small number might cause unnecessary failovers.

The hold down timer for the hello mechanism is two updates. If the standby unit does not see a hello packet from the active PIX over two consecutive hello periods, the standby unit will initiate failover tests on its interfaces in order to determine which unit has failed—the active or standby unit—and if the active PIX has failed, the standby unit will promote itself. The following section covers the failover tests performed.

Detecting Failures

As I mentioned in the previous section, if the standby PIX misses two consecutive hello messages from the active PIX, it will start the failover process by running some tests. Likewise, if you are using the serial-based failover cable to allow the two PIXs to communicate with each other, and there are cable errors detected on the serial cable, the standby PIX will also start the failover process. In a situation where you have a bad serial failover cable, the standby PIX might end up promoting itself to an active state while the other PIX is still active. In other words, the cable itself might have failed, but the first PIX is still functioning normally.

Causes of Failover

There are actually many things that can cause your PIXs to go through a failover process. Here is a list of some of the more common ones:

- You turn off the active PIX.
- You reboot the active PIX.
- You manually force a failover by executing the `failover active` command on the standby PIX.
- An interface on the active PIX goes down for longer than twice the poll period.
- The active PIX experiences a block memory exhaustion condition for more than 15 seconds.

What's interesting about the failover process is that a change in state can be initiated by *either* PIX. For instance, the active PIX might determine that one of its interfaces has failed and thus have the standby PIX take over the active role. Or, the standby PIX might detect that the active PIX has lost power and thus the standby PIX will promote itself to an active state.

Failure detection is based on one of the three following criteria:

- There are cable errors on the serial failover cable.
- There are missed hellos from a peer PIX.
- There is a loss of power on the active PIX.

Cable errors can be caused by a PIX being turned off, the cable becoming disconnected, or a physical failure in the cable, like a crimp. Typically, if the cable is unplugged, a failover will not occur. However, there is one exception to this. If the cable is not plugged into the PIXs when you power them up, the standby unit will promote itself to an active state. The problem with this scenario is that the primary PIX will also be in an active state. As you will see later in this chapter, both PIXs will be using the same IP address when they are in an active state, creating a duplicate IP address problem.

NOTE When using the serial cable for failover, make sure that the serial-based failover cable is plugged in when you power up the PIXs.

By default, the PIX generates hello messages every 15 seconds on both the network interfaces as well as the failover interface (serial- or LAN-based). When two consecutive hello messages are missed on an interface, the PIXs assume that a failure has possibly taken place. Therefore, after 30 seconds, the PIX(s) will perform further testing to determine whether or not a failure has occurred.

If a failure is due to a loss of power on the active PIX and the serial cable is used for failover, the standby unit begins a change of state within a 15-second period. The standby unit is able to detect the failure because one of the leads of the cable goes to an off state. However, if any other problem occurs, both PIXs will run through a series of tests to determine which PIX, or component of the PIX, has failed. These tests typically begin when two consecutive hello messages are not seen from the peer PIX. The following sections cover the tests that the PIXs perform in order to determine whether or not a failure has occurred. Table 12-1 lists some typical time lengths to detect a failure.

Interface Tests

After missing two consecutive hello messages from a peer PIX, one set of tests each PIX runs is for the physical interfaces that they use for connectivity. Once a failure condition occurs, the PIX will notify its peer about the issue and then begin running its interface tests. Cisco refers to this state as *test mode*. The assumption here is that if the PIX is not seeing hello messages, and the interface tests pass, then the peer PIX must have failed. Of course, by running the tests, the PIX might find out that its own interface has failed. In either case, the appropriate failover will take place, if necessary.

These interface tests include the following:

- Link up/down
- Network activity
- ARP (Address Resolution Protocol)
- Broadcast ping

These tests are non-intrusive to the interface. When each of the interface tests begin, the PIX clears the received packet count for each interface, runs the test, and then checks this count at the end of the test to determine if any traffic was received on the interface. If traffic was received, the PIX assumes that the interface is operational—if not, the PIX flags itself as failed and tells the other PIX to assume the active role (if this isn't the case already). Of course, this is just one set of tests. In any case, if just one of the interfaces on the active PIX fails, the standby PIX will promote itself to an active role and the first PIX will demote itself to a standby role.

Type of Problem	Time Length to Detect
Power failure (serial cable)	Up to 15 seconds
Communication error with missed hellos	Up to 30 seconds
Network error with missed hellos	Up to 30 seconds

Table 12-1.   Time Periods for Detecting Failures

Link Up/Down Test   With the link up/down test, the PIX tests the physical and data link layer connection and operation. If there is no cable plugged into an active interface, the PIX will assume that the interface is bad and initiate a failover. Likewise, if the hub or switch that the interface is connected to fails, the PIX will trigger a failover. When connecting to a switch, you must disable STP (Spanning Tree Protocol) for the connected PIX port. Otherwise, when a change occurs in the VLAN that this interface is connected to, the switch port will go through three or four of its STP states before being placed into a forwarding state. This process will cause the PIX to assume that the interface has failed and initiate a failover.

TIP   Make sure that you disable Spanning Tree on the port of the switch that the PIX's interface is connected to in order to ensure that any recalculation of STP will not cause the PIX to initiate a failover. Cisco refers to this feature as PortFast on their Catalyst switches.

Also, if you are not using an interface, it is imperative that you disable it with the `interface` command by specifying the `shutdown` parameter, discussed in Chapter 3.

Network Activity Test   The PIX also looks at network activity on the interface for a period of five seconds. During this second test, the PIX examines the data link layer frames to see if they are good or bad. If any valid frames are received during this time frame, the interface is considered to be operational. If not, the PIX will proceed to the third test.

ARP Test   The third interface test that the PIX performs is an ARP test. In this test, the PIX generates an ARP request for the last IP address that it queried. The PIX expects an ARP reply back within a five-second period. After this five-second period, the PIX checks to see if any valid frames were received, including the ARP reply. If a valid frame was seen, the interface is considered operational, and no further testing is performed. If a valid frame wasn't seen, the PIX will send an ARP request to the next IP address— it will perform this process for the last ten IP addresses that it most recently acquired. If no traffic is seen on the interface, the PIX will proceed to the fourth test.

Broadcast Ping Test   The fourth test that the PIX performs is a broadcast ping, in which the destination IP address is 255.255.255.255. In this test, the PIX is expecting at least one device to respond back from the subnet connected to the interface. As long as one valid frame is received in this test, the interface is considered operational.

Other Tests

During the interface tests, as long as the PIX sees a valid frame received on an interface, the interface is deemed operational. Upon completion of each interface test, the PIX will share the results with its peer. If one PIX receives traffic while the other doesn't, then the one that doesn't is considered to have failed. Or, if a PIX doesn't receive the results from its peer PIX, it will assume that the peer has failed. Of course, both units might not have received traffic during the interface tests. In this situation, a state change will not take place as long as the PIXs can "see" each other via the failover cable.

When you enable failover, the PIX will automatically send an ARP to itself on every interface periodically. The ARP poll period is the same as the hello timer—by default this is every 15 seconds. This process is used for testing purposes.

When Failover Occurs

Whenever a failover occurs, a syslog message is generated by both the active and standby PIXs. The standby PIX then promotes itself to an active state. When the standby unit takes the role of the active PIX, it assumes *both* the IP and MAC addresses of the first PIX. Any communications directed at the first PIX can now be seamlessly handled by the standby (now active) PIX. Likewise, the first PIX assumes the addressing information of the standby PIX. Therefore, you do not have flush any ARP tables of devices that the two PIXs are connected to.

Switched Environments

If your PIXs are connected to switches, then there are two issues that you need to be aware of that might create problems. A layer-2 switch performs three main functions:

- Learns which devices are on which ports
- Intelligently switches traffic
- Runs Spanning Tree Protocol (STP) to remove loops

The first issue deals with the learning and switching functions of a switch. The problem with a standby PIX assuming the IP and MAC addresses of the primary PIX is that the switch might not know about this, and might still switch the traffic to the port that the failed PIX is connected to. To solve this problem, each PIX advertises its new addressing information out of each of its respective interfaces. This ensures that the switch will learn the new location of the MAC addresses.

The second issue deals with STP. When a switch is running STP, it stops traffic traveling to its ports for about 30 seconds—the time it takes to transition from a listening to learning state, and from a learning to forwarding state. During this period, the PIXs will not be able to see each other's hello messages on their respective interfaces, and if you are using a LAN-based failover connection, the PIXs won't be able to see each other at all. This issue can cause unnecessary failovers.

To deal with this issue, you should enable the portfast feature for all ports on a switch that your PIX interfaces are connected to. Portfast is a feature that basically keeps the switch's port in a forwarding state when it runs STP. You should only use portfast on a switch's interfaces that are connected to non–layer 2 devices: that is, don't enable portfast on connections to other switches or bridges.

You should make sure that you follow these recommendations when configuring the ports on the switch that are connected to your PIX firewall:

- Make sure that portfast is enabled on the switch port(s) to the PIX.

- Make sure that trunking is disabled on the switch port(s) to the PIX.
- Make sure that channeling is disabled on the switch port(s) to the PIX.

Failed State

The unit that was the active PIX and is now demoted to a *failed* role automatically disables its network interfaces. The failed PIX waits 15 seconds and then tries to transition to a standby state. In order to make this transition, all of the PIX's interfaces must be operational. Therefore, if one of the interfaces on this PIX has failed, it will not assume a standby status.

You can manually set the PIX from a failed state to a standby state with the `failover reset` command. However, if you have not fixed the physical problem, the PIX will transition to a failed state again. In a failed state, the PIX cannot participate as a standby PIX.

For example, a physical interface failure, where the NIC is no longer operational, will cause the PIX to remain in a failed state. However, if you unplug a cable from a PIX's interface, it will transition to a failed state, and when you plug the cable back in, it will transition from a failed to a standby state.

When you are using a LAN connection for the failover cable, and this connection fails, the PIXs use their other interfaces to communicate with each other. However, if the LAN failover interface of the active PIX fails, the standby unit will be promoted.

Two Active PIXs

It is possible for both PIXs to be placed into an active state. This can occur if both the active and standby PIXs lose complete communication with each other. This can happen if all the PIXs' connections are going to the same switch or hub. To ensure that this doesn't happen, you should have the failover connection go through one switch or hub and the other interfaces through another switch or hub.

Returning to an Original State

Once a failover occurs, the active PIX is demoted to either a failed or standby state and the standby PIX is promoted to an active state. When the problem that caused the failover process is fixed, the PIXs do *not* automatically revert to their original states. Actually, there is no need for the PIXs to revert because this would cause disruption with the users' connections.

You can manually force a failover by executing one of the two commands in Table 12-2.

PIX to Execute on	PIX Command
Standby	`failover active`
Active	`no failover active`

Table 12-2.   Reverting to the Original Failover Configuration

The `failover active` command should be executed on the PIX in a standby state—this forces this PIX to become the active PIX. The `no failover active` command, when executed on the active PIX, causes the other PIX to take on the active role.

Please note that if you don't have stateful failover configured, the users will lose their connections during the cutover process. If you have stateful failover configured, then the users shouldn't lose their current connections.

Initial Bootup

When you have two PIXs configured for failover, and you turn them both on simultaneously, both PIXs are in an off state for failover. Once power is enabled, the PIXs can automatically detect the serial-based failover cable and enable failover. However, if you are using a LAN-based failover cable, the PIXs will have to establish IP connectivity before assuming that failover is functioning.

Both units assume a standby status and request the MAC addresses of the other unit. If the other unit does not move to an active state within the hello poll period (15 seconds), the PIX assumes an active state. This assumption is based on the fact that the other PIX doesn't send a reply back as to what state it is in. Assuming that the other PIX is operational, it will respond back with its state. When both PIXs boot up simultaneously, the PIX configured as the primary PIX assumes the active state, and the other PIX assumes a standby state.

If one of the PIXs has already booted up and is in an active state, the newly booted-up PIX will learn of the other's active state, and the new PIX will assume a standby state. This is true even if the newly booted-up PIX was originally configured as the primary PIX. Therefore, when you are booting up your PIXs, you should always boot up the primary PIX first, and the standby PIX second, to ensure that they assume their configured roles. Of course, you can always manually force a failover to put the PIXs into their configured roles.

FAILOVER CONFIGURATION

Like many of the features of the PIX firewall, configuring failover is a simple process involving only a handful of commands. In addition to enabling failover, you need to specify some additional parameters. The next section covers the basic failover commands. The two sections following the basic commands shows you how to set up failover if you are using the failover serial-based cable or LAN-based cable.

Command Overview

This section is an overview of the failover commands that you'll use to set up failover. Listing 12-1 shows these commands:

Listing 12-1
```
pixfirewall(config)#  failover [active]
pixfirewall(config)#  failover ip address interface_name IP_address
```

```
pixfirewall(config)#  failover lan enable
pixfirewall(config)#  failover lan unit primary|secondary
pixfirewall(config)#  failover lan interface interface_name
pixfirewall(config)#  failover lan key secret_key
pixfirewall(config)#  failover link [stateful_interface_name]
pixfirewall(config)#  failover mac address interface_name
                          active_PIX_MAC standby_PIX_MAC
pixfirewall(config)#  failover poll seconds
pixfirewall(config)#  failover replicate http
pixfirewall(config)#  failover reset
pixfirewall#  show failover [lan [detail]]
```

Table 12-3 contains a description of the commands shown in Listing 12-1.

Command	Description
failover [active]	Enables failover and specifies the active PIX—executing the `failover active` command on the standby PIX causes the standby PIX to become the active PIX.
failover ip address	Specifies the IP address for the standby unit for the specific standby interface.
failover lan enable	Enables failover using a LAN-based connection instead of the serial cable.
failover lan unit	Specifies which PIX is the primary PIX and which one is the standby when using a LAN-based failover cable (secondary).
failover lan interface	Specifies which interface is to be used for the LAN-based connection.
failover lan key	Specifies the encryption key to use to protect failover messages between the active and standby PIXs.
failover link	Specifies the interface to use for stateful failover—use the `mtu` command to ensure that the maximum transmission unit (MTU) size for the stateful failover link is at least 1,500 bytes in length.
failover mac address	Specifies the MAC addresses to use for the primary and standby PIXs' interfaces. This allows you to override the burnt-in address (BIA) of the primary PIX and assign a virtual address. However, if you are using LAN-based failover, you cannot use this command for the link used for the LAN-based failover connection. It is also recommended that you reboot your PIX if you change the MAC address of one of its interfaces.
failover poll	Specifies the hello interval, which can range from 3 to 15 seconds (defaults to 15).
failover replicate http	Allows stateful replication of HTTP connections (disabled by default).
failover reset	Forces the PIXs back to an unfailed state.
show failover	Shows the status of the failover connection as well as which unit is in an active state.
show failover lan	Shows the status of a LAN-based failover connection.

Table 12-3.   Failover Commands

To remove any of the commands in Listing 12-1 and Table 12-3, precede them with the `no` parameter. If you want to complete disable failover, execute the `no failover` command on the active PIX. The following sections discuss some important items that you should check when setting up the failover feature on your PIX firewalls.

Unused Interfaces

If you will not be using an interface on your PIX, make sure you either do one of the following to notify the PIXs in the failover configuration that the interface is not to be used:

- Assign a 127.0.0.1 IP address to the primary unit's interface using the `ip address` command, and assign a 0.0.0.0 IP address with the `failover ip address` command for the standby unit's interface.

- Disable the interface with the `shutdown` parameter by using the `interface` command—this command was discussed in Chapter 3.

If you do not perform one of these two actions, the PIXs will assume that the interface is in use—and if the interface is not operational, this can cause unnecessary failovers between the two PIXs.

Interface Configurations

It is highly recommended that you do not use autosensing on your interfaces when you configure the failover feature. If you use autosensing, you might run into problems that can cause unnecessary failovers between the two failover PIXs.

If you decide to implement stateful failover, you are precluded from using autosensing for your interfaces—you must manually configure the speeds and duplexing in order for stateful failover to function correctly. To hard code the speed or duplexing of a physical interface on your PIX, use the `interface` command discussed in Chapter 3.

Verifying Failover Configuration

There are four basic ways that you can verify the operation of failover on your PIXs:

- Examine the ACT LED on the front of the chassis.
- Use the `show ip` command
- Use the `show failover` command.
- Use the `debug fover` command.

Examining the LEDs

The first method, examining the ACT LED on the front of the PIX chassis, is valid for the 515, 525, and 535 PIX models. On the front of these chasses, you will find an ACT LED indicator. When failover is enabled, the active PIX's LED is green, and the standby PIX's LED is off.

Verifying the IP Address Configuration

To verify the configuration of the IP addresses on the two failover PIXs, use the `show ip` command. This is an example of the command for the primary PIX shown in Figure 12-1:

```
pixfirewall#  show ip
System IP Addresses:
        ip address outside 192.168.1.2 255.255.255.0
        ip address inside 172.16.1.1 255.255.255.0
Current IP Addresses:
        ip address outside 192.168.1.2 255.255.255.0
        ip address inside 172.16.1.1 255.255.255.0
```

The *System IP Addresses* are the IP addresses assigned to the active PIX when you have failover configured. If this PIX were the standby unit, it would assume these addresses on its interface when a failover occurred. The *Current IP Addresses* are the IP addresses currently being used on the interface. In this example, this PIX happens to be the active PIX.

   If you execute this command on the standby PIX, the output would look like this:

```
pixfirewall#  show ip
System IP Addresses:
        ip address outside 192.168.1.2 255.255.255.0
        ip address inside 172.16.1.1 255.255.255.0
Current IP Addresses:
        ip address outside 192.168.1.3 255.255.255.0
        ip address inside 172.16.1.2 255.255.255.0
```

As you can see from this example, the *System* and *Current* addresses are different, indicating that this unit is in a standby state.

`show failover` Command

If you are not in front of the PIXs, you can also use the `show failover` command. This command allows you to see the status of the failover connection between the PIXs, the status of each of the PIXs' interfaces, as well as stateful information, if this has been enabled. The following sections go over some examples of the `show failover` command.

Example of No Failover Configured   Here is an example of the use of the `show failover` command where failover has *not* been configured:

```
pixfirewall#  show failover
Failover Off
Cable Status: My side not connected
Reconnect timeout: 0:00:00
```

As you can see from this output, the failover status is *Off* and the serial-based failover cable has not been connected.

Example of a Serial-Based Non-stateful Configuration   Let's look at an example output of the `show failover` command where two PIXs are using a serial-based connection for communications in a non-stateful configuration. Listing 12-2 shows an example of the `show failover` command in this situation:

Listing 12-2
```
pixfirewall(config)# show failover
Failover On
Cable status: Normal
Reconnect timeout 0:00:00
Poll frequency 15 seconds
     This host: Primary - Active
             Active time: 257 (sec)
             Interface outside (192.168.1.2): Normal
             Interface inside (172.16.1.1): Normal
     Other host: Secondary - Standby
             Active time: 0 (sec)
             Interface outside (192.168.1.3): Normal
             Interface inside (172.16.1.2): Normal
```

In Listing 12-2, the display line shows the failover status, which is *On*. Below this is the *Cable status*. Table 12-4 lists these three statuses. In the example shown in Listing 12-2, the cable status shows that the two failover PIXs are in an operational state.

Following this is the status of the interfaces for the two PIXs. In this example, this PIX is the active PIX and the other PIX is the standby PIX. You can view the configuration (IP address) and status of each interface. Table 12-5 shows the different

Status	Description
Normal	The active and standby unit are operational.
Waiting	This PIX has not yet begun to monitor the other PIX's interfaces.
Failed	This PIX is in a failed state.
My side not connected	The serial-based cable is not plugged into this PIX.
Other side is not connected	The serial-based cable is not plugged into the other PIX.
Other side is powered off	The serial-based cable indicates that the other PIX is powered off.
Unknown	The serial-based cable status is not known—you'll typically see this when you are using a LAN-based connection for failover communications.

Table 12-4.   Cable Status

Status	Description
Normal	The interface is operational.
Waiting	The PIX has not yet begun monitoring the other PIX's interface.
Shut Down	The interface has been manually disabled.
Failed	The interface has failed.
Link Down	The interface's data link layer is down.
Unknown	The IP address for this interface has not been configured and thus the PIX cannot determine the status of the interface.

Table 12-5. Interface Status

interface statuses that you might see. In Code Listing 12-2, all of the interfaces are operational.

Example of a Serial-Based Stateful Configuration   Let's look at an example output of the show failover command where two PIXs are using a serial-based connection for communications in a stateful configuration. I'll use the primary PIX in the network shown in Figure 12-4. Listing 12-3 shows an example of the show failover command in this example:

Listing 12-3
```
pixfirewall(config)# show failover
Failover On
Cable status: Normal
Reconnect timeout 0:00:00
Poll frequency 15 seconds
     This host: Primary - Active
             Active time: 257 (sec)
             Interface state (172.16.2.1): Normal
             Interface outside (192.168.1.2): Normal
             Interface inside (172.16.1.1): Normal
     Other host: Secondary - Standby
             Active time: 0 (sec)
             Interface state (172.16.2.2): Normal
             Interface outside (192.168.1.3): Normal
             Interface inside (172.16.1.2): Normal

Stateful Failover Logical Update Statistics
        Link : state
        Stateful Obj    xmit       xerr       rcv        rerr
        General         0          0          0          0
```

Listing 12-3
```
        sys cmd       0           0           0           0
        up time       0           0           0           0
        xlate         0           0           0           0
        tcp conn      0           0           0           0
        udp conn      0           0           0           0
        ARP tbl       0           0           0           0
        RIP Tbl       0           0           0           0
    Logical Update Queue Information
                    Cur       Max       Total
        Recv Q:       0         0         0
        Xmit Q:       0         0         0
```

The first thing to point out in Listing 12-3 is that there is an additional interface called *state* on each PIX and that each of these interfaces has a *Normal* status. The major difference between the example in Listing 12-2 and Listing 12-3 is the bottom part of Listing 12-3: The bottom part shows the stateful failover information.

The first line under the *Stateful Failover Logical Update Statistics* is the *Link* connection—this defines which interface is being used to communicate the state information between the two PIXs. In this example, this is the interface called *state*.

Below this line are five columns. Table 12-6 explains these columns.

Table 12-7 describes the entries under the `Stateful Obj` column from Listing 12-3.

Below this information is a section entitled *Logical Update Queue Information*. This section displays the information waiting in the PIX's queues to be transmitted to the other failover PIX.

Example of a LAN-Based Non-Stateful Configuration   Let's look at an example output of the `show failover` command where two PIXs are using a LAN-based connection for

Name of Column	Description
Stateful Obj	Groups together the stateful objects beneath it
Xmit	The number of packets transmitted to the other PIX for this stateful object
Xerr	The number of errors that have occurred when transmitting packets to the other PIX for this stateful object
Rcv	The number of packets received from the other PIX for this stateful object
Rerr	The number of errors that have occurred when receiving packets from the other PIX for this stateful object

Table 12-6.   Columns of State Information

Stateful Object	Description
General	A summary of all of the stateful objects in this display
sys cmd	The update system commands
up time	The amount of time the active PIX has been up, which is passed to the standby PIX
Xlate	The address translation information
Tcp conn	The TCP connection information
Udp conn	The UDP connection information
ARP tbl	The ARP table of the PIX
RIP tbl	The routing table of the PIX

Table 12-7.   Shared Stateful Objects

communications in a non-stateful configuration. I'll use the primary PIX in the network shown in Figure 12-3:

```
pixfirewall(config)#  show failover
Failover On
Cable status: Unknown
Reconnect timeout 0:00:00
Poll frequency 15 seconds
    This host: Primary - Active
            Active time: 257 (sec)
            Interface failcable (172.16.2.1): Normal
            Interface outside (192.168.1.2): Normal
            Interface inside (172.16.1.1): Normal
    Other host: Secondary - Standby
            Active time: 0 (sec)
            Interface failcable (172.16.2.2): Normal
            Interface outside (192.168.1.3): Normal
            Interface inside (172.16.1.2): Normal

Lan Based Failover is Active
        Interface failcable (172.16.2.1): Normal, peer (172.16.2.2) Normal
```

The first thing to point out in this example is that the *Cable status* is listed as *Unknown*—the reason for this is that this information refers to a configuration using a serial-based cable for failover communications, which these PIXs are not using—they're using a LAN connection where the interface on each side is called *failcable*.

The rest of the output is the same as a serial-based set up with one exception: At the bottom of the display is a line entitled *Lan Based Failover is Active*. This line indicates that LAN-based failover has been enabled. Below this is a line indicating the name of the interface that is used for the LAN-based failover connection as well as the status for this interface.

You can also use the `show failover lan` and `show failover lan detail` commands to display information related to only the LAN-based failover connection itself. The `show failover lan` command displays the very last part of the display in the last code display, the section entitled *Lan Based Failover is Active*. So you would only see two lines in your output of this command, as shown here:

```
pixfirewall#  show failover lan
Lan Based Failover is Active
        Interface failcable (172.16.2.1): Normal, peer (172.16.2.2) Normal
```

The `show lan failover detail` command displays debug output related to the LAN-based connection:

```
pixfirewall#  show failover lan detail
Lan Failover is Active
This Pix is Primary
Command Interface is failcable
Peer Command Interface IP is 172.16.2.1
My interface status is 0x1
Peer interface status is 0x1
Peer interface downtime is 0x0
Total msg send: 1035, rcvd: 1031, droped: 0, retrans: 13, send_err: 0
Total/Cur/Max of 2:0:2 msgs on retransQ if any
LAN FO cmd queue, count: 0, head: 0x0, tail: 0x0
Failover config state is 0x5c
Failover config poll cnt is 0
Failover pending tx msg cnt is 0
Failover Fmsg cnt is 0
```

As you can see from this output, this command is really for Cisco engineers to troubleshoot difficult problems with LAN-based connections. Cisco hasn't officially published what each of the hexadecimal values are for this information.

`debug fover` Command

Like Cisco IOS-based routers, the PIX supports some debug capabilities. Debug is a feature that allows you to tell the PIX to display certain events, or certain packet contents, as information is flowing through the PIX. This is a very useful tool when troubleshooting problems. Unlike the router IOS `debug` command, however, the PIX command has three major differences over its IOS cousin:

- You must execute it in *Configuration* mode.

- There is not a command that will disable all debug processing like on the router—you must disable each `debug` command individually be preceding it with the no parameter.

- The number of parameters is limited and the output is not as detailed.

Given these differences, though, this command is still a very powerful tool. If you are experiencing problems with the failover operation of your PIXs, or the failover communication between them, you can use the `debug fover` command to help troubleshoot these problems. When you enable this command with one of the failover options, whenever the PIX sees an event, condition, or packet information that matches the debug failover option, the PIX will display a message on the console port (these can also be logged to the PIX's internal buffer or a syslog server) pertaining to the event. This is real-time information.

Here is syntax of the `debug fover` command:

```
pixfirewall(config)#  debug fover debug_option
```

Table 12-8 lists the parameters that you can use for the `debug_option`.

Debug Option	Description
cable	Displays information related to the status of the failover cable.
fail	Displays information whenever an internal exception occurs for failover.
fmsg	Displays the contents of failover messages between the PIXs.
get	Displays a summary of when an IP packet is received by the PIX.
ifc	Displays information on the status of a PIX's network interface.
lanrx	Displays information when receiving LAN-based failover information.
lanretx	Displays information when LAN-based failover messages have to be retransmitted.
lantx	Displays information when transmitting LAN-based failover information.
lancmd	Displays information about the LAN-based failover process running on the PIX.
open	Displays information concerning the access of a failover PIX.
put	Displays information when the PIX transmits an IP packet.
rx	Displays information when a message is received on the failover cable.
rxdmp	A cable RECV message dump is displayed on the console only.
rxip	Displays information when an IP packet with failover information is received.
tx	Displays information when a message is transmitted on the failover cable.
txdmp	A cable XMIT message dump is displayed on the console only.
txip	Displays information when an IP packet with failover information is transmitted.
verify	Displays information when a failover verification message is received.
switch	Displays information about the switching status for failover.

Table 12-8.   Parameters for the `debug fover` Command

EXAMPLE CONFIGURATIONS

To help illustrate the configuration of failover, I have included two different scenarios in this chapter. This first scenario assumes that the PIXs are using a serial-based failover connection for communications and the second scenario assumes that the PIXs are using a LAN-based connection. The next two sections cover the configuration for these two scenarios.

Cable-Based Failover Configuration

For the serial-based failover connection example, I'll use the network shown in Figure 12-5 to help illustrate the configuration. I'll assume that the LAN connections presented here are *logical* connections—in other words, the LAN connections are really connected to LAN switches, even though these switches are not shown. In the following sections, I will lead you step-by-step through the process that you'll go through in setting up your two PIXs.

Preparation Tasks

Before you begin your configuration, make sure that both PIXs are the same model number and have the same amount of RAM and flash, as well as the same version of the FOS. Next, make sure that you execute the `write erase` command on the *standby* PIX.

Once you have executed the `write erase` command on the standby PIX, turn it off. After this, plug in all of the LAN interfaces for both PIXs, as well as the serial

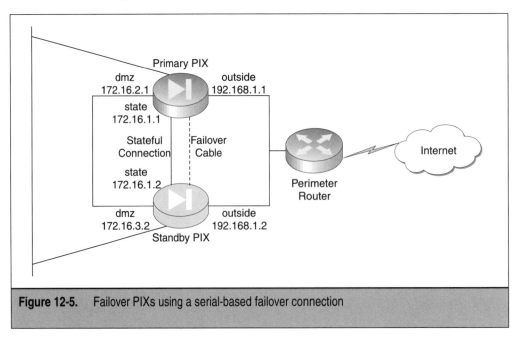

Figure 12-5.   Failover PIXs using a serial-based failover connection

failover cable between the two PIXs—make sure that the end marked primary is plugged into the primary PIX and the end marked standby is plugged into the standby PIX. Remember that the stateful connection must be a dedicated connection via a hub, switch, or crossover cable. Once you have completed these tasks, you are now ready to proceed with the configuration of the primary PIX.

Primary PIX Configuration

In the configuration of the primary PIX, I'm going to focus on just the commands necessary to set up failover. Once you have completed your failover configuration and tested it, you should only make configuration changes on the active PIX.

Set the Time   The first thing that you should do on the primary PIX is to set the time and date with the `clock` commands. I discussed these commands in Chapter 10. Once the standby unit is booted up (don't boot it up yet!), the standby PIX will acquire the correct date and time information from the active PIX. Here is an example of this configuration:

```
primary(config)#  clock set 15:00:00 May 23 2002
```

You might also want to configure the time zone and summertime settings in addition to setting the time and date. Instead of manually configuring the time, you might want to use NTP to dynamically acquire your timing information. I also discussed NTP in Chapter 10.

Configure the LAN Interfaces   After setting the time, hardcode the interface settings for your LAN connections. As I mentioned earlier in this chapter, you should not use autosensing. Therefore, examine your configuration and make sure that you do not see `auto` or `1000auto` for an interface setting for the LAN interfaces that you'll be using. If you see these settings, hardcode the setting to the correct speed and duplex setting with the `interface` command. Also, remember that the MTU size for the stateful connection must have an MTU size of at least 1,500 bytes (this is the default for all Ethernet interfaces). In our network, I'll assume that all of the interfaces are 10/100 Ethernet interfaces. Here is an example of setting up these interfaces:

```
primary(config)#  interface ethernet0 100full
primary(config)#  interface ethernet1 100full
primary(config)#  interface ethernet2 100full
primary(config)#  interface ethernet3 100full
primary(config)#  nameif ethernet0 outside sec0
primary(config)#  nameif ethernet2 dmz sec50
primary(config)#  nameif ethernet3 state sec75
primary(config)#  nameif ethernet1 inside sec100
primary(config)#  clear xlate
```

In this example, I've hard-coded the interface settings to 100 Mbps full-duplex. I've also given each of the interfaces an appropriate name. Remember that after you change any configuration on your interfaces, you should always clear the xlate table.

Configuring IP Addresses   After setting up your interfaces, you'll need to assign your IP addresses to the interfaces on the primary PIX with the `ip address` command:

```
primary(config)# ip address outside 192.168.1.1 255.255.255.0
primary(config)# ip address dmz 172.16.2.1 255.255.255.0
primary(config)# ip address state 172.16.1.1 255.255.255.0
primary(config)# ip address inside 172.16.3.1 255.255.255.0
primary(config)# show ip
System IP Addresses:
    ip address outside 192.168.1.1 255.255.255.0
    ip address inside 172.16.3.1 255.255.255.0
    ip address state 172.16.1.1 255.255.255.0
    ip address dmz 172.16.2.1 255.255.255.0
Current IP Addresses:
    ip address outside 192.168.1.1 255.255.255.0
    ip address inside 172.16.3.1 255.255.255.0
    ip address state 172.16.1.1 255.255.255.0
    ip address dmz 172.16.2.1 255.255.255.0
```

After setting up your addressing, make sure you verify it with the `show ip` command. The *System IP Addresses* and *Current IP Addresses* should be the same for the primary PIX.

Enabling Failover   Once you have set up the primary's IP addresses, you are now ready to proceed with the configuration of failover on the primary PIX. Here are the necessary commands to set up and verify failover for the example:

```
primary(config)# failover active
primary(config)# show failover
Failover On
Cable status: Other side powered off
Reconnect timeout 0:00:00
Poll frequency 15 seconds
    This host: primary - Active
                Active time: 45 (sec)
                Interface dmz (172.16.2.1): Normal (Waiting)
                Interface state (172.16.1.1): Normal (Waiting)
                Interface outside (192.168.1.1): Normal (Waiting)
                Interface inside (172.16.3.1): Normal (Waiting)
    Other host: secondary - Standby
                Active time: 0 (sec)
                Interface dmz (0.0.0.0): Unknown (Waiting)
                Interface state (0.0.0.0): Unknown (Waiting)
```

```
Interface outside (0.0.0.0): Unknown (Waiting)
Interface inside (0.0.0.0): Unknown (Waiting)
```

Notice that the `failover active` command is used on the primary PIX to make it the active PIX. When using the `show failover` command to verify your configuration, notice that the failover status is On and that the `Cable Status` indicates that the standby unit is not powered on. The display output indicates that this PIX is the active PIX, and that you have only configured IP addresses for the primary PIX's interfaces.

Configuring Standby PIX's IP Addresses   Now that you have configured the primary PIX's IP addresses, you need to tell the primary what IP addresses the standby unit should have configured on its LAN interfaces. Here is the configuration to do this with the `failover ip address` command:

```
primary(config)#  failover ip address dmz 172.16.2.2
primary(config)#  failover ip address state 172.16.1.2
primary(config)#  failover ip address outside 192.168.1.2
primary(config)#  failover ip address inside 172.16.3.2
primary(config)#  show failover
Failover On
Cable status: Other side powered off
Reconnect timeout 0:00:00
Poll frequency 15 seconds
    This host: primary - Active
                Active time: 197 (sec)
                Interface dmz (172.16.2.1): Normal (Waiting)
                Interface state (172.16.1.1): Normal (Waiting)
                Interface outside (192.168.1.1): Normal (Waiting)
                Interface inside (172.16.3.1): Normal (Waiting)
    Other host: secondary - Standby
                Active time: 0 (sec)
                Interface dmz (172.16.2.2): Unknown (Waiting)
                Interface state (172.16.1.2): Unknown (Waiting)
                Interface outside (192.168.1.2): Unknown (Waiting)
                Interface inside (172.16.3.2): Unknown (Waiting)
```

Notice that when I verify the PIX's configuration, the standby's IP addresses show up in the output of the `show failover` command; however, the status is Unknown—this is because the standby unit is powered off.

Configuring Stateful Failover   Now that you have configured the standby PIX's IP addresses on the primary PIX, you are now ready to enable stateful failover (remember that this feature must be purchased from Cisco and is optional). This shows the configuration of stateful failover:

```
primary(config)#  failover link state
primary(config)#  show failover
```

```
Failover On
Cable status: Other side powered off
Reconnect timeout 0:00:00
Poll frequency 15 seconds
    This host: primary - Active
                Active time: 242 (sec)
                Interface dmz (172.16.2.1): Normal (Waiting)
                Interface state (172.16.1.1): Normal (Waiting)
                Interface outside (192.168.1.1): Normal (Waiting)
                Interface inside (172.16.3.1): Normal (Waiting)
    Other host: secondary - Standby
                Active time: 0 (sec)
                Interface dmz (172.16.2.2): Unknown (Waiting)
                Interface state (172.16.1.2): Unknown (Waiting)
                Interface outside (192.168.1.2): Unknown (Waiting)
                Interface inside (172.16.3.2): Unknown (Waiting)

Stateful Failover Logical Update Statistics
        Link : state
        Stateful Obj    xmit        xerr        rcv         rerr
        General         0           0           0           0
        sys cmd         0           0           0           0
        up time         0           0           0           0
        xlate           0           0           0           0
        tcp conn        0           0           0           0
        udp conn        0           0           0           0
        ARP tbl         0           0           0           0
        RIP Tbl         0           0           0           0
    Logical Update Queue Information
                    Cur     Max     Total
        Recv Q:     0       0       0
        Xmit Q:     0       0       0
```

The failover link command specifies that the interface called state will be used for transmitting the state information between the two PIXs. Also, notice the output from the show failover command—the bottom half of the display indicates that the interface used for the stateful connection is called state by looking at the Link value.

Enabling the Standby PIX   Now that you have finished the mandatory configurations for the primary PIX, you can go ahead and power up the standby PIX. On the console of the primary PIX, you should see two messages appear in sequence: Sync Started and Sync Completed. Once you see these messages, you can use the show failover command on either PIX to verify the operational status of the failover feature. Here is an example of the display of the show failover command on the primary PIX:

```
primary(config)#  show failover
Failover On
Cable status: Normal
Reconnect timeout 0:00:00
Poll frequency 15 seconds
    This host: primary - Active
                Active time: 388 (sec)
                Interface dmz (172.16.2.1): Normal
                Interface state (172.16.1.1): Normal
                Interface outside (192.168.1.1): Normal
                Interface inside (172.16.3.1): Normal
    Other host: secondary - Standby
                Active time: 47 (sec)
                Interface dmz (172.16.2.2): Normal
                Interface state (172.16.1.2): Normal
                Interface outside (192.168.1.2): Normal
                Interface inside (172.16.3.2): Normal

Stateful Failover Logical Update Statistics
        Link : state
        Stateful Obj    xmit        xerr        rcv         rerr
        General         0           0           0           0
        sys cmd         0           0           0           0
        up time         0           0           0           0
        xlate           0           0           0           0
        tcp conn        0           0           0           0
        udp conn        0           0           0           0
        ARP tbl         0           0           0           0
        RIP Tbl         0           0           0           0
    Logical Update Queue Information
                        Cur     Max     Total
        Recv Q:         0       0       0
        Xmit Q:         0       0       0
```

Notice that the Cable status is `Normal` and that the status for all of the standby PIX's interfaces is also `Normal`.

NOTE   Remember that once you have made any changes on the active PIX, use the `write memory` command on the active PIX to save the configuration changes to flash on both PIXs.

LAN-Based Failover Configuration

For the LAN-based failover connection example, I'll use the network shown in Figure 12-6 to help illustrate the configuration. I'll assume that the LAN connections presented in

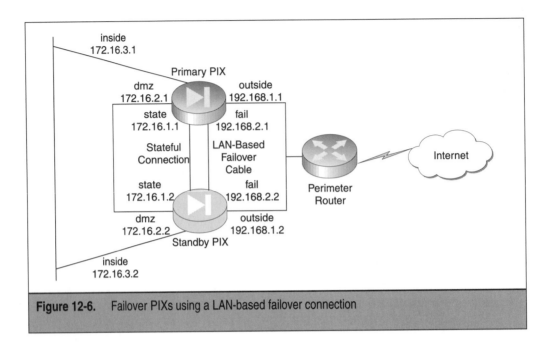

Figure 12-6. Failover PIXs using a LAN-based failover connection

Figure 12-6 are *logical* connections—in other words, the LAN connections are really connected to LAN switches, even though these switches are not shown in Figure 12-6. With LAN-based failover, you *cannot* use a crossover connection for the LAN-based failover connection—the connection must be through a switch. This connection must be a dedicated connection, so make sure that the LAN-based connection from each PIX is placed into the same VLAN, and that there are no other devices in this VLAN. In the following sections, I will lead you step-by-step through the process that you'll go through in setting up the primary and standby PIXs for the LAN-based failover connection.

Preparation Tasks

Before you begin your configuration, make sure that both PIXs have the same hardware configuration as well as the same version of the FOS. Remember that LAN-based failover is new in FOS 6.2, so you need at least this version of software on your PIXs. Also, you need at least a dedicated 100 Mbps connection between the two PIXs for the failover connection. Next, make sure that you execute the following commands on the standby PIX:

```
standby#  write erase
standby#  reload
```

After executing these commands on the standby PIX, plug in all of the LAN interfaces for both PIXs, but *not* the LAN-based failover cable between the two PIXs (via a switch or hub). The LAN-based connection will be added *after* completing the configuration on both the primary and standby PIXs. Also, if the serial-based failover cable is connected between the two PIXs, *disconnect* it. Once you have completed these tasks, you are now ready to proceed with the configuration of the primary PIX.

Primary PIX Configuration

In the configuration of the primary PIX, I'm going to focus on just the commands necessary to set up failover. Once you have completed your failover configuration and tested it, you should only make configuration changes on the active PIX.

Set the Time   The first thing that you should do on the primary PIX is to set the time and date with the `clock` commands (Chapter 10). Once the standby unit is set up for failover, the standby PIX will acquire the correct date and time information from the primary PIX:

```
primary(config)#  clock set 16:00:00 May 23 2002
```

You might also want to configure the time zone and summertime settings beside setting the time and date. Instead of manually configuring the time, you might want to use NTP.

Configure the LAN Interfaces   After setting the time, hardcode the interface settings for your LAN connections. As I mentioned earlier in this chapter, you should not use autosensing. Therefore, examine your configuration and make sure that you do not see `auto` or `1000auto` for an interface setting for the LAN interfaces that you'll be using. If you see these settings, hard-code the setting to the correct speed and duplex setting with the `interface` command. Also, remember that the MTU size for the stateful connection must have an MTU size of at least 1,500 bytes (this is the default for all Ethernet interfaces). In our network, I'll assume that all of the interfaces are 10/100 Ethernet interfaces. Here is an example of setting up these interfaces:

```
primary(config)#  interface ethernet0 100full
primary(config)#  interface ethernet1 100full
primary(config)#  interface ethernet2 100full
primary(config)#  interface ethernet3 100full
primary(config)#  interface ethernet4 100full
primary(config)#  nameif ethernet0 outside sec0
primary(config)#  nameif ethernet2 dmz sec25
primary(config)#  nameif ethernet3 state sec50
primary(config)#  nameif ethernet4 fail sec75
primary(config)#  nameif ethernet1 inside sec100
primary(config)#  clear xlate
```

In this configuration, I've hard-coded the interface settings to 100 Mbps full-duplex. I've also given each of the interfaces an appropriate name. It is very important that you configure the LAN-based connection to the correct hardware settings. Remember that after you change any configuration on your interfaces, you should always clear the xlate table.

Configuring IP Addresses After setting up your interfaces, you need to assign your IP addresses to the interfaces on the primary PIX with the `ip address` command:

```
primary(config)#  ip address outside 192.168.1.1 255.255.255.0
primary(config)#  ip address dmz 172.16.2.1 255.255.255.0
primary(config)#  ip address state 172.16.1.1 255.255.255.0
primary(config)#  ip address fail 192.168.2.1 255.255.255.0
primary(config)#  ip address inside 172.16.3.1 255.255.255.0
primary(config)#  show ip
System IP Addresses:
      ip address outside 192.168.1.1 255.255.255.0
      ip address inside 172.16.3.1 255.255.255.0
      ip address state 172.16.1.1 255.255.255.0
      ip address dmz 172.16.2.1 255.255.255.0
      ip address fail 192.168.2.1 255.255.255.0
Current IP Addresses:
      ip address outside 192.168.1.1 255.255.255.0
      ip address inside 172.16.3.1 255.255.255.0
      ip address state 172.16.1.1 255.255.255.0
      ip address dmz 172.16.2.1 255.255.255.0
      ip address fail 192.168.2.1 255.255.255.0
```

After setting up your addressing, make sure you verify it with the `show ip` command. The *System IP Addresses* and *Current IP Addresses* should be the same for the primary PIX.

Enabling Failover Once you have set up the primary's IP addresses, you are now ready to proceed with the configuration of failover on the primary PIX:

```
primary(config)#  failover active
primary(config)#  show failover
Failover On
Cable status: My side not connected
Reconnect timeout 0:00:00
Poll frequency 15 seconds
    This host: primary - Active
                Active time: 48 (sec)
                Interface dmz (172.16.2.1): Normal (Waiting)
                Interface state (172.16.1.1): Normal (Waiting)
                Interface fail (192.168.2.1): Normal (Waiting)
                Interface outside (192.168.1.1): Normal (Waiting)
                Interface inside (172.16.3.1): Normal (Waiting)
    Other host: secondary - Standby
                Active time: 0 (sec)
                Interface dmz (0.0.0.0): Unknown (Waiting)
```

```
Interface fail (0.0.0.0): Unknown (Waiting)
Interface state (0.0.0.0): Unknown (Waiting)
Interface outside (0.0.0.0): Unknown (Waiting)
Interface inside (0.0.0.0): Unknown (Waiting)
```

Notice that the `failover active` command is used on the primary PIX in order to make it the active PIX. When using the `show failover` command to verify your configuration, notice that the failover status is On and that the `Cable Status` indicates `My side not connected`—this is because you have disconnected the serial-based failover cable. The output indicates that this PIX is the active PIX and that you have only configured IP addresses for the primary PIX's interfaces.

Configuring Standby PIX's IP Addresses   Now that you have configured the primary PIX's IP addresses, you need to tell the primary what IP addresses the standby unit should have configured on its LAN interfaces. Here is the example that shows you how to do this with the `failover ip address` command:

```
primary(config)#  failover ip address dmz 172.16.2.2
primary(config)#  failover ip address state 172.16.1.2
primary(config)#  failover ip address fail 192.168.2.2
primary(config)#  failover ip address outside 192.168.1.2
primary(config)#  failover ip address inside 172.16.3.2
primary(config)#  show failover
Failover On
Cable status: My side not connected
Reconnect timeout 0:00:00
Poll frequency 15 seconds
    This host: primary - Active
                Active time: 177 (sec)
                Interface dmz (172.16.2.1): Normal (Waiting)
                Interface state (172.16.1.1): Normal (Waiting)
                Interface fail (192.168.2.1): Normal (Waiting)
                Interface outside (192.168.1.1): Normal (Waiting)
                Interface inside (172.16.3.1): Normal (Waiting)
    Other host: secondary - Standby
                Active time: 0 (sec)
                Interface dmz (172.16.2.2): Unknown (Waiting)
                Interface state (172.16.1.2): Unknown (Waiting)
                Interface fail (192.168.2.2): Unknown (Waiting)
                Interface outside (192.168.1.2): Unknown (Waiting)
                Interface inside (172.16.3.2): Unknown (Waiting)
```

Notice that when you verify the PIX's configuration, the standby's IP addresses show up in the output of the `show failover` command; however, the status is Unknown—this is because the standby unit has not been correctly set up yet.

Remember that LAN-based failover uses IP for failover communications and that you did a write erase on the standby unit, so the primary cannot make any connections to the standby unit; plus, you have not told the primary unit which interface is to be used for the LAN-based failover connection, and the serial cable is not, and should not be, connected.

Configuring the LAN-Based Failover Connection   You are now ready to tell the primary PIX which connection, and its parameters, that it will use for LAN-based failover communications:

```
primary(config)# no failover
primary(config)# failover lan unit primary
primary(config)# failover lan interface fail
primary(config)# failover lan key secretkey
primary(config)# failover lan enable
primary(config)# failover
primary(config)# show failover
Failover On
Cable status: My side not connected
Reconnect timeout 0:00:00
Poll frequency 15 seconds
    This host: primary - Active
                Active time: 262 (sec)
                Interface dmz (172.16.2.1): Normal (Waiting)
                Interface state (172.16.1.1): Normal (Waiting)
                Interface fail (192.168.2.1): Normal (Waiting)
                Interface outside (192.168.1.1): Normal (Waiting)
                Interface inside (172.16.3.1): Normal (Waiting)
    Other host: secondary - Standby
                Active time: 0 (sec)
                Interface dmz (172.16.2.2): Unknown (Waiting)
                Interface state (172.16.1.2): Unknown (Waiting)
                Interface fail (192.168.2.2): Unknown (Waiting)
                Interface outside (192.168.1.2): Unknown (Waiting)
                Interface inside (172.16.3.2): Unknown (Waiting)

Lan Based Failover is Active
        Interface fail (192.168.2.1): Normal, peer (192.168.2.2) Unknown
```

In this example, the first thing that you must do is temporarily disable failover with the no failover command. Then you set up your LAN-based failover configuration and, once that is done, reenable failover. In this example, the interface to be used for failover communications is fail and the encryption key is secretkey. When you examine the output of the show failover command, notice that LAN-based failover is enabled (`Active`) and that the interface used is `fail`—you can see this at the bottom of the display. Also, notice that the peer status at the bottom is listed as `Unknown`—this is because you haven't configured the standby unit yet.

TIP   If you are switching from serial-based failover communications to LAN-based failover communications, follow the above steps and then make sure you disconnect the serial failover cable between the two PIXs. You also have to set up LAN-based failover on the standby unit, which I cover later in this chapter.

Configuring Stateful Failover   Now that you have configured the LAN-based failover connection on the primary PIX, you are ready to enable stateful failover (remember that this feature must be purchased from Cisco, and it is optional). Here is the configuration of stateful failover:

```
primary(config)#  failover link state
primary(config)#  show failover
Failover On
Cable status: Other side powered off
Reconnect timeout 0:00:00
Poll frequency 15 seconds
    This host: primary - Active
                Active time: 281 (sec)
                Interface dmz (172.16.2.1): Normal (Waiting)
                Interface state (172.16.1.1): Normal (Waiting)
                Interface fail (192.168.2.1): Normal (Waiting)
                Interface outside (192.168.1.1): Normal (Waiting)
                Interface inside (172.16.3.1): Normal (Waiting)
    Other host: secondary - Standby
                Active time: 0 (sec)
                Interface dmz (172.16.2.2): Unknown (Waiting)
                Interface state (172.16.1.2): Unknown (Waiting)
                Interface fail (192.168.2.2): Unknown (Waiting)
                Interface outside (192.168.1.2): Unknown (Waiting)
                Interface inside (172.16.3.2): Unknown (Waiting)

Stateful Failover Logical Update Statistics
        Link : state
        Stateful Obj    xmit        xerr        rcv         rerr
        General         0           0           0           0
        sys cmd         0           0           0           0
        up time         0           0           0           0
        xlate           0           0           0           0
        tcp conn        0           0           0           0
```

```
     udp conn          0           0           0           0
     ARP tbl           0           0           0           0
     RIP Tbl           0           0           0           0
Logical Update Queue Information
                       Cur       Max       Total
     Recv Q:           0         0         0
     Xmit Q:           0         0         0
```

```
Lan Based Failover is Active
        Interface fail (192.168.2.1): Normal, peer (192.168.2.2) Unknown
```

The `failover link` command specifies that the interface called `state` will be used for transmitting the state information between the two PIXs. Also, notice the output from the show `failover` command—the bottom half of the display indicates that the interface used for the stateful connection is called `state` by looking at the `Link` value.

Standby PIX Configuration

Now that you have configured the primary PIX with the necessary failover setup, you are ready to set up the standby PIX. At the beginning of this section on configuring LAN-based connections, I had you erase the configuration on the standby PIX. Once you have completed your failover configuration on the standby PIX and tested it, you should only make configuration changes on the primary PIX.

Configure the Standby Interface   The first thing that you should do on the standby unit is set up the interface *fail* for IP connectivity. Here are the commands to accomplish this:

```
standby(config)# interface ethernet4 100full
standby(config)# nameif ethernet4 fail sec75
standby(config)# ip address fail 192.168.2.2 255.255.255.0
```

Notice that the physical interface that you configure must be the same one on the primary PIX that will be used for the LAN-based failover connection. Whatever hardware settings you configured on the primary PIX's interface need to be the same on this interface. One difference between the configuration of the two interfaces is the IP address—each of the two PIXs needs a unique IP address on their respective interfaces.

Configure Failover   Now that you have set up the interface for the standby PIX, you are ready to configure the its `failover` commands, as shown here:

```
standby(config)# failover ip address fail 192.168.2.2
standby(config)# failover lan unit secondary
standby(config)# failover lan interface fail
standby(config)# failover lan key secretkey
standby(config)# failover lan enable
standby(config)# failover
```

One item to point out about this configuration is that the IP address specified is the standby's IP address for the *fail* interface. The primary PIX initiates the connection to the standby PIX, and through this process, learns the primary PIX's IP addresses. You also do not need the second command—failover lan unit secondary—because the standby PIX will learn this from the primary (I've included the first two commands for reference). You must tell the standby PIX which interface to use for communicating to the active PIX (*fail*). Remember that the encryption key, secretkey, must match the key configured on the primary.

Save and Reload   Now that you have set up the standby PIX, you need to save and reboot it:

```
standby(config)#  write memory
standby(config)#  reload
```

Final Tasks for LAN-Based Failover Configuration

Once the standby PIX has rebooted, you are now ready to complete the LAN-based failover configuration. You can go ahead and cable up the LAN-based connection. In this example, connect the ethernet4 interfaces together via a switch (in the same VLAN). Once you do this, the two PIXs should be communicating with each other. You can verify this by using the show ip on the standby PIX or the show failover command on either PIX. Here is the output from the primary (active) PIX:

```
primary(config)#  show failover
Failover On
Cable status: Other side powered off
Reconnect timeout 0:00:00
Poll frequency 15 seconds
   This host: primary - Active
                 Active time: 683 (sec)
                 Interface dmz (172.16.2.1): Normal
                 Interface state (172.16.1.1): Normal
                 Interface fail (192.168.2.1): Normal
                 Interface outside (192.168.1.1): Normal
                 Interface inside (172.16.3.1): Normal
   Other host: secondary - Standby
                 Active time: 0 (sec)
                 Interface dmz (172.16.2.2): Normal
                 Interface state (172.16.1.2): Normal
                 Interface fail (192.168.2.2): Normal
                 Interface outside (192.168.1.2): Normal
                 Interface inside (172.16.3.2): Normal

Stateful Failover Logical Update Statistics
        Link : state
```

Stateful Obj	xmit	xerr	rcv	rerr
General	0	0	0	0
sys cmd	0	0	0	0
up time	0	0	0	0
xlate	0	0	0	0
tcp conn	0	0	0	0
udp conn	0	0	0	0
ARP tbl	0	0	0	0
RIP Tbl	0	0	0	0

```
Logical Update Queue Information
                    Cur    Max     Total
     Recv Q:        0      0       0
     Xmit Q:        0      0       0
```

```
Lan Based Failover is Active
        Interface fail (192.168.2.1): Normal, peer (192.168.2.2) Normal
```

As you can see from this example, the interfaces on the active and standby PIXs are in a `Normal` state, and so is the LAN-based failover connection, seen at the bottom of the display.

FURTHER STUDY

Web Sites

The following is an excellent Cisco document that explains how failover works: www.cisco.com/warp/customer/110/failover.html. You will need a CCO from Cisco account to access this web site.

For more information about configuring your PIX, visit: www.cisco.com/univercd/cc/td/doc/product/iaabu/pix/pix_62/config/index.htm.

CHAPTER 13

*Password Recovery
Procedure*

In the last chapter, I talked about how to set up the failover feature of the PIX firewall to provide redundancy for your network. In this chapter, I cover a common problem that many network administrators have had to face one time or another—accessing a networking device when you have either forgotten the password, or do not know the password. As you will see, the process of breaking into your PIX to bypass the configured password has a few similarities to Cisco's IOS-based router's password recovery procedure; however, there are some major differences between the two methods.

PASSWORD RECOVERY OVERVIEW

Actually, the term *password recovery* is misleading, even though Cisco uses this term to describe the process. A better term to use would be *password bypass*. The function of the password recovery procedure is to bypass the configured passwords on your PIX. You cannot, however, recover the passwords on your PIX firewall and see what was previously configured.

As I mentioned in Chapter 3, there are two passwords that you can configure on your PIX: one for telnet access and one for *Privilege EXEC* access. When you configure these passwords, the PIX automatically encrypts them. Therefore, when you view your active or saved configuration file, you will only see a string of random characters, like this:

```
enable password 8Ry2YjIyt7RRXU24 encrypted
passwd 2KFQnbNIdI.2KYOU encrypted
```

As you can see, both the *Privilege EXEC* and telnet passwords are encrypted. There is no known program that you can use to reverse-engineer the encrypted information that will result in the actual password. Therefore, if you don't know the password to access the PIX, you will have to break into it and clear the configured passwords.

When to Use the Password Recovery Procedure

There are three situations when you might be locked out of your PIX:

- You have forgotten the configured password.
- You have inherited the PIX firewall from another administrator and do not know the configured password.
- You are only using AAA for authentication and the AAA server is not reachable.

The third problem is the easiest one to deal with. As I mentioned in Chapter 11, if you are using AAA to secure access to your PIX, and the AAA server is not available, you can still access your PIX on the console port by entering a username of *pix* and the *Privilege EXEC* password that you have configured. However, if you don't know the *Privilege EXEC* password, you will have to perform the password recovery procedure.

Approaches

Cisco has developed two approaches to their password recovery procedure. Based on the hardware configuration of your PIX, you will use only one. The two approaches are:

- When the PIX has a floppy drive
- When the PIX doesn't have a floppy drive

Actually, the first approach is only valid for the 520 and some very old PIX models. All the PIX models that Cisco is currently shipping do not have a floppy drive.

Here are some important items to point out regarding the password recovery procedure of the PIX:

- You must have console access to the PIX.
- You will need to download a special file(s) from Cisco.
- Passwords are erased, not recovered.
- The process requires some downtime.

The following sections cover these issues in more depth.

Console Access

During the password recovery procedure, you need physical access to the console port on the PIX—in other words, you cannot execute this procedure remotely. This is a safety feature that Cisco has developed for this process. You wouldn't want anyone from a remote location to attempt the password recovery procedure for your PIX firewall.

Software Image

In addition to console access to the PIX, you also need to download, from Cisco's web site, a file or files that will be used for the password recovery procedure. The files that you must download are based on whether or not the PIX has a floppy drive and what version of software is currently running on your PIX firewall.

Erasing Passwords

When the password recovery procedure has completed, the PIX will have erased both the telnet password and *Privilege EXEC* password from the PIX's configuration. Remember that the default telnet password for the PIX is *cisco*. As I mentioned earlier, there is no way of figuring out what the configured passwords are—your only option is to erase them.

SECURITY ALERT!   When the PIX erases the passwords, they are set back to the factory default: No password for *Privilege EXEC* access and *cisco* for telnet access. You will want to change these passwords.

Downtime

To perform the password recovery procedure, you will have to reboot your PIX. This procedure has two different flavors based on the type of PIX that you have.

For a PIX that doesn't have a floppy drive, the procedure is actually performed from *Monitor* mode. As I mentioned in Chapter 3, *Monitor* mode is similar to rommon mode on an IOS-based router. On the PIX, when you are in *Monitor* mode, the PIX is not running the FOS and thus is not passing traffic between its interfaces. However, you can use *Monitor* mode to perform some basic troubleshooting as well as to perform software upgrades (in older versions of the software) and the password recovery procedure.

For a PIX that has a floppy drive, you copy the software image to a floppy and reboot the PIX with this floppy in the floppy drive. Therefore, no matter which type of PIX you have, you should schedule some downtime when you perform the password recovery procedure.

PASSWORD RECOVERY FOR PIXS WITHOUT A FLOPPY DRIVE

All of the following PIXs do *not* have a floppy drive: 501, 506, 506E, 515, 515E, 525, and 535. If you have one of these PIXs, you need to perform the password recovery procedure for PIXs that lack a floppy drive. Here are the basic steps that you will have to go through in order to execute the password recovery procedure:

1. Get the appropriate password image file from Cisco.
2. Place this file on a TFTP server.
3. Break into *Monitor* mode on your PIX.
4. Configure the PIX in *Monitor* mode.
5. Pull in the file from the TFTP server.
6. Reboot your PIX firewall.

The following sections will cover these steps in more depth.

Password Recovery Requirements

As I mentioned earlier in this chapter, you need console access to the PIX, and you will have to reboot the PIX when performing the password recovery procedure. Before you begin the password recovery process, you'll need a special software image from Cisco called np*xy*.bin, where the *xy* value represents the version of software that the PIX is running. Table 13-1 lists the names of the files and what version of software they are used for when executing the password recovery procedure.

Image Name	FOS Version
nppix.bin	4.3 and earlier
np44.bin	4.4
np50.bin	5.0
np51.bin	5.1
np52.bin	5.2
np53.bin	5.3
np60.bin	6.0
np61.bin	6.1
np62.bin	6.2

Table 13-1.   Software Images for Password Recovery

Note that these software images are *not* the FOS—they only contain code to find the password commands in the configuration file stored in flash and set the passwords back to the factory default. You must use the correct image, or else the password recovery procedure might not work, or, in the worse case, your configure file in flash may become corrupted.

NOTE   If you do not know what version of software your PIX is running, reboot it and examine the bootup display—the PIX will display the version of the FOS that it is loading before you get the *User EXEC* prompt. An example of this bootup process is shown in Chapter 3.

At the time of this writing, these binary files were located at the following URL: www.cisco.com/warp/public/110/*image_name*. However, Cisco tends to change the structure of their web site every few months. If you cannot find the files at this URL location, do a search on the file name with Cisco's web search feature. Once you have downloaded the correct np*xy*.bin file from Cisco's web site, you should place this image on an internal TFTP server. The password recovery process will have the PIX load this file from the TFTP server.

Accessing Monitor Mode

Once you have copied the password recovery file to your internal TFTP server, you are now ready to begin the actual password recovery process. Remember what I mentioned earlier in this chapter—you should schedule some downtime to perform the recovery process. You will have to reboot your PIX twice—once to break into *Monitor* mode, and once to load the FOS image located in flash. The password recovery process should only take 10 or 15 minutes to complete, so budget your downtime appropriately.

To access *Monitor* mode, you first need to reboot your PIX. As the PIX boots up, you'll see a message that states "Use BREAK or ESC to interrupt flash boot". Press one of these control sequences within 10 seconds of seeing this message and you'll be taken into *Monitor* mode, shown here:

```
CISCO SYSTEMS PIX-501
Embedded BIOS Version 4.3.200 07/31/01 15:58:22.08
Compiled by morlee
16 MB RAM
←output omitted→
Use BREAK or ESC to interrupt flash boot.
Use SPACE to begin flash boot immediately.
Flash boot interrupted.
0: i8255X @ PCI(bus:0 dev:17 irq:9 )
1: i8255X @ PCI(bus:0 dev:18 irq:10)

Using 1: i82557 @ PCI(bus:0 dev:18 irq:10), MAC: 0008.e3c7.f7a2
Use ? for help.
monitor>
```

Notice that the prompt now reads monitor>, indicating that you are in *Monitor* mode.

NOTE While in *Monitor* mode, the PIX does not pass any traffic between interfaces: you must have the PIX load the FOS to accomplish this.

Configuring Your PIX in Monitor Mode

Now that you are in *Monitor* mode, you are ready to proceed with the password recovery procedure. The PIX is not passing any traffic between its interfaces. The reason for this is that the PIX is not running the FOS and thus is not using the configuration file stored in flash. In other words, there is no configuration on the PIX. In order to download the password recovery file from the TFTP server, you will need to put a basic configuration on the PIX within *Monitor* mode.

You will probably have to perform most of the following tasks to configure your PIX correctly within *Monitor* mode:

- Define which interface the TFTP server resides on, with the interface command.
- Define the IP address for this interface, with the address command.
- Define a default gateway if the TFTP server is more than one hop away, with the gateway command.
- Define the IP address of the TFTP server, with the server command.

- Define the name of the software image to use on the TFTP server, with the `file` command.

- Test the connection to the TFTP server, with the `ping` command.

- Start the download process with the `tftp` command.

Here is the syntax for these commands:

```
monitor>  interface [interface_number]
monitor>  address interface's_IP_address
monitor>  gateway router's_IP_address
monitor>  server TFTP_server's IP_address
monitor>  file name_of_BIN_file
monitor>  ping destination_IP_address
```

The `interface` command is used to specify which interface the PIX should use when accessing the TFTP server. The `interface_number` parameter is the number of the interface, such as 0, 1, or 2. If you omit the number of the interface, it defaults to the inside interface (1).

NOTE   One restriction with the use of interfaces in *Monitor* mode is that on the PIX 535, you cannot use an interface in a 64-bit slot, because *Monitor* mode doesn't recognize these cards—you must use an interface in a 32-bit slot. Refer to Chapter 2 to determine which slots are 32-bit versus 64-bit.

The `address` command specifies the IP address that the PIX will use for the interface on the PIX. Note that there is no subnet mask. If you don't configure the IP address, it defaults to 0.0.0.0, which means the PIX will not process any type of IP packet. You must configure this command.

The `gateway` command specifies the IP address of the router's interface that the PIX should use for a default gateway. This command is optional and only necessary if the TFTP server is more than one router hop away from the PIX.

The `server` command specifies the IP address of the TFTP server that has the password recovery file on it. If you don't configure this address, the PIX will use a destination address of 255.255.255.255. This address will work if the TFTP server is on the same network segment as the PIX itself.

The `file` command specifies the name of the password recovery image on the TFTP server. This is a required command—if you don't configure this file name, the PIX will not be able to download the image from the TFTP server.

Once you have configured these commands (or you are in the process of configuring them), you can test IP connectivity by using the `ping` command. Please note that any ICMP echoes that the PIX generates will only exit the interface specified by the `interface` command. You should use this command if you are experiencing connectivity problems to the TFTP server.

Password Recovery Process

Once you have configured your PIX from within *Monitor* mode and tested IP connectivity to the TFTP server, you are now ready to start the download process of the password recovery file. To start the download process, execute the `tftp` command:

```
monitor> tftp
tftp np62.bin@192.168.1.1.............................................
......................................................................
..........
Received 73728 bytes

Cisco Secure PIX Firewall password tool (3.0) #0: Wed Mar 27 11:02:16 PST 2002
Flash=E28F640J3 @ 0x3000000
BIOS Flash=E28F640J3 @ 0xD8000

Do you wish to erase the passwords? [yn] y
The following lines will be removed from the configuration:
        enable password 8Ry2YjIyt7RRXU24 encrypted
        passwd 2KFQnbNIdI.2KYOU encrypted

Do you want to remove the commands listed above from the configuration? [yn] y
Passwords and aaa commands have been erased.

Rebooting....
```

When you execute the `tftp` command, the PIX attempts to download the file specified by the `file` command from the TFTP server specified by the `server` command. In this example, the server is *192.168.1.1* and the file name is *np62.bin*. Notice that the size of the password recovery file that was pulled into the PIX is very small—only 73,728 bytes.

The PIX will then execute this file. The first question the PIX asks is whether or not you wish to erase the passwords. If you type **n**, you are aborting the password recovery procedure. If you type **y**, the procedure will continue. After this, the PIX displays the commands in flash that it will erase. These commands include the *Privilege EXEC* password and the telnet password commands. Also, if you have any AAA authentication commands for PIX access, these commands will be displayed also.

You are then asked if you want to remove these commands from the configuration. Actually, this is somewhat misleading. If you have AAA commands on the PIX, these will be removed (this is a new feature starting in FOS 6.2); however, the two password commands will still be in your configuration when you are done with the password recovery process—the passwords are simply set to their factory defaults. If you answer **n** to this question, the PIX will leave the commands alone in the flash's configuration file and reboot the PIX; otherwise, the PIX will perform the password recovery procedure and reboot. As you can see from this process, the password recovery procedure is straightforward.

NOTE   Once the PIX reboots, any configuration that you performed within *Monitor* mode is gone. Also, the process described in this section might differ slightly based on the password recovery image file that you are using.

PASSWORD RECOVERY FOR PIXS WITH A FLOPPY DRIVE

Only the PIX 520 and older models have a floppy drive. If you have one of these PIXs, the password recovery process will be different than for PIXs that don't have a floppy drive. Here are the basic steps that you will have to go through to execute the password recovery procedure:

1. Get the appropriate password software image from Cisco.

2. Copy the software image to a floppy diskette.

3. Place the diskette into the floppy drive.

4. Reboot your PIX firewall.

If you would like the specifics on the password recovery procedure for PIXs with a floppy drive, please visit my web site at http://home.cfl.rr.com/dealgroup/.

PASSWORD RECOVERY EXAMPLE

To help illustrate how the password recovery process is performed, I'll assume that I'm locked out of the PIX 501 shown in Figure 13-1.

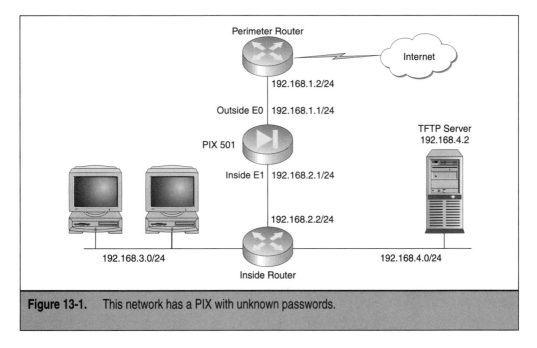

Figure 13-1.   This network has a PIX with unknown passwords.

In this example, I've just been hired by a company whose network administrator quit his job and left no documentation. I need to access the PIX in order to make some configuration changes, but I don't know what the configured passwords are. Therefore, I need to execute the password recovery procedure.

The first thing that I do is to figure out what version of software this PIX is running. To accomplish this, I need to reboot the PIX and watch the console to determine the appropriate version of software. In this example, I'll assume that the software version is FOS 6.2. Once I know the version of software, I visit Cisco's web site, download the image called np62.bin, and place this on the TFTP server (192.168.4.2).

Now that I have the password recovery file on the TFTP server, I'm ready to begin the password recovery process. I reboot the PIX 501, break into *Monitor* mode, and set up the appropriate configuration, as shown here:

```
CISCO SYSTEMS PIX-501
Embedded BIOS Version 4.3.200 07/31/01 15:58:22.08
Compiled by morlee
16 MB RAM
PCI Device Table.
Bus Dev Func VendID DevID Class            Irq
  00  00   00   1022   3000  Host Bridge
  00  11   00   8086   1209  Ethernet         9
  00  12   00   8086   1209  Ethernet        10

Cisco Secure PIX Firewall BIOS (4.2) #6: Mon Aug 27 15:09:54 PDT 2001
Platform PIX-501
Flash=E28F640J3 @ 0x3000000

Use BREAK or ESC to interrupt flash boot.
Use SPACE to begin flash boot immediately.
Flash boot interrupted.
0: i8255X @ PCI(bus:0 dev:17 irq:9 )
1: i8255X @ PCI(bus:0 dev:18 irq:10)
Using 1: i82557 @ PCI(bus:0 dev:18 irq:10), MAC: 0008.e3c7.f7a2
Use ? for help.
monitor> interface 1
monitor> address 192.168.2.1
monitor> gateway 192.168.2.2
monitor> server 192.168.4.2
monitor> file np62.bin
monitor> ping 192.168.4.2
Sending 5, 100-byte 0xf8d3 ICMP Echoes to 192.168.4.2, timeout is 4
seconds:
!!!!!
Success rate is 100 percent (5/5)
monitor>
```

Notice that the first thing that I did was hit the ESC key to break into *Monitor* mode.

Once in *Monitor* mode, I configure the PIX for TFTP connectivity. The TFTP server is on interface 1, the *inside* interface. This is the default interface if you don't specify it, but I've included it here for clarity. I configure the IP address of the *inside* interface (192.168.2.1) and specify the IP address of the internal router (192.168.2.2) as the default gateway. After this, I configure the IP address of the TFTP server (192.168.4.2) and the name of the password recovery file (np62.bin). Once I configure the connectivity for the PIX, I test the connection to the TFTP server with the ping command, which is shown at the end of the example.

Now that I've established connectivity, I'm ready to proceed with the password recovery process by executing the tftp command:

```
monitor> tftp
tftp np62.bin@192.168.4.2......................................................
..............................................................................
..........
Received 73728 bytes
Cisco Secure PIX Firewall password tool (3.0) #0: Wed Mar 27 11:02:16 PST 2002
Flash=E28F640J3 @ 0x3000000
BIOS Flash=E28F640J3 @ 0xD8000

Do you wish to erase the passwords? [yn] y
The following lines will be removed from the configuration:
        enable password 8Ry2YjIyt7RRXU24 encrypted
        passwd 2KFQnbNIdI.2KYOU encrypted
Do you want to remove the commands listed above from the configuration? [yn] y
Passwords and aaa commands have been erased.
Rebooting....
```

After I execute the tftp command, the PIX downloads the binary file and executes it, prompting me to erase the passwords. Once I complete the process, the PIX automatically reboots.

FURTHER STUDY

Web Sites

For more information on the PIX password recovery procedure, visit www.cisco.com/warp/public/110/34.shtml.

CHAPTER 14

Upgrading Your PIX Firewall

In the last chapter, I talked about how to use the password recovery procedure to break into your PIX when you had either forgotten your passwords, inherited a PIX with unknown passwords, or you are using AAA and your AAA server is unreachable. This chapter focuses on how to upgrade the software on your PIX firewall. Interesting enough, one method of the upgrade process is very similar to the password recovery method that used *Monitor* mode, which I discussed in the last chapter. Therefore, upgrading your PIX should be a simple step forward. To make it even easier, Cisco has recently included FOS commands similar to the IOS-based routers for performing upgrades.

Based on the type of PIX that you have and the version of the FOS it is running, the upgrade process will be different. I will make no assumptions about what kind of PIX you have or what version of the FOS is running on your PIX. Instead, I will cover all the software upgrade methods available on the PIX, as well as some new enhancements in FOS 6.2.

UPGRADING YOUR PIX

There are a handful of ways of upgrading your FOS, which can make the process seem somewhat confusing. Table 14-1 shows the possible ways of upgrading your PIX firewall and the version of the FOS that they were available in.

Of course, the FOS is not the only software image that might be installed in your PIX's flash. Starting with 6.0 of the PIX FOS, Cisco introduced the PIX Device Manager (PDM), discussed in Chapter 9, to provide a GUI-based management solution. PDM is installed in flash and is upgradeable.

Another item that you might upgrade on your PIX is its activation key. The PIX's activation key is used to activate features on your PIX firewall, like 3DES. Until version 6.2 of the FOS, you had to reinstall your software image to enter a new activation key. Now in 6.2, you can install new activation keys in your PIX with a simple *Configuration* mode command. The following sections cover each of these topics.

UPGRADING YOUR FOS

As I mentioned in Table 14-1, there are a handful of ways to upgrade your PIX's operating system. Some are easy, and some are more involved. To give you an appreciation of the

Method	FOS Version
Monitor mode	5.0 and earlier
`copy tftp flash` command	5.1 and later
`copy http flash` command	6.2
Auto Update	6.2

Table 14-1. Methods to Upgrade your PIX's FOS

upgrade process, I will start with Cisco's older upgrade method using *Monitor* mode on the PIX and progress to Cisco's newer methods.

One important item to point out is that in order to upgrade from one version of the FOS to another, you might have to perform an incremental upgrade. Therefore, it is very *important* that you read the release and installation notes included for a particular version of the FOS. Cisco will point out any issues with the upgrade process and methods of getting around these issues.

TIP   Before upgrading your FOS, make sure you back up your PIX's configuration to a TFTP server. In some instances, the PIX will make a change to your configuration file when it upgrades the FOS, which might present difficulties if you need to go back to the older FOS version.

FOS Version 5.0 and Earlier

Before version 5.1 of the FOS, the `copy tftp flash` command didn't exist. Instead, you had to boot your PIX into *Monitor* mode and perform the software upgrade from this mode. Therefore, to upgrade your PIX with this method, you need console access to your PIX firewall—without console access, this upgrade method is not possible. As you will see later on, if you are running FOS 5.1 or later, you can use the `copy tftp flash` command to perform an upgrade on your PIX via any access method, including telnet, SSH, and PDM, as well as from the console port.

The following sections discuss the files that you need in order to perform the operating system upgrade as well as the method that you need to use for a PIX without a floppy drive, and one with a floppy drive.

Software Requirements

Before you begin your upgrade, you should download the release notes for the FOS that you want to install on your PIX. Read these carefully, looking for issues regarding upgrading from specific releases of the FOS to the new release. Once you are sure that there aren't any upgrade issues, download the FOS version that you want to upgrade to.

The upgrade process is similar to the process I discussed in Chapter 13 concerning the password recovery procedure using *Monitor* mode. You need to download the files in Table 14-2.

PIX FOS Image   You need a special Cisco Connection Online (CCO) account to download these files. Cisco uses CCO accounts to restrict the kinds of software that

File Type	File Nomenclature	PIX without a Floppy Drive	PIX with a Floppy Drive
FOS image	`pixxyz.bin`	Yes	Yes
Boothelper	`bhxyz.bin`	No	Yes (FOS 5.1 and later)
Disk Copier	`rawrite.exe`	No	Yes

Table 14-2.   Files to Upgrade a PIX Running FOS 5.0 and Earlier

you download. Cisco's web page that contains all of the PIX's FOS and PDM images, help files, and other images can be seen at `http://www.cisco.com/cgi-bin/ tablebuild.pl/pix`. Cisco's naming nomenclature for their FOS images is: `pixxyz.bin`. All PIX FOS images begin with the word *pix*. The *xyz* represents the version, the release of the version, and the subrelease. For instance, `pix602.bin` would be the FOS image for version 6, release 0, subrelease 2. You need to download the appropriate FOS image for your PIX firewall. Currently, Cisco has the PIX FOS images on their web site specified in Table 14-3.

If you see an ED designation following the FOS image, this indicates *Early Deployment*. Cisco recommends that these FOS images be installed only to solve specific security problems or to gain access to added or enhanced features. Cisco has tested these images to the best of their ability, including tests at some customer sites, but these images still might have some operational issues. In other words, if you are happy with your current release, and don't need added features of a new release, you are better off waiting for the other type of release—GD, or *General Deployment*. GD releases have been used and tested by many of Cisco customers. These are typically ED releases with patches—you will not find any new enhancements in a GD release.

Also, make sure that your PIX has the appropriate amount of RAM and flash before installing your new FOS. If you buy a brand new PIX today, you shouldn't have to worry about this because almost all of Cisco's new PIXs have a minimum of 32MB of RAM and 8MB of flash; however, this might not be true for older PIXs or older models.

FOS Image	Release and Designation	Memory Requirements	Flash Requirements
pix448.bin	FOS 4.4.8 GD	16MB	2MB
pix449.bin	FOS 4.4.9 GD	16MB	2MB
pix523.bin	FOS 5.2.3	32MB	8MB
pix527.bin	FOS 5.2.7	32MB	8MB
pix528.bin	FOS 5.2.8 GD	32MB	8MB
pix529.bin	FOS 5.2.9 ED	32MB	8MB
pix533.bin	FOS 5.3.3	32MB	8MB
pix534.bin	FOS 5.3.4 ED	32MB	8MB
pix602.bin	FOS 6.0.2	32MB	8MB
pix603.bin	FOS 6.0.3 ED	32MB	8MB
pix604.bin	FOS 6.0.4 ED	32MB	8MB
pix612.bin	FOS 6.1.2	32MB	8MB
pix613.bin	FOS 6.1.3 ED	32MB	8MB
pix614.bin	FOS 6.1.4 ED	32MB	8MB
pix621.bin	FOS 6.2.1	32MB	8MB
pix622.bin	FOS 6.2.2 ED	32MB	8MB

Table 14-3.   Current FOS Images and Hardware Requirements

NOTE Make sure that you never TFTP FOS version 4.4 or earlier to your PIX—doing so will corrupt the flash memory on the PIX. If you make this mistake, you will have to contact Cisco to recover from this problem.

Boothelper Image The boothelper image is only necessary for PIXs that have a floppy drive, like the 520, where the FOS image that you are loading is 5.1 or higher. If you are loading an FOS image older than 5.1, then you do not need this image. The software upgrade process for older versions of the FOS for PIXs with floppy drives is to copy the PIX FOS image to a floppy drive and then boot up your PIX from this floppy—a straightforward process. However, starting with FOS 5.1, the FOS image would not fit on a single floppy. Cisco circumvented this problem by creating a boothelper image that contains *Monitor* mode.

One problem with PIXs with a floppy drive is that they do not have a *Monitor* mode. The function of the boothelper image is to provide *Monitor* mode for these PIXs. You need to download the appropriate boothelper image from Cisco's web site, and there are a few of them. Boothelper images have a nomenclature of bh$xy(z)$.bin. They x and y represent the version and release numbers. Some boothelper images (those specifically for FOS 6.x) only have two numbers, whereas older images have three numbers, where the third number (z) represents the subrelease number. Download the boothelper image that is appropriate for the version of FOS that you will be upgrading to.

Disk Copier Image The rawrite.exe program is only necessary for PIXs that have a floppy drive. This is used to copy the FOS image or the boothelper image to a blank, formatted floppy diskette. I discussed the use of this program on my web site for the password recovery procedure on a PIX 520: http://home.cfl.rr.com/dealgroup/.

TFTP Server Software If you have a PIX without a floppy drive, you must have a TFTP server for PIXs currently running FOS 5.0 and earlier. You will place the FOS image that you downloaded from Cisco's web site onto this server. If you are using the boothelper program to load a FOS onto a PIX with a floppy drive, you also need to place the downloaded FOS on a TFTP server. Any TFTP-compliant server will suffice.

PIX without a Floppy Drive

This section covers the process to upgrade your PIX if it is running FOS 5.0 or earlier and doesn't have a floppy drive, such as the PIX 515 or 525. To perform the upgrade, you need the following items: the FOS image to install, a TFTP server, and console access to your PIX. Once you have these items, you need to follow these steps in the upgrade process:

1. Place the new FOS image file on a TFTP server.

2. Break into *Monitor* mode on your PIX.

3. Configure the PIX in *Monitor* mode.

4. Pull in the FOS image from the TFTP server.

5. Reboot your PIX firewall.

Accessing Monitor Mode   Once you have copied the new FOS image to your internal TFTP server, you are now ready to begin the upgrade process. Because you are accessing *Monitor* mode and the PIX doesn't pass traffic in this mode, you should schedule some downtime to perform the upgrade. You have to reboot your PIX twice—once to break into *Monitor* mode, and once to load the new FOS image you copied to flash. The upgrade process should take less than 15 minutes to complete.

To access *Monitor* mode, you first need to reboot your PIX. As the PIX boots up, you'll see a message that states "Use BREAK or ESC to interrupt flash boot." Press one of these keys within 10 seconds of seeing this message and you'll be taken into *Monitor* mode. This process is described in Chapter 13 for using the password recovery procedure.

NOTE   While in *Monitor* mode, the PIX does not pass any traffic between interfaces; you must have the PIX load the FOS to pass traffic.

Configuring Your PIX in *Monitor* Mode   Now that you are in *Monitor* mode, you are ready to proceed with the upgrade procedure. As I mentioned, the PIX is not passing any traffic between its interfaces. The reason for this is that the PIX is not running the FOS, and thus is not using the configuration file stored in flash. In other words, there is no configuration on the PIX. To download the new FOS image from the TFTP server, you need to put a basic configuration on the PIX within *Monitor* mode. The following listing shows the syntax for these commands.

```
monitor>    interface [interface_number]
monitor>    address interface's_IP_address
monitor>    gateway router's_IP_address
monitor>    server TFTP_server's IP_address
monitor>    file name_of_BIN_file
monitor>    ping destination_IP_address
monitor>    tftp
```

These commands are described in Chapter 13. Once you have set up your PIX's configuration in *Monitor* mode, you need to execute the tftp command to start the download process.

NOTE   One restriction with the use of interfaces in *Monitor* mode is that on the PIX 535, you cannot use an interface in a 64-bit slot, because *Monitor* mode doesn't recognize these cards—you must use an interface in a 32-bit slot. Refer back to Chapter 2 to determine which slots are 32-bit versus 64-bit on a PIX 535.

Upgrade Example   To help illustrate the upgrade, process, I'll use the network shown in Figure 14-1.

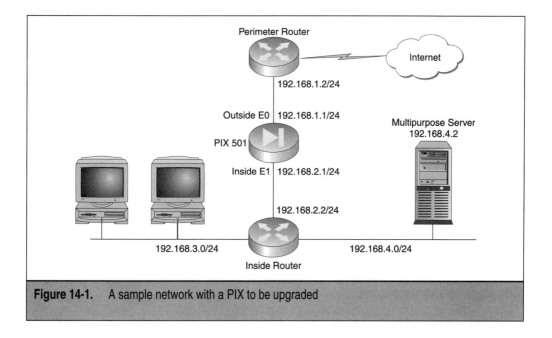

Figure 14-1. A sample network with a PIX to be upgraded

The actual upgrade process for the PIX is in the following listing.

```
CISCO SYSTEMS PIX-501
Embedded BIOS Version 4.3.200 07/31/01 15:58:22.08
Compiled by morlee
16 MB RAM

<--output omitted-->

Use BREAK or ESC to interrupt flash boot.
Use SPACE to begin flash boot immediately.
Flash boot interrupted.
0: i8255X @ PCI(bus:0 dev:17 irq:9 )
1: i8255X @ PCI(bus:0 dev:18 irq:10)

Using 1: i82557 @ PCI(bus:0 dev:18 irq:10), MAC: 0008.e3c7.f7a2
Use ? for help.
monitor> address 192.168.2.1
monitor> gateway 192.168.2.2
monitor> server 192.168.4.2
monitor> file pix621.bin
monitor> ping 192.168.4.2
Sending 5, 100-byte 0x9cb6 ICMP Echoes to 192.168.4.2, timeout is 4 seconds:
!!!!!
Success rate is 100 percent (5/5)
monitor> tftp
tftp pix621.bin@192.168.4.2....................................
```

```
Received 1640448 bytes

<--output omitted-->

Do you wish to copy the install image into flash? [n] y

Installing to flash
Serial Number: 406091733 (0x183477d5)
Activation Key: bbdb185f c57ebacc 5c47ef1b 59a2a66e

Do you want to enter a new activation key? [n] n
Writing 1531960 bytes image into flash...
###################################################################
 <--output omitted-->
```

The first part of the listing shows the PIX booting up and breaking into *Monitor* mode. Once in *Monitor* mode, the PIX is configured to access the TFTP server (192.168.4.2).

The upgrade is then started with the `tftp` command, which causes the PIX to download the FOS image to RAM. You are then asked if you want to install (copy) the new FOS image to flash: answer **y** or **n**. Please note that the PIX is smart enough to detect if this image is an FOS image or another type of file. After this, you are asked if you have a new activation key for your PIX—if you are not adding any features, accept the default value of **n**. Once you answer these two questions, the PIX will copy the FOS image downloaded from the TFTP server into flash memory. Upon completion of this copy process, the PIX will reboot. As you can see, the upgrade procedure is very similar to performing the password recovery procedure.

PIX with a Floppy Drive

This section covers the process to upgrade your PIX with a floppy drive, like the 520, if it is running FOS 5.0 or earlier. To perform the FOS upgrade process, you need the following items:

- FOS image to install
- `rawrite.exe` file
- Boothelper file (only necessary if the FOS image that you are loading is 5.1 or later)
- TFTP server (only necessary if the FOS image that you are loading is 5.1 or later)
- Console access to your PIX

Installing 5.0 or Earlier Images   Once you have these items, you need to follow these steps if you are upgrading to an FOS version that is 5.0 or earlier.

1. Use the `rawrite.exe` program to copy the FOS image to a blank, formatted floppy diskette. The use of this program is covered on my web site (http://home.cfl.rr.com/dealgroup/).

2. Place the floppy into the diskette drive of your PIX.

3. Reboot your PIX.

4. Answer **y** to proceed with the flash installation.

5. Enter a new activation key, if this is necessary.

6. Take the floppy out of the diskette drive and reboot the PIX.

As you can see, the installation process is straightforward.

Installing 5.1 or Later Images   If you want to install an FOS version that is 5.1 or later, you cannot use the process described in the preceding section because the FOS image will not fit on a diskette. Instead, you'll need to use the following steps:

1. Copy the FOS image to a TFTP server.

2. Use the `rawrite.exe` program to copy the boothelper program to a blank, formatted floppy diskette.

3. Place the floppy into the diskette drive of your PIX.

4. Reboot your PIX.

5. You are now in *Monitor* mode—use the upgrade process discussed previously in the section on PIXs without a floppy drive.

When you are in *Monitor* mode, the PIX's prompt will change to the following:

```
pixboothelper>
```

Remember that PIXs with a floppy drive do not have a *Monitor* mode—the boothelper image performs this process. The boothelper image only installs FOS versions 5.1 and later. If you try to install FOS 5.0 or earlier using this method, you'll get a "Checksum verification on flash image failed" message, and the PIX will reboot without actually loading the new FOS into flash. If you are installing an earlier image, use the process described in the previous section.

FOS Version 5.1 and Later

Starting in FOS 5.1, Cisco has made your job easier by allowing you to copy your FOS image from an external TFTP server directly to flash with the `copy` *Configuration*-mode command. The command syntax is similar to the IOS-based routers in version 12.0 and later. There are actually two methods of upgrades that you can use: TFTP and HTTP. Also, you can use the `copy` command to download two different types of images to flash: FOS and PDM. If you want to install PDM on your PIX (assuming that you are running FOS 6.0 or later), your only option is to use the `copy` command. The following two sections cover the TFTP and HTTP upgrade methods.

TFTP Upgrade

One option for upgrading your PIX firewall is to place your FOS or PDM images on a TFTP server and use the `copy tftp` command to load these images into your PIX's flash:

```
pixfirewall(config)# copy tftp[:[[//TFTP_location][/file_name]]]
                          flash[:[image|pdm]]
```

If you only type in `copy tftp flash`, the PIX will do a few things. First, it will prompt you for the IP address of the TFTP server as well as the name of the image that you want to download. Second, the PIX will assume that the image that you are downloading is a FOS image—in other words, the default flash parameter is `image`, not `pdm`.

Instead of being prompted for the IP address and file name, you can include them in the command line, like this:

```
pixfirewall(config)# copy tftp://192.168.4.2/pix621.bin flash:image
```

In this example, the TFTP server is 192.168.4.2, and the FOS image is `pix621.bin`.

NOTE   Unlike IOS-based routers, the `copy` command is executed from *Configuration* mode. Also, to install and use PDM, your PIX must currently be running FOS 6.*x*.

FOS Upgrade Example   For this example, I'll use the network shown in Figure 14-1. Here's an example of upgrading the FOS using TFTP.

```
pixfirewall(config)# copy tftp flash
Address or name of remote host [127.0.0.1]? 192.168.4.2
Source file name [cdisk]? pix621.bin
copying tftp://192.168.4.2/pix621.bin to flash:image
[yes|no|again]? y
!!!!!!!!!!!!!!!!!!!!!!!!!!!!!!!!!!!!!!!!!!!!!!!!!!!!!!!!!!!!!!!!!!!!
Received 1640448 bytes
Erasing current image
Writing 1531960 bytes of image
!!!!!!!!!!!!!!!!!!!!!!!!!!!!!!!!!!!!!!!!!!!!!!!!!!!!!!!!!!!!!!!!!!!!!
Image installed
pixfirewall(config)#
```

Here, I was prompted for the TFTP server's IP address, the FOS image name, and whether or not I wanted to proceed. When I answered **y**, the PIX copied the FOS image to RAM (not flash), erased the current FOS in flash, and then copied the FOS from RAM to flash. Once you have completed the upgrade, you have to reboot your PIX to use the new FOS.

PDM Upgrade Example The following shows an example of upgrading PDM using TFTP (see Figure 14-1).

```
pixfirewall(config)# copy tftp flash:pdm
Address or name of remote host [127.0.0.1]? 192.168.4.2
Source file name [cdisk]? pdm-201.bin
copying tftp://192.168.4.2/pdm-201.bin to flash:pdm
[yes|no|again]? y
Erasing current PDM file
Writing new PDM file
!!!!!!!!!!!!!!!!!!!!!!!!!!!!!!!!!!!!!!!!!!!!!!!!!!!!!!!!!!!!!!!
PDM file installed.
pixfirewall(config)#
```

Notice that the `flash` parameter in the `copy` command specifies `pdm`. After entering the command, I was prompted for the TFTP server's IP address, the PDM image name, and whether or not I wanted to proceed. When I answered **y**, the PIX erased the PDM image in flash, and then copied the PDM image from the TFTP server to flash. Unlike an FOS upgrade, you do *not* have to reboot the PIX to use the new PDM image.

HTTP Upgrade

The second `copy` option of upgrading your PIX firewall is to place your FOS or PDM images on an HTTP server, and use the `copy http` command to load these images into your PIX's flash memory (new in FOS 6.2):

```
pixfirewall(config)# copy http[s]://[username:password@]
                         web_server_IP_address
                         [:port_number][/file_name]]]
                         flash[:[image
```

You have your option of using HTTP or HTTPS for the web connection: HTTPS uses SSL (Secure Socket Layer) to provide for a secure connection. If you have password protection set up on your web server, you need to specify a username and password. The username and password are not stored in clear text in the PIX's configuration—they are always displayed as **********. Otherwise, you need to specify the IP address of the web server. If you omit the name of the FOS or PDM image, you'll be prompted for it. And last, the PIX assumes that the image that you are downloading is an FOS image. Here is an example of this command's format:

```
pixfirewall(config)# copy http://192.168.4.2/pix621.bin flash:image
```

NOTE In addition to using HTTP to load FOS and PDM images, you can also use it to restore your PIX's configurations with the `configure http` command.

FOS Upgrade Example   This is an example of upgrading the FOS using a web server (see Figure 14-1 for the network layout).

```
pixfirewall(config)# copy http://192.168.4.2/pix621.bin flash:image
copying http://192.168.4.2/pix621.bin to flash:image
!!!!!!!!!!!!!!!!!!!!!!!!!!!!!!!!!!!!!!!!!!!!!!!!!!!!!!!!!!!!!!!!
Received 1640448 bytes
Erasing current image
Writing 1531960 bytes of image
!!!!!!!!!!!!!!!!!!!!!!!!!!!!!!!!!!!!!!!!!!!!!!!!!!!!!!!!!!!!!!!!
Image installed
pixfirewall(config)#
```

Here, I entered the full syntax for the upgrade. After I entered this command, the PIX copied the FOS image to RAM (not flash), erased the current FOS in flash, and then copied the FOS in RAM to flash. Once you have completed the upgrade, you have to reboot your PIX in order to use the new FOS.

PDM Upgrade Example   The following shows an example of upgrading PDM using a web server (see Figure 14-1 for the network layout).

```
pixfirewall(config)# copy http://192.168.4.2/pdm-201.bin flash:pdm
copying http://192.168.4.2/pdm-201.bin to flash:pdm
Erasing current PDM file
Writing new PDM file
!!!!!!!!!!!!!!!!!!!!!!!!!!!!!!!!!!!!!!!!!!!!!!!!!!!!!!!!!!!!!!!!
PDM file installed.
pixfirewall(config)#
```

Notice that the flash parameter in the copy command specifies pdm. After I entered the command, the PIX erased the PDM image in flash and then copied the PDM image from the web server to flash. Unlike an FOS upgrade, you do not have to reboot the PIX to use the PDM image.

Upgrading Failover Configurations

In Chapter 12, I discussed how to set up a failover configuration for your PIX firewalls to provide redundancy. One item that I did not discuss was how to upgrade PIXs that are in a failover configuration. This section covers the steps necessary to successfully upgrade your PIXs in a failover configuration.

Use these steps to upgrade your failover PIXs.

1. Set up console connections to your primary and standby PIXs.

2. Reboot both the primary and standby PIXs into *Monitor* mode—for PIXs without a *Monitor* mode, use the boothelper program.

3. Configure the primary PIX in *Monitor* mode to access your TFTP server.

4. Load the FOS image on the primary PIX and reboot it.

5. After rebooting, use the `show failover` command to verify your PIX's failover configuration (remember, at this point the standby unit is still in *Monitor* mode).

6. Configure the standby PIX in *Monitor* mode to access your TFTP server.

7. Load the FOS image on the standby PIX.

8. Boot the standby PIX—it should synchronize with the primary. When it is finished booting, use the `show failover` command to verify your failover configuration.

The actual FOS upgrade process has already been described earlier in this chapter (the process for 5.0 FOS images and earlier).

DOWNGRADING YOUR FOS

Throughout this chapter, I have discussed how to upgrade your PIX firewall. However, there might be a case where you have loaded a new version of the FOS and experienced problems with this new release—possibly because it was an ED release and Cisco has not ironed out all of the bugs in it. In this instance, you need to downgrade the FOS on your PIX.

Unfortunately, the PIX does not have the same capabilities of IOS-based routers. IOS-based routers, assuming that you have enough flash memory, allow you to store more than one IOS image. This comes in handy if you have a problem with a new IOS image—you can easily go back to the earlier image already in flash. With the PIX firewall, however, you have to reinstall the old image.

When you downgrade to an older FOS image, the PIX displays the following message alert when you reboot the PIX firewall:

```
Configuration Compatibility Warning:
 The config is from version 6.2(1).
 but the image is version 6.1(2).
```

 SECURITY ALERT!   When you downgrade to a previous FOS version, there may be commands in your PIX's configuration from the current FOS that the downgraded FOS version may not understand. Therefore, whenever you downgrade to an earlier FOS version, back up your configuration file, write down your activation key, and then *always* check your PIX's configuration after it boots up.

If you are downgrading to FOS versions 5.2 or later, you do not have to do anything special—just download the older FOS software and reboot your PIX. However, if you are downgrading to an older version of the FOS than the ones I just mentioned, you first need to tell your PIX what the version number is that you are downgrading to, as shown here:

```
pixfirewall(config)#  flash downgrade version_number
```

The version number in the `flash downgrade` command can be `4.2`, `5.0`, or `5.1`.

AUTO UPDATE FEATURE

In FOS 6.2, Cisco introduced a new feature called *Auto Update*. Auto Update allows a remote management device (Cisco refers to this as an *Auto Update Server*) to download FOS and PDM images and configuration files to a PIX (running 6.2), as well as perform basic monitoring and troubleshooting tasks. The PIX firewall can also poll the remote management device to determine if there are downloads available. You can even have the Auto Update Server tell the PIX to execute a polling.

Configuring Auto Update

There are three configuration tasks you need to perform on your PIX when you set up a connection to use an Auto Update Server:

- Specify the location of the Auto Update server
- Enable Auto Update
- Configure the polling parameters

The following three sections cover these configuration tasks.

Specifying the Location of the Auto Update Server

The first thing that you should do when setting up the Auto Update feature is specify the location of the Auto Update server—this is the device that contains the FOS and PDM images, as well as the configuration files, that the PIX will be downloading. Here is the command to specify the Auto Update server's location:

```
pixfirewall(config)#  auto-update server
                      [http[s]://][username:password@]
                          server's_location[:port]/path
                      [verify-certificate]
```

Currently, you can only have one Auto Update server configured on your PIX firewall.

You can omit the `http` reference in the `auto-update server` command, because this is the default; however, if you want to use SSL, which is more secure, you need to specify `https`. Following this is an optional username and password—you should probably configure this to restrict who accesses the Auto Update Server. The username and password are not stored in clear text in the PIX's configuration—they are always displayed as **********.

After the username and password is the Server's location information, such as its fully-qualified domain name or IP address—you can specify a port number if the server is using a port other than 80. After this is the directory path where the PIX's files are stored.

At the end of the command is the optional `verify-certificate` parameter. Using HTTPS causes the PIX to verify the Auto Update Server's certificate information before continuing with any type of file transaction. I discuss certificates in Chapter 16.

You can remove an `auto-update server` command by preceding it with the `no` parameter. This disables any polling performed by the PIX.

Enabling Auto Update

Once you have configured the location of the Auto Update Server, you must enable the Auto Update feature on the PIX firewall. Enabling this feature will cause the PIX to poll the Auto Update server. To enable Auto Update, use the `auto-update device-id` command:

```
pixfirewall(config)# auto-update device-id
                         hostname|
                         mac-address [interface_name]|
                         ipaddress [interface_name]|
                         hardware-serial|string text_string
```

You have a handful of options regarding how the PIX will be identified on the Auto Update Server. These options are shown in Table 14-4. The PIX uses the specified identifier (`device-id`) when communicating with the Auto Update server. You can remove this command by preceding it with the `no` parameter.

Parameter	Device ID Descriptions
hostname	The name of the PIX, given to it with the `hostname` command.
mac-address	The MAC address of a PIX's interface. If you omit the interface name, it defaults to the interface of the PIX where the Auto Update server resides.
ipaddress	The IP address of a PIX's interface. If you omit the interface name, it defaults to the interface of the PIX where the Auto Update server resides.
hardware-serial	The serial number of the PIX firewall.
string	A text string that describes the PIX firewall—this cannot contain a space or any of the following characters: ' " > ? and &.

Table 14-4. Parameters for the `auto-update device-id` Command

Configuring Polling Parameters

By default, the PIX polls the Auto Update server every 720 minutes (12 hours). If the PIX is unsuccessful in polling the server, it will continually retry every 5 minutes. You can change these polling parameters with the `auto-update poll-period` command:

```
pixfirewall(config)# auto-update poll-period polling_period
                         [times_to_retry [time_between_retries]]
```

All the timing parameters in the `auto-update poll-period` command are specified in minutes. If you configure the `times_to_retry` parameter to be 0, the PIX will continually retry the polling of the server—you can restrict the number of retries by putting a number greater than 0 in this position. To reset these values back to the factory defaults, use the `no auto-update poll-period` command.

If you are concerned about the PIX operating without the latest configuration, you can use the `auto-update timeout` command. The function of this command is to ensure that the PIX has the latest updates—if it is not able to retrieve the latest updates from the Auto Update server within a defined time period, your PIX will not allow any new user connections. This is a nice security feature if you are paranoid about the security of your network; but the downside is that if the Auto Update server fails, using this command you could stop all of your traffic through the PIX, because you are not allowed to have a backup server when using the Auto Update feature. Here is the syntax of the `auto-update timeout` command:

```
pixfirewall(config)# auto-update timeout minutes
```

If your PIX is not able to contact the Auto Update server in the specified time interval (in minutes), the PIX stops accepting new user connections. If this situation occurs, the PIX generates a log message. You can remove this command be preceding it with the no parameter.

Verifying Auto Update

Once you have configured the Auto Update feature, you can verify your configuration and operation with the `show auto-update` command:

```
pixfirewall# show auto-update
Server: https://*******@192.168.4.2:443/management.cgi?1276
Certificate will be verified
Poll period: 720 minutes, retry count: 5, retry period: 5 minutes
Timeout: none
Device ID: host name [pixfirewall]
Next poll in 4.02 minutes
Last poll: 12:02:38 EST Fri Jun 7 2002
Last PDM update: 11:22:02 EST Fri Jun 7 2002
```

In this example, the PIX is using HTTPS for the connection (SSL). The polling period is 720 minutes, and the PIX will retry five times, once every 5 minutes, to access the

Auto Update server (192.168.4.2). In this example, Auto Update was used on June 7, 2002 to upgrade the PDM image on the PIX.

TIP   If you want to remove all Auto Update commands on your PIX, use the `clear auto-update` command.

ENTERING AN ACTIVATION KEY

Activation keys are used on PIX firewalls to enable special features, like 3DES and unlimited throughput. Each key is unique to each PIX, tied to the hardware components on the PIX's motherboard. Therefore, if your PIX fails and you have to replace it, you would need a new activation key.

This process is very different from how Cisco deals with their IOS router-based images. Given the right type of account from TAC, you can download virtually any type of IOS-based image. When you use your CCO account to download images, you have access to all of these images (except for the 3DES images, which require special access because of export restrictions). Cisco sells the IOS based on the features that you want, like SNA, desktop protocols like AppleTalk and IPX, firewall functions, and so on. Cisco uses the honor system with the download process—Cisco assumes that you will only download the IOS image sets that you purchased when you upgrade your router.

Cisco has taken a different approach with the PIX. With the correct type of CCO account, you can download any PIX image. Each PIX image contains all of the features and functions; however, many of these features are disabled. You need an appropriate activation key to turn on some, or all, of these functions. To get this key, you have to give Cisco some information about your PIX, including its serial number. Cisco takes this information and runs it through a proprietary program that produces a unique activation key for your PIX that will activate the features you have purchased. Your only task is to then enter this activation key.

NOTE   This activation key is only good for the serial number of the PIX that it was generated for—the key will not work on any other PIX.

Of course, when you buy a PIX, it already has an activation key installed on it. You only have to worry about reentering this key if you upgrade the features on your PIX, or you have to replace the PIX motherboard because of a failure. The following two sections cover the two processes that you can use to enter a new activation key.

FOS 6.1 and Earlier

Before version 6.2 of the FOS, you had to reinstall your FOS when you entered a new activation key. What made this worse was that you could not use the `copy tftp` command discussed earlier in this chapter. Instead, you had to use the *Monitor* mode method discussed earlier and reload the same FOS image back into flash. Of course, this is not a simple process just to enter a single parameter in order to activate a new feature on your PIX, like 3DES. Unfortunately, this was the only method available to you in FOS 6.1 and earlier. I will not discuss this process here because I previously discussed it thoroughly.

FOS 6.2 and Later

One really handy feature introduced in FOS 6.2 is the ability to enter your activation key from within *Configuration* mode with the `activation-key` command. This greatly simplifies the process of activating new features on your PIX firewall. If you are upgrading your FOS as well as activating new features, Cisco recommends that you use the following process:

1. Upgrade the FOS first (preferably using the `copy` command).
2. Reboot your PIX.
3. Enter the new activation key.
4. Reboot your PIX.

It is important that you follow these steps. Activation keys are backward-compatible with FOS versions. In other words, an activation key entered for the currently running FOS will work with older versions of the FOS; however, it will not work with new versions of the FOS unless you perform an upgrade process. Therefore, you should always upgrade your FOS first and then enter the PIX's activation key. If you are downgrading your FOS, the PIX will be able to use the newly entered activation key. The following sections show you how to enter your activation key and verify the activation key that your PIX is using.

NOTE   Always upgrade your FOS first, and then enter your new activation key.

Entering Your Activation Key

As I mentioned in the previous section, you should first upgrade your FOS and reboot your PIX before you enter a new activation key. Once you have completed these steps (if they are necessary), you can go ahead and enter your key with the `activation-key` command:

```
pixfirewall(config)#  activation-key your_activation_key
```

The activation key is actually a set of four different hexadecimal numbers. This is an example of entering the same activation key using a hexadecimal and decimal numbering scheme:

```
pixfirewall(config)#  activation-key 0x12345678 0x12345678
                                      0x12345678 0x12345678
pixfirewall(config)#  activation-key 12345678 12345678
                                      12345678 12345678
```

When you enter the activation key, you can precede it with 0x, indicating that this is a hexadecimal number. As you can see, this is optional—the PIX assumes that the number is hexadecimal.

When you have entered your new key, and the PIX accepts the new key, the message shown in the following listing will be displayed.

```
pixfirewall(config)# activation-key 0xbbdb185f 0xc57ebacc
                                     0x5c47ef1b 0x59a2a66e
Serial Number: 406091733 (0x183477d5)

Flash activation key: 0xbbdb185f 0xc57ebacc 0x5c47ef1b 0x59a2a66e
Licensed Features:
Failover:             Disabled
VPN-DES:              Enabled
VPN-3DES:             Disabled
Maximum Interfaces:   2
Cut-through Proxy:    Enabled
Guards:               Enabled
URL-filtering:        Enabled
Inside Hosts:         10
Throughput:           Limited
ISAKMP peers:         5

The flash activation key has been modified.
The flash activation key is now DIFFERENT than the running key.
The flash activation key will be used when the unit is reloaded.
pixfirewall(config)#
```

Notice that at the end of the listing, the PIX sees a difference between the activation key in flash and the one that it is currently using. Make sure you save the PIX's current configuration and then reboot your PIX to have it use the newly entered key.

The most important part of this display is the message that appears at the bottom of the previous listing. Table 14-5 shows the possible results and explanations of these messages.

Message	Explanation
The flash activation key is now DIFFERENT than the running key.	You have entered a valid, but different key from the one the PIX is currently using.
The activation key you entered is the SAME as the flash activation key.	The activation key has already been entered previously on the PIX.
ERROR: The requested key was not saved because it is not valid for this system.	You entered an invalid key—reenter it or contact Cisco for the correct key.

Table 14-5. Messages When Entering an Activation Key

When you enter an activation key, there may be issues with the key and the version of the FOS that resides in flash, assuming that you just completed an upgrade with the `copy tftp` method. If this is the case, you need to enter a new activation key. Or, if the activation key you entered is an invalid key, you have to reenter the old key value or call Cisco for assistance in generating a new key.

Examining Your Activation Key

To examine your PIX's activation key, use the `show activation-key` command, as shown here:

```
pixfirewall#  show activation-key
Serial Number: 406091733 (0x183477d5)

Running Activation Key: 0xbbdb185f 0xc57ebacc 0x5c47ef1b 0x59a2a66e
Licensed Features:
Failover:           Disabled
VPN-DES:            Enabled
VPN-3DES:           Disabled
Maximum Interfaces: 2
Cut-through Proxy:  Enabled
Guards:             Enabled
URL-filtering:      Enabled
Inside Hosts:       10
Throughput:         Limited
IKE peers:          5

The flash activation key is the SAME as the running key.
pixfirewall#
```

With this command, you can see which features are enabled on the PIX using this activation key, as well as the status of the key, which you can see at the bottom of the display. In this example, I've entered a new activation key and rebooted the PIX. This means the activation key in flash and what the PIX is using will be the same.

FURTHER STUDY

Web Sites

For information on upgrading your PIX firewall, visit www.cisco.com/warp/ public/ 110/upgrade.shtml and www.cisco.com/univercd/cc/td/doc/product/iaabu/pix/ pix_62/config/ upgrade.htm.

For information on installing PDM, visit www.cisco.com/univercd/cc/td/doc/ product/iaabu/pix/pix_62/pdm_ig/pdm_inst.htm.

For information on downgrading from FOS 6.1, visit www.cisco.com/univercd/ cc/td/doc/product/iaabu/pix/pix_61/relnotes/61dwngrd.htm.

For information on upgrading the hardware components in a 515 or 520, like the RAM, cards, or lithium battery, visit www.cisco.com/univercd/cc/td/doc/ product/ iaabu/pix/pix_60/install/openbox.htm.

For information on installing memory in a 515 or 520, visit www.cisco.com/ univercd/cc/td/doc/product/iaabu/pix/pix_v52/install/memory.htm.

CHAPTER 15

SOHO Environments: DHCP and PPPoE

In the last chapter I talked about upgrading the software on your PIX firewall. This chapter focuses on two of the features of the PIX firewall that are helpful in SOHO and branch office environments: The Dynamic Host Configuration Protocol (DHCP) and PPP over Ethernet (PPPoE). In many instances, you'll want to use DHCP in small offices to eliminate the manual assigning of IP addresses. On Microsoft Windows machines, DHCP is enabled by default when you enable TCP/IP—this simplifies the addition of new machines to an office. Likewise, many of your offices might be using cable modem or xDSL access, where your ISP might be using PPP to perform authentication and DHCP to assign your PIX a dynamic address. The rest of this chapter focuses on these topics.

DHCP

DHCP is used to dynamically assign addressing information to client devices. The PIX started supporting DHCP in version 5.2 of the FOS. The PIX supports both client and server DHCP functions. The PIX is not a full-functioning DHCP product, though. Typically, the PIX is used to provide these functions in a SOHO environment. Therefore, you might see a DHCP configuration on a PIX 501 or 506(E), but not typically on a higher-end PIX.

When a client is configured for DHCP, it generates a local broadcast (destination IP address of 255.255.255.255) requesting addressing information. This assumes that the DHCP client and server are on the same segment. If they are not on the same segment, some mechanism must be used to forward the client requests to the DHCP server. In a SOHO environment, you typically do not have this problem; however, in larger environments that use VLANs and routers, your routers will have to perform this function. On Cisco's IOS-based routers, you can use the ip helper-address command to do this. If your DHCP clients are on one interface of your PIX, and the DHCP server is on another interface, DHCP will fail because the PIX does not forward local broadcasts.

Assignable Attributes

The PIX can assign the following addressing information to DHCP clients: IP address, subnet mask, default gateway address, domain name, DNS server address, WINS server address, and the length of address lease. Two limitations of the PIX are that it does not support DHCP scopes or the BOOTP protocol.

Using the PIX as a DHCP Server

In SOHO environments, you can use your PIX firewall as a DHCP server, removing the need for a file server to perform this process. Imagine that you have a small office with only five users and no file server—this situation doesn't warrant placing a server in this office just to handle addressing functions. Instead, you can use your PIX firewall to solve this problem. The following shows the commands that you can use to set up your addressing information:

```
pixfirewall(config)#   dhcpd address IP_address_1[-IP_address_2]
                          [interface_name]
pixfirewall(config)#   dhcpd domain domain_name
pixfirewall(config)#   dhcpd dns 1st_DNS_Server [2nd_DNS_Server]
pixfirewall(config)#   dhcpd wins 1st_WINS_Server [2nd_WINS_Server]
pixfirewall(config)#   dhcpd lease length_in_seconds
pixfirewall(config)#   dhcpd option 66 ascii server_name
pixfirewall(config)#   dhcpd option 150 ip server_IP_1 [server_IP_2 ]
pixfirewall(config)#   dhcpd ping_timeout length_in_milliseconds
pixfirewall(config)#   dhcpd enable [interface_name]
pixfirewall(config)#   clear dhcpd
```

NOTE The PIX must have an IP address on an interface where the DHCP server will be serving addressing information.

DHCP Server Address Commands

To create your pool of IP addresses that your PIX will assign, use the dhcpd address command. For a range of addresses, specify the first and last address separated by a hyphen, such as 192.168.1.5-192.168.1.254. There is an option to specify a name of an interface. If you omit this, it defaults to *inside*. Note, however, that the current FOS versions only allow you to specify the *inside* interface. Cisco may allow you to specify other interfaces in future FOS releases. The PIX uses the subnet mask of its interface when sending addressing information to DHCP clients. Note that there are some addressing restrictions with Cisco's DHCP server, which are listed in Table 15-1.

DHCP Server Address Resolution Commands

There are three commands related to address resolution. The first command, dhcpd domain, assigns the domain name to the client, like me.com or OleDrews.com. The second command, dhcpd dns, assigns up to two DNS servers to a client. If you have two servers, specify them with a space separating the IP addresses of the DNS servers. The third command, dhcpd wins, is only used in Microsoft environments that have

FOS Version	PIX Model	Maximum Addresses
5.2	All models	10
5.3-6.0	506/506E	32
	All other models	256
6.1+	501 (10-user)	32
	501 (50-user)	128
	All other models	256

Table 15-1.   DHCP Server Addressing Restrictions

deployed WINS for address resolution. You can specify a maximum of two WINS server addresses.

DHCP Server and IP Phones

Starting in FOS 6.2, Cisco has added some extensions to the PIX's DHCP server function to allow it to deal with Cisco IP Phones that use CallManager. As I mentioned in Chapter 7, Cisco's IP Phones can dynamically acquire their IP addressing as well as download their configuration via a TFTP server.

When a Cisco IP Phone boots up and doesn't have an IP address, it uses DHCP to acquire its address as well as sending an option within DHCP. There are actually many supported (and non-supported) options, or extensions, to have a DHCP server assign other items to a client. DHCP option 66 is part of RFC 2132 and allows the assignment of a single TFTP server. DHCP option 150 (not part of the RFC) assigns a list of TFTP servers. Cisco IP Phones actually put both of these options in their DHCP request to the server. Cisco's DHCP server enhancements allow their IP Phones to perform these processes.

With the dhcpd option 66 ascii command, you specify the name of the TFTP server. With the dhcpd option 150 ip command, you specify either one or two TFTP server IP addresses.

DHCP Server Management Commands

When the PIX assigns an IP address to a client, the address is on loan. In other words, the client isn't necessarily given this address to use indefinitely. You can use the dhcpd lease command to specify the duration of the leased address. The default lease length of an assigned IP address is 3600 seconds (one hour). The minimum lease length is 300 seconds (five minutes) and the maximum is 2,147,483,647 seconds (which is a *very* long time … over 68 years!).

Of course, before the PIX assigns a particular IP address to a client, the PIX must first verify that the address is not currently being used by another device on the segment. The PIX performs a ping test to verify this. By default, the PIX waits 750 milliseconds for an echo reply. If it doesn't see an echo reply, the PIX will assume that the address is not being used and will go ahead and assign this address to the client. You can change this ping waiting period with the dhcpd ping_timeout command, which was introduced in FOS 5.3. The minimum wait period that you can specify is 100 milliseconds, and the maximum is 10,000.

DHCP Server Activation, Verification, and Removal

Even though you have configured the previous DHCP server commands, the PIX will not serve out addressing information until you enable the server with the dhcpd enable command. There is an optional parameter with this command that allows you to specify the interface where the DHCP server will be active, which defaults to *inside*. Note, however, that only the *inside* interface can have a DHCP server running on it in current FOS versions; but Cisco might enable this ability for other interfaces in future FOS releases.

To view your DHCP server configuration, use the show dhcpd command. This command only displays the command configuration for the DHCP server on your PIX:

```
pixfirewall#  show dhcpd
dhcpd address 192.168.2.10-192.168.2.126 inside
dhcpd lease 3600
dhcpd ping_timeout 750
dhcpd dns 192.168.2.2
dhcpd wins 192.168.2.3
dhcpd enable inside
```

There are two optional parameters to the show dhcpd command: binding and statistics. If you execute the show dhcpd binding command, all leasing information is displayed. The show dhcpd statistics command shows all DHCP statistics with the exception of the lease lengths. Here is an example of the show dhcpd binding command:

```
pixfirewall#  show dhcpd binding
IP Address      Hardware Address      Lease Expiration  Type
192.168.2.10   0100.a0c2.a3e2.2a81 3549 seconds       automatic
```

In this example, there is one assigned IP address, and it expires in 3549 seconds. To see the actual DHCP server statistics, use the show dhcpd statistics command, shown here:

```
pixfirewall#  show dhcpd statistics
Address Pools 1
Automatic Bindings 1
Expired Bindings 1
Malformed messages 0

Message Received
BOOTREQUEST 0
DHCPDISCOVER 1
DHCPREQUEST 1
DHCPDECLINE 0
DHCPRELEASE 0
DHCPINFORM 0
 <--output omitted-->
```

As you can see from this output, the show dhcpd statistics command displays the DHCP packets that the PIX, as a DHCP server, has seen and responded to.

If you are having problems with the DHCP server functions, like clients not getting addressing information, you can troubleshoot this problem with the debug dhcpd event and debug dhcpd packet commands. The first command shows DHCP server events as they are happening on the PIX, and the second command displays part of the packet information for DHCP server requests and responses.

If you make a mistake and want to remove a single DHCP server command, precede it with the no parameter. To remove your DHCP server configuration completely, use the clear dhcpd command. There are two optional parameters to the clear dhcpd command: `bindings` and `statistics`. If you execute the `clear dhcpd bindings` command, all leasing information is immediately expired. The `clear dhcpd statistics` command resets all DHCP statistics with the exception of the lease lengths.

DHCP Server Example Configuration

To better help you understand the configuration of your PIX as a DHCP server, let's look at an example. I'll use the network shown in Figure 15-1 as an illustration. In this example, the PIX is a DHCP server for the clients off of the *inside* interface. The domain name is dealgroup.com, and there is a DNS and a WINS server. The addresses assigned to the clients by the PIX range from 192.168.2.10 to 192.168.2.126. The lease period is expanded to two hours. In this example, I'll only focus on the commands related to the DHCP server configuration.

The following shows the sample configuration for this network:

```
pixfirewall(config)#  ip address inside 192.168.2.1 255.255.255.0
pixfirewall(config)#  dhcpd address 192.168.2.10-192.168.2.126
pixfirewall(config)#  dhcpd dns 192.168.2.2
pixfirewall(config)#  dhcpd wins 192.168.2.3
pixfirewall(config)#  dhcpd lease 7200
pixfirewall(config)#  dhcpd domain dealgroup.com
pixfirewall(config)#  dhcpd enable inside
```

As you can see, the DHCP server configuration is straightforward.

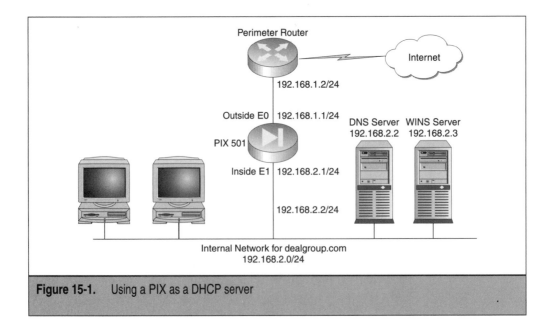

Figure 15-1.   Using a PIX as a DHCP server

Using the PIX as a DHCP Client

Cisco's PIX firewalls can also become DHCP clients, dynamically acquiring their addressing information when you connect them to an xDSL or cable modem. This modem, in turn, is directly connected to your ISP, and your ISP uses DHCP to assign your PIX an IP address.

NOTE   One limitation of using the DHCP client feature is that when it is enabled, you cannot use the failover feature on your PIX.

Configuring Your PIX DHCP Client

To configure the PIX to become a DHCP client, use `ip address` command:

```
pixfirewall(config)#   ip address interface_name dhcp [setroute]
                             [retry count]
```

I discussed the use of the `ip address` command in Chapter 3. You'll notice that the syntax of this command is different than what I covered in Chapter 3. The first parameter that you need to specify is the name of the logical interface that will be acquiring its addressing information. Currently, Cisco only supports the DHCP client feature for the *outside* interface. As I mentioned in Chapter 4, you can still use PAT in this scenario—you can configure your PIX to use the IP address that is either statically or dynamically assigned to an interface by using the `interface` parameter in the `global` command.

The second parameter that you must specify is `dhcp`. The last two parameters are optional. The `setroute` command causes the PIX to use the default gateway address returned by your ISP—in most instances you will want to enable this command. When you use this command, do not also configure a static default route. The `retry` parameter specifies the maximum number of times that the PIX will query the ISP for its addressing information. This parameter defaults to 4, but you can change it to any value from 4 to 16.

Renewing, Verifying, and Troubleshooting Your PIX DHCP Client

If you want your PIX to release its current IP address on its interface and get a new one (or renew its lease), enter the `ip address` command. If you use the `clear ip address` command, your PIX will also acquire a new address; however, this will also clear the IP addressing on all the other PIX interfaces.

To verify your addressing information, use the `show ip address dhcp` command:

```
pixfirewall#   show ip address outside dhcp
Temp IP Addr:200.200.200.2 for peer on interface:outside
Temp sub net mask:255.255.255.0
DHCP Lease server:200.200.199.2, state:3 Bound
DHCP Transaction id:0x4123
```

```
Lease:7200 secs, Renewal:1505 secs, Rebind:7000 secs
Temp default-gateway addr:200.200.200.1
Next timer fires after:6809 secs
Retry count:0, Client-ID:cisco-0000.0000.0000-outside
```

Cisco also supports `debug` commands for troubleshooting the DHCP client on the PIX. Here are the debug commands that you can use:

- `debug dhcpc packet`   Displays the partial contents of DHCP client packets.
- `debug dhcpc error`   Displays DHCP client error information.
- `debug dhcpc detail`   Displays all information related to DHCP client packets.

DHCP Autoconfiguration

Cisco supports an enhanced feature for its DHCP client and server functions called *DHCP Autoconfiguration*. With DHCP Autoconfiguration, the PIX uses the DHCP client to acquire its IP address and subnet mask for the *outside* interface, and the DHCP server to assign addressing information to devices on the *inside* interface. One major difference between DHCP Autoconfiguration and manually configuring DHCP server and client is that DHCP Autoconfiguration takes the other DHCP parameters that your ISP passes to your *outside* interface and has the DHCP server on the *inside* interface use this information, like the DNS server and domain name, if you so choose.

Command Syntax

To use DHCP Autoconfiguration, use the `dhcpd` command:

```
pixfirewall(config)#  dhcpd auto_config [client_interface_name]
```

Even though there is an option to specify which interface the PIX is using the DHCP client feature, currently Cisco only supports the *outside* interface. Remember that you must still create a DHCP address pool for your inside interface as well as any other DHCP information that you want to manually configure—information that you do not configure will be passed from the ISP to your internal clients. One item that the PIX does not pass to the internal clients is the IP address and subnet mask that the ISP assigns to the PIX itself on the *outside* interface.

Autoconfiguration Example

To help illustrate the configuration of DHCP Autoconfiguration, I'll use the network shown in Figure 15-2. The following is an example configuration for this network:

```
pixfirewall(config)#  ip address inside 192.168.1.1 255.255.255.0
pixfirewall(config)#  ip address outside dhcp setroute
pixfirewall(config)#  dhcpd address 192.168.1.10-192.168.1.126
pixfirewall(config)#  dhcpd lease 3600
pixfirewall(config)#  dhcpd domain dealgroup.com
pixfirewall(config)#  dhcpd enable inside
pixfirewall(config)#  dhcpd auto_config inside
pixfirewall(config)#  global (outside) 1 interface
pixfirewall(config)#  nat (inside) 1  0.0.0.0  0.0.0.0
```

In this example, the PIX is both a DHCP client and server. The second `ip address` command allows the PIX to use DHCP to acquire its IP address, subnet mask, and default gateway address from the ISP. The `dhcpd address` command specifies the addresses to assign to the internal clients. The lease length is one hour, and the domain name is dealgroup.com. Remember that you must enable the DHCP server with the `dhcpd enable inside` command. The last `dhcpd` command enables Autoconfiguration for the *inside* interface.

I've added two commands at the bottom of the example to show you how to set up PAT using the dynamically acquired interface on the PIX. The `global` command specifies to use the IP address assigned (manual or dynamic) on the *outside* interface. The `nat` command specifies that all internal addresses will have PAT performed on them as their traffic leaves the network.

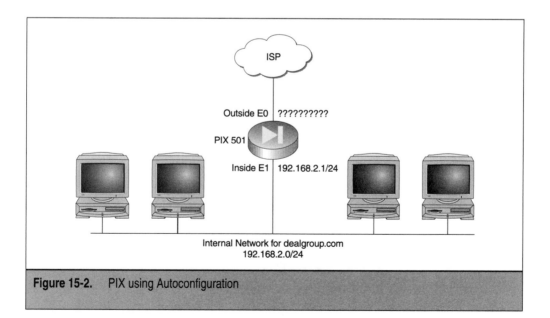

Figure 15-2. PIX using Autoconfiguration

PPPoE

Because this chapter focuses on SOHO environments, I thought it prudent to discuss PPPoE, because it is becoming more popular in small- to medium-sized offices. Most people think that PPP is a WAN protocol; however, in the last few years, there have been many extensions to PPP, including its use over a LAN medium. PPP over Ethernet allows devices to authenticate and connect to each other across a bridged access device to a remote Access Concentrator. With the widespread use of xDSL and cable modems, the media connectivity used is Ethernet. Some ISPs are even setting up direct Ethernet connections to their customers. One problem with Ethernet is that there is no authentication or billing mechanism built into the protocol. Therefore, PPP was enhanced to incorporate other media besides serial or ISDN.

Overview of PPPoE

PPPoE goes through two separate stages when it builds a connection: Discovery and Session. In the Discovery stage, a client that wishes to initiate a PPPoE session must first discover the Ethernet MAC address of the remote peer. Typically this process is initiated by the company device (like the PIX) wishing to connect to the ISP (Access Concentrator). Even though PPP was developed as a point-to-point protocol, in Ethernet, there could be more than one device (more than one Access Concentrator) that the client is connected to. During the Discovery stage, the client discovers all of the Access Concentrators and then uses one of these to establish the PPP connection. One of the things assigned to this connection is a Session ID, which uniquely identifies the PPPoE client to the Access Concentrator.

Once the discovery stage has completed, the Session stage starts. This stage involves the mechanics of PPP using LCP and NCP. Parameters like authentication are negotiated and validated. Upon completion of the Session stage, the two devices can start sending Ethernet frames containing data back and forth.

PPPoE on the PIX

PPPoE client support is new in FOS 6.2. Before this feature, it was sometimes impossible to directly connect your PIX to your ISP if you had a xDSL or cable modem—you had to use a PPPoE-aware router instead, which increases the price of the connectivity solution. However, starting with FOS 6.2, you can now enable PPPoE client functionality on the *outside* interface of your PIX firewall. The following sections discus the configuration and verification of PPPoE on your PIX firewall.

NOTE When using PPPoE, the MTU for the interface is automatically adjusted to 1,492 bytes, which allows PPP information to be encapsulated in an Ethernet frame. With some ISPs, you might have to set this to a smaller value (using the `mtu` command). You will also want to change the MTU setting on your internal desktops to prevent fragmentation.

Setting Up the PPPoE Session Parameters

The first thing you must specify is a group name that you will use to bind together your PPPoE configuration information. This name is similar to the function of an ACL name with the PIX `access-list` command. The syntax of this command is:

```
pixfirewall(config)# vpdn group group_name request dialout pppoe
```

The name of the group needs to be unique among all PPPoE groups on your PIX. Of course, the PIX only supports one interface (*outside*) and thus you only need one group for PPPoE. However, this command is also used for L2TP and PPTP for VPN connections, which I discuss in Chapters 16 and 17.

The second thing that you need to do is configure the type of PPP authentication:

```
pixfirewall(config)# vpdn group group_name
                          ppp authentication pap|chap|mschap
```

Remember to use the same group name to group your PPPoE information together. You have three choices for authentication: PAP, CHAP, or MSCHAP—ask your ISP which authentication method you should configure.

The third step is to configure the usernames and password to use during the authentication phase. The ISP will assign your PIX a personal username and will tell you the remote username and password to use:

```
pixfirewall(config)# vpdn group group_name localname PIX_username
```

To configure the ISP's username and password, use this command:

```
pixfirewall(config)# vpdn username ISP_username password ISP_password
```

If you specify CHAP or MSCHAP for authentication, the username that you specify in the `username` parameter is typically the device name of the ISP's Access Concentrator.

Enabling PPPoE on the Outside Interface

Now that you have performed the initial PPPoE configuration, you need to tell your PIX that it will use PPPoE on the *outside* interface. There are two methods of enabling PPPoE depending on whether you have manually assigned an IP address to the outside interface or you are using PPP to acquire an address from the ISP.

NOTE   You must first create your PPPoE group configurations before enabling PPPoE on the PIX's *outside* interface.

Configuring an IP Address Manually   If your ISP has manually assigned you an IP address and subnet mask, but you still need to configure PPPoE, use the `ip address` command shown here to set up your access:

```
pixfirewall(config)# ip address interface_name IP_address
                     subnet_mask pppoe [setroute]
```

Currently, you can only specify *outside* for the logical name of the interface. Next, specify the IP address and subnet mask assigned by your ISP, and then the pppoe parameter. As you can see, this command is very similar to the one discussed in Chapter 3. Like the DHCP client configuration, you can also use the default route assigned by the ISP by specifying the setroute parameter.

Acquiring an IP Address Dynamically   In most cases your ISP will dynamically assign you an IP address using PPP—notice that I did not say DHCP. Actually the two methods are not compatible. You must use one or the other. As in the previous section, you use the ip address command to enable PPPoE:

```
pixfirewall(config)#  ip address interface_name pppoe [setroute]
```

Use the ip address command shown here to enable PPPoE, and to dynamically acquire an address. You can also reenter this command to clear and restart a PPPoE session to the ISP's Access Concentrator. The setroute parameter creates a default route. You should either use this method or manually create a static default route with the route command, but not both.

By default, the PIX does not pass any other PPP configuration information to inside clients, like the IP address of a DNS or WINS server. You can have these parameters passed to internal clients by using the dhcpd auto_config command discussed earlier in this chapter.

Verifying and Troubleshooting PPPoE

Once you have configured PPPoE, use these show commands for verification:

- show ip address outside pppoe—displays the IP addressing for the outside interface.
- show vpdn [session pppoe]—displays the PPPoE session information.

The first show command displays the PIX's PPPoE client configuration information. Its output is similar to the show ip address outside dhcp command. The show vpdn command shows a brief overview of the PPPoE sessions:

```
pixfirewall#  show vpdn
Tunnel id 0, 1 active sessions
    time since change 1209 secs
   Remote Internet Address 192.168.1.1
   Local Internet Address 200.200.200.1
    12 packets sent, 12 received, 168 bytes sent, 0 received
Remote Internet Address is 192.168.1.1
    Session state is SESSION_UP
<--output omitted-->
```

In this example, there is one active PPPoE session. You can restrict the output of this command by adding the `session pppoe` command—this will only display PPPoE information, and not any VPN information.

For detailed troubleshooting of PPPoE, use the `debug` command:

```
pixfirewall(config)#  debug pppoe event|error|packet
```

The `event` parameter displays protocol event information concerning PPPoE. The `error` parameter displays any PPPoE error messages. The `packet` parameter displays the partial contents of PPPoE packets. To disable the `debug` command, precede it with the `no` parameter.

FURTHER STUDY

Web Sites

For information on DHCP, examine RFC 2131 and 2132 at www.ietf.org/rfc/rfc2131.txt and www.ietf.org/rfc/rfc2132.txt.

For information on PPPoE, examine RFC 2516 at ftp://ftp.isi.edu/in-notes/rfc2516.txt.

For more information about configuring your PIX, visit www.cisco.com/univercd/cc/td/doc/product/iaabu/pix/pix_62/config/index.htm.

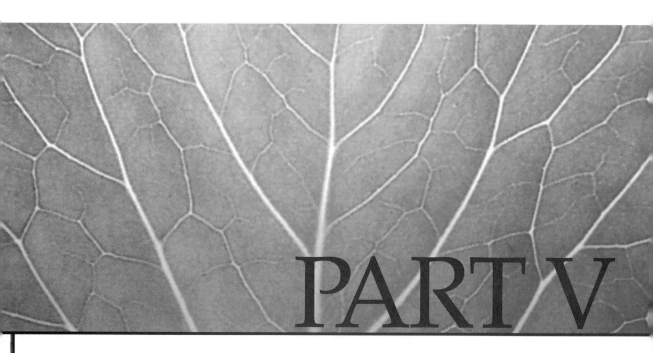

PART V

VPNs and the PIX Firewall

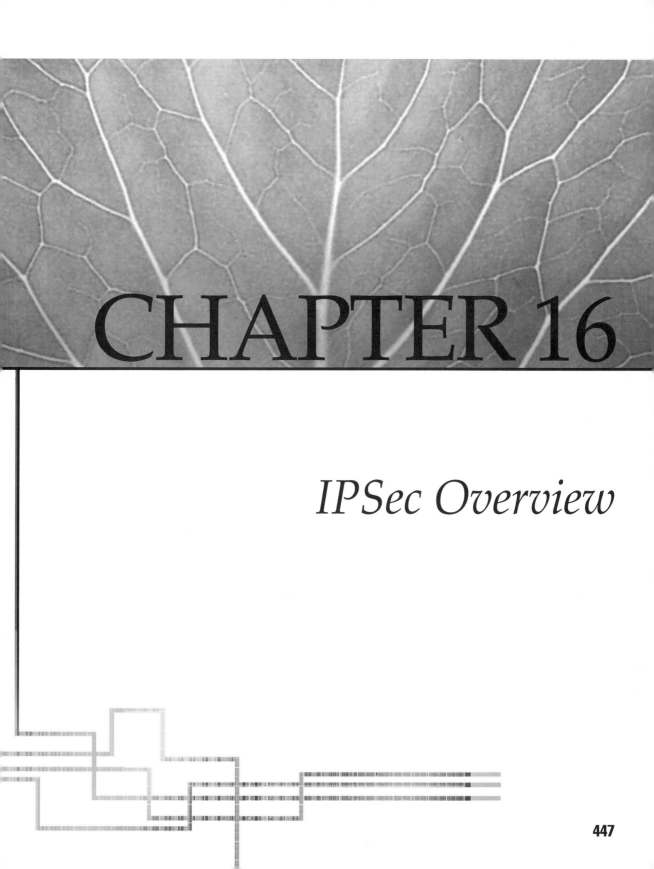

CHAPTER 16

IPSec Overview

The last few chapters of this book focused on management functions and advanced features of the PIX firewall. The last two chapters of this book focus on the PIX firewall's Virtual Private Network (VPN) features. This chapter provides an overview of VPNs and the IPSec standard, and the next chapter discusses how to terminate VPNs on your PIX firewall.

VPN OVERVIEW

A VPN is basically a protected connection between two devices, two networks, or a device and a network. This connection is typically not a direct connection, but a virtual connection. In other words, there are usually many networking devices between the two devices that are terminating the endpoints of the VPN connection. VPNs are very popular when you need to protect information as it is being sent across a public network, like the Internet. Many people often think that when the word *protected* is used to describe the function of a VPN, the traffic is being encrypted. As you will see later on in this chapter, however, VPNs can provide other types of protection, including identity verification and packet validation.

Devices that support VPNs come in many flavors, including routers, firewalls, VPN gateways, servers, and even PCs. Generally, though, VPNs come in two varieties: *site-to-site* and *remote access*. These two types of connections are shown in Figure 16-1.

In a site-to-site connection, two devices provide a VPN connection between two networks. An example of a site-to-site VPN is shown in the top part of Figure 16-1, where the VPN connection is between the router at the corporate site and the router at the branch office. These two routers are responsible for protecting the traffic between these two networks. What is interesting about the site-to-site connection is that the users sitting behind the routers are unaware that their traffic is being protected—the VPN is transparent to them.

A remote access connection involves a single end-user device and some type of VPN gateway, as shown in the bottom part of Figure 16-1. In this example, a DSL user has a VPN connection to the router, where the traffic between this user and the router is protected. An interesting point to make about this type of connection is that the user can still use this VPN to send information to devices behind the router, and this information will still be protected, while traffic to other sites can be sent unprotected. This process is referred to as *split tunneling*.

Functions of a VPN

VPNs provide a variety of protection services to you and your networking devices. To provide these services, there are three key functions built into any VPN: confidentiality method, encapsulation method, and defining the traffic that should be protected.

The first, and most important, function of a VPN is to provide confidentiality—to protect the information that is transmitted between two devices. There are different methods available in the market place to accomplish this. However, one of the most common standards used by companies is IPSec, short for IP Security. IPSec's biggest

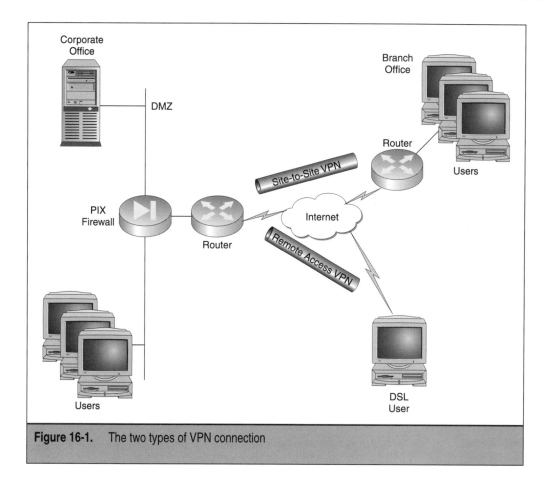

Figure 16-1. The two types of VPN connection

shortcoming is that it was developed to protect only IP traffic, but because most networks are IP-based, this is usually not a problem. There are other methods, though, that support other protocols like IPX and AppleTalk. The focus of this chapter and the next, though, will be on IPSec itself. As you will see in later sections, IPSec is actually a group of interoperable standards that provide confidentiality.

The second function of a VPN is to use an encapsulation method to package information that is to be protected into a packet format that can be forwarded to the VPN endpoint. This process includes not only how information is encapsulated (like what the headers should look like, and the protocol numbers assigned to the encapsulation methods), but also how to tell the remote VPN peer the method of protection, like the encryption algorithm, so the remote peer can verify and validate the encapsulated information.

The third function of a VPN is to define which traffic should be protected between two devices. One problem with using encryption to provide confidentiality is that it is very resource-intensive. For devices built for this function, like Cisco's 3000 series VPN appliances, or Cisco PIX firewalls with a VPN accelerator card, handling the encryption is not an issue. However, for devices that use software to provide encryption, like your PC, encryption can cause a noticeable delay in the transmission of information. Therefore, you will need to determine what traffic needs to be protected and configure this on your VPN device. For example, if you have a SOHO user with an Internet connection, you probably do not want to protect all of their traffic. Of course, any traffic between the user and the corporate office should be protected, but traffic from the user to other Internet destinations shouldn't be protected.

Encapsulation Methods

As I mentioned in the last section, one of the functions of a VPN is to specify an encapsulation method that will be used to encapsulate protected traffic. There are actually quite a few encapsulation methods available, including the following:

- Generic Route Encapsulation (GRE)
- Layer 2 Forwarding (L2F)
- Point-to-Point Tunnel Protocol (PPTP)
- Layer 2 Tunneling Protocol (L2TP)
- Authentication Header (AH) and Encapsulation Security Payload (ESP)

Each of these methods has advantages and disadvantages.

GRE is a Cisco proprietary protocol. It defines an encapsulation method of placing other types of information into an IP packet and using IP to transport this information to a destination. The protocols that can be encapsulated in GRE IP packets include AppleTalk, Apollo, CLNP, DECnet, IP (yes, IP encapsulated in IP), IPX, SDLC, Vines, and XNS. Many companies use GRE to connect noncontiguous networks together, like the one shown in Figure 16-2. In this example, two noncontiguous IPX networks are connected together. The tunnel itself appears as a logical IPX network and can be used to carry IPX packets between the two noncontiguous networks. Actually, the GRE tunnel is transparent to the users in the IPX network. From their perspective, this is an IPX segment that is used to transport IPX packets. In actuality, however, the IPX packets between the two routers are encapsulated in an IP packet and IP is used to transport the encapsulated information back and forth.

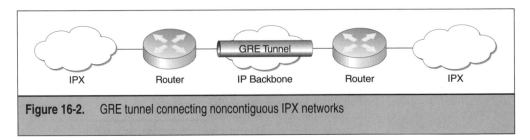

Figure 16-2. GRE tunnel connecting noncontiguous IPX networks

The biggest drawback with GRE is that it lacks confidentiality—there is no inherent method within the GRE protocol to protect your packets. Another limitation of GRE is that it lacks any scalability—it can only be used between Cisco routers and not other devices. Because of these limitations, Cisco developed the L2F encapsulation method, which is a prestandard of IPSec. L2F provides confidentiality, but is, for the most part, still restricted to being used by networks that have Cisco devices.

Microsoft also has their own proprietary solution, called PPTP, to provide VPN functions. This solution is used to protect information between Windows clients, like a PC running Windows 95 or 98 to a Remote Access Server (RAS) running Windows NT. However, just like Cisco's two initiatives, Microsoft's solution is not an open standard, and thus causes issues when integrating it with non-Microsoft devices. I discuss PPTP and its configuration in more depth on my web site (http://home.cfl.rr.com/dealgroup/).

To provide an open, integrated solution, Cisco, Microsoft, Ascent, and 3Com developed the L2TP standard, defined in RFC 2661. L2TP is basically a combination of Cisco's L2F and Microsoft's PPTP. It supports the encapsulation of three protocols: IP, IPX, and AppleTalk. IP is used as the transport protocol to move the encapsulated information between two networks. L2TP supports multiple tunnels to the same destination, which can be used for load balancing and also support per-user authentication. One of the initial limitations of IPSec using AH and ESP was that only the device, and not the user using the device, could be authenticated. I discuss L2TP and user authentication in more depth on my web site (http://pages.prodigy.net/richard.deal).

The last two encapsulation methods mentioned in the list at the beginning of this section are AH and ESP. IPSec uses these two protocols to prevent packet tampering and eavesdropping. These two protocols define how information that is to be protected are encapsulated in either an IP packet (AH) or a segment (ESP).

Interestingly enough, Cisco actually supports all of these tunneling protocols, but not necessarily on every Cisco VPN-capable device. Typically, when you have an IP-only network, you will use IPSec for your VPN solution. If you have non-IP protocols, like IPX, you'll typically use L2TP. This chapter will focus strictly on IPSec, because IPSec is what most companies use when building VPNs; however, on my web site (http://home.cfl.rr.com/dealgroup/), I discuss how to configure PPTP and L2TP VPNs on your PIX firewall.

IPSEC OVERVIEW

There are other methods available to protect traffic besides IPSec. One example is Secure Shell (SSH) for console connections and Secure Sockets Layer (SSL) for Web connections. The problem with these two solutions is that they solve a security issue with a specific application—they don't solve security issues with other applications. IPSec, on the other hand, works at the network layer. Therefore, any information at the network layer and higher is protected. Also, because IPSec functions at the network layer, no modifications are required to any of your IP applications, making it non-intrusive. IPSec is defined in RFC 2401, and is compatible with both IPv4 and IPv6.

Functions of IPSec

There are many kinds of network attacks, including eavesdropping, spoofing, session hijacking, and man-in-the-middle attacks. To prevent man-in-the-middle attacks, you can use certificate authorities to validate a peer's identity. To prevent eavesdropping attacks, you can use encryption to protect your data. To prevent spoofing and session hijacking attacks, you can use hashing functions to provide packet integrity.

To help deal with these kinds of network threats, IPSec provides three critical functions: authentication, confidentiality, and integrity. The authentication function is responsible for validating the identity of the remote IPSec peer. Either digital signatures with certificates or pre-shared keys are used to perform the authentication function. Or authentication function is the responsibility of the Internet Key Exchange protocol (IKE), which I'll discuss later in this chapter.

The confidentiality function is responsible for guaranteeing that any intermediate devices between the two IPSec peers cannot decipher the contents of the protected packet stream. Encryption is used to implement the protection. DES and 3DES are the encryption algorithms that Cisco currently supports. ESP is responsible for the encryption function. I will discuss encryption algorithms later in this chapter.

The integrity function is responsible for verifying that the protected packets have not been tampered with by an intermediate device. Hashing functions are used to verify that the originator of the packet was the remote VPN peer as well as whether or not the packet contents have been changed by an intermediate device. AH and, possibly, ESP are responsible for the integrity function. Cisco supports MD5 and SHA hashing functions. I'll discuss hashing functions later in this chapter.

Main Components of IPSec

To actually perform the three functions I mentioned in the previous section, IPSec uses three standards: IKE, ESP, and AH. IKE's main function is to set up a secure connection between two IPSec peers and come up with keying information that will be used to encrypt the packets as well as digital signatures to provide for integrity and authentication. ESP is responsible for encrypting packets, and AH is responsible for verifying that the packet contents have not been tampered with. The following sections will cover the actual items needed in order to provide authentication, confidentiality, and integrity.

Keys

A key is similar to a password or PIN number that you use at an ATM machine to withdrawal money. In security, keys are used to encrypt or protect information to provide confidentiality, authentication, and integrity. Typically, the longer the length of the key, the more secure your information is. This makes it more difficult for a hacker to implement man-in-the-middle attacks, like eavesdropping, session hijacking, and masquerading. There are two basic types of keys:

- Symmetric—a single key is used for encryption and decryption
- Asymmetric—one key is used for encryption and the other used for decryption

Symmetric Keys

With symmetric keys, a single key is used to encrypt and decrypt the information. Because a single key is used for both processes, the algorithm used for the encryption and decryption process is simpler than an algorithm that uses separate keys for each process. Therefore, performing encryption and decryption is very fast. Because of this speed advantage, symmetric keys are used to solve confidentiality problems—encrypting data between two peers.

One issue with symmetric keys is that because both the source and destination use the same key, sharing the key securely becomes an issue. You have two options—if you are using pre-shared keys, you could share the key out-of-band, perhaps through a telephone conversation with the administrator of the remote VPN device. The problem with this solution, though, is that it doesn't scale very well—every time you need to change the key (to ensure the security of your connection), you would have to call the remote administrator to make the change. Multiply this by 100 VPN devices, and this becomes a management nightmare. Your other solution would be to use an already created encrypted connection to share the key across. This is somewhat of a catch-22 situation—how do you create a secure connection *and* securely share the keying information? I'll discuss this later when I talk about IKE and Diffie-Hellman.

There are many different types of algorithms, many of which are standards, that use symmetric keys, including the ones listed in Table 16-1.

Table 16-1 is by no means all-inclusive, but gives you an idea as to some of the more popular symmetric key algorithms. The IPSec standard has adopted the DES and 3DES algorithms for ESP to provide confidentiality services (encryption of data). Cisco now includes a free DES license for every PIX sold—if you have an older PIX without a DES license, you can obtain one free from Cisco if you are currently under warranty or have an up-to-date maintenance contract with Cisco. Cisco's 3DES license, however, is a purchasable option.

Algorithm	Key Length in Bits	Description
DES	40, 56	Developed by the National Institute of Standards and Technology (NIST). The 56-bit key is the most commonly used key length, but is weak by most of today's standards. DES is the fasted encryption algorithm.
3DES	168	This is the slowest encryption algorithm, but is one of the most secure: it's much more secure than DES.
CAST	128, 256	Similar to DES, less secure than 3DES, but faster.
IDEA	128	Developed by the Swiss Institute of Technology—second most secure encryption algorithm, but also the second slowest.
RC6	<= 2,048	Developed by the RSA (named after its founders, Ronald Rivest, Adi Shamir, and Leonard Adleman).
Skipjack	80	Developed by the National Security Agency (NSA) and, until recently, classified as secret by the U.S. government.

Table 16-1.   Symmetric Key Algorithms

Asymmetric Keys

Asymmetric key algorithms use two keys for encryption and decryption: a public key and a private key. Each of these keys is different from the other. One key is used for encryption and the other for decryption. Typically, the public key is used for encryption and the private key is used for decryption. One advantage that asymmetric keys have over symmetric keys is the sharing of the keys. You can freely share the public key with other peers and hold the private key to yourself—the advantage of this is that only the private key can decrypt the information, so it's not too much of a concern that a man-in-the-middle sees the public key as it is being shared with other remote VPN peers. Of course, you should always be security conscious—I'll discuss a way to enhance your security later on in this chapter where you can hide the sharing of the public key from prying eyes as it is sent across a public network to a remote peer or peers.

Asymmetric keys are typically used for authentication with digital signatures and setting up an initial, secure connection to share symmetric and asymmetric keys across it. Because only one key encrypts and one key decrypts, the encryption algorithm used to encrypt and decrypt the information is much slower—about 1,500 times slower than symmetric keys. Therefore, asymmetric keys are typically not used to protect data (confidentiality), but instead to provide authentication functions, like digital signatures. Authentication happens at the beginning of the setting up of a VPN connection and is only performed once, or periodically if you want to regenerate keys to ensure the security of the connection. Because authentication is not performed very often, it is not a big issue that its process is slower. However, protection of data, which could include millions of packets in a data transfer, would greatly suffer in performance if an asymmetric key algorithm was used to provide encryption.

There is one exception to this. In many instances, a temporary connection is built with encryption using asymmetric keys. This connection is used to transfer symmetric keys securely. Once the symmetric keys are shared across the secured connection, the symmetric keys are used to securely share data because their encryption algorithm is much faster.

Table 16-2 shows the more common asymmetric key algorithms—there are many more asymmetric key algorithms than the ones I listed.

Algorithm	Key Length in Bits	Description
RSA public key	512, 768, 1,024	Used by both digital signatures and encryption purposes; 100 times slower than DES
Diffie-Hellman (DH)	768, 1,024	Used by IKE to securely exchange keys—cannot be used for encryption purposes, only key exchange
KEA	160	Advanced version of Diffie-Hellman
Digital Signature Standard (DSS)	1,024	Used to create digital signatures (typically by certificate authorities)

Table 16-2. Asymmetric Key Algorithms

Integrity with Hashing Functions

Hashing functions are typically used to verify the integrity of information received—in other words, that the information wasn't tampered with while in transit. A hashing function takes variable-length input, which includes user data and a key value, and creates a fixed-length output, sometimes referred to as a *checksum*. Hashing Message Authentication Code (HMAC) functions are a subset of hashing functions. HMACs were specifically designed to deal with authentication and integrity validation. The fixed-length output that an HMAC function produces is commonly called an *Integrity Check Value* (ICV), or a digital signature.

Both AH and ESP, discussed later in this chapter, can use HMAC functions to ensure that the packet contents were not tampered with. When HMAC is used with either of these protocols, a random key needs to be generated and securely shared with each side. Before the source device sends information to a destination, it takes the data, along with the shared secret key, and processes it through the HMAC function, producing the ICV output. This ICV output is then included with the user data. When the destination receives the data, it takes the data, along with the same shared secret key, and repeats the HMAC process, creating an ICV. The destination then compares its own ICV with the one the source put in the packet—if the two values match, the destination can be assured that no one changed the contents of the packet. If a man-in-the-middle wanted to change the packet contents, he would need to know the secret key in order to correctly compute a new ICV.

The main problem with hashing functions is the key—somehow it must be securely shared between the source and the destination. You have two basic choices. First, you can share the key out-of-band, which is not very manageable. Second, you can create a secure (encrypted) connection first and share the key across the secure connection—I'll discuss how this is done later using Diffie-Hellman.

The main advantage of HMAC functions is that they use a one-way process. Both the source and destination use the same information to compute the ICV—this is different from encryption algorithms that must work their way backwards when decrypting the information. Therefore, HMAC functions are very fast and add little overhead when computing a value for each packet that you send to a remote peer. Also, unless you know the secret key, it is practically impossible to work your way backwards from the ICV value to come up with the original data.

There are two hashing functions that IPSec uses to provide for integrity validation: Message Digest 5 (MD5) and Secure Hashing Algorithm (SHA), shown in Table 16-3.

Authentication with Digital Signatures

Authentication is provided by the use of digital signatures. A digital signature is similar to a hand-written signature, a finger print, or a retinal scan—it's a unique item used to authenticate the destination device. Hashing functions are used to create digital signatures. Text or graphical information is taken, along with a private key, and fed through the hash function, producing a fixed-length digital signature. The signature is

Algorithm Name	RFC	ICV length	Comparison	Used By
MD5	1321	128-bit	Fast, but less secure	PPP's CHAP, IPSec's AH and ESP, OSPF, EIGRP, BGP, RIPv2
SHA	2404	160-bit	Slow, but more secure	IPSec's AH and ESP

Table 16-3.   Comparison of MD5 and SHA

then attached to information sent to a peer, who can use this information to validate the source's identity. Digital signatures use two keys to create the signature: a public and private key. The private key is used by the source to create the signature, and the public key is used by the destination to validate the signature. The main difference between a digital signature and an ICV is that a digital signature uses two keys, but an ICV uses one key.

One problem with authentication and digital signatures is the sharing of the public key with other peers. If a man-in-the-middle attack occurs, the hacker (in the middle) could create their own public and private key combination, and share his public key with the remote peers and have the remote peers set up connections to him instead of the real source. Because of this problem, the public key is either sent to the remote peers out-of-band, or a trusted third party is used to hold the keys, called a Certificate Authority (CA). When peers use a CA, they contact the CA to verify the validity of a peer's signature. I'll discuss CAs later in this chapter.

Types of Digital Signatures

You have a choice of three types of digital signatures to provide authentication: pre-shared keys, RSA encrypted nonces (a nonce is a time-variant parameter, like a time stamp or counter, that is used in security protocols to protect you against message replay and other types of attacks), and RSA signatures. Pre-shared keys use symmetric keys that are shared out-of-band in order to perform authentication. When peers need to authenticate each other, they do it directly with the pre-shared keys. Out of the three types of digital signatures, pre-shared keys are the easiest to configure, as you will see in Chapter 17; however, their two main drawbacks are the secure sharing of the key and the management of the key on an ongoing basis. Because you manually have to enter this key on both IPSec peers, every time you change the key, you have to change it on all peers that use the same key. Of course, you could simplify this process by using the same key on every peer, but this is not a very secure approach to authentication, especially if one of the peers becomes compromised—then every IPSec peer is compromised. Therefore, pre-shared keys are typically used when you have a small number of site-to-site connections, where you are responsible for managing all of the sites.

RSA encrypted nonces use asymmetric keys to create a digital signature. You must manually create a public and private key on each peer, and then share the public keys with all of the other peers. When peers need to authenticate each other, they do it with the private and public keys—the source uses the private key to create a signature and the destination uses the public key to verify the signature. Again, like pre-shared keys, this sharing process requires manual configuration by you. Because you are using two keys, however, this is a more secure authentication method than pre-shared keys, but does require more configuration on your part. Again, because of the amount of manual configuration, this method scales even less well than pre-shared keys, and is only used for site-to-site connections.

RSA signatures, like RSA encrypted nonces, use asymmetric keys. The major difference between these two methods is that the IPSec device uses the private key to create a digital signature, which, in turn, is placed on a certificate held by a Certificate Authority (CA). When authenticating a remote peer, your IPSec device will acquire its peer's certificate from the CA and use the information in the certificate to validate the peer's identity. Because of the complexity of using a CA, I will cover this information in the next section. Because there is a central device handling the certificates, the use of RSA signatures is more scalable than pre-shared keys and encrypted nonces, and is typically used for remote access connections where you might have to handle thousands of clients.

I should also point out that the IPSec standard has been updated to provide user authentication. One limitation of the three methods mentioned in the last paragraphs is that they provide *device* authentication—they don't identify the user who is using the device. XAUTH is an extension of the IPSec standard that allows peers to perform additional authentication by prompting the user for a username and password. Typically, XAUTH is used in remote access connections when you might want to simplify the user's connection by providing a single login connection for the user—the user authenticates once and is allowed to complete the VPN connection as well as access resources behind the remote VPN gateway, like a Windows domain.

Certificate Authority

A CA is similar to a notary—it is a trusted third party that provides identity verification between two parties. A notary is an individual who validates the identity of an individual. He does this by examining your government identification, like a driver's license, passport, or military ID. He compares both your picture and signature on your identification document to the signature that you sign in front of him. If the picture ID matches what you look like and the signature on the ID matches the signature that you sign, the notary then puts his seal of approval as well as his signature on your document, thus validating your identity.

A CA, in the computer world, is used to validate the identity of networking devices. It provides proof that when two devices are going to set up a VPN connection between themselves, that the connection is really between themselves and not a man-in-the-middle device performing IP Spoofing. To provide this identity checking, instead of using a driver's license or military ID, a CA uses a *digital certificate*. Digital certificates are defined in ITU-T's X.509 standard. A digital certificate contains the following information:

- The CA's digital signature, signed with the CA's private key
- A networking device's identity
- A networking device's digital signature, signed by the device's private key

To prevent man-in-the-middle attacks, you should obtain the CA's public key out-of-band. When your networking device receives a certificate from a CA, it will verify the CA's signature by using the CA's public key. This allows you to verify the authenticity of the certificate to ensure that the certificate came from the CA and not someone pretending to be the CA.

When a networking device is given its own certificate, the certificate is only valid for a specific period of time. A CA keeps a list of expired certificates in a *Certificate Revocation List* (CRL). Devices can request a CRL to determine if a peer's certificate has expired. And to provide redundancy, CAs support *Registration Authorities* (RAs). An RA provides backup services to a CA—it handles certificate authentication services if the CA is not available. One limitation of an RA is that it cannot be used to register new certificates—only a CA can do this.

There are many CA products available on the market. Cisco doesn't have their own CA product; however, they do support the following CA products: Baltimore Technologies, Entrust, Microsoft, Network Associates, and VeriSign. Not every Cisco product supports these CA products. Many companies use Microsoft's CA product to manage their own certificates—this is included with your purchase of Windows 2000 Server or Advanced Server products. This product is very easy to install and use (I have used it on many occasions). Of course, if you are setting up VPN connections to many different companies, these other companies might not *trust* your management of the CA. In this case, you would contract a neutral party to provide CA services. Baltimore Technologies and VeriSign are the most well known in the certificate business. Many companies that sell products and services through the Internet use these companies, like American Express.

Each of your networking devices that use RSA signatures for authentication needs its own unique certificate. There are two basic methods of obtaining a certificate for your networking device: manual or dynamic, using the Simple Certificate Enrollment Protocol (SCEP). The following two sections will discuss these enrollment methods.

Manual   If you are using the manual method, you need to manually create your digital certificate information and forward this, out-of-band, to the CA. Typically, you copy this information to a floppy drive and mail this to the CA administrator. The CA administrator then uses this information to create a certificate for your device, which the administrator then sends to you, out-of-band, and you load the certificate into your networking device. Obviously, this method is not manageable if you have hundreds of devices that need certificates, or if the devices you have either change a lot or need to regenerate certificate information often.

SCEP If you have either of these two situations in your network, you might be better off using SCEP to dynamically register your certificate information and have the newly created certificate downloaded to your networking device. Currently, SCEP is in a draft state, and Cisco and Microsoft are two of the main companies pushing this standard. There are two RSA standards included in SCEP:

- Public Key Cryptography Standard (PKCS) #7 This standard defines how certificate enrollment messages are encrypted and signed.

- PKCS #10 This standard defines how a CA will handle certificate requests sent by a networking device.

When your networking device obtains its own certificate using SCEP, the following steps occur:

1. You have your networking device request the CA's and RA's (if it exists) certificates.

2. You verify these certificates out-of-band with the CA administrator.

3. Your networking device can then request its own certificate from the CA.

4. The CA sends your networking device its certificate—this may or may not require manual intervention by the CA's administrator.

5. Your networking device stores these certificates locally (a PIX would store this information in flash).

Of course, when you use SCEP to obtain a certificate for your networking device, there is a question concerning the identity of your device that is registering certificate information. When you use SCEP to enroll and obtain a new certificate, the CA will either use one or two methods of authentication (to verify your identity):

- **Manual** The CA administrator will verify the certificate information out-of-band, typically by calling you and verifying the information; until the certificate is manually approved, your device will not be able to use the CA for authentication.

- **Pre-shared secret key** The CA administrator assigns your device a secret key, which is used when enrolling to validate your identity; one advantage of this method is that it doesn't require manual intervention by the CA administrator to obtain a certificate, which is ideal when you have to create certificates for 1,000 SOHO users in your network.

Using either of these two methods allows the CA administrator to verify your device's identity before giving it a certificate.

Authentication Process   Now that you understand how your networking device can get a certificate, how does your device use this certificate? Remember that one of the concerns when setting up a VPN connection to a remote peer is how to verify the remote peer's identity. Certificates and a CA are one method that you can use to perform this validation.

Two peers that wish to establish a VPN connection go through the following steps when using certificates:

1. The peers exchange their own personal certificates with each other.

2. Each peer then requests the other peer's certificate from the CA.

3. When peers receive the certificate from the CA, they validate the digital signature of the CA on the peer's certificate (received from the CA) to ensure that the source of the certificate is the CA.

4. After verifying the authenticity of the certificate, each peer validates the other peer's signature on the certificate it received from the CA to the certificate it received from the remote peer.

5. If the remote peer's digital signature can be validated, then the two devices can proceed with setting up an IPSec connection. If the certificate can't be validated, one of two things is true: the certificate they received is invalid (possibly expired), or the certificate has been forged by a man-in-the-middle device.

METHODS OF IPSEC DATA PROTECTION

IPSec incorporates two standards to provide data confidentiality and integrity: Authentication Header (AH) and Encapsulation Security Payload (ESP). The following two sections cover these protocols, and then I will discuss how IPSec connections are set up between two IPSec peers.

Authentication Header

AH is defined in RFC 2402, and is an IP protocol. As an IP protocol, it has been assigned a protocol number of 51 (TCP is 6 and UDP is 17). AH is used to verify the integrity of the packets received from an IPSec peer. In other words, AH is used to digitally sign each packet sent so that if a man-in-the-middle device tampers with the packets, you'll be able to detect the tampering by examining the digital signature. You might have noticed that I didn't mention anything about encryption—AH only provides data integrity, *not* data encrytpion. To resolve this limitation, you can use AH in combination with ESP, which *does* provide encryption abilities.

To help you better understand the type of integrity that AH provides, take a look at the packet diagram shown in Figure 16-3. This example shows how AH is encapsulated within an IP packet. The top part of the figure shows the contents of an IP packet. At the beginning of the packet is the IP packet header, which contains the source and

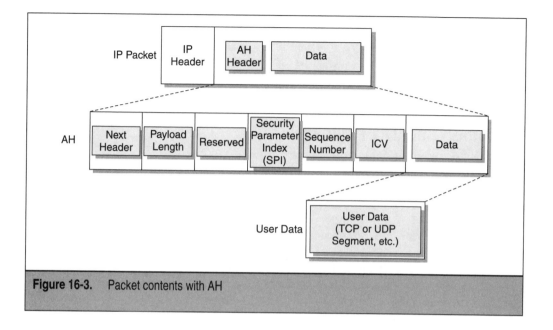

Figure 16-3. Packet contents with AH

destination IP addresses, the IP protocol field (AH uses 51), the TTL field, and other information. To the right of this is the AH encapsulation.

The middle part of Figure 16-3 shows the AH segment that is encapsulated in the IP packet. The *Next Header* field denotes the IP protocol that is encapsulated in the AH payload (for example, 6 for TCP or 17 for UDP). The *Payload Length* field contains the length of the AH header, in bytes (this doesn't include the length of the data payload). The *Reserved* field is currently not used. The *Security Parameter Index* (SPI) contains a value that is used to uniquely identify this IPSec connection compared to other IPSec connections from this IPSec device. The *Sequence Number* field contains a number indicating the order of the packets as they are being sent to the remote peer; this is used to prevent session replay attacks. The *Integrity Check Value* (ICV) field is an authentication/data integrity field that contains a digital signature created by the source IPSec peer.

There are a couple of important items to point out about AH and the protection that it provides. When the source IPSec peer creates the ICV value, it takes a secret key (which is shared with the remote peer), all the IP header fields that are not mutable (those values that don't change, like the IP addresses), the AH header contents itself, and the AH encapsulated user data, and runs them through a hashing algorithm to create the digital signature (ICV). The hashing algorithms supported are MD5 and SHA. The destination IPSec peer can run the same information through the hashing function, with the shared secret key, to check if the packet contents were tampered with.

An important item to point out is that AH cannot protect all of the contents of the IP header. For example, the Time to Live field (TTL) is a mutable field—its value is decremented by every router that the packet passes though.

NOTE   Another important item concerning AH is that it does not work through a NAT or PAT device. A NAT device changes the IP addresses in the IP header and a PAT device changes port numbers. Either of these situations would invalidate the digital signature. Therefore, you need to ensure that no NAT or PAT devices are performing address translation on these protected packets. To get around this problem, use NAT or PAT on the packets first, and then use AH on them.

Encapsulation Security Payload

One of the limitations of AH is that it doesn't provide data confidentiality. ESP, on the other hand, provides confidentiality by using encryption as well as data integrity through hashing functions. ESP is defined in RFC 2406 and has an IP protocol number of 50 assigned to it. Cisco currently supports the DES and 3DES encryption algorithms for data confidentiality with ESP. As I mentioned earlier, these algorithms use symmetric keys.

To help you better understand what ESP is doing, take a look at an IPSec packet using ESP, as shown in Figure 16-4. This figure shows how ESP is encapsulated within an IP packet. The top part shows the contents of an IP packet. At the beginning of the packet is the IP packet header, which contains the source and destination IP addresses, the IP protocol field (50 in the case of ESP), the TTL field, and other information. To the right of this is the ESP encapsulation.

The middle part of Figure 16-4 shows the ESP segment that is encapsulated in the IP packet. Here is a description of each of these fields in the ESP header: the *Security Parameter Index* (SPI) field contains a value that is used to uniquely identify this IPSec connection compared to other IPSec connections. The *Sequence Number* field contains a number indicating the order of the packets as they are being sent to the remote peer; this is used to prevent session replay attacks. The *Encrypted Data* field contains

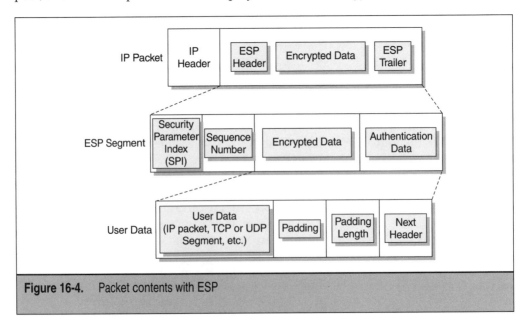

Figure 16-4.   Packet contents with ESP

the encrypted data (like the TCP or UDP segment) created by DES or 3DES. The *Authentication Data* (ICV) field is an authentication/data integrity field that contains a data signature created by the source IPSec peer.

The bottom of Figure 16-4 shows the data that is encrypted. Another feature of ESP is that before performing encryption, it will pad the user data to help prevent hackers from guessing what the transmission type is. Remember that many IP applications are fairly predictable—a hacker could guess the type of transmission by performing eavesdropping and examining the length of the encrypted data. The byte length of the padding is then denoted in the *Padding Length* field following the user data and the padding. After this is the *Next Header* field, indicating what the user data is (like the TCP or UDP protocol number).

There are a couple of important items to point out about ESP and the protection that it provides. When the source IPSec peer creates the ICV value, it takes a secret key and all of the ESP segment contents, with the exception of the Authentication Data, and runs them through a hashing algorithm to create the digital signature (ICV). The hashing algorithms supported are MD5 and SHA. The destination IPSec peer can run the same information through the hashing function, with the secret key, to check if the packet contents were tampered with.

Notice that the ESP *Authentication Data* field does not compute an ICV value by including the contents of the IP packet header. Therefore, if you were only using ESP for data integrity, a hacker could spoof IP packets and your IPSec device wouldn't be able to detect this because the IP source address is not included in the ICV calculation. If you need this kind of protection, you could use AH authentication instead of ESP authentication. You could even use both types of authentication, but this would be, for the most part, redundant.

However, ESP authentication does provide one advantage over AH—because the IP packet header information, like the source and destination IP addresses, are not included in the ICV calculation, these packets *can* have a NAT device perform network address translation on them.

ESP support two different modes for protecting your data:

- Transport—the real source and destination IP addresses are placed in the IP packet header

- Tunnel—the original IP packet is encapsulated into an ESP segment, which is encapsulated into another IP packet with a different IP address for the source and destination

Transport mode is typically used for point-to-point connections, where the source and destination only need to share information securely with each other, but not with other devices. The problem with transport mode is that it is not very scalable—the more devices a peer needs to share information with securely, the more unmanageable the security solution becomes. Tunnel mode is typically used for site-to-site connections, where the two devices performing ESP are the devices at the exit points of a network, as shown in Figure 16-5. In this example, there are two networks using private IP addresses. The two routers (VPN devices) connected to the Internet provide the ESP tunnel between

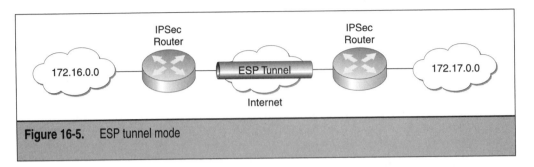

Figure 16-5. ESP tunnel mode

the two sites. This tunnel is a logical connection between the two sites. Therefore, if a device from 172.16.0.0 sends traffic to 172.17.0.0, this device wouldn't have to worry about securing the data—this has been centralized by the ISP-connected router. This single IPSec connection can be used for all traffic between these two sites.

One nice feature of ESP tunnel mode is that the original *IP packet* is encapsulated in an ESP segment, and this segment is encapsulated in a new packet. In Figure 16-5, if 172.16.1.1 sends something to 172.17.1.1, this packet would be encapsulated in an ESP segment by the ISP-connected router, and placed into a new IP packet where the source IP address is this router's address, and the destination address is the destination router's IP address. When the destination router receives this IPSec packet, it verifies the contents and decrypts the packet, and then removes the original IP packet and forwards it to the destination. Actually, this process is similar to a GRE tunnel, which I discussed earlier.

One advantage of ESP tunnel mode is that your internal hosts can use private IP addresses. Another advantage is that the real source and destination devices are hidden from any eavesdroppers in the public network—the original IP packet is encrypted and thus the original IP addresses are hidden. And, you can easily add, change, and remove hosts from your internal network without having to make changes to your IPSec configuration.

SETTING UP AN IPSEC VPN CONNECTION

Setting up an IPSec connection is not a simple process—there are many configuration tasks that you'll have to perform as well as decisions you'll have to make about how much security that you want for your connection. The following sections discuss the details of setting up a connection. Before I can begin discussing how a connection is set up, you'll first need to gather some information about the kind of security you'll want for your IPSec connection.

Gathering Information

There are many choices that you have to make when securing your data connection: What protocols you are going to use, what traffic is going to be protected, what algorithms and functions are going to be used, and more. The following is a basic list of items you should decide upon before you start your configuration process:

- You need to decide which traffic is going to be protected. Remember that if you are going to use encryption, the amount of traffic that has to be encrypted may cause a performance problem for your VPN device.
- You need to determine which IPSec security protocols you are going to use: ESP, AH, or both.
- For ESP or AH authentication, you need to choose either MD5 or SHA as a hashing function—MD5 is quicker, but SHA is more secure.
- For ESP encryption, you need to choose an encryption algorithm—DES or 3DES.
- For ESP, you need to choose your mode—transport or tunnel.
- You need to determine what initial authentication method you'll use— pre-shared keys, RSA encrypted nonces, or RSA signatures (CA).
- You need to use Diffie-Hellman (DH) to set up a temporary secure connection and need to specify a key size for DH. I'll discuss DH later in this chapter.

These are some of the most important items. As you'll see, there are other items you'll have to address when building your IPSec connection.

Steps For Setting Up an IPSec Connection

There are certain steps a VPN device will go through when establishing an IPSec connection. I've generalized this process into five basic steps:

1. You need to define what traffic is to be protected by the IPSec connection.
2. Your IPSec device needs to build a management connection that will be used for setting up any data connections.
3. Your IPSec device builds any necessary secure data connections.
4. Once the data connection is built, you can send your data across it—protected, of course.
5. Once networking devices are done sending data and the IPSec connection is no longer needed, your IPSec device will tear down the IPSec data connection.

For the first step, a networking device needs to send traffic through the IPSec device. The IPSec device compares this traffic to what is to be protected—if the traffic isn't supposed to be protected, the IPSec device forwards it normally; if it is supposed to be protected, the IPSec device checks to see if there is already a protected connection to the destination. If there is a protected connection, the IPSec device uses this connection; if not, the IPSec device starts the process of setting one up.

NOTE: Cisco uses ACLs on their PIXs to define the traffic that is to be secured.

The first connection built between the two IPSec peers is what I refer to as a *management connection*. This connection is not used to transmit user data, like telnets and FTPs, but is used for management purposes: building, maintaining, and tearing down user VPN connections.

Across this management connection, the IPSec peers negotiate the parameters for a secure data connection (the protected connection for user traffic). I commonly refer to this as a *user* or *data connection*. Once this second connection is built, your IPSec device can start using this connection to transmit user data securely. Generically, an IPSec connection is referred to as a *session*, and all of the parameters associated with securing the session are referred to as *Security Association* (SA).

Both the management and user connections typically have a default lifetime associated with them. Once this lifetime expires, the IPSec peers tear down the connection and reestablish the secure connection. This process is done to ensure the security of your IPSec connections since new encryption keying and hashing material is generated for the new connections. One important item to point out is that user connections are only established when the IPSec peer sees traffic coming from the user. Once this occurs, the IPSec device builds the user connection and then keeps it up for the lifetime of the connection (whether or not there is more user traffic to be sent).

As you can see from these five steps, the setting up of an IPSec connection seems to be a straightforward and simple process. However, as the rest of this chapter will explain, setting up an IPSec connection and its ongoing management is a complicated process.

ISAKMP and IKE

The Internet Security Association and Key Management Protocol (ISAKMP), defined in RFC 2408, specifies the message format used for the IPSec management connection, as well as the mechanics of a key exchange protocol and negotiation process used to build the management and data connections. A key exchange protocol is necessary to exchange keys securely between IPSec peers, and, of course, the actual negotiation of security parameters, like encryption algorithms and hashing functions, that are needed to secure the connections. ISAKMP, however, has two limitations—it doesn't define *how* keys should be shared between the peers, nor how the keys should be managed (how often they should be changed to increase your security).

Because of these two limitations, the Internet Key Exchange (IKE) protocol is used. The three main functions of IKE are to securely exchange keys between peers, negotiate the security protocols for an IPSec connection, and manage the keys for IPSec peers on an ongoing basis. IKE is defined in RFC 2409. Actually, IKE is a hybrid protocol, combining ISAKMP and the Oakley and Skeme key exchange methods. Oakley and Skeme support five different key groups. Cisco's PIX firewall supports two of these groups: group 1, which has a 768-bit key length, and group 2, which has a 1,024-bit key length. IKE actually fills in the gaps of the ISAKMP protocol. ISAKMP and IKE are, therefore, responsible for setting up and maintaining IPSec connections. Some people refer to these protocols as *ISAKMP*, or sometimes people refer to the two phases of IKE—Phase 1 and 2—when differentiating between the different setup processes. Through the rest of this chapter and the next, I'll use the latter nomenclature.

One of the difficulties that the IPSec standards body faced was how to share keys securely in a public network to build a secure connection. When you look at this last statement, it presents a catch-22 situation. You need keys to secure a connection, so if you share these keys across a public network, then you've compromised your security. One method of dealing with this problem is to pre-share the keys out-of-band. Of course, this creates management problems if you have hundreds of devices that you need to share keys with.

A more scalable, as well as ingenious, solution to this catch-22 situation was the development of the Diffie-Hellman (DH) protocol. DH is used to securely exchange keying material that will be used to encrypt the management session in IKE Phase 1. I'll discuss the DH protocol later in this chapter.

Functions of IKE

As I mentioned in the previous section, IKE is a hybrid protocol that is used to set up management and user connections to remote IPSec peers. One of the functions of IKE is to authenticate the remote peer's identity. As I mentioned earlier in this chapter, there are three ways to do this: pre-shared keys, RSA encrypted nonces, and RSA signatures (in use with a CA). IKE supports all three of these authentication methods.

Once a peer is authenticated, IKE uses DH to set up a temporary, yet secure, connection that it uses to negotiate the security protocols, encryption algorithms, and keying information for the management connection.

After the management connection is built, IKE is used again to negotiate the same parameter for the user connection. Note that the keying information, encryption algorithms, and hashing functions can be different between the user and management connections. For remote access clients, IKE can even assign a dynamic IP address to the remote peer. Once IPSec connections are built, IKE is responsible for maintaining these connections—once these connections expire, IKE is responsible for rebuilding them.

IKE is actually broken into two phases: Phase 1 is responsible for building the management connection, and Phase 2 is responsible for building the user connection. The following sections cover both of these phases in more depth.

IKE Phase 1

Of the two phases, IKE Phase 1 is the more complicated one because more events happen in Phase 1 than in Phase 2. During IKE Phase 1, any connections built between the IPSec peers are *not* used to send user traffic. Instead, they are used for management purposes.

As I mentioned in the previous section, IKE is responsible for authenticating the remote peer's identity. IKE Phase 1 handles this process to prevent man-in-the-middle attacks. For a small number of site-to-site connections, administrators typically use pre-shared keys. For a large number of site-to-site connections, or for remote access connections, administrators typically use digital certificates.

Modes   IKE Phase 1 has two modes that can be used to set up the bidirectional management connection: *main* and *aggressive*. When using main mode in IKE Phase 1, there are three two-way exchanges of six packets. During the exchange, the identities of the peers are hidden from prying eyes. During main mode, three steps occur. In the first step, the IPSec security policies that are to be used for the management connection are negotiated. These policies include the DH key groups that will be used for the DH algorithm. Once this is complete, DH is used to securely exchange keys between the two peers for protecting the management connection. And last, the peer's identities are authenticated.

Aggressive mode sets up the management connection in IKE Phase 1 more quickly than main mode. However, one difference between aggressive and main mode is that where main mode hides the identity of the two peers, aggressive exposes the peers' identities. In aggressive mode, there are two exchanges. In the first exchange, the IKE policies are negotiated, a DH public key is exchanged, and the identity of each peer is shared. The second exchange is basically used for acknowledgment purposes—verifying the contents of the first exchange.

Policies   Policies are the components used to secure an IPSec connection. During Phase 1 of IKE, the peers negotiate the following security policies for the management connection:

- Type of authentication: pre-shared keys, RSA encrypted nonces, or RSA signatures
- Encryption algorithm: DES or 3DES
- Hashing function: MD5 or SHA
- DH key group: group 1 or group 2
- Lifetime of the management connection

These items are not configured automatically on Cisco's PIX firewall. Even though these policies are dynamically shared via ISAKMP, you must still manually configure them on your PIX. The next chapter, Chapter 17, is dedicated to this subject.

Diffie-Hellman   Before I get ahead of myself, I want to discuss how DH is used by IKE Phase 1 to share this information securely so that the peers can set up a secure management connection. DH is used to set up a *temporary* secure connection between the two peers so that they can share their keying information across this connection. The following basic steps occur through IKE:

1. The two peers use an authentication process to verify each other's identity.
2. Each peer creates a public and private key (asymmetric) using a DH key group: 1 or 2.
3. Each peer shares their public key with the other peer.
4. Each peer takes their own private key, the other peer's public key, and runs it through the DH hashing algorithm, coming up with a fixed-length value.
5. Interestingly enough, the value that the algorithm creates is the same on *both* peers. This new secret key is then used to build the management connection between the two IPSec peers.

Figure 16-6 shows an example of these five steps. The first step is actually not part of DH, but steps 2 through 5 are. As to the last step, an amazing function of the algorithm DH uses allows for different inputs creating the same output; however, the inputs have to have a relation—in this example, the relation is the public and private key combination where each peer uses its own private key but the other peer's public key. Once a secret key is generated, the two peers use this key for encryption purposes in order to set up their management connection in Phase 1 of IKE.

The main strength of DH is that it defeats man-in-the-middle attacks concerning the sharing of keying information. In order to create the *secret* key, a hacker would need to not only know the public key (which the hacker can see), but also the other peer's private key (which is not shared). One weakness of DH is that it doesn't perform any authentication; however, as I already mentioned, IKE Phase 1 allows for authentication by using pre-shared keys, RSA encrypted nonces, or RSA signatures.

IKE Phase 2

IKE Phase 1 is responsible for building a secure IPSec management connection. IKE Phase 2 uses this management connection to negotiate the security protocols and keying information for the actual IPSec *user connections*. These user connections are unidirectional; this means that each peer builds a separate IPSec connection to the destination peer that it will use when sending protected user traffic. Therefore, if you have two peers, you will have two unidirectional connections: PeerA to PeerB, and PeerB to PeerA.

IKE Phase 2 has two main functions. Its first function is to negotiate the security protocols and keying information that the user connection will use. Its second function is to periodically generate new keying information; you can use DH to enhance the security of this function. If you already have an encrypted user connection between

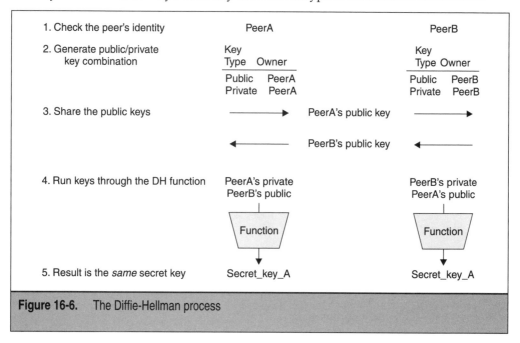

Figure 16-6. The Diffie-Hellman process

two IPSec peers, you can use this connection to share your newly generated keys securely. However, if you are paranoid, you can use DH a second time to ensure perfect forward secrecy (PFS) or by refreshing the original DH secret shared key by running this through the DH hash algorithm again (the first of these is more secure, but the second is faster). Because the DH key groups when you use PFS are longer than the keys that you use for DES or 3DES encryption, PFS is more secure, but adds an additional delay in the key regeneration process.

Although IKE Phase 1 has two modes, IKE Phase 2 only has a single mode: *quick* mode. Quick mode is responsible for negotiating the security parameters for the user connection. These parameters include the following information:

- The security protocol used: AH, ESP, or both

- The encryption algorithm used for ESP: DES or 3DES

- The authentication method used: AH, ESP, or both

- The authentication hashing function for AH or ESP: SHA or MD5

- The ESP mode used: tunnel or transport

- The lifetime of the user connection—can be specified in seconds or kilobytes of information transmitted

Typically, ESP encryption is used for securing the user connection. Remember, that if you are using NAT, you should not use AH for authentication because AH protects most of the IP header, including the IP addresses. The grouping of the AH and ESP parameters is called a *transform set*.

Each IPSec connection is treated as a unique SA and each peer will assign a different SPI value to differentiate between the various IPSec SAs that the device has open. As I mentioned in the AH and ESP sections of this chapter, the SPI value is placed in the headers of these packets so that the destination can determine which encryption algorithm it should use to decrypt the packet contents as well as which hashing algorithm it should use to check the integrity of the packet contents.

OVERVIEW OF THE CONNECTION SETUP PROCESS

I'll now review the whole IPSec process so that you can see how all of these components work together. Understanding this process is very important, especially when two peers are having problems establishing an IPSec connection and you must troubleshoot the problem:

1. IKE Phase 1

    A. Initial exchange: main or aggressive mode

    B. Identity authentication

    - Pre-shared keys

    - RSA encrypted nonces

    - RSA signatures

    C. Diffie-Hellman

    D. Exchange of management transform sets

    E. Creation of management connection

  2. IKE Phase 2

    A. Exchange of user transform sets using quick mode

    B. Creation of user connection

    C. Periodically refreshing keys for connections

The first step is that the two peers start IKE Phase 1. Within IKE Phase 1, the peers either use main or aggressive mode to perform an initial exchange. Two of the items shared here are the type of authentication and the DH key group to use for the DH algorithm.

Once this initial exchange has taken place, the peers validate each other's identity using RSA signatures, RSA encrypted nonces, or pre-shared keys. With RSA signatures, a CA is used as a trusted third party. Each peer shares their own certificates with the other and then each peer obtains the other peer's certificate from the CA. This information is then compared and validated. With RSA encrypted nonces, each peer generates its own public and private key. The public key is then shared, out-of-band, with the remote peer and configured on the remote peer. When performing validation, the peer creates a digital signature with its private key and sends this to the remote peer. The remote peer uses the source peer's public key to verify the signature. If you are using pre-shared keys, a single secret key is shared out-of-band between the two peers. This key is then used to create a signature, which the other verifies with the same key. Of these three methods, RSA signatures are the most scalable, but pre-shared keys are the easiest to configure.

Once authentication has been performed, DH is used to create a temporary, secure connection. Each peer creates its own unique public and private key combination. Each peer shares its public key with the other peer. Each peer then takes their own private key and the remote peer's public key and runs this through a hash function, creating the same secret key. This secret key is then used to protect the *exchange* of information for the management connection.

Once DH has completed and a secret key has been generated, this secret key is used to protect the negotiation of the parameters of the management connection, including the transform set and keying information. These parameters include the authentication method (MD5 or SHA), the encryption algorithm (DES or 3DES), and the lifetime of the management connection. Once these parameters have been negotiated and the peers agree upon a common parameter set and generate the necessary keys, the management connection is built. A unique SPI value is then assigned to this SA. This now completes IKE Phase 1.

In IKE Phase 2, user connections can be built to this remote peer using the secure management connection built in IKE Phase 1. IKE Phase 2 only has one mode, quick mode, which is used to negotiate the parameters, including the transform set, for the user connection. The transform set includes the following parameters: the security protocol (AH, ESP, or both), the authentication method (MD5 or SHA), the encryption algorithm (DES or 3DES), and the ESP mode (tunnel or transport). The lifetime of the user connection (in seconds, kilobytes, or both) is also shared. Once a common set of parameters has been negotiated, an SPI value is assigned and the user connection is built. Remember that this is a unidirectional connection, so there are two connections built in this part of IKE Phase 2—one connection from PeerA to PeerB and one from PeerB to PeerA.

Once these two SAs have been built, user traffic can be sent across these secured connections. Another function of IKE Phase 2 is to maintain the user connections and to rebuild them once the connection lifetime has expired. DH can be used to provide PFS, or the current secure user connection can be used for this negotiation process.

This was a real quick summary of the steps involved in the setup of an IPSec connection. As you will see in the next chapter, there are a lot of commands that you have to configure on your PIX firewall to set up site-to-site and remote access connections.

FURTHER STUDY

Web Sites

For information on IPSec, examine RFC 2401 at www.ietf.org/rfc/rfc2401.txt.

For information on DES and 3DES, visit csrc.nist.gov/publications/fips/ fips46-3 /fips46-3.pdf.

For information on MD5, see RFC 1321 at www.ietf.org/rfc/rfc1321.txt.

For information on SHA, see RFC 2404 at www.ietf.org/rfc/rfc2404.txt.

For information on AH, see RFC 2402 at www.ietf.org/rfc/rfc2402.txt.

For information on ESP, see RFC 2406 at www.ietf.org/rfc/rfc2406.txt.

For information on ISAKMP, see RFC 2408 at www.ietf.org/rfc/rfc2408.txt.

For information on IKE, see RFC 2409 at www.ietf.org/rfc/rfc2409.txt.

For information on Diffie-Hellman, see RFC 2631 at www.ietf.org/rfc/rfc2631.txt.

CHAPTER 17

IPSec Configuration

In the last chapter, I introduced you to VPNs and the IPSec standard. Most VPNs that you'll set up will use IPSec. The focus of this chapter is on the setup and maintenance of IPSec connections on your PIX. I'll first discuss site-to-site connections, and then remote access. If you already have experience configuring IPSec on Cisco routers, the configuration of IPSec on PIX firewalls is similar—many of the commands are similar, if not the same.

PREPARING FOR IPSEC CONNECTIONS

I can clearly remember my first experience with setting up IPSec between two routers. A few years ago I was tasked to build an encrypted connection using IPSec between two Cisco routers. Configuring IPSec was completely new to me, and for that matter, so was the IPSec standard itself. I looked at the boilerplate examples that Cisco has on their web site, but that wasn't much help when the configuration that I put on the two routers didn't work. Of course, having no experience with the configuration and mechanics of IPSec made matters worse when I was trying to troubleshoot the problem. From this hair-pulling experience, I sat down and learned the mechanics of IPSec. This not only helped in this particular situation, but also when implementing IPSec with other vendors' products. I learned from this situation that the configuration and setup of an IPSec connection can be broken down into simple steps.

Preparation Steps

Before you begin configuring IPSec on your PIX firewall, there are some preparation tasks that you should complete:

1. Address any design and policy issues.
2. Specify protected traffic with an ACL configuration on your PIX.
3. Determine your configuration policies for IKE Phase 1.
4. Determine your configuration policies for IKE Phase 2.
5. Verify your PIX's configuration.
6. Check the status of the IPSec connection.

If you break down the configuration and setup process of IPSec, your job will be much easier. In the last chapter, you saw that IPSec is not a simple protocol. And as you will see in this chapter, there are many ways of setting up an IPSec connection, with many parameters and many commands. Therefore, by following the six steps in this list, you'll make the setup of your IPSec connection a simple process.

Allowing IPSec Traffic into Your Network

When you're dealing with design and policy issues, one of the items that you need to determine is which device or devices will be sending or receiving IPSec traffic. For example, you might have an internal VPN concentrator that is the termination point for VPN traffic. If you have a PIX in front of the concentrator, you need to permit the IPSec traffic from outside devices to reach the VPN concentrator. If the PIX itself is the termination point, you will still need to permit IPSec traffic to the PIX itself—the PIX, by default, denies all traffic that originates on a lower security level interface. When you're dealing with IPSec, you'll need to permit three connections:

- **ISAKMP/IKE**   uses UDP port 500
- **AH**   an IP protocol with a protocol number of 51
- **ESP**   an IP protocol with a protocol number of 50

With a PIX firewall, you need to either set up conduits or ACL statements to allow this traffic or use the `sysopt` command. If you are using ACLs, here is the syntax for these commands if the PIX is terminating the IPSec connection:

```
pixfirewall(config)#  access-list list_name permit udp
                         outside_source_address source_subnet_mask
                         host PIX_outside_interface_IP_address eq isakmp
pixfirewall(config)#  access-list list_name permit ah
                         source_address source_subnet_mask
                         host PIX_outside_interface_IP_address
pixfirewall(config)#  access-list list_name permit esp
                         source_address source_subnet_mask
                         host PIX_outside_interface_IP_address
```

If you don't know the source address (the remote peer), which may be true for remote access clients that receive their IP address dynamically from their ISP, use 0.0.0.0 0.0.0.0 for the address and mask. If the PIX is not the termination point for the IPSec connection, but an internal IPSec device is, then you need to list the internal device's global IP address as the destination (internal) address when permitting IPSec traffic into your network (instead of the PIX's interface address). Also, remember to activate this ACL on your PIX's *outside* interface.

Your other option is to use the `sysopt` command shown here:

```
pixfirewall(config)#  sysopt connection permit-ipsec
```

The advantage of this command is that it performs the same process as the three previous ACL commands. The one downside of the `sysopt` command, however, is that you cannot be specific about which source or destination devices are allowed to set up inbound IPSec connections—from the PIX's perspective, any outside device can perform this function. My personal preference is to use the ACL configuration: it's more configuration-intensive, but gives you more control over inbound IPSec traffic.

SITE-TO-SITE CONNECTIONS

To simplify the setup of IPSec connections, I've broken this chapter into two major sections: the first part covers site-to-site connections, and the second part covers remote access. As I mentioned in Chapter 16, a site-to-site connection is where two intermediate devices handle the IPSec protection of traffic between two networks. For example, these could be two PIX firewalls, or two perimeter routers, or a perimeter router and a PIX firewall (actually the number of potential combinations is very great). With site-to-site connections, the devices terminating the IPSec tunnel are typically not the recipients of the traffic, but the devices behind them are.

Configuring Authentication

Before you can begin your IKE Phase 1 configuration, you need to determine what type of authentication you will use. Authentication is used at the beginning of IKE Phase 1 to verify the identities of the two peers establishing an IPSec connection. As I mentioned in the last chapter, IKE supports four types of authentication: pre-shared keys, RSA encrypted nonces, RSA signatures, and XAUTH. XAUTH is only used for remote access connections and doesn't apply to site-to-site connections. I'll discuss XAUTH in the second part of the chapter in the remote access section. Of the three remaining authentication methods, the PIX supports only pre-shared keys and RSA signatures (certificates).

Pre-Shared Keys

Typically pre-shared keys are used when you have a small number of site-to-site connections. As you will see in this section, configuring pre-shared keys is very simple.

Specifying the Identity Type   The first item I need to point out is that when you use many of the IPSec commands on the PIX, you must specify the identity of the remote peer. There are actually two ways that you can specify a peer's identity: by their IP address or their hostname. Cisco assumes that you will be specifying a peer by IP address. If you wish to use a hostname instead of an IP address, you must change that behavior with the `isakmp identity` command:

```
pixfirewall(config)# isakmp identity address|host
```

If you specify `host`, you either need to build a static host table on your PIX or use DNS to resolve names. If you do not create a manual resolution entry or use DNS, IKE will not be able to look up the IP address, and thus will not be able to resolve the identity, causing IKE Phase 1 to fail. Remember that DNS is susceptible to spoofing. My preference is to use the default (`address`). If you are creating a static host table, use the `names` and `name` commands:

```
pixfirewall(config)# names
pixfirewall(config)# name remote_peer's_IP_address peer's_hostname
```

The first command, `names`, enables the use of name functions on the PIX. With the second command, `name`, you first specify the IP address of the remote peer and then the hostname. The name cannot exceed 16 characters and cannot begin with a number. To list your static naming, use the `show names` command.

NOTE   The identity type you specify is global—you can only use one method.

Configuring Your Pre-Shared Key   Once you have determined the identity type that you will use when accessing a remote peer, you are now ready to configure the pre-shared key. This key value must be the same on the remote peer, otherwise authentication will fail. The syntax for configuring a pre-shared key is

```
pixfirewall(config)#  isakmp key key_string address peer's_IP_address
                               [netmask subnet_mask]
```
or
```
pixfirewall(config)#  isakmp key key_string hostname peer's_hostname
```

The first command specifies the pre-shared key if the peer identity type is `address` in the `isakmp identity` configuration. You can optionally enter a subnet mask to specify a range of devices that use the same key. If you omit the mask, it defaults to 255.255.255.255. A key can be up to 128 bytes in length and consists of alphanumeric characters. Use the second command if you are specifying your peer by a hostname. Once you have configured your keys, you can verify your configuration with the `show isakmp` command.

SECURITY ALERT!   If you are setting up IPSec connections to devices that you manage, you might want to use the same key value for all peers. Do this by using an IP address of 0.0.0.0—this eliminates you from having to type in an `isakmp key` command for each peer. The drawback of this method, however, is that if a key on one peer is compromised, all of the peers are compromised.

Configuring RSA Signatures

As you saw in the last section, configuring a pre-shared key is very simple. Unfortunately, using a CA to perform authentication definitely complicates your PIX configuration. However, using a CA provides a more scalable security solution. There are almost a dozen commands that you need to configure in order to have your PIX use a CA. Currently Cisco's PIXs support the following CA products (which also include SCEP support):

- Baltimore Technologies' UniCERT v 3.05—requires FOS 5.2 or later
- Entrust Technologies' Entrust/PKI 4.0—requires FOS 5.1 or later
- Microsoft Windows 2000 Certificate Services 5.0—requires FOS 5.2 or later
- VeriSign's OnSite 4.5—requires FOS 5.1 or later

Because configuring CA support on your PIX is not a simple process, I've created the following steps to assist you with your configuration:

1. Examine the amount of flash in your PIX.
2. Set the date and time.
3. Set the hostname and domain name.
4. Create an RSA public and private key pair for the signature on your PIX's certificate.

5. Specify the CA that your PIX will use.

6. Download and verify the CA's certificate.

7. Retrieve your PIX's personal certificate from the CA.

8. Save the PIX's configuration (this requires two commands).

9. Check your PIX's certificate configuration.

10. Monitor and maintain your PIX's CA authentication configuration.

Step 1: Examine Flash Usage   As I mentioned in the last chapter, an IPSec device will store certificate information locally. The PIX stores this information in flash, which includes: The RSA public and private keys used to sign the PIX's personal certificate, the PIX's personal certificate, the CA's certificate, two certificates for the RA (if the CA has an RA), and one or two CRLs (if the CA has an RA). You need to ensure that there is enough flash on your PIX to store this information; otherwise, authentication using a CA will not function. Use the show flashfs command to verify the amount of free flash on your PIX.

Steps 2 and 3: Set the Date and Time and the PIX Name   As I mentioned in the last chapter, certificates are assigned an expiration date—they are given a beginning and ending time by CA creating the certificates. Therefore, it is of utmost importance that your PIX have the current date and time. I discussed the date and time in Chapter 10. You can manually assign the date and time with the clock set command or you can acquire the time automatically by configuring the PIX as an NTP client.

Each IPSec device also needs a unique identity. The PIX uses a fully-qualified domain name (FQDN) to provide a unique identity. To configure a FQDN, use these commands:

```
pixfirewall(config)# hostname name_of_the_PIX
pixfirewall(config)# domain-name domain_name_of_the_PIX_organization
```

NOTE   Make sure that the clock on your PIX firewall is set to GMT, to the same month, day, and year, that is configured on the CA. Otherwise, the CA might reject your certificate request or give you a certificate based on an invalid time period.

Step 4: Create Your RSA Keys   Once you have completed the previous steps, you are now ready to create your RSA public and private keys. These keys are used to create a digital signature for your PIX's certificate, as well as to verify the signature on the certificate. Use the ca generate rsa command to create your public and private key combination:

```
pixfirewall(config)# ca generate rsa key|specialkey modulus_of_the_key
```

If you use the key parameter, only a single public and private key combination is created. These keys are referred to as *General Purpose* keys. If you specify specialkey, two sets of keys are created: General Purpose and Encryption. The last part of this command is the modulus (between 512 and 2,048 bits)—the larger this value is, the more secure your keys will be. However, the larger the modulus, the longer it will take to compute your new keys.

Once you have created your keys, use the `show ca mypubkey rsa` command to view your PIX's public key (you can't view your private key):

```
pixfirewall(config)#  show ca mypubkey rsa
        % Key pair was generated at: 19:18:51 August 29 2001
        Key name: pixfirewall.dealgroup.com
            Usage: General Purpose Key
            Key Data:
             1123311D 04039B36 7898F70D 01010A05 D078EB00 2043CBA5 8123E239
             5CDEAB21 15AEF6B0 8DCE18A6 93210BC5 C29D99EF 14947826 747EABC0
             03214E9C 85179D72 6914A849 3A602D12 1034F6F8 EEDD6C28 DBDEF22A
             A58BD7AC D102D301 E20F
```

In this example, the public key of the PIX called *pixfirewall.dealgroup.com* is shown—this is the hexadecimal output following the *Key Data* heading.

Steps 5 and 6: Connect to the CA and Verify its Certificate   After you have created your RSA public and private keys, you are now ready to configure the connectivity parameters to the CA and obtain the CA's certificate:

```
pixfirewall(config)#  ca identity name_of_the_CA CA's_IP_address
                              [:ca_script_location] [LDAP_IP_address]
pixfirewall(config)#  ca configure name_of_the_CA ca|ra retry_period
                              retry_count  [crloptional]
pixfirewall(config)#  ca authenticate name_of_the_CA [fingerprint_of_CA]
```

The `ca identity` command specifies the location of the CA. You typically must give it the FQDN of the CA as well as the CA's IP address; however, if you are setting up your own internal CA, you can just use the name configured on the CA itself. Optionally, you can specify the CGI BIN script location—the default is `/cgi-bin/` and the name of the script is `pkiclient.exe`. Your CA administrator will tell you what these values are—specify these in the `ca identity` command by using a colon, and immediately proceeding this with the directory location. If the CA supports an LDAP server, you can also specify this at the end of the command. You can use the `show ca identity` command to verify your configuration. If you are using Microsoft 2000's CA product, the syntax of the `ca identity` command would look like this:

```
pixfirewall(config)#  ca identity caserver
                              200.200.200.3:/certserv/mscep/mscep.dll
```

The `ca configure` command allows you specify an RA, if the CA supports an RA, and then the connection parameters to the CA, RA, or both. The *retry_period* specifies how often the CA or RA should be tried when contacting it. This value can range from 0 to 60 minutes, and defaults to one minute. The *retry_count* parameter specifies how many times the CA or RA should be contacted when you're trying to establish a connection. This parameter can range from 0 to 100, where 0 is the default. When you use 0 for the number of retries, the PIX keeps on trying to contact the CA or RA indefinitely. The `crloptional` parameter is an optional parameter that is used to influence how the PIX reacts when it cannot retrieve a Certificate Revocation List (CRL) from the CA. A VPN device, once it establishes an IPSec connection to a remote peer, will eventually tear down this connection upon reaching the expiration timer for the SA. When this occurs for the IKE Phase 1 management connection, the device requests the CRL from the CA and compares this information to the remote peer's certificate it has cached. If the peer's certificate is still valid, the device does not have to request the remote peer's certificate from the CA—the process of getting a CRL is actually quicker than retrieving a particular certificate. The problem with CRL, however, is that if the VPN device cannot retrieve the CRL, it will fail the authentication for the remote peer. This will happen when the CA is not reachable, obviously. The `crloptional` parameter tells the PIX that it should attempt to retrieve the CRL from the CA; however, if the CA is not reachable, the PIX will use the remote peer's certificate that it has cached and continue with IKE Phase 1 authentication. You can use the `show ca configure` command to verify your CA configuration parameters.

TIP   When you are using VeriSign's CA, always specify the `crloptional` parameter—if you don't you'll receive an error message when the PIX attempts to verify a certificate during main mode of IKE Phase 1.

Once you have configured access to the CA, you'll need to download the CA's certificate and verify it by using the `ca authenticate` command. Make sure that you use the same CA name that you specified in the `ca identity` command. You can optionally include the CA's fingerprint (digital signature) to have the PIX validate the CA, or you can perform the process manually. If you include the fingerprint, and the received fingerprint doesn't match the entered fingerprint, the PIX will discard the CA's certificate that you received. Here is an example:

```
pixfirewall(config)#  ca authenticate caserver
Certificate has the following attributes:
Fingerprint: 12345678 87654321 aabbccdd ddccbbaa
```

In this example, you'll notice that the certificate was retrieved and that there is a `Fingerprint` value, which is the CA's signature. You need to call the administrator of the CA and verify that this is the correct signature and that it hasn't been tampered with.

Step 7: Retrieve Your PIX's Personal Certificate   Upon completing step 6, you are now ready to obtain a certificate for your PIX:

```
pixfirewall(config)#  ca enroll name_of_the_CA challenge_password
                      [serial] [ipaddress]
```

The first parameter of the `ca enroll` command is the name of the CA, followed by a challenge password, which can contain up to 80 alphanumeric characters. If you ever need to revoke a certificate, the CA administrator will ask you for this password—make sure you write this down and keep it in a safe place. The CA can also use this password to validate the identity of the requestor. Optionally, you can have the PIX specify its serial number, its IP address, or both to be included in the certificate for identification purposes. If you are using the PIX failover feature, Cisco recommends that you not use either of these two options. Remember that the administrator of the CA might have to manually approve your certificate request, so you might not get a certificate immediately.

NOTE If you generated two RSA public/private key combinations, you only need to execute the `ca enroll` command once—the PIX requests two certificates for you.

To view the certificates on your PIX, use the `show ca certificate` command:

```
pixfirewall#  show ca certificate
Subject Name
    Name: pixfirewall.quizware.com
IP Address: 201.201.201.1
  Status: Available
  Certificate Serial Number: 8765432a
  Key Usage: General Purpose
 RA Signature Certificate
  Status: Available
  Certificate Serial Number: 8765432b
  Key Usage: Signature
<--output omitted-->
```

If you have connectivity problems with the CA, use the `debug crypto ca` command.

NOTE If your PIX reboots before retrieving a certificate, you'll need *re-execute* the `ca enroll` command.

Step 8: Save Your CA Configuration   Now that you have retrieved the CA's certificate and your PIX's certificate, you are ready to save your configuration, which is a two-step process:

```
pixfirewall(config)#  ca save all
pixfirewall(config)#  write memory
```

The `ca save all` command saves the RSA key pairs, the CA and RA certificates, the PIX's certificate, and the CRL to flash. The `write memory` command saves the rest of the CA configuration to flash. Note that the `write memory` command does not save the key and certificate information—only the `ca save all` command can do this.

NOTE Steps 9 and 10, which are based on using `show` and `debug` commands, have been covered throughout the first eight steps.

Miscellaneous CA Commands If your PIX's private key has become compromised, you can remove the public and private key combination with the `ca zeroize rsa` command. If you do this, you'll also need to revoke the certificate that was using these keys for your PIX's digital signature, and then generate new keys and request a new certificate.

If you change CAs, you can use the `no ca identity` command to remove the old CA configuration. When putting in a new CA configuration, remember to remove your PIX's old certificate and request a new one from the new CA. To remove all of the certificate information in flash, use the `no ca save` command—this removes the CA's certificate as well as the PIX's personal certificate.

Configuring IKE Phase 1

Now that you have configured your authentication method (pre-shared keys or RSA signatures), you are ready to proceed with configuring the parameters for IKE Phase 1. These parameters affect how the management connection will be established. The following sections covers IKE Phase 1's configuration components for the PIX.

Enabling ISAKMP/IKE

By default, ISAKMP/IKE is enabled on your PIX, assuming that you have installed either a DES or 3DES license. In FOS 5.0 and earlier, you were limited to using IPSec on the PIX's *outside* interface. However, starting with FOS 5.1, any interface on the PIX supports IPSec. ISAKMP/IKE is enabled on every interface. It is recommended that you disable IPSec on the interfaces where you are not using it. Typically you'll use IPSec on just the *outside* interface, which is connected to the public network. However, there may be situations where more than one interface of the PIX is connected to a public network, possibly for redundancy, and you need to set up more than one set of VPN connections. In this case, leave IPSec enabled on those respective interfaces, but disable it on the rest of the PIX's interfaces.

To enable or disable ISAKMP/IKE on an interface, use the following command:

```
pixfirewall(config)#  [no] iskamp enable name_of_interface
```

Specifying Your IKE Phase 1 Policies

Use the following commands to define your IKE Phase 1 policies:

```
pixfirewall(config)#  isakmp policy priority_number authentication
                        pre-share|rsa-sig
pixfirewall(config)#  isakmp policy priority_number hash md5|sha
pixfirewall(config)#  isakmp policy priority_number encryption des|3des
```

```
pixfirewall(config)#  isakmp policy priority_number group 1|2
pixfirewall(config)#  isakmp policy priority_number lifetime seconds
```

All IKE Phase 1 commands begin with `isakmp policy`, and then are followed by a priority number. This number, just like an ACL number, is used to group your policies together. This number can range from 1 to 65,534. Typically, if all of your remote IPSec peers have the same abilities, like supporting DES for encryption, SHA for a hash function, and group 2 DH keys, you only need to set up one group of policy statements. However, if your peers have different capabilities, like some peers support DES while others support 3DES, you should set up two sets of polices, one for each group of peers.

The number you use for the policy is very *important*—when peers are negotiating during IKE Phase 1, they exchange all of their policy configuration. If you have two policy groups, the PIX shares both of these. Each peer processes these top-down, starting with the lowest number (1 is the lowest number and has the highest priority). Because the lowest numbered policy is always processed first, you should always make sure that this policy has the most secure parameters, like RSA signatures for authentication, SHA for a hash function, 3DES for an encryption algorithm, and group 2 keys for DH. Your least secure set of policies should have the physically highest priority number (lowest priority).

Table 17-1 lists the parameters, a description, and the default value, if the specified IKE parameter is not configured.

One thing to point out about the parameters in Table 17-1 is that the default parameters will not be displayed if you execute the `write terminal` or `show config` commands; however, if you use the `show isakmp [policy]` command, they will be displayed.

> **SECURITY ALERT!** Make sure your most secure policy is assigned the lowest policy number (like 1), because policies are processed from the lowest to highest number. Also, if you do not create an IKE policy, the PIX uses a default policy, which is set to the lowest policy number (65,535). This policy contains the default parameters in Table 17-1.

Parameter	Default	Description
authentication	rsa-sig	Defines the type of authentication to perform (RSA signatures or pre-shared keys)
hash	sha	Defines the hashing function to use for checking data integrity
encryption	des	Defines the encryption algorithm to use
group	1	Defines the DH key group to use
lifetime	86,400	Defines the lifetime of the management Security Association (SA) in seconds

Table 17-1. IKE Phase 1 Parameters

For the management connection to be built, the two peers must have the following parameters in common in at least one policy grouping: authentication, hash function, encryption algorithm, and DH key group. If there is not a match, then IKE Phase 1 will fail and no IPSec connections will be set up. Depending on the vendor's implementation of IPSec, the `lifetime` parameter might or might not have to match the remote peer. The IPSec standard states that they don't have to match, and the lowest time period configured between the two peers should be used; however, some vendors do not follow this part of the standard. In Cisco's implementation of IKE Phase 1, Cisco will negotiate the lifetime value and use the lowest time period.

Verifying Your IKE Phase 1 Policies

Use the `show isakmp policy` command to view your IKE Phase 1 policies:

```
pixfirewall#  show isakmp policy
Protection suite priority 1
        encryption algorithm: DES - Data Encryption Standard (56 bit keys)
        hash algorithm: Message Digest 5
        authentication method: Pre-Shared Key
        Diffie-Hellman group: #2 (1024 bit)
        lifetime: 7200 seconds, no volume limit
```

In the output in this example, there is only one IKE Phase 1 policy (number 1). It uses DES for an encryption algorithm, MD5 for a hash function, pre-shared keys for authentication, group 2 keys for DH, and a lifetime of 2 hours for the management connection.

Configuring IKE Phase 2

Now that you have completed your configuration tasks for building the management connection to an IPSec remote peer, you are now ready to proceed with the setup of your data connection to the remote peer. The following sections cover the setup of the data connection. The items that you have to configure are to define which traffic is to be protected, your transform set, and your crypto map.

Specifying the Traffic to be Protected

One of the first items you need to configure is to specify which traffic is to be protected between your PIX and the remote IPSec peer. To accomplish this, you use an ACL on the PIX. This ACL is often referred to as a *crypto ACL*. I discussed ACL commands in Chapter 5, so please review that chapter for the syntax of ACLs. Use `permit` parameters in your ACL statements to specify traffic that is to be protected and `deny` statements for traffic that is not to be protected (remember that there is an implicit deny at the end of the ACL). Note that the ACL is not used for filtering purposes, and is only used to specify which traffic is to be protected or not protected. Here are the rules for the PIX's actions when comparing traffic to crypto ACLs:

- If outbound traffic doesn't match any of the statements in the crypto ACL, the PIX will not protect the traffic.
- If outbound traffic matches a crypto ACL, the PIX will protect the traffic.

- For inbound traffic, if the traffic matches a crypto ACL, and the traffic is not protected, the PIX will *drop* the traffic.

- For inbound traffic, if the traffic matches a crypto ACL and the traffic is protected, the PIX will use the transform set information to decrypt it and verify the packet integrity.

- For inbound unprotected traffic, if the traffic doesn't match a crypto ACL, the PIX will process it normally.

- For inbound protected traffic, if the traffic doesn't' match a crypto ACL, the PIX will process it normally (this might be the case if an internal device is the IPSec termination point).

If you change a crypto ACL, any current SAs using the crypto ACL will not automatically reinitialize—you have to either clear those SAs or reapply the crypto map (I'll discuss this shortly) on the PIX's interface.

NOTE   If you have different security requirements for different types of traffic, you'll need to create a separate crypto ACL for each set of security requirements.

Another important item to point out is that you might have a situation like that shown in Figure 17-1. In this example, the two networks are using private addresses. The two networks are actually part of the same company, and the network administrator wants to use ESP tunnel mode to make the Internet appear transparent. In this situation, you do not want your PIX to perform address translation when traffic travels back and forth between the two private networks. To accomplish this, use the nat 0 command.

The following is a simple example of this configuration for the PIX on the left of Figure 17-1:

```
pixfirewall(config)#   access-list NONAT permit ip 172.16.0.0
                            255.255.0.0
                            172.17.0.0 255.255.0.0
pixfirewall(config)#   nat (inside) 0 access-list NONAT
```

Actually, the ACL called *NONAT* in this example can be used both for the disablement of NAT between these two networks as well as for identifying the traffic to be protected by

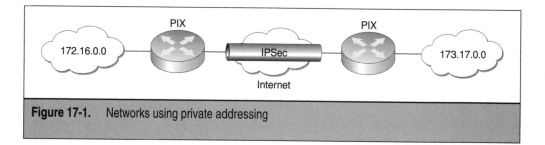

Figure 17-1.   Networks using private addressing

IPSec. However, Cisco highly recommends that you use one ACL to disable address translation and another ACL to specify the traffic to protect...even if the ACL parameters will be the same between the two ACLs.

 SECURITY ALERT!   Do not use the keyword `any` in a crypto ACL `permit` statement, because this will force the PIX to protect all of the outbound source or destination traffic, or drop inbound traffic if it is not protected.

Creating Your Transform Sets

The next step in the setup of your IPSec data connection is to create your transform set or sets. A transform set defines how your data or user traffic is to be protected using IPSec. It contains the security protocols and security algorithms that you will use for your data SA(s). You can configure the following four items in a single transform:

- ESP encryption: DES or 3DES
- ESP authentication: MD5 or SHA
- AH authentication: MD5 or SHA
- Mode: tunnel or transport

When you set up your transform set, you can only choose one configuration option from each of these four items. For example, a transform that specifies both DES and 3DES encryption algorithms would be an invalid transform set. If you have peers with different security needs, you can create a unique transform set for each group of peers. For example, you might have one set of peers that uses tunnel mode with ESP DES encryption and ESP MD5 authentication, and another set of peers that uses tunnel mode with ESP 3DES encryption and ESP SHA authentication. In this example, create two transforms (with unique names), including the appropriate security protocols and algorithms.

To create your transform set, use the `crypto ipsec transform-set` command:

```
pixfirewall(config)#  crypto ipsec transform-set name_of_transform_set
                            transform1 [transform2 [transform3]]
pixfirewall(config)#  crypto ipsec transform-set name_of_transform_set
                            mode tunnel|transport
```

The first command specifies the protection parameters. You must give the transform set a unique name among all transform sets on your PIX. Following this are the actual transforms. Here is a list of transforms that you can enter:

- `ah-md5-hmac` or `ah-sha-hmac`
- `esp-md5-hmac` or `esp-sha-hmac`
- `esp-des` or `esp-3des`

Remember that you can only use one parameter from each of these sets, but you can have up to three protection transforms in a transform set.

The default connection mode for the IPSec data connection is set to `tunnel`. You can change the mode with a second command. Typically, you'll use tunnel mode for site-to-site connections. Use the `show crypto ipsec transform-set` command to view your IPSec transform sets.

NOTE   If you change the parameters in a transform set, the change will not affect any existing SAs—you need to clear the SAs, which I discuss later in the chapter.

Changing Global SA Timeouts

Each data SA has two default timeouts, or expirations periods. By default, the PIX uses a timeout period of 28,800 seconds (8 hours) or 4,608,000 kilobytes worth of traffic, whichever is reached first. When either of these limits is almost reached, the PIX builds a new data connection using its existing management connection, and tears down the old one. These parameters are negotiated with the remote IPSec peer.

To change your global data SA timeout values, use the following two commands:

```
pixfirewall(config)#  crypto ipsec security-association lifetime
                             seconds seconds
pixfirewall(config)#  crypto ipsec security-association lifetime
                             kilobytes kilobytes
```

Configuring these commands is optional. The first command specifies a length, in seconds, of the lifetime of the data SA. The minimum lifetime is 120 seconds, and the maximum is 86,400 seconds—the default is 28,800 (8 hours). The second command specifies the data SA lifetime based on the amount of traffic that has traversed the connection. The default lifetime in kilobytes per second is 4,608,000. Whichever of these lifetimes is reached first will cause the PIX to start building a new connection, and then tear down of the old connection.

If you change the global lifetimes, these changes will not affect any existing SAs—you'll need to either manually clear the existing SAs or reapply the crypto map to the PIX's interface. Use the `show crypto ipsec security-association lifetime` command to view the configured lifetime parameters.

NOTE   When you use these timeout values, whenever the PIX reaches within 30 seconds of the seconds lifetime or 256KB of the kilobytes lifetime values, the PIX starts the negotiation process for a new connection.

Creating Your Crypto Maps

The function of a crypto map is to bind together the necessary information to establish a data SA. The crypto map binds together the following information:

- The identity of the remote peer
- How the SAs are to be established using either manual or dynamic ISAKMP/IKE

- The crypto ACL to use that specifies what traffic is to be protected
- The transform set to use that defines how the traffic is to be protected
- Whether or not PFS (perfect forward security) should be used when rebuilding an SA
- The lifetime of the data SA
- The IP address on the PIX to use for IPSec communications

Listing 17-1 lists the crypto map commands used to bind your IPSec components together:

Listing 17-1
```
pixfirewall(config)#  crypto map map_name sequence_number set peer
                          peer's_IP_adddress|peer's_host_name
pixfirewall(config)#  crypto map map_name sequence_number
                          ipsec-isakmp|ipsec-manual
pixfirewall(config)#  crypto map map_name sequence_number set session-key
                          inbound|outbound ah SPI_number key_string
pixfirewall(config)#  crypto map map_name sequence_number
                          set session-key
                          inbound|outbound esp SPI_number
                          cipher key_string [authenticator key_string]
pixfirewall(config)#  crypto map map_name sequence_number
                          match address crypto_ACL_name
pixfirewall(config)#  crypto map map_name sequence_number
                          set transform-set transform_set_name
pixfirewall(config)#  crypto map map_name sequence_number
                          set pfs group1|group2
pixfirewall(config)#  crypto map map_name sequence_number
                          set security-association
                          seconds seconds | kilobytes kilobytes
```

The first thing to point out about the creation of your crypto map is that each crypto map needs a unique name. Later on I'll discuss how to activate a crypto map on the PIX's interface; however, you should know that there can only be one crypto map per interface. Within this crypto map, though, you can have many entries—one for each peer or set of peers that you'll use to establish data SAs to. Each grouping of crypto map commands is given a unique priority number. You should create multiple crypto map entries if

- You have different data flows that need to be handled by separate peers
- You have different security requirements for different peers (or traffic to the same peer)
- You are using manual ISAKMP/IKE—each crypto ACL is restricted to a single statement

If you are using manual ISAKMP/IKE, you can only have a single `permit` statement in a crypto ACL. If you need more than one `permit` statement, you'll need to create a different ACL for each `permit` entry. This means you'll *also* need separate crypto map entries for each ACL.

When IPSec peers share their crypto maps in IKE Phase 2, they process these from the lowest to highest sequence number when looking for a matching set of crypto map entries to use when setting up an IPSec data connection. Therefore, you should place the most secure entry at the top of the crypto map (give it the lowest sequence number, like 1) and the least secure at the bottom (the highest sequence number). When the PIX and the remote peer are comparing their respective crypto map entries, at least one entry must be in common between the two devices—if there is no common entry, then a data SA will not form. The following, at a minimum, should be in common between the two peers in a crypto map entry:

- The identity of the other peer
- Mirrored crypto ACLs—the addresses in the ACL should be reversed for the remote peer
- A common transform set

One of the first items you'll configure is the identity of the remote peer. You'll use the `peer` parameter to define the peer (the first command in Listing 17-1). Based on your identity type configured on the PIX (defaults to the IP address), you'll either specify the IP address or hostname of the peer. I discussed the configuration of this option earlier in this chapter.

Another important item you need to specify is the type of ISAKMP/IKE you'll use to set up the IPSEC connections. Cisco supports three options—I'll discuss two here and one in the section relegated to remote access connections. Normally, you want to use ISAKMP/IKE to negotiate all of your parameters, including your keying information. To accomplish this, use the second command in Listing 17-1 and specify the `ipsec-isakmp` parameter. However, there may be a situation where the remote peer cannot dynamically share its keying information. If this is the case, you'll specify the `ipsec-manual` parameter. Note that if you use manual ISAKMP/IKE, you must use pre-shared keys—the PIX does not support CA authentication with manual ISAKMP/IKE. Typically, if you have a small number of peers that require manual ISAKMP, you'll create a crypto map entry for these peers while creating other dynamic ISAKMP crypto map entries for the other peers.

If you specify the `ipsec-manual` parameter, you'll need to use the `crypto map` commands with the `set session-key` parameter to define your encryption or authentication keys. These commands are the third and fourth commands in Listing 17-1. Remember that data SAs are unidirectional, so you must specify the direction (`inbound` or `outbound`) for the definition of the key values. Actually, you have to configure each of the `set session-key` commands twice—one command for each direction.

If you are using AH, use the `ah` parameter. Follow this with the SPI value—this value is used to uniquely identify this data SA. For the number you specify here for the `outbound` parameter, the remote peer must configure the same number for the `inbound` parameter (this is also true for the keying material). The SPI value can range from 256 to 4,294,967,295. After the SPI value, you need to specify the hexadecimal key string, which can be up to 80 characters in length. Remember that this key must match the remote peer's configured key.

If you're using ESP, specify the `esp` parameter in the `set session-key` command. Again, remember that you need two commands—one for each unidirectional connection. Because ESP supports both encryption and authentication, you can specify two sets of keys. The `cipher` parameter is used to specify the encryption key and the `authenticator` parameter is used to specify the authentication (integrity validation) key.

Another required item in your crypto map is the specification of the traffic you wish to protect. The command with the `match address` parameter is used. Specify the crypto ACL that you created after this parameter. Likewise, you must also specify the transform set to use for protecting your data SAs. Use the sixth command, the one with the `set transform-set` parameter, to specify your transform sets. You can list up to six transform sets within a single priority number grouping in a crypto map—just separate them by a space on the command line.

The commands that I just discussed—the peer's identity, ISAKMP type, the crypto ACL, and the transform set—are *required* for a site-to-site connection. The rest of the commands in Listing 17-1 are optional. The command with the `set pfs` parameter specifies that PFS should be used when rebuilding an expired data SA—this says that DH should be used instead of the existing SA for sharing keying material. With this command, you have two parameters—`group1` and `group2`—that specify the DH key group to use. The `set security-association` command allows you to change the lifetime for the data SA associated with any peers that use this crypto map entry. This command allows you to override the globally configured timers. If you are using manual ISAKMP/IKE, you cannot configure SA lifetimes or PFS, because these are only used with dynamic ISAKMP/IKE.

Activating Your Crypto Map

Once you have created your crypto map, it must be applied to an interface on the PIX in order for the PIX to start protecting IPSec traffic:

```
pixfirewall(config)#  crypto map map_name interface interface_name
```

Typically, you activate your crypto map on the *outside* interface of your PIX. Of course, if you are using an interface like *cust1* to connect to a remote customer and want to use IPSec to connect to this customer, you would create a crypto map with the appropriate information, and activate this map on the *cust1* interface.

When the PIX sends traffic to a destination, it first examines its crypto map entries to determine if the traffic is to be protected or not. If the traffic is not supposed to be protected, the PIX forwards the traffic normally. If the traffic is to be protected, it uses the appropriate crypto map entry in order to build a secure SA to the remote peer.

When the PIX receives traffic it again compares this information to its crypto map entries. If the PIX does not find a match, the PIX forwards the traffic normally (based on its inbound ACL or conduits). Note that the traffic could be protected, or could be completely unprotected. If the PIX finds a match, however, it looks for a corresponding SA (using the SPI value) to verify the packet, decrypt it, or both. If the PIX doesn't find an existing SA for this traffic, it drops the packet. This is a security feature of the PIX: if the traffic is supposed to be protected, and it isn't, the PIX will not forward the packet into your network.

TIP If you modify a crypto map, you can either clear your existing data SAs to use the new information, or reapply the crypto map to the PIX's specified interface.

Verifying Your IKE Phase 2 Configuration

Now that you have applied your crypto map, you should check your configuration:

- `show access-list`   view your configured crypto ACLs
- `show crypto ipsec transform-set [tag transform_set_name]`   view your configured transform sets
- `show crypto map [interface interface_name|tag crypto_map_name]`   view your configured crypto maps
- `show crypto ipsec security-association lifetime`   view your PIX's SA lifetime expiration values

This example displays the crypto maps on your PIX:

```
pixfirewall#  show crypto map
Crypto Map: "pixmap" pic: outside local address: 201.201.201.1
Crypto Map "pixmap" 10 ipsec-isakmp
    Peer = 202.202.202.1
    access-list cryptoacl permit ip 172.16.0.0 255.255.0.0
                                    172.17.0.0 255.255.0.0
    Current peer: 201.201.201.1
    Security-association lifetime: 4608000 kilobytes/3600 seconds
    PFS (Y/N): N
    Transform set={DES-and-SHA, DES-and-MD5}
```

In this output, there is one crypto map named *pixmap*, and it is applied to the *outside* interface with an IP address of 201.201.201.1. There is one entry in the crypto map—priority 10—and it uses dynamic ISKAMP/IKE. The peer is 202.202.202.1, and the protected traffic is between the two private networks (172.16.0.0 and 172.17.0.0). The lifetime of the data SA has been changed to one hour and PFS is not to be used to rebuild expired SAs. Two transform sets can be used between this PIX and the remote peer—*DES-and-SHA* and *DES-and-MD5*.

Troubleshooting IPSec Connections

Once you have activated your crypto map on your PIX's interface, your PIX and any configured remote peers should establish IPSec SAs (assuming that there is user traffic that triggers the setup of the SAs). The following two sections can be used to examine and troubleshoot your IPSec SAs.

Viewing Your SAs

To view the management connections on your PIX that were built in IKE Phase 1, use the show isakmp sa command:

```
pixfirewall#  show isakmp sa
dst               src               state     pending   created
202.202.202.1  201.201.201.1  QM_IDLE   0         1
```

The state column lists the status of the management connection. Table 17-2 lists the states, the IKE modes that the state refers to, and the description of the connection state.

If you want to remove the management SAs and have the PIX rebuild them, use the clear [crypto] isakmp sa command—the crypto parameter is optional and has no affect on the actual result of the command.

Use the show crypto ipsec sa command to view the IKE Phase 2 data SAs:

```
pixfirewall#  show crypto ipsec sa
interface: outside
    Crypto map tag: mymap, local addr. 201.201.201.1
   local ident (addr/mask/prot/port): (201.201.201.1/255.255.255.255/0/0)
   remote ident (addr/mask/prot/port): (202.202.202.1/255.255.255.255/0/0)
   current_peer: 202.202.202.1
     PERMIT, flags={origin_is_acl,}
    #pkts encaps: 12, #pkts encrypt: 12, #pkts digest 12
    #pkts decaps: 12, #pkts decrypt: 12, #pkts verify 12
    #send errors 12, #recv errors 0

    local crypto endpt.: 201.201.201.1, remote crypto endpt.: 202.202.202.1
    path mtu 1500, media mtu 1500
    current outbound spi: 20890A6E

    inbound esp sas:
     spi: 0x257A1038(628756536)
       transform: esp-des esp-sha-hmac ,
       in use settings ={Tunnel, }
       slot: 0, conn id: 20, crypto map: mymap
       sa timing: remaining key lifetime (k/sec): (4607102/3562)
       IV size: 8 bytes
       replay detection support: Y
    inbound ah sas:
    outbound esp sas:
     spi: 0x20890A6E(545852014)
<--output omitted-->
```

In this example there is a crypto map called *mymap* that has been activated on the *outside* interface. There is one remote peer configured with a connection to it (202.202.202.1). You can see that some packets have been encapsulated and deencapsulated using IPSec, some packets have been encrypted and decrypted (ESP encryption), and some packets have had a digital signature attached to them and verified (ESP authentication). Below this

State	IKE mode	State Description
MM_NO_STATE	Main	Nothing has been negotiated yet.
MM_SA_SETUP	Main	The peers have negotiated the management parameters.
MM_KEY_EXCH	Main	The peers have exchanged keys using DH and have created the secret key.
MM_KEY_AUTH	Main	The IKE Phase 1 finished authentication and the process will move into quick mode.
AG_NO_STATE	Aggressive	Nothing has been negotiated yet.
AG_INIT_EXCH	Aggressive	The peers have negotiated the IKE Phase 1 parameters and have exchanged keys.
AG_AUTH	Aggressive	The IKE Phase 1 finished authentication and the process will move into quick mode.
QM_IDLE	Quick	IKE Phase 2 has completed.

Table 17-2. IKE/ISAKMP Status Options

section is a section that begins with *local crypto endpt*, which gives a brief overview of the data SA, including the outbound SPI value for identifying the connection. After this are the inbound ESP and AH and outbound ESP and AH information. In this example, the connection is using ESP SHA authentication and DES encryption in tunnel mode, but is not using AH.

There are some optional parameters to the show crypto ipsec sa command:

```
pixfirewall#  show crypto ipsec sa [map map_name|address|identity] [detail]
```

You can restrict the SAs listed by using the map parameter and giving it a crypto map name—this assumes that you have more than one interface with different crypto maps applied. The output of the display is sorted based on the interfaces of the PIX. The address parameter overrides the default sorting behavior, and sorts the information based on the source and destination address. The identity parameter sorts information based on the remote peer's identity. The detail parameter lists detailed information concerning the SAs.

If you want to remove your data SAs, use the clear crypto ipsec sa command. This command causes your PIX to remove all existing data SAs, which is necessary if you have made configuration changes that will affect the SA, and you want all SAs to use these new changes. You can also reapply the crypto map to the PIX's interface with the crypto map interface command. To delete a specific SA, use this command:

```
pixfirewall(config)#  clear [crypto] ipsec sa entry
peer's_IP_address IPSec_protocol SPI_number
```

You need to specify the peer's IP address, the IPSec protocol name (like ah or esp), and the SPI number of the connection. Remember that IPSec data connections are unidirectional; therefore, to completely delete a data SA, you need to use this clear command twice: once for the inbound connection and once for the outbound connection. To clear the statistical counters for a data SA, use the clear [crypto] ipsec sa counters command—the crypto parameter is optional and has no effect on the result of the command.

Debugging Your SAs

If you cannot determine your IPSec problem with the PIX's show commands, you can resort to using the following *Configuration*-mode debug commands:

- debug crypto isakmp [*level*]   troubleshoots ISAKMP/IKE connectivity issues
- debug crypto ipsec [*level*]   troubleshoots the IPSec process
- debug crypto ca [*level*]   troubleshoots CA authentication problems

If an IPSec connection is set up correctly, you should see the following message in the debut output: return status is IKMP_NO_ERROR.

With these debug commands, you can specify an optional *level* parameter, which affects how much information the PIX will show you. Here are the three levels that you can specify:

1. Events that are interesting (default; only important events)
2. Events that are interesting as well as normal events
3. Events that are interesting, normal, or inconsequential

To disable debugging, precede the debug command that you entered with the no parameter. Remember that debugging is process-intensive and will affect the performance of your PIX.

Example Pre-Shared Key Configuration

To help you understand the IPSec configuration using pre-shared keys, I'll use the network shown in Figure 17-2 and Listing 17-2 to build a site-to-site connection between PIX1 and PIX2.

```
Listing 17-2  PIX1(config)#  access-list PROTECT permit ip 172.16.0.0 255.255.0.0
                                        172.17.0.0 255.255.0.0
              PIX1(config)#  nat (inside) 0 access-list PROTECT
              PIX1(config)#
              PIX1(config)#  access-list IPSEC permit udp host 201.201.201.1
                                        host 202.202.202.1 eq isakmp
              PIX1(config)#  access-list IPSEC permit ah host 201.201.201.1
                                        host 202.202.202.1
              PIX1(config)#  access-list IPSEC permit esp host 201.201.201.1
                                        host 202.202.202.1
              PIX1(config)#  access-group IPSEC in interface outside
```

Listing 17-2
```
PIX1(config)#
PIX1(config)#   isakmp policy 10 authentication pre-share
PIX1(config)#   isakmp policy 10 encryption des
PIX1(config)#   isakmp policy 10 group 2
PIX1(config)#   isakmp policy 10 hash md5
PIX1(config)#   isakmp key PIXaccess address 202.202.202.1
PIX1(config)#
PIX1(config)#   crypto ipsec transform-set PIX2transform
                             esp-md5-hmac esp-des
PIX1(config)#   crypto map CRYTPO_MAP 10 ipsec-isakmp
PIX1(config)#   crypto map CRYPTO_MAP 10 set peer 202.202.202.1
PIX1(config)#   crypto map CRYPTO_MAP 10 match address PROTECT
PIX1(config)#   crypto map CRYPTO_MAP 10 set transform-set PIX2transform
PIX1(config)#   crypto map CRYTPO_MAP interface outside
```

This example only focuses on the IPSec configuration components. The *PROTECT* ACL is used for two purposes in this configuration—to specify which traffic is to be protected, and to disable NAT between 172.16.0.0/16 and 172.17.0.0/24. Remember

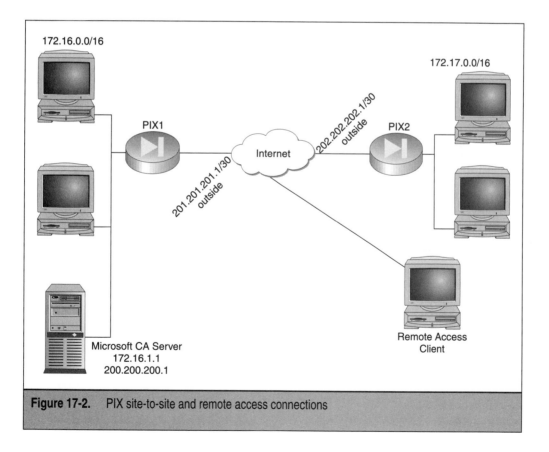

Figure 17-2.   PIX site-to-site and remote access connections

that Cisco recommends that you use two different ACLs for these functions. The *IPSEC* ACL is used to allow IPSec traffic destined to the PIX into the PIX.

The ISAKMP policies for IKE Phase 1 specifies that pre-shared keys, DES encryption, group 2 DH keys, and MD5 integrity checking should be used. The pre-shared key is *PIXaccess* (this needs to be configured exactly the same on PIX2). One transform set, *PIX2transform*, was created, with ESP authentication using MD5 and ESP encryption using DES. There is one crypto map, called *CRYPTO_MAP*, that specifies the data connection information. Dynamic ISAKMP/IKE is being used to the 202.202.202.1 peer, and the *PROTECT* ACL specifies the traffic to be protected. The transform set *PIX2transform* is to be used to secure the connection and the crypto map is applied to the *outside* interface. PIX2's configuration is similar to PIX1. The main difference is that the addressing in the crypto ACLs needs to be reversed.

Example CA Configuration

To help you understand using a CA for authentication, I'll use the network previously shown in Figure 17-2 to build a site-to-site connection between PIX1 and PIX2. This is basically the same setup, but I'll use a CA for authentication instead of pre-shared keys. In this example, I'm using an internal CA (Microsoft 2000's CA software). I'll just focus on the IPSec code in the configuration and only show PIX1's configuration (PIX2 is very similar).

Listing 17-3 shows the configuration for PIX1:

Listing 17-3
```
pixfirewall(config)#  hostname PIX1
PIX1(config)#  domain-name dealgroup.com
PIX1(config)#
PIX1(config)#  access-list PROTECT permit ip 172.16.0.0 255.255.0.0
                           172.17.0.0 255.255.0.0
PIX1(config)#  nat (inside) 0 access-list PROTECT
PIX1(config)#  nat (inside) 1 0 0
PIX1(config)#  global (outside) 1 200.200.200.10-200.200.200.254
PIX1(config)#  static (inside, outside) 200.200.200.1 172.16.1.1
                           netmask 255.255.255.255
PIX1(config)#
PIX1(config)#  access-list IPSEC permit udp host 201.201.201.1
                           host 202.202.202.1 eq isakmp
PIX1(config)#  access-list IPSEC permit ah host 201.201.201.1
                           host 202.202.202.1
PIX1(config)#  access-list IPSEC permit esp host 201.201.201.1
                           host 202.202.202.1
PIX1(config)#  access-list IPSEC permit tcp any host 200.200.200.1 eq 80
PIX1(config)#  access-group IPSEC in interface outside
PIX1(config)#
PIX1(config)#  ca generate rsa key 512
PIX1(config)#  ca identity caserver 172.16.1.1
```

```
                                   172.16.1.1:/certsrv/mscep/mscep.dll
PIX1(config)#  ca configure caserver ra 1 5 crloptional
PIX1(config)#  ca authenticate caserver
PIX1(config)#  ca enroll caserver mychallenge
PIX1(config)#  ca save all
PIX1(config)#
PIX1(config)#  isakmp policy 10 authentication rsa-sig
PIX1(config)#  isakmp policy 10 encryption des
PIX1(config)#  isakmp policy 10 group 2
PIX1(config)#  isakmp policy 10 hash md5
PIX1(config)#
PIX1(config)#  crypto ipsec transform-set PIX2transform
                                   esp-md5-hmac esp-des
PIX1(config)#  crypto map CRYTPO_MAP 10 ipsec-isakmp
PIX1(config)#  crypto map CRYPTO_MAP 10 set peer 202.202.202.1
PIX1(config)#  crypto map CRYPTO_MAP 10 match address PROTECT
PIX1(config)#  crypto map CRYPTO_MAP 10 set transform-set PIX2transform
PIX1(config)#  crypto map CRYTPO_MAP interface outside
```

In this configuration, the first thing that I did was assign a host and domain name. I then defined the crypto ACL, which specifies which traffic is to be protected. Even though 172.16.1.1 is included in the source address, it will be excluded from protection to non-172.17.0.0/16 addresses—this will allow the remote IPSec peers, like 202.202.202.1, to authenticate to the CA without any protection issues. Notice that the nat command disables NAT between 172.16.0.0/16 and 172.17.0.0/16, including the CA (but not for any other type of connection).

Following this is a static command for the CA server. Internally, the CA has an IP address of 172.16.1.1, but a global address of 200.200.200.1. There is an ACL applied to the *outside* interface that allows IPSec traffic as well as web (certificate) traffic to the CA.

After the ACL is the CA configuration. Notice that the CA server is called *caserver*, and also notice the URL location for the CA. Because the PIX is connected to the internal network, I used the private address (172.16.1.1). For PIX2, however, you would use the CA's global IP address. Within the ISAKMP policy, I changed the authentication type from pre-shared keys to RSA signatures; otherwise, the configuration is basically the same as the pre-shared key example in Listing 17-2.

REMOTE ACCESS CONNECTIONS

In the first part of the chapter, I discussed how you can use the PIX firewall for site-to-site connections. In addition to site-to-site IPSec connections, the PIX also supports remote access connections. The PIX can perform the function of a concentrator by terminating VPN connections from remote clients, as well as connecting to a concentrator as a remote client itself. The following sections cover both aspects of the PIX's remote access for VPNs. I've also included a handful of examples showing you some typical VPN connections used.

Dynamic Crypto Maps

The PIX uses *dynamic* crypto maps to handle incoming connections from remote access clients. Dynamic crypto maps are similar to normal crypto maps, or what I like to refer to as *static crypto maps*. With a static crypto map, you must manually specify all of your configuration and connection parameters, like the remote peer's IP address. This poses a problem with remote access clients, which, in many cases, dynamically acquire an IP address from their ISP. In this situation, a static crypto map will not suffice. Instead, dynamic crypto maps give you more flexibility in setting up your IPSec connections, including the ability to assign an IP address to the client for an IPSec tunnel connection.

Overview of Dynamic Crypto Maps

Dynamic crypto maps can only be used when a remote VPN client establishes a connection to the PIX—not vice versa. Dynamic crypto maps are very similar to static crypto maps. Of course, many of the items that you configured for static crypto maps are usually not configured in a dynamic crypto map. For instance, you typically don't know the IP address of the client or the traffic that is to be protected until the client initiates the connection.

Basically, a dynamic crypto map is a template with some things that are defined and some things that will be discovered when the client connects to the PIX. This allows remote access clients to connect and allow the PIX to learn the necessary connection components, yet still gives you control over important items of the connection, like the method of authentication and the security parameters (AH and ESP).

A dynamic crypto map is actually a separate crypto map embedded within a static crypto map. You need to create a static crypto map and place a reference in the static crypto map pointing to the dynamic crypto map entries to use. Because a dynamic crypto map doesn't define all of the connection parameters, which makes it less secure than a static crypto map entry that does, you should always place the reference for the dynamic crypto map at the *end* of a static crypto map—in other words, you assign this entry the highest crypto map sequence number. You want site-to-site connections to use the specified connection parameters, like the crypto ACL that specifies what traffic is to be protected. To do this, these crypto map entries must appear before a dynamic entry, because a dynamic entry doesn't define these. If you place a dynamic entry before a static entry, *all* traffic to and from the remote peer in a site-to-site connection would be protected, which would probably cause connection problems.

Just like static crypto maps, dynamic crypto maps are a group of crypto map entries that are grouped together by a sequence number. When you set up a dynamic crypto map, the only required configuration command is the `transform-set` command. As I mentioned earlier in this chapter, this command specifies the transform sets to use in the IKE Phase 2 negotiation to set up a secure data SA. Remember that if a match is not found in a crypto map during the negotiation, a data SA will not form. Once a connection is established with the remote peer, the items that you did not specify in the dynamic crypto map will be negotiated and filled in by the two peers to create the data SA. Basically, the PIX creates a temporary crypto map entry for the SA, which it removes when the SA expires.

Creating Dynamic Crypto Maps

Creating a dynamic crypto map is very similar to creating a static crypto map. You go through two steps in configuring dynamic crypto maps:

1. Create the dynamic crypto map
2. Place it as the last entry in a static crypto map

Listing 17-4 shows the commands to create a dynamic crypto map:

Listing 17-4
```
pixfirewall(config)# crypto dynamic-map map_name sequence_number
                         set transform-set transform_set_name(s)
pixfirewall(config)# crypto dynamic-map map_name sequence_number
                         match address ACL_name
pixfirewall(config)# crypto dynamic-map map_name sequence_number
                         set security-association lifetime
                         seconds seconds|kilobytes kilobytes
pixfirewall(config)# crypto dynamic-map map_name sequence_number
                         set pfs group1|group2
pixfirewall(config)# crypto dynamic-map map_name sequence_number
                         set peer hostname|IP_address
```

Notice that all dynamic crypto map commands begin with `crypto dynamic-map`. This is followed by the name of the dynamic crypto map—this name must be unique among all dynamic *and* static crypto maps. The name is followed by a sequence number. The sequence number performs the same function as in a static map—it is used to group statements together and to separate the different remote access policy groupings. The lower the sequence number, the higher the priority.

The first command in Listing 17-4, the one with the `set transform-set` parameter, specifies the transform set or sets to use in the IKE Phase 2 negotiation. You can specify up to six transform names, each separated by a space. This is the only command that is required within a dynamic crypto map.

The second command in allows you to specify the traffic to be protected with the `match address` parameter. Normally, you would not specify what traffic to protect because you wouldn't necessarily know the traffic to be protected until the peer makes the connection. If you omit this parameter, all traffic to and from the remote peer is expected to be protected.

The `set security-association lifetime` is also optional—if you omit this command, the PIX uses the globally configured values for the data SA. Likewise, if you omit the `set pfs` command, DH will not be used when renegotiating an expired data SA. Normally you would not specify the peer's identity with the `set peer` command, since the peer will acquire its address via DHCP or PPP; but you do have this option within the dynamic crypto map.

You can view your newly created dynamic crypto map with the `show crypto dynamic-map` command. This command displays all the dynamic crypto maps on your PIX. You can display a specific map by adding the `tag` parameter to the previous command and follow this with the name of the dynamic crypto map.

Once you have created your dynamic crypto map, you must add it as an entry in a static crypto map. Use the following command to do this:

```
pixfirewall(config)#  crypto map static_map_name sequence-number
                               ipsec-isakmp dynamic dynamic_crypto_map_name
```

You must put the dynamic entry as the last (highest sequence number) entry in the static map. You must also use dynamic ISAKMP/IKE with a dynamic crypto map. With this command, you just need to put the name of the dynamic crypto map after the `dynamic` parameter.

 SECURITY ALERT!   Always assign a dynamic crypto map entry the highest sequence number for a priority (making it the last entry) because a dynamic crypto map does not define all of the connection parameters.

Dynamic Crypto Map Example

To help you understand how to set up your PIX to handle incoming remote access connections, I'll use the network previously shown in Figure 17-2. This is the same PIX shown in the last example with a site-to-site CA configuration. I'll assume that a CA is used for authentication, and that these commands have already been configured on PIX1. I'll concentrate on only the remote access commands. Listing 17-5 shows the configuration:

```
Listing 17-5  PIX1(config)#  isakmp policy 10 authentication rsa-sig
              PIX1(config)#  isakmp policy 10 encryption des
              PIX1(config)#  isakmp policy 10 group 2
              PIX1(config)#  isakmp policy 10 hash md5
              PIX1(config)#
              PIX1(config)#  crypto ipsec transform-set PIX2transform
                                     esp-md5-hmac esp-des
              PIX1(config)#  crypto ipsec transform-set remoteaccess
                                     esp-sha-hmac esp-des
              PIX1(config)#  crypto ipsec transform-set remoteaccess mode transport
              PIX1(config)#  crypto dynamic-map DYN_MAP 10
                                     set transform-set remoteaccess
              PIX1(config)#  crypto map CRYTPO_MAP 10 ipsec-isakmp
              PIX1(config)#  crypto map CRYPTO_MAP 10 set peer 202.202.202.1
              PIX1(config)#  crypto map CRYPTO_MAP 10 match address PROTECT
              PIX1(config)#  crypto map CRYPTO_MAP 10 set transform-set PIX2transform
              PIX1(config)#  crypto map CRYPTO_MAP 99 ipsec-isakmp dynamic DYN_MAP
              PIX1(config)#  crypto map CRYTPO_MAP interface outside
```

In this example, as I mentioned, I am assuming that the PIX will be using a CA for authentication, as is shown with the first `isakmp policy` command (I've omitted the commands for the CA configuration). There is one entry in the dynamic crypto map called *DYN_MAP*. This entry specifies that the transform set called *remoteaccess* is to be used. This transform specifies that ESP SHA should be used for authentication and DES for encryption. Also, the ESP mode is transport, indicating that the real IP address of the client will be used for the connection parameters. Notice that the static crypto map called *CRYPTO_MAP* has two sets of entries. Entry 10 was used for the site-to-site connection and 99, which is at the bottom, specifies the use of the dynamic crypto map. These entries allow the PIX to handle both the site-to-site and remote access connections. And of course, you also need to activate the static crypto map on the PIX's external interface. As you can see from this example, the configuration is not too different from setting up a site-to-site connection.

Assigning IP Addresses to Remote Peers

The previous section on dynamic crypto maps is actually the basis of building remote access connections. You'll typically have to set up other information, though, when setting up a remote access connection. For instance, in the previous example, the client was in ESP transport mode. One problem with this is that from devices on the internal side of the PIX, it is obvious that the remote client is external to the network.

You can, however, simulate a site-to-site connection to a stand-alone remote client. Cisco calls this process *IKE Mode Config*—by using IKE Mode Config, you can make the remote access client appear as an internal client to the internal devices behind your PIX firewall. This process is accomplished by using ESP tunnel mode to the client and having the PIX assign an internal IP address that the client will use inside the tunnel.

Understanding IKE Mode Config

IKE Mode Config allows your PIX firewall to assign an IP address to a remote access client that it will use within an ESP tunnel. Figure 17-3 shows a generic example of IKE Mode Config. In this example, an ESP tunnel exists between the PIX and the remote access client. When IPSEC IP packets are sent from the client to the PIX, the client first creates an IP packet with a source address of 172.16.254.1 (assigned by the PIX) and a destination address of 172.16.0.0/16 (internal network resource). The client then encapsulates this IP packet in an ESP segment, and then within an IP packet, where this second, external IP packet has a source address of 64.1.1.1 and a destination address of 201.201.201.1. When the PIX receives this packet, it authenticates it, decrypts it, and forwards the encapsulated packet with the private addresses to the appropriate internal client. From the internal resource's perspective, the received packet looks like the source is part of the internal network, which is obviously not true. IKE Mode Config allows you to make a logical network extension between the remote access clients and the internal network by using ESP tunnel mode.

There are actually two different types of IKE Mode Config that the PIX implements:

- **Client initiation** In this mode, the client initiates the IKE Mode Config and the PIX assigns the IP address, from a pool, to the remote client.

- **Gateway initiation** In this mode, the PIX initiates the IKE Mode Config—no address is given to the client, but any packets received by the client have the source address changed to make it appear that the client is a logical extension of the internal network.

NOTE If you are using IKE Mode Config on your PIX firewall, and the firewall is connected to a router, which, in turn, is connected to your ISP, your intermediate router must also support IKE Mode Config. Otherwise, you may experience connection problems. Cisco routers with IOS 12.0(7)T and later support this.

Configuring IKE Mode Config

This section focuses on the configuration of IKE Mode Config. There are three configuration steps that you have to perform, above and beyond the normal IPSec configuration, to set up IKE Mode Config:

- Create an IP address pool that the PIX will use to assign addresses.
- Have IKE reference this pool.
- Specify which crypto map the PIX should use to assign addresses to the client.

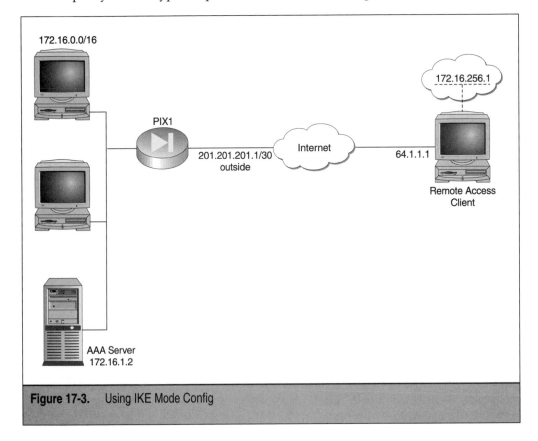

Figure 17-3. Using IKE Mode Config

Required Commands The first thing that you should do is create an address pool that your PIX can use to assign IP addresses to the clients. Here is the syntax of this command:

```
pixfirewall(config)#  ip local pool pool_name
                          beginning_address[-ending_address]
```

You must assign a unique pool name to the address pool. You must then specify a beginning address. Optionally you can specify a dash followed by an ending address—if you omit this, there is only one address in the pool. If a client requests an address and there are no more addresses in the pool, you will see the following message: %PIX-4-404101: ISAKMP: Failed to allocate address for client from pool "poolname". If you see this message, you need to add more addresses to your PIX's pool.

To view your address pool, use the show ip local pool command—you can optionally add the pool name at the end of this command to view a single address pool. This command displays the addresses assigned as well as those available to clients.

Once you have created your address pool, you must reference it in your ISAKMP configuration by using the command:

```
pixfirewall(config)#  isakmp client configuration address-pool
                          local pool_name [interface_name]
```

Notice that this command does not reference a specific ISAKMP policy grouping, but instead is for the PIX itself. The name that you specified in the ip local pool command must be listed here. You can limit which interface the pool can be used on by listing one of the PIX's interface names—if you omit this, it defaults to whatever interfaces ISAKMP is enabled on.

The last required command is to place an entry in your crypto map that will have the PIX assign addresses to the clients. Use the command shown here to do this:

```
pixfirewall(config)#  crypto map map_name client configuration
                          address initiate|respond
```

The initiate parameter has the PIX try to set an IP address for each peer (gateway initiation), and the respond parameter has the PIX accept IP address requests from any requesting remote access client (client initiation).

Optional Commands There are two optional commands that you can configure for IKE Mode Config. One of the problems with the previous setup is the assumption that all peers are remote access clients. Of course, you might have a mixture of remote access clients and site-to-site connections on your PIX. In this situation, you don't need to assign an IP address to the peer at the other end of the site-to-site connection. Actually, if your PIX attempts to do this, the site-to-site connection might not be able to be established.

Therefore, you will want to make exceptions to assigning addresses to the site-to-site peers. Cisco allows you to do this with the following two commands in Listing 17-6:

Listing 17-6
```
pixfirewall(config)#  isakmp key key_string address IP_address
                           [netmask netmask]
                           no-config-mode
pixfirewall(config)#  isakmp peer fqdn FQDN no-config-mode
```

The first command, isakmp key, is used to make exceptions to clients that will be using pre-shared keys for authentication. I discussed the use of this command previously in the site-to-site section—the only difference is the no-config-mode parameter, which disables IKE Mode Config for the peers that use this pre-shared key. The second command disables IKE Mode Config for the specified peers using RSA signatures (CAs) for authentication. You must list the fully-qualified domain name of each peer that you are making exceptions for.

IKE Mode Config Example

To help illustrate how to assign IP addresses to remote access clients, I'll use the network shown previously in Figure 17-3. Listing 17-7 shows an excerpt of the configuration to set up the assignment of addresses to remote access clients:

Listing 17-7
```
PIX1(config)#  access-list IPSEC permit udp any host 201.201.201.1 eq isakmp
PIX1(config)#  access-list IPSEC permit ah any host 201.201.201.1
PIX1(config)#  access-list IPSEC permit esp any host 201.201.201.1
PIX1(config)#  access-group IPSEC in interface outside
PIX1(config)#
PIX1(config)#  access-list NONAT ip 172.16.0.0 255.255.0.0
                             172.16.254.0 255.255.255.0
PIX1(config)#  nat (inside) 0 access-list NONAT
PIX1(config)#
PIX1(config)#  ip local pool remotePCs 172.16.254.1-172.16.254.254
PIX1(config)#  crypto isakmp client configuration address-pool local
                           remotePCs outside
PIX1(config)#
PIX1(config)#  isakmp policy 10 authentication rsa-sig
PIX1(config)#  isakmp policy 10 encryption des
PIX1(config)#  isakmp policy 10 group 2
PIX1(config)#  isakmp policy 10 hash md5
PIX1(config)#
PIX1(config)#  crypto ipsec transform-set remoteaccess
                             esp-sha-hmac esp-des
PIX1(config)#
PIX1(config)#  crypto dynamic-map DYN_MAP 10
                             set transform-set remoteaccess
PIX1(config)#
PIX1(config)#  crypto map CRYPTO_MAP client configuration address initiate
PIX1(config)#  crypto map CRYPTO_MAP client configuration address respond
PIX1(config)#  crypto map CRYPTO_MAP 99 ipsec-isakmp dynamic DYN_MAP
PIX1(config)#  crypto map CRYTPO_MAP interface outside
```

The first part of the example is an ACL that allows IPSec traffic into the PIX—notice that I used the keyword any as the source, because the source is typically unknown in remote access situations. After this, I disabled NAT for traffic traversing the IPSec tunnel. The ip local pool command specifies the range of addresses to assign the clients and the crypto isakmp client command specifies the IP address pool. Below this I have the ISAKMP policies. In this example, I am assuming that only remote access connections are terminated on the PIX—not a mixture of remote access and site-to-site. I've created a dynamic crypto map called *DYN_MAP* for the remote access transform sets and enabled both IKE Mode Config modes—client and gateway—with the configuration address parameters. I have one entry in the static crypto map, referencing the dynamic map. Finally, I enabled the static crypto map on the *outside* interface of the PIX. If this network also had site-to-site connections, you would want to exclude them from dynamic address assignment by using the commands in Listing 17-6.

User Authentication with XAUTH

The last section discussed how to assign addresses to remote clients. Another problem with remote access is authentication. The methods that I described previously—pre-shared keys and RSA signatures—only provide device authentication. If someone else uses the device instead of the intended user, they have the same access privileges to your internal network via IPSec. You can use Extended Authentication, an enhancement to IPSec authentication, to deal with this issue. Extended Authentication, often referred to as *XAUTH*, provides user-level authentication by prompting the user to give both a user name and password in addition to the device-level authentication of pre-shared keys or RSA signatures. XAUTH is even compatible with token card servers. Actually, this process is transparent to XAUTH—the AAA server passes the PIN entered by the user (as the password) and forwards it to the token card server for authentication.

Using AAA for Authentication

When PIX firewalls employ XAUTH for VPNs, the firewalls cannot handle the actual user authentication themselves. Instead, the PIX firewall has to pass off the username and password to an AAA security server, which performs the authentication and sends the results back to the PIX. The PIX, as I mentioned in Chapter 11, can use the TACACS+ and RADIUS security protocols to secure the transmission of user information to the AAA server. XAUTH is actually performed before IKE Mode Config, which I discussed in the last section. If XAUTH fails, an SA does not form to the destination remote access client.

Many VPN clients support XAUTH, including Cisco client products. Cisco recommends that you use their client products, shown here, when connecting to a PIX firewall:

- Cisco Secure VPN Client version 1.1
- Cisco VPN 3000 Client version 2.5/2.6
- Cisco VPN 3000 Client version 3.*x*

Of the three clients, Cisco recommends that you use their newest client software, Cisco VPN 3000 Client version 3.*x*, if you're using XAUTH to connect to your PIX firewalls. Note that you do not have to use Cisco VPN clients for remote access connections—other IPSec-compliant client are supported, including Microsoft's 2000 VPN client software.

XAUTH is not a required component, but does add an additional layer of authentication and security to your network. When you use XAUTH you will need to configure your `aaa-server` commands, which I discussed in Chapter 11.

Configuring XAUTH

When you choose to use XAUTH for an additional layer of authentication, you need to complete the following steps:

- Set up your AAA commands.
- Specify XAUTH client authentication in your crypto map.

If you have a combination of remote access and site-to-site connections, you will also need to disable XAUTH for the site-to-site connections. The following two sections cover the necessary commands for enabling or disabling XAUTH.

Required Commands   The first thing you need to do is set up your AAA configuration. You will need to specify the AAA security protocol that you'll be using (TACACS+ or RADIUS) and the security server or servers that your PIX will use for XAUTH authentication:

```
pixfirewall(config)# aaa-server group_tag protocol tacacs+|radius
pixfirewall(config)# aaa-server group_tag (interface_name)
                          host AAA_server_IP_address AAA_key
                     [timeout value_in_seconds]
```

I covered these commands in Chapter 11—the first command specifies the security protocol, and the second command specifies the AAA server and security key. The *group_tag* value ties these commands together.

After you have set up your AAA configuration, you are now ready to add XAUTH authentication to your crypto map setup. Use the `crypto map` command to accomplish this:

```
pixfirewall(config)# crypto map map_name client authentication group_tag
```

The *group_tag* value that you specify in this command refers to the AAA configuration that the PIX should use when performing user authentication.

Optional Commands   As you can see from the previous section, adding user authentication to your IPSec setup is a simple process. However, one important item to point out is that with the `client authentication` parameter in the `crypto map` command, any IPSec peer that uses this crypto map will have to perform user authentication. Normally, you will

only use XAUTH for remote access authentication. However, the previous command forces
the PIX to perform user authentication for any IPSec connection—remote access and
site-to-site. In most instances, you will want to disable XAUTH for site-to-site connections.

To disable XAUTH for site-to-site connections, use one of these two commands:

```
pixfirewall(config)#  isakmp key key_string address IP_address
                            [netmask netmask] no-xauth
pixfirewall(config)#  isakmp peer fqdn FQDN no-xauth
```

These are the same commands I covered in Code Listing 17-7 for IKE Mode
Config—the only difference is the `no-xauth` parameter. You can disable IKE Mode
Config and XAUTH in the same command by specifying both the `no-xauth` and
`no-config-mode` parameters. The first command disables XAUTH for site-to-site
connections that use pre-shared keys, and the second command disables XAUTH for
site-to-site connections that use RSA signatures.

XAUTH Example

To help illustrate how to use XAUTH to provide user authentication for remote access
clients, I'll use the network shown previously in Figure 17-3. I'll build upon Code
Listing 17-7, which assigned an IP address to the remote access client. I'll assume that
the AAA server is using TACACS+. Here is a listing that shows just the code necessary
for XAUTH (see Listing 17-7 for the remainder of the configuration).

```
PIX1(config)#  aaa-server SECURITY protocol tacacs+
PIX1(config)#  aaa-server SECURITY (inside) host 172.16.1.2 secretkey
PIX1(config)#  crypto map CYRPTO_MAP client authentication SECURITY
```

The first two commands show the security connection to the AAA server (172.16.1.2).
The `crypto map` command specifies that XAUTH authentication will take place via the
172.16.1.2 AAA server. If this network also had site-to-site connections, you would want
to exclude them from XAUTH authentication by using the `isakmp key` or `isakmp peer`
commands by specifying the `no-xauth` parameter.

Cisco VPN 3000 Client Configuration

If your remote access clients use the Cisco Secure VPN 1.*x* software for IPSec, you can
use the previous remote access configurations to set up your remote access connection.
However, if your remote access clients are using the Cisco VPN 3000 2.5, 2.6, or 3.*x*
software, there are some additional commands that you need to configure for the client
to successfully build an IPSec connection to your PIX. These Cisco clients support both
IKE Mode Config as well as XAUTH. However, you can also have your PIX firewall
download additional configuration information to these Cisco clients, including the
domain name of the client, the DNS and WINS server addresses, the split tunnel mode
attributes, and many other items.

Split tunnel mode determines which traffic should and shouldn't be protected
between the client and the PIX. This allows you to protect traffic between the client and

networks behind your PIX, but to not protect traffic between the client and other Internet sites. This ability allows the remote access client to access other Internet sites directly without having to use the IPSec tunnel to send all traffic to your corporate site, before forwarding it out to the Internet.

Configuring the VPN 3000 Client Parameters

All of the 3000 Client commands begin with vpngroup. The vpngroup commands are shown in Listing 17-8:

Listing 17-8
```
pixfirewall(config)#  vpngroup group_name password pre_shared_key
pixfirewall(config)#  vpngroup group_name address-pool address_pool_name
pixfirewall(config)#  vpngroup group_name default-domain domain_name
pixfirewall(config)#  vpngroup group_name dns-server primary_DNS_server
                          [secondary_DNS_server]
pixfirewall(config)#  vpngroup group_name split-dns domain_name_1
                          [domain_name_2...domain_name_8]
pixfirewall(config)#  vpngroup group_name wins-server primary_WINS_server
                          [secondary_WINS_server]
pixfirewall(config)#  vpngroup group_name split-tunnel ACL_name
pixfirewall(config)#  vpngroup group_name pfs
pixfirewall(config)#  vpngroup group_name idle-time seconds
pixfirewall(config)#  vpngroup group_name max-time seconds
```

The group_name parameter is something that the 3000 clients also configure on their desktop and is sent to the PIX so that the PIX knows what group parameters to assign to the client. This gives you the ability to separate your remote access clients into different groups, with different access configurations and privileges. Each group has an assigned password, which is configured with the password parameter. If you are only setting up one group, Cisco recommends that you don't assign a password to this group; however, you should assign passwords if you have multiple groups. The group name can be up to 63 characters in length. You can configure a group called *default*, which allows you to create a default group policy configuration. The PIX will use this if there is not a policy match for another group. When you save your configuration, the PIX will display-protect the password from view by showing the password as a bunch of asterisks (*******).

You have two methods of assigning addresses to the 3000 clients: IKE Mode Config or the vpngroup address-pool command. If you are only using one set of IP addresses for all of your remote access clients, use the IKE Mode Config method. One limitation of this method is that you can only have one address pool. If you want to have different address pools for different groups of people, use the vpngroup address-pool parameter. You must create your address pool with the ip local pool command discussed previously.

To assign a domain name, use the default-domain parameter. You can assign two DNS server addresses with the dns-server parameter and two WINS server addresses with the wins-server parameter. The split-dns parameter specifies the IP addresses of split DNS servers. Split DNS is used when you need to have queries for internal names to be handled by one DNS server (primary DNS server) and queries for external names to be handled by a different server (secondary servers)—you can specify one primary and up to seven secondary servers.

The `split-tunnel` parameter sets up split tunneling on the client. Split tunneling allows you to specify what traffic between the PIX and the client should be protected, and what traffic shouldn't be protected. The traffic that is to be protected is specified by `permit` statements in an ACL, which is referenced in the `vpngroup split-tunnel` command. If you do not configure this command, the PIX assumes that all traffic from the client should be protected and sent to the PIX.

The `pfs` parameter specifies that the client should use PFS when rebuilding an expired connection. The `idle-time` parameter specifies the amount of idle time, in seconds, the VPN connection is allowed before the PIX tears it down. This defaults to 1800 seconds (30 minutes) if you omit it. The `max-time` parameter allows you to limit the amount of time a client is allowed to connect to the PIX. Once this time limit is reached, the PIX tears down the connection and forces the client to reestablish it. The default for this parameter is no time limit. The `idle-time` and `max-time` parameters take precedence over the global or crypto map timeout values: the `isakmp policy lifetime` and `crypto map set security-association lifetime` commands.

VPN 3000 Client Example

To help you understand the configuration for the Cisco VPN 3000 series clients, I'll use the network diagram shown in Figure 17-4.

I'll assume that the remote access client is running version 3.5 of the Cisco VPN 3000 client software. This example uses XAUTH and TACACS+ authentication. Listing 17-9 shows an excerpt of the PIX1's configuration:

Listing 17-9
```
PIX1(config)#  access-list IPSEC permit udp any host 201.201.201.1 eq isakmp
PIX1(config)#  access-list IPSEC permit ah any host 201.201.201.1
PIX1(config)#  access-list IPSEC permit esp any host 201.201.201.1
PIX1(config)#  access-group IPSEC in interface outside
PIX1(config)#
PIX1(config)#  access-list NONAT permit ip 172.16.0.0 255.255.0.0
                           172.16.254.0 255.255.255.0
PIX1(config)#  nat (inside) 0 access-list NONAT
PIX1(config)#
PIX1(config)#  ip local pool ADDRESS 172.16.254.1-172.16.254.254
PIX1(config)#  vpngroup USERS password SeCrEt
PIX1(config)#  vpngroup USERS address-pool ADDRESS
PIX1(config)#  vpngroup USERS default-domain dealgroup.com
PIX1(config)#  vpngroup USERS dns-server 172.16.1.3
PIX1(config)#  vpngroup USERS wins-server 172.16.1.4
PIX1(config)#
PIX1(config)#  isakmp policy 10 authentication rsa-sig
PIX1(config)#  isakmp policy 10 encryption 3des
PIX1(config)#  isakmp policy 10 group 2
PIX1(config)#  isakmp policy 10 hash sha
PIX1(config)#
```

Listing 17-9
```
PIX1(config)#  crypto ipsec transform-set remoteaccess
esp-sha-hmac esp-3des
PIX1(config)#  crypto dynamic-map DYN_MAP 10
                        set transform-set remoteaccess
PIX1(config)#
PIX1(config)#  aaa-server SECURITY protocol tacacs+
PIX1(config)#  aaa-server SECURITY (inside) host 172.16.1.2 secretkey
PIX1(config)#
PIX1(config)#  crypto map CRYPTO_MAP client authentication SECURITY
PIX1(config)#  crypto map CRYPTO_MAP 99 ipsec-isakmp dynamic DYN_MAP
PIX1(config)#  crypto map CRYTPO_MAP interface outside
```

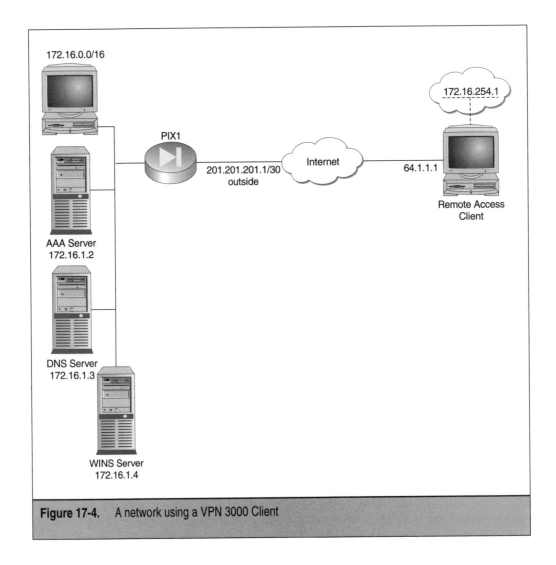

Figure 17-4. A network using a VPN 3000 Client

In this example, I'm assuming that the CA configuration for RSA signatures has already been performed. I first allowed IPSec traffic into the PIX with the *IPSEC* ACL. I then created an address pool for the remote access clients called *ADDRESS*. After this I entered my `vpngroup` commands for the VPN 3000 clients.

There are a few things I would like to point out. First, because I didn't specify split tunneling, all traffic from the client must be sent to the PIX. Second, because the traffic to 172.16.0.0/16 is to be protected, I used the private addresses when assigning the DNS and WINS server, since the client will tunnel these queries. This is followed by the transform set and dynamic crypto map entry. The AAA configuration for XAUTH is configured with the `aaa-server` commands and the `crypto map client authentication` command. And last, a static crypto map entry is created referencing the dynamic map, and the static map is activated on the PIX's outside interface.

As you can see from this example, the configuration tasks for the VPN 3000 clients are in addition to the features I mentioned earlier in this chapter, like dynamic crypto maps and XAUTH. The only new thing in this configuration is the `vpngroup` commands.

The PIX as a Remote Access Client

Cisco has developed a remote access solution called *Easy VPN*. Actually, this is a new name for an old technology, which was developed for the Cisco VPN 3000 and 5000 concentrators and the Cisco VPN client. Easy VPN is broken into two components: *Easy VPN Server* and *Client*. Easy VPN Server is responsible for terminating the client connections—Cisco VPN 3000 and 5000 concentrators, Cisco routers, and PIX firewalls support the Server function. The Client function is used as a remote access connection to the Server. Clients include the Cisco VPN software client, 3002 hardware client, Cisco routers, and PIX firewalls.

With the introduction of FOS 6.2, the PIX can function as a remote access client, sometimes referred to as a *hardware client*. A hardware client is different from a software client in that a software client typically protects traffic from a single machine, whereas a hardware client protects traffic from more than one machine. A hardware client would seem like a VPN concentrator like a VPN 3000; however, as a hardware client, the VPN functions of the PIX are limited. Typically, only lower-end PIXs, like the 501, 506, and 506E, would be configured as remote access clients.

Connectivity and Modes

Before you can begin your configuration, you need to determine two things: how your remote access PIX will acquire its IP address, and what mode of connectivity the PIX will use when accessing a VPN concentrator, like the VPN 3000, a Cisco IOS-based router, or another PIX firewall in server mode. There are three ways that a PIX can acquire its IP address: static IP address, DHCP client, or PPPoE client.

One of the problems of using dynamic addresses is that you cannot use a site-to-site connection with static crypto maps—a static crypto map requires you to specify the IP address of the remote peer. To overcome this, you can use dynamic crypto maps. However, dynamic crypto maps provide less scalability than static maps. As a remote access client, though, the PIX provides an advantage over dynamic crypto maps: it can perform XAUTH for user authentication, providing an additional layer of authentication, as well as defining exactly what traffic is to be protected, and other connection parameters.

Once you have determined how your PIX will acquire an IP address, you need to determine the mode of connectivity for the VPN connection. There are two modes of connectivity to choose from: *client* and *network extension* mode. Client mode has the PIX use NAT or PAT on the devices on in its internal interfaces when sending traffic to a VPN Server (which could be another PIX). In this mode, the PIX must act as a DHCP server on the inside interface and assign IP addressing information to the internal clients. The IPSec connections are built on-demand to the VPN Server.

Network extension mode, unlike client mode, does not apply NAT or PAT to any of the internal addresses. Instead, the internal devices are seen as an extension of the network where the VPN Server is located. One advantage of this mode is that the PIX client sets up and maintains the single IPSec connection to the VPN concentrator. In client mode, an IPSec connection is brought up when a client wants to communicate; and if you are using NAT, your PIX will have to handle multiple IPSec connections to the VPN Server.

Configuring the PIX as a Remote Access Client

When you set up the PIX as a remote access client, you have to use the vpnclient commands. If you are using network extension mode, you also have to set up your PIX as a DHCP server for your internal clients by using the dhcpd commands.

Listing 17-10 shows the commands to set up the PIX as a remote access client:

Listing 17-10
```
pixfirewall(config)#   vpnclient vpngroup group_name
                                 password group_key
pixfirewall(config)#   vpnclient username xauth_username
                                 password xauth_password
pixfirewall(config)#   vpnclient server primary_IP [secondary_IP]
pixfirewall(config)#   vpnclient mode client-mode|network-extension-mode
pixfirewall(config)#   vpnclient enable
pixfirewall(config)#   show vpnclient
```

The vpngroup parameter assigns the VPN group and group key to use for client access—this helps the VPN concentrator (remote IPSec device) determine what security parameters to use to secure the connection, as well as the pre-shared key to protect the connection. The group name can be up to 63 characters in length. The username parameter assigns the username and password used by XAUTH. Both of these parameters can be up to 127 characters in length. The server parameter assigns the IP address of the VPN concentrator—you can list a primary and secondary address. The mode parameter assigns the connection mode: client or network extension. If you are using network extension mode, you need to configure the PIX as a DHCP server on its internal interface where the internal clients are located. Finally, you must enable the remote access client on the PIX with the vpnclient enable command. To verify your configuration, use the show vpnclient command. If you want to remove all of your VPN Client commands from your PIX, use the clear vpnclient command.

PIX Client Configuration Example

To help you understand the remote access client configuration of a PIX, I'll use the network shown in Figure 17-5. In this example, I'll assume that the PIX is using a statically assigned IP address on its *outside* interface and that the connection mode is network extension.

Listing 17-11 shows the remote access client commands to set up this IPSec connection:

```
Listing 17-11  PIX1(config)#  dhcpd address 172.16.254.10-172.16.254.254 inside
               PIX1(config)#  dhcpd domain quizware.com
               PIX1(config)#  dhcpd lease 3600
               PIX1(config)#  dhcpd ping_timeout 750
               PIX1(config)#  dhcpd enable inside
               PIX1(config)#
               PIX1(config)#  vpnclient vpngroup remotegroup password secretkey
               PIX1(config)#  vpnclient username pix1 password letmein
               PIX1(config)#  vpnclient server 202.202.202.1
               PIX1(config)#  vpnclient mode network-extension-mode
               PIX1(config)#  vpnclient enable
```

In this example, the first part of the configuration deals with the DHCP server commands. The two required commands are the dhcpd address command, which assigns the address pool for the internal clients, and the dhcpd enable command, which enables the DHCP server on the *inside* interface. The other dhcpd commands are optional.

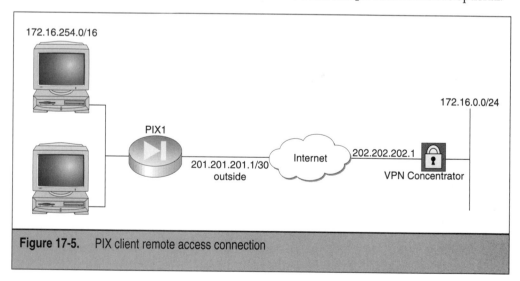

Figure 17-5. PIX client remote access connection

NOTE Because of space constraints, I have omitted L2TP and PPTP connectivity for the PIX. However, I have an excellent explanation and example configurations for both of these protocols and their configuration on a PIX. Please visit my web site at http://home.cfl.rr.com/dealgroup/ for more information.

FURTHER STUDY

Web Sites

For information on configuring site-to-site IPSec connections on a PIX firewall, visit: www.cisco.com/univercd/cc/td/doc/product/iaabu/pix/pix_62/config/ipsecint.htm.

For some simple examples of PIX site-to-site connections, visit: www.cisco.com/univercd/cc/td/doc/product/iaabu/pix/pix_62/config/sit2site.htm.

For information on L2TP, examine RFC 2888 at www.faqs.org/rfcs/ rfc2888.html.

For an example of configuring L2TP on a PIX firewall, visit: www.cisco.com/warp/public/110/l2tp-ipsec.html.

For information on PPTP, examine RFC 2637 at www.ietf.org/rfc/rfc2637.txt.

For an example of configuring PPTP on a PIX firewall, visit: www.cisco.com/warp/public/110/pptpcrypto3.html and www.cisco.com/warp/public/110/ pix_pptp.html.

For information on the PIX to accept remote access connections, visit: www.cisco.com/univercd/cc/td/doc/product/iaabu/pix/pix_62/config/basclnt.htm.

To set up your PIX as an Easy VPN Client, visit: www.cisco.com/univercd/cc/td/doc/product/iaabu/pix/pix_62/config/pixclnt.htm.

For an example of configuring a PIX as a VPN Client in network extension mode, visit: www.cisco.com/warp/customer/471/pix501506_vpn3k.html. You need a CCO account from Cisco to access this link.

For all kinds of example PIX VPN configurations, visit: www.cisco.com/warp/customer/471/top_issues/vpn/pixvpn_index. You need a CCO account from Cisco to access this link.

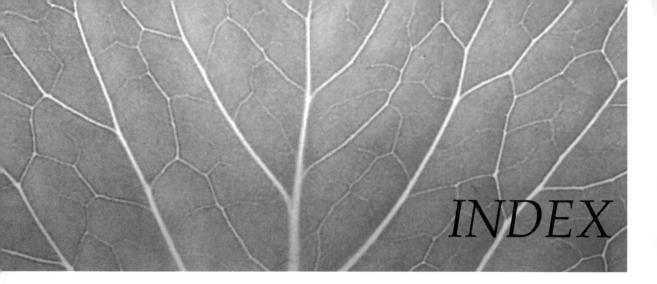

INDEX

❖ D

❖ G

❖ X

INTERNATIONAL CONTACT INFORMATION

AUSTRALIA
McGraw-Hill Book Company Australia Pty. Ltd.
TEL +61-2-9900-1800
FAX +61-2-9878-8881
http://www.mcgraw-hill.com.au
books-it_sydney@mcgraw-hill.com

CANADA
McGraw-Hill Ryerson Ltd.
TEL +905-430-5000
FAX +905-430-5020
http://www.mcgraw-hill.ca

**GREECE, MIDDLE EAST, & AFRICA
(Excluding South Africa)**
McGraw-Hill Hellas
TEL +30-210-6560-990
TEL +30-210-6560-993
TEL +30-210-6560-994
FAX +30-210-6545-525

MEXICO (Also serving Latin America)
McGraw-Hill Interamericana Editores S.A. de C.V.
TEL +525-117-1583
FAX +525-117-1589
http://www.mcgraw-hill.com.mx
fernando_castellanos@mcgraw-hill.com

SINGAPORE (Serving Asia)
McGraw-Hill Book Company
TEL +65-6863-1580
FAX +65-6862-3354
http://www.mcgraw-hill.com.sg
mghasia@mcgraw-hill.com

SOUTH AFRICA
McGraw-Hill South Africa
TEL +27-11-622-7512
FAX +27-11-622-9045
robyn_swanepoel@mcgraw-hill.com

SPAIN
McGraw-Hill/Interamericana de España, S.A.U.
TEL +34-91-180-3000
FAX +34-91-372-8513
http://www.mcgraw-hill.es
professional@mcgraw-hill.es

**UNITED KINGDOM, NORTHERN,
EASTERN, & CENTRAL EUROPE**
McGraw-Hill Education Europe
TEL +44-1-628-502500
FAX +44-1-628-770224
http://www.mcgraw-hill.co.uk
computing_europe@mcgraw-hill.com

ALL OTHER INQUIRIES Contact:
McGraw-Hill/Osborne
TEL +1-510-420-7700
FAX +1-510-420-7703
http://www.osborne.com
omg_international@mcgraw-hill.com